The Legal System of Scotland: Cases and Materials

AUSTRALIA
LBC Information Services—Sydney

CANADA and USA
Carswell—Toronto

NEW ZEALAND
Brooker's—Auckland

SINGAPORE and MALAYSIA
Sweet & Maxwell Asia
Singapore and Kuala Lumpur

The Legal System of Scotland: Cases and Materials

FOURTH EDITION

A.A. PATERSON,
LL.B. (Edin.), D.Phil. (Oxon), Solicitor

*Professor of Law,
University of Strathclyde*

T. ST J. N. BATES,
M.A., LL.M. (Cantab.)

*Clerk of Tynwald,
Secretary to the House
of Keys and Counsel to the
Speaker, Isle of Man*

*Professor of Law,
University of Strathclyde*

&

MARK R. POUSTIE,
M.A., LL.B., Dip.L.P. (Edin.), Solicitor

*Senior Lecturer in Law,
University of Strathclyde*

W. GREEN/Sweet & Maxwell Ltd
EDINBURGH
1999

First edition 1983
Second edition 1986
Third edition 1993
Fourth edition 1999

Published in 1999 by W. Green & Son Ltd
21 Alva Street
Edinburgh EH2 4PS

Phototypeset by LBJ Typesetting Ltd of Kingsclere
Printed and bound in Great Britain by Redwood Books Ltd,
Trowbridge, Wiltshire

No natural forests were destroyed to make this product;
only farmed timber was used and replanted

A CIP catalogue record for this book is available from the British Library

ISBN 0 414 01273 9

To our families from whom the time was stolen

Alison, Jane and Jacqueline

Christopher, Rachel, Michael, David and Helen

PREFACE

A legal system is the product of its time, yet it must draw on the past and prepare for the future. It thus behoves those concerned with the Scottish legal system not only to honour its past achievement but also to examine its present operation and respond to future needs. In this book emphasis is placed on a critical analysis of some of the contemporary aspects of the Scottish legal system and its future development.

At the fore of these must be the establishment of the new Scottish Parliament and the impact of the Human Rights Act 1998. In addition, there is a new chapter designed to highlight some of the key issues in dispute resolution, including the development of ADR and moves towards judicial case management.

That it has remained possible to maintain this approach is a measure of the continuing work of others. As this is still to a major extent a cases and materials book, our primary debt is to those on whose work we have drawn, and to colleagues who have read and commented on selected drafts of earlier editions of the book. For their assistance with the fourth edition we are particularly grateful to Ms. Trudi Overman, Mrs. Gill Whiteside, Mr. Liam McMonagle, Mr. Andrew Horne, Ms. Annalee Crowe, Ms. Tracy Milligan, Ms. Arlene Carruthers, Mr. Peter Demick and Ms. Katharine Nisbet.

We also wish to thank the following for permission to use copyright materials in the more extended extracts: Allen & Unwin Ltd, All Souls College Oxford, Basil Blackwell Ltd, Messrs Butterworth & Co. Ltd, Castlemilk Law Centre, the Controller of Her Majesty's Stationery Office, Deborah Charles Publications, Edinburgh University Press, the Faculty of Advocates, Glasgow University Press, W. Green & Son Ltd, Justice, the Incorporated Council of Law Reporting for England and Wales, the Law Book Co. of Australia, the Law Centres' Federation, the Law Society of Scotland, the Legal Action Group, Levy & McRae, Martin Robertson & Co., Oceana Publications Inc., Octagon Books, the Office of Parliamentary Counsel, Oxford University Press, S.L.S. Legal Publications, Scottish Academic Press Ltd, the Scottish Association of Citizens' Advice Bureaux, the Scottish Council of Law Reporting, the Scottish Courts Administration, the Scottish Office, the Stair Society, Stevens & Sons Ltd, Sweet & Maxwell Ltd; the publishers and editors of the *British Journal of Law and Society*, the *Journal of Social Policy*, the *Journal of Social Welfare Law*, the *Journal of the Society of Public Teachers of Law, the Law Quarterly Review, Legal Action*, the *Modern Law Review*, the *New Law Journal*, the *Liverpool Law Review*, the *Northern Ireland Law Quarterly, Public Law, SCOLAG Bulletin*, the *Statute Law Review*; Professor J.W.G. Blackie; Professor A.W. Bradley; the Hon. Lord Cameron; Professor C.M. Campbell; Lord Devlin; Professor T.C. Hartley; Mr. P.

Lewis; Professor D.R. Miers; Mr. A.D. Miller; Professor W.L. Twining; Professor B. Schwartz; Mr. E. Sutherland; Professor H.W.R. Wade and Professor M. Zander.

September 1999

A. A. P.
T. St.J. N. B.
M. R. P.

CONTENTS

TABLE OF CASES

TABLE OF STATUTES

TABLE OF STATUTORY INSTRUMENTS

TABLE OF EUROPEAN LEGISLATION, TREATIES AND CONVENTIONS

Table of Directives

Table of Decisions

Table of Treaties

EXCERPTS OF BOOKS, ARTICLES AND REPORTS

Abel-Smith, B. and Stevens, R., *In Search of Justice* (Allen Lane: 1968), **159**

Abraham, H.J., *The Judicial Process* (4th ed.) (O.U.P.: 1980), **223**

Allen, F., "CABx and legal services in Scotland" (1976) 4 SCOLAG Bul. 41, **292–293, 294–295**

Annual Report of the Council on Tribunals 1991–92, H.C. 316 (1992–93), **192–193**

Annual Report of the Scottish Committee of the Council on Tribunals 1996–97, **194–197**

Benson Commission [*Royal Commission on Legal Services* (Chairman: Sir Harry Benson), Final Report, vol. 1, Cmnd. 7648 (1979)], **303–304**

Black, R., "Review of Stair's *Institutions* (1981 ed.)", 1981 S.L.T. (News) 283, **465–466**

Blackie, J.W.G., "Stair's later reputation as a jurist" [in *Stair Tercentenary Studies* (ed. D.M. Walker) (Stair Society: 1981)], **463–464**

Burns, P., "A day in the stipendiary court", from "Professional Justice" (1985) 29 J.L.S. 13, **117–118**

Cairns, "Managing Civil Litigation: an Australian Adaption of American Experience" (1994) *Civil Justice Quarterly* 50, **3**

Cameron (Lord), "The superior courts" [in *A Guide to the Scottish Legal System*, published for R.I.P.A. (Edinburgh and East of Scotland group) (C.J. Cousland & Sons: 1957)], **56, 120**

Campbell, C.M., "Judicial selection (and judicial impartiality)" 1973 J.R. 254, **228**

Campbell, C.M., "Law centres and legal services" (unpublished: 1980), **343–344**

Castlemilk Law Centre (unpublished paper by the Castlemilk Law Centre: 1985), **345**

Castlemilk Law Centre's Statement of Intent (Castlemilk Law Centre: 1981), **339**

Cavenagh, R. and Sarat, A., "Thinking about courts" (1980) 14 Law and Society Review 394, **40**

Cavenagh, W.E. and Newton, D., "Administrative tribunals: how people become members" (1971) 49 Pub. Admin. 197, **165**

Central Research Unit, "Debt Recovery" [Doig, B., *Debt Recovery through the Scottish Sheriff Courts* (C.R.U., Scottish Office: 1980)], **39–40**

Central Research Unit, "The Dundee Small Claims Experiment" (A. Connor with B. Doig, *A Research-Based Evaluation of the Dundee Small Claims Experiment* (C.R.U., Scottish Office: 1983)], **41–42**

Central Research Unit, "Small Claims in the Sheriff Courts in Scotland" (1991), 46–47

Clancy, R., Murray, A. and Wadia, R., "The New Commercial Cause Rules" 1997 S.L.T. (News) 45, 53, **72**

Clark, B. and Mays, R., "Funding ADR in Scotland" 1997 S.L.T. (News) 29, **22–23**

"Complaints against solicitors" (1976) J.L.S. 179, **278–279**

"Conciliating Complaints" (1997) J.L.S.S. 151, **274**

Constitution Unit, *Scotland's Parliament—Fundamentals for a New Scotland* Act (1996), **84**

Cooper, J., "Structure and management of law centres" [in Cooper, *Public Legal Services in three countries*, doctoral dissertation, Florence, 1981], **341**

Cooper (Lord), "The common law and the civil law" [in Cooper, *Selected Papers* (Oliver & Boyd: 1957)], **459–460**

Cross, Sir Rupert, *Precedent in English Law* (3rd ed.) (Clarendon Press: 1977), **418**

Cross, Sir Rupert, "The ratio *decidendi* and a plurality of speeches (in the House of Lords)" (1977) 93 L.Q.R. 378, **443–444**

Crown Office and Procurator Fiscal Service Annual Report 1997–98, **104–105**

Cutts, Martin, "Unspeakable acts?', **363**

Daily Record and Mail, August 14, 1909, **219**

Dale, Sir William, *The European Legislative Scene*, **358**

Dale, Sir William, *Principles, Purposes and Rules*, **359–360**

Devlin (Lord), "Judges and Lawmakers' (1976) 39 M.L.R. 1, **458–459**

Devlin (Lord), *The Judge* (O.U.P.: 1979, **455–458**

Devlin (Lord), "The judge and case law" [in Devlin, *The Judge* (O.U.P.: 1979)], **409, 424**

Devlin (Lord), "Who is at fault when injustice occurs?" [in Zander, M. (ed.), *What's wrong with the* law? (B.B.C. Publications: 1970)], **423**

Diplock (Lord), "A.L.G.: a judge's view" (1975) 91 L.Q.R. 457, 459–460 Drewry, G., "Leapfrogging (—and a Lord Justice's eye view of the final appeal)" (1973) 89 L.Q.R. 260, **82, 100**

Duff, P., "The Fiscal Fine: How Far can it be Extended?" 1996 S.L.T. (News) 167, **109**

East End Community Law Centre Newsletter No. 2, **343**

Economides, K., "Small claims and procedural justice" (1980) 7 B.J.L.S. III, **40–41,** 44

Edmund-Davies (Lord), "Judicial Activism" (1975) 28 C.L.P. 1, **424**

Erskine, J. *An Institute of the Law of Scotland* (new ed. by J. Badenach Nicolson) (Bell & Bradfute: 1871), **410, 467–468**

Faculty (of Advocates) Evidence to the Hughes Commission (Mem. of Ev. 144) (unpublished), **233, 234, 252**

Finnie, W., "The European Court of Human Rights and Criminal Legal Aid in Scotland" 1995 S.L.T. (News) 271, **148**

Flockhart, R., "Some aspects of tribunal membership" [in Adler, M. and Bradley, A.W. (eds.) *Justice, Discretion and Poverty* (Professional Books: 1975)], **165–166**

Folberg & Taylor, *Mediation: a Comprehensive Guide to Resolving Disputes without Litigation* (1984), **14**

Franks Committee [*Report of the Committee on Administrative Tribunals and Enquiries* (Chairman: Rt. Hon. Sir Oliver Franks) Cmnd. 218 (1957)], **156, 157–158**

Gamble, A.J., "Advocates' Liability" (1979) 28 SCOLAG Bul. 4, **252–253**

Genn, H. and Genn, Y., *The Effectiveness of Representation at Tribunals*, **175–176, 176–180**

Gibb, A.D., *Law from over the Border* (W. Green & Son: 1950), **77–78, 87–88**

Glanville Williams, *Learning the Law* (11th ed.) (Stevens & Sons: 1982), **419–420, 422**

Gordon, G.H., "Criminal Proceedings in Scotland" (1968) 19 N.I.L.Q. 249, **106**

Goriely, T. and Paterson, A.A., *Introduction to Resourcing Civil Justice*, 286, **314**

Grant Report [*The Sheriff Court*, report by Committee appointed by the Secretary of State for Scotland (Chairman: Rt. Hon. Lord Grant) Cmnd. 3248 (1967)], **32, 37–38, 60–61**

Griffiths, J.E., "The distribution of legal services in the Netherlands' (1977) 4 B.J.L.S. 260, **287**

Harari, A., *(The place of) Negligence in the law of Torts* (Law Book Co. of Australasia: 1962), **419**

Harper, J.R., "Plea negotiation" [in Harper, *My Client, My Lord* (Law Society of Scotland: 1981)], **128**

Harris, L., "The life of a procurator fiscal" (1976) 6 SCOLAG Bul. 93, **107–108**

Hartley, T.C. *The Foundations of European Community Law* (Clarendon Press: 1981), **212–213**

Hughes Commission [*Royal Commission on Legal Services in Scotland* (Chairman: Rt. Hon. Lord Hughes) Cmnd. 7846 (1980)], **38, 40, 134–135, 158–159, 181–183, 240–241, 242, 246, 247–248, 248–249, 259–260, 270, 287–288, 289, 292, 296, 306–307, 317, 351**

Hunter, R.L.C., "The courts and the legal profession" [in Grant, J.P. (ed.), *Independence and Devolution: the legal implications for Scotland* (W. Green & Son: 1976)], **41**

Jackson, G.J., "Devolution and the Scottish legal Institutions" [in Bates, T. StJ. N. (ed.), *Devolution for Scotland: the Legal Aspects*, **103–104**

Jackson, R.H., *The Struggle for Judicial Supremacy* (Octagen Press, N.Y.: 1979), **423**

Justice, *The Judiciary* (Justice/Stevens & Sons: 1972), 233–234 *Justice-All Souls Review (of Administrative Law in the United Kingdom* (Justice/All Souls, Oxford: 1981), **170–171, 172–173, 180–181**

Kelly, P. and Lorber, S., "The Medway: unmet need for legal services" (1975) 4 Praxis 8, **289–290**

Kincraig Committee on Personal Injuries Litigation [*Committee on Procedure in the Court of Session in Personal Injuries Litigation* (Chairman: Hon. Lord Kincraig), *consultative document*, April 1979], **68–69**

Law Centres' Federation, "The role of management committees" [in *Law centres —a practical guide* (L.C.F., London: 1980)], **340**

Law Centres' Working Group, Evidence to the Benson Commission (L.C. Wkg. Grp.: 1976), **340–341**

Law Society of Scotland, *Response to Crime and Punishment*, (Law Society of Scotland: 1996), **140–141**

Law Society Report on women in the profession [Law Society of Scotland Future of the Profession Committee, *Report on its survey of women members of the Society* (Law Society of Scotland: 1985)], **263**

Legal Action Group, *A Strategy for Justice* (report by LAG: 1992), **351–354**

Legal Aid Annual Report, 34th 1983–84, **317–318**

Lewis, P., "Unmet legal needs" [in Morris, P. *et al, Social Needs and Legal Action* (Martin Robertson: 1973)], **283–284, 285**

Llewellyn, K.N., "Case Law" [in *Encylopaedia of Social Science*, vol. III (Macmillan: 1931), **409**

Llewellyn, K.N., *The Bramble Bush* (Oceana Pub. Inc.: 1950), **417, 419–421**

MacCormick, D.N., "Can *stare decisis* be abolished?" 1966 J.R. 197, **461**

MacCormick, D.N., *Legal Reasoning (and Legal Theory)* (Clarendon Press: 1978), **417–418**

MacQueen, H.L., "Mackenzie's Institutions in Scottish Legal History" (1984) 29 J.L.S. 498, **467**

Maher, G., "*Cessante ratione cessat ipsa lex*" 1978 S.L.T. (News) 161, **432–433, 437–438**

Maher, G., "Statutory interpretation and overruling in the House of Lords" (1981) Stat. L.R. 85, **427–428**

Manson-Smith, D., *The legal system of* Scotland (H.M.S.O.: 1995), **28**

Martin, F.M., *et al., Children out of Court* (Scottish Academic Press: 1981), **184–186**

Maxwell, D., *The practice of the Court of* Session (Scottish Courts Administration: 1980), **62**

Mays, R., "Frying Pan, Fire, or Melting Pot?—Reforming Scottish Civil Justice in the 1990s" 1997 J.R. 91, **4–5**

Mellick, J., "Legal Aid (and legal advice and assistance) in Scotland" [in *Proceedings and Papers of the Fifth Commonwealth Law Conference* (1977)], **309–310**

Miller, A., "Sole practice in Scotland" (unpublished: 1981), **269**

Mnookin, R.H., "Bargaining in the shadow of the law: the case of Divorce" (1979) 32 C.L.P. 65, **65**

Monopolies and Mergers Commission, *Advocates' Services*, H.C. 513 (1975–76), **239, 243, 244–245, 246–247**

Monopolies and Mergers Commission, *Services of Solicitors*, H.C. 558 (1975–76), **299**

Moody, S.R., "An Overview of Alternative Dispute Resolution in Scotland" [in Moody, S.R. and Mackay, R.E., *Alternative Dispute Resolution in Scotland* (W. Green & Son, 1995), **1, 2–3, 8, 13–14, 14–16**

Moody, S.R. and Tombs, J., "Plea negotiations" [in Moody and Tombs, *Prosecution in the Public Interest* (Scottish Academic Press:1982)], **127**

Moran, J.M., "The parliamentary draftsman" (1974) 19 J.L.S. **364–365**

Morrison, N., "The Cullen Report" 1996 S.L.T. (News) 93, **5, 10, 13**

Morrison, N., "Reform of Civil Procedure" 1998 S.L.T. (News) 137, **12, 43, 52**

Myers, P., "The future of legal aid in Scotland" (1974) 19 J.L.S. 312, **313**

Nicholson, C.G.B., *The Law and Practice of Sentencing in Scotland* (W. Green & Son: 1981), **125**

Nicholson, C.G.B., *Sentencing Law and Practice in Scotland* (2nd ed.), **126**

Normand (Lord), "The Scottish judicature and legal procedure" (address to the Holdsworth Club, University of Birmingham, 1941), **464**

Norrie, K. McK., Children's Hearings in Scotland (W. Green & Son, 1997), **187–188**

O'Carroll, D., "Civil jurisdiction limits: proposed increases" (1998) 254 SCOLAG 129, **48, 52**

"Opinions delivered before the Select Committee" (1856) 2 Macq., **89–90**

Paterson, A.A., "Appellate decision-making in the Common law world" (unpublished: 1981), **94–97**

Paterson, A.A., *Contingent Fees and their Rivals*, **323–325**

Paterson, A.A., *Financing Legal Services*, **319, 320–321, 326–328, 330–331**

Paterson, A.A., "Judges: a political elite?" (1974) 1 B.J.L.S. 118, **64–65, 91**

Paterson, A.A. and Goriely, T., *Introduction to Resourcing Civil Justice*, **286, 314**

Paterson, A.A., "Legal services for all?" (1980) J.S.W.L. 321, **316–317**

Paterson, A.A., "Lord Reid's unnoticed legacy—a jurisprudence of overruling" (1981) 1 O.J.L.S. 375, **428–431**

Paterson, A.A., "Paying for legal services" (1979) 24 J.L.S. 237, **322–323, 328–330**

Paterson, A.A., *The Law Lords* (Macmillan: 1982), **91–92, 444–445**

Paterson, A.A., "The Purpose of Legal Aid" 1985 S.L.T. (News) 232, **315–316**

Phillips, J. and Hawkins, K., "(Some economic aspects of) the settlement process" (1976) 39 M.L.R. 497, **63–64**

Podmore, D., "The sole practitioner—a declining species" (1979) 129 New L.J. 356, **267–268**

Practice Statement (Judicial Precedent) [1966] 1 W.L.R. 1234, **425–426**

The Preparation of Legislation, Cmnd. 6053 (1975), **361–362**

Reed, R.J., "Judicial Review of errors of law" 1979 S.L.T. (News) 241, **188–191**

Reid (Lord), "The judge as law maker" (1972) XII J.S.P.T.L. 22, **100, 424, 444, 455, 462**

Report of the Clerk to the Discipline Tribunal 1979/80 (unpublished), **277**

Rodger, A., "At risk" (1978) 23 J.L.S. 463, **253–254**

S.A.C.A.B., *Annual Report 1981–82* (Scottish Association of Citizens' Advice Bureaux: 1982), **294**

SAFCOS, "Family [Mediation] Services" (Scottish Association of Family Conciliation Services), **19–22**

Sainsbury, *Social Security Appeals: In Need of Review?*, **159–161, 161–162**

Salisbury and Winchester Journal, December 6, 1779, **298**

Scottish Office, "Crime and Punishment" (Cm. 3302, 1996), **137, 139**

Scottish Office, "Criminal Legal Aid Review" (Consultation Paper) (1993), **132–133**

Scottish Courts Administration, "Proposals to increase jurisdiction limits in the Sheriff Court (including privative jurisdiction limit)", **52**

Sheehan, A.V., *Criminal Procedure in Scotland and* France (H.M.S.O.: 1975), **102–103, 104, 125**

Sheriff Court Rules Council, "The New Ordinary Cause Rules" 1993 J.L.S.S. 334, **35**

Sherr, A. and Domberger, S., "Measuring legal work" (1982) 132 New L.J. 80, **348–350**

Shetreet, S., *Judges on Trial* (North-Holland: 1976), **237–238**

Simon (Lord), "Some judicial processes in England" (1979) 1 Liverpool L.R. 1, **457**

CHAPTER 1

KEY ISSUES IN DISPUTE RESOLUTION

I. DISPUTE RESOLUTION

This chapter provides an overview of the role of dispute resolution in society and the variety of dispute resolution mechanisms available. It then considers litigation in particular, the perceived problems of litigation such as delay and expense, and measures taken to address these. Finally, it focuses on the merits, current use and potential role of one response to the perceived problem of litigation, namely Alternative Dispute Resolution (ADR).

S.R. Moody, "An Overview of Alternative Dispute Resolution in Scotland" in S.R. Moody and R. E. Mackay, *Alternative Dispute Resolution in Scotland* (W. Green, 1995), p. 1

> "1.1.1 The satisfactory resolution of disputes is a key issue for any society. International conflicts, disputes between the citizen and government, conflicts between citizens and disputes within families each threaten the maintenance of social order. Parties will seek to find the most satisfactory way of resolving their particular dispute but it is also in the interests of the wider community to assist in the shaping of dispute resolution methods. Inevitably the ways in which disputes are managed will vary, depending on the nature of that society. . . ."

Litigation has traditionally been regarded as the dispute resolution procedure *par excellence*. Indeed provision of courts for citizens or businesses to settle disputes and access to those courts as of right is seen as a fundamental function of government.

***Bremer Vulkan v. South India Shipping* [1981] AC 909 per Lord Diplock at p. 977**

> "Every civilised system of government requires that the state should make available to all its citizens a means for the just and peaceful settlement of disputes between them as to their respective legal rights. The means provided are courts of justice to which every citizen has a constitutional right of access in the role of plaintiff to obtain the remedy to which he claims to be entitled in consequence of an alleged breach of his legal or equitable rights by some other citizen, the defendant. Whether or not to avail himself of this right of access to the court lies exclusively within the plaintiff's choice; if he chooses to do so, the defendant has no option in the matter; his subjection to the jurisdiction of the court is compulsory."

Yet in truth there are a wide variety of dispute resolution options; indeed the vast majority of disputes are resolved without any recourse to the courts.

However, the outcome of litigation in the courts does have the advantage of being binding and enforceable.

S.R. Moody, "An Overview of Alternative Dispute Resolution in Scotland" in S.R. Moody and R. E. Mackay, *Alternative Dispute Resolution in Scotland* (W. Green, 1995), pp. 2–4

"METHODS OF DISPUTE RESOLUTION

1.2.1 Parties in dispute in Scotland already have a variety of dispute resolution methods open to them. They may practice avoidance, accept the other party's imposed solution, take part in negotiations (either through lawyers or unaided) submit their disputes to arbitration or choose litigation. Each of these processes has certain advantages and disadvantages for the parties, their advisers and for the community at large. These different forms of dispute resolution vary significantly in relation to the cost and time of processing disputes, the key players in managing disputes, the formality of the process, the possible outcomes and their legal standing.

Avoidance and acquiescence

1.2.2 Avoidance and acquiescence, for instance, can be cheap, speedy and entirely informal. One party or group takes and retains control of the process, which generally produces an unsatisfactory result for the other party or parties. There is no dialogue or discussion between the parties and no agreement. The outcome, while it may act as a bar to subsequent legal proceedings, in general has no legal standing. Avoidance, according to research, is the form of dispute resolution which is most frequently used in modern societies.

Negotiation

1.2.3 Negotiation is another form of dispute resolution which can be informal, economic and quick, and which encourages the parties to work out a resolution for themselves. However, unlike avoidance it is bilateral. While the outcome of negotiation itself has no legal status it may meet the requirements of a valid contract. There are numerous variants within negotiation, including, for instance, the use of professional advisers to negotiate on behalf of each party, and these may increase the cost, time and formality of the process.

Arbitration

1.2.4 Arbitration has flourished in Scotland since at least the thirteenth century. The Crown and the Church encouraged the early development of arbitration and today in many respects it represents a parallel legal system. While there are significant differences between different kinds of arbitration in terms of their cost, speed and formality, arbitration can be expensive, time consuming and highly structured. Any party may relinquish their role in appearing before the arbiter to a professional adviser, and in some cases will always do so. The arbiter has an adjudicatory, not merely an advisory role, and arbitral awards are binding on the parties. It is usual to insert a clause by which the parties consent to registration for preservation and execution of the award so that it becomes an order of court.

Litigation

1.2.5 Litigation is generally a formal procedure in which legal representatives and judges are the key players. It is frequently slow and costly and produces an outcome which favours one party only. The outcome of litigation is binding on the parties and can be enforced by the court through, for instance, diligence procedures in civil cases.

1.2.6 These dispute resolution processes occupy points on a continuum, ranging from the very informal, low cost, speedy solutions which result when one party uses avoidance or acquiescence to the highly formal situation of traditional litigation. However, the idea of a continuum does not truly reflect the weight which is given to these processes in terms of their status, both in law and in the public mind. Only litigation and certain forms of arbitration have the force of law and litigation is seen by many as the form of dispute resolution *par excellence*. Yet, in numerical terms, only a fraction of all disputes are taken to litigation, less than 10 per cent of civil matters and five per cent of criminal issues."

II. OUTLINE OF THE SYSTEM OF CIVIL LITIGATION

Cairns, "Managing Civil Litigation: An Australian Adaption of American Experience" (1994) *Civil Justice Quarterly 50* at p. 50

"Ordinary adversary system notions mandate that the parties initiate and prosecute civil litigation. The plaintiff decides whether to sue and sets out the material facts in a statement of claim. Pleadings define the boundaries of the dispute. When the parties are ready for trial the court allocates a hearing date, hears the evidence and gives judgment. The court's role is therefore passive. All interlocutory steps are the parties' responsibility. Where a disagreement arises, a party may apply to the court for a ruling. Times are prescribed in the rules of court for interlocutory steps to be completed. Generally, if the plaintiff fails to meet the prescribed time for delivering the statement of claim, or entering the action for trial, the defendant has a ground for applying to the court to have the action struck out for want of prosecution. Similarly, if the defendant fails to enter an appearance or deliver a defence within the time allowed, the plaintiff may enter a default judgment."

Although the above extract from Cairns relates to Australia, with appropriate changes to terminology, it nonetheless outlines the key features of the system of civil litigation as they apply in Scotland. The key features are (1) the system is adversarial; (2) written pleadings define the areas of dispute; (3) the parties are responsible for the progress of cases; and (4) the court functions largely as a passive referee in a contest between the parties rather than as an active manager of the litigation. A period is usually provided for parties to adjust the written pleadings. Lord Justice-Clerk Thomson describes the role of the judge in the adversarial system in the following extract:

***Thomson v. Corporation of Glasgow* 1961 SLT 237 per Lord Justice-Clerk Thomson at p. 246.**

> "A litigation is in essence a trial of skill between opposing parties conducted under recognised rules, and the prize is the judge's decision. We have rejected inquisitorial methods and prefer to regard our judges as entirely independent. Like referees at boxing contests they see that the rules are kept and count the points."

III. DEVELOPMENTS IN DISPUTE RESOLUTION: PROBLEMS WITH LITIGATION

In recent years there has been considerable dissatisfaction expressed with the civil justice system, particularly in relation to delay in and the expense of litigation. This has not been confined to Scotland: similar concerns have been voiced, for example, in England and Wales, the United States of America and Australia. The following extract deals with England and Wales but is equally applicable to Scotland.

Lord Woolf, *Access to Justice, Final Report*, HMSO, 1996, Section I, para.2

> "The defects I identified in our present system were that it is too expensive in that the costs often exceed the value of the claim; too slow in bringing cases to a conclusion and too unequal: there is a lack of equality between the powerful, wealthy litigant and the under-resourced litigant. It is too uncertain: the difficulty of forecasting what litigation will cost and how long it will last induces the fear of the unknown; and it is incomprehensible to many litigants. Above all it is too fragmented in the way it is organised since there is no-one with clear overall responsibility for the administration of civil justice; and too adversarial as cases are run by the parties, not by the courts and the rules of court, all too often, are ignored by the parties and not enforced by the court."

Delay has also been identified as a problem in Scotland as the following extract illustrates in relation to the sheriff court.

R. Mays, "Frying Pan, Fire, or Melting Pot?—Reforming Scottish Civil Justice in the 1990s" 1997 J.R. 91 at p. 93

> "Prior to modifications to the ordinary cause procedure in 1993, the whole pace of litigation in the sheriff court was substantially in the hands of the parties. Research in Scotland disclosed that the average time for disposal of an ordinary cause was 83 weeks. In many instances, cases (particularly reparation cases) would remain active for several years. Cases were repeat-

edly calling in court on minor, often undisputed, interlocutory issues. Only 5 per cent of cases were resolved by way of proof hearings in court. Substantial numbers of actions were sisted for, on average, 28 weeks."

See also Chapter 2, pp. 35–36. Cost and delay have also been identified as problems in litigation in the Court of Session:

N. Morrison, "The Cullen Report" 1996 SLT (News) 93

"Lord Cullen has unearthed some disturbing statistics about the current conduct of civil business in the Court of Session. The cost of actions rose by almost 20 per cent from the year 1992–93 to 1994–95, a period in which solicitors' fees did not increase. The rise in cost must, therefore, be due to delay and expense.

The basic period from service of a summons to the closing of the record under the time limits in the Rules of the Court of Session 1994 (RCS), is 15 weeks. In the 218 actions in Lord Cullen's study sample (300 cases) which continued to the closing of the record, the average period from service of the summons was a staggering 38 weeks. . . ."

The *Report of the Working Party on Commercial Causes* (Chairman Lord Coulsfield, November 1993) also provided evidence that delay and expense in civil litigation involving business in Scotland was seen as a major problem by commercial organisations. See also Chapter 3, pp. 71–72 below.

However, it could be argued that many of these problems are not always problems at all—at least for litigants. They may be problems for the efficient administration of the court since late settlement and use of procedural rules as tactical devices may result in wasted court resources but the resources of the parties may not be wasted at all. It may be that existing court procedures work well in terms of facilitating settlement. Aside from the evidence produced in the said *Report of the Working Party on Commercial Causes*, there has been little attempt to ascertain the views of litigants about the length and cost of civil litigation. In Lord Cullen's more fundamental *Review of the Business of the Outer House of the Court of Session* (1995) there was little attempt to analyse whether costs and length of proceedings were actually perceived to be unnecessary or unreasonable by the parties.

R. Wadia, "Judicial Case Management in Scotland—Indecision and Indigestion" 1997 SLT (News) 255, pp. 256–258

"Unnecessary expense?

In the Court of Session 20 per cent of cases are supported by legal aid (46 per cent in the sheriff court). These form the only collated information on case costs. The Scottish Legal Aid Board annual reports show that over the last five years, during a time when controlled fee structures have been relatively static in the Court of Session, total civil legal aid expenses have risen from £4.4 million to £6.3 million (43%) while cases have dropped 14 per cent. The 1997 Legal Aid Board Report attributes this continuing trend to a significant rise in individual case costs (7 per cent), which have almost doubled in the past five years. Lord Cullen argued that cost increases reflected the length of time that cases remained within the litigation system (report, para.3.2). Recent insinuations of feeing abuse resulted in calls for increased scrutiny, controlled fee structures and franchising (Grant McCulloch (1997) 42 J.L.S. 199). There is little research on privately funded litigation, or hidden costs of litigating, although uncertainty over expense can become a powerful weapon in negotiating settlement and controlling the flow of business through the courts.

Undue delay?

Delay is a relative concept, and is not necessarily an evil, allowing conditions to develop and costs to be spread. Comparing published studies with raw data supplied for the Cullen review, it can be shown that at least two procedures which were intended to provide fast track resolutions have succeeded in becoming procedural superhighways (although it would be naïve to suggest that speed is a sole measure of success). A sample of cases using the optional procedure for personal injuries showed that the average time to disposal was 36 weeks, compared to 72 weeks on the ordinary roll (personal injuries) in the Court of Session. The average time under the commercial cause rules was 26 weeks. These all compare favourably with the Cullen sample, where the average time to resolution was 94 weeks. Given the distorting effects of averages, the span of time taken within the litigation process is more relevant:

Procedure	*Longest time to resolution*
Optional procedure for personal injuries	111 weeks (excluding one case)
Court of Session ordinary personal injuries	191 weeks
Commercial case procedures	65 weeks
Cullen review Court of Session (mixed procedures)	317 weeks (excluding one case of 439 weeks)

The longest time to a judicial decision in the Cullen sample was four years while cases which eventually settled (94.3 per cent) stretched over almost nine years. A closer analysis of the data shows that there was a loose correlation with the number of adjustments and amendments of pleadings, but sisting a case was a large contributor to the length of process, a trend also noted in other Scottish research studies. Without intervention cases do seem to fall asleep in procedural abyss. It is usually in one party's interest to delay, and the time taken to resolve some disputes may support the argument that unlimited access to legal procedure is used tactically for settlement by exhaustion or strategic bargaining in a contest of skill and brinkmanship. Is it just that the court should tolerate these practices? The answer strikes at the heart of the purpose of a civil justice system and the responsibility for the abuses within that system.

Efficient administration?

It is noteworthy that in almost all adversarial legal systems, where control of the presentation and progress of a case lies solely with the parties, around 95 per cent of cases normally settle on the way to trial. It is a client's inalienable right to resolve his/her dispute informally at any point and it is not a failure of the litigation process that it facilitates settlements. But the unpredictability of the stage and timing of settlements repeatedly hinders the efficient administration of the court's timetable, and forms the main cause of delay, wasted preparation, wasted administrative resources and unnecessary court attendances (Cullen review, paras.3.38–3.41), consequentially affecting those queuing for court time.

In the Cullen sample the majority of cases were settled prior to a substantive hearing—either before procedure roll (13 per cent) or before proof (51 per cent). The vast majority of commercial settlements are at the preliminary hearing stage (75 per cent) where emphasis is placed on flushing out substantive issues. One conclusion would seem to be that imminence of a substantive hearing focuses the parties' minds on the risk/benefit analysis of progressing their case. Lord Cullen's recommendations for early hearings, earlier disclosure and therefore earlier preparation are aimed at pre-empting unpredictable settlement patterns, cutting down on delays and supervising procedural tactics to improve both the effectiveness and efficiency of a public resource while protecting the development of Scots legal principles."

There is also a concern that if procedures are not streamlined, potential litigants, particularly commercial organisations, will opt for dispute resolution fora that are cheaper and have abbreviated procedures. These might be courts south of the border where procedural reforms to tackle the problems of cost and delay have progressed further (although not without being subjected to considerable criticism—see below pp. 10–12) or potential litigants might opt for non-litigation solutions, particularly Alternative Dispute Resolution (ADR) (see below, pp. 13–26).

IV. REFORM OF CIVIL PROCEDURES IN THE COURTS

A. SCOTLAND—INITIAL STEPS

With the potential competitive challenge of ADR and the possibility of litigants forum shopping for the most efficient civil justice system, the Scottish courts began to respond with a variety of initiatives. Principally, these involve abbreviated written pleadings, enhanced disclosure/discovery of evidence to narrow down issues in dispute well in advance and judicial case management. The latter seeks to transfer control of the progress of the case from the parties to the judiciary; the idea being that this will reduce delays and hence in turn reduce costs.

S.R. Moody, "An Overview of Alternative Dispute Resolution in Scotland" in S.R. Moody and R. E. Mackay, *Alternative Dispute Resolution in Scotland* (W. Green, 1995), pp. 3–4

> 1.2.7 As a relatively non-litigious nation Scotland has encouraged the growth of dispute resolution processes which seek to provide compromise solutions and avoid the win/lose dichotomy which characterises litigation. More recently efforts have been made in civil cases to encourage early settlement or at least to produce agreement on non-contentious issues through the use of options hearings at which "the sheriff shall seek to secure the expeditious progress of the cause by ascertaining from the parties the matters in dispute". [See Chapter 2, pp. 35–36.] In addition, matters of fact may be referred to "any person of skill" by the sheriff on a joint motion or motion by any party and "the report of such person shall be final and conclusive with respect to the subject-matter of the remit". The new Commercial Cause procedure is also intended to speed up case processing and encourage early agreement on non-contentious issues. [See Chapter 3, pp. 71–72]. Proposals have been made to reduce delays in criminal cases through greater use of intermediate diets and, more controversially, restrictions on the accused's right to silence [See Chapter 5].

In the Court of Session the optional procedure for personal injury cases has also been introduced, which provides for abbreviated pleadings, a shortened period for adjustment and earlier and fuller disclosure to try to reduce the areas of dispute. The commercial cause procedure mentioned by Moody involves a similar approach with the added ingredient of judicial case management to keep the case moving along. Both these procedures are discussed in more detail in Chapter 3 (pp. 69–72).

B. ENGLAND & WALES—THE WOOLF REPORT

However, in England and Wales the process has been taken much further with Lord Woolf being commissioned by the Government to examine the whole of the civil justice system. His report, *Access to Justice, Final Report* was published in July 1996. Lord Woolf's key proposals were:

(1) people should be encouraged to view litigation as a last resort and to use other more appropriate means when these are available with information on ADR being provided at all civil courts;
(2) litigation should be less adversarial and more co-operative with greater pre-trial disclosure of evidence, the use of single expert witnesses when practicable and with the courts encouraging use of ADR by the parties;
(3) litigation should be less complex with a single set of rules applying to the High Court and the county court and all litigation commenced in the same way and a single point of entry to the court system with cases allocated to one of three tracks: small claims (up to £3,000), fast-track (£3,000–£10,000) and multi-track (over £10,000);

(4) there should be judicial case management to progress cases expeditiously with fixed timetables for fast track cases and sanctions for parties not complying with procedures or timetables;
(5) there should be more predictable costs for litigation with fixed costs for fast-track cases and estimates of costs for multi-track cases published by the court or agreed by the parties and approved by the court; and
(6) that a variety of administrative measures should be put in place to ensure that the new system functions efficiently.

Lord Woolf's recommendations are being implemented although the value of claims in each of the tracks has been increased with the small claims track now including claims up to £5,000, the fast-track claims between £5,000 and £15,000 and the multi-track claims over £15,000 (see the Civil Procedure Rules 1998 (S.I. 1998 No.3132).

C. SCOTLAND—THE CULLEN REVIEW AND SHERIFF COURT DEVELOPMENTS

In Scotland, there has been no comparable systematic review of the whole civil justice system. However, at sheriff court level, the Sheriff Court Rules Council examined ordinary procedure in the sheriff court, as a result of which the ordinary court rules were revised to try to reduce delay in cases partly by giving judges a greater role through case management in options hearings. This is discussed in more detail in Chapter 2 (pp. 35–36). At Court of Session level Lord Cullen was commissioned to review the manner in which the business of the Outer House was administered, conducted and allocated with a view to making recommendations about improvement. His report, *Review of the Business of the Outer House of the Court of Session* was published in 1995. The recommendations contained in Lord Cullen's review were similar but not identical to those in Lord Woolf's report. Lord Cullen essentially proposed that the optional procedure would be made the ordinary procedure in the Court of Session. Abbreviated pleadings, an element of case management and greater and earlier disclosure of evidence in order to minimise areas of dispute were the key findings. Lord Cullen rejected any form of court-annexed ADR. However, the key aspects of Lord Cullen's proposals still remained unimplemented in mid-1999.

What might strike one immediately about the Scottish approach to reform of civil procedure is that, in contrast to England and Wales, it has been piecemeal: there has been no attempt to consider reform of the sheriff court, Outer House and Inner House procedures together. Indeed there is no overall body which is responsible for recommending proposals for reform of procedures in the sheriff court and the Court of Session. Harmonisation of all civil procedure rules in Scotland seems very distant although more recently, a small step towards this, the harmonisation of the small claims and summary cause rules in the sheriff court has been proposed, *A Consultation Paper on Proposed New Rules for Summary Cause and Small Claims in the Sheriff Court* (1998); see also Chapter 2, p. 43).

Should the Cullen Review's proposals for fuller and earlier disclosure of evidence be implemented they would certainly lead to a reduction in areas of dispute and might result in shorter more focused written pleadings.

N. Morrison "The Cullen Report" 1996 S.L.T. 93

"Under our present procedures, there is no means of discovering a latent ambiguity in pleadings, and there is no procedural means for requiring parties to indicate the scope of what they intend to challenge or establish. Present rules are not well adapted to achieve early settlement. Lord Cullen notes that our system of pleading is not well suited to dealing with complaints that defenders are being less than candid."

D. WILL JUDICIAL CASE MANAGEMENT RESULT IN REDUCED COSTS?

However, aside from such a development the implementation of the Cullen (and Woolf) reforms may not be as desirable as may at first be thought. Major criticism has in particular been directed at the supposed benefits of judicial case management, notably in relation to Lord Woolf's reforms although the same criticisms could be and have been to a lesser extent levelled at Lord Cullen's proposals. Although there are obviously questions about the ability of judges to move away from the traditional "referee" approach to a new hands-on managerial role and the cost of training judges for such a role, the key criticism is that while the Woolf reforms may reduce delay, they are nonetheless likely to increase costs and may not produce justice for the litigant.

Zander, "The Woolf Report: Forwards or Backwards for the New Lord Chancellor" (1997) 16 C.J.Q. 208 at pp. 219–221

"(7) . . . The proposition that judicial case management will reduce costs has the ring of common-sense plausibility about it. But, commonsense is often wrong. It may be that in large and untypical cases like the Lloyds' litigation it is true. But in ordinary run-of-the-mill cases it is not true. Judicial case management does not save money, it positively adds to the costs. The recent RAND study [A five-year study of 10,000 cases in 20 federal courts in 16 states of the United States of America, see J. S. Kakalik *et al. Just, Speedy and Inexpensive? An Evaluation or Judicial Case Management under the Civil Justice Reform Act* (RAND, 1996)] both establishes that as a fact and explains the reason. 'Early judicial case management [also] is associated with significantly increased costs to litigants, as measured by attorney work hours'. The reason? Case management generates more work for lawyers:

'Lawyer work may increase as a result of early management because lawyers need to respond to a court's management—for example, talking to the litigant and to the other lawyers in advance of a conference with the judge, and updating the file after a conference'.

Even shortening the time to trial, as Lord Woolf proposes with his Fast Track, does not necessarily reduce costs. RAND estimated that even when case management cuts time to trial it increased costs. It added: 'These results debunk the myth that reducing time to disposition necessarily reduces litigation costs'.

Experiments were conducted by RAND to see whether it made any difference if early case management were earlier or later. It made no difference. The RAND Report said:

'This finding suggests that the fact of management adds to the lawyer work hours, not the 'earliness' of the management'.

Of course, the earlier the case management comes in the life of a case, the more cases are brought into the system and the more costs will be front-loaded onto cases that would have settled anyway.

In my view, the Woolf Report gives wholly insufficient attention to this crucial point. According to Woolf, case management should apply to all cases where a defence is entered—but almost all such cases will settle anyway and most do not need case management.

Lord Woolf has said that too many cases settle at the door of the court and early case management may cause some of them to settle earlier. That may or may not prove to be the case. But even if it does, far more cases settle much earlier anyway and will incur extra and often useless extra cost by reason of the imposition of unneeded case management.

It is true that many cases that are set down for trial are disposed of after trial or by settlement at or near to the door of the court. But the overwhelming majority of actions commenced do not reach the stage of being set down for trial. Yet all cases which get as far as a defence being entered (and unfortunately, no one knows the number of these) will be subject to the extra cost of Woolf-generated case management. This point is obvious and I believe devastating for the credibility of the Woolf package of reforms. It is a mystery to me how anyone can believe that case management could do anything other than increase costs for the mass of cases that are settled before being set down. But now the RAND study has demonstrated that judicial case management tends to increase costs also for the cases that do get as far as the door of the court. The fact that it may reduce costs in a few untypical long cases is clearly no consolation. (A case management regime could be introduced for long complicated cases.) But the increase in cost for the many is not balanced by the decrease in cost for the few.

Lord Woolf's answer may be that at least in Fast Track cases costs will be reduced by being fixed. But that is on the assumption that the lawyers do less work than now. If, as the RAND study shows, judicial case management causes them actually to do more work than now, reduced fees are patently unfair. If the lawyers are not paid for their work they will not take the cases. . . .

(8) If judicial case management will tend to increase rather than reduce cost, will it at least reduce delay? The answer is that it may. The RAND study tells us that early case management can cut time to disposition. It also reports that the most effective device to achieve that result is the simple one of giving the parties a trial date from a very early stage and then adhering to that date, as Lord Woolf proposed. RAND also reports that having the lay client present at settlement conferences speeds disposition—another Woolf proposal. The Australian data also suggest that delay can be cut by case management—though the effect may only be temporary. . . .

(9) This leads to what ought to be our main focus—justice for the litigant. An earlier study by RAND found that, contrary to what one might think,

litigants are not primarily concerned about cost and delay. What they are primarily concerned about is a fair process. One aspect of a sense of fair process is having one's day in court, feeling that one has been able to present one's story. Lord Woolf's Fast Track abbreviated procedure is consciously designed to inhibit the client's opportunities to tell his story. Thus, in particular, the evidence at trial is generally restricted to three hours for both sides together and experts will not be allowed to testify orally at all. This may make sense in terms of economy but for the litigants, perhaps the litigants on both sides, it may provoke a sense of frustration. Claims involving sums of £3,000 to £10,000 [now £5,000 to £15,000] may seem like relatively small beer for practising lawyers and judges—justifying somewhat summary procedures. But £3,000 to £10,000 [now £5,000 to £15,000] is not small beer for most ordinary citizens and I am not sure that they will appreciate being fobbed off with what is bound to be thought of as a restricted, second-class service—neither cheap nor cheerful.

I am therefore concerned that Lord Woolf's Fast Track may turn out to be more of a minus than a plus. A rushed pre-trial stage is to culminate in a rushed trial. I am sceptical as to whether litigants will regard that as better or even adequate justice. The same issue will occur equally in Multi-Track cases when the court's case management decisions appear unreasonable to the litigants."

Support for Zander's critical approach may also be found in M. Mears' "Too late for carbon dating?" (1997) 147 N.L.J. 1597 who points out that Lord Woolf has not responded directly to these criticisms except for criticising Zander for being an academic. However, more persuasive criticism of Zander's arguments has come from a U.S. source who has pointed out that the RAND report on which Zander bases many of his arguments has itself been the subject of criticism in the U.S., for example, on the basis that its conclusions are simply not justified by the data gathered (see S. Flanders, "Case Management: Failure in America? Success in England and Wales?" (1998) 17 C.J.Q. 308, pp. 312–315). Flanders also notes that the U.S. reforms which led to the RAND research were also arguably much less radical than those proposed in England and Wales as judicial case management has developed in the federal courts in the U.S. since the 1950s. The reforms there mandated by the Civil Justice Reform Act 1990 simply required more case management rather than a fundamental switch from the traditional judicial role described above at p. 4 to a hands-on case management role in the first place.

In Scotland too, there has been criticism of Lord Cullen's proposals. For example, it has been argued that abbreviated pleadings may well require greater judicial involvement to identify the issues in dispute. This would in turn increase judicial workload and will ultimately raise costs for the parties as the courts are moving towards a pay-as-you-litigate system which has already been implemented in the sheriff court.

N. Morrison, "Reform of Civil Procedure" 1998 SLT (News) 137 at p. 143

"A danger of case management is that instead of the parties at their own expense preparing a case for court, it is handed over to judges to do it for them at judicial expense".

Abbreviated pleadings and judicial case management are already in operation for cases brought under the Commercial Cause Rules in the Court of Session so the operation of those rules provides some evidence as to whether costs will be increased or not.

N.Morrison, "The Cullen Report" 1996 SLT (News) 93 at p. 95

> "It will no doubt be pointed out that the rules for commercial actions in Chap[ter] 47 of the RCS [Rules of the Court of Session] 1994, which permit abbreviated pleadings, are successful. It has to be pointed out, however, that an action in the commercial court is very expensive for the court to service, a cost not yet borne by the litigants. The lessons would appear to be that abbreviated pleadings and case management are expensive options and may not be cost effective without increases in court fees. . . . "

Morrison argues that case management should not be used in Scotland to identify the issues in dispute but only to ensure that actions are dealt with expeditiously and without unnecessary expense. However, whether it is possible to separate these aspects of judicial case management remains unclear.

On the Woolf reforms see Lord Woolf, *Access to Justice*, *Interim Report*, June 1995; *Access to Justice*, *Final Report*, July 1996. For criticisms of the Woolf reforms see Zander "The Woolf Report: Forwards or Backwards for the New Lord Chancellor?" (1997) 16 C.J.Q. 208; Zander, "The Government's Plans on Civil Justice" [1998] 61 M.L.R. 382; Zander, "How does judicial case management work?" (1997) N.L.J. 353. On the Cullen Review see N. Morrison, "The Cullen Report" 1996 S.L.T. (News) 93; Upton "The Cullen Review" (1996) 41 J.L.S.111. On reform of Scottish civil procedures more generally see Lord Gill, "The Case for a Civil Justice Review" (1995) 40 J.L.S. 129; R. Wadia, "Judicial Case Management in Scotland" 1997 S.L.T. (News) 255; R. Mays, "Frying Pan, Fire, or Melting Pot?—Reforming Scottish Civil Justice in the 1990s" 1997 J.R. 91; N. Morrison, "Reform of Civil Procedure" 1998 S.L.T. (News) 137; and R. Mays, "Case Management in the Scottish Civil Courts—Whose Case is it Anyway?" (1998) 3 SLPQ 65. Further reading on new ordinary procedure in the sheriff court is given in Chapter 2 on p. 35 and on the optional and Commercial Cause procedures in the Court of Session in Chapter 3 on pp. 69–72.

V. ALTERNATIVE DISPUTE RESOLUTION

A. INTRODUCTION

S.R. Moody, "An Overview of Alternative Dispute Resolution in Scotland" in S.R. Moody and R. E. Mackay, *Alternative Dispute Resolution in Scotland* (W. Green, 1995), p. 4

> "1.2.8 In spite of these efforts to improve the administration of justice there appears to be a growing dissatisfaction with existing dispute resolution procedures. This has led to a search for other ways of dealing with conflicts, either complementary or alternative to current processes. Much of the

impetus for this had been pragmatic, with rising concern about the cost of litigation and the length of time taken to conclude even those cases which are non-contested. Some disquiet has a more principled basis, reflecting concerns about access to justice, the lack of control exercised by the parties when more formal processes are invoked and the limited and sometimes inappropriate solutions offered by such procedures. In the 1960s these criticisms led to the development, primarily in the United States, of Alternative Dispute Resolution."

B. DEFINITIONS OF ADR

First, it would be helpful to attempt to define what is meant by Alternative Dispute Resolution (ADR). Unfortunately, it is not easy to provide a comprehensive definition. Indeed, to some extent ADR is not "alternative" to court procedures at all; rather it is complementary. For example, in Scotland, the sheriff court has the power to refer parties to family mediation and may give to any settlement reached the force of law (see pp. 20–21 below). It has been suggested that "appropriate" would more properly reflect what ADR involves. Nonetheless some of the key features of ADR can be identified. For example, Folberg & Taylor have argued in *Mediation: A Comprehensive Guide to Resolving Disputes without Litigation* (1984), p. 7, that ADR entails

> "the process by which participants, together with the assistance of a neutral person or persons, systematically isolate dispute issues in order to develop options, consider alternatives, and reach a consensual settlement that will accommodate their needs."

Moody and Mackay note that there are three key elements present in this definition: (1) the role of the parties in resolving their disputes; (2) the role of the neutral third party; and (3) the particular approach of ADR.

S.R. Moody, "An Overview of Alternative Dispute Resolution in Scotland" in S.R Moody and R. E. Mackay, *Alternative Dispute Resolution in Scotland* (W. Green, 1995), pp. 6–8

Party Control over Dispute Resolution

1.3.6 In the majority of ADR procedures the parties exercise some measure of control. The decision to engage in ADR, the process to be adopted, venue, duration and cost, the nature and scope of documentary and other evidence and the range of possible outcomes may all be matters for the parties themselves to decide. The degree of party control will inevitably depend on the nature of the dispute and the ADR procedure applied to that dispute. Parties involved in commercial mediation, for instance, will have the opportunity to exercise much more control over the process than parents referred to family mediation. They may seek advice from an agency providing expertise in ADR but they may vary or veto aspects of the package offered to them by that agency. For example, parties involved in a dispute may decide to submit it to mediation and agree where and when the process will take place. They may accept that each party submits a very limited amount of documentation and agree the order in which parties will present their case and the length of time which they will be allocated so to do.

The only procedural rule of any substance, accepted by the parties in advance, may be that the parties must not interrupt each other and that intemperate language may lead to the premature closure of the mediation. Parties may agree also that the process will include "caucusing" where the ADR neutral confers with each party separately. Issues about confidentiality will also be agreed in advance. A successful outcome may take a wide variety of forms, including financial compensation, payment in kind, deletion, amendment or expansion of contractual terms governing future dealings, security for future compliance, waiver of contractual requirements, the involvement of a trade association as watchdog, an apology or a combination of these solutions. Crucially, of course, ADR does not result in the win/lose dichotomy which characterises litigation but frequently leads to each party incurring both obligations and benefits.

1.3.7 Contrast this with even the most informal of court proceedings where very little will be within the control of the parties. Even trivial matters, like seating arrangements or timetabling of sessions, are entirely outwith the remit of either party. The court decides on the presentation of documentary and oral evidence and sessions are timetabled primarily to fit in with the demands of the administration of justice and not at the convenience of the parties.

The Role of the ADR Neutral

1.3.8 . . . ADR processes involve an additional element, and one which research suggests is crucial to their success, the presence of a neutral third party. The neutral works with the parties to facilitate a solution but usually cannot impose an outcome and has no judicial authority. He or she seeks to assist both parties to reach a mutually acceptable outcome and is not there to represent the interests of one side in the dispute. The neutral's skills lie in encouraging a climate of openness within the ADR process while responding to the parties' desire for confidentiality, exploring the key issues with both parties, identifying obstacles to co-operation and showing the parties alternative ways of viewing the dispute (including the view of the opposing party), providing impetus for the parties to move towards a solution and not to become locked in analysing past discord and assisting in the framing of an agreement which is satisfactory to all the parties. This offers great scope for flexibility and innovation.

1.3.9 The ADR neutral may be known as a mediator, conciliator or facilitator depending on the particular substantive area with which the dispute is concerned and the specific ADR process which is applied. In most ADR procedures the neutral does not adjudicate and has none of the formal, traditional authority enjoyed by judges. The parties may accord neutral parties certain powers in deciding the form of and limits to the preferred ADR process but they do not exercise these as of right. Neither can the neutral invoke legislative provisions or precedent to circumscribe procedure or outcome. On the other hand, the impartiality which characterises the judicial function is essential to the role of the ADR neutral. In most ADR procedures parties may decide whether they wish to involve their legal representatives in the process. The neutral also plays a crucial role in assisting the parties in 'reality testing'. Testing the strengths and weaknesses of one's own and one's opponent's case, with the benefit of input from a neutral expert where required can help bring a sense of realism into the matter and into settlement negotiations. ADR neutrals can be drawn from any discipline or none and be assisted through training and accreditation procedures to develop appropriate skills which can be applied to any kind of dispute.

The Particular Approach of ADR to Dispute Resolution

1.3.10 The emphasis on party control and the inclusion of third party assistance are not simply devices designed to appeal to potential users of ADR processes. They are grounded in a particular approach to dispute resolution at all levels which focuses on generating mutual benefits rather than a stark all or nothing result. The encouragement of communication between the parties, the development of trust, focusing on the future rather than the past, the desire to sustain continuing relationships, the efforts to give parties some autonomy and authority within ADR are all reflections of this underlying ethos. . . .

C. ADR MECHANISMS

A variety of ADR mechanisms are available. These include mediation, mini-trial, summary jury trial, private judging and mediation-arbitration.

M. Upton, "ADR in Perspective" 1993 SLT 75 at pp. 75–76

"Mediation

. . . 'Mediation' is the simplest and most popular form of ADR, whereby the parties lay their arguments before a mediator at a joint session, in the light of which the mediator discusses the matter in confidence with both sides and shuttles between them, until, through his good offices, an agreement is reached—or one side walks out. The mediator's role in the private sessions is to clarify the issues, to play devil's advocate, and to assist the parties to assess the merits of a compromise against the prospects of litigation. . . .

The advantage of using a lawyer as a mediator is that he can assess the strength of the opposing cases. However, views differ over whether a mediator should express his own opinions, rather than simply act as a channel of communication. The terms 'mediation' and 'conciliation' are sometimes used to distinguished such 'evaluative' and merely 'facilitative' processes; unfortunately, there is no agreement over which term equates with which, and in practice 'mediation' and 'conciliation' are synonyms. What matters is that the mediator be clear in his own mind as to the nature of his role, and as to the danger of losing the confidence of one side by associating himself with the other's arguments.

Mini-trial

The 'mini-trial' or 'executive tribunal' assumes that the antagonists are corporate bodies. The tribunal comprises a senior representative from each side (who, ideally, has not been directly involved in the dispute) and a neutral chairman. In US practice, the parties are usually represented by their law agents, who make submissions on both fact and law, whereafter the tribunal retires for private discussion. In practice, the closed session is rarely a judicial conference on the merits of the submissions, but more usually develops into a negotiation mediated by the chairman. It is popular, apparently often successful, and suited for disputes between companies between whom a dispute has blown up at the grass roots but whose executives mutually desire to maintain a working relationship.

Summary jury trial

This is another American concept, similar to a 'mini-trial'; however, the submissions are made to a mock jury of impartial outsiders—often laymen coaxed in from the street. . . . The parties, or senior executives thereof, sit in on the submissions, and the verdict is followed by a mediation session in which the parties' positions are supposedly informed by the jury's 'award'. In practice, it is not successful; unsurprisingly, the 'losing' party dismisses the verdict as a product of the caprice of juries. . . .

Private judging

In ADR, the parties do not submit to the decision of the third party; thus, the hiring of a respected individual to decide a case is truly arbitration. Nevertheless, in America, such 'private-judging' or 'rent-a-judge' has developed in parallel with ADR as an alternative to traditional fora. The parties make brief submissions to their chosen arbiter, who is commonly a retired, or even a practising judge. . . .

Mediation-arbitration

'Med-arb' refers to a process which begins as a conventional mediation, but where a time limit is set for the voluntary discussions; if no agreement is reached, the parties agree that the mediator may then proceed to act as an arbiter, and make a binding award. The extent to which this provides an incentive to settle may be balanced by a reluctance to be as candid with the mediator in the private discussions as the parties might be in a true mediation. . . ."

D. DEVELOPMENT OF ADR IN SCOTLAND

Research conducted by Mays and Clark has demonstrated that there have been a number of initiatives to promote ADR in Scotland (Mays & Clark, *Alternative Dispute Resolution*, Scottish Office Central Research Unit, 1996). For example, in 1987 the Scottish Association of Family Conciliation Services (now Family Mediation Scotland)(FMS) was established to promote and support regional family mediation services in Scotland. In December 1994 the Comprehensive Accredited Lawyer Mediators (CALM) was established by the legal profession to offer mediation in family law issues and at the time of the research, there were 45 accredited lawyer mediators. In addition, commercial mediation initiatives have been taken both by the Faculty of Advocates which set up a panel of 9 accredited advocate mediators in April 1994 and the Law Society of Scotland which promoted established ACCORD to offer solicitor mediator services for commercial disputes (there were 57 solicitor mediators at the time of the Mays and Clark research). Citizens Advice Scotland has also set up a free pilot mediation service for consumer disputes in Edinburgh.

However, aside from the area of family mediation, the research conducted by Mays and Clark has demonstrated that there has been little ADR activity in Scotland. For example, while FMS handled 3,669 case referrals in 1994–95, the 32 ACCORD mediators who responded to the research survey had handled only 17 cases and indeed 24 out of the 32 had had no experience of mediation in practice at all.

The reasons for this are considered further below at pp. 24–25.

E. ADR IN FAMILY DISPUTES

Why then is there such a contrast between the take-up of ADR in the family sphere and other areas? There is no doubt that family mediation schemes (formerly known as conciliation schemes) have been one of the most successful forms of ADR and have been operating in Canada, the United States of America and Australia for some years. England and Wales, too, have seen numerous conciliation schemes established in recent years. In Scotland there are now schemes providing a service in each sheriffdom but not in some of the remoter, rural districts. The oldest scheme, the Lothian Family Conciliation Service, opened its doors in March 1984.

Wright, Matrimonial Conciliation, p. 432

> "Matrimonial conciliation . . . takes as its starting-point the recognition that the marriage has broken down, and then goes on to recognise that there is more to disputed divorce than can be dealt with by ordinary court proceedings between the spouses. The breakdown of the peculiarly close relationship of marriage often produces emotional upset, bitterness and distrust. While some of these features may arise in other disputes, a peculiar feature of divorce is that often a form of contact requires to be maintained after the proceedings are concluded. This is the situation, of course, where children, particularly children under sixteen, are involved. At a time when a party's own emotional

problems have to be faced, the material and emotional needs of his or her children also need attention. Conciliation offers assistance in this situation, in two interrelated ways: first, by helping parties to understand and sort out their feelings; second, by helping parties to reach agreement on all or some of the issues about which they are in dispute.

Conciliation therefore involves both counselling and mediation. The conciliator requires a degree of experience in counselling in the area of personal interaction together with training in the art of mediation. It may well be suggested that a party's own lawyer can fulfil these functions, and indeed this often happens up to a point. But there are several reasons why lawyers are not able to achieve nearly as much along these lines as conciliators, and the experience of conciliation schemes bears this out. First, the individual lawyer is in an adversarial situation—as research shows, his client expects him to fight, not to be conciliatory (although, paradoxically, the same research also shows most clients acknowledging in general terms the need for a more conciliatory approach to the divorce process); second, in any case, the lawyer usually hears only one side of the case in person; third, the lawyer does not have all the necessary training and is not necessarily inclined towards a conciliatory approach; and, finally, the lawyer often does not have the time to spend on conciliation sessions. In many cases, it is understandably difficult for the solicitor to give priority consideration to the interests of the children of the marriage."

Although the following extract was originally written in relation to family conciliation services it is still highly relevant and may be read as if it referred to family mediation as it does demonstrate how family mediation services work.

SAFCOS, "Family [Mediation] Services", p. 187

"**Update on family [mediation].**
Few tasks are less rewarding for a solicitor than dealing with disputes over custody and access. No matter how sensitively a solicitor handles the situation, his professional role is to try to win the case for his client; little can be done to meet the instinctive wish to reach the best outcome for the children. It is likely to be in the children's best interests to achieve a compromise outcome which both parents can accept, and for which they are both responsible. This also serves the client's best interest as he or she will be more likely to abide by an arrangement achieved through agreement. Experience shows clients are more satisfied when solicitors support [mediation].

Family [mediation] is very effective at helping parents to settle arrangements together, especially access. The [mediator] can reframe their opposing positions into common interests as the parties always share the common goal of wanting the best for the children. When this is openly acknowledged, although they may not agree on what is best, compromise can be achieved. By focusing on the children, on future arrangements rather than recriminations on the past, parties can move from their apparently entrenched positions. They can work out arrangements that meet the children's need to continue to have a loving relationship with each of their parents and their need for their parents to stop fighting.

There are now [mediation] services available throughout Scotland, although not in every sheriff court district. Very many solicitors are already referring their clients to the services.

The importance of [mediation] to the children of separating and divorcing parents and its value to the legal profession is recognised. The [Law] Society has agreed with . . . [Family Mediation Scotland (FMS), formerly the] Scottish Association of Family Conciliation Services (SAFCOS) on a code of practice for [mediators] and solicitors. A rule of court has been introduced to enable judges and sheriffs to refer parties to [mediation].

This article emphasises the importance of solicitors to the [mediation] process, gives brief details of the code of practice and rule of court, describes the growth of [mediation] services and the need for resources for further development.

The importance of the solicitor's role

The solicitor's role vis-a-vis [mediation] is crucial. Research shows that where solicitors encourage their clients to attend [mediation] there is a greater likelihood of agreement being reached.

Solicitors also have a vital role to play in referring their clients to [mediation] at as early a stage as possible, before animosity escalates.

Solicitors have the opportunity to explain to their clients that [mediation] is not to be confused with reconciliation, that it is not about getting couples back together again but proceeds on the basis that the relationship is over. People can be advised to contact the service for advice at any stage, even before they have actually separated if, for example, they want advice on how to tell the children they are going to separate. Solicitors can also explain that [mediation] is not about counselling. If clients need long-term in-depth counselling then marriage guidance or other counselling agencies should be recommended, although it can be said that parties might come to the [mediation] service later.

It can be explained by the solicitor that [mediation], in a relatively informal environment with an impartial third party, enables couples to discuss the practical arrangements for their children following separation or divorce. Parties will be encouraged by the [mediator] to focus on their shared interest for the well-being of the children rather than on their disputes.

The main topic discussed in [mediation] is usually access. Research shows that there is a very high success rate in reaching agreement on this issue in [mediation]. Parents are motivated to work towards [mediation] because they want the best for their children. [Mediation] helps them to achieve their own solution rather than having one imposed on them by the court.

New rules of court—referral to family [mediation] services

Judges and sheriffs have been convinced by the success of the family [mediation] services in Scotland. On 9th April [1992] new rules were introduced into the Court of Session and sheriff court to allow the judiciary to refer parties to specified family [mediation] services. Sheriffs will have the power to direct disputing couples to [mediation]; judges in the Court of Session may do this if the parties agree.

A remit to the service will give parties an opportunity to be informed of the benefits to them and to their children of [mediation]. They can then decide whether they wish to use the service or return to the court process. It is intended that the use of the rule will be educative rather than coercive. To force people to [mediate] would be a contradiction in terms. We know from experience elsewhere, for example in Australia and California, that a high proportion of couples attending information sessions on [mediation] subsequently go on to [mediate].

Solicitors are asked to recognise that the [mediation] process may take a few weeks. Time is required to set up appointments and perhaps to try out various options before making a final decision on what seems to be the best arrangement for the family. This need not necessarily disadvantage say a father who has not seen his children for some time and who is trying to re-establish contact. The sheriff may award interim access at the same time as remitting to a [mediation] service. Also the [mediation] service may, for example, enable the couple to restart access during the [mediation] process before final arrangements are made. Family [mediation] can avoid delay in making access arrangements as it can take place while legal aid applications are processed.

Funding of [mediation] services

The services in Scotland are already dealing with about 1,750 referrals a year from all over Scotland and the new rule of court will increase the workload. This will serve to highlight the present piecemeal and unsatisfactory funding of [mediation] throughout Scotland. The national body, [FMS], is 75% funded by the Scottish Office; the services in [the former] Strathclyde and Central Regions are funded under the urban aid programme; and the other services receive very different amounts from their local authorities with grants ranging from a few hundred pounds in Dumfries and Galloway to approximately £49,000 in Lothian.

All services have . . . a paid co-ordinator. This post is full-time only in Fife, Lothian, Strathclyde and Tayside. [Mediators] are paid in areas where there is an adequate budget; in other areas [mediators] are volunteers.

Standards of practice of [mediation] are high in Scotland. All [mediators] are carefully selected according to criteria laid down by [FMS] and trained and/or accredited by [FMS].

In order that all sheriffs may fully use the rule of court [mediation] should be locally available in every sheriff court district. To make this possible far greater resources than are at present made available to the [mediation] services would be required. [FMS] would like to see some sort of block grant system. At present, services have to spend a significant proportion of their time in raising money to top up grants. The quality of service provided throughout Scotland is recognised to be high, but there cannot be a comprehensive spread of services until the funding is placed on a regular basis.

Widespread support for [mediation]

Many judges and sheriffs strongly support [mediation], seeing it as a better way to reach a conclusion on what some of them say can be their most agonising decisions. As one said: 'It is often surprising how the bitterly irreconcilable can come to focus on the best interests of their children, despite their personal antagonisms, when afforded the space, understanding and objectivity which independent [mediation] can provide. Agreements reached by parents are more likely to last and be in the best interests of the children than any solution imposed by a court.'

An impressive list of organisations and individuals in the legal and other professions supports [mediation] and there is political support from MPs in all parties. Support for [mediation] comes from many solicitors who refer clients, from those who have been and are directly involved in steering groups to set up services and also from those who are on management committees to run the services."

More recently research has been conducted into the operation of mediation in family law cases (Lewis, *The Role of Mediation in Family Disputes in Scotland*, Scottish Office Central Research Unit, 1999). Lewis found that mediation could be used successfully in resolving family disputes with oral or written agreement being reached on all the issues in dispute in 57 per cent of the cases involved and on some of the issues in 21 per cent of the cases. In only 22 per cent did mediation end without agreement. She found that issues relating to children were more likely to be agreed than those relating to finances or divorce. However, Lewis found that parties appeared to enter mediation with very little understanding of what would be involved regardless of whether they were referred through the legal system or referred themselves. Most parties referred themselves (53 per cent) with 24 per cent being referred by a solicitor and 22 per cent by sheriffs under Rule of Court 33.22. Interestingly, in cases where parties referred themselves agreement was reached in 66 per cent of the cases whereas if they were referred by solicitors this dropped to 48 per cent and to 43 per cent if referred by the court. Difficulties in mediation identified by Lewis included the degree of control exercised by mediators over the conduct of the mediation, the ability of mediators to redress power imbalances between the parties and arrangements for disclosing abuse and ensuring clients' safety.

There is a considerable amount of evidence that mediation may not be appropriate in cases where there has been abuse or violence in the relationship and hence a power imbalance and may only be acceptable where specialist strategies are deployed by highly trained mediators (see e.g. F.E. Raitt, "Mediation as a Form of Alternative Dispute Resolution—A Rejoinder" (1995) 40 J.L.S. 182; J. Auerbach, *Justice without Law?*, (New York, 1983, ch.5 and conclusion).

For further discussion of conciliation and mediation in Scotland see J. Ross, *The Challenge of Conciliation*, 1987 J.L.S. 457; CRU, *Family Conciliation in Scotland* (Scottish Office: 1990); A. Dick, "Court or Conciliation: War and Peace?", 1991 S.L.T.(News) 209 and Lord Ross, "Family Conciliation: The Child's View and Confidentiality", 1991 J.L.S. 20; Semple, "Mediation as a Form of Alternative Dispute Resolution" (1994) 39 J.L.S. 406; Raitt, "Mediation as a Form of Alternative Dispute Resolution—A Rejoinder" (1995) 40 J.L.S. 182; S. Matheson, "Family Mediation in Scotland" in S.R. Moody & R. E. Mackay, *Alternative Dispute Resolution in Scotland*, W. Green, 1995; J. Lewis, *The Role of*

Mediation in Family Disputes in Scotland (Scottish Office Central Research Unit, 1999). On divorce mediation see L. Parkinson, *Divorce Mediation—The Future*, 1993 J.L.S. 85. On the benefits of lawyer-mediators, see A. Dick and M. Jeffrey, "Lawyer Mediator—Interface or Interloper?", 1995 S.L.T. (News) 305.

F. FUNDING OF ADR IN SCOTLAND

Funding for family mediation services is increasingly a major concern.

B. Clark and R. Mays, "Funding ADR in Scotland" 1997 SLT (News) 29 at pp. 31–32

> "Funding is a major concern for a number of the regional family mediation services affiliated to FMS. These regional bodies, although affiliated to the umbrella organisation FMS, are financially autonomous. The Scottish Office has donated a substantial part of FMS's budget since 1986 and also given grants to Borders, Central, Highland, Tayside and Western Isles affiliated mediation services. The balance of funding for FMS and the regional mediation services is raised through a combination of trust moneys, commercial donations, fees, sales and proceeds from seminars and conferences. . . .
>
> It is clear that the insecure and piecemeal nature of the funding provisions for FMS and the affiliated bodies is a major concern. As a representative of FMS stated: 'funding is a problem for FMS: after 1999 [FMS] don't know what [the] position will be . . . Four affiliated services are in the last year of their Scottish Office grant and others are in their second last year. The two biggest services in Grampian and Strathclyde are facing closure or at least cut-backs to half-time. . . .
>
> . . . FMS are currently examining the possibility of charging for their mediation services, or at least suggesting to participating parties that they pay a donation for the service on trust.
>
> What FMS have been advocating for some time is the establishment of a state sponsored national family mediation service, offering a free mediation service to parties throughout Scotland. . . .
>
> It was recognised, though, that if a state sponsored service were to be established, it would need to be proven that family mediation was a cost effective dispute resolution mechanism . . .".

As we saw above, Lewis' research has demonstrated that family mediation has a fairly high success rate and would appear to be a fairly cost effective dispute resolution mechanism.

It should be noted that legal aid has been made available on a pilot basis for parties using a CALM mediator to resolve their disputes. Although this may lead to a more cost effective deployment of legal aid funds, it has been recognised that there is a danger that mediation might be made a pre-requisite of resorting to litigation in family matters which would effectively deprive parties of an automatic right to litigate (see B. Clark and R. Mays, "Funding ADR in Scotland" 1997 SLT (News) 29 at p. 31). The funding of legal services is considered in more detail in Chapter 12 below.

Funding for commercial mediation is not a problem as parties are expected to bear their own costs. However, for certain other areas such as mediation in consumer disputes and community mediation, funding is a concern.

G. WHERE NEXT FOR ADR IN SCOTLAND?

The research conducted by Mays and Clark (see p. 18 above) suggests that ADR is principally used in family disputes in Scotland. Lewis' research and the extract from SAFCOS above (see pp. 18 and 19 above) suggest that generally ADR is very suitable for family disputes except in cases where there is or has been abuse or violence. It is unclear why ADR has not developed in other areas, for example, commercial and community disputes to the same extent. It is perhaps most surprising that it has not developed to a greater extent in both these areas where there are many of the same factors present as there are in family disputes For example, the parties might wish the dispute to remain private and confidential whereas the court proceedings are public; and they might wish to retain a business—or neighbour—relationship which the win/lose approach of litigation might destroy. Lack of funding may be the problem in the case of community mediation schemes. To date there have only been a small number of pilot schemes including urban aid projects in Dundee and Edinburgh and their future funding remains uncertain (see R. Mackay and A. Brown, *Community Mediation in Scotland*, Scottish Office Central Research Unit, 1999). In commercial disputes, however, funding is not likely to be such an issue as the parties would be expected to pay their own costs.

Several factors for the lack of development of ADR outside the family sphere may be relevant. At least until recently ADR had not featured widely on the curricula of Scottish Law Schools—the exceptions being the Universities of Dundee and Strathclyde. New entrants to the profession might therefore be unaware of the potential for ADR in a range of disputes. Existing lawyers might also be unwilling to refer disputes to ADR because it is something new and because there is little evidence about how successful it can be. Likewise clients might perceive that they are being asked to act as "guinea pigs" and hence be reluctant to try ADR. There might also be an entrenched adversarial culture amongst lawyers (and possibly also their clients to an extent) with use of ADR being seen as a weak option.

Publication of research by the Scottish Office Central Research Unit into the operation of ADR in various sectors should assist in providing existing lawyers with evidence that ADR can be successful (see e.g. J. Lewis, *The Role of Mediation in Family Disputes in Scotland*, (Scottish Office Central Research Unit, 1999) and R. Mackay and A. Brown, *Community Mediation in Scotland—A Study of Implementation*, (Scottish Office Central Research Unit, 1999). Greater emphasis on ADR in university law school curricula may also encourage a move towards a legal culture which is more willing to embrace ADR. More publicity about ADR for potential litigants might also assist. To that end, Scottish Courts Administration has published a free booklet entitled "Resolving Disputes Without Going to Court" which attempts to explain to members of the public what alternatives there are for resolving a dispute without the need to go to court. It provides an introductory guide to community and business mediation, trade association conciliation, arbitration schemes, employment disputes, ombudsmen and regulator schemes as well as family disputes.

A number of other problems remain to be overcome before ADR has a wider role to play in Scotland. These include regulation of standards of ADR practitioners to ensure consistently high standards, and confidentiality of ADR proceedings. As Clark and Mays' research (see pp. 22 and 23 above) has noted, security of funding appears to be essential. While this is not a significant issue in relation to commercial disputes where organisations would be expected to meet their own expenses, it is clearly a problem in relation to family, consumer and community disputes. However, provision of legal aid for parties in using ADR to resolve such disputes brings its own problems (see p. 23 above).

Furthermore, given the whole approach of ADR is voluntary it would be highly inappropriate for it to be made compulsory in any way. The present court rules in relation to family matters which enable the sheriff court to refer parties to mediation and the Court of Session to refer parties with their consent are probably satisfactory and no further powers are required by the courts. It is noteworthy that cases referred to mediation by the sheriff court were significantly less likely to result in agreement than those where the parties themselves opted to try out ADR (see above p. 22). This suggests that the powers of the sheriff court in this regard perhaps even go too far and that the consent of the parties should be required as in the Court of Session. Provision of additional information about ADR in the courts would be beneficial but it would defeat the whole purpose of ADR if the courts had a general power to direct parties to ADR without their consent. It is also questionable whether legal aid for litigation should be made dependent upon parties trying out ADR as a prerequisite as this would undermine a party's right to bring a dispute before the courts and hence access to a remedy.

M. Upton, "ADR in Perspective" 1993 S.L.T.(News) 75 at p. 79

> "There is no right without a remedy. A remedy postponed by a court that declines to hear you until you have hired a mediator and submitted to his ministrations is a remedy denied. A remedy denied is a right denied. What is being advanced from some quarters is the paternalistic idea that the state—in the form of the court—should be able to require litigants to assert their rights only in a reasonable way. That is to say that people cannot be trusted with the prerogative of asserting their rights at their own option."

ADR should also not be seen as a panacea for all disputes. It has already been pointed out that ADR may be inappropriate in family cases where there is a power imbalance resulting from abuse or violence. In the criminal sphere also, although mediation may be appropriate between a victim and an offender in cases of vandalism or petty theft, it would not appear suitable for cases involving violence against persons. It would also be inappropriate in cases where an interdict was required to preserve the status quo pending the ascertainment of the respective rights of the parties or where a party was seeking to assert a right, for example, to housing from a local authority under the Housing (Scotland) Act 1987.

On ADR generally, see M. Upton, "ADR in Perspective", 1993 S.L.T. (News) 75; A. Bevan, "ADR: The Story Since 1989" 1993 S.L.T. (News) 80; the *Modern Law Review Special Issue on Dispute Resolution* (1993) 56 M.L.R. 277; S.R. Moody and R. E. Mackay, *Greens Guide to Alternative Dispute Resolution in Scotland* (W. Green, 1995); R. Mays and B. Clark, "Alternative Dispute Resolution and the Courts" (1997) 2 SLPQ 57.

CHAPTER 2

THE SHERIFF COURT

I. STRUCTURE AND ADMINISTRATION

Courts are normally classified according to their powers, their area of operation or the types of case they are permitted to handle. As the Grant Report observed (p. 7) the principal distinguishing features of the sheriff court are that it is local, it is presided over by professional judges and it has an extensive jurisdiction in both civil and criminal cases as well as possessing a wide range of administrative functions.

While the history of the court stems back to the 12th century its structure and administration in modern times is controlled by the Sheriff Courts (Scotland) Acts of 1907 and 1971. Thus, Scotland is now divided into six sheriffdoms which largely consist of groupings of local authority areas. The sheriffdoms are (1) Grampian, Highland and Islands; (2) Tayside, Central and Fife; (3) Lothian and Borders; (4) Glasgow and Strathkelvin; (5) North Strathclyde; and (6) South Strathclyde, Dumfries and Galloway. The six sheriffdoms are subdivided into sheriff court districts of which there are currently 49, each of which has its own sheriff court building (see also http://www.scotcourts.gov.uk/). Each sheriffdom has a sheriff principal who in addition to his judicial duties is under a duty "to secure the speedy and efficient disposal of business in the sheriff courts of that sheriffdom" (Sheriff Courts (Scotland) Act 1971, s. 15).

In addition to sheriffs principal there are 112 or so full-time sheriffs who act as the judges at first instance in the sheriffdoms. They are usually appointed to serve in a particular sheriff court district although there are a number of floating sheriffs. There are also a large number of temporary sheriffs (see also Chapter 8). Sheriffs, too, have wide-ranging administrative duties.

As a result of the devolution arrangements introduced by the Scotland Act 1998, the Secretary of State for Scotland's responsibility for the staffing, overall organisation and administration of the sheriff court has been transferred to the Scottish Ministers. In pursuance of this responsibility they may create or abolish sheriffdoms and sheriff court districts or alter their boundaries. They may also create temporary sheriffs and sheriffs principal or transfer sheriffs from one sheriffdom to another if this is required by illness, pressure of business or other like cause. In fact, since 1971 the functions now exercised by the Scottish Ministers in this area have been delegated to a civil service department known as Scottish Courts Administration (see also http://www.scotcourts.gov.uk/). A further body, the Sheriff Courts Rules Council, which consists of sheriffs principal, sheriffs, sheriff clerks, practitioners in the sheriff court and consumer representatives is responsible for monitoring the operation of procedure and practice in civil proceedings in the court and for suggesting reforms.

II. CIVIL JURISDICTION

The civil jurisdiction of the sheriff court—those cases which it has the power to try and dispose of—is unusually wide for a local (or inferior) court.

D. Manson-Smith, *The Legal System of Scotland*, H.M.S.O., 1995, pp. 17–18

"4.1 The sheriff court deals with the bulk of civil litigation in Scotland. It is a local court, presided over by the sheriff who is a legally-qualified judge and exercises a very wide jurisdiction. . . . In common law, the sheriff is 'judge ordinary of the bounds', that is, the judge with jurisdiction in all cases arising in his or her sheriffdom that are not allocated to other courts. The sheriff court also deals with appeals from, or review of, many local authority and administrative decisions, for example, licensing appeals. . . .

The sheriff court has exclusive jurisdiction in actions for sums of £1,500 or less and in many statutory applications and appeals. The value of the subject matter that the court may deal with has, with very few exceptions, no upper limit, and a wide range of remedies may be granted."

For a civil court to have jurisdiction in a particular case it must (a) have authority over the defender, or the subjects in respect of which the remedy is sought, (b) have the power to grant the remedy sought, and (c) have the power to entertain the cause in question.

A. AUTHORITY OVER DEFENDER OR SUBJECT MATTER

This is primarily a geographical limitation on the courts' powers. The general rule is that a case must be raised in the forum of the defender. This is partly an equitable requirement and partly a pragmatic one. Scottish courts are reluctant to grant a decree which is unenforceable. (See *Ford v. Bell Chandler*, 1977 S.L.T. (Sh.Ct.) 90.)

Sheriff Courts (Scotland) Act 1907, s. 4

"4. *Jurisdiction*.—The jurisdiction of the sheriffs, within their respective sheriffdoms, shall extend to and include all navigable rivers, ports, harbours, creeks, shores, and anchoring grounds in or adjoining such sheriffdoms. And the powers and jurisdictions formerly competent to the High Court of Admiralty in Scotland in all [civil] maritime causes and proceedings . . . including such as may apply to persons furth of Scotland, shall be competent to the sheriffs, provided the defender shall upon any legal ground of jurisdiction be amenable to the jurisdiction of the sheriff before whom such cause or proceeding may be raised . . . Provided always that where sheriffdoms are separated by a river, firth, or estuary, the sheriffs on either side shall have concurrent jurisdiction over the intervening space occupied by water."

Domicile and Matrimonial Proceedings Act 1973, s. 8(2)

"8.—(2) The court shall have jurisdiction to entertain an action for separation [or separation and aliment or divorce] if (and only if)—

(a) either party to the marriage in question—
   (i) is domiciled in Scotland at the date when the action is begun, or
   (ii) was habitually resident there throughout the period of one year ending with that date; and
(b) either party to the marriage—
   (i) was resident in the sheriffdom for a period of forty days ending with that date, or
   (ii) had been resident in the sheriffdom for a period of not less than forty days ending not more than forty days before the said date, and had no known residence in Scotland at that date."

The sheriff court has jurisdiction in actions of declarator of death under the Presumption of Death (Scotland) Act 1977, s. 1(4), which contains provisions on the lines of s. 8(2).

In other cases the position is governed by the Civil Jurisdiction and Judgments Acts 1982 and 1991. The former Act gives effect to the E.C. (Brussels) Conventions on jurisdiction and the enforcement of judgments in civil and commercial matters. The latter Act implements the closely paralleling Lugano Convention which extends essentially the same jurisdiction and enforcement rules to those E.F.T.A. countries which choose to ratify it. (The Conventions do not cover status, matrimonial property rights, succession, bankruptcy, liquidation, social security, arbitration, revenue or administrative cases.) Nowadays defenders are subject to four slightly different sets of rules on jurisdiction, although the basic rule that the case must follow the defender is still retained. Defenders domiciled in the territory of a contracting E.F.T.A. state whose cases fall within the Lugano Convention are governed by Schedule 1 to the 1991 Act. Defenders from other E.C. countries whose cases fall within the Brussels Conventions are governed by Schedule 1 of the 1982 Act, similarly placed defenders from other U.K. countries are governed by Schedule 4 to the 1982 Act and defenders in all other cases except those relating to status, capacity, custody, liquidation/sequestration, admiralty matters, commissary proceedings and appeals/review of tribunal decisions are governed by Schedule 7 to the 1982 Act.

In essence all defenders covered by the Acts may be sued in the courts for the place where they are resident and with which they have a substantial connection. In addition they may be sued in a particular sheriff court:

(1) if the case relates to a contract which is to be performed within the jurisdiction of that court;
(2) if the case relates to delict or quasi-delict and the harmful event took place within the jurisdiction of that court;
(3) if the case relates to a civil claim for damages arising from events which are the subject of criminal proceedings before that court:
(4) if the case relates to maintenance and the maintenance creditor is habitually resident within the jurisdiction of that court or if the matter is ancillary to proceedings relating to status and that court has jurisdiction under the Domicile and Matrimonial Proceedings Act 1973;
(5) if the case arises out of the operations of a branch, agency or other establishment located within the jurisdiction of that court;

(6) if there are a number of defenders and one of them is resident and has substantial ties with a place within the jurisdiction of that court;
(7) if the case is a counter claim arising from the same contract or facts which have given rise to a case which is pending before that court;
(8) if the case relates to the ownership or tenancy of immoveable property which is situated within the jurisdiction of that court;
(9) if the defenders have prorogated, *i.e.* accepted, the jurisdiction of that court by express agreement or by entering appearance before the court to oppose the action;
(10) if the case relates to a consumer contract completed in Scotland and the consumer or the defender resides in, and has substantial ties with a place within the jurisdiction of that court.

In cases where Schedule 7 applies defenders may also be sued in a particular sheriff court:

(1) if they have no fixed residence and they have been personally cited within the jurisdiction of that court;
(2) if they have no fixed residence in the United Kingdom and moveable property belonging to them has been arrested, or they own moveable property situated within the jurisdiction of that court;
(3) if the proceedings relate to moveable property situated within the jurisdiction of that court;
(4) if the proceedings are for interdict and it is alleged that the wrong is likely to be committed within the jurisdiction of that court;
(5) if the proceedings concern a debt secured over immoveable property situated within the jurisdiction of that court.

For further details on the history and intention of the 1982 Act see the Report of the Scottish Committee on Jurisdiction and Enforcement (H.M.S.O.: 1980). For a further exposition of the provisions of the Acts see A.E. Anton and P. Beaumont, *Civil Jurisdiction in Scotland: the Brussels and Lugano Conventions* (W. Green & Son: 2nd, ed 1995).

The geographical limitations contained within these provisions are not as restrictive as they may appear. Sheriffs acting under the Sheriff Courts (Scotland) Act 1907, Schedule 1, rule 26.1 may, upon cause shown, remit a case to another sheriff court.

Wilson v. Hay 1977 S.L.T. (Sh. Ct.) 52

SHERIFF PRINCIPAL REID: "I respectfully adopt the view expressed in Fyfe on Sheriff Court Practice, para. 154: 'The theory of the transfer rules seems to be that the whole Sheriff Courts of Scotland are to be regarded practically as one system, that the hard and fast jurisdiction rules which have hitherto prevailed are to be relaxed, and that a Sheriff Court cause, in whatever district it is initiated, may be tried in that Sheriff Court which affords the maximum of convenience, at the minimum of expense, to all concerned.' . . . Rule 20 [the predecessor of the current rule 26.1] is expressed in terms sufficiently wide to enable causes to be transferred between courts having concurrent jurisdiction: or from a court having no jurisdiction to a court possessing jurisdiction; or vice versa (cf. Dobie, *Sheriff*

Court Practice, p. 45) . . . . It is hardly necessary to say that it is essential that either the transferring court or the court to which the cause is transferred should have jurisdiction over the defender. Otherwise, the matter is one for the sheriff's discretion."

B. POWER TO GRANT THE REMEDY

Sheriffs can grant a number of remedies. These include: petitory remedies (*e.g.* for payment, delivery or implement of a contract), actions of declarator (except declarators of marriage or nullity of marriage, and actions the direct or main object of which is to determine the personal status of individuals), actions for damages, possessory actions, suspensions and interdicts. (See the Sheriff Courts (Scotland) Act 1907, s. 5.) However, sheriffs cannot grant the remedy of reduction which is exclusive to the Court of Session (*Brown v. Hamilton District Council* 1983 S.C. (H.L.) 1).

C. POWER TO ENTERTAIN THE CAUSE

On policy grounds it is commonplace for the inferior courts in a country to be denied the more important cases. The sheriff court is unusual in this respect, since it has considerable breadth of jurisdiction. Some causes may only be heard in the sheriff court. These are its privative or exclusive jurisdiction. Thus, under the Sheriff Courts (Scotland) Act 1907, s. 7 (as amended by the Privative Jurisdiction and Summary Cause Order 1988, S.I. No. 1993):

> "All causes not exceeding one thousand five hundred pounds in value exclusive of interest and expenses competent in the sheriff court shall be brought and followed forth in the sheriff court only, and shall not be subject to review by the Court of Session:. . .".

The privative jurisdiction limit of the sheriff court is currently under review. The Scottish Courts Administration consultation paper, *Proposals to Increase Jurisdiction Limits in the Sheriff Court (including Privative Jurisdiction Limit)* (1998) canvasses views on raising the privative jurisdiction limit to £3,000, £5,000, £10,000, £15,000, £20,000 or even £50,000. This would potentially result in a considerable number of relatively low value cases being removed from the Court of Session, hence freeing up more of its time to deal with higher value, more complex cases. Of course, the fact a case is of low value does not necessarily mean that it is without legal complexity. Although the power exists to remit cases to the Court of Session (see below) it cannot be used to remit cases which fall within the privative jurisdiction (see Sheriff Court (Scotland) Act 1971, s.37(1)(b)).

Again, the sheriff court alone can entertain actions for summary removing (eviction from heritable property) and sequestration for non-payment of rent.

Duncan v. Lodjensky (1904) 6 F. 408

LORD MCLAREN: "I never heard of an action of sequestration for rent being brought in the Court of Session. In the institutional writers reference is made to a class of actions in which the Judge Ordinary of the bounds has privative jurisdiction. It is hardly necessary to give instances, but there is a class of cases which are only competent in the Sheriff Court, and in which an action brought to the Court of Session would be dismissed as incompetent. The general character of such cases is that they relate to questions as to property within the sheriffdom in which there is a necessity for immediate decision, such, for example, as warrants for the sale of a pledge or for the sale of perishable articles when the right of possession is disputed. There can be no doubt that cases between the landlord and tenant of property situated within the Sheriff's territory have always been regarded as specially suited for decision in the Sheriff Court."

On the other hand there are remarkably few areas where the jurisdiction of the sheriff court is now excluded. The principal exclusion long related to actions affecting personal status. However, divorce actions (Divorce Jurisdiction, Court Fees and Legal Aid (Scotland) Act 1983) and declarator of death actions (Presumption of Death (Scotland) Act 1977) have become competent in the sheriff courts. Indeed, the great majority of divorce actions are now brought in the sheriff courts rather than the Court of Session (which formerly had exclusive jurisdiction in such cases). Thus in 1983 90% of family actions were heard in the Court of Session and only 10% in the sheriff court. By 1988 the ratio had been more than reversed with 7% in the Court of Session and 93% in the sheriff court. Somewhat anomalously there are still certain actions affecting personal status which are privative to the Court of Session.

Court of Session Act 1830, s. 33

> "33. All actions of declarator of marriage, and of nullity of marriage, and all actions of declarator of legitimacy and of bastardy . . . shall be competent to be brought and insisted on only before the Court of Session."

Secondly, petitions for the liquidation of a limited company with a paid up share capital exceeding £120,000 can only be heard in the Court of Session (Companies Act 1985, s. 515).

The Grant Report, p. 24

> "Also exclusive to the Court of Session are actions of reduction, actions for proving the tenor of lost documents, adjudications and inhibitions. There are also some actions which are exclusive to courts other than the Court of Session: thus, the Court of the Lord Lyon deals with questions of right to bear arms, the Lands Valuation Appeal Court with appeals against rateable valuations, and the Restrictive Practices Court with monopolistic practices."

These limitations apart, the sheriff court has a broad-ranging concurrent or overlapping jurisdiction with the Court of Session. Thus in contrast with the position in the English county court, there are no financial limits to the cases which a sheriff may hear (with the sole exception of certain liquidation petitions, as we have seen.) Cases worth over a million pounds have been brought before the court. The Grant Committee considered whether such limits should be imposed but decided against the change. As the Committee noted, "the importance and difficulty of an action need not be directly related to the sum sued for." What was needed, they felt, was a flexible remit procedure between the sheriff court and the Court of Session.

The rules governing remits from the sheriff court to the Court of Session were eventually simplified under s.16 of the Law Reform (Miscellaneous Provisions) (Scotland) Act 1980 which amended s.37 of the Sheriff Courts (Scotland) Act 1971. Section 37(1)(b) now permits a sheriff to remit a case on the motion of one of the parties "if he is of the opinion that the importance or difficulty of the cause make it appropriate to do so." See *Mullan v. Anderson* 1993 S.L.T. 835. Only if the action relates to parental responsibilities or rights in relation to a child or guardianship or adoption may the sheriff remit the action of his own accord (Sheriff Courts (Scotland) Act 1971, s.37(2A) as amended by the Children (Scotland) Act 1995). Under section 44 of the Crown Proceedings Act 1947, proceedings raised against the Crown in the sheriff court must be remitted to the Court of Session if the Lord Advocate certifies that the proceedings may involve an important question of law, or may be decisive of other cases, or are for other reasons more fit for trial in the Court of Session.

It is unclear whether the flexibility which the Grant Report was seeking has been achieved. The reforms abolished the power of either party to insist that a case be remitted and restricted the freedom of sheriffs to remit a case of their own accord.

The provisions as to remits raise the longstanding question as to whether the division of labour between the sheriff court and the Court of Session is a rational one. This is not a question that appears to have received much attention in recent years in Scotland (with the exception of the legislative decision to restrict judicial review to the Court of Session) although the English county court has been the subject of numerous reviews. In each, the jurisdiction of the county court has been expanded—though it remains considerably narrower than that of the sheriff court. In the light of the most recent developments concerning status actions it must be questionable whether the sheriff court should not now have parallel jurisdiction with the Court of Session in all status actions.

The Court of Session has made it clear that where actions are raised in that court which should, because of the size of the awards sought and the straightforwardness of the action, more appropriately have been raised in the sheriff court; then the expenses awarded will be modified to the ordinary sheriff court scale. See *Smith v. British Rail Engineering Ltd.*, 1985 S.L.T. 463, *McPherson v. British Railways Board*, 1985 S.L.T. 467, *Banks v. D.R.G. plc*, 1988 S.L.T. 825 and *McIntosh v. British Railways Board (No. 1)*, 1990 S.L.T. 637.

The sheriff court may now also refer devolution issues (see Chapter 4, p. 9 for a definition) to the Inner House of the Court of Session for determination (Scotland Act 1998, Sched. 6, para. 7; see Chapter 3, pp. 20 and 21).

III. PROCEDURE AND CASELOAD

A. ORDINARY CAUSE PROCEDURE

1. Scope of Ordinary Procedure

There are now four procedures in civil sheriff court cases, the ordinary, summary cause, small claims (technically a form of summary cause) and summary application procedure. The latter is dealt with in section V, Miscellaneous and Administrative Functions below. The great majority of types of actions which are competent within the sheriff court must be raised under the ordinary procedure. Such actions are heard by a sheriff sitting on his or her own or (occasionally) with an assessor. Civil jury trials are no longer competent in the sheriff court. The range of ordinary actions is considerable. It extends from actions for payment or delivery in excess of £1,500 to racial discrimination cases (outside the field of employment), from succession to copyright and from landlord and tenant (*e.g. Holiday Flat Co. v. Kuczera*, 1978 S.L.T. (Sh. Ct.) 47) to contravention of lawburrows. Lawburrows is a remedy akin to requiring caution for good behaviour. If a defender who has been ordained to find caution does any harm of the kind specified in the original application, a civil action of contravention of lawburrows can be raised against him. See W. J. Stewart, "Lawburrows: Elegant Remedy or Absurd Form", 1988 S.L.T. (News) 181 and the case of *Morrow v. Neil*, below. Divorce actions must also be raised under the ordinary procedure, but where (1) the divorce is evidenced by separation (whether for two or five years), (2) there are no children of the marriage under 16 and (3) no financial claims, a simplified "do-it-yourself" procedure may be used.

TABLE 2.1

Number of ordinary causes initiated and disposed of by nature of action, and whether the action was defended, during 1997

			Defended actions				
Nature of Action	Initiated during year	For pursuer undefended	Defended	Dismissal	Absolviter	Remits	Total
Aliment (Child)	41	9	16	4	1	–	30
Aliment (Spouse)	80	7	25	24	–	–	56
Aliment (Top-up)	3	–	2	1	1	–	4
Custody	1,127	260	336	231	14	–	841
Damages	1,101	134	64	38	295	–	531
Debt	20,607	12,858	1,191	826	1,698	4	16,577
Delivery	1,256	851	53	43	35	–	982
Divorce	8,038	6,100	1,132	301	7	–	7,540
Furthcoming	98	40	3	5	3	–	51
Interdict	2,442	750	149	208	44	1	1,152
Land/Heritable	994	707	72	51	50	1	881
Mortgage Lender	5,381	4,065	159	55	26	–	4,305
Other	1,482	255	216	325	64	–	860
Personal Injury	1,698	77	73	76	612	3	841
Variation of Court of Session Decree	18	8	9	1	–	–	18
Grand Total	44,366	26,121	3,500	2,189	2,850	9	34,669

[Source: Scottish Courts Administration, *Civil Judicial Statistics* 1997, table 3.7.]

Table 2.1 reflects a pattern which has held true for many years, namely, that money claims, and debt actions in particular, predominate. There are, however, substantial numbers of divorce actions and mortgage lender cases. The high proportion of ordinary debt actions which are unopposed reveals that even under the ordinary cause procedure debt actions are largely "administrative" (*i.e.* a rubber-stamp en route to diligence) rather than adversarial in character.

2. The New Ordinary Cause Rules

In the last decade the number of ordinary actions raised in the sheriff courts has more than doubled, largely because of the transfer in divorce jurisdiction. The increase led to a major reconsideration of the ordinary cause procedure designed to eliminate unnecessary delays, complexity and expense. The result was the introduction of new Ordinary Cause Rules from 1st January 1994 (SI 1993 No. 1956).

Sheriff Court Rules Council, "The New Ordinary Cause Rules" 1993 JLS 334

> "The policy developed by the Rules Council as the result of their research and the consultation process was that:
>
> (a) cases should call in court only when necessary;
> (b) the number of callings should be kept to a minimum;
> (c) rules should prescribe periods for completion of the various stages of the procedure;
> (d) control and management of cases should be vested in the court rather than leaving the parties free to litigate at their own pace;
> (e) procedures of the Court of Session and the Sheriff Court should be harmonised wherever possible."

The new rules lay down a fixed timetable within which adjustments to pleadings are to be made. The first calling in court is a new procedural hearing called the Options Hearing. It is usually fixed for a time 13 weeks after the receipt by the sheriff clerk of a Notice of Intention to Defend. At this hearing the sheriffs are given a new interventionist role in deciding on the future progress of the case: "At the Options Hearing the sheriff shall seek to secure the expeditions progress of the cause by ascertaining from the parties the matters in dispute . . ." (Rule 9.12(1)). The new rules also provide for sanctions for parties failing to meet the timetable. The principal aim is to reduce delay and the number of times a case calls in court.

Scottish Courts Administration commissioned research to make an evaluative comparison between ordinary procedures prior to the implementation of the new rules (see S. Morris, D. Headrick, *Pilgrim's Progress? Defended Actions in the Sheriff's Ordinary Court*, Central Research Unit, 1995) and after their implementation (see E. Samuel & R. Bell, *Defended Ordinary Actions in the Sheriff Court: Implementing Ordinary Cause Rules 1993*, Central Research Unit, 1995). The 1995 research found that on balance the new rules had been successful in reducing delays in most cases although this occurred principally because of the fixed period for adjustment. The new rules had also reduced the number of court appearances in most cases. For example the average length of defended actions reduced from 48 weeks to 41 weeks. Furthermore, in only 4% of cases where defences were lodged were Options Hearings called more than twice compared to 57% of cases calling more than twice on the adjustment roll prior to the implementation of the new rules. However, the 1995 research also found that some of the policy objectives for the new rules did not support each other. In particular, it found that by reducing the number of times a case calls in court, the opportunities for the court to control and manage the case were also reduced. The new rules also did not always result in reduced delays because practitioners often used court hearings to expedite the progress of cases and, with reduced opportunities for hearings, delays might actually increase. The research also found that the Options Hearings had not been as effective as anticipated, particularly in relation to family cases and recommended that procedures needed to be put in place to ensure that cases were effectively handled after the Options Hearing as there was no fixed timetable at present after that hearing.

However, other factors, particularly the new "pay as you go" fee structure for the sheriff court may have contributed to the number of times cases called in court. Indeed the 1995 research noted that in 1994, the first full year of the new fee structure as well as the new rules, the number of ordinary actions initiated dropped by over 20%.

3. Appeals

Sheriff Courts (Scotland) Act 1907, ss. 27–29

> "27. Appeal to sheriff principal—Subject to the provisions of this Act an appeal to the sheriff principal shall be competent against all final judgments of the sheriff and also against interlocutors—
>
> (a) Granting or refusing interdict, interim or final;
> (b) Granting interim decree for payment of money other than a decree for expenses, or making an order *ad factum praestandum*;
> (c) Sisting an action;
> (d) Allowing or refusing or limiting the mode of proof;
> (e) Refusing a reponing note; or
> (f) Against which the sheriff either *ex proprio motu* or on the motion of any party grants leave to appeal."

In addition to section 27 there is a general right of appeal to the sheriff principal against an interlocutor of the sheriff which is incompetent.

> "28. Appeal to the Court of Session—(1) Subject to the provisions of this Act, it shall be competent to appeal to the Court of Session against a judgment either of a sheriff principal or a sheriff if the interlocutor appealed against is a final judgment; or is an interlocutor—
>
> (a) Granting interim decree for payment of money other than a decree for expenses; or
> (b) Sisting an action; or

(c) Refusing a reponing note; or
(d) Against which the sheriff principal or sheriff, either *ex proprio motu* or on the motion of any party, grants leave to appeal."

In addition, there is a general right in the Court of Session to intervene in respect of any incompetent or irregular proceedings in the sheriff court, or failure by a sheriff principal or sheriff to exercise jurisdiction, or excess of jurisdiction by the sheriff court.

"29. Effect of appeal—An appeal shall be effectual to submit to review the whole of the interlocutors pronounced in the cause . . . "

These provisions create two alternative routes of appeal from a sheriff's decision, one to the Inner House of the Court of Session direct, the other to the Inner House by way of the sheriff principal. There is a further appeal on points of law to the House of Lords.

TABLE 2

Appeal from sheriffs 1996

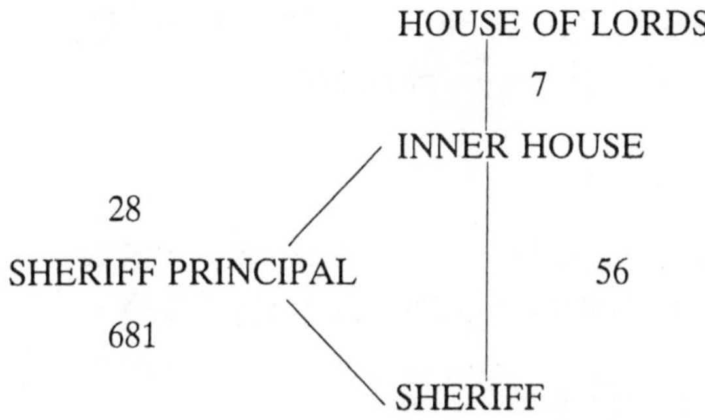

[Source: Scottish Courts Administration, *Civil Judicial Statistics* Scotland 1996]

For examples of appeals from a sheriff reaching the House of Lords by way of a sheriff principal and the Inner House, see *R.H.M. Bakeries Ltd. v. Strathclyde Regional Council*, 1985 S.L.T. 214 and *Laing v. Scottish Grain Distillers Ltd.*, 1992 S.L.T. 435.

The Grant Report, pp. 104–105

"Appeals
347. No one denied that the appeal to the sheriff principal is cheap, quick and popular. Some, however, suggested that apparent advantages of the appeal are in fact defects. Cheapness may be achieved by the appeal being conducted by the solicitor who handled the case at first instance. Also, it was argued that the appeal is rather too convenient, and that there is something to be said for making an appeal difficult when judgment has been given by a competent court. The main objection we heard was that it is wrong in principle that an appeal should lie from a single judge to a single judge . . . We were also told that the appeal grew up by accident, that it makes

possible an undesirable multiplicity of appeals,—and that by diverting appeals from the Court of Session it deprives the sheriff courts of guidance that they should receive from the Supreme Court. It was suggested that an appellate decision should have wider currency than that of the sheriff principal, which is valid only within the sheriffdom . . .

348. While recognising the theoretical defects of the appeal to the sheriff principal, we are of the opinion that it has worked well, is undeniably popular, and should if possible be retained. It is cheaper than an appeal to the Court of Session because it can be conducted by a solicitor, there is no necessity to print or duplicate papers, and travelling expenses to Edinburgh are avoided since the appeal is almost invariably heard locally. The time taken to dispose of an appeal in the sheriff court is somewhat shorter than in the Court of Session. The popularity of the appeal to the sheriff principal particularly in interlocutory matters, is self-evident; over ten times as many appeals are taken from sheriffs to sheriffs principal as from sheriffs to the Court of Session, and less than one-tenth of the appellate decisions of sheriffs principal are further appealed. We are impressed by the fact that almost all of our witnesses favoured the retention, in some form or other, of the appeal to the sheriff principal."

B. SUMMARY CAUSE PROCEDURE

1. Outline

Summary causes are regulated by the Sheriff Courts (Scotland) Act 1971, ss. 35–38 and by Act of Sederunt (Summary Cause Rules, Sheriff Court) 1976 (S.I. 1976 No. 476 (S. 44)) (as amended).

The Hughes Commission, p. 174

"11.11 The present summary cause procedure in the sheriff court was introduced in 1976 in the light of the recommendations of the Grant Committee. The main purpose of its introduction was to provide a procedure that was both efficient and cheap. The summary cause does not normally involve written pleadings and the lengthy procedure of adjustment that goes with the ordinary cause; there is no recording of evidence at the hearing itself. In most actions for the payment of money, the procedures can easily be carried through without the parties being required to appear in court—a considerable advantage in preventing loss of wages and travelling expenses. Appearance is required only when the action is defended, or when there is some dispute about the method of payment. Broadly speaking, the actions which may be brought by the summary cause procedure include most consumer claims, actions by corporate bodies for the recovery of debts, claims for the recovery of heritable property (for example repossession by commercial landlords or local authorities following non-payment of rent) and claims for damages where the sum involved does not exceed [£1,500]. The rules setting out the procedure and forms are complex and extend to some fifty pages."

Act of Sederunt (Summary Cause Rules, Sheriff Court) 1976, r. 17

"*Representation*

17.—(1) Except as hereinafter provided a party who does not elect to conduct his own cause shall be represented by an advocate or solicitor.

(2) A party shall be entitled to be represented by a person other than an advocate or solicitor at the first calling of a summary cause, and, unless the court at that calling otherwise directs, at any subsequent diet where the cause is not defended on the merits or on the amount of sum due:

Provided that the court in that cause is satisfied that the person is a suitable representative and is duly authorised to represent the party."

Section 37 of the Sheriff Courts (Scotland) Act 1971 confers powers on sheriffs in certain circumstances to remit cases from the ordinary to the summary cause and vice versa.

2. Problems With Summary Cause Procedure

The limits on the type of case which can be raised under the summary cause procedure are such that the overwhelming majority of summary cause actions raised since its introduction in 1976 have been debt related. Most have been straightforward debt actions with almost a quarter relating to the non-payment of rent. Despite the provision for lay representation, in the great majority of summary cause actions the defender is unrepresented and no defence is entered. Unsurprisingly, over 90% of pursuers are public utilities or businesses with the great bulk of defenders being individuals. It follows that the summary cause procedure is even more administrative in character than the ordinary procedure.

Central Research Unit, "Debt Recovery", pp. 53–54

"6.11 . . . The court stage is largely an administrative procedure, and this is highlighted by the fact that in most cases the defender did not dispute the claim against him; only a small portion of cases went to proof (less than 1 per cent of summary cause payment actions) or were continued for several callings (4 per cent of summary cause payment actions continued at the first calling) thereby indicating an element of dispute about liability or delay in coming to an arrangement for payment for some reason or other. The majority of actions were undefended and only 3 per cent of defenders in summary cause payment actions were represented in court and only 8 per cent of pursuers.

6.12 . . . However, the court stage, from the delivery of the summons to the defender to the granting of decree, appears to play an important constructive role in the process of debt recovery as well as being the legal precursor of the doing of diligence. The court stage does this mainly by acting as a channel of, or spur to, communication between the debtor and creditor. The raising of court action itself may result in full settlement of the debt to the pursuer or may encourage the debtor to make an informal instalment arrangement for repayment; this is generally the background to the relatively large number of actions which were dismissed following receipt of the summons by the defender (30 per cent). It also may stimulate the resolution of disputes about, *e.g.* the amount owed, or defective goods and services."

The cheap and efficient procedure favoured by the Grant Committee simply transformed the sheriff court into a streamlined debt-collecting agency. This exactly replicated the experience in the United States.

Cavenagh and Sarat, "Thinking about Courts", p. 389

"In theory, small claims courts were courts for the 'ordinary person'; in theory, their informal procedures promoted access to justice for consumers, tenants, and others supposedly disadvantaged through market transactions.

In fact, many small claims courts were quickly recognized by creditors as the happy equivalent of state-subsidized debt collection agencies. The result: high volumes of debt actions in the state courts most conveniently available to creditors, typically resulting in default judgments for plaintiffs. 'In major cities, 75 per cent of all contract claims filed in courts of limited jurisdiction may end in default judgments' . . . Yngvesson and Hennessey (1975) . . . drew from a review of fourteen empirical studies of small claims courts a common theme: 'all of the studies point to the high number of business plaintiffs, the high number of non-business "individual" defendants (frequently identified as low-income consumers), and a high default rate.'"

The Hughes Commission, pp. 175–176

"11.15 The summary cause serves a useful purpose in disposing of routine cases of undisputed debt but it does not appear to encourage individuals to pursue claims—either individual claims for debt or consumer and other claims. There seems to be substantial public ignorance of the summary cause procedure. In our survey of legal needs some 99 per cent of respondents had no knowledge or only inaccurate knowledge of the summary cause procedure. This public ignorance is no doubt compounded by the uninformative name of the summary cause procedure. Another reason, however, appears to be the complexity of the procedure. . . . It is doubtful whether many people would be willing or competent to conduct their own cases in summary cause, even if they had heard of it or understood what it was. Indeed, the formalities make it impossible for the party litigant to conduct the whole case himself without professional assistance. A solicitor or sheriff officer must be employed to effect service and solicitors may not be willing to perform the task unless they are engaged for the whole case. It follows that where claims for small sums of money are at issue, the cost of legal representation is a significant disincentive to taking legal action. In addition, the expenses of a summary cause case which are borne by the losing party can be considerable, particularly where an action is defended. Indeed, in actions for small sums, expenses can exceed the value of the claim involved."

Economides, "Small Claims and Procedural Justice", p. 113

"At a very basic level, the problem can be viewed as the result of 'process costs' exceeding the amount in controversy and perceived gains. It is simply uneconomic, not only for individuals but also for society at large, for parties to involve themselves and others in the litigation, adjudication or arbitration of disputes over small amounts of money. The most common response then, is to avoid or endure the grievance which gives rise to the dispute."

Hunter, "The Courts and the Legal Profession", pp. 212–213

"It may be asked why consumers rarely bring actions against the suppliers? The main reason is probably that the game is not usually worth the candle. Economies of scale make it possible for the supplier to litigate even where each individual action is for a relatively small, to him even quite trivial, sum; but the citizen as a consumer is only rarely placed in a situation in which he might reasonably consider legal proceedings against a supplier. In addition, many citizens are not aware of their legal rights and are not in the habit of consulting legal advisers. The voice of the consumer is now heard quite loudly in Parliament but is hardly more than a whisper in the ordinary courts."

The complexity of the summary cause procedure which undoubtedly inhibits party litigants can be gauged from the fact that there are some 95 rules, many of which would be difficult for most laymen to comprehend. Rule 68A (contained in S.I. 1980 No. 445) is one such rule.

"*Actions against Persons in Possession of Heritable Property without Right or Title*

68A. In an action for recovery of possession of heritable property against a person in possession *vi clam aut precario* and without right or title to possess or occupy that property, the sheriff may in his discretion and subject to rule 81A, shorten or dispense with any period of time provided anywhere in these rules. An application by a party under this rule to shorten or dispense with any such period may be made verbally and the provisions in rule 93(1) and (2) shall not apply, but the sheriff clerk shall enter details of any such application in the Book of Incidental Applications."

Further evidence of the complexities of the summary cause procedure comes from another report produced by the Central Research Unit where it discussed summary cause contested proofs.

Central Research Unit "The Dundee Small Claims Experiment", paras. 6.12, 6.19

"The people who attended a proof found it to be complicated and even more formal than they had anticipated. People who were not legally represented had difficulties in putting questions to witnesses, and found it difficult to explain their case in a way which was acceptable to the Sheriff, although most people said that the Sheriff had tried to help them, and had himself asked the witnesses questions. Almost all of the people who had been required to give evidence in court said that they had found it difficult to answer the questions put to them by solicitors, and many people expressed the view that solicitors asking questions was an unnecessarily complicated way of establishing straightforward facts" (para. 6.12).

. . . [I]n cases in which a contested adjudication took place more dissatisfaction was expressed by summary cause defenders and particularly personal defenders in actions brought by firms:

> "The common view was that under summary cause it was presumed that the money claimed was owed, and that it was up to the defender to prove that he did not owe the sum or that he had withheld payment for good reasons ('guilty till able to prove self innocent'). This was considered by them to be extremely unfair and to run contrary to everything which the courts were supposed to do. A few people said that they had not had an opportunity to explain their side of a disputed case to the Sheriff, and they considered this to be very unfair. Each of these people had lost the action, and was certain that if the Sheriff had heard both sides of the case the outcome would have been different. However they stressed that even if the outcome had not altered they would have been prepared to accept a decision made by the Sheriff" (para. 6.19).

The procedure's complexities have also ensured that, with the exception of a few eviction actions, the provision for lay representation has been little utilised.

3. Appeals

Sheriff Courts (Scotland) Act 1971, s. 38

> "38. *Appeal in summary causes*. In the case of any summary cause an appeal shall lie—
>
> (a) to the sheriff principal on any point of law from the final judgment of the sheriff, and
>
> (b) to the Court of Session on any point of law from the final judgment of the sheriff principal, if the sheriff principal certifies the cause as suitable for such an appeal,
>
> but save as aforesaid an interlocutor of the sheriff or the sheriff principal in any such cause shall not be subject to review."

Appellants request the sheriff to draft a stated case setting out his findings in fact and law. Where necessary he may add a narrative of the proceedings before him and a note stating the reasons for his decision in law. The stated case, which forms the basis of the appeal before the sheriff principal, also includes the question of law stated by each of the parties. In 1991, 101 summary cause appeals to sheriffs principal were disposed of; most of them were unsuccessful. In 1997 37 summary cause appeals were disposed of.

4. The Future of Summary Cause Procedure

To address some of the shortcomings of the summary cause procedure, a small claims procedure was introduced. It was designed to be more accessible to people without legal representation; less formal and complex although research indicates that these aspirations have not been met. The introduction of the small claims court has had a considerable impact on the number of cases raised as summary causes. In 1977, the first full year of the summary cause procedure, approximately 87% of actions for payment raised in the sheriff court were raised as summary causes. However, in 1989, the first full year of the small claims procedure, approximately 60% of payment actions were raised as small claims and 22% as summary causes. In 1996 of payment actions raised in the sheriff court, 62% were raised as small claims, 14% as summary causes and 24% as ordinary causes.

There has been considerable pressure for harmonisation of the summary cause and small claims rules if not an outright demand that summary cause procedure be abolished entirely.

Sheriff N.M. Morrison, Q.C., "Reform of Civil Procedure" 1998 SLT 137 at p. 140

> "We do not need and cannot have three sets of general rules for civil causes in the sheriff court. One or other of the Small Claims Rules and the Summary Cause Rules must be abolished. I do not much mind which it is; but I suppose to avoid a political and public outcry from those who fought for the introduction of small claims, it may have to be the summary cause.
>
> . . .
>
> In my limited experience, there is little to choose between them in practice. In Edinburgh, the procedural, interlocutory and other business, such as proofs or hearings, relating to both summary causes and small claims are dealt with in the same court on the same day at the same time. In a summary cause one may have party litigants, and in a small claim one may have solicitors, appearing. One advantage the latter has over the former is that the sheriff has to note the issues. At a small claim proof, therefore, the court is supposed to have some idea what the issues are."

If the summary cause procedure were to be replaced by small claims, this would have the effect of removing legal aid from cases where it was previously available under the summary cause procedure as legal aid is not available for small claims. Thus, while proceedings may become less complex, there would be less likelihood of assistance or representation being available to potential litigants.

In 1998 the Sheriff Court Rules Council issued a consultation paper (*A Consultation Paper on Proposed New Rules for Summary Cause and Small Claim in the Sheriff Court*, 1998). While the paper does not propose the abolition of the summary cause procedure, it proposes harmonisation of the two sets of rules within a single set of rules. A draft set of harmonised rules appears in the paper. Most of the proposed rules are common to both procedures while some apply to one or the other only. The proposed harmonised rules are more closely related to the existing small claims procedure although that too is to be simplified. In addition they would enable sheriffs to determine cases without a hearing on the basis of the summons and response from the defender and no first calling in court would be required.

C. SMALL CLAIMS

1. The Need for a Small Claims Procedure

The deficiencies of the summary cause procedure stem from the fact that it retains most of the features of a fully adversarial procedure. Yet around the world there has been a near universal movement in the past 30 years away from adjudication in small claims and towards such alternatives as conciliation, mediation and arbitration. Scotland has now begun tentatively to follow this path but the crucial problem is to determine how far the relaxation in formalities should go.

Economides, "Small Claims and Procedural Justice", p. 118

> "In deciding whether, and to what degree, a dispute is to be resolved by reference to legal norms it can be noted that legal informality in procedure possesses the advantage of being relatively cheap, accessible and simple, and hence easily understandable to the disputants. On the other hand, fundamental principles of procedural natural justice stand in danger of being eroded. Where safeguards derived from legal formality are absent, the weaker party may feel inclined to compromise or settle for something less than he would receive were he to rely on the full enforcement of his legal rights. Conversely, legal formality, although safeguarding these core principles, does so in only a limited number of cases because it is relatively expensive, complex and hence inaccessible. The most promising approach to finding a solution to the small claims problem would appear to lie in a synthesis of both formal and informal justice."

Some countries have opted for a modified adversary procedure in their small claims courts, with the judge adopting a semi-inquisitorial role. In England and in many states in the U.S.A. an arbitration model has been favoured, while in other parts of the U.S.A. neighbourhood justice centres have relied on mediation and conciliation to resolve small claims disputes. In Queensland and New South Wales the referees who handle small claims are even enjoined not to give decisions according to the law but to make orders which are "fair and equitable to the parties to the proceedings concerning the dispute."

In 1978 the Scottish Consumer Council put forward proposals for an experimental small claims scheme which was subsequently introduced (though not in the form favoured by the Council) in Dundee Sheriff Court for the years 1979, 1980 and 1981. The adjudicators (sheriffs) were urged to make hearings "as relaxed and informal as possible." An inquisitorial approach was adopted by adjudicators and the strict rules of evidence were dispensed with—adjudicators were even permitted to accept evidence by telephone. Unlike the summary cause, the rules were few (14), short (3 pages) and simple.

Although defects in the nature of the experiment led to only 52 claims being lodged under it in the three years, it was accepted to be a success both by the consumer groups and the researchers evaluating the experiment ("A Research-

Based Evaluation of the Dundee Small Claims Experiment" by Anne Connor with Barbara Doig, Central Research Unit, Edinburgh, 1983). The Government agreed and produced a Consultation Paper on *Summary Cause and Small Claims Procedures in Sheriff Courts* in 1984. After discussions with interested parties the Government's proposals were considerably modified. The skeletal form of the new procedure for small claims is contained in s. 18 of the Law Reform (Miscellaneous Provisions) (Scotland) Act 1985. The full details of the small claims procedure (which is technically a new form of summary cause procedure) are contained in the Small Claims (Scotland) Order 1988 (S.I. 1988 No. 1999) and the Act of Sederunt (Small Claims Rules) 1988 (S.I. 1988 No. 1976). Small claims are defined as actions for payment for £750 or less or actions for delivery or recovery of possession of moveable property or for the implement of an obligation (actions *ad factum praestandum*) where there is an alternative claim for less than £750. In 1989, the first full year of the new procedure, 73,946 small claims were raised in Scotland. More than 99% of them were payment actions. In 1997, 56,551 small claims were raised in Scotland.

2. What Should the Ground Rules Be?

Joint research by the Central Research Unit of the Scottish Office and the law faculties of Strathclyde and Dundee Universities which was published in 1991, *Small Claims in the Sheriff Courts in Scotland* ("the 1991 Research"), monitored the operation of the new procedure in its first 18 months. In the six courts studied by the researchers 92% of claims were raised by large businesses or public utilities. In the great majority of these cases there was no dispute that the money was owed and decree was obtained without a hearing. At first sight this might suggest that there would be merit in following the lead provided in numerous states in America where business and commercial organisations are barred from the small claims courts. However, such a move would exclude "reverse consumer" cases (*e.g.* where the consumer declines to meet the full cost of a product on the grounds that it is defective).

The real areas of dispute in defining small claims have proved to be whether it was correct to include personal injury cases and whether the upper limit should be above £750. As to the former, critics from widely different sectors of the legal profession have argued that it was an error to include such potentially complex cases in the procedure. They have been fortified in their argument by the fact that cases which are included under the small claims procedure are not eligible for legal aid.

As to the proper upper limit, the Scottish Consumer Council and more recently Scottish Courts Administration in their consultation paper, *Proposals to Increase Jurisdiction Limits in the Sheriff Court* (June 1998), have suggested that it should be higher than £750 (so that second hand cars and three piece suites would be covered). However, others have objected to any increase in the upper limit since it would have the effect of excluding significantly greater numbers of litigants from legal aid and thus legal representation. (See D. O'Carroll and P. Brown, "Small Claims" (1991) 181 SCOLAG 154 and D. O'Carroll (1998) 254

SCOLAG 129.) These issues are explored further in the section on possible reforms below.

To some extent the problems caused by the cut-off level have been offset by s. 37 of the Sheriff Courts (Scotland) Act 1971 (as amended) which permits small claims to be remitted by the consent of both parties or by the sheriff on his or her own accord if the case is complex, to the summary or ordinary cause. Conversely, cases over the limit can be treated as small claims if the parties so agree.

As to the format of small claims hearings, it was accepted by all involved with the introduction of the procedure that it should be informal and that the strict rules of evidence should not apply. The 1985 Act specifically provided that rules of law relating to admissibility or corroboration of evidence were not to be binding in small claims hearings. The Act and the Rules, however, are silent as to whether sheriffs should adopt an inquisitorial approach to hearings in small claims. As a result the 1991 Research found that the majority of sheriffs continued to wear their wigs and gowns and made no attempt to adopt an inquisitorial approach.

3. Preliminary Hearings

One of the major features of the English small claims procedure to date has been the provision for a pre-trial review at which the judge ascertains the nature of the dispute, advises the parties as to evidence which may be required at the proof and occasionally acts as a conciliator. Ironically, just as preliminary hearings were being introduced as part of the Scottish procedure to perform a very similar function, the English Civil Justice Review recommended that pre-trial review be dispensed with except in housing, personal injury and other particularly complex or difficult cases.

The 1991 Research indicated that in practice, of actions raised by individuals, 59% were concluded without a hearing of any kind, 25% were concluded at the preliminary hearing stage with only 16% of cases going beyond a preliminary hearing. In cases which went no further than a preliminary hearing, the pursuer attended the hearing in person in only 20% of cases and represented him or herself in only 10%. Few problems were reported in relation to these largely uncontested preliminary hearings. However, in contested cases which went beyond a preliminary hearing there was widespread dissatisfaction with preliminary hearings amongst both litigants and advisers.

Small Claims in the Sheriff Court in Scotland, pp. 28–9, 43–4, 63

> "In all but one of the sample courts, small claims preliminary hearings were scheduled for the same time and in the same courtroom as other civil business. In most courts, these other cases involved procedural matters for ordinary actions or first callings for summary causes which were frequently heard before small claims. This meant that parties to small claims had to sit around the court for a considerable period of time before their cases were called. No prior notification of this practice appeared to be given to small claims litigants in court correspondence nor was the order of precedence of

court business explained to the parties when they arrived in court. Thus, on a number of occasions, party litigants were left to sit in the public benches without necessarily understanding what was going on and wondering when their cases would be called . . . .

So far as litigants were concerned, over half of those with experience of preliminary hearings were alienated or made nervous by their attendance at court, even although they were only required to speak a little. The time that litigants had to wait for their cases to be called and the presence of solicitors and members of the public in court all contributed towards this feeling. Further, party litigants often seemed to have difficulty in following the proceedings. This was not only a function of their lack of legal knowledge but often was because it was difficult to hear what was being said in court due to the acoustics of the courtroom, the noise made by solicitors and others entering or leaving the court and the tendency for sheriffs and solicitors to discuss issues in very soft voices as if they were having a private conversation. Some party litigants even appeared not to hear what was being said during the course of their own preliminary hearing. This happened frequently when asides were made by the sheriff to the sheriff clerk or a solicitor. Also, although sheriffs did make efforts to avoid the use of legalistic language, it was clear that there were occasions when party litigants were unable to understand what was being said. This was most likely to arise when the other party was represented by a solicitor. Despite these difficulties many party litigants commented positively on the role of the sheriff when the time came for their case to be called; they felt that the sheriff had tried to put them at their ease in a basically alien environment . . . .

The lay advisers' views on preliminary hearings were uniformly unfavourable. Again and again they reiterated the same complaints about formality, inaudibility and exclusivity:

'The consumer doesn't have a chance to put their case properly. They are left standing near the table not knowing what to do, while the solicitors sit sniggering.'

'The sheriffs have been helpful or think that they are, but it is still terrifying. Sheriffs don't understand the difficulty for people not used to it. It is like a closed shop. They do not understand the concept of user friendliness.'"

In 1998 the Sheriff Court Rules Council issued a consultation paper (*A Consultation on Proposed New Rules for Summary Cause and Small Claim in the Sheriff Court*, 1998) which proposed that preliminary hearings should be done away with in most small claims. This is considered further below in section 7, Possible Reforms.

4. Representation

There is a continuing debate as to whether legal representation should be permitted in small claims hearings since lawyers tend to add to the formality of proceedings. While most systems do permit such representation it is usually discouraged by the limits that are placed on the expenses that can be recovered from the other side and the fact that legal aid is not available for representation in small claims cases. The Law Societies of Scotland and England favour the retention of the profession's right of audience in these cases, though some reformers do not. Others have argued that banning legal representation would not greatly affect business organisations but it might disadvantage inarticulate party litigants. One solution to this might be to encourage lay representation or, as the National Consumer Council has proposed, to permit legal representation if the interests of justice require it because of the size and complexity of the claim or the respective capacities of the parties.

The Small Claims Rules permit representation by laypersons and lawyers and provide for the service of the summons by the sheriff clerk in small claims cases where the pursuer is not a partnership or a body corporate or acting in a representative capacity. Only 31% of pursuers interviewed in the 1991 Research project took advantage of this facility, the other 69% using a solicitor to serve the summons. Indeed 56% of pursuers and defenders had a legal representative at hearings (preliminary or full). Very few used a lay representative and indeed it appears that the experience of lay representatives in the sheriff court is far from positive:

O'Carroll, "Civil jurisdiction limits: proposed increases" 1998 254 SCOLAG 129 at p. 130–1

> "The very recent report from Citizens' Advice Scotland on the experience of lay representatives in the small claims court was extremely critical of the intimidatory nature of the procedure even from the point of view of those lay representatives whose job it is to represent litigants in the small claims court.
>
> It may be that this explains the relatively small number of CABx who regularly appear in the small claims court. . . . Mike Dailly . . . concludes from the CAS report that *in the whole of Scotland*, only 3 CABx representatives are involved in small claims "often", 13 in the eviction court "often" and 45 in industrial tribunals "often" or "very often".
>
> For many lay representatives, the relative complexity and difficulty of different dispute resolution forums can be expressed in a hierarchy beginning with Social Security Appeals Tribunals at the bottom going through Disability Appeal Tribunals then Employment Tribunals [sic] with Small Claims full hearings as the most intimidating and difficult to advise on, prepare and represent."

For the minority of individuals who were not represented, the two most common reasons given for non-representation were that they thought it was unnecessary and because of the expense of using a solicitor. While figures of this magnitude are a little discouraging, it should be remembered that in England and Wales where small claims have been going for nearly 15 years longer than in Scotland, 34% of plaintiffs and 21% of defendants are still legally represented in small claims hearings. Both the English and the Northern Irish experience suggest that the need for representation will decline over time.

5. Expenses

The Dundee experiment revealed that the fear of substantial and unpredictable expense was a major disincentive to individuals using the summary cause procedure. In most small claims schemes there are reasonable maximum limits to recoverable expenses. Thus it is normal for such litigants to have to meet their own lawyers' fees, though other expenses, *e.g.* court fees, witness expenses and travel costs may be awarded at the discretion of the adjudicator/arbiter. The 1985 Act and the Small Claims Rules provide that for cases below £200 no expenses will be recoverable. In other small claims expenses may be awarded up to £75. In cases where the debt is admitted, the rules limiting awards of expenses do not apply (1) where no defence is stated or (2) where one is stated but it is not proceeded with or (3) where one is stated and proceeded with but the defender is considered not to have acted in good faith as to the merits of the defence. Fears that these provisions might lead to sheriffs routinely awarding expenses beyond the set limits have proved to be groundless. The 1991 Research found very few cases where expenses had been awarded because of frivolous conduct by the defender. Indeed the research found that the expenses rules had worked well subject to two caveats. First, the fact that court dues are not refunded to successful pursuers in cases worth less than £200 was felt by many to be unfair. Secondly, there was some feeling that expert witnesses' costs ought to be recoverable in whole or in part, in cases where such evidence was genuinely felt to be necessary.

More recent research (E. Samuel, *In the Shadow of the Small Claims Court*, Scottish Office, Central Research Unit 1998) has demonstrated that in personal injury litigation where cases are often complex and the other party, usually an insurance company, often represented, the very low level of recoverable expenses deters lawyers from assisting parties with the result that unassisted litigants are rarely successful. The impact of raising the small claims limit on expenses is considered further on p. 17.

6. Appeals

If small claims schemes provided an unrestricted right of appeal, defenders might simply appeal every case they lost. For this reason some schemes contain no right of appeal, while others permit appeal only on a point of law, or on certification by the adjudicator. The small claims procedure provides for appeal to the sheriff principal on any point of law from the final judgment of the sheriff (s. 38(a) of the Sheriff Courts (Scotland) Act 1971 (as amended)). However, s. 38(b) excludes a further right of appeal on to the Court of Session. Fears that this relatively generous provision for appeal might lead commercial defenders to appeal every case in which they had lost have also proved to be groundless. Of the 73,946 small claims raised in Scotland in 1989, only 46 went to an appeal. Of the 56,551 raised in 1997, only 39 went to an appeal with only 20 of those being disposed of by judgment.

7. Possible Reforms

The conclusion of the 1991 Research was that the small claims procedure had been only partially successful. While it was generally thought to be cheap and relatively quick there was less consensus as to its simplicity and informality, particularly in contested cases. The full hearings were considered by consumers and lay advisers to be almost as formal as the preliminary hearings and not particularly simple for litigants who were unrepresented. Although the court staff were of the opinion that sheriffs had made an effort to make the procedure more informal than in other procedures in the sheriff court, from the layperson's perspective they have not gone far enough. The 1991 Research establishes once again how difficult it is for lawyers to appreciate that their daily world is an alien one for most laypersons. Nevertheless it should be stressed that a clear majority of the parties interviewed in the research felt that they had been fairly treated by the sheriffs.

The 1991 Research report and the consultation paper from Scottish Courts Administration which accompanied its publication raised a number of issues for consideration as potential reforms. The principal ones included:

(a) **Doing away with the requirement of a preliminary hearing in all or many cases.**

As we have seen this proposal is in line with the recommendations of the English Civil Justice Review in 1988. It would remove perhaps the most unsatisfactory feature of the procedure (except in complex or difficult cases). The Sheriff Court Rules Council's Consultation Paper (*A Consultation Paper on Proposed New Rules for Summary Cause and Small Claim in the Sheriff Court*, 1998) proposes new rules which would do away with preliminary hearings. Instead they require the sheriff to note the issues in dispute on the basis of the summons and any written response lodged. It is only if the sheriff is unable to note the issues in dispute on the basis of these documents that a preliminary hearing would be fixed. The sheriff is also placed under a duty to seek to resolve the dispute without the matter proceeding to a hearing at which evidence is led. This means that the sheriff may dispose of the matter simply on the basis of the summons and the response lodged.

(b) **Holding full hearings at more convenient times for party litigants, *e.g.* fixed appointments, or evenings or Saturday mornings.**

Since the publication of the report there have been limited (but successful) experiments designed to implement each of these proposals in particular sheriff courts. For example, evening hearings were held in Dumbarton Sheriff Court.

(c) **Endeavouring to achieve a more informal and less adversarial approach to the hearing of small claims through a series of practice notes.**

This proposal might lead to more sheriffs adopting an inquisitorial approach and being willing to remove their wigs and gowns and come down from the bench. Preliminary indications are that this proposal will not meet favour with a significant number of sheriffs. For a depressing illustration of shrieval resistance to informality in small claims, see *Kuklinski v. Hassell*, 1993 S.L.T. (Sh. Ct) 23. The draft rules for small claims contained in the Sheriff Court Rules Council's 1998 Consultation Paper address this issue. They provide that the hearing must be conducted as informally as the circumstances of the case permit and that the sheriff must adopt a procedure which he considers fair, best suited to the clarification and determination of the issues before him; and which gives each party a sufficient opportunity to present his case. Having regard to whether or not the parties are represented, the sheriff is empowered to assist parties putting questions to them and to witnesses and enjoined to explain any legal terms or expressions which are used if it appears necessary for the fair conduct of the hearing.

(d) **Making provision for in-court lay advisers.**

The consumer movement is particularly supportive of this proposal which would provide advice and possibly representation by lay advisers based in courthouses. Such schemes exist in a number of courts in England and Wales though they are not without problems as to training, funding and mode of operation. A pilot in-court advice project was introduced in Edinburgh Sheriff Court for one year from April 1997. Research into the project demonstrated a large demand for its services, that it helped to promote a level playing field in court and strong client satisfaction. See E. Samuel, *Supporting Court Users: The Pilot In-court Advice Project in Edinburgh Sheriff Court,* Central Research Unit, 1999.

(e) **Small claims and personal injury actions.**

Research has been conducted on the appropriateness of the small claims procedure for personal injury actions (E. Samuel, *In the Shadow of the Small Claims Court*, Central Research Unit, 1998). The main findings of the report are outlined in the Scottish Courts Administration consultation paper, *Proposals to increase jurisdiction limits in the Sheriff Court (including privative jurisdiction limit)*, pp. 6–7. As the case is likely to be as complicated as one of higher value, the report noted that at the very outset, it is unlikely that a potential pursuer could assess the wisdom of legal action without seeking legal advice. When advice was sought, it was found that many lay advisers referred such cases to legally qualified persons, many of whom were unwilling to take the case due to the restriction of expenses to £75. Negotiation was also problematic given the imbalance between unrepresented individuals and powerful, well-resourced insurance companies. Where parties were funded by legal expenses, insurance or trade unions, however, their experience was much more positive. Unassisted litigants were also often unaware of the legal basis of their action and found preliminary hearings both intimidating and unhelpful. Unassisted litigants also found it difficult to pursue their action at full hearings and were rarely successful when they did so, particularly because they were more likely to come up against litigation and reparation specialists at such hearings. Sheriffs were also reluctant to play an interventionist role where one party was represented, which was normally the case in personal injury litigation. The report also found that although the procedure reduced access to advice, negotiation and other pre-litigation assistance, it did provide some claimants with the opportunity to litigate by reducing financial risk. The Scottish Courts Administration consultation paper considered the research inconclusive although it sought views on whether the suggestion that an "option of forum" be given to personal injury litigants and, in view of the proposed raising of the small claims limit, a further tier of expenses for claims in excess of £750.

(f) **Raising the jurisdictional limits.**

Scottish Courts Administration produced a consultation paper in 1998 (*Proposals to Increase Jurisdiction Limits in the Sheriff Court (including private jurisdiction limit*)). The paper notes that in 1996, 62% of actions for payment in the sheriff court were raised under the small claims procedure, 14% under summary cause and 24% as ordinary actions. If the small claims limit were raised to £1,500 and summary cause to £10,000, 76% of cases would be raised under small claims, 18% under summary cause and 6% under ordinary procedure on the basis of the 1996 figures. If the limits were raised to £3,000 and £15,000 respectively, 85% of actions would be raised as small claims, 11% as summary causes and 4% as ordinary actions. With limits of £5,000 and £20,000 respectively the figures change to 90%, 6.5% and 3.5% respectively.

Scottish Courts Administration, Proposals to increase jurisdiction limits in the Sheriff Court (including privative jurisdiction limit), p. 5

> "12. To facilitate the necessary access to justice, demanded by litigants who wish to conduct their own litigation, it is considered appropriate to increase the jurisdiction limit which applies to Small Claim in the Sheriff Court. It is considered that an increase to the present limit is required to reflect the value of the majority of consumer goods which may give rise to litigation".

However, a very significant side effect would be that at the same time, legal aid would be denied to more litigants as legal aid is not available in the small claims procedure. Although the following extract refers to the proposed increase of the small claims limit in England and Wales, it has equal force in relation to the proposed increase in Scotland:

Sheriff N.M.P. Morrison, Q.C., "Reform of Civil Procedure" 1998 SLT 137

> "There is a Government proposal to raise the small claims limit in England and Wales from £3,000 (yes, £3,000 not £750 as in Scotland) to £5,000. This has met with opposition from at least the English Law Society. That body says that poorer litigants would be hardest hit because they would not be able to get legal aid. They would not be able to get legal representation or expert witnesses in cases for which the small claims procedure was not designed, such as landlord and tenant disputes or cases involving legal issues where the public have to face organisations which are powerful and with substantial resources".

D. O'Carroll, "Civil jurisdiction limits: proposed increases" (1998) 254 SCOLAG 129 at p. 131

> "Extending the reach of the Small Claims Procedure without either making legal aid available or ensuring some other means of legal support including representation will effectively shut out large numbers of ordinary citizens from the court process."

See further on small claims, C. Ervine, *Small Claims Handbook* (W. Green: 1992), Ervine, "Small Claims: A Progress Report", 1992 S.L.T. (News) 33, C. Whelan (ed.) *Small Claims Courts: A Comparative Study* (Oxford University Press: 1990), J. Baldwin, *Small Claims in the County Courts in England and Wales* (Clarendon Press: 1997).

IV. MISCELLANEOUS AND ADMINISTRATIVE FUNCTIONS

Sheriffs also have not a few miscellaneous and administrative functions, some of considerable importance. Most of them take the form of summary applications as defined by s. 3(p) of the Sheriff Courts (Scotland) Act 1907:

> "(p) 'Summary application' means and includes all applications of a summary nature brought under the common law jurisdiction of the sheriff, and all applications, whether by appeal or otherwise, brought under any Act of Parliament which provides, or, according to any practice in the sheriff-court, which allows that the same shall be disposed of in a summary manner, but which does not more particularly define in what form the same shall be heard, tried, and determined."

The procedure is governed by s.50 of the 1907 Act:

> "In summary applications (where a hearing is necessary) the sheriff shall appoint the application to be heard at a diet to be fixed by him, and at that or any subsequent diet (without record of evidence unless the sheriff shall order a record) shall summarily dispose of the matter and give his judgment in writing:. . ."

More detailed provision is made by the Sheriff Court Summary Application Rules 1993 (SI 1993 No 3240).

TABLE 2.3

Miscellaneous and Administrative Applications in 1997

Name of application	Number disposed of
Adoption	392
Freeing orders	111
Bankruptcy	12,040
Child Support	252
Civil imprisonment	17
Civil Jurisdiction, section 12 applications	370
Conveyancing and Feudal Reform actions	459
Fatal Accident Inquiries held	175
Human Fertilisation and Embryology Act	3
Judicial Factors	
-Appointments	210
-Discharge	35
-Judicial taxations lodged	1,347
Liquidations	1,216
Maintenance Orders Act 1950	66
Mental Health (Scotland) Act 1960, Part V	1,034
Presumption of Death (Scotland) Act 1977	6
Social Work (Scotland) Act 1968	
-Applications under section 16	90
-Applications under section 42	1,531
-Applications under sections 49 & 50	227
Other miscellaneous applications	6,518
Total	26,099

[Source: Scottish Courts Administration, *Civil Judicial Statistics Scotland* 1997, Table 3.12.]

Apart from the applications set out in Table 3 sheriffs also hear applications under the Heritable Securities (Scotland) Act 1894 (*Prestwick Investment Trust v. Jones*, 1981 S.L.T. (Sh. Ct.) 55), the Fair Trading Act 1973 (*Director General of Fair Trading v. Boswell*, 1979 S.L.T. (Sh. Ct.) 9) and statutory nuisance applications by individuals under s.82 of the Environmental Protection Act 1990 (*Anderson v. Dundee City Council*, 1999 S.C.L.R. (Notes) 518). Under the Licensing (Scotland) Act 1976 (as amended by the Law Reform (Miscellaneous Provisions) (Scotland) Act 1990, Part III) appeal lies to sheriffs from the decisions of licensing boards. Such appeals, of which there were 117 in 1991, are dealt with as summary applications. Likewise appeals against contaminated land remediation notices served by local authorities under s.78L of the Environmental Protection Act 1990 lie to the sheriff. It is not always entirely clear whether a sheriff is hearing an appeal in an administrative or a judicial capacity. Thus in *Rodenhurst v. Chief Constable, Grampian Police*, 1992 S.L.T. 104 an Inner House of five judges had to be convened to overrule a 1958 case which had held that a sheriff in hearing an appeal against the revocation of a firearm certificate by a chief constable was exercising a judicial as opposed to an administrative function. Also it is not always entirely clear if it is intended that there should be an appeal from the sheriff in a summary application. The statute providing for the summary application may prescribe the mode of appeal. If it does not, then the same appeal rights as are available in the ordinary cause procedure will apply (Sheriff Courts (Scotland) Act 1907, ss.27 and 28) unless the statute expressly or by necessary implication excludes appeal rights (see Holligan, "Aspects of Appeals from the Sheriff Court" 1997 SLT (News) 40).

Amongst the more unusual applications made to sheriffs are those which relate to lawburrows (*Morrow v. Neil*) and to burial grounds (*Sister Jarlath, Petitioner*).

Morrow v. Neil 1975 S.L.T. (Sh. Ct) 65

> "A widow living in a tenement flat claimed that members of a family from a neighbouring flat had injured and threatened to injure her and her children and that she was afraid that they would commit further assaults upon her. She, accordingly, brought an action of lawburrows against these neighbours with the concurrence of the procurator-fiscal. The neighbours lodged defences and, after sundry procedure, a proof was heard. The sheriff considered, inter alia, the nature of the remedy sought, the procedure to be followed, what the pursuer had to prove in order to succeed, the standard of proof incumbent upon the pursuer, and the weight to be attached to corroboration.
>
> *Held* (1) that the concurrence of the procurator-fiscal was unnecessary; (2) that defences should not have been lodged; (3) that the pursuer had to establish that she had reasonable cause to apprehend that the defenders would harm the person or property or herself or her family, tenants or servants, and that although she genuinely believed that the defenders were likely to harm her, her belief was not based on rational grounds; (4) that the standard of proof incumbent on the pursuer was proof on a balance of probabilities; and (5) that in the circumstances, where corroboration was available, the presence or absence of corroboration was an important

consideration for the court in deciding whether or not a fact had been proved; and defenders *assoilized*."

Sister Jarlath, Petitioner 1980 S.L.T. (Sh. Ct.) 72

"A private burying place belonging to trustees for a religious order contained 46 bodies, the last of which had been interred in 1972. In order to carry out the reconstruction of their convent (which adjoined the said burying ground), the Mother Superior presented a petition to the sheriff principal for authority to disinter the 46 bodies and reinter them in a private cemetery elsewhere. Evidence was put before the sheriff principal to the effect that disintegration of all the bodies would be virtually complete.

Held that there was no reason in principle why the court should not grant the order sought in a suitable case; and prayer of the petition *granted*."

Although the sheriff is directed to dispose of such applications summarily, there has been strong criticism from the bench that summary application procedure is unsuited to certain complex applications such as statutory nuisances which might be more suited to ordinary cause.

Anderson v Dundee City Council, 1999 S.C.L.R. (Notes) 518 at 522

SHERIFF STEWART: "I think it is proper for me to observe that this case gives rise to the question whether the summary application procedure is really appropriate to proceedings of this sort. I heard evidence over ten days between February and July 1998. . . . I then heard detailed submission over two days. These had been preceded at my request, by draft findings in fact and summaries of submissions. Since hearing submissions I have taken the opportunity to read through the whole of the evidence and consider the submissions, both written and oral, in detail. It is fair to say that the amount of work put into this case by counsel and solicitors on each side as well as myself really makes a mockery of describing the proceedings as summary".

CHAPTER 3

THE COURT OF SESSION

I. STRUCTURE AND COMPOSITION

The Court of Session is the highest civil court based in Scotland. It is a central court, sitting only in Edinburgh.

Lord Cameron, "The Superior Courts," p. 23

> "The Court of Session, which was established in 1532 by James V of Scotland and grew out of the King's Council, derives its name from the fact that when established it sat, and was required to sit, in one determined place—Edinburgh—thus obviating the necessity of litigants following the King's Council wherever it might move about the country. The Court itself sits in the Parliament House, Edinburgh, and with brief intermissions occasioned by civil convulsions has sat there continuously since at least the completion of the new Parliament House in 1640. It forms part of the College of Justice and members of the Court are still officially styled 'Senators of The College of Justice.' Within the College of Justice are included, Advocates, Clerks of Session, Writers to the Signet and certain others of the officers and officials of the court."

From 1532 until 1808 the whole court sat as one body. Understandably, counsel found it an unwieldy body to appear before; one contemporary newspaper editor referred to it as "a regular bear garden." See also Henry Cockburn, *Memorials of His Time* (Black: 1856), pp. 245–246.

During this period one of the 15 judges sat in the "Outer House" of the court to deal with preliminary issues in cases which would subsequently come before the whole court. In 1808 the court was divided into two Divisions, the First Division consisting of the Lord President and seven Ordinary Judges and the Second Division of the Lord Justice-Clerk and six Ordinary Judges. As before, one of the Ordinary Judges sat by rotation in the Outer House to handle preliminary issues.

The court as we know it today emerged from the Court of Session Act 1825. This provided that the seven junior Ordinary Judges of the court should normally sit as Lords Ordinary in the Outer House. The eight remaining members of the court formed the Inner House and sat in two Divisions, the First and Second Divisions consisting respectively of the Lord President and the Lord Justice-Clerk each sitting with three senior Lords Ordinary. Since that date the number of Senators of the College of Justice (known also as Lords of Council and Session) has been increased. Under the Maximum Number of Judges (Scotland)

Order (1993) (No. 3154) up to 27 Senators can be appointed. At present there are 27, one of whom (Lord Gill) is the part-time Chairman of the Scottish Law Commission. Nineteen are in the Outer House (and are primarily responsible for deciding cases at first instance), and eight are in the Inner House (the work of which is mainly appellate). In addition there are now a number of temporary judges appointed in terms of s. 35(3) of the Law Reform (Miscellaneous Provisions) (Scotland) Act 1990 and retired judges appointed in terms of s. 22 of the Law Reform (Miscellaneous Provisions) (Scotland) Act 1985.

Despite the hierarchical and divided structure of the court in modern times it is still collegiate in its essence. A number of consequences flow from this:

1. All decrees, though pronounced by a single judge are decrees of the Court of Session, and the judge who pronounces them exercises only a delegated jurisdiction. (*Purves v. Carswell* (1905) 8 F. 351 per Lord McLaren at p. 354.)
2. If necessary, an Outer House judge can be asked to sit in the Inner House to make up a Division. Equally, an Inner House judge can sit in the Outer House to relieve the pressure of business (*Purves v. Carswell*).
3. Where questions of difficulty or importance render it expedient, or the judges of a Division are equally divided, the judges may require a case to be reheard before such a larger court as is necessary to dispose of the case (Court of Session Act 1988, s. 36). This may be a Court of Seven (see *e.g. Reiley v. Kingslaw Riding School* 1975 S.C. 28 and *Collie and Buyers* 1981 S.L.T. 191) or, at least in theory, the Whole Court. The last reported case where this occurred was *Bell v. Bell* 1940 S.C. 229. In it the judges split 7:6 with the deciding vote being that of the Lord Ordinary from whom the original reclaiming motion (appeal) came. In practice it is almost inconceivable that we will ever again see a decision of the Whole Court. This is because in any one week nowadays up to ten of the judges will be presiding in High Court trials. The combined pressure of the civil and criminal caseload would make a Whole Court hearing impractical and uneconomic.

Nevertheless there have been several small reforms to the Court which may, inadvertently, have begun to erode the collegiate nature of the Court. Thus it is no longer possible for a Lord Ordinary faced with a difficult question to refer a case to the Inner House for disposal or guidance nor for a Division of the Court to "seek the opinions" of the judges of the other Division or all the other judges of the Court on difficult or important points of law. Secondly, the senior judge in an Extra Division no longer automatically presides in an appeal—the Lord President directs who will preside. Again, promotion to the Inner House from the Outer House is no longer by seniority alone, now promotion is through selection by the Lord President and the Lord Justice-Clerk with the consent of the Scottish Ministers (see the Law Reform (Miscellaneous Provisions) (Scotland) Act 1990, s. 35(2) and Schedule 4, para. (4)). Finally, as we have seen there is now provision for temporary judges to sit who may well never become permanent members of the College of Justice.

II. JURISDICTION

A. AUTHORITY OVER DEFENDER OR SUBJECT MATTER

As in the sheriff court the general rule is that a case must be raised in the forum of the defender. The territorial jurisdiction of the Court of Session is the whole of Scotland and the territorial waters including parts of the Continental Shelf. For further details, see W.A. Wilson, *Introductory Essays on Scots Law* (2nd ed.) (W. Green & Son: 1984) at pp. 32–35.

Domicile and Matrimonial Proceedings Act 1973, s. 7(2), (3)

"(2) The Court shall have jurisdiction to entertain an action for divorce, separation or declarator of freedom and putting to silence if (and only if) either of the parties to the marriage in question—

(*a*) is domiciled in Scotland on the date when the action is begun; or

(*b*) was habitually resident in Scotland throughout the period of one year ending with that date.

(3) The Court shall have jurisdiction to entertain an action for declarator of marriage or declarator of nullity of marriage if (and only if) either of the parties to the marriage—

(*a*) is domiciled in Scotland on the date when the action is begun; or

(*b*) was habitually resident in Scotland throughout the period of one year ending with that date; or

(*c*) died before that date and either—

(i) was at death domiciled in Scotland, or

(ii) had been habitually resident in Scotland throughout the period of one year ending with the date of death."

Presumption of Death (Scotland) Act 1977, s. 1(3)

"(3) The Court of Session shall have jurisdiction to entertain an action of declarator [of death] if and only if—

(*a*) the missing person was domiciled in Scotland on the date on which he was last known to be alive or had been habitually resident there throughout the period of one year ending with that date; or

(*b*) the pursuer in the action—

(i) is the spouse of the missing person, and

(ii) is domiciled in Scotland at the date of raising the action or was habitually resident there throughout the period of one year ending with that date."

Note that in actions of status the forum of the pursuer can be used as well as the forum of the defender.

In other cases the position is regulated by the Civil Jurisdiction and Judgments Acts 1982 and 1991. The jurisdiction of the court varies slightly depending whether the defender falls within the ambit of Schedule 1, Schedule 4 or

Schedule 7 of the 1982 Act or Schedule 1 of the 1991 Act (see Chapter 2, pp. 3 and 4 above and A.E. Anton and P. Beaumont, *Civil Jurisdiction in Scotland: the Brussels and Lugano Conventions* (W. Green & Son, 2nd ed, 1995).

In essence all defenders covered by the Acts may be sued in the courts for the place where they are resident and with which they have a substantial connection. In addition they may be sued in the Court of Session:

(1) if the case relates to a contract which is to be performed within the territorial jurisdiction of the court;
(2) if the case relates to delict or quasi-delict and the harmful event took place within the jurisdiction of the court;
(3) if the case is brought against them in their capacity as trusters, trustees or beneficiaries of a Scottish trust;
(4) if the case relates to maintenance and the maintenance creditor is habitually resident within the jurisdiction of the court or if the matter is ancillary to proceedings relating to status and the court has jurisdiction under the Domicile and Matrimonial Proceedings Act 1973;
(5) if the case arises out of the operations of a branch, agency or other establishment located within the jurisdiction of the court;
(6) if there are a number of defenders and one of them is resident and has substantial ties with a place within the jurisdiction of the court;
(7) if the case is a counter claim arising from the same contract or facts which have given rise to a case which is pending before the court;
(8) if the case relates to the ownership or tenancy of immoveable property which is situated within the jurisdiction of the court;
(9) if the proceedings are concerned with the validity of the constitution, the nullity or the dissolution of Scottish or Scottish controlled companies, partnerships or associations or the decisions of such bodies;
(10) if the defenders have prorogated, *i.e.* accepted, the jurisdiction of the court by express agreement or by entering appearance before the court to oppose the action;
(11) if the case relates to a consumer contract completed in Scotland and the consumer or the defender resides in, and has substantial ties with a place within the jurisdiction of the court.

In cases where Schedule 7 applies defenders may also be sued in the Court of Session:

(1) if they have no fixed residence and they have been personally cited within the jurisdiction of the court;
(2) if they have no fixed residence in the United Kingdom and moveable property belonging to them has been arrested, or they own immoveable property situated, within the jurisdiction of the court;
(3) if the proceedings relate to moveable property situated within the jurisdiction of the court;
(4) if the proceedings are for interdict and it is alleged that the wrong is likely to be committed within the jurisdiction of the court;
(5) if the proceedings concern a debt secured over immoveable property situated within the jurisdiction of the court;

(6) if the proceedings concern an arbitration which is conducted in Scotland or which is governed by Scots law;

(7) if the proceedings are principally concerned with the registration in the United Kingdom or the validity in the United Kingdom of patents, trade marks, designs or other intellectual property. The Court of Session may now also make a declaration that a United Kingdom Act of Parliament is incompatible with the rights secured under the Human Rights Act 1998 (s. 4) or quash an Act of the Scottish Parliament as being *ultra vires* or in contravention of E.C. law or rights secured under the Human Rights Act 1998 (Scotland Act 1998, s. 29).

B. POWER TO GRANT THE REMEDY

Like the sheriff court, the Court of Session can grant a variety of possessory and petitory (payment, multiplepoinding, accounting, delivery and specific implement) remedies as well as declarator, damages, reduction, adjudication, suspension, interdict, petitions to the nobile officium and special cases.

C. POWER TO ENTERTAIN THE CAUSE

Generally the Court of Session has jurisdiction in all causes connected with Scotland unless excluded by statute. Its privative jurisdiction includes most actions of adjudication, reduction, proving the tenor, petitions for the liquidation of a limited company with a paid up share capital exceeding £120,000, petitions to the nobile officium, judicial review, special cases (see below at pp. 74 and 75), summary trials (Court of Session Act 1988, s. 26) and certain actions of status.

The Grant Report, pp. 38–39

"**Reductions**

119. Except for [some] very limited sheriff court powers . . . the Court of Session has privative jurisdiction in reductions, in which the Court orders that a document, agreement, decision or court decree shall be of no effect. It may for instance reduce a will, contract or interlocutor, or the administrative decision of a public authority such as government department or local authority. Actions of reduction are rare, and a substantial proportion involve the reduction of sheriff court decrees, particularly where the decree was granted in error . . .

120. It was put to us that the sheriff court might have jurisdiction in all actions of reduction, but we do not feel able to endorse this proposal. A reduction is sometimes used as a kind of appeal against the decision of a sheriff court and we think it inappropriate that a sheriff court should have power to reduce its own decrees. As regards other reductions which are not now competent in the sheriff court, we consider that they frequently raise questions of great legal difficulty and importance which ought to be handled in the Court of Session . . .

Adjudications

121. The title 'adjudication' is applied to two types of actions. An adjudication in implement is an action in which a person who has paid for heritable

property, but has not received a title, moves the court to grant him one. The second type, adjudication for debt, is a form of diligence in which heritable property is attached for debt. The decree of adjudication in this case vests the adjudged land in the creditor, subject to a right of redemption by the debtor within a period of ten years known as 'the legal'. Further action may become necessary after this period to exclude the debtor's right of redemption . . .

Actions for Proving the Tenor of Lost Documents

136. An action for proving the tenor of a lost document is at present privative to the Court of Session. No witness expressly suggested to us that actions for proving the tenor should be competent in the sheriff court, but we have considered whether this change might be made. The number of applications to the Court of Session for this purpose is, we understand, very small and they tend to raise difficult questions of fact and law. Having regard to the need for uniformity of decision in a very small field, and the unlikelihood of hardship or serious inconvenience to any number of litigants, we have concluded that actions for proving the tenor of lost documents should remain privative to the Court of Session."

For a case on proving the tenor see *Crichton v. Wood* 1981 S.L.T. (Notes) 66.

In most other cases the Court of Session has concurrent jurisdiction with the sheriff court. For details of the privative jurisdiction of the sheriff court see pp. 31 and 32 above. This raises the question as to why, when confronted with a choice of courts, some pursuers and their advisers prefer the sheriff court and some the Court of Session. In the absence of research, any answer to this question is necessarily speculative. Normally, the sheriff court will be more convenient, more accessible, cheaper and will often involve fewer delays than the Court of Session. Sometimes the choice will effectively be made by the Scottish Legal Aid Board, sometimes the perceived strengths and weaknesses of the local sheriff court will determine the pursuer's choice and sometimes potential problems of enforcement may tip the scales in the direction of the Court of Session. While some pursuers will be influenced by the simple and cheap appeal procedure available from the sheriff court others may be tempted to raise their actions in the Court of Session to avoid publicity or because of the higher levels of legal expenses awardable in that court. Pursuers who are minded to adopt the latter course in an attempt to put pressure on the defender to settle the action may find to their cost that they are only awarded expenses on the sheriff court scale. See *Smith v. British Rail Engineering Ltd.* 1985 S.L.T. 463 and *McPherson v. British Railways Board* 1985 S.L.T. 467. As in the sheriff court there is provision for an action raised in the Court of Session to be remitted by the Court at its own instance or on the application of one or both parties to the appropriate sheriff court (Law Reform (Miscellaneous Provisions) (Scotland) Act 1985, s. 14). See *e.g. Gribb v. Gribb* 1993 S.L.T. 178.

III. PROCEDURE AND CASELOAD

A. THE OUTER HOUSE

The Outer House consists of 19 Lords Ordinary who sit singly (or occasionally with a civil jury of 12). The pressure of business today is such that it has become necessary to also call on the services of temporary judges.

Maxwell, The Practice of the Court of Session, p. 7

"The jurisdiction of a Lord Ordinary is both original and, to a limited extent, appellate. By virtue of his original jurisdiction, he is a judge of first instance in cases above [£1,500] in value, and in cases where the Court of Session has privative jurisdiction. His appellate jurisdiction includes jurisdiction to entertain at common law processes for the suspension and reduction of decrees of lower courts, and a statutory jurisdiction in causes arising under administrative law."

Cases are initiated in the Outer House in two ways; as actions and as petitions.

Civil Judicial Statistics Scotland 1983, p. 8

"The Court of Session

2.6 An action is initiated in the general department by the signeting of the summons (thus allowing it to be served on the defender) whereafter it is called in court not earlier than the fourteenth day after service. The defender has 14 days from calling to lodge defences, and failure to do so may result in a decree of absence (and expenses) for the pursuer. If defences are lodged the pursuer's representative draws up a consolidated record of claim and defence which is then adjusted by the representatives of both parties over about the following four months. The action then appears before the court to be disposed of. In defended consistorial (marriage, divorce and separation) actions the period between lodging defences and adjusting the record is shorter: in undefended actions, proof (the submission of evidence) may be made by affidavit. Petitions in the Court of Session specify parties affected by the cause: the process of adjustment of the petition (if answers are lodged) is, again, shorter than for actions initiated by summons."

1. ACTIONS

TABLE 3.1

Civil Actions disposed of by final judgment 1997

	Sheriff Court Ordinary	*Outer House*
Payment (debt)	16,577	299
Land or heritable estate	881	50
Personal injury	841	1,297
Damages	531	246
Husband and wife (including divorce)	8,471	267
Other (excluding divorce)	7,368	434
Total	34,669	2,593

[Source: Scottish Courts Administration, *Civil Judicial Statistics Scotland* 1997.]

Table 3.1 demonstrates that the Outer House, like the ordinary procedure in the sheriff court, is dominated by personal injury, debt (payment) and consistorial actions albeit in different proportions.

(1) Adjudication: Non-consistorial Causes

It is worth stressing that the figures in Table 3.1 are only the tip of an iceberg. Many unpaid debts never reach a debt collection agency or a solicitor's office. Of those that do, many more are settled by correspondence without a writ being issued. See Scottish Office Central Research Unit paper, "Debt Recovery" 1981.

Similarly the Pearson Commission (Cmnd. 7054, 1978) estimated that of 250,000 personal injury claims in the United Kingdom in a year, only 1% actually reach the courts. Very few of those non-consistorial causes where an action has been raised in court, actually get to a proof (trial).

TABLE 3.2

Completed Debt and Damages actions in the Outer House 1991

	1 *Withdrawn*	2 *Decree in absence of defences*	3 *Decree without evidence*	4 *Proof*	*Total*
Debts	388	712	155	34	1,289
Damages	402	59	1,124	72	1,657

[Source: Scottish Courts Administration.]

While there are clearly differences between debt and damages actions as Table 3.2 reveals (*e.g.* a far higher proportion of debt cases are undefended and thus decree is granted in absence), the overall picture is largely the same. The great majority of debt and damages cases where a writ has been served are disposed of by out of court settlement (column 1), by the court giving its stamp of approval to such a settlement (column 3) or by the court approving the pursuer's unopposed action without hearing evidence (column 2). In short, the role of the court in non-consistorial cases is mainly "administrative" in nature. In fairness it should be admitted that the figures in Table 3.2 do not contain reference to the motions and debates in defended cases (which relate to interim or incidental matters), which usually take the form of an adversarial contest.

This conclusion prompts the question: why do so many cases settle? A partial answer is because a settlement ensures that a pursuer will get something, while if he goes to trial he may get nothing. Thus, a survey of Scottish personal injury cases conducted for the Pearson Commission in 1974 suggested that in almost 90% of cases which were disposed of without a proof (columns 1–3) some payment was made to the pursuer.

Phillips and Hawkins, "The settlement process," p. 497 et seq.

> "'A settlement,' Atiyah says, 'is a business bargain in which the plaintiff sells his claim . . . for what he can get and the buyer buys for as little as he has to pay.' One important consequence of the commercial nature of this transaction is that what is received in a claim in settlement is by no means what

the courts would necessarily award. Moreover, claimants in minor cases of personal injury receive a much higher proportion of their losses than those involved in more serious cases . . .

There are two major reasons why the great majority of claims are settled rather than resolved by judgment of a court: the cost to the individual who wishes to pursue a claim for damages to its ultimate conclusion in the courts, and the risks involved in doing so.

Delay

One of the most important factors likely to affect a claimant's perception of the value of pursuing the case further is the delay likely to be involved. So far as the ordinary plaintiff is concerned, delay is costly since he receives no compensation until the case is settled (except sick pay or social security benefits or, occasionally, an interim payment where liability is not in dispute), while as a result of his injury his various expenses may be increased and his earning power possibly reduced. 'Even the most meritorious claims,' according to the Winn Committee, 'weaken in geometrical progression with the passage of time.' In contrast, the defendant's insurance company may not find it costly to delay settlement, depending on the rate of interest to be charged. [T]he existence of risk . . . encourages claimants to accept offers that are unfair in the actuarial sense. American insurance adjusters themselves openly exploit it, [and are taught to do so in their training] . . . 'In discussing the merits of a settlement the adjuster should always be specific and, if possible, pinpoint those areas that will most likely create doubt and uncertainty on the opposing side . . . Creating doubt . . . is the focal point of good claim negotiations'."

Paterson, "Judges: a political elite?" pp. 129–130

"[In] the Thalidomide case (*Att. Gen. v. Times Newspapers Ltd.* [1974] A.C. 273) . . . at first all the bargaining counters seemed to be on the side of Distillers. The parents were disunited and financially far weaker than the company. Their position in law was uncertain and counsel indicated that they were unlikely to win their case without being fought all the way to the House of Lords. This would involve delay and expense. Therefore efforts were made to settle the actions. However time was also against the parents since as the deformed children grew up the special equipment and facilities which they required, imposed an increasing financial burden on the parents. Accordingly, the incentive to compromise for a lower figure than they might otherwise receive also increased. Distillers on the other hand were getting the interest on the money which they might eventually have to pay out, for as long as they could stave off a settlement. Therefore, there was little incentive for Distillers to settle. When they did make an offer to the parents in November 1971, they insisted that it was accepted by all the parents. Although this offer was a poor one judged by the standards of what the company finally offered, eventually all but five sets of parents were prepared (albeit reluctantly in many cases) to settle for the 1971 offer. When these five still held out, one of the majority tried to have them removed as the representatives of the children on the grounds that they were being unreasonable.

It was only after this move had been defeated that the *Sunday Times* began its campaign on September 24th 1972. Yet when the *Sunday Times* was taken to the House of Lords over their right to publish an article in this campaign the Law Lords held if they did so they would be in contempt of court for bringing unfair influence on a litigant and thus perverting the course of justice. The point here is not that this decision was wrong, but that according to the . . . Law Lords, pressure placed on the parents by delay, anxiety, financial hardship, despair, disunity and the uncertainty of their legal rights, was not unfair but the exercise of their one effective weapon, newspaper publicity, was."

As these extracts suggest, although negotiation takes place in almost every contested case, as a method of resolving cases it can sometimes yield unfair results. This is not simply because negotiation may involve compromising legal rights but because the party with the stronger bargaining counters (including delay, anxiety and expense factors) can impose an unfair "settlement" on the other party and the adversarial system encourages the stronger party to do just that. The cruel pressure exerted by a defence offer or "tender" of an inadequate but not totally derisory sum just before a proof, with its accompanying threat that the pursuer will have to meet all the expenses of the proof for both sides if he or she fails to "beat the tender", is but one case in point. See J. Robertson, "Learning to play the legal game of brinkmanship," *The Scotsman*, 28th September 1990.

(2) Adjudication: Consistorial Causes

Almost exactly the same processes are at work in consistorial causes as in non-consistorial ones. The high number of consistorial cases which reach "final judgment" is not an indication that negotiated settlements do not take place in divorce cases. It is simply that to obtain a divorce the court must grant a decree, and that decree cannot be granted without written or oral evidence from the pursuer. Approximately 60% of divorce cases are probably opposed at one stage or another, most commonly in relation to money (periodical allowance, capital sum and aliment) and to a lesser extent in relation to parental rights and responsibilities, *e.g.* custody of the children or the grounds of the divorce. These disputes are settled in a very similar fashion to personal injury cases.

Mnookin, "Bargaining in the shadow of the law," p. 76

"[There are] four factors that would seem to be important influences or determinants of the outcomes of bargaining . . . (1) the preferences of the divorcing parents; (2) the bargaining endowments created by legal rules that allow the imposition of a particular allocation if the parties fail to reach agreement; (3) the degree of uncertainty concerning the legal outcome if the parties go to court, and the parties' attitudes towards risk; (4) transaction costs, and the parties' respective abilities to bear these costs."

As an all-party group of M.P.s stated in 1980:

> "All too often the courts are simply rubber-stamping arrangements made by the parents as part of the bargaining over financial and property matters in which the children are used as pawns."

Once the settlement is reached the cases go ahead undefended and the court grants approval to the settlement and the divorce usually on the basis of affidavit evidence (sworn documentary statements). The court is usually not concerned with the fairness or otherwise of the settlement nor to check the accuracy of the facts contained in the affidavit. As in the case of non-consistorial actions the work of the court is largely "administrative". Again it has to be conceded that it is not unusual in consistorial cases for the court to be required to make rulings on incidental and interim matters following a contested hearing on an opposed motion. Few cases remain defended to the last and in only a small minority of cases does the pursuer not get decree.

Negotiated settlements in consistorial causes, therefore, can suffer from similar flaws to those that can arise in non-consistorial causes. Furthermore, "defensive lawyering" and the adversarial approach of solicitors emphasise rather than reduce the area of conflict between the parties, thus leading to unnecessary suffering and bitterness. One answer to these problems would be to reduce the scope for bargaining. This may be done by exploring the possibilities for alternative dispute resolution (ADR) including: simplifying the grounds for divorce, by reducing the cost of divorce, or by encouraging conciliation. These possibilities are explored in more detail in Chapter 1.

Following the Report of the Working Party on Divorce Procedure (chaired by Lord Cowie) in 1980 a simplified and cheap "do-it-yourself" divorce procedure was introduced in January 1983. The procedure is competent in both the Court of Session and the sheriff court. Litigants who are eligible to raise their actions under this procedure do not require corroborated evidence (the evidence of a witness other than the pursuer). Having paid a fee (from which recipients of Income Support, Family Income Supplement or Legal Advice and Assistance are exempt) the pursuer simply sends in a completed form and a sworn statement (affidavit) to the court. Costing less than a tenth of the expense of a normal undefended divorce and having a simplicity which obviates the necessity of employing a solicitor (although over a third of applicants consult a solicitor in practice) the procedure has been well received by participants. See Scottish Office Central Research Unit paper, "The Simplified Divorce Procedure" 1984. While there is no doubting the popularity of the procedure (about a quarter of those seeking a divorce invoke the simplified procedure) its impact in reducing unnecessary conflict and bitterness is limited. This is because applicants are only eligible to use the procedure where the spouses have lived apart for at least two years (and both consent to the divorce) or for at least five years, there are no children of the marriage under 16 and neither spouse is seeking a financial award against the other from the court. A recent working party chaired by Lord Cowie recommended that contrary to the practice in England and Wales, the simplified procedure should not be extended to other forms of divorce. It is perhaps unfortunate that there were no lay-persons on the working party. In short, parties with children or who cannot agree on all financial matters or who have only recently separated cannot use the procedure. For them, mediation schemes may be an answer (see Chapter 1, pp. 18–22).

(3) Jury Trials

Civil jury trials have become relatively scarce in modern times (in the ten years to 1991 there has been an average of 4.5 jury trials per annum in the Outer House). Such trials have once before fallen into desuetude in Scotland, only to be re-introduced from Westminster. How long they will continue to survive in the future must be an open question. Although once theoretically available in sixteen types of action ranging from furiosity and idiotcy to life insurance under the 1825 Court of Session Act, by the 1980s jury trials were almost exclusively reserved for personal injury actions. Even in these cases its efficacy as a means of deciding cases was coming under attack. For a rare case of a jury trial in a defamation case in modern times see *Winter v. News Scotland Ltd.* 1991 S.L.T. 828.

Watt, "The News Reporter's Role," p. 495–496

> "**Jury Trial**
>
> Take . . . the diminution of the jury trial. In 1955 there was a total of 104 actions tried by that method. In 1960 the figure was up to 114. But five years later the total had dropped to 67, in 1970 it was 49, in 1975 18, and by 1978 it had dropped to a mere five cases.
>
> This very remarkable change took place not as the direct result of any legislative intent affecting the rights of parties to civil actions to have their disputes determined by juries. It . . . occurred, as I see it, because juries were out of favour not only with the legal profession, or at least a majority of it, but also with insurance companies. It is this circumstance which has wrought another important but silent revolution in the conduct of reparation litigation in Scotland.
>
> No statistics are available to establish the point, but it must be widely recognised that it is no longer judges and juries but insurance companies who determine in the majority of cases how much, if anything, an injured party should receive. Precedent has increasingly become available not from judicial opinion but from the tables kept in insurance offices. It is a development no doubt derived from the motive to save expense by avoiding a hearing in court, but it is a trend which causes some misgivings. I say so, not because it has necessarily had any deleterious effect on the doing of justice—I have no means of knowing that—but because it has been brought about without public consultation or any deliberate act of reform through the usual methods, and purely as a matter of expediency as seen from the viewpoint of practitioners in the fields of law and insurance."

In June 1988 the Scottish Courts Administration published a Consultation Paper on the Jury Trials in the Court of Session. Its tenor was to suggest that civil jury trials were no longer popular with litigants and would become increasingly inappropriate with the growth in admissibility of hearsay evidence following the introduction of the Civil Evidence (Scotland) Act 1988. Although the then Lord President and a number of his colleagues favoured abolition of the civil jury (as did members of the Scottish Law Commission, the Sheriffs' Association and the Association of British Insurers), the majority of respondents (including the Law Society, several leading court firms and the consumer lobby) favoured retention. Rather to the surprise of the commentators the Lord Advocate subsequently announced that civil jury trials would be retained but suggested a number of possible reforms on which he invited comment: (1) restriction of the right to jury trial to cases which do not raise difficult questions of law or factual issues of exceptional complexity; (2) the "right" to jury trial should become a privilege available only at the discretion of the court on special cause being shown; (3) further guidance should be provided to the jury on appropriate levels of damages awards; and (4) reduction in the size of the civil jury to seven. (See (1989) 152 SCOLAG 66.) Subsequently, the Court of Session Act 1988, s. 11 restricted civil jury trials to personal injury, defamation, delinquency and reduction actions but, that apart, none of the proposed reforms have been implemented.

(4) Delay

One factor which plays a part in out-of-court negotiations as we have seen is the delay involved in litigation. Such delays are a perennial source of complaint. The Pearson Commission's study of personal injury cases in Scotland in 1974 cast some light on the problem.

TABLE 3.3

Delays in Personal Injury Cases

	Months
Average interval	
From injury to writ	26
From writ to fixing proof	12
From fixing of proof to disposal	6

[Source: Pearson Report (1974) Table 147.]

These figures were broadly confirmed by G.Cameron and R. Johnston, in their 1995 report, *Personal Injury Litigation in the Scottish Courts: A Descriptive Analysis* (Scottish Office Central Research Unit, 1995). Cameron and Johnston found that the average median interval from injury to service of summons in Court of Session ordinary procedure was approximately 28 months and from summons to final disposal 17 months. As can be seen the lengthiest delay occurs between the injury and the issuing of the writ. This is a product of Scottish legal rules and practice.

The Kincraig Committee on Personal Injuries Litigation, p. 8

"The present practice of having the issue on the merits and the issue on quantum decided at the same time and the rule that a pursuer can obtain no more than he concludes for, involve having to conclude for a specific sum as representing the maximum he can obtain. This can delay determination of the merits of a case because in many instances the medical condition of the claimant is not sufficiently static to enable reasonably accurate assessment of quantum to be made at an early stage."

The committee's findings (published in 1979) suggested that the delay between the signeting of the summons and the fixing of a proof (caused by the Scottish system of pleading) had been reduced since 1974. So too had the period between fixing a proof and the date of the trial. In the years following the Kincraig Committee, however, a rise in criminal work in the High Court led to greater calls on the Court of Session judiciary. This in turn led to the delay between fixing a proof and the actual hearing rising to 15 months by 1986. Indeed, it was partly on the strength of these delays that the government was persuaded to increase the number of judges in the Court of Session in 1985. Moreover, as the Kincraig Committee observed, the high incidence of settlements of actions in the week before and on the day of the trial (over one in two cases) causes a loss of judicial time which could otherwise be devoted to hearing cases which are not settled. The Maxwell Report on the "Use of Judicial Time in the Superior Courts of Scotland" (1986) concluded that only 60% of the available judge time in the Court of Session was utilised—primarily because of the problems caused by late settlements.

Although there are the occasional lengthy hearings (the evidence alone in *McColl v. Strathclyde Regional Council*, 1983 SLT 616 concerning the latter's proposal to add fluoride to the public water supply lasted for 143 days in 1981/82) the average personal injury case lasts less than two days. Delay at the hearing stage is therefore minimal.

(5) Tackling delay

The increases in delay in the mid-eighties were compounded by a steady rise in the number of ordinary actions (excluding consistorial cases) and criminal cases at this time. Faced by a Government and a Treasury which were reluctant to expand the existing judicial complement to resolve the problem, a series of steps were initiated to confront the problem of delay head-on.

In 1984 rule of court 89B (now Chapter 21 of the Rules of the Court of Session 1994) was introduced. It enables the court to grant a motion by the pursuer for "summary decree" if it is satisfied that the defences as lodged by the defender indicate that there is no defence to the action or any part of it. See "Summary Decree in the Court of Session," 1987 S.L.T. (News) 93.

In the following year, in an endeavour to tackle the problem of delay in personal injury cases—particularly delays attributable to the Scottish system of pleading—the optional procedure was introduced in the Court of Session (see now rules 43.18–43.28 of the Rules of the Court of Session 1994). Where the pursuer elects to adopt this procedure a streamlined and simplified form of pleadings is used and witness lists and documents are exchanged. The new procedure proved popular with pursuers as a means of putting pressure on defenders. By 1988 the average duration of an optional procedure case was 8.5

months as compared with an average of 20 months for ordinary or jury trials (see SCA Consultation Paper on Jury Trials in the Court of Session, 1988). By 1993, the median period for duration of an optional procedure case was an average of approximately 8 months as compared with an average of approximately 17 months for a case brought under the ordinary procedure in the Court of Session and 11 months for cases brought under the ordinary procedure in the sheriff court (see G. Cameron & R. Johnston, *Personal Injury Litigation in the Scottish Courts: A Descriptive Analysis*, Scottish Office Central Research Unit, 1995, pp. 34–38).

The Maxwell Report on *Use of Judicial Time in the Superior Courts of Scotland* (1986). Its Report in 1986 suggested guide times for the key intervals in civil litigation which were about a third of the then current intervals. The average interval between the allowance of a hearing by way of proof or jury trial and the completion of the hearing was 15 months—Maxwell considered it should be between four and six months. By careful overloading of the court rolls (listing many more cases for each day than the court could hear) on the assumption that most cases would be settled and by devising more accurate methods for assessing the likely length of hearings together with the use of retired and temporary judges (Law Reform (Miscellaneous Provisions) (Scotland) Act 1985, s. 22 & Law Reform (Miscellaneous Provisions) (Scotland) Act 1990, s. 35(3)), the court has managed to attain the Maxwell target figures. (See Lord Hope, "Judicial Business," 1991 J.L.S. 266.) The pace of litigation in the court is now such that the optional procedure has begun to lose some of its initial popularity.

The success of these measures has paralleled the success of another measure designed to streamline procedures within the Court. Following critical comments by Lord Fraser in the House of Lords in *Brown v. Hamilton District Council*, 1983 S.L.T. 397, Lord President Emslie set up a working party under Lord Dunpark to devise a simple and quick judicial review procedure for the Court of Session in cases alleging *ultra vires* action or failure to perform a statutory duty. The Act of Sederunt (1985 No. 500 (S. 48)) implementing (at least in part) the Dunpark Report recommendations provides petitioners with an expeditious form of judicial review (see now Chapter 58 of the Rules of the Court of Session 1994). It provides for an accelerated first hearing, a panel of judges with expertise in the relevant branches of law and a limited scope for appeals. Research conducted between April 1985 and April 1987 has shown that the new procedure has led to a substantial increase in applications for judicial review and that these applications have been dealt with extremely expeditiously—25% of petitions were disposed of in four weeks and 68% within two months (see A. Page, "Judicial Review in the Court of Session" in M. Adler and A. Millar (eds.), *Socio-Legal Research in the Scottish Courts*, Volume 2 (Scottish Office Central Research Unit, 1991)). More recently, further research has confirmed a rising trend in the number of judicial review petitions being presented as Table 3.4 illustrates.

TABLE 3.4

Judicial review petitions presented 1988–1997

1988	*1989*	*1990*	*1991*	*1992*	*1993*	*1997*
66	86	62	78	117	151	152

[Sources: Mullen, Pick and Prosser, *Judicial Review in Scotland* (Wiley & Son, 1996), Table 3.1, p. 18 and Scottish Courts Administration, Civil Statistics Scotland 1997, Table 2.10].

This research has also demonstrated that petitions continue to be dealt with expeditiously with 21% between 1988 and 1993 concluding within 2 months and 49% within 5 months (Mullen, Pick and Prosser, *op. cit.*, p. 43). On judicial review generally see T. Mullen, *Guide to Judicial Review* (W. Green & Son: 1987), *West v. Secretary of State for Scotland*, 1992 S.L.T. 636 and W. Finnie, "Triangles as Touchstones of Review," 1993 S.L.T. (News) 51.

Not the least interesting point about the comparative success of these recent initiatives in relation to delay in the Court of Session is the fact that the three procedures existing in the Court of Session prior to 1985 for expediting hearings have remained relatively unused. The first, summary trial (now governed by section 26 of the Court of Session Act 1988) permits parties to bring before the Lord Ordinary of their choice, for no extra payment, any actions competent in the Outer House except those relating to status. The hearing and the preliminary proceedings are expedited and the judge's decision is final. Secondly, under s. 17 of the Law Reform (Miscellaneous Provisions) (Scotland) Act 1980 any Senator of the College of Justice can act as an arbiter or oversman in a commercial dispute when the state of business in the court warrants it. The third procedure is the special case before the Inner House (see pp. 19 and 20 below).

The court returned to the problem of ensuring expeditious procedures in 1988 when a new Act of Sederunt for Commercial Actions was introduced. A revised procedure was introduced in 1994 (Act of Sederunt (Rules of the Court of Session 1994 Amendment No.1 (Commercial Actions) 1994 (S.I. 1994 No. 2310) following recommendations of the Report of the Working Party on Commercial Causes (Lord Coulsfield, Chairman, November 1993) (see now Chapter 47 of the Rules of the Court of Session 1994). Commercial actions could include (i) the construction of a commercial contract, (ii) the export or import of merchandise, (iii) the carriage of goods by land, air or sea, (iv) insurance or (v) commercial leases. The new rules were introduced as a result of the Working Party's report that commercial organisations were highly critical of existing civil court procedures on the grounds of delay, expense and lack of judicial expertise. Their introduction was designed to enable the court to meet these criticisms and to compete effectively with other dispute resolution fora that are available such as courts in other jurisdictions, particularly England and arbitration and alternative dispute resolution.

Stirling Aquatic Technology Ltd v Farmocean AB 1993 SLT 713, Lord President Hope at 715

> "One of the principal objects of the procedure on the commercial roll is to enable disputes of a business or commercial nature to be dealt with as quickly as possible under the close supervision of the court."

To facilitate this object, written pleadings are abbreviated and the judge is given the power to direct the case to a speedy conclusion. The new rules are designed to promote early and full disclosure of relevant evidence to facilitate agreement on as many issues as possible so as to narrow down the areas of dispute and hence speed up litigation on those points.

In addition, a full-time commercial judge has been appointed and two other judges are also available. The full-time commercial judge is relieved from High Court of Justiciary trial work and most other Outer House commitments. This is designed to ensure the development of judicial expertise, continuity in dealing with cases and to facilitate case management. Judicial case management is considered in more detail in Chapter 1.

There is evidence from research conducted between September 1994 and April 1996 that the new rules are reducing delay very considerably.

R. Clancy, A. Murray and R. Wadia, "The New Commercial Cause Rules" 1997 SLT (News) 45, 53 at p. 46

> "A major objective of the new arrangements then is to speed up proceedings, and this has to a large extent been achieved. Of the completed actions 87 per cent (81 in number) were disposed of within 12 months of being raised or transferred, with 55 per cent (51 in number) being disposed of within six months. The average time taken to dispose of defended cases in our study was 26.6 weeks after initiation or transfer to the commercial roll. This compares very favourably with personal injury cases conducted as ordinary actions in the Court of Session where the median estimate of time to disposal was 72 weeks, although the figure for cases conducted on the optional procedure roll was 36 weeks (see Personal Injury Litigation in the Scottish Courts, Scottish Office Central Research Unit, 1995)."

See also Lord Hamilton, "Commercial actions in the Court of Session" (1999) 44 J.L.S.S. 20 and Chapter 1.

Continuing dissatisfaction with apparent delay and expense involved in civil litigation procedures led the then Lord Chancellor, Lord Mackay of Clashfern, to appoint Lord Woolf to consider English and Welsh civil justice. The outcome of Lord Woolf's review is considered in Chapter 1. This increased calls for a similar review in Scotland (see *e.g.* Lord Gill, "The Case for a Civil Justice Review" (1995) 40 J.L.S.S. 129). In response to these developments the then Lord President, Lord Hope appointed Lord Cullen to conduct a review of Outer House procedure. His report, *Review of the Business of the Outer House* (1995, "the Cullen Report") recommended the use of abbreviated pleadings, earlier and wider disclosure of evidence, the introduction of case management hearings and administrative measures to reduce delays in proofs and civil jury trials (see *e.g.* N. Morrison, "The Cullen Report" 1996 S.L.T. (News) 93; M. Upton, "The Cullen Review: Reform of Procedure in the Court of Session" (1996) 41 J.L.S.S. 111; A.D. Murray, "Court of Session Procedure: Past, Present and Future" 1997 S.L.T. (News) 259). The current Lord President, Lord Rodger committed himself in his installation speech to carrying forward procedural reforms in the Court of Session in the light of the Cullen report. Subsequently two further reviews have been undertaken by Lord

Macfadyen and Lord Coulsfield but these remain unpublished and although some of the minor Cullen proposals have been implemented, the principal proposals relating to abbreviated pleadings and case management remain unimplemented (see Lord Macfadyen, "Existing and Future Reforms in Court of Session Practice", unpublished paper for Law Society Conference on Court of Session Practice and Procedure, March 1997). The Cullen Report is considered in the wider context of developments in dispute resolution in Chapter 1.

2. PETITIONS

Causes initiated by petition are often non-contentious as will be apparent from the figures in Table 3.5. Where the petition is opposed, the respondent is almost invariably successful. There is a sense, therefore, in which it could be said that much of the petition work of the Outer House is also "administrative" in character.

TABLE 3.5

Outer House Non-administrative petitions ended by final judgment 1997

Nature of petition	*Petition opposed*	*Petition unopposed*	*Total*
Suspension, interdict and liberation	30	17	47
Factors, curators, etc.	3	16	19
Companies Acts	16	46	62
Sequestration	140	270	410
Trusts Acts	3	16	19
International child abduction	9	4	13
Other	51	155	206
Total	252	524	776

[Source: Scottish Courts Administration, Civil Judicial Statistics Scotland *1997*].

In addition to the non-administrative petitions discussed above, there are also administrative petitions, for example, petitions for caveats and fiats. Lodging a caveat prevents a certain course of action being taken without first informing the petitioner. Fiats simply prevent certain courses of action, for example the disposal of heritage by a debtor or the pledging of a husband's credit by a wife.

B. THE INNER HOUSE

The Inner House, as we saw earlier, consists normally of two Divisions. The usual quorum is three and only occasionally is a full Division of four judges convened. This enables the remaining judges to go on criminal circuit, to sit in the Outer House or to form an Extra Division (with the help of a Lord Ordinary or retired judges) to assist with Inner House business. In recent times an Extra Division has been sitting almost continuously, with the help of retired judges. The Divisions are of equal authority and competence, though in some areas there is by custom a division of labour between them. Thus, the First Division hears most tax cases except capital gains tax cases which are heard by the Second Division.

1. ACTIONS

The Inner House hears both actions and petitions. Its jurisdiction in respect of actions is overwhelmingly appellate. Although the appeal may sometimes be on fact as well as law, fresh evidence is rarely taken. The original transcript usually suffices. This nevertheless places the court hearing the appeal at a disadvantage as compared with the judge of first instance. As Lord Sumner observed in *Hontestroom v. Sagaporack* [1927] A.C. 37 at p. 47:

> "Not to have seen the witnesses puts appellate judges in a permanent position of disadvantage as against the trial judge, and, unless it can be shown that he has failed to use or has palpably misused his advantage, the higher Court ought not to take the responsibility of reversing conclusions so arrived at, merely on the result of their own comparisons and criticisms of the witnesses and of their own view of the probabilities of the case."

TABLE 4.6

Inner House Actions disposed of by final judgment 1997

Debt	3
Land/heritable estate	10
Personal injury	28
Damages	19
Husband and wife (excluding divorce)	—
Others (including divorce)	40
Total	100

[Source: Scottish Courts Administration, *Civil Judicial Statistics Scotland 1997*.]

There are three main sources of appellate jurisdiction in the Inner House:

(1) By reclaiming motion from decisions taken in the Outer House. This is the biggest single source of appeals.

(2) Appeals from the sheriff court (usually direct from sheriffs, see pp. 36 and 37 above).

(3) Appeals from administrative tribunals, the Land Court, and other courts of special jurisdiction, and also stated cases on a point of law in arbitrations (for which see, Administration of Justice (Scotland) Act 1972, s. 3). See, *e.g. John G. McGregor (Contractors) Ltd. v. Grampian Regional Council*, 1991 S.L.T. 365.

In addition, The Inner House now has an important jurisdiction in determining the devolution issues referred by the sheriff court or Outer House under the Scotland Act 1998 (see below, pp.75 and 76).

The most celebrated source of original jurisdiction in actions is special cases on a point of law under the Court of Session Act 1988, s. 27:

"**Special cases**

27.—(1) Where any parties interested, whether personally or in some fiduciary or official capacity, in the decision of a question of law are agreed upon the facts, and are in dispute only on the law applicable to those facts, it shall be competent for them without raising any proceeding, or at any stage of any proceeding, to present to the Inner House a case (in this section referred to as a special case) signed by their counsel setting out the facts upon which they are so agreed and the question of law arising from those facts; and the parties may ask the Court either for its opinion or for its judgment on that question of law. . . .

(5) Any judgment pronounced by the Court by virtue of this section shall be liable to review by the House of Lords unless such review is excluded by consent of all the parties to the special case."

See, *e.g. Carnegie Trustees v. University of St. Andrews* 1968 S.C.(H.L.) 27 and *Spencer's Trustees v. Ruggles* 1982 S.L.T. 165.

2. PETITIONS

Very few Inner House petitions are opposed. Indeed only 9 of the 35 petitions disposed of in 1997 were opposed (see also Table 3.7).

TABLE 3.7

Non-administrative petitions ended by final judgment, 1997

Nobile officium	4
Trusts	9
Company petitions	4
Other	18
Total	35

Source: Scottish Courts Administration, *Civil Judicial Statistics Scotland 1997.* For petitions on the nobile officium see Chap. 16 below.

3. DEVOLUTION ISSUES

The sheriff court and the Outer House may refer any devolution issue (see Chapter 4, p. 85 for a definition) to the Inner House for determination (Scotland Act 1998, Sched.6, para.7). Reference of devolution issues from the Outer House is to take the form of a report to the Inner House for a ruling (rules 25A.7 and 34 of the Rules of the Court of Session 1994). A tribunal from which there is no appeal must refer such an issue to the Inner House and any other tribunal may make such a reference (Scotland Act 1998, Sched.6, para.8). Where the Inner House makes a determination on a devolution issue under the above provisions there is a right of appeal to the Judicial Committee of the Privy Council (Scotland Act 1998, Sched.6, para.12) (see also Chapter 4, pp. 85 and 86 below).

If a devolution issue arises in a court consisting of 3 or more judges of the Court of Session (which could be either a large Outer House bench or the Inner House) otherwise than by way of a reference under the above provisions, the Court may refer the matter to the Judicial Committee of the Privy Council (Scotland Act 1998, Sched.6, para.10). An appeal against a determination of a devolution issue by a court consisting of 3 or more judges of the Court of Session from which there is no appeal to the House of Lords shall lie to the Judicial Committee of the Privy Council but only with leave of the court concerned or with special leave of the Judicial Committee itself (Scotland Act 1998, Sched.6, para.13).

On the Judicial Committee of the Privy Council, see Chapter 4 below.

C. COURTS OF SPECIAL JURISDICTION

These include the Court of the Lord Lyon, the Court of Teinds, the Restrictive Practices Court, the Registration of Voters Appeal Court, the Election Petition Court, the Valuation Appeal Court, the Lands Tribunal for Scotland and the Scottish Land Court. Only the last three handle a sizeable caseload. It is the last which is perhaps the most interesting for reformers since it contains a number of innovative features. It is peripatetic, it consists of a legal chairman (having the status of a judge of the Court of Session) and four expert lay assessors including at least one Gaelic speaker, it encourages party litigants, its procedure is simplified and semi-inquisitorial and the formal rules of evidence are relaxed. The court deals primarily with agricultural and crofting tenancies.

TABLE 3.8

Cases Disposed of by the Scottish Land Court, 1986 to 1997

Nature of case	1986	1987	1988	1989	1990	1991	1992	1993	1994	1995	1996	1997
Holdings revalued/ Fix fair rents etc.	196	30	57	63	15	13	4	6	6	—	5	7
Applications by landlords for resumption of part holdings	220	237	293	234	219	226	230	194	196	202	164	120
Applications under Crofting Reform (Scotland) Act 1976 (purchase of croft)	19	25	18	6	—	—	10	20	—	—	—	—
Other applications	90	92	71	52	56	48	68	28	26	31	33	48
Total	525	384	439	355	290	287	312	248	228	233	202	175

[Source: Scottish Courts Administration, *Civil Judicial Statistics Scotland 1994, 1997.*]

CHAPTER 4

THE HOUSE OF LORDS AND THE JUDICIAL COMMITTEE OF THE PRIVY COUNCIL

I. JURISDICTION

A. HOUSE OF LORDS

The House of Lords has no original jurisdiction in Scots cases. It has appellate jurisdiction in fact and law in the case of final judgments of the Inner House of the Court of Session, except where appeal is excluded by statute. If the case originated in the sheriff court the appeal is limited to points of law. The House also has jurisdiction to entertain appeals against interlocutory judgments of the Inner House if the Division is not unanimous or if the Division itself grants leave to appeal.

1. CIVIL APPEALS

(I) THE TREATY OF UNION 1707, ARTICLE XIX

"That the Court of Session or College of Justice do after the Union and notwithstanding thereof remain in all time coming with in Scotland as it is now constituted by the laws of that kingdom and with the same authority and privileges as before the Union subject nevertheless to such regulations for the better administration of justice as shall be made by the Parliament of Great Britain . . . And that no causes in Scotland be cognoscible by the Court of Chancery Queen's Bench Common Pleas or any other Court in Westminster Hall and that the said Courts or any other of the like nature after the Union shall have no power to cognosce review or alter the acts or sentences of the judicature within Scotland or stop the execution of the same . . ."

Since the House of Lords did not sit in Westminster Hall the Treaty of Union is silent on the question whether there were to be appeals to the British Parliament from the Court of Session after the Union.

Gibb, *Law from over the Border*, p. 3

"It is a historical mystery as yet unsolved what the Commissioners for negotiating the Union really intended to do about the right of appeal. Under Article XIX of the Treaty of Union it was agreed that no causes in Scotland should be 'cognoscible' by the Courts of Chancery, Queen's Bench, Common Pleas or any other Court in Westminster Hall. Language such as this of course leaves a loop-hole for the intrusion of the jurisdiction of the House of Lords and ingenious authors have suggested that the ambiguity of the article was not unintentional but was dictated by statesmanlike considerations. These learned authors state that if it had been made plain to the people of Scotland that an appellate jurisdiction in the Lords was contemplated, the proposal would have inflamed the opposition of patriotic Scotsmen. A plan indeed was advanced by the English Commissioners for the erection, in Scotland, of a branch of the House of Lords, so to call it, composed of peers of Great Britain, but this came to nothing, as did a suggestion that the Scottish peers should be allowed to choose the court for the hearing of appeals from Scotland."

The Earl of Roseberie v. Inglis, House of Lords, 1708, *unreported*

Several months after the start of the Union the cause of *The Earl of Roseberie v. Sir John Inglis*, which had been decided by the Court of Session in 1695, was appealed to the House of Lords. The case is unreported. But Gibb in *Law from over the Border* describes the proceedings, as follows:

> "In the year 1708 the Earl of Roseberie (sic) . . . decided to appeal against a decision of the Court of Session given before the Union in favour of Sir John Inglis. It would be interesting to have any record at all of what passed at the consultation of Lord Roseberie's advisers with their client before the launching of this appeal. It required a good deal of fortitude in an appellant to brave not only the obstacle of an adverse decision but that also of persuading a foreign tribunal that henceforth it was seised of a new jurisdiction, for which no statutory provision whatsoever had been made. It appears indeed that when the appeal was presented the officers of the House of Lords did not know what to do with it. The officers of the Court of Session, for their part, were unwilling to give the appellant copies and extracts for use in the House of Lords and had to be ordered to do so. On March 27, 1708, the Earl of Rochester reported 'that it was the opinion of the Committee that the respondents in this and all other cases of appeal from Scotland do put in their answers as respondents do in cases of appeal from the courts in England . . . and that the Clerk-Register and his deputies the principal clerks of session shall give authentic copies of the proofs and extracts of the proceedings' for the use at the Bar of the House. This appeal was finally dismissed for want of prosecution, but the ice was broken and a course of practice for handling Scots appeals was entered upon."

The first reported appeal from the Court of Session was *Greenshields v. Magistrates of Edinburgh* (1710–11) Rob. 12. The following extract is taken from the fuller English report in Colles 427 (1710).

> "The appellant protested against the Lords of Session, and appealed to the Queen's Majesty, and the Lords; and . . . the Lords having declared by their order, that the prosecutors should be at liberty to argue in the first place,

whether this appeal be regularly and properly before them or not, [the] respondents contended it was not, because . . . [*inter alia*] before the late Union of the two nations, it was never known that any appeal from the ecclesiastic judicatory of the Church, lay properly or regularly to the Parliament of *Scotland*; nor could any precedent be produced of such an appeal brought . . . After reading the extracts and transcripts of the orders and proceedings delivered, it was ordered by the Lords, that the petition and appeal be received . . . that [the] respondents answer before the first day of [the] session of Parliament, and that their counsel be at liberty to argue in the first place, whether this appeal be regularly and properly before this House or not. And, on 1st March, 1710, after hearing counsel to that point, it was resolved, that the petition and appeal [was] regularly and properly before the House."

For a detailed account of contemporary events which shows that the Union commissioners did envisage that civil appeals would go from the Court of Session to the House of Lords and an explanation as to why the Articles of Union are silent on the point, see A.J. MacLean, "The 1707 Union" (1983) 4 Journal of Legal History 50.

(II) Court of Session Act 1988, s. 40

"(1) Subject to the provisions of any other Act restricting or excluding an appeal to the House of Lords and of sections 27(5) and 32(5) of this Act, it shall be competent to appeal from the Inner House to the House of Lords—

(a) without the leave of the Inner House, against a judgment on the whole merits of the cause, or against an interlocutory judgment where there is a difference of opinion among the judges or where the interlocutory judgment is one sustaining a dilatory defence and dismissing the action;

(b) with the leave of the Inner House, against any interlocutory judgment other than one falling within paragraph (a) above.

(2) An interlocutor of the Court granting or refusing a new trial, on an application under section 29 of this Act, shall be appealable without the leave of the Court to the House of Lords; and on such an appeal the House of Lords shall have the same powers as the Court had on the application and in particular the powers specified in sections 29(3) and 30(3) of this Act.

(3) It shall be incompetent to appeal to the House of Lords against an interlocutor of a Lord Ordinary unless the interlocutor has been reviewed by the Inner House.

(4) On an appeal under this section all prior interlocutors in the cause shall be submitted to the review of the House of Lords."

Ross v. Ross, 1927 S.C. (H.L.) 4

The defender's plea of no jurisdiction having been sustained by the Lord Ordinary but repelled unanimously by the First Division on appeal, the defender endeavoured to appeal to the House of Lords. The Appeal Committee, applying s. 15 of the Court of Session Act 1808 [now s. 40 of the Court of Session Act

1988] dismissed the appeal as incompetent. In the course of his opinion (with which his colleagues concurred) Lord Dunedin set out the following four propositions:

> "(1) The disability imposed on this House, which forbids the hearing of appeals against interlocutory judgments when there has been no difference of opinion in the Court below and no leave to appeal has been granted, is statutory, and cannot be got over either by the action of this House or by consent of parties. (2) The right to grant an appeal against an interlocutory judgment is confined to the Court of Session, and their discretion cannot be controlled by this House. (3) The right of appeal remains where the judgment, though interlocutory in form, is final in substance. (4) The test of finality in substance is to see whether the case would have been equally decided in substance whether the interlocutor under discussion had been pronounced as it was or had been pronounced to the opposite effect. Applying those propositions to the case in hand, it is a clear case for refusing the leave to appeal."

Since 1934 English civil appeals have only gone to the House of Lords with leave from the Court of Appeal or the Appeal Committee of the House. At first sight, therefore, it seems anomalous that Scottish civil appeals against final judgments still lie to the House as of right. In practice the emphasis on interlocutory matters which arises from the Scottish system of pleading, means that s. 40 of the 1988 Act acts as a substantial curb on appeals to the House.

(III) Appeals Originating in the Sheriff Court

Since the Court of Session Act 1825 appeals originating in the Sheriff Court which come to the House of Lords are restricted to matters of law only (see now the Court of Session Act 1988, s. 32(5)).

This seemingly clear position is subject to a number of caveats.

Sutherland v. Glasgow Corporation, 1951 S.L.T. 185

LORD REID: "My Lords, as the proof in this case was led in the Sheriff Court section 40 of the Judicature Act, 1825, applies to the case and we are bound to accept the findings of fact set out in the interlocutor of the Second Division of 14th July 1949, which is now under appeal. But that is subject to two qualifications. In the first place, as explained by Lord Dunedin in *Owners of the 'Bogota' v. Owners of the 'Alconda'* . . . it is legitimate to go to the opinions of the Judges of the Division to explain any ambiguity there may be in the findings. And, secondly, if it appears that what purports to be a finding in law is really a finding in fact I think that it must be treated as a finding in fact. It has more than once been pointed out that if what purports to be a finding in fact is really a finding in law it should be treated as such: I need only refer to the speech of Lord Watson in *Gilroy Sons & Co. v. Price & Co.*, 20 R. (H.L.) 1. I think that the same principle must apply in the converse case."

Even where the House is entitled to hear appeals on a question of fact (which it always is, unless it is expressly excluded by statute) it will be slow to overturn the findings of fact in the lower courts.

As Lord Jauncey observed in *Higgins v. J. & M. Smith (Whiteinch) Ltd.*, 1990 S.L.T. 663 at p. 665:

> "A lower appellate court will examine the transcript of evidence and reach its own conclusions as to the facts which have been established and the inferences which should be properly drawn therefrom. This review of the evidence is, however, subject to the important qualification that the appellate court will be slow to interfere with findings of primary fact based upon an assessment of credibility or reliability of witnesses. In this connection I draw no distinction between credibility in the narrow sense involving truth and untruth and reliability embracing quality of recollection and accuracy of description. The advantage possessed by the judge of first instance in relation to both these matters of seeing and hearing the witnesses is not to be lightly disregarded. Where there are concurrent findings of fact in the courts below, generally this House will interfere with those findings only where it can be shown that both courts were clearly wrong. It is nothing to the point that this House might on the evidence have reached a different conclusion which, as was said by Lord Chelmsford in *Gray v. Turnbull* at p. 54, was 'just as likely to be wrong' as was the conclusion of the lower courts. Lord Watson expressed a similar view in *The Owners of the 'P. Caland' and Freight v. Glamorgan Steamship Co. Ltd.* at p. 217. This is a salutary principle whose purpose is to prevent this House, as the ultimate court of appeal, from being flooded with cases which depend not upon important questions of law but upon pure questions of fact."

On the other hand, where the question at issue relates not to credibility or reliability but to inferences properly to be drawn from primary facts by the trial judge the House is less reticent about stepping in. See Lord Keith, *Stair Memorial Encyclopaedia*, Vol. 6 at para. 830.

(IV) Two-Tier Civil Appeals and Leapfrogging

It follows from the above that for most Scottish civil cases there is a two-tier appellate structure and that for some there can be three tiers: *e.g.* sheriff court (ordinary)—sheriff principal—Inner House—House of Lords. (In the period 1952–68, 15 per cent of Scottish appeals to the House of Lords originated in the sheriff courts: L. Blom-Cooper and G. Drewry, *Final Appeal* (1972) p. 379. In England there has long been a body of opinion against even a second tier of appeal. Proponents of this view secured the abolition of appeals to the House of Lords in the 1870s only for the House's judicial functions to be restored at the eleventh hour. Part II of the Administration of Justice Act 1969 introduced a compromise which retained the two tiers of appeal but permitted certain categories of appeal to by-pass the Court of Appeal and "leapfrog" directly to the Lords. All parties to the case must consent to a "leapfrog" and both the trial judge and an Appeal Committee of the House must consider that the case involves a point of law of general public importance which is either wholly or mainly one of statutory construction, or one in respect of which the trial judge is bound by a decision of the Court of Appeal or of the House of Lords. A similar provision exists in New Zealand permitting appeals to "leapfrog" direct from the Supreme Court to the Judicial Committee of the Privy Council, missing out the Court of Appeal. Such appeals are at the discretion of the Supreme Court alone and the consent of all the parties is not required. The court must, however, consider that the question involved is one which by reason of its "great general or public importance or of the magnitude of the interests affected or for any other reason," ought to be submitted to the Judicial Committee of the Privy Council.

In practice the New Zealand provision has been little used and the forebodings that the 1969 Act might emasculate the Court of Appeal have proved groundless (the English "leapfrog" procedure has only been successfully invoked in five or so cases a year). As Gavin Drewry commented in "Leapfrogging" (1973) 89 L.Q.R. 260:

> "[T]he appellate process tends to involve a sifting of a more or less complex body of fact, case-law and statutory construction, in varying proportions, and to be geared (at the highest level of 'general public importance' and legal complexity) to a two-stage process in which the Court of Appeal and the House of Lords play mutually complementary roles. One gains the clear impression that in many cases the Law Lords rely heavily upon the spadework done by the Court of Appeal, though it is difficult to estimate this quantitatively since it is seldom explicitly stated in the Lords' opinions (apart from a few instances where judgements below are expressly adopted)."

2. Criminal Appeals

The House of Lords has no jurisdiction to hear criminal appeals from Scotland. There was no right of appeal from the Court of Justiciary to the Scottish Parliament prior to the Union and largely because of this the House of Lords in a series of cases in the eighteenth and nineteenth centuries steadfastly refused to entertain criminal appeals from the Court of Justiciary. In the last of these cases, *Mackintosh v. Lord Advocate* (1876) 3 R. (H.L.) 34, the Lord Chancellor (Cairns) stated at p. 36:

> "Your Lordships have now the experience of upwards of one hundred and seventy years since the Union. Is there any instance produced of any appeal from an order of the Court of Justiciary during that time? No instance has been found, notwithstanding the diligence used by the learned counsel for the appellant. On the contrary, your Lordships have a most exhaustive and conclusive argument, delivered in this House by Lord Mansfield in Bywater's case, upon this very point. Lord Mansfield went through every case that was supposed to bear upon the question up to the time at which he spoke, and he shewed that there was no case of an appeal from an order of the Court of Justiciary, and that the one or two cases, the case of Mr Dempster and the earlier case of Elgin, which were supposed to bear an appearance to an appeal of that kind, really were no authorities whatever for holding that an appeal would lie. With regard to one of those cases, the case of Dempster, it

appears to me to afford the strongest possible argument that an appeal would not lie, for that was a case in which, if this House could have exercised an appellate jurisdiction, it was obviously extremely well inclined to do so. But it found that it could not do so, and it therefore resorted to a very singular proceeding, which Lord Mansfield describes, and which was quite inconsistent with any assertion of an appellate right by this House.

From the time of Bywater's case down to the present day there is no instance of any appeal to this House from the Court of Justiciary, and it would be somewhat strange to imagine that during the period up to the Union, and during the period of nearly two centuries which have elapsed since the Union, down to the present time, there should during all that time have been slumbering a right to maintain an appeal from the Court of Justiciary, either to the Scottish Parliament in the first period, or to this House since the Union, and that right should never have been resorted to by any of the hundreds and thousands of those persons to whose interest it would have been to resort to it."

For a fuller account of the history of the House's reluctance to hear Scottish criminal appeals see A.J. MacLean, "The House of Lords and Appeals from the High Court of Justiciary, 1707–1887," 1985 J.R. 192.

This position was endorsed in the Criminal Procedure (Scotland) Act 1887 by s. 72, which provides that "all interlocutors and sentences pronounced by the High Court of Justiciary . . . shall be final and conclusive, and not subject to review by any court whatsoever."

A similar provision relating to appeals from cases tried on indictment appears in s. 17(1) of the Criminal Appeal (Scotland) Act 1926.

3. Devolution Issues

The Scotland Act 1998 does not alter the role of the House of Lords as Scotland's supreme civil court. However, it does generally provide for the final determination of "devolution issues" by Judicial Committee of the Privy Council (see below, pp. 84–85). However, there is an important exception to this in relation to proceedings in the House of Lords.

Scotland Act 1998, Sched.6, para.32

"32. Any devolution issue which arises in judicial proceedings in the House of Lords shall be referred to the Judicial Committee unless the House of Lords considers it more appropriate, having regard to all the circumstances, that it should determine the issue."

There is perhaps the possibility that the Judicial Committee and the House of Lords might take divergent approaches to devolution issues but if there is Judicial Committee authority on a point, it will bind even the House of Lords by virtue of s.103(1) of the Scotland Act 1998:

Scotland Act 1998, s.103

"(1) Any decision of the Judicial Committee in proceedings under this Act shall be stated in open court and shall be binding in all legal proceedings (other than proceedings before the Committee)".

B. JUDICIAL COMMITTEE OF THE PRIVY COUNCIL

The Judicial Committee of the Privy Council was historically the supreme court of appeal for British colonies, dependencies and other overseas territories and latterly of many Commonwealth countries. However, in most states which enjoyed a final right of appeal to the Judicial Committee that right has now been abolished and this has resulted in a much reduced jurisdiction for the Judicial Committee.

Constitution Unit, Scotland's Parliament—Fundamentals for a New Scotland Act, 1996, p. 49

> "141. . . . the judicial role of the Privy Council is in decline, and the time may not be so far off when it comes to an end altogether. Appeals will no longer lie from Hong Kong after 1997, and New Zealand may follow. There is also some dissatisfaction with appeals arising from Caribbean countries."

For an example of the Judicial Committee's role in Caribbean death penalty cases, see *Earl Pratt v. Attorney-General for Jamaica* [1993] 3 W.L.R. 995.

It also has a role, for example, as an appeal court for the Channel Islands courts, for the English ecclesiastical courts, and from the General Medical Council.

For the purposes of the devolution arrangements, there was a need to decide which court should act as court of final appeal in relation to disputes about devolution issues. Essentially the choice was between the House of Lords and the Judicial Committee of the Privy Council. Although the Constitution Unit was in favour of making the House of Lords the final court for devolution issues largely to avoid the risk of conflict between the House of Lords and the Judicial Committee at the top of the hierarchy and in recognition of the decline of the Judicial Committee, the Government nevertheless decided that the Judicial Committee of the Privy Council was to be the court of last resort for determining devolution issues. Despite its opposition, the Constitution Unit set out clearly the case in favour of the Judicial Committee:

Constitution Unit, Scotland's Parliament—Fundamentals for a New Scotland Act, 1996, p. 49

> "140. Against these arguments is the fact that the Privy Council enjoys the weight of precedent as a final court of appeal for devolution issues. For nearly a century it heard appeals on jurisdictional disputes between the federal and provincial governments in Canada, and it was the final court of appeal for the determination of constitutional issues under the Government of Ireland Act 1920. The 1978 Act [*i.e.* Scotland Act 1978] followed this precedent."

There is also the argument that although the Judicial Committee is largely staffed by the same judges as the House of Lords (see below), it is distinct from the Westminster Parliament and in that sense it is more politically acceptable for it to deal with devolution issues than the House of Lords which is, after all, part of the Westminster Parliament.

Accordingly, the Scotland Act 1998 provides, firstly, that the Judicial Committee may be required by one of the Government Law Officers specified below to determine whether a Scottish Parliament Bill is within its devolved competence. This is known as pre-Assent scrutiny.

Scotland Act 1998, s.33

> "(1) The Advocate General, the Lord Advocate or the Attorney General may refer the question of whether a Bill or any provision of a Bill would be within the legislative competence of the Parliament to the Judicial Committee for decision."

Where the Judicial Committee determines that the provision or whole Bill is not within the Parliament's legislative competence, s.32(3)(a) of the Scotland Act 1998 requires that it must not be submitted for Royal Assent without amendment.

Secondly, acting as a court of last resort the Judicial Committee may be required to determine "devolution issues" including post-Assent challenges to the validity of an Act of the Scottish Parliament.

Scotland Act 1998, s.98, Sched.6.

> "1. In this Schedule "devolution issue" means—
>
> (a) a question whether an Act of the Scottish Parliament or any provision of an Act of the Scottish Parliament is within the legislative competence of the Parliament,
>
> (b) a question whether any function (being a function which any person has purported, or is proposing to exercise) is a function of the Scottish Ministers, the First Minister or the Lord Advocate,
>
> (c) a question whether the purported or proposed exercise of a function by a member of the Scottish Executive is, or would be, within devolved competence,
>
> (d) a question whether the purported or proposed exercise of a function by a member of the Scottish Executive is, or would be, incompatible with any of the Convention rights or with Community law,
>
> (e) a question whether a failure to act by a member of the Scottish Executive is incompatible with any of the Convention rights or with Community law,
>
> (f) any other question about whether a function is exercisable within devolved competence or in or as regards Scotland any other question arising by virtue of this Act about reserved matters."

A devolution issue may arise in any proceedings in Scotland, England, Wales or Northern Ireland. Any member of the public may bring proceedings to determine a devolution issue subject to the applicable rules on title and interest or raise a devolution issue as part of a defence. In addition Schedule 6 to the Scotland Act 1998 provides that in Scotland proceedings for determination of a devolution issue may be started by the Advocate General or the Lord Advocate, while in England and Wales such proceedings may be raised by the Attorney

General and in Northern Ireland by the Attorney General for Northern Ireland. If a devolution issue arises in a court of first instance, it may be referred to the Inner House of the Court of Session or the High Court of Justiciary as appropriate for determination. However, appeals against such decisions will lie to the Judicial Committee:

Scotland Act 1998, s.98, Sched.6

> "12. An appeal against a determination of a devolution issue by the Inner House of the Court of Session on a reference under paragraph 7 or 8 shall lie to the Judicial Committee.
>
> 13. An appeal against a determination of a devolution issue by—
>
> (a) a court of two or more judges of the High Court of Justiciary (whether in the ordinary course of proceedings or on a reference under paragraph 9), or
>
> (b) a court of three or more judges of the Court of Session from which there is no appeal to the House of Lords,
>
> shall lie to the Judicial Committee, but only with leave of the court concerned or, failing such leave, with special leave of the Judicial Committee."

Where a devolution issue arises in proceedings before three or more judges of the Court of Session or two or more judges of the High Court of Justiciary, Sched.6, paras.10–11 to the Scotland Act 1998 enable those courts to refer the issue to the Judicial Committee for determination. Similar provision is made by Parts III and IV for proceedings in England and Wales and Northern Ireland respectively. Devolution issues arising in the House or Lords may but need not be referred to the Judicial Committee for determination (Sched.6, para.32 to the Scotland Act 1998; see p. 83 above). The Judicial Committee (Devolution Issues) Rules Order 1999 (SI 1999 No. 665) sets out the procedural rules governing the determination of devolution issues by the Judicial Committee.

To ensure its effectiveness as the court of last resort in this context, the judgments of the Judicial Committee, which are otherwise of persuasive value only in the courts, were made binding in relation to devolution issues by s.103(1) of the Scotland Act 1998 (see p. 83 above).

II. CASELOAD—HOUSE OF LORDS

Once established, the appellate jurisdiction of the House of Lords in Scottish cases soon attained a dominance which it was not to lose until the 1860s. Although the published statistics for eighteenth-century appeals are unreliable, it is clear from contemporary writings that Scottish litigants very quickly acquired a taste for appeals to the House—a development which was not welcomed by the Court of Session or by the commentators. By 1712 Fountainhall in his *Journal of Decisions* (Vol. 2, p. 734) was complaining that Scots appeals to the Lords "increased every year, to the great impoverishing and detriment of the Nation." In 1786 six times as many Scots appeals were presented as from England, and in the period 1794–1807 84 per cent (419 out of 501) of the appeals presented were Scots.

A number of explanations have been given for the prevalence of Scots appeals to the House in the eighteenth century. Most commonly, the English rule that an appeal to the House operated as a stay of execution of the judgment of the lower court, is blamed. This rule was applied by the House of Lords in Scots appeals from 1709 onwards. Since this was a reversal of the existing Scottish procedure, because appeals could take several years in the Lords and because it was possible to appeal directly from the interlocutory judgments of the Lords Ordinary it is very likely that the new ruling did encourage unsuccessful litigants in Scotland to appeal, simply as a delaying tactic. (It is not clear why this tactic was not equally popular in England.) Secondly, although in theory the House was sitting as a Scottish court when it heard Scots appeals, in reality such cases were usually argued by English counsel, using English law and terms of art, before lay peers and judges with no training or knowledge of Scots law. The forensic lottery thus produced (the House was more likely to reverse the Court of Session than to affirm it in the eighteenth century), coupled with the expense and inconvenience of appeals to the Lords must have "coerced" many respondents into settling even where they had a strong case. On the other hand the expenses incurred by an appellant who abandoned his appeal to the House even after a number of years, were minimal. Frivolous appeals were the order of the day.

Nevertheless, it was not until the Court of Session Act 1808 that Parliament responded to the Scottish appeals which were threatening to swamp the House of Lords. Section 15 [now s. 40 of the Court of Session Act 1988] provided (see p. 79 above) that in future appeals could only come from the First or Second Divisions and that interlocutory appeals from the Divisions would require leave (from the Divisions) except where the decisions were not unanimous. The Act also tackled the problem of the 1709 ruling by providing (s. 17) that the Divisions could give interim effect to their decrees pending the outcome of the appeal to the Lords. Despite these reforms the flood of Scots appeals continued unabated. Thus, of the 266 appeals pending before the House in 1811, 76 per cent were Scots. By 1827 the percentage of Scots appeals pending had only dropped to 64 per cent. It was not until the professionalisation of the House in the middle of the century (see Robert Stevens, *Law and Politics* (1979), Chap. 2), with the "abolition" of the lay peers' rights to vote on appeals and the elevation of several judges to the peerage, that the stature of the House as a court increased sufficiently to attract as many English appeals as Scottish ones. Only since the 1860s have the number of English appeals presented to the House consistently exceeded the number of Scottish appeals. (Even then there have been aberrant years, *e.g.* 1890 when 47 Scottish appeals were presented and only 30 English ones.)

Why Scottish appeals remained so numerous despite the reforms designed to curb them which were contained in the various Court of Session Acts of the first quarter of the nineteenth century, is still something of a mystery. Perhaps the habit had become engrained. Other, less charitable explanations have been put forward.

Gibb, *Law from over the Border*, p. 65

> "Bethell, who later became Chancellor as Lord Westbury, was firmly persuaded of the litigiousness of the Scots. He spoke of their miserable ingenuity as soon as they became engaged in litigation when, so he said, there ensued an entire absence of prudence, sound sense and discretion."

The witnesses who gave evidence to the Select Committee on the Appellate Jurisdiction which reported in 1856 failed to agree on the matter.

Stevens, *Law and Politics*, p. 43

> "On the question of why there were so many Scottish appeals, views varied. The Lord Advocate suggested that the Scots regarded appeals to the Lords as a lottery; Mr Anderson, Q.C. (Scotland), denied that the Scots were more litigious than the English, 'but when they go to law they are more persevering in their litigation'; and John Rolt, Q.C. (Scotland), claimed, 'It is the consistency of our character; having taken up a view, we maintain it'."

Whatever is the true explanation, a substantial flow of Scots appeals continued until the 1930s. Since then the number of Scots appeals has rarely exceeded ten a year—sometimes it has been much less.

TABLE 4.1

Appeals heard and disposed of in the House of Lords

Year	*Scots Appeals*	*English, Welsh and Northern Irish Appeals*
1860	18	27
1870	31	19
1880	12	22
1890	16	30
1900	8	56
1910	13	59
1920	23	45
1930	11	38
1939	4	41
1950	0	31
1960	9	29
1970	5	29
1980	4	69
1981	9	63
1982	7	72
1983	9	64
1984	3	56
1985	4	55
1986	5	46
1987	9	98
1988	2	67
1989	10	55
1990	3	47
1991	3	63
1992	7	53

1993	5	58
1994	6	51
1995	7	47
1996	6	38
1997	11	46

[Sources: *Final Appeal; Law and Politics*; Lord Chancellor's Department, *Judicial Statistics*, England & Wales Annual Reports up to 1997.]

Although the introduction of legal aid for appeals to the House of Lords in 1960 led to a small increase in Scots appeals in the next ten years, since then they have dropped by a third. It seems probable that the high cost of such appeals even where legal aid is available will keep the House's Scottish caseload low. This might suggest that free legal aid should be available to facilitate appeals on important points of law. The Hughes Commission seems to have favoured such a proposal. See R.8.30.

III. COMPOSITION

A. HOUSE OF LORDS

Despite the overwhelming preponderance of Scottish appeals to the House of Lords in the 100 years following the Act of Union it was not until 1867 that the first judge with a training in Scots law began to sit consistently in the House. Understandably, legal scholars in recent times have attributed the anglicisation which took place in Scots law in the eighteenth and nineteenth centuries partly to the lack of Scots-trained judges in the Lords. Yet, curiously, the Scottish legal profession during this period was not as opposed to the absence of such judges as might have been anticipated. The quality of the Court of Session's decisions in the eighteenth century was not always of the highest (they were often given without reasons). The Scottish witnesses who gave evidence to the Select Committee on the appellate jurisdiction of the House of Lords in 1856, were convinced as to the value of retaining the "right" of appeal to the House in Scottish cases, but divided as to the merit of a proposal that a Scots-trained judge should be promoted to the House of Lords. The Lord Advocate, the Dean of Faculty, the majority of the Bar and the Writers to the Signet all appeared to favour such an appointment. But the Lord Justice-Clerk was but one of a number of dissenting voices.

"Opinions delivered before the Select Committee" (1856) 2 Macq. at p. 664

> "The Right Hon. LORD JUSTICE CLERK OF SCOTLAND: I always believed the suitors to be exceedingly unfavourable to any such notion as that of a Scotch Judge being placed upon the Court of Appeal. The present feeling, as far as my knowledge goes of the Faculty of Advocates, is quite new. I never heard the subject broached, during the eleven years I was Dean of Faculty; and I can speak from my positive knowledge that Lord

Corehouse, Lord Moncrieff, Lord Murray, and others, who were seniors to me, thought that it was quite an essential feature of the Court of Appeal that there should be no Scotch lawyers, but that it should be composed entirely of English Judges. There are a great many benefits I think resulting from that."

The present-day provisions as to who may sit and vote in appeals to the House of Lords are contained in the Appellate Jurisdiction Act 1876, s. 5,

"An appeal shall not be heard and determined by the House of Lords unless there are present at such hearing and determination not less than three of the following persons, in this Act designated Lords of Appeal; that is to say,

(1) The Lord Chancellor of Great Britain for the time being; and
(2) The Lords of Appeal in Ordinary to be appointed as in this Act mentioned; and
(3) Such Peers of Parliament as are for the time being holding or have held any of the offices in this Act described as high judicial offices."

One of the first two Lords of Appeal in Ordinary to be appointed pursuant to the Act was Scots, thereafter there was always at least one Scottish Lord of Appeal and, since 1947, always at least two.

TABLE 4.2

Scots-trained Law Lords active from 1867–1998

Lords of Appeal		*Judicial Peers*
		Colonsay, 1867–74
Gordon, 1876–79		
Watson, 1880–99		Shand, 1892–1904
Robertson, 1899–1909		Kinnear, 1900, 1909–17
		Dunedin, 1905–09
Shaw, 1909–29	Dunedin, 1913–32	
Thankerton, 1929–48	Macmillan, 1930–39, 1941–47	Alness, 1934–37
Reid, 1948–75	Normand, 1947–53	
	Keith, 1953–61	
	Guest, 1961–71	
Fraser, 1975–85	Kilbrandon, 1971–77	Wheatley, 1975–88
	Keith, 1977–1996	Emslie, 1980–
Mackay, 1985–87	Hope 1996–	Mackay, 1987–97
Jauncey, 1988–1996		McLuskey, 1990–
Clyde, 1996–		

As can be seen from Table 4.2, although there have been several periods during this century when there have been three "active" Scots-trained Law Lords (indeed between 1930–32 three of the seven Lords of Appeal were Scots-trained), these periods have been the exception rather than the rule. Because Appellate Committees normally sit with five Law Lords, Scots-trained judges have rarely constituted a majority of those sitting in a particular case. In fact, there are still Scottish appeals where only one, or sometimes no, Scots-trained judge is sitting. Between 1952–68, 24% of the Scots appeals to the House were heard by an Appellate Committee including only one or no Scots-trained Law Lord (*Final Appeal*, p. 381). In 1975 the Lord Advocate, in response to a parliamentary question from Mrs. Winifred Ewing, stated:

> "*The Lord Advocate*: Of the nine Lords of Appeal in Ordinary two are always appointed from the Scottish Bench or Bar.
>
> Appeals are normally heard by five Lords of Appeal, and I understand that every effort is made to ensure that the two Scottish Lords of Appeal are present in the case of a Scottish appeal. Both Scottish Lords of Appeal sat in 15 of the 18 Scottish appeals heard during the period 1970–74; one sat in two of the remaining three, and in one case no Scottish Lord of Appeal was present"—893 H.C. Deb., col. 115 (W.A.), 10 June 1975.

When Halsbury was Lord Chancellor there is reason to believe that in at least one important Scottish appeal the "exclusion" of a Scots-trained judge was improperly motivated. Halsbury was not averse to "packing" the House where it suited him. This seems to have occurred in the *Free Church of Scotland* case ((1904) 7 F. (H.L) 1).

Paterson, "Judges: A Political Elite?" p. 123

> "This momentous Scots Appeal involved over £2 million and turned on a knowledge and understanding of Scottish ecclesiastical history and practice. It was decided unanimously in favour of the United Free Church by the five Scottish judges in the Court of Session. In the House of Lords Halsbury favoured the Free Church but the six Law Lords split evenly. By tradition the Appeal should therefore have been dismissed but fortunately for Halsbury, one of his opponents (Shand) died before judgement could be delivered. Halsbury had the grace to order a rehearing but despite press suggestions declined to invite Kinnear (the obvious Scottish Judge) to sit in the increased court, inviting two English judges instead. Halsbury's side won the rehearing but the political storm which resulted led the government to appoint a Committee chaired by Kinnear to reverse the impact of the decision. Two of the English judges admitted afterwards that had they had the guidance of a Scots judge familiar with the ecclesiastical position they would have voted the other way."

Nevertheless, even in Halsbury's time the exigencies of running an Appellate Committee in the House and a Judicial Committee in the Privy Council imposed limitations on the Lord Chancellor's room for manoeuvre in panel selection. In recent years the logistical problems have considerably increased.

Paterson, *The Law Lords*, pp. 87–89

> "Selection for Appellate Committees although theoretically in the hands of the Lord Chancellor, is actually delegated to his Permanent Secretary who

consults the Lord Chancellor in cases of difficulty. Lord Hailsham described the guidelines which operated in his first period as Lord Chancellor, in the following way,

> 'Obviously cases which have party political implications should normally be adjudicated by non-political judges. Also the composition of the panel must take account of the nature of the problems to be adjudicated upon, an expert in each of the relevant fields being made available where possible. A Scottish Law Lord should usually sit in all Scottish cases. These special considerations are, however, exceptional. The normal practice is to select the most convenient panel available.'

In practice the Permanent Secretary often has remarkably little room for manoeuvre. At the end of each legal term he meets with the Principal Clerk of the Judicial Office and the Judicial Clerk to the Privy Council. Together they compile a provisional list setting out the order for hearings of appeals in the following term in the House and in the Privy Council and the two Clerks brief the Permanent Secretary as to the talents needed in the various appeals. If there is a Chancery appeal in the Lords and a commercial case before the Privy Council then other things being equal the Chancery Law Lords will sit in the Lords. Equally, Chancery Law Lords tend not to sit on criminal appeals. When a Scots appeal comes to the Lords strong efforts are made to ensure that one, if not both, Scottish Law Lords will sit. But of course other things never are equal. If the Law Lord is Scottish he may be wanted to head a strong team in the Privy Council or to preside in an English appeal before a second Appellate Committee. A balance has to be struck to ensure that junior Law Lords are not relegated to the Privy Council for more than 50% of the year. Judges who have sat in an appeal in the Court of Appeal or in the Court of Session and since become Lords of Appeal, have to be excluded when that appeal comes before the Lords. On top of this, because of the difficulty in synchronising the hearing in the Appellate Committee and the Judicial Committee of the Privy Council, there is a tendency to keep the same or almost the same panel of Law Lords together for several appeals on end.

As if the logistical problems of organising suitable panels for the House and the Privy Council several weeks or months in advance were not enough, the Lord Chancellor's Office has to cope with subsequent developments—often at the last minute. A case may drastically overrun its estimate, a judge can fall ill, or decline to sit because of an interest in a case, he may want to attend a conference in a foreign country or be asked to serve as Chairman of a Royal Commission or a Public Inquiry. Such complications go a long way to ensuring that any present day Lord Chancellor would find it exceedingly difficult to 'pack the court' in cases of a particular type, even if he were minded to do so. They are also the explanation of the occasional 'freak' panel of Law Lords which is thrown up, *e.g.* one with five common law Lords of Appeal or one which contains no Scottish Law Lord in a Scots Appeal."

For a rare example of refusal and judicial disqualification on a significant scale in the House of Lords, see *In re Lonrho plc* [1990] 2 A.C. 154. See also *R. v. Bow*

Street Stipendiary Magistrate, ex parte Pinochet Ugarte (No. 2) [1991] 1 All E.R. 577.

Of the members of the Appellate Committee the presiding judge can exercise the most influence over the course and length of the argument presented to the court by counsel. Indeed, his leadership role in the exchanges between the Bench and counsel can often be greater in this phase of the decision-making process than in the drafting of the final decision. [See Paterson, *The Law Lords*, Chaps 4 and 5 and Paterson, "Scottish Lords of Appeal, 1876–1988" (1988) J.R. 235.] Possibly in recognition of the fact that experience is not synonymous with expertise when it comes to chairing Appellate and Appeal Committees, the rules on judicial precedence governing the right to preside at meetings of these Committees were changed in 1984. As Lord Hailsham announced to the House of Lords:

> "As your Lordships know, the practice is that at sittings in the House itself, if present, the Lord Chancellor presides on the Woolsack. If he is not present . . . the Woolsack is taken by the senior Lord of Appeal present, seniority being reckoned from the date of first appointment. . . . Nevertheless, the position is still not ideal, in that the duty of presiding is still governed by the order in appointment of the Lords of Appeal in Ordinary. . . . This has persuaded me that the time has now come to bring the arrangements in the House and in the Appeal and Appellate Committees into line with what is now the normal practice in other parts of the judicial system.
>
> I have therefore advised Her Majesty that it would be appropriate for her in future to appoint the senior and second senior Law Lords who, between them, normally preside over two sittings of Committees, or of the House and the Judicial Committee of the Privy Council. . . . In the absence of either or both of them, precedence among the Lords of Appeal in Ordinary will thereafter continue to be governed as before, by the date of first appointment without regard to rank in the peerage."
>
> LORD DIPLOCK: "My Lords . . . I hope that it will not be thought to be out of place if, as the longest serving, by many years, of the current Law Lords, I were to express my full support for the changes which my noble and learned friend upon the Woolsack proposes to make with regard to the office of presiding over the Appellate Committee and the Judicial Committee of the Privy Council.
>
> Twenty-three years of sitting in appellate courts, both as a member and during the last nine years habitually as a presider, have taught me that the task of presiding over a plurality of judges in such a way as to promote an efficient and expeditious way of dealing with appeals is not the same as producing judgments which clarify and develop the law. The tasks call for different qualities. They may be combined in the same judge, but also they may not. To preside is a more taxing task, and increasing age may well render a judge less fit to undertake it, though still leave unimpaired his ability to produce judgments which clarify and develop the law.
>
> For efficient administration of justice in the highest court in the United Kingdom seniority ought not to be the sole criterion to preside. No

reflection is intended on any appellate judge that he should sit in a court presided over by one appointed later than himself."—453 H.L. Deb., col. 915–18, 27 June 1984.

The necessity for this change can be questioned, especially since its practical effect to date has been limited—other than to cause gratuitous offence north of the Border. See Paterson, "Scottish Lords of Appeal 1876–1988" (1988) J.R. 235 at p. 251.

B. COMPOSITION—JUDICIAL COMMITTEE OF THE PRIVY COUNCIL

In relation to its non-devolution business the composition of the Privy Council includes the Lords of Appeal in Ordinary, the Lord Chancellor, the Lord Justices of Appeal and the members of the Privy Council who have been judges in the higher courts of Commonwealth states. However, for devolution purposes the composition of the Judicial Committee is defined thus:

Scotland Act 1988, s.103

"(2) No member of the Judicial Committee shall sit and act as a member of the Committee in proceedings under this Act unless he holds or has held—

(a) the office of a Lord of Appeal in Ordinary, or

(b) high judicial office as defined in section 25 of the Appellate Jurisdiction Act 1876 (ignoring for this purpose section 5 of the Appellate Jurisdiction Act 1887)."

Although this excludes from membership Commonwealth judges it includes serving and retired Lords of Appeal in Ordinary, the Lord Chancellor, judges of the Court of Session and judges of the English and Northern Irish High Court and Court of Appeal.

IV. DECISION-MAKING IN THE LORDS AND THE JUDICIAL COMMITTEE OF THE PRIVY COUNCIL

Paterson, "Appellate Decision-Making in the Common Law World," pp. 1–3, 5–9

This extract is derived from the author's interview-based research on the Law Lords.

"It is a truth commonly neglected by scholars, that judicial decision making in the higher appellate courts in the Anglo-American world is typically a collective enterprise—a group activity rather than a multiplicity of individual efforts. The size and content of the 'group' varies from court to court. Usually, it includes the counsel or the brief-writers as well as the sitting judges; sometimes, it extends to other judges or to law clerks; very occasionally, it includes legal academics or other 'outsiders.' Again, the form and nature of the exchanges between 'group-members' varies between courts. Thus, in the U.S. Supreme Court the bulk of the interchanges in the decision making process, whether between counsel and the Bench, Justice and law clerk or Justice and Justice, are in writing. In the House of Lords and the Privy Council they are mainly oral. Insignificant as such variations may seem, they entail that the role of the appellate judge in the Anglo-American world is far from homogeneous. . . .

In the House of Lords counsel and Law Lord alike consider that a predominantly oral approach, with the consequent flexibility which it gives to arguments, has advantages which cannot be matched in a written brief. Counsel can, and are expected to, respond to the thoughts expressed by the Court and to adjust their arguments accordingly. Lord Reid told me,

> '[Counsel] have got to know their stuff and know it backwards and they have got to be a little bit, taking a hint, you know. A man who simply reads out his stuff from his notes and will not take a hint is not a good advocate.'

Thus a case can change course in mid-stream as a result of a point thrown up in the debate. As another Law Lord remarked,

> 'I have known cases in which when the case started I was convinced that the appellant was either right or wrong and during the course of the case a point made either by me or by one of my colleagues has completely changed one's view.'

Moreover, oral argumentation, at least in the House of Lords and the Privy Council, both restricts the range of judicial creativity and exercises a persuasive influence on the decision ultimately reached, in a way that written briefs, at least in the U.S. Supreme Court, do not. As Lord Scarman recently observed,

> 'The judge, however wise, creative and imaginative he may be, is "cabin'd cribb'd, confined, bound in" not, as was Macbeth, to his "saucy doubts and fears" but by the evidence and arguments of the litigants. It is this limitation, inherent in the forensic process, which sets bounds to the scope of judicial law reform.'

Gillis Wetter in *The Styles of Appellate Judicial Opinions* concludes from this limitation that,

> 'the most notable effect of a court considering the primary function of its opinions to be the rendering of conclusive answers to the allegations of counsel . . . is that of shifting the responsibility for judicial law-making from the courts to the Bar . . .'

I think that Wetter is overstating his case, for the interchange between Bench and Bar is not all one way. It is a dialectic to which each side contributes. Each may borrow from the other. Nevertheless, it is clear that counsel's part in the decision making process in the Lords is a significant one even though it has been overlooked in much of the recent jurisprudential writing on judicial creativity. A scrutiny of *The Brethren*, of judicial diaries and other research, however, reveals that in the U.S. Supreme Court, despite occasional flattering references to counsel's arguments by Justices, the oral and written arguments of counsel contribute considerably less to the decision making process than is the case in the United Kingdom. This is in part due to the inflexibility of written briefs, in part to the lack of a specialist Supreme Court Bar and in part to the fact that Justices may (if they so desire) use their law clerks to assist them in researching the relevant law.

In the House of Lords or the Privy Council . . . there are constant discussions between the judges outside the Committee Rooms—at lunch, at the end of the day's hearing, in each other's rooms and in the mornings before the hearing resumes. Once the hearing comes to an end a formal conference is held. Thereafter, the presiding judge (in the Privy Council) assigns who is to write the opinion of the Court. In the House of Lords it is sometimes collectively agreed that a Law Lord will write the leading opinion but more often than not it is still unclear at the end of the conference who will write an opinion.

The Law Lords are divided as to the merits of the Privy Council practice of having a single majority judgment. One retired Law Lord commented,

> 'The people who were accustomed to being in the Privy Council got rather good at rendering one judgment that reflected the opinions of the others. There was a sort of tradition that you didn't take a strong line unless it was one which could be shared by the others.'

Other Law Lords were less enthusiastic. As one put it,

> 'We all know that in the Privy Council it gave quite a bit of weakness over the centuries to a Privy Council judgment that sentences were put in for the man who thought the appeal was doubtful as to whether it should succeed, and felt that it was more likely it should fail, as against the man who wrote it, who was certain it should succeed, and so he would put in the sentences. . . . You are getting a compromise judgment in a sense.'

Composite judgments of this sort are much rarer in the Lords, though there are some famous, not to say notorious, examples. As a result, the 'bargaining' over the content of the opinion of the court which is so prevalent in the U.S. Supreme Court is much less common in the House of Lords.

Yet, curiously, there are probably as many private discussions between individual Law Lords concerning an appeal as take place between Justices in the U.S. Supreme Court. This is largely due to two instititutional factors. First, the Justices have their own chambers with several law clerks, secretaries and a messenger. Each functions as a small, independent law firm. The Justice relies on his law clerks for discussion in a case and collaborates with them while drafting his opinion. Thus he has less need to confer with his colleagues on difficult points than his transatlantic counterpart. Justice Powell has even gone so far as to assert that,

> 'The [Supreme] Court . . . is perhaps one of the last citadels of jealously preserved individualism. . . . The informal interchange between chambers is minimal, the most exchanges of views being by correspondence or memoranda. Indeed, a Justice may go through an entire term without being once in the chambers of all of the other eight members of the Court.'

Secondly, while the Justices frequently write comments on, or memoranda in response to, a colleague's circulated opinion, in the House of Lords this is practically never done. Either the Law Lord will comment orally to his colleagues on the opinion or he will simply adjust his speech to take account of the points made in the circulated opinion. As one Law Lord put it,

> 'At the stage where the opinions are circulated one's colleagues are very polite. If there is an obvious omission you draw attention to it, but you would seldom re-argue the merits.

Another commented,

> 'Generally you'd leave it alone unless it was a case where you'd agreed that only one judgment would be delivered or if you were going to follow a particular man you might go to him and say, "Look, I'm really almost in entire agreement with you so I just propose to say, 'I agree,' but I'm a bit stuck about this [phrase] . . ." You might do that.'

Of course, some judges participate in the exchanges which I have been describing, with greater effectiveness than others. Small group analysis of the U.S. Supreme Court has shown that both 'social leaders' (judges who endeavour to reduce tensions and to reconcile differences amongst their brethren) and 'task leaders' (judges who use their personality, intelligence, technical competence, esteem within the Court and persuasive ability to lead their brethren to a particular outcome in an appeal) exist on the Court. They are also to be found in the House of Lords and the Privy Council. The acid test for the 'group-orientated' Law Lord, however, is not how often he influences his colleagues. Some Law Lords have found to their cost that, if they 'lobby' their colleagues too persistently (particularly if they are not open to persuasion in return), they are very likely to have a negative influence on their colleagues. The acid test is whether he can influence a majority of his colleagues to share his point of view, particularly where this will result in a voting switch or even a reversal of the existing majority position. Such successes do occur but are remarkably hard to document. The final judgment cannot be taken at face value. A unanimous decision may emerge from a Court divided at the first conference. Equally, there have been 3: 2 decisions where none of the participants have ever felt any doubt. My researches revealed that in the Lords most changes of mind take place at the hearing stage, but that they also occur between the first conference and the final judgment. In the U.S. Supreme Court, perhaps because of the pervasiveness of 'bargaining,' Justices frequently change their positions after the initial conference. Nevertheless, it is very difficult to establish that such changes in the House of Lords are the outcome of effective lobbying by 'group-orientated' Law Lords. What can be said is that the Law Lords with such an orientation have usually ended up on the majority side in cases in the past twenty years and where the House has been heavily divided."

The conclusion that appellate decision-making in the House of Lords is a collective activity has two implications. First, that the role of counsel in the decision-making process has hitherto been insufficiently recognised. Secondly, the traditional measure of success in an appellate judge, *i.e.* the long-term standing of his judgments, is incomplete. A judge who exercises "leadership" in his court may appear very little in the Law Reports, though profoundly influencing the outcome of the cases in which he sits.

Decision-making in the House of Lords has undergone a number of changes in the last 15 years largely as a result of reforms initiated by Lords Diplock and Wilberforce. First, the House has endeavoured to cut the cost of appeals to the Lords by introducing measures designed to curtail the length of the oral argument before the House.

M.V. Yorke Motors (a firm) v. Edwards [1982] 1 All E.R. 1024 at 1025 and 1026

LORD DIPLOCK: "The length of time required for counsel's opening addresses at hearings of appeals to the House of Lords has been significantly reduced by the practice adopted over the last seven years under which all the members of the Appellate Committee who will be sitting on an appeal will have read in advance at least the judgments in the courts below and the written cases lodged by the parties. This practice of which the purpose is to reduce the length and consequently the cost of appeals to the House of Lords is one of which by now the Bar should be well aware. Signs are, however, now appearing that this awareness may be giving rise to a tendency to expand the written cases lodged by the parties so as to incorporate and develop in them detailed written arguments supported by lengthy citations from and references to numerous authorities, much on the same line as the written 'briefs' submitted by the parties in appeals to appellate courts in the United States which have resulted in oral argument playing a relatively insignificant role in the decision-making process adopted by appellate courts in that country.

The practice of this House whereby members of the Appellate Committee read in advance the judgments in the courts below and the parties' written cases is not intended to reduce the importance of the role played by oral argument in the decision-making process. Its purpose is to add to the cogency of the oral argument by eliminating the necessity for vocal exposition of facts already stated in the judgments below and the reading out of those judgments in extenso. Counsel are thus enabled from the outset to concentrate their arguments on what are the real issues in the appeal. A written case lodged by a party, which itself contains long and elaborate argument and citations from and references to numerous authorities, does nothing to serve this purpose that is not better done by a written case that follows the guidance contained in . . . the Directions as to Procedure applicable to Civil Appeals to the House of Lords . . . On the contrary, it defeats one of the principal objects of the practice by adding substantially to the costs of the appeal which the shortening of the oral hearing is designed to reduce. . . .

The case should set out the heads, but no more than the heads, of the argument on each of the issues which it is intended should be advanced by counsel for the party at the oral hearing to challenge or support, as the case may be, the decision on that issue of the court from which the appeal is brought. Detailed or elaborate argument added unnecessarily to the costs of preparing the case and is seldom helpful or time saving at the oral hearing. Reference to authorities relied on in support of the argument on any issue should be limited to key authorities (seldom numbering more than one or two on any one issue) which lay down the principle which it is contended is applicable, and the particular passage or passages in the judgments in which the principle is stated should be identified and, unless unduly lengthy, may helpfully be quoted verbatim. But references to numerous other cases in which that principle has been previously applied by courts to particular facts which it is claimed may be regarded as presenting some analogies to the facts of the case under appeal, are usually out of place in the written case and, I may add, more often than not turn out to be time wasting in oral argument also. Where, however, it is intended to rely, as persuasive authority, on cases decided by courts in other countries or legal writings such as the American Restatement, it is of assistance to their Lordships if specific reference is made to these in the written case."

There is evidence that the effect of written cases has not helped to reduce unnecessary argument.

Maclaine Watson v. Department of Trade [1989] 3 All E.R. 523 at 531e

LORD TEMPLEMAN: "For the conduct of these appeals, there were locked in battle 24 counsel supported by batteries of solicitors and legal experts, armed with copies of 200 authorities and 14 volumes of extracts, British and foreign, from legislation, books and articles. Ten counsel addressed the Appellate Committee for 26 days. This vast amount of written and oral material tended to obscure three fundamental principles: . . . In my opinion the length of oral argument permitted in future appeals should be subject to prior limitation by the Appellate Committee."

Secondly, there has been a marked shift in the attitude of the House of Lords towards the issue of multiple judgments. Single judgments in the name of one Law Lord with concurrences from the other four Law Lords who have heard the appeal have become the norm rather than the exception, especially in cases involving statutory construction. In 1974 25% of appeals to the Lords resulted in single judgments, by 1983 the figure had reached 68%. A. Bradney, "The Changing Face of the House of Lords" (1985) J.R. 178.

Re Prestige Group plc [1984] I.R.L.R. 166 at 167

LORD DIPLOCK: "[It] has become a frequent practice in this House when dealing with questions of statutory construction . . . [to have] only [one] reasoned speech; the other Law Lords [limiting] themselves to expressing their agreement with it. Because for historical reasons a decision of the House of Lords in the exercise of its judicial functions takes the form of a motion passed at the close of a debate between those Law Lords by whom the appeal was heard, the single reasoned speech (although of recent years it has not been read out viva voce but made available instead in written form) cannot accurately be termed 'the judgement of the court'. Nevertheless, lest there be any continuing misapprehension among litigants or their lawyers, it should be clearly understood that at the drafting stage what later emerges as a single reasoned speech has been the subject of prior consultations between all members of the appellate committee by whom the appeal was heard, which frequently result in the making of revisions that are incorporated in the final draft. Indeed, connoisseurs of judicial literary styles may find it possible in some cases to identify particular passages in the single speech of which the authorship is not that of the Law Lord by whom the first draft of the main body of the speech was prepared."

There are indications that already this shift towards single judgments has achieved the increased certainty within the legal community as to the meaning of decisions of the House, which was its aim. But critics of these developments would argue that the gain in certainty has been purchased at too great a price. Because the legal community tends to treat single judgments from the House of Lords as though they were statutes, the flexibility of the common law which has been its hallmark, is being curtailed. Single judgments freeze the development of the law—the incremental "trial and error" progress of the common law is being abandoned for the "stop-go" model of the log-jam. Future judges will find their room for manoeuvre has been much reduced by the actions of the present Law Lords. For a powerful critique of single judgments in the Lords see F.A. Mann, "The Single Speech" (1991) 107 L.Q.R. 519.

Since 1966 it has been possible for dissenting opinions to be given in the Judicial Committee of the Privy Council (Judicial Committee (Dissenting Opinions) Order in Council 1966; see also *Madzimbamuto v Lardner-Burke* [1968] 3 All ER 561.)

V. THE ROLE OF THE HOUSE OF LORDS

Drewry, "Leapfrogging," p. 263

"The role of the House of Lords as a final court of appeal . . . can be broken down into two closely related but ultimately quite different elements, review and supervision. The former is the process whereby mistakes at first instance are corrected and some kind of continuity and certainty maintained in the administration of justice. Supervision is the process of laying down fresh precedents and up-dating old ones for the guidance of lower courts in the hierarchy and of resolving that small percentage of cases embodying legal problems of a peculiarly high order both of difficulty and of public importance. These two functions cannot be separated if only because . . . points of law of general public importance cannot be decided in the abstract but must arise in the course of litigation. But the emphasis is different: review is principally to do with achieving justice in the instant case while supervision has primarily to do with solving legal problems in the wider public interest."

Lord Reid (Interview, 1972)

"Well, the first . . . that comes to mind is that you've got to keep the laws of England and Scotland in line, and if you've got any United Kingdom statutes somebody's got to mediate and I think this is the best way of doing it. You can't have a sort of joint meeting at York. Then I think our function is twofold—(a) to clear up the messes, of which there are many, and (b) occasionally to be a bit bold and innovate a bit."

Stevens, *Law and Politics*, p. 627

"The future will lie in an acceptance of the element of discretion in the final appeal process, coupled with a responsibility to articulate the purposes and goals of different branches of the law. The courts in Britain are never likely to compete with the legislature; such a possibility runs counter to four hundred years of political and intellectual history. Complementarity with the legislature is, however, essential; and complementarity involves intelligent creativity. The next decade will show whether the appeal judges are capable of providing a rationale that will at a minimum make them an essential element in the British Constitution and, ideally, raise the issue of whether they might not appear as the junior partners of Parliament in the lawmaking process."

See further on the role of the Lords, Lord Fraser of Tullybelton, "The House of Lords as Court of Last Resort for the United Kingdom" 1986 S.L.T. (News) 33.

CHAPTER 5

CRIMINAL COURTS

In Scotland there are three levels of criminal court: the district court, the sheriff court, and the High Court of Justiciary. District courts handle primarily minor offences (mainly statutory) committed within their territorial jurisdiction (one of the local authority areas). Sheriff courts may deal with a wide range of offences (minor or serious) committed within the sheriffdom, including all those that can be raised in the district court and most that can be heard in the High Court. As in the district court, the sentencing powers of the sheriff court are limited. The High Court's jurisdiction extends throughout Scotland and sometimes beyond. Like the sheriff court its case jurisdiction is almost universal. It has exclusive jurisdiction with respect to certain grave offences and in practice all the most serious cases are tried in the High Court.

Criminal cases are conducted in two ways in Scotland. Under the solemn procedure serious crimes are tried by judge and jury either in the High Court or the sheriff court. The trial proceeds on the basis of charges contained in a document called an indictment and severe penalties are available on conviction. All other offences are dealt with under the summary procedure and trial is by a judge or judges without a jury, either in the sheriff or the district court. In summary trials the charges against an accused are set out in a document called a summary complaint.

I. THE PROSECUTION PROCESS

The prosecution of crime in Scotland is almost exclusively the prerogative of the Crown. The right to private prosecution though still extant is rarely invoked.

A. PUBLIC PROSECUTION

Sheehan, *Criminal Procedure in Scotland and France*, p. 109 *et seq.*

> "**The Public Prosecutor**
> 132 Prior to 1587, most prosecutions were left in the hands of the injured party, although the King's Advocate, otherwise known as the Lord Advocate usually joined the prosecution for the King's interest partly in order to preserve law and order, and partly out of financial interest as any fines went to the royal treasury. The instigation of criminal proceedings was however in the hands of the victim. In 1587, the Lord Advocate was empowered by an Act of Parliament to instigate criminal proceedings 'although the parties be silent or would otherwise privily agree'. This power of the Lord Advocate to prosecute without the concurrence of any private party made him the master

of the instance, giving him an almost absolute right to decide who should be prosecuted, and, in the absence of legal provision to the contrary, in which court the case should be tried. The Lord Advocate is responsible for and directs all public prosecutions in Scotland. He is assisted by the Solicitor General for Scotland and [13] Advocate Deputes. The Lord Advocate and the Solicitor General are known as the Law Officers of the Crown, and the Advocate Deputes as Crown Counsel.

133 The Lord Advocate and the Solicitor General . . . are selected from among the leading senior counsel, and since they are political appointments, change office every time there is a change in government. The Advocate Deputes are advocates appointed . . . by the Lord Advocate . . ." [on a part time basis but do not now demit office following a change in government. All prosecutions in the High Court are conducted by Advocate Deputes or occasionally, in cases of exceptional importance, by one of the Law Officers of the Crown.]

Formerly appointed by the Queen on the recommendation of the Prime Minister, with the advent of devolution, both the Lord Advocate and Solicitor General have become Law Officers to the Scottish Executive rather than Scottish Law Officers of the U.K. Government, necessitating a change in the manner of their appointment.

Scotland Act 1998, s.48

"(1) It is for the First Minister to recommend to Her Majesty the appointment or removal of a person as Lord Advocate or Solicitor General for Scotland; but he shall not do so without the agreement of Parliament."

The Lord Advocate's independence as head of the prosecution system in Scotland is guaranteed by the Scotland Act 1998.

"(4) Any decision of the Lord Advocate in his capacity as head of the systems of criminal prosecution and investigations of deaths in Scotland shall continue to be taken by him independently of any other person."

This is reinforced by s.29(2)(e) of the 1998 Act which provides that it is outwith the legislative competence of the Scottish Parliament to remove the Lord Advocate from the above positions. These and certain other provisions protect the Lord Advocate's position from political interference by other members of the Scottish Executive even though he will himself be a member of the Executive. As head of the criminal prosecution system in Scotland, the Lord Advocate will have responsibility for prosecutions in relation to a number of criminal matters over which the U.K. Parliament retains control such as firearms offences, misuse of drugs offences and consumer protection offences. This may cause difficulties.

G.J.Jackson, Q.C. "Devolution and the Scottish Legal Institutions" in T.StJ.N. Bates (ed.), *Devolution to Scotland: The Legal Aspects*, p. 56

"If [prosecution of these offences] is to be at the instance of the Lord Advocate, that will mean that he will be ordering and conducting prosecutions on matters which are within the legislative competence of a parliament to which he is not responsible (either directly or as a member of the government which is responsible to that parliament) and in which he does not sit. This has at least the potential to cause problems, particularly if the two governments are quite different in their politics and policies."

The success of such arrangements may well depend on the effectiveness of liaison and co-operation between the U.K. and Scottish governments and more particularly between the Advocate General for Scotland, the new Scottish officer responsible to the U.K. parliament created by s.87 of the Scotland Act 1998 and the Lord Advocate.

Sheehan, *Criminal Procedure in Scotland and France*, p. 109 *et seq.*

"**The Procurator Fiscal**

135 The procurator fiscal is the prosecutor in the sheriff [and district] court, although his duties range much further. The office of procurator fiscal was known in the 16th century when he was an officer employed by the sheriff with the duty of collecting fines imposed by the court. Such fines were paid into a fund known as 'The Fisk', and the procurator fiscal appeared at the trial just before sentence was imposed. While the sheriff acted both as prosecutor and judge in his own court, the prosecuting duties were taken over by the procurator fiscal by the time of the 17th century . . . In 1927 the appointment of procurators fiscal was placed in the hands of the Lord Advocate and since then all procurators fiscal and their deputes have been whole-time civil servants. [Nowadays most of them are also solicitors. Such has been the increase in criminal work in the past decade that there are now nearly 300 procurators fiscal in Scotland and over 60 in Glasgow alone.] . . .

140 The procurator fiscal is subject to the direction of and control by the Lord Advocate, who issues general instructions in a Book of Regulations to all procurators fiscal concerning the conduct of their duties. In addition, from time to time the Lord Advocate issues instructions concerning specific matters by means of Crown Office circulars. The advantage of this system is that it promotes a high degree of uniformity of procedure and practice. The Lord Advocate may also issue instructions concerning the conduct of any particular case. Such instructions however do not derogate from the important functions of the procurator fiscal, who has been described as 'central to the criminal administration of Scotland'."

A considerable amount of information about public prosecution in Scotland is now available from the *Annual Reports of the Crown Office and the Procurator Service* which have been published since 1992. For a critical appraisal of the first report see S.R. Moody, "The Silent Service Speaks" 1992 S.L.T. (News) 293. The 1997–98 Annual Report provides information on the strategic aim and key objectives of the organisations:

Crown Office and Procurator Fiscal Service Annual Report 1997–98, pp. 5–6

"Our Strategic Aim

To play a pivotal role in the achievement of the purpose of the criminal justice system of maintaining the security and confidence of the community by providing just and effective means by which crimes may be investigated, and offenders brought to justice. . . .

Our key objectives in our new Strategic Plan are—

- to provide the sole public prosecuting authority in Scotland, which, in the public interest, ensures that all crimes made known to the Procurator Fiscal, including cases of serious and complex fraud, are investigated and that effective and consistent use is made of the range of prosecution options and alternatives to prosecution;
- to investigate all sudden deaths made known to the Procurator Fiscal and, in appropriate cases, conduct public inquiries;
- to investigate independently all complaints of criminal conduct by police officers;
- through the Scottish Charities Office to supervise charities and investigate alleged misconduct and mismanagement in the voluntary sector;
- through the office of the Queen's and Lord Treasurer's Remembrancer to administer property falling, as *bona vacantia* or treasure trove, to the Crown as *ultimus haeres*.

Our values
The ways in which we seek to achieve our objectives are driven by our values:
Impartiality
Decisions will be impartial, fair and timely, and taken on an independent, objective and professional assessment of the evidence available.
Thoroughness
The investigation, preparation and presentation of cases will be carried out thoroughly, critically and accurately.
Integrity
The professional integrity of our staff will be maintained by, *inter alia*:

- being open with the court and fair and dispassionate in the prosecution of cases in court;
- disclosing to the defence any information considered material to the defence; and
- preserving the confidentiality of reports and investigations.

Sensitivity
We will be sensitive and responsive to the needs of the public, including victims, next of kin and witnesses.
Co-operation
We will seek to maintain effective working relationships with other agencies in the criminal justice system.
Professionalism
We are committed to maintaining high quality performance by all staff."

Procurators fiscal thus have a number of duties, including the investigation of all sudden or suspicious deaths, all deaths in the course of employment, all suicides, all anaesthetic and road traffic fatalities, and all serious fires and explosions occurring within their district. Their major functions, however, are the investigation of all crimes committed in their district, the prosecution of all cases taken to the district or sheriff court and the initial investigation and preparatory work for cases going to the High Court.

Gordon, "Criminal Proceedings in Scotland," pp. 253–254

> "In practice much of the investigation is done by the police, who obviously have the organisation, training, experience and technical facilities which the procurator fiscal lacks, but once the fiscal is informed of an investigation he personally directs it, acting in frequent personal contact with the detective constables concerned, and giving instructions as to what enquiries are to be made and what information sought. In most cases the procurator fiscal may not know about the offence until the police have charged someone, but he is frequently consulted at an early stage, and he is called out personally to the locus of all suspected murders."

After conducting their investigations the procurators fiscal must decide whether or not a prosecution is warranted. In so doing they will take account of a number of factors.

Gordon, "Criminal Proceedings in Scotland," p. 274

> "Perhaps the most important decision in the whole process is the decision whether to put on trial or not. Renton & Brown's *Criminal Procedure* gives some general principles to act as a guide to a prosecutor in making this decision. He should take account, of course [of whether the facts uncovered constitute a crime known to Scots law] . . . of whether there is sufficient evidence to justify proceedings—this is important in Scotland where a crime may clearly have been committed by someone but there may be no corroborative evidence and therefore no prospect of conviction; of whether the act is sufficiently important to be made the subject of criminal proceedings; of whether there is reason to suspect malice on the part of the informant . . . of whether there is sufficient excuse for the conduct of the accused to warrant abandonment of the proceedings; and of whether the case is more suitable for civil proceedings. The courts have also indicated that it is the prosecutor's duty not to enforce statutory regulations which are unrelated to modern conditions. These considerations guide both the procurator fiscal in his initial decision and the Crown Office in issuing instructions in reported cases, but the Crown Office may also take account of wider questions of policy."

The guidelines contained in Renton and Brown were quoted with approval by the Crown Office in its evidence to the Hughes Commission, but not elaborated on. It is somewhat surprising in the era of the Justice Charter that we should still be in the dark as to whether Scottish prosecutors follow the English Director of Public Prosecution's approach to sufficiency of evidence if a prosecution is brought—is there a better than 50% chance of a conviction? Where there is sufficient evidence, the D.P.P. also asks himself whether it is in the public interest that a prosecution be brought. It seems likely the Crown Office expects Scottish prosecutors to ask themselves the same question. Unfortunately, the production of Annual Reports by the Crown Office and Procurator Fiscal Service since 1992 has done nothing to shed light on the basis for proceeding with a prosecution in Scotland.

It is at the stage of this initial decision of whether or not to prosecute that the significance of the Scottish system of independent prosecution is most clearly apparent. As one procurator fiscal has written:

Harris, "The Life of a Procurator Fiscal," p. 95

> "Once the case is in the Procurator Fiscal's office, it is looked at by someone who has had no knowledge of the case until it lands up in front of him, and moreover by someone who has in no way been concerned with the police investigations into the case. Therefore preconceived notions of guilt or otherwise are less likely to affect that person's judgement. Because the police have charged a person with committing a crime, (this charge is contained in the police report) it does not mean the person will automatically be prosecuted by the Procurator Fiscal . . .
>
> This highlights an important aspect of the work of the Procurator Fiscal—the separate identities of the police and the Procurator Fiscal. They are not, as is so often thought in league with each other against the criminals in an area. The duties of each are quite separate, and although in the majority of cases they take the same view of a case, their approach to a particular case will be from a different angle. . . ."

1. Alternatives to Prosecution

One factor of increasing significance in relation to the decision as to whether to initiate a prosecution or not, is the range of options available to the fiscal other than prosecution in the courts. Over the 15 years up to the beginning of the 1990s the number of recorded crimes rose by over 70%. Inevitably, there was a similar rise in the number of police reports to the fiscal service. Some commentators went so far as to say that the criminal justice system in Scotland was in crisis. Although the number of recorded crimes in 1997 was 15.9% lower than the number recorded for 1994 when compared with that figure and the number of reports to the procurator fiscal fell by 4.2% over the same period, the pressure on the criminal justice system remains very considerable. Just as ADR is increasingly being talked of as a possible solution to the problems of the civil justice system (see Chapter 1, pp. 13–26), so increasingly we find the prosecution service relying on non-court methods of disposal to tackle the growing caseload with which they are confronted. These include: no proceedings, warnings, conditional offers, fiscal fines and diversions (including forms of ADR). Thus in 1976, 93% of police reports resulted in a prosecution in court—the comparable figure for 1991 was only 53% although by 1997/98 the figure had risen again to 67% (see Table 5.2).

Obviously, if the fiscal concludes that there is insufficient evidence to warrant a prosecution he or she may determine to mark the report as a "no pro" (no proceedings). But the decision to take no proceedings may also be taken if the case is a trivial one, one in which the fiscal considers that no useful purpose would be served by a prosecution or because of certain mitigating factors, *e.g.* the length of time which has passed since the offence was committed, age or other factors relating to the accused and the attitude of the victim.

Harris, "The Life of a Procurator Fiscal," p. 96

> "It may be felt inappropriate to prosecute a person for a small theft if that person has already been punished—for example by losing his job, or by having to leave the neighbourhood and the likelihood of recurrence is small. Or, if a person feels so provoked by the behaviour of another over a period that he takes the law into his own hands, and commits a minor assault, without having instant provocation which would be recognised by the law, then prosecution of the person for assault would only aggravate an already raw situation, and the best thing that can be done is to let sleeping dogs lie. If a Procurator Fiscal decides to take no proceedings, then he need communicate that decision to no-one. It is not normal practice to send a formal intimation of this decision to the accused."

In 1986, "no pro-ing" was the most commonly used non-court disposal. However, for some time thereafter it took second place behind conditional offers of fixed financial penalties—a trend that was accelerated as "no pro-ing" became more contentious following the publication of a report by the National Audit Office in 1989, *Prosecution of Crime in Scotland*, which, *inter alia*, highlighted the considerable variations between areas in terms of "no pro" percentages. Not the least curious feature was that it was not always the busiest courts which had the highest percentages and vice versa. Thus a table published in 1990 showed that whilst the "no-pro" rate in Glasgow was 23% the figures for Edinburgh and Aberdeen were 10% and 6% respectively. Equally while Stornoway had a rate of 2% Rothesay's was 16% [see 1990 S.L.T. (News) 275]. However, as Table 5.1 demonstrates the no "pro-ing" rate between sheriffdoms in 1997/98 had subsequently equalised to an extent, with Lothian and Borders the lowest at 10%, Glasgow at 12% and Tayside, Central and Fife the highest at 14%. However, it may be that wider variations between individual sheriff courts still persist but because the Crown Office and Procurator Fiscal Service Annual Reports aggregate the figures for each sheriffdom such variations may be masked. Furthermore, it is clear from these Annual Reports that since 1993/94, "no pro-ing" has again become the most commonly used non-court disposal.

Alternatively, the fiscal may determine that the case requires some action short of prosecution or an administrative penalty and issue a formal warning to the accused either personally or by letter. Such warnings cannot be referred to in any subsequent court proceedings although it appears that lists of those who have been so warned are retained by fiscals. Warnings are most commonly used in shoplifting, speeding and breach of the peace cases. Another commonly used alternative to court proceedings is the use of conditional offers of fixed financial penalties by fiscals to accused persons in a wide range of road traffic cases.

A majority of the Stewart Committee in their report, *Keeping Offenders Out of Court: Further Alternatives to Prosecution* (Cmnd. 8958: 1983) recommended that fiscals should be able to impose a fine of up to £50 on offenders, without reference to a court. However, there were powerful opponents to this proposal. Nevertheless, fiscal fines were introduced in 1988 under s. 56 of the Criminal Justice (Scotland) Act 1987 in relation to cases which could be prosecuted in the District Court (other than motoring offences). The fiscal offers the offender an opportunity of paying a fixed sum (then £25) either as a lump sum or by instalment, to the court. If payment is made no prosecution is brought. Moreover payment is not a tacit admission of guilt and accepted fines are not recorded as convictions. In 1993–94 the government canvassed expanding the role of the fiscal fine as part of a more general review of the criminal justice system in the consultation paper, *Sentencing and Appeals*, 1993, ch.2 and the White Paper, *Firm and Fair* (Cm.2600, 1994, paras.8.7–8.12). The Government's proposals were that all statutory offences should be triable in the district court, hence making the fiscal fine available in such cases and that a scale of penalties envisaged as being £25, £50, £75 and £100 should be introduced. These proposals were subsequently implemented by ss.60 and 61 of the Criminal Justice (Scotland) Act 1995 which were consolidated in ss.302 and 303 of the Criminal Procedure (Scotland) Act 1995. Figures from Table 5.2 below reveal that the use of fiscal fines remained very constant from 1993/94 to 1996/97 with between 5.2% and 5.7%. However, following the implementation of the Government's proposals discussed above, the 1997/98 figures in Table 2 show a slight increase in use of fiscal fines to 6.5% of disposals. However, although there are advantages in an extended fiscal fine, there might also be dangers.

P. Duff, "The Fiscal Fine: How Far can it be Extended?" 1996 S.L.T. (News) 167, at p. 170

> "There is little doubt that the prosecutor fine has proved a highly successful method of easing the pressure of work upon prosecution services and courts. (It should not be forgotten that it also has certain humanitarian advantages—for instance, it avoids stigmatising first time offenders with a criminal record.) The extent to which the use of the fiscal fine could—and should—be expanded is a difficult issue. The measure clearly represents a move towards a bureaucratic/administrative type of criminal justice and there is a consequent danger of diluting the moral content of the criminal law. . . . Unfortunately, it is virtually impossible to test, far less quantify, whether indeed a fiscal fine carries a less forceful message than a criminal conviction and court imposed fine. Nevertheless, the prosecutor fine does seem to represent a move away from the expressive moralism of a court appearance towards disinterested administrative efficiency."

On fiscal fines see See *K. Meechan*, "Extrajudicial Punishment and Procurator Fiscal Fines," 1991 S.L.T. (News) 1; P. Duff, K. Meechan, M. Christie & D. Lessels, "The Fiscal Fine" 1994 S.L.T. (News) 151 and P. Duff, "The Fiscal Fine: How Far can it be Extended?" 1996 S.L.T. (News) 167.

The police are also now able to offer "on the spot" fixed penalties to alleged road traffic offenders.

The Stewart Committee was united in its support for pre-trial diversion schemes in terms of which minor offenders in suitable cases are referred to agencies which can offer help to the offender. Social Work diversion is perhaps the best known and most successful of these. Following a pilot scheme in Ayr such schemes have been introduced throughout Scotland. Under them alleged offenders who are considered to be likely to respond positively to social work assistance and who agree to participate are referred to a social work department rather than prosecuted in court. See I. Willock, "Diversion to Social Work Assistance" (1987) 131 SCOLAG 124. Under pressure from Scottish Women's Aid it is being increasingly accepted that diversion schemes are inappropriate in domestic violence or child abuse cases. Diversion may also be to outside agencies like Councils on Alcoholism or to detoxification centres for persons arrested for being drunk in public. The labour intensiveness and thus the expense of such centres means that regrettably there are only two such centres in Scotland. See S. Lloyd and A. Taylor, "Alternatives to Custody for Drunken Offenders" (1985) 101 SCOLAG 24 and "Inverness gets new centre for drunken offenders" (1991) 179 SCOLAG 118.

Diversion may also take the form of reparation and mediation (recompensing the victim for the damage done) or a non-harassment agreement in neighbourhood disputes. The one sustained mediation and reparation project in Scotland has been run by the Scottish Association for the Care and Resettlement of Offenders (SACRO) since 1987. The procurator fiscal does not waive prosecution; rather the project operates on the basis of deferred prosecution. A final decision on prosecution depends upon the outcome of the mediation.

S.R. Moody and R.E. Mackay (eds.), *Alternative Dispute Resolution in Scotland* (W.Green, 1995), p. 20

[See the following page.]

Procedure

Procedure for Mediation and Diversion

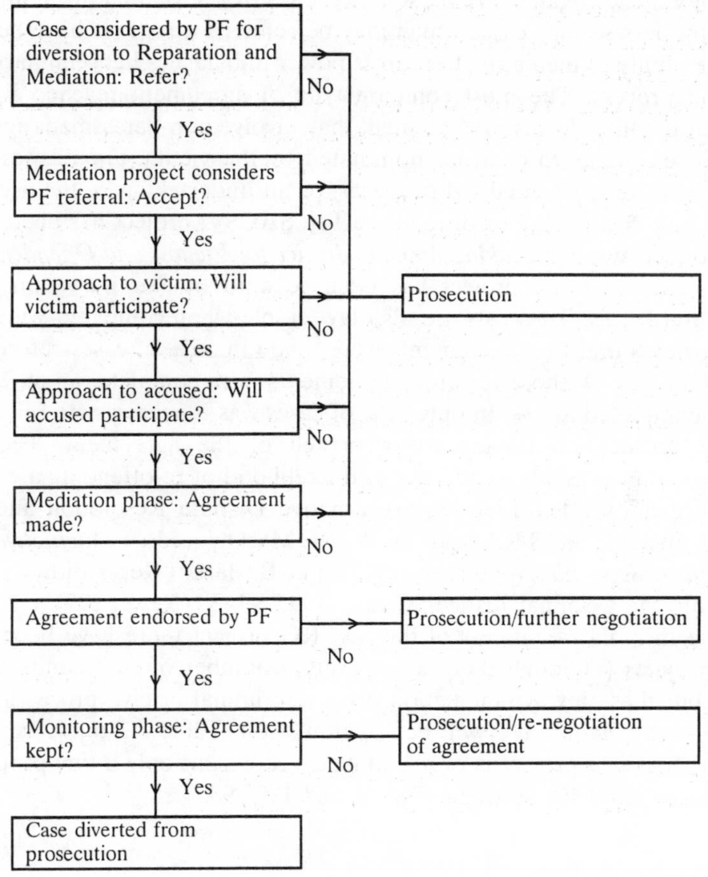

The types of cases which have been referred have mainly been assaults, assaults to injury, breaches of the peace, thefts and malicious mischief. However, it is unlikely that this project would be appropriate for cases involving a greater degree of violence against the person or crimes of a sexual nature. Furthermore, even in the less serious cases which may be referred questions have been raised about the ability of mediators to redress power imbalances between parties in the mediation process. The most common type of agreement reached is financial recompense. Other forms of agreement may involve non-harassment agreements, apologies, payments to charities nominated by the victim, unpaid work for the victim (*e.g.* to repair vandalised property) or an undertaking by the accused that he seeks help for alcohol or drug abuse.The SACRO project has been positively evaluated (see Warner, *Making Amends: Justice for Victims and Offenders* (1992)). Warner notes that the project has been seen to be fair by victims, accused persons and fiscals. The costs are also favourable when compared with prosecution. Warner found that agreements were made in 55% of cases referred to the SACRO project. Of those referred, agreements were completed in 69% of cases, partially completed in 6%. In only 11% of cases was it necessary to refer the case back for prosecution because of a breach of the agreement. The benefits including victim satisfaction and reduced likelihood of re-offending are considerable. See generally R.E.Mackay, "Alternative Dispute Resolution and Scottish Criminal Justice" in S.R.Moody and R.E.Mackay (eds.), *Alternative Dispute Resolution in Scotland* (W. Green, 1995) and B.Clark, "Reparation and Mediation Within the Criminal Justice System" 1995 S.L.T. (News) 225).

Despite the relative success of the SACRO project there have been no other similar projects (although there are a limited number of community mediation projects but these involve mediation prior to criminal or civil proceedings being initiated—see Chapter 1, it will be apparent from Table 5.2 that diversions—of which the SACRO project is only one type—represent only a tiny proportion of disposals around 0.4% between 1993/94 and 1997/98.

TABLE 5.1

Prosecutions in Scottish Sheriffdoms in 1997/98

Sheriffdom	Total Received	No Pros	Warnings	Conditional Offers	Fiscal Fines	Diversions	To Reporter etc.	% of Reports Received
N.Strathclyde	39,595	13%	8%	2%	7%	0.6%	1%	48%
S.Strathclyde	51,439	13%	7%	4%	8%	1%	1%	50%
Lothian	40,613	10%	4%	2%	4%	0.4%	1%	55%
Glasgow	69,117	12%	13%	3%	8%	0.1%	1%	41%
Grampian	40,624	12%	5%	2%	5%	1%	1%	53%
Tayside	49,995	14%	6%	3%	6%	0.1%	1%	53%

[Source: *Crown Office and Procurator Fiscal Service Annual Report 1997/98* (1998).]

TABLE 5.2

Non-Court Disposals in Scotland

	1993/94	1994/95	1995/96	1996/97	1997/98
Total number of reports received	301,140	288,584	279,147	281,439	291,383
No proceedings	41,120	40,614	37,553	36,631	36,701
Warnings	15,330	17,135	17,694	19,898	22,421
Conditional Offers*	23,652	8,966	10,354	7,220	7,559
Fiscal Fines*	15,580	16,046	16,054	15,138	18,961
Diversions	1,082	971	1,083	1,224	1,209
To reporter etc.	n/a	n/a	4,092	4,375	9,153
Total	96,764	83,732	88,825	84,486	96,044
% of total reports received	32%	29%	32%	30%	33%

* From April 1996, the figures recorded relate to cases closed.

[Sources: *Crown Office and Procurator Fiscal Service Annual Reports 1995/96* (1996), *1996/97* (1997) and *1997/98* (1998).]

As can be seen from these Tables there is a fair degree of variation between regions in the use of all types of non-court disposals. In the absence of research the causes of these variations must remain a matter for conjecture.

2. Prosecution Proceedings

Once the procurator fiscal has decided that an offence has been committed and that a prosecution be initiated in respect of it, the next decisions to be made are by what procedure and in what court should the action be raised. It is the prosecution which makes these choices and the defence have no say in them. Thus the accused cannot elect to be tried by a jury (solemn procedure) rather than by a judge alone (summary procedure). If the fiscal considers that the offence warrants trial on indictment he must make a report to the Crown Office. Crown counsel will then determine whether the case should proceed by indictment in the High Court or in the sheriff court or that the case be taken summarily or that no further proceedings should be taken. The usual test to be applied in determining whether to use the solemn or the summary procedure is whether, having regard to the gravity of the offence, an adequate sentence can be imposed by a summary court in the event of conviction.

For further details concerning the operation of public prosecution today see the Crown Office and Procurator Fiscal Service Annual Report for 1997/98.

B. PRIVATE PROSECUTION

Apart from the Crown, summary prosecutions in Scotland can also be brought by certain public bodies for particular statutory offences (*e.g.* education authority actions against parents for permitting truancy), and by private landowners against daytime trespassers in pursuit of game (though actions of either sort are rare). Rarest of all are private prosecutions under the common law brought by victims of offences or their relatives. As we saw earlier, such private prosecutions were once the norm. By the nineteenth century they had become unusual and could only be brought with the concurrence of the Lord Advocate or the High Court. Until recently, the last successful attempt to raise such a prosecution was *J. & P. Coats Ltd. v. Brown* (1909) 6 Adam 19. There the Lord Advocate had refused to prosecute a coal exporter on a charge of fraud and the victims of the fraud were granted permission by the High Court to institute a prosecution in the High Court by way of criminal letters (the private equivalent of an indictment). After a number of unsuccessful attempts to invoke the procedure since then, it had been thought that it had become obsolete in all but name. However, in April 1982 the High Court granted a Bill for Criminal Letters at the instance of a woman who had been raped and severely slashed with a razor: *H. v. Sweeney*, 1983 S.L.T. 48. The Lord Justice-General (Emslie) stated in the course of his opinion:

> "The rights of a private prosecutor in our system of criminal jurisprudence have grown up alongside those of the Lord Advocate and indeed, historically, bulked larger in earlier times than those of the King's Advocate. These rights still exist and there seems to be no good reason in principle for saying that they should not be available in any case in which the Lord Advocate has, for any reason, declined to prosecute an offender to a conclusion."

The test applied by the High Court in this case was the test most clearly set out in *McBain v. Crichton*, 1961 J.C. 25. In that case a Glasgow chartered accountant, who was a vice-president of a union of boys' clubs, an office which gave him a particular interest to prevent the corruption of youth, sought to prosecute a Glasgow bookseller for exposing for sale (and selling) *Lady Chatterley's Lover* by D.H. Lawrence, which he alleged was obscene. Lord Justice-General (Clyde) stated in his opinion (pp. 29–30):

> "This Court can permit, and on rare occasions has permitted, a private prosecutor to proceed without the Lord Advocate's concurrence. But to entitle a private prosecutor to do so, he must be able to show some special personal interest in the matter which, notwithstanding the Lord Advocate's decision in the public interest, satisfies us that a private prosecution in respect of this special personal interest may proceed. Hume on Crimes, vol. ii, at p. 119, puts it thus: 'To support his instance the individual complainer must be able therefore to show some substantial and peculiar interest in the issue of the trial; an interest arising out of some injury which he, beyond others, has suffered on the occasion libelled, and at which he is entitled to feel more than the ordinary indignation, with which his fellow citizens will regard it. It is not therefore sufficient, that he has some feeble and remote concern in the issue, or one of a general nature, in common with a whole neighbourhood, or with all of the same order or class of society.'
>
> But, in the present case, the wrong complained of, if it is a wrong . . . is of a quite general and public nature, committed against a whole neighbourhood or perhaps against the whole country, and, in its very nature, devoid of that personal and peculiar interest without which no private prosecution ever has been sustained in Scotland. [The complainer's interest to prevent

> the corruption of youth] . . . does not partake of that essential quality without which the prosecution could not proceed at the instance of a private party, because it does not show that the complainer personally and beyond all others has suffered owing to the wrong libelled. At the highest it would only invest him with an interest as protector of the morals of a class of persons in the community—namely the younger members of it. This is in its very nature a public and not a private or personal interest."

It remains a moot point whether the retention of private prosecution is justified or, as some have said, is an historical anachronism. See further on private prosecution, *McDonald v. H.M. Advocate*, 1988 S.L.T. 713.

C. REVIEW

The fact that prosecution in Scotland is almost exclusively in public hands raises the question whether a decision by a public prosecutor to prosecute or not to prosecute in a particular case is reviewable or one for which the prosecutor can be called to account. It appears that in the case of a decision by a procurator fiscal not to prosecute, a complaint can be made to the Lord Advocate who may instruct the fiscal to make a report to him, after which the Lord Advocate will make the decision. Again, where a procurator fiscal has prosecuted summarily and the accused has been imprisoned and the sentence subsequently quashed, the fiscal may be found liable in damages to the accused if he can be shown to have acted with malice or without probable cause.

On the other hand, the Lord Advocate by constitutional convention is not required to give reasons to the courts or Parliament to justify any decision to prosecute or not to prosecute taken by him or by Crown counsel, though, as in the 1982 case, he will sometimes answer questions in Parliament and in the media in relation to such decisions. Nor can the Lord Advocate, Crown counsel or procurators fiscal in cases tried on indictment, be sued for their actings as public prosecutors. In *McDonald v. H.M. Advocate*, 1988 S.L.T. 713 the High Court observed that the Lord Advocate was criminally responsible for his own actings and he was not vicariously responsible for the actings of Crown Counsel, the Crown Office and procurators fiscal. See further, J. Edwards, *The Law Officers of the Crown* (Sweet & Maxwell: 1964) p. 177.

McBain v. Crichton 1961 J.C. 25

> LORD JUSTICE-GENERAL (Clyde): The Lord Advocate . . . in this country is the recognised prosecutor in the public interest. It is for him, in the exercise of his responsible office, to decide whether he will prosecute in the public interest and at the public expense, and under our constitutional practice this decision is a matter for him, and for him alone. No one can compel him to give his reasons . . . the decision whether or not to prosecute is exclusively within his discretion."

In this context a declarator by the Court of Session in a civil action that certain conduct is criminal could not require the Lord Advocate to bring criminal proceedings:

Law Hospital NHS Trust v Lord Advocate 1996 S.L.T. 848 at p. 855 per Lord President Hope

"... I am clearly of the opinion that it would be undesirable for the Court of Session to attempt to define what does or does not amount to criminal conduct unless this is essential in order to decide an issue which a party has an interest to raise in this court. There are strong reasons of policy for leaving the definition of what amounts to criminal conduct to the courts. Any declaration which we might make would not be binding on the High Court of Justiciary. Nor would any declarator which we might authorise be binding on the Lord Advocate, who would be entitled in the public interest, irrespective of what we might say, to bring the matter before the criminal courts, to which the issue clearly belongs because the function of the criminal law is to regulate conduct by the imposition of criminal sanctions."

However, the Human Rights Act 1998 may have a considerable impact on the traditional Scots Law position. Since the Lord Advocate clearly constitutes a "public authority" in terms of s. 6 of the 1998 Act, it is unlawful for him to act in contravention of one of the rights contained in the European Convention on Human Rights which are incorporated into Scots Law by the 1998 Act. This could involve either a decision to prosecute or not to prosecute. Although the *Law Hospital NHS Trust* case (see above) suggests that the Court of Session would be unwilling to deal with such challenges, it may be that it has no choice especially in relation to decisions not to prosecute where judicial review would appear to be the only possible remedy. Judicial review is only available in the Court of Session. Judicial review of prosecutorial discretion is not uncommon in England and Wales where the High Court has dealt with such issues. If it is a decision to prosecute that is being challenged the High Court of Justiciary may be the appropriate venue with the accused arguing that the decision to prosecute constitutes oppression because it infringes a Convention Right (see C. Gane, "Bound to have a profound effect" (1998) 43 J.L.S. 22).

II. COMPOSITION AND JURISDICTION OF THE COURTS

A. THE DISTRICT COURT

There is a district court in each local authority area. Each consists of one or more justices of the peace (lay magistrates) sitting with a legal assessor (the clerk of the court—who must be legally qualified, District Courts (Scotland) Act 1975, s. 7; Criminal Procedure (Scotland) Act 1995, s.6(2); see also J. Hyslop, "The Role of the District Court Clerk" 1994 S.L.T.(News) 285) or, in four courts in Glasgow, a stipendiary magistrate (a judge of at least five years' standing as a solicitor or an advocate (District Courts (Scotland) Act 1975, s. 5).

The jurisdiction of criminal courts (the cases which they have the power to try and to dispose of) like that of their civil counterparts has three aspects, namely, limitations as to territory, power and competence. These aspects are governed by the place where the offence was committed and by the type of offence involved.

In relation to the first aspect, for a district court to have jurisdiction the offence must have been committed within the local authority area in which the court is situated. As to the second, in an effort to reduce congestion in the sheriff court the jurisdiction of the district court was expanded by the Criminal Justice (Scotland) Act 1980 to cover any statutory offence for which the maximum penalty does not exceed 60 days' imprisonment, a fine of £2,500 or both (Criminal Procedure (Scotland) Act 1995, s. 7(6)). These are the maximum penalties which can be imposed in the district court for common law or statutory offences unless a stipendiary magistrate is sitting when the maximum sentence becomes up to six months' imprisonment or a fine of £5,000 or both (Criminal Procedure (Scotland) Act 1995, s.7(5)). The court has the discretion to remit the case to a higher court (Criminal Procedure (Scotland) Act 1995, s.7(9)–(10)).

As to competence, the jurisdiction of the court includes breach of the peace, drunkenness, minor assaults, petty theft, and offences under the Civic Government (Scotland) Act 1982 (*e.g.* soliciting, loitering and being a known thief). Indeed the district court may now try all statutory offences which are triable summarily unless it is precluded by any enactment (Criminal Procedure (Scotland) Act 1995, s.7(3)). This is designed to relieve pressure on the sheriff court. Again, in a bid to relieve pressure in the sheriff court the Criminal Justice (Scotland) Act 1980, as amended, conferred jurisdiction on the district court in cases of theft, reset, fraud, breach of trust or embezzlement where the amount does not exceed £2,500 (see now Criminal Procedure (Scotland) Act 1995, s.7(4)) and s. 48 of the Transport Act 1982 confers jurisdiction on the court in relation to endorsable road traffic offences provided their maximum penalty is within the district court limits.

Burns, "A Day in the Stipendiary Court," p. 14

> "The system only works because everyone has confidence in the professionalism of the others. Of none is this more true than the stipendiary. If he knows his business and is consistent, many cases can be properly dealt with in a few sentences. It is almost a litany. The fiscal's eloquence may not extend beyond 'Usual thing, your Honour'. The defence may rest on 'He has a fixed address and money in his possession'. Almost as an aside from the bench comes 'Fined twenty pounds at two pounds a week'. Thus ends a saga that all began when he had come home, and, to let you understand, he had a bit to drink, and when his mother-in-law said to him, and to let you understand . . .
>
> It would be a mistake . . . to do down the importance of the district court. Quantitative judgments do not apply to law cases. The district court is the court that any citizen appearing in court is most likely to appear in. It is the first experience of court for people about to go off the rails. It has an overlap with social work to a greater extent than any other court. Without in any way wishing to diminish the importance of other courts, I have often thought that in human terms the determination of guilt or innocence of a middle-aged shoplifter carries at least equal weight with whether Slasher McGrew gets eight or ten years one hundred yards down the road at the High Court. The most unfortunate of society have their last lifeline, quite literally, in this court.

> The miscellany of cases is astonishing. There is, of course, what the police officers call the 'heavy bevvy' brigade. In government circles, these are the 'male, single homeless', but the euphemism conceals the reality. To interview this lot calls for a stout stomach and preferably nasal catarrh of a robust sort. Mostly they are cheerful. Each has a face like an unshaved pound of mince with two poached eggs in the middle. They all appear to be on first-name terms with the stip and wish the compliments of the season to be extended to him. 'Ah plead guilty to havin' a drink, surr,' they usually say, as if letting one into a greatly guarded secret. Sometimes as they are called from the detention cell to the dock they will give a few bars of a song, or have difficulty with ragged trousers that are trying to fall down, or come to attention in the dock and endeavour a salute that pokes an eye. In the public benches the serried ranks of Tuscany can scarce forbear to cheer these performances. Even the stern demand for silence from the bench cannot still the smiles. Now and again what appears to be a party breaks out in the detention room and the police have to open the door and demand silence. An old-timer will come out of the room singing the HL1 song and stagger to attention in the dock with a cheery 'God bless ye, surr'. As the good Sheriff Ian Hamilton has remarked, it is not difficult to picture them hidden behind a hillock chucking boulders at Roman soldiers. The stips monitor their flock with a kindly firmness. Every so often a fine will do. Other times admonition is right. Sometimes prison is needed if only to save them. It is a great pity that the detoxification centres so bravely and piously legislated for in 1980 have vanished like the euphoria of the night before.
>
> Sometimes prison seems the objective. 'The accused thereafter took a brick, your honour, and smashed the public house window. He stood around for some time, but nothing happened. Accordingly, he went to the nearest police station and reported what he had done. Officers came round with him to the pub where they found the brick and the damage and duly arrested him. Cautioned and charged he replied, 'I done it to get away from the wife' . . .
>
> Unpaid fines are obviously a problem. A long and weary means enquiry court is intertwined with quiet moments of the day's business. The excuses are all the same. 'Ah forgot.' 'The wean had measles.' Occasionally, 'Ah'd nae money', or, from women, 'The rent needed payin'."

See further on district courts Z. Bankowski, N. Hutton and J. McManus *Lay Justice* (T. & T. Clark: 1987).

B. THE SHERIFF COURT

The sheriff court is without doubt the more important "inferior" criminal court both in terms of jurisdiction and of caseload (see Table 5.3 below). Criminal proceedings in the sheriff court are heard either before the sheriff principal or sheriff alone (summary proceedings) or together with a jury of 15 (solemn proceedings).

The territorial jurisdiction of the court in criminal cases is regulated by s.4(1) of the Criminal Procedure (Scotland) Act 1995:

> "... the jurisdiction of the sheriffs within their respective sheriffdoms shall extend to and include all navigable rivers, ports, harbours, creeks, shores and anchoring grounds in or adjoining such sheriffdoms and includes all criminal maritime causes and proceedings (including those applying to persons furth of Scotland) provided the accused is, by virtue of any enactment or rule of law, subject to the jurisdiction of the sheriff before whom the case or proceeding is raised."

While sitting summarily the sheriff can impose a £5,000 fine or six months' imprisonment or both and twelve months' imprisonment in the case of certain re-offenders (Criminal Procedure (Scotland) Act 1995, s.5(2)–(3)(as amended by the Crime and Punishment (Scotland) Act 1997)). On indictment the sheriff may impose a sentence of up to five years' imprisonment, an unlimited fine or both (Criminal Procedure (Scotland) Act 1995, s.3(3) (as amended by the Crime and Punishment (Scotland) Act 1997). The significant increase in the sheriff's sentencing powers effected by the Crime and Punishment (Scotland) Act 1997 was designed to implement proposals initially canvassed in the consultation paper, *Sentencing and Appeals* (1994). That paper noted that the number of persons prosecuted in the High Court of Justiciary had more than doubled between 1980 and 1992 while at the same time the number prosecuted summarily in the sheriff court had decreased markedly and the number proceeding against in the district court had remained relatively constant over the same period. The paper also noted that the High Court should be dealing with the most serious cases but that it was apparently dealing with many cases that might appropriately have been sentenced in the sheriff court. Thus, in order to relieve the High Court of the pressure of dealing with less important cases, the paper canvassed increasing the sentencing powers of the sheriff court and district court. While the subsequent White Paper, *Firm and Fair* (Cm.2600, 1994) did not propose implementing the higher sentencing powers, nonetheless the then government again proposed implementing these increased sentencing powers in a further White Paper, *Crime and Punishment* (Cm.3302, 1996) and they were ultimately implemented by the Crime and Punishment (Scotland) Act 1997. If the sheriff feels the case should be heard in a higher court he may remit it to the High Court at any stage (Criminal Procedure (Scotland) Act 1995, s. 7(9)–(10)). In addition, if he feels that his sentencing powers in a solemn case are inadequate he can remit it to the High Court for sentence (s. 195) and in certain cases the sheriff may be required to remit the case to the High Court for sentence (s. 219(8)).

In relation to competence the sheriff court has concurrent jurisdiction with district courts in its sheriffdom (Criminal Procedure (Scotland) Act 1995, s. 4(4)) and a wide concurrent jurisdiction with the High Court for offences committed within its sheriffdom. Its case jurisdiction, in fact, is almost universal, though a few serious crimes are within the exclusive jurisdiction of the High Court (Criminal Procedure (Scotland) Act 1995, s.3(6)). The Thomson Committee considered a proposal that sheriff courts should be competent to try all cases except murder and treason but found little support for the suggestion (paras. 13.08–9).

C. THE HIGH COURT OF JUSTICIARY

Lord Cameron, "The Superior Courts," p. 30

> "The High Court of Justiciary is the supreme criminal court in Scotland, taking its title from the ancient office of the Justiciar. Since 1887 the members of the court are the same as the members of the Court of Session, but instead of being officially designed as Senators of the College of Justice, they are known as Commissioners of Justiciary . . . The head of the court is the Lord Justice General, who also holds the office of Lord President of the Court of Session, while the second senior judge is now the Lord Justice Clerk."

Unlike the Court of Session, the High Court of Justiciary goes on circuit (and has done since its constitution in the 17th century). At present there are four circuits, Home (Edinburgh), West (Glasgow, Stirling and Oban), North (Perth, Dundee, Aberdeen and Inverness) and South (Ayr, Dumfries and Jedburgh). The court is not restricted to these towns, however, and may sit anywhere in Scotland. In practice there is an almost permanent sitting of the court in Glasgow.

As a trial court the High Court normally consists of one Lord Commissioner and a jury of 15. In cases of difficulty or importance two or more judges in the court can sit with the jury (Criminal Procedure (Scotland) Act 1995, s. 1(5)) but this happens only infrequently (see, *e.g. HM. Advocate v. McKenzie*, 1970 S.L.T. 81). A larger court can be convened to consider points of difficulty if the presiding judge so requests (see, *e.g. Hay v. H.M. Advocate*, 1968 S.L.T. 334) and must be so convened when a petition to the *nobile officium* is heard (*Milne v. McNicol*, 1944 J.C. 151). It should be noted that the trial of the two Libyans accused in the Lockerbie bombing case (which involved the destruction of a Pan-American airliner over Lockerbie) is to be held in the Netherlands before three judges, together with an alternate judge to replace a trial judge if one should become ill or die, sitting without a jury.

The territorial jurisdiction of the High Court extends to crimes committed anywhere in Scotland or in Scottish territorial waters. It can also deal with certain crimes committed furth of Scotland, *e.g.* murder or hi-jacking by a Scots person anywhere in the world or piracy or offences against the Geneva Convention Act 1957 committed outside the United Kingdom. This is known as the High Court's extraterritorial jurisdiction. For a full account of the extraterritorial jurisdiction of the High Court see Renton and Brown's *Criminal Procedure*, paras. 1–22—1–40. See also Upton & Poustie, "The War Crimes Act 1991" in *Justice and Crime* (T & T Clark, ed. R.F.Hunter, 1993). The court can impose the death sentence for treason and possesses unlimited powers of imprisonment and fine in other cases.

Unless expressly excluded by statute the High Court's original case jurisdiction is unlimited. It has exclusive jurisdiction regarding certain crimes namely, treason, murder, rape, breach of duty by magistrates (Criminal Procedure (Scotland) Act 1995, s.3(6)). The High Court alone can remedy extraordinary or unforeseen occurrences in criminal cases through the exercise of its *nobile officium* (see Chapter 16 below).

III. CASES

In 1996 the number of persons proceeded against in solemn and summary cases was 174,844 of whom 36% (63,727) were charged with crimes and the remainder (111,117) with offences. Almost all offences (as opposed to crimes) were proceeded against summarily. In about 9% of cases (mostly summary ones) the charges are withdrawn or a plea of not guilty is accepted. This may be for a variety of reasons, *e.g.* because the fiscal has re-assessed the case, because a key witness is not available or fresh evidence becomes available which suggests that the accused is innocent, or because the accused has absconded or is unavailable for trial due to illness or some other reason. This is proportionately far fewer than the percentage of civil cases which are taken out of court. The difference is more apparent than real since withdrawals in criminal cases are equivalent only to civil actions which are abandoned by the pursuer. Criminal cases which are disposed of following negotiations are rarely withdrawn in the way that their civil counterparts are.

TABLE 5.3

Cases called for trial

	1986	*1991*	*1996*
High Court[1]	1,183	1,227	1,420
Sheriff court	108,434	100,013	100,928
District Court	77,728	87,186	62,485
Stipendiary magistrates	16,976	11,522	9,973
Unknown court type	—	54	38
Overall total	204,321	200,002	174,844

1. Includes remits from the sheriff court.

This table demonstrates the significance of the sheriff court as an inferior court, and the growth in High Court cases in the past decade. The decline in district court and stipendiary magistrate cases must be set in a context where approximately one third of the charge reports received by Fiscals are disposed of out of court (see Table 5.2 above, p. 113 and more generally pp. 107–114).

In general the more serious the charge the greater the likelihood that the accused person will plead "not guilty". On the other hand the greater the case of proof, the more likely the accused will plead "guilty", *e.g.* speeding offences. Table 5.4 suggests that once proceedings have begun an accused's chances of escaping a conviction of some sort are low—particularly in the case of motor vehicle offences (94% chance of conviction). On the other hand if the case goes to trial (proof) the chances of an acquittal (not guilty or not proven) are dramatically higher (between 30 and 50%). The reason for the high conviction rate in Table 5.4 is the high number of cases in which the accused pleads guilty at or before trial. In 1982 75% of those accused of a crime pled guilty (and 84% of those charged with offences). By 1991 only 59% of those charged with a crime in the sheriff court (and 78% of those charged with offences) were pleading guilty. (See: *Review of Criminal Evidence and Criminal Procedure* (Scottish Office, 1993) at p. 8.) Why do so many accused persons plead guilty?

TABLE 5.4

Cases called for trial and disposed of in 1996

	% *PGNA*[1,2] *or deserted*	% *Acquitted not guilty*	% *Acquitted not proven*	% *Charge proved*
1. Non-sexual crimes of violence	11	10	4	75
2. Crimes of indecency	4	7	4	85
3. Crimes of dishonesty	12	3	1	84
4. Fire-raising, vandalism etc.	9	5	1	84
5. Other crimes	19	4	1	77
Total crimes	14	4	1	81
6. Miscellaneous offences	8	4	1	87
7. Motor vehicle offences	4	1	0	94
Total offences	6	2	1	91
Total crimes and offences	9	3	1	88

1. Plea of not guilty accepted.
2. Includes cases where proceedings are dropped after a person has been called to court *e.g.* if witnesses cannot be traced.

[Source: Scottish Office Statistical Bulletin Criminal Justice Series, *Criminal Proceedings in Scottish Courts*, March 1998.]

A. WHY PLEAD GUILTY?

Part of the answer is that in many cases, particularly where a minor offence is involved, *e.g.* a parking violation or drunkenness, the accused does not deny the offence. This is equivalent to the many civil debt actions where decree in absence is taken because the defender does not deny the debt.

Secondly, it has been suggested that the high conviction rate in summary cases, particularly in the district court, discourages those who might otherwise plead not guilty. Thus McBarnet has attacked the simpler, cheaper procedures of summary courts for encouraging an "ideology of triviality" which ill accords with the media image of the "ideology of justice" derived from the higher courts where a jury determines issues of fact, a record of the proceedings is kept and the accused is almost always represented. See D. McBarnet, *Conviction* (Macmillan: 1981) and "Magistrates Courts and the Ideology of Justice" (1981) 8 *British Journal of Law and Society* 181.

The third, and perhaps the most significant reason for the high level of guilty pleas is the widespread practice of "plea bargaining" or plea negotiation. Just as in civil cases (see Chapter 3 above, pp. 63–65) many criminal cases are "resolved" between the parties by negotiation prior to coming before the court for judgment. Nevertheless the analogy is not complete because the outcome of the case, the sentence, ultimately depends on the judge in a way that civil settlements generally do not.

B. PLEA NEGOTIATION

The term plea negotiation covers a wide variety of informal and formal processes which take place in many legal systems. In Scotland it takes the form of plea adjustment, *i.e.* the reduction of a charge, the dismissal of one or more charges where the accused is charged on several counts or the exclusion of information about the criminal incident or accused person in a charge, in return for an admission of guilt by the accused. The parties involved include the public prosecutor, the accused's legal adviser and the accused. Judges are not involved in the process in Scotland and are not permitted to be so in England, although they take part in plea negotiations over sentences as a matter of course in the United States. The process, however informal, usually involves two stages: the discussion between the prosecutor and the legal representative for the accused, and that between the legal representative and his client.

The phenomenon of plea negotiation or plea adjustment, far from being officially frowned on, has received approval in high places. Chief Justice Burger of the United States Supreme Court in 1971 described it as "an essential element in the administration of justice". In 1981 the Solicitor-General for Scotland in a written answer in the House of Commons (14 H.C. Deb., col. 452, 10 Dec. 1981) commented:

> "The practice of plea adjustment is set out in para. 21.02 of the second report of the Thomson committee which was set up to examine criminal procedure in Scotland. It reads:
>
> > 'There is no statutory authority for plea adjustment but it is accepted as proper practice for either the accused's legal adviser or the prosecutor to approach the other and negotiate the acceptance of a partial plea. Normally such an approach comes from the defence but it is perfectly proper for the prosecutor to intimate to the defence that he would be willing to accept a plea of guilty to some of the charges in an indictment or complaint and drop the others or to accept a plea of guilty to less than the full extent on any particular charge. An offer of this sort, made by the prosecutor or the defence, cannot be founded upon by the other if not accepted.'
>
> I approve of this practice which is confined to discussion between the defence and the prosecutor. The judge is not involved and therefore there can be no discussion as to the sentence to be imposed. All that is agreed is the plea which the defence will offer and which the prosecutor will accept.
>
> If satisfactory pleas can be adjusted, valuable court time is freed to permit other cases to be heard. This creates speedier justice, which is in my opinion a very desirable aim."

It is difficult to gauge the frequency of plea adjustment from the published statistics. Table 5.5 indicates the number of summary proceedings which were disposed of by the sheriff court prior to or following trial. It provides some indication of the extent of plea negotiation although obviously some cases may be disposed of at the first court appearance (or subsequently) by the Crown dropping the case against the accused rather than because the accused pled guilty.

TABLE 5.5

Sheriff Court Summary Disposals

	1993/94	1994/95	1995/96	1996/97	1997/98
Case disposed of at first court appearance	47,585	49,013	43,816	44,004	42,246
Pled guilty at an intermediate diet	2,783	5,616	6,343	11,013	11,636
Pled guilty on day of trial	25,206	22,265	22,829	20,162	17,340
Number which went to trial	11,815	10,550	10,424	10,953	10,004
Total disposals prior to trial diet	50,368	54,629	50,159	55,017	53,882
Total cases disposed of	87,389	87,444	83,412	86,132	81,226

[Sources: *Crown Office and Procurator Fiscal Service Annual Reports 1995–96, 1996–97* and *1997–98*.]

Crown Office statistics show that in a third of all solemn cases and a tenth of all summary cases the accused changes his original plea of not guilty to a guilty plea at a later stage. The 1993 consultation paper on *Criminal Evidence and Procedure* suggested that the figures were even higher. In many of these cases plea negotiations will have taken place. In many more, such negotiations will occur before any plea has been tendered. A study conducted by Susan Moody and Jacqueline Tombs (1982) has shown, however, that there are considerable regional variations and that prosecutors in the busy urban courts feel under more pressure to negotiate with the defence than their rural colleagues. Such variations are also attributable to the lack of Crown Office guidelines on the situations in which and the ways in which plea adjustment should take place.

A procedural measure which is partly designed to encourage the accused to change his plea to guilty in summary proceedings is the intermediate diet. Intermediate diets were introduced in 1980. The purpose of such diets is to ascertain whether a case was likely to proceed to trial. It thus provides an opportunity for the accused to plead guilty before the trial took place and hence avoids the waste of resources which occurs when the accused pleads guilty on the day of the trial. Section 148 of the Criminal Procedure (Scotland) Act 1995 now governs intermediate diets. The previous administration's White Paper, *Crime and Punishment* (Cm. 3302, 1996) noted that mandatory intermediate diets were operating in 64 of Scotland's 78 courts dealing with summary cases and that courts which were then exempt from holding mandatory intermediate diets would be subjected to the mandatory requirement in 1997. The court must now ascertain the parties' state of preparation for the trial at the intermediate diet and whether the case is to proceed to trial. If the matter is to proceed further, the court may set a new trial date or indeed another intermediate diet. As Table

5.5 demonstrates, the introduction of mandatory intermediate diets has resulted in a considerable reduction in the number of cases where there is a guilty plea on the day of trial, which should presumably result in a consequent saving of resources.

1. Why Do Plea Negotiations Occur?

A number of reasons have been put forward to explain why plea negotiation is as prevalent as it is.

Sheehan, *Criminal Procedure in Scotland and France*, p. 119

> "The advantages to the prosecutor of a plea of guilty are that he need not proceed to trial, his onus of proof is discharged, and the accused will be convicted (of which there can be no guarantee if the matter goes to trial). The advantages to the defence are that they may obtain some concessions such as a reduced charge, the dropping of certain charges and the possibility of a lighter sentence (the accused being able to maintain in mitigation that he had never sought to deny his guilt and repented of his actions—an attitude which is more difficult to explain if the accused had denied his guilt by pleading not guilty)."

The position is rather more complicated than Sheehan makes out. The argument that a guilty plea and a contrite accused will attract a lesser sentence is accepted by some defence agents—particularly in indecency cases where it protects the victim from the embarrassment and the tribulations of the witness box. Nevertheless the English practice of allowing an almost automatic discount in sentence for those pleading guilty (which has been approved in the Court of Appeal) has no Scottish counterpart.

Nicholson, *The Law and Practice of Sentencing in Scotland*, pp. 218–219

> "There is no comparable, approved, practice in Scotland . . . In a legal system which presumes innocence and which permits every accused person to go to trial if he wishes, there can be nothing of a mitigating nature in the fact that many people nonetheless plead guilty; and, of course, it would be quite unacceptable that a person who was found guilty after trial should be punished more severely simply because he had not pled guilty . . . [The] reason . . . for not accepting a plea of guilty as being a mitigating circumstance in itself is that, if there were a regular practice to that effect, it might easily be seen as the court offering an inducement to accused persons to plead guilty rather than go to trial."

This was just the criticism that the High Court did indeed launch against the English practice in the case of *Strawhorn v. McLeod*, 1987 S.C.C.R. 413. Moreover, as the Court observed such a practice might disable judges from exercising their discretion fully and freely in a particular case. Some commentators have, nevertheless, been somewhat ambivalent about the possible breadth of the ruling in the *Strawhorn* case.

Nicholson, *Sentencing Law and Practice in Scotland* (2nd ed.), para. 9–36

> "It is to be noted, however, that what the High Court described as objectionable in the case of *Strawhorn* was a *practice* of giving a discount for a plea of guilty. That does not, it is submitted, mean that a court must never impose a lower sentence on account of a plea of guilty. Whether that will be appropriate, however, will always depend on the circumstances of a particular case and, it is suggested, on the extent to which a plea of guilty is itself a reflection of a mitigating circumstance, such as genuine remorse, or has truly mitigating consequences, such as avoiding the need for young children to give evidence in court."

Sheriff Gordon notes in his Commentary on the *Strawhorn* case in 1987 S.C.C.R. at p. 416 that by offering the Crown a certain conviction, less inconvenience for witnesses and a saving of court time and resources, accused persons are likely to feel that they should at least have a hope of more lenient treatment in suitable cases. Sheriff Gordon adds that if this is not the case then guilty pleas might become rarer—an outcome "that would not necessarily be to the overall benefit of the criminal justice system."

Following consultation the then government announced that it intended to introduce a statutory provision enabling but not requiring the courts to take account of a guilty plea and the circumstances in which it was made.

Scottish Office Home and Health Department, *Firm and Fair*, Cm. 2600, June 1994, paras.4.11–4.13

> "4.11 . . . many respondents asserted that in practice Scottish judges often do impose lesser sentences on those who have pled guilty than on those who go to trial. However, these respondents and most others were opposed to any formal system of sentence discounting or any requirement to reduce sentences in such circumstances. This was generally on the grounds that such a system would penalise accused persons who exercised their right to go to trial. It was also argued that the weight that should be attached to a plea of guilty for sentencing purposes varies widely from case to case and that the courts should not be constrained from deciding the appropriate weight to attach to such a plea in the circumstances of each case.
>
> 4.12 For most, although not all, respondents, these considerations outweighed any benefit which might be obtained if a system of sentence discounting were to reduce the number of late pleas of guilty, and therefore reduce the waste of time and inconvenience suffered by witnesses, jurors and others involved in criminal proceedings, who turn up expecting a trial which is then cancelled.
>
> 4.13 Having considered the various arguments, the Government has decided against the introduction of a formal or mandatory approach to sentence discounting in Scotland. Nevertheless there appears to be considerable acceptance of the principle that it may be right in many cases to reduce sentence for those who plead guilty early. At present, it is possible that some courts are inhibited from reducing sentences where they see justification for doing so by their perception of the effect of the judgment in *Strawhorn v*

McLeod (1987) which proscribed "a declared practice of discounting". Similarly, accused persons may not realise that it is in fact open to the court to take account of an early guilty plea by imposing a reduced sentence. The Government therefore intends to introduce a statutory provision to make it clear that the courts *may* take into account a guilty plea, and the circumstances in which it was made, as a mitigating factor in considering the appropriate sentence."

This proposal was implemented in s.196 of the Criminal Procedure (Scotland) Act 1995. See also Judge Ian McLean, "Judicial Discretion in Sentencing: (2) Discount for Plea of Guilty" 1995 S.L.T. (News) 339.

Sheehan is correct to point to the prosecutor's interest in a negotiated plea but as the Moody and Tombs study has shown the picture is again more complex than at first appears. First, prosecutors are not in general neutral as to whether a prosecution should succeed—the survey found that most fiscals considered that if proceedings have been instituted their implicit assumption was that the accused was guilty of some or all of the charges. The unpredictability of trials, particularly jury trials, and the defence's chances of acquittal (see Table 5.4 above) encourages the prosecutor to agree to a plea which will guarantee a conviction. As in civil cases a negotiated "settlement" ensures that the pursuer/prosecutor is at least partly successful. Secondly, prosecutors regard some cases, *e.g.* assaults on the police, as unsuitable for a negotiation, while in others the prosecutor considers that the accused would be sufficiently punished by a plea to a lesser charge and is therefore willing to accept the plea. The third and major factor is caseload pressures.

Moody and Tombs, "Plea Negotiations," pp. 120–121

"The major reason for negotiation of pleas offered by fiscals is to cut down on the number of trials, particularly at summary level. Neither the fiscal service nor the sheriff and district court personnel are equipped to deal with the volume of cases which would go to trial if pleas were not negotiated: 'it saves judicial time, fiscal time, defence time and very particularly it saves expense to the state in paying witnesses'; 'it is undoubtedly useful for the court and for the public . . . if every person who pled not guilty initially went to trial there would be a lot more folks coming into the court as witnesses—at vast expense to the Exchequer.' . . . The feeling that they are bound by constraints on time and money which makes them more vulnerable to offers from the defence is strongly expressed by some fiscals: 'it was my intention not to appear to be a person who was prepared to negotiate pleas but the system beats me'; 'I think we have to concede quite often . . . although we are not supposed to. I am being honest about this, other fiscals might not acknowledge it. I am sure we all do it'; 'you should be taking every trial on its merits and negotiating any pleas in that trial on their merit but you cannot help but think of the other ten trials."

Curiously, studies have shown that there is no correlation in America between caseload pressure and the percentage of cases going to trial, and that in the 1930s plea bargaining existed when there was no overload in the courts. See the *Law and Society Review* special issue on plea bargaining, Volume 13 (1979), pp. 189–582.

For the accused a suitable plea can hopefully avoid the risk of a heavy sentence, the uncertainties of trial and minimise the economic loss caused by the delay in waiting for trial. For the accused's solicitor it can also be advantageous if a guilty plea is tendered rather than the case going to trial, for he too may be subject to intolerable pressures of work.

2. The Merits of Plea Negotiation

At first glance plea negotiation seems to be in the interests of all the participants as well as the state. There are, however, some indicators to suggest that the process has its drawbacks. First, unlike judges in England, Scottish judges are bound to accept guilty pleas tendered by the defence and accepted by the prosecutor, since the Crown is the master of the instance. As in the civil cases therefore, the judges will accept the negotiated settlement without investigation of the circumstances to see if the settlement is a fair one. The significance of this is highlighted by the findings of the Moody and Tombs study. This study showed that some fiscals include extra charges which are unlikely to stand up in court because they are hoping for a plea to the lesser charge. Most fiscals disapproved of including charges as bargaining counters only but they not infrequently included charges which they could not prove, for evidential reasons or in an effort to show a course of conduct. The study also showed that many fiscals assert, and some defence agents accept, that the deletion of a few minor charges has very little effect on the sentence of the court. Thus in some cases an accused will have been persuaded to plead guilty in exchange for little in return from the prosecution.

The dangers of defence agents in England persuading their reluctant clients to make a guilty plea were the theme of John Baldwin and Michael McConville's *Negotiated Justice* (Martin Robertson: 1977). Ross Harper makes the same point in his booklet *My Client, My Lord* (Law Society of Scotland: 1981), but most of his chapter on plea negotiation relates to how to persuade a client to accept a guilty plea.

Harper, "Plea Negotiation," pp. 44–45

> "You have a duty to relate to your client the likely consequences of his going to trial as against those of a well-adjusted plea. If you put forward options in a disinterested manner, nine times out of ten your client will decide, in those dreadful words, to 'give it a run'. You are entitled—indeed you have a duty—to use reasonable persuasion without hectoring and forcefulness without threatening. Your client should be told the odds for and against conviction or acquittal and the likely result of conviction . . .
>
> If a client pleads not guilty at the outset he is not likely to change his mind without good reason. After evidence is obtained, an interview in the office may lead to a plea. More often than not in the security of an office the client will persist in his denial.
>
> The psychological time is on the morning of the court. Civil practitioners know well that a tender consistently refused may well be accepted in an

> action for damages on the morning of proof. The imminence of the case concentrates the mind wonderfully. As one moves towards the time of the trial the plea becomes that much more negotiable."

If these arguments suggest that plea negotiations do not always work to the benefit of the accused, Ross Harper's final paragraph hints at why plea negotiation has its drawbacks for the administration of justice. The Thomson Committee's main criticism of plea adjustment (para. 21.04) was the fact that so much of it occurs at the last minute. This was also a criticism made by the Sheriffs' Association in their evidence to the Hughes Commission, who pointed to the disruptions caused by such last-minute pleas to witnesses, jurors, prosecutors and judges. These issues lay at the heart of the 1993 Review of Criminal Evidence and Procedure which noted with alarm that about 80% of trials do not go ahead when programmed. Attempts by court administrators to tackle the problem of late pleas by setting down more summary trials for any one day than could possibly be heard, either exacerbate the problem by encouraging fiscals to "settle" cases by accepting a plea or lead to chaos when less than the anticipated 50% of trials go off. Such disruptions may be the price for avoiding the crippling overload if all cases went to trial but late changes of plea produce unnecessary delays for cases which are definitely going to trial.

However, the obvious solution of encouraging fiscals and defence agents to negotiate at an early stage (put forward by the Thomson Committee and endorsed by the Crown Office in a note published in 1980 S.L.T. (News) 42) is unlikely to work without some additional changes. The 1993 Review called for mandatory intermediate and first diets, routine disclosure of prosecution witness statements to the defence and far greater efforts to agree uncontentious evidence. The subsequent introduction of mandatory intermediate diets (see p. 124 above) has clearly resulted in earlier guilty pleas and far fewer guilty pleas on the day of the trial (see Table 5.5 above). This is because, as the Moody and Tombs study showed, defence agents are in a much better bargaining position if they approach the harassed fiscal at the last minute. Without time for reflection, or to take advice and faced with an impracticable caseload on the date of trial fiscals are more prone to accept a negotiated plea. It is also easier for the agent to persuade his client to change his plea at this stage as Harper indicates.

It remains a matter for debate how defensible plea negotiation is. Those who object to the "behind the scenes" way in which it currently operates may be attracted by the argument recently aired in England and Wales by the Bar Council and the Director of Public Prosecutions and since endorsed by the English Royal Commission on Criminal Justice, 1993 (R.156) that plea agreements should be formalised and clear sentence discounts offered for early guilty pleas. To many Scots lawyers this will be anathema which may have accounted for the greater caution of the 1993 Review, the 1994 White Paper and the subsequent minimal legislative changes on the topic. But how else might the practice be improved? Moreover it is unclear whether the prevalence of guilty pleas suggests that it is not in the interests of justice that all cases go to trial or that the ideal of the adversarial system cannot be achieved, or merely that society is not prepared to devote sufficient resources to enable it to be achieved. See further on plea negotiation in Scotland A.V. Sheehan, *Criminal Procedure* (Butterworths: 1990) pp. 74ff.

C. DELAY

It has been said that justice delayed is justice denied. In recognition of this, Scottish criminal procedure contains a number of devices designed to reduce delay. First, there is provision both in summary and in solemn cases for an accelerated guilty plea (if the prosecutor agrees). In solemn cases a letter signed by the accused intimating a complete or partial plea of guilty in terms of the Criminal Procedure (Scotland) Act 1995, s. 76 can lead to the case being disposed of by the sheriff or the High Court on remit within two weeks or so of the letter being received. Ironically this can put pressure on the accused to plead guilty to get the case over quickly, as the Royal Commission on Criminal Procedure recognised (Cmnd. 8092: 1981, p. 185).

Secondly, sections 65 and 147 of the Criminal Procedure (Scotland) Act 1995 provide that in solemn and summary cases where the accused is being held in custody, he must be brought to trial within 110 or 40 days respectively, otherwise he will normally be immune from prosecution for the offence, unless the delay was not the fault of the prosecution. Section 65 further provides that if a solemn trial has not been commenced within 12 months of the accused's first appearance on petition, he will normally be immune from prosecution for the offence, unless the delay was not the fault of the prosecution. (Contrast *McGinty v. H.M. Advocate*, 1985 S.L.T. 25 with *H.M. Advocate v. Swift*, 1985 S.L.T. 26.) The Thomson Committee proposed that a similar rule should be introduced in summary cases (the period being six months) but this has not so far been implemented. Nevertheless, if there has been "undue delay" by the Crown in raising proceedings in a summary case which results in "gross or grave prejudice" to the accused, then the complaint will be dismissed on the grounds of *mora* (delay). (See *Tudhope v. McCarthy*, 1985 S.L.T. 392.) It appears likely that these provisions comply with art.6(1) of the E.C.H.R. which requires that "In the determination of . . . any criminal charge against him, everyone is entitled to a fair and public hearing *within a reasonable time* by an independent and impartial tribunal established by law" (emphasis added).

See further on delay in criminal cases, the statistics contained in parliamentary answers reported in 1990 S.L.T. (News) 282 and 1991 S.L.T. (News) 205, and K. Miller *et al*, *Delay in Summary Criminal Proceedings* (CRU: 1989).

IV. REPRESENTATION

A. THE E.C.H.R. CONTEXT

The importance of representation in criminal cases seems now to be taken for granted. Article 6 of the European Convention on Human Rights and Fundamental Freedoms (E.C.H.R.) underpins this:

European Convention on Human Rights and Fundamental Freedoms, Art.6

"1. In the determination of . . . any criminal charge against him, everyone is entitled to a fair and public hearing within a reasonable time by an independent and impartial tribunal established by law. . . .

. . .

3. Everyone charged with a criminal offence has the following minimum rights:

. . .

(c) to defend himself in person or through legal assistance of his own choosing or, if he has not sufficient means to pay for legal assistance, to be given it free when the interests of justice so require; . . ."

The European Court of Human Rights has reinforced the importance of this aspect of article 6 in its rulings. For example, in *Granger v. United Kingdom* (1990) 12 E.H.R.R. 469 the court held that free legal aid should be available in an appeal involving complexity and the liberty of the accused. Even in cases not involving complexity, the court has held that where an appellant facing a heavy penalty is left to present his own defence to the appeal court, there is a breach of article 6 of the European Convention on Human Rights (E.C.H.R.) (see *Boner v United Kingdom* (1994) 19 E.H.R.R. 246; *Maxwell v United Kingdom* (1994) 19 E.H.R.R. 97 and also W.Finnie, "The European Court of Human Rights and Criminal Legal Aid in Scotland" 1995 S.L.T. (News) 271). In this context article 6 and the jurisprudence of the European Court are of paramount importance given the implementation of the E.C.H.R. in Scotland by virtue of the Human Rights Act 1998 and the prohibition on the Scottish Parliament enacting legislation contrary to the E.C.H.R. This will enable arguments based on article 6 and the jurisprudence of the court to be raised directly in criminal proceedings in Scotland. However, given the dramatic rise in the criminal legal aid budget, the problem facing the Treasury is how to pay for the existing provision far less any expansion. One response to the above decisions of the European Court therefore has been to withdraw the automatic right of appeal in Scottish criminal cases (see below pp. 146 and 148) in an attempt to cut the amount of legal aid spent on appeals, given that such a right is not a requirement of the E.C.H.R. Leave to appeal must now be sought.

B. THE GROWTH IN CRIMINAL LEGAL AID

The criminal legal aid budget has grown enormously in recent years (see Table 5.6). The Scottish Legal Aid Board's 1996–97 Annual Report revealed that the total cost of legal aid had risen from £47.2 million in 1987–88 to £143.1 million in 1996–97, a 200% increase.

TABLE 5.6

Criminal Legal Aid Applications and Expenditure

	1987–88	*1988–89*	*1989–90*	*1990–91*	*1991–92*	*1992–93*	*% change 1987–88—1992–93*
Total no. of grants	212,005	189,992	192,341	198,734	223,196	244,468	15.3%
Total expenditure (£)	27,215,862	35,012,676	37,285,701	43,560,056	52,739,475	70,259,206	158.2%

[Source: Figures derived from *Criminal Legal Aid Review—Consultation Paper*, 1993.]

Even though the growth in grants of legal aid has been quite small, overall expenditure has grown dramatically indicating an increase in the cost per case.

TABLE 5.7

Expenditure on Criminal Legal Aid

	1987–88 (£)	1988–89 (£)	1989–90 (£)	1990–91 (£)	1991–92 (£)	1992–93 (£)	% increase 1987–88—1992–93
Criminal Advice and Assistance	911,002	2,911,691	2,642,222	3,425,135	4,469,855	6,241,983	585.2%
ABWOR[1]	538,871	486,855	1,057,242	1,003,981	1,299,054	1,770,336	228.5%
Duty Solicitor	714,542	820,480	824,104	911,668	890,459	988,565	38.3%
Summary	16,344,543	18,771,786	21,207,623	24,736,525	31,287,496	40,786,470	149.5%
Solemn	8,498,404	11,585,481	11,065,347	12,745,245	14,019,698	19,289,103	127.0%
Criminal Appeals	208,500	436,383	489,163	737,502	772,913	1,182,749	467.3%
Total	27,215,862	35,012,676	37,285,701	43,560,056	52,739,475	70,259,206	158.2%

1 Advice by Way of Representation

[Source: *Criminal Legal Aid Review—Consultation Paper*, 1993, Table 4].

Table 5.7 illustrates that in terms of overall expenditure, summary legal aid absorbs more than 50% of the total resources although criminal advice and assistance, appeals and ABWOR have seen the largest percentage increases.

However, even more serious is the problem for the public that criminal legal aid expenditure is beginning to so dominate the overall legal aid bill that its continued rise is having destructive knock-on effects on non-criminal legal aid. Criminal legal aid (including Advice and Assistance and ABWOR) has accounted for a sizeable majority of all net legal aid expenditure in the last decade (in 1991/92 it was 70% and in 1996/97 it was 67%). The savage cuts in legal aid which were announced in the Autumn of 1992 have, in Scotland, impacted almost entirely on the civil legal aid budget which has already fallen in real terms by 28% over the five years up to 1992. The decisions of the European Court of Human Rights discussed above (see p. 30) have simply encouraged governments in the United Kingdom to protect criminal legal aid expenditure at the expense of persons of modest or moderate incomes with divorce, housing or employment cases.

C. ADMINISTRATION OF LEGAL AID IN SCOTLAND

Legal aid in Scotland is governed by the Legal Aid (Scotland) Act 1986 which created the Scottish Legal Aid Board ("SLAB") as a non-departmental public body to be responsible for the administration of legal aid in Scotland (see Chapter 12 below).

Given concerns about achieving value for money from public funds, there has been considerable focus on the possibility of introducing quality standards for solicitors providing criminal legal aid services. In England and Wales, a system of franchising was introduced to ensure adherence to quality standards (see Chapter 12). The following extract from a Scottish Office consultation paper explains why the introduction of quality standards was considered necessary.

Scottish Office, *Criminal Legal Aid Review—Consultation Paper*, 1993, para.5.34

"5.34 At present there are no minimum standards or experience requirements set out in relation to solicitors who wish to undertake legal aid work.

The volume of work varies substantially between firms of solicitors. Some may handle as few as 1 or 2 cases per year, while for others criminal legal aid represents the majority, or even the totality of their business. Research has shown that solicitors who have considerable experience of handling legal aid cases can frequently provide a better level of service at the same cost as solicitors with less experience, thus resulting in better value for money. In some cases, the quality of applications provided by solicitors may be low, leading to the need for further administrative input by SLAB in processing the application. Research commissioned by the Scottish Office also indicates that those solicitors with significant experience of criminal legal aid are more comfortable in dealing with the administrative requirements of the system and have fewest difficulties in explaining it to their clients and that there is already a degree of specialisation within the legal aid system by particular firms of solicitors."

Subsequently, radical changes were made by the Crime and Punishment (Scotland) Act 1997 to the Legal Aid (Scotland) Act 1986 to introduce quality standards. The 1986 Act now provides that only solicitors and firms registered with SLAB may provide criminal legal assistance (which covers all the types of criminal legal aid available—see below) and that such solicitors and firms must comply with a Code of Practice issued by SLAB. Compliance with the Code is a prerequisite to registration. The Code may include provisions on professional training, the standards expected of a solicitor providing criminal legal assistance, the manner in which a solicitor should conduct a case and represent his client, the manner in which applications for criminal legal assistance are to be made, the monitoring of a solicitor's performance to check whether he should continue to be registered, and the manner in which records are to be kept. SLAB has been given extensive powers to monitor compliance with the provisions of the Code (Legal Aid (Scotland) Act 1986, ss.35A–B as inserted by the Crime and Punishment (Scotland) Act 1997). Where it appears to SLAB that a registered firm or solicitor is not complying with the Code, it must investigate the matter and must give the firm or solicitor the chance to make representations. Ultimately, however, if SLAB is satisfied that the firm or solicitor is not complying with the Code, the firm and any registered solicitors connected with the firm or the solicitor from the register (Legal Aid (Scotland) Act 1986, s.25D). The register must be made available for inspection by the public free of charge (s.25F). In accordance with the requirements of the legislation, SLAB issued a consultation paper, Registration and Code of Practice under the Crime and Punishment (Scotland) Act 1997 in October 1997 which contained a draft Code of Practice.

D. TYPES OF CRIMINAL LEGAL AID

Legal aid is available to accused persons under three different headings: advice and assistance (for initial advice) and advice by way of representation (ABWOR) (following a guilty plea/up to the intermediate diet); the duty solicitor scheme which provides advice for those in custody or attending an identification parade; and criminal legal aid which covers the preparation prior to trial, the trial itself and any appeal arising therefrom.

1. Advice and Assistance—Assistance by way of Representation

Assistance by way of representation (ABWOR) was introduced as part of Advice and Assistance (see Chapter 12 below) in 1987 to simplify summary criminal legal aid procedure and to encourage earlier plea changes (from not guilty to guilty). Research has shown that it has largely succeeded in the first objective but failed in the second. See F. Rutherdale, *The Impact of "Assistance by way of Representation"* (CRU: 1990). The intention of ABWOR was originally that it should be available in summary criminal cases where an accused person, who is not in custody, has pled guilty or changed his or her plea to guilty within 14 days of the original "not guilty" plea. However, this time limit appeared to be encouraging the maintenance of a "not guilty" plea and hence entitlement to full legal aid. Therefore, following consultation in *Criminal Legal Aid Review—Consultation Paper*, 1993, para.5.34, the then government proposed in its White Paper, *Firm and Fair* (Cm. 2600, 1994) to extend the provision of ABWOR to the intermediate diet or if there was no intermediate diet to a set period in advance of the trial. This was subsequently implemented to encourage more accused to change their pleas before any trial diet and hence save public funds. To be eligible for ABWOR the accused must meet the same financial tests as for Advice and Assistance. In addition the offence must be such that, if proved, it would be likely to lead to a sentence involving loss of liberty or livelihood of the accused. Alternatively, ABWOR can be extended to accused persons who are financially eligible but who are unable to understand the proceedings or make a plea in mitigation because of age, inadequate knowledge of English, mental illness or other mental or physical disability or incapacity. The research suggested that although loss of liberty was the criterion most frequently cited by solicitors using the scheme (64%), in only 6% of cases in the research project was a custodial sentence imposed. Despite the recent furore in England and Wales over the introduction of fixed fees for some criminal legal aid work, the Scots solicitors interviewed in the research project approved of the standard block fee arrangement which already exists for ABWOR work in Scotland.

2. The Duty Solicitor Scheme

Under this scheme (originally introduced in 1967) and now governed by the Legal Aid (Scotland) Act 1986, s. 22 (and accompanying regulations) in all sheriff and district courts a "duty solicitor" drawn from the solicitors undertaking criminal legal aid work in these courts is available on a rota basis, for every day of the year.

The Hughes Commission, p. 89

> "8.11 When the duty solicitor is informed that a person has been taken into custody charged with murder, attempted murder or culpable homicide and that he wishes the duty solicitor's services, he is required to visit that person in custody and to advise him and act for him until he is brought to a sheriff court for his judicial examination. In all cases where the accused is in

custody and is dealt with under solemn procedure (those tried with a jury), the duty solicitor is required to visit the accused before his judicial examination and represent him at that examination. In summary cases, the duty solicitor is required to interview any accused person in custody who wishes his services and to represent that accused up to the first diet at which he is called on to plead. If a plea of guilty is tendered, the duty solicitor will continue to act for the accused until the case is terminated. Typically, this will involve the presentation of a plea in mitigation."

The duty solicitor's services are also available to represent accused persons at identification parades. The services are provided free of charge and the solicitor is reimbursed out of state funds. In 1996/97 duty solicitors represented 20,160 accused persons in custody at their initial appearance in the sheriff court and 6,445 in the district court.

3. Criminal Legal Aid

Criminal legal aid since its inception has been granted by the court both in solemn and in summary cases—normally the court before which the accused makes his or her first appearance. In solemn cases all that the court requires to be satisfied is that the accused person's financial circumstances are such that the expenses of the case cannot be met without undue hardship to the accused or his or her dependants. In Scotland, unlike England, accused persons who are granted legal aid are not required to pay a contribution. In summary cases the same financial test was and is applied but in addition the judge had to determine whether it was in the interests of justice that legal aid be granted in the case. This criterion ensured that legal aid was not available for many minor cases heard before the sheriff and district courts. The "interests of justice" test was controversial for several reasons. First, it was considered by many to be inappropriate that the same body that was determining the case should also decide beforehand where the interests of justice in the case might lie. Secondly, research established that there were widespread variations between courts in interpreting the eligibility criteria for legal aid in summary proceedings. This in turn led to substantial differences between courts in the success rate of applications for legal aid in summary cases (in 1984 the range extended from 60% to 99%). Certainly, when SLAB was established it was given the responsibility for awarding legal aid in summary cases partly as a bid to ensure greater consistency in the application of the "interests of justice" test. To assist SLAB the Legal Aid (Scotland) Act 1986, s. 24(3) lays down the factors to be taken into account by SLAB in applying the "interests of justice" criterion:

"(a) the offence is such that if proved it is likely that the court would impose a sentence which would deprive the accused of his liberty or lead to loss of his livelihood;

(b) the determination of the case may involve consideration of a substantial question of law, or of evidence of a complex or difficult nature;

(c) the accused may be unable to understand the proceedings or to state his own case because of his age, inadequate knowledge of English, mental illness, other mental or physical disability or otherwise;

(d) it is in the interests of someone other than the accused that the accused be legally represented;

(e) the defence to be advanced by the accused does not appear to be frivolous;

(f) the accused has been remanded in custody pending trial."

SLAB has published guidance expanding on what it is looking for in relation to each of these factors (see *Criminal Legal Aid Review—Consultation Paper*, 1993, Annex B).

For the time being the courts have been left with the responsibility of awarding legal aid in solemn cases and in summary cases where the accused has been convicted and is facing a sentence of imprisonment or detention for the first time (Legal Aid (Scotland) Act 1986, s. 23). While there is no appeal against a court's decision not to award legal aid it is possible to apply to SLAB in summary cases where legal aid has been refused to ask for a review. Almost 50% of reviews result in a grant of legal aid. Since 1990 in cases where legal aid has been refused by SLAB for a criminal appeal and the appeal is ultimately successful it has been possible to recover the expenses of the action from SLAB.

Consistently over the last decade about 99% of applications for legal aid in solemn cases have been granted. In 1996/97 93% of applications in sheriff court summary cases and 79% of applications in district court cases were granted. However, this leaves a misleading impression in that although almost all those who stand trial under solemn procedure do so with legal aid, only a minority of accused persons in summary cases are so aided (approximately 20%). It is not clear how many persons plead guilty in summary cases because they are refused legal aid or because they are convinced that they would not be granted legal aid in any case, and so do not apply. Certainly, very few accused persons in summary cases are unrepresented at trial. Nevertheless, a significant majority of persons accused of summary offences are not legally aided, fall outwith the scope of the duty solicitor scheme and plead guilty.

It should be noted that the statutory test for criminal legal aid in appeals has been changed from "substantial grounds" to "interests of justice". This was proposed in the White Paper, *Firm and Fair* (Cm.2600, 1994, para.7.7), partly to ensure consistency with article 6(3)(c) of the European Convention on Human Rights (see above). See now s.25 of the Legal Aid (Scotland) Act 1986 as amended by the Criminal Procedure (Consequential Provisions) (Scotland) Act 1995.

E. FIXED FEES

As Table 5.7 reveals, legal aid expenditure in Scotland, particularly in summary cases has expanded enormously. In England and Wales a similar situation has led to fixed fees in criminal cases and franchising (see Chapter 12 below) of legal aid firms which meet certain quality assurance standards. Quality standards have now been introduced in Scotland also but by means of the Code of Practice rather than by franchising (see p. 32 above). The previous administration also canvassed the introduction of standard or fixed fees in Scotland to control this expenditure (see *Criminal Legal Aid Review—Consultation Paper*, 1993, paras.5.25–5.31; and *Firm and Fair* (Cm.2600, 1994), para.7.9).

Scottish Office, *Crime and Punishment* (Cm.3302, 1996)

"6.10 The costs of legal aid have risen in all areas. These rises are evident not only in overall costs but also in individual case costs. . . . [Case costs for summary criminal legal aid] have increased by 134% since 1987–88 compared with 47% for the cost of living generally Although overall costs have slightly reduced in the last year, case costs have continued to rise.

6.11 The majority of expenditure is on summary criminal legal aid, and it is in this area particularly that the Government considers urgent action is required. The historical upward trend on summary criminal legal aid simply cannot be sustained. It is pre-empting resources that could more usefully be devoted to the fight against crime and the protection of victims.

6.12 A number of criticisms have been made of arrangements for summary criminal legal aid. These are set out below.

6.12.1 The current system provides no incentive to solicitors to address at an early stage with their clients whether an effort should be made to negotiate a realistic plea with the Crown. On the contrary, any extra work which the solicitor undertakes will be paid for even though, in the event of a change of pleas, it turns out to be unnecessary. Provided the work constitutes a valid charge against the Legal Aid Fund, it tends to be carried out. In some instances, of course, the work is necessary, in other instances less so and in some not at all. There is no mechanism for questioning the necessity of the work or for stipulating that it should be done to a particular standard.

6.12.2 When the question of adjourning trials arises, such adjournments are proposed or agreed to without any regard to the additional costs involved. The more work that is done in preparing for and attending trials which do not take place, the greater are the charges against the Legal Aid Fund. The intention of intermediate diets to encourage early case preparation will not be achievable unless both sides have an incentive to undertake early preparation.

6.12.3 Comparative research into cost in different jurisdictions appears to show that costs per summary case are higher in Scotland than in England and Wales and the Netherlands. One possible explanation is that the present system allows solicitors to provide a very full service to accused persons, since each separate activity will attract remuneration. It might also be that our type of legal aid system encourages considerable "hand-holding" of clients, without necessarily achieving better outcomes for them.

6.12.4 Lastly, the present system of remuneration requires detailed compilation of accounts by solicitors and detailed scrutiny by SLAB. This too involves resources that might be better used in other parts of the system."

It is clear that the Government's case for fixed fees is based on the argument that solicitors are doing too much work that is really unnecessary because they get paid for it and that the system provides no incentive for them to get their clients to focus at an early stage on pleading guilty. However, although the comparative research mentioned above, T. Goriely, C. Tata and A. Paterson,

Expenditure on Criminal Legal Aid: Report of a Comparative Pilot Study of Scotland, England and Wales and the Netherlands, Scottish Office Central Research Unit, HMSO, 1997 noted that the way in which legal aid was paid in Scotland was a relevant factor in the increase of summary case costs, nonetheless it concluded that there was inadequate evidence to support the contention that lawyers themselves were responsible for the increases in case costs. However, it did conclude that there was evidence that the system of standard fees adopted in the Netherlands for legal aid payments was an effective means of controlling the costs of summary legal aid albeit that questions remained as to the impact that the system had on quality.

Further research by Stephen that was commissioned by the Law Society of Scotland postulated that if the demand for solicitors' other legal services were declining, they might be more willing to spend additional time on criminal defence work, thus increasing the average costs of such cases (F.H. Stephen, *Legal Aid Expenditure in Scotland: Growth, Causes and Alternatives*, 1998, p. 23). However, following detailed statistical analysis Stephen rejected this explanation and concluded that the statistical evidence supported the view that the increase in the average cost of legally-aided summary cases in the sheriff courts in the 1990s had actually been caused by the increase in the number of cases tried there (pp. 24–25). The congestion this had caused led to delay, lengthening of cases which in turn has increased costs (see also F.H. Stephen, "Legal aid comes under the microscope" (1998) 43 J.L.S. 18). Therefore the research would tend to support the view that while fixed fees will control costs, the increased costs are not necessarily being caused by lawyers to any extent but rather by delay in the courts resulting from an increased caseload.

Nonetheless the government has introduced fixed fees by the Criminal Legal Aid Fixed Payments (Scotland) Regulations 1998 made under s.33(3A)–(3B) of the Legal Aid (Scotland) Act 1986 which was inserted by s.51 of the Crime and Punishment (Scotland) Act 1997 (see "Criminal Legal Aid Fixed Payments Consultation" 1998 S.L.T. (News) 261). There has been consternation in the legal profession about the impact of fixed fees on the legal profession, (see, *e.g.* R.Mackenzie, "Redundancy fears over fixed fees" (1999) 44 J.L.S. 26). Concerns have been expressed in particular about the impact on legal services in the far north of Scotland and the islands where the cost of travel and lost revenue during travelling and waiting time for a solicitor travelling, for example, to Wick from Inverness or a trip to one of the islands (which might of necessity take two or three days) cannot be adequately catered for by fixed fees. Indeed the Mackenzie article reveals that all Inverness solicitors on the duty roll for Wick Sheriff Court have resigned their services because of this.

F. CONTRACTING

In England and Wales one means of ensuring value for money in the legal aid system has been franchising (see also Chapter 12). Registration and the Code of Practice now provide a means of ensuring quality standards in Scotland but the Government has also introduced legislation enabling SLAB to enter into contracts with registered firms for the provision of criminal legal assistance

(Legal Aid (Scotland) Act 1986, s.33A as inserted by the Crime and Punishment (Scotland) Act 1997). In its White Paper, *Crime and Punishment*, the then government explained that it did not consider that fixed fees could by themselves provide the degree of control over criminal legal aid expenditure that was necessary.

Scottish Office, *Crime and Punishment*, Cm.3302, 1996

> "6.27 . . . The Government believes that competition amongst suppliers is normally the best means of providing services to the public in an efficient and cost effective way.
>
> 6.28 As against this, it is clear that there are no such disciplines in place at present to drive down costs as far as summary criminal legal aid is concerned. Legal aid is already a public sector activity, because it is entirely funded by the taxpayer. There is no real competition or search for efficiency, because the client, who chooses which firm to approach, has no financial stake in the cost, while the Board must grant legal aid to all who qualify.
>
> 6.29 A move to contracting would eventually provide an element of competition among legal aid suppliers. However it will be some time before that takes place. Meanwhile SLAB will require to gather as much benchmark information as possible (in addition to experience of controlled [*i.e.* fixed] fees) about what the proper price of a contract for summary criminal legal aid should be. That information is not available from records of what the cost historically has been. The year on year rise in costs suggests that criminal legal aid now costs considerably more than it should if the service were efficiently and economically organised."

One way of gathering such "benchmark information" would be "for SLAB to employ on fixed salaries a small number of solicitors to provide criminal legal aid on a pilot basis" (para.6.31). This is the public defender scheme.

G. PUBLIC DEFENDER SCHEME

The Royal Commission on Legal Services in Scotland (the Hughes Commission) proposed experimenting with public defenders (state salaried lawyers who would act for accused persons) along the lines of schemes in Australia, Canada and the United States (r. 8.29). Although the Commission proposed this in 1980, it was not until the consultation paper *Criminal Legal Aid Review—Consultation Paper* in 1993 that the then government began to canvass the idea of introducing a public defender scheme (see paras.5.45–5.48). The idea was finally taken up in the White Paper, *Crime and Punishment* (Cm.3302, 1996) where the government proposed the establishment of a pilot public defender scheme involving lawyers employed by SLAB to provide legal advice and representation for accused persons. The government explained that while it did not envisage that it was appropriate for all criminal legal aid work to be provided through a salaried service, nonetheless a pilot public defender scheme would enable SLAB to obtain "as much benchmark information as possible (in addition to experience of controlled [*i.e.* fixed] fees) about what the proper price of a contract for summary criminal legal aid should be" (para.6.29) for the purposes of developing legal aid contracting (see above).

The Law Society of Scotland's response to this proposal was overwhelmingly negative but it does highlight some areas of real concern, particularly in relation to resources provided for the public defender and the potential for conflict of interest

Law Society of Scotland, *Response to Crime and Punishment*, 1996, pp. 13–15

> "The Society has deep concerns about the possibility of the establishment of a public defender scheme.
>
> The Society has undertaken a broad research of the public defender systems applicable in the United States and Canada.
>
> In the United States the total expenditures for the criminal justice system in both the state and federal systems display an inequity in the distribution of resources.
>
> Across the US the bulk of criminal justice funds go to the police, prosecutors and jails. In the fiscal year 1990, approximately $74 billion was spent in the US on criminal justice. Only 2.3% of this amount was spent on providing assistance to indigent defendants, while 7.4% was provided for prosecution, 12.5% on courts, 33.6% on corrections and 42.8% on police protection. However, the number of defendants unable to afford an attorney has risen dramatically from 48% in 1982 to 80% today. Public defenders handle over 11 million of the 13 million criminal cases which are tried annually. Yet, as of 1990, the United States Department of Justice found that nationally, public defenders are receiving less than 1/3 of the resources provided to the prosecution. Prosecutors' offices received $5.5 billion dollars from federal, state, local, county and municipal governments as opposed to the $1.7 billion provided for public defence by the same government sources. This kind of resource disparity is just one of the reasons why many believe indigent criminal defendants are not competing on a fair playing field, and why their lawyers are often unable to provide them an adequate defence.
>
> The representation provided by a number of public defenders has been found unconstitutional due to lack of resources. Richard Teisser, a New Orleans public defender filed suit against himself demanding that the judge declare his work inadequate and order the state to provide adequate resources. The judge agreed and found the state's indigent defence system unconstitutional. Other suits have been filed in at least five states which also challenge the funding and staffing of indigent defence programs.
>
> An ABA study on the quality of indigent criminal defence found that problems in the system are reaching crisis proportions. There is a clear and present danger that innocent people are going to jail because public defenders are so overworked and have so few resources that their cases cannot be thoroughly investigated and defended. . . .
>
> There are few positions as laden with tension and contradiction as that of the public defender. He is typically a government employee and yet functions as private counsel. In most instances, he is paid and staffed by the

very entity—the state—he opposes in his client representations. He is sometimes appointed by the very judges before whom he argues in court. . . .

To compound matters, the indigent defendant does not specifically choose the public defender assigned to his case. Consequently, public defenders can have difficulty with establishing client confidence. Not uncommonly, clients provide public defenders with unreliable information or behave unpredictably. Mistrust is also engendered when the client perceives, as he often does, that the publicly-funded defender is merely a cog in the very court bureaucracy that is processing and convicting him. . . .

The Society is fearful that if a public defender system were established in Scotland it would create an assembly line or bureaucratic system of defence in which the vast bulk of cases would be disposed of without trial by a guilty plea. This need not be the fate of Scottish justice which after all has had provision for legal aid since 1424.

The Society is of the view that:-

1. The failure of the public defender to be perceived as an independent body will result in it being fundamentally and constitutionally unacceptable.
2. The conflict between the duty to the client and to the employer is irreconcilable.
3. The current system, when operated fairly and reasonably, is an effective means of providing representation.
4. There are serious questions as to whether the service would attract the right calibre of lawyer who could make the service work efficiently and achieve the requisite quality of service.
5. The denial of Legal Aid to a person for the solicitor of his or her choice is not in the interests of justice.
6. The public defender system is likely to be less work intensive, less efficient, and therefore much more costly than the expense currently incurred by SLAB.
7. The need for the client to be independently advised especially in cases involving more than one accused renders the Public Defender system flawed."

However, research conducted by Henry and Fleming (A. Henry & A. Fleming, *A Literature Review of Public Defender or Staff Lawyer Schemes*, Scottish Office Central Research Unit, 1999) provides evidence that public defender schemes can provide excellent value for money. The study found that information available from the United States was of limited value because the research there had been carried out in a less strategic manner and that the system was so fragmented that it was impossible to arrive at a consistent overall view on the merits or demerits of public defender schemes there. Likewise in Australia, although the system was less fragmented than the US, there were only a small number of individual studies which were hampered by methodological problems. However, Henry and Fleming's study found Canadian research particularly valuable.

The key finding that emerged from a study of the Canadian research is that public defenders are capable of providing cheaper legal aid services than private sector lawyers. Research in Nova Scotia, Quebec, British Columbia and Manitoba—provinces in which both private sector lawyers and public defenders provide criminal legal assistance—demonstrated that the average case costs incurred by private sector lawyers were roughly double the costs incurred by public defenders (in Nova Scotia the figure was no less than 7 times higher!). The study noted that various hypotheses had been put forward in the Canadian research to explain this. First it was postulated that public defenders provided an inferior service to private sector lawyers. However, the evidence demonstrated that clients of public defenders were neither more nor less likely to be convicted than clients of private sector lawyers and indeed were given consistently fewer custodial sentences than the latter. The evidence did not support the second hypothesis, that private lawyers handled more difficult cases. The third hypothesis was that the way in which private lawyers applied for and were paid for legal aid work made them more expensive. Work conducted by the Canadian Department of Justice concluded that private sector lawyers received higher hourly rates of remuneration than public defenders and that this was partly caused by "strategic billing", by which private solicitors maximised their billable hours. The fourth hypothesis, which was linked to the third was that private sector lawyers spent more time on cases. This was borne out by the evidence (in Manitoba private sector lawyers spent almost double the time on cases as did their public defender counterparts) but interestingly the evidence also indicated that this extra time did not improve the service received by clients. Indeed public defenders usually achieved slightly better outcomes. The fifth hypothesis was that public defenders tended to conclude cases at an earlier stage. The research demonstrated that public defenders tended to plead their clients guilty at an earlier stage and that charges were likely to be withdrawn at an earlier stage. It was suggested that this was because public defenders were more active in engaging in constructive negotiations with prosecutors. The final hypothesis was that public defenders processed cases to the benefit of the court, not their clients. While the research suggested that public defenders did spend more time negotiating with the prosecution and that this benefited the government in terms of more effective use of legal aid and court time, there was no evidence to indicate that this compromised clients' interests. Indeed as noted above, public defenders actually achieve slightly better outcomes for their clients, particularly in terms of custodial sentencing.

Henry and Fleming's study concludes that Scotland's pilot public defender project has much to learn from the Canadian experience which demonstrates that such schemes can bring clear benefits, including more cost effective provision of legal aid services, fewer and shorter custodial sentences for convicted clients, the provision of legal services that are as satisfactory as those offered by the private sector and the resolution of cases at an earlier stage resulting in fewer expensive trials. It does appear that this research provides a more rigorous evaluation of the public defender elsewhere than the Law Society's "broad research" noted above and that many of the Law Society's concerns may prove to be groundless. Certainly, we have now reached the situation where it will be necessary to demonstrate that society is getting value for money from its ever rising criminal legal aid bill. The Henry and Fleming study appears to demonstrate that without a doubt public defender schemes can provide value for money in contrast to private sector lawyers. See also B. Clark "Who's afraid of the Public Defender?" (1997) 147 N.L.J. 1629 and A. Watson, "Public Defender Schemes in the United States: Lesson for Britain" (1997) 161 J.P. 1031.

Section 50 of the Crime and Punishment (Scotland) Act 1997 inserted a new s.28A into the Legal Aid (Scotland) Act 1986 empowering SLAB to employ solicitors for the purpose of providing criminal legal assistance. The provision is framed to allow a limited pilot public defender scheme for a period of five years. The provision enables the Scottish Ministers to designate areas where the scheme will operate (the pilot scheme has been established in Edinburgh) and enables SLAB to require persons seeking criminal legal assistance in that area to instruct the public defender (in practice those with birthdays in January and February are being directed to the public defender). This is partly designed to ensure that data is available for comparison with the performance of private sector lawyers. The government has given an assurance that the scheme will be evaluated by independent researchers commissioned by the Central Research Unit after three years. The Public Defence Solicitors' Office (PDSO) came into being in October 1998 with six full-time salaried lawyers including its director, Alistair Watson. Where there is a potential conflict of interest such as where two co-accused are to be represented by the PDSO, the director may waive referral to the service. Referrals may also be waived on applications from clients' solicitors on the basis that the issue before the court is a new matter related to an existing case (see Reg McKie, "The Interview: Alistair Watson" (1998) 43 J.L.S. 34).

V. SENTENCING POWERS

A. THE RANGE OF SENTENCING OPTIONS

Apart from the power to imprison or to fine, criminal courts have a wide variety of measures open to them where an accused is found guilty. The range of measures has been increased considerably in recent years with the addition of, for example, confiscation and forfeiture orders. For the government's case for extending the range of possible disposals, see *Firm and Fair* (Cm.2600, 1994, paras. 4.15–4.18) and *Crime and Punishment* (Cm.3302, 1996, ch.9). A court may:

(a) Discharge the offender absolutely (under summary procedure, no conviction is recorded) or, following a deferral of sentence, make no order.
(b) Admonish the offender or make an order to find caution.
(c) Place the offender on probation (with or without a community service requirement) under the supervision of a social worker for one to three years (under summary procedure, no conviction is recorded).
(d) Impose a community service order requiring the offender to undertake unpaid work.
(e) Defer sentence subject to conditions (see L.Nicholson, "Deferment of Sentence in Scotland" 1993 S.L.T.(News) 1).
(f) Sentence a young offender as follows:

(i) to a detention centre for between four weeks and four months (not available as a sentence in district courts);
(ii) to a young offenders' institution for a period not exceeding that of imprisonment which the court could have imposed on an adult.

(g) Sentence a child to a period of detention in a place and on such conditions that the Scottish Ministers may direct.
(h) Make a hospital or guardianship order if the accused is suffering from mental disorder (no conviction is recorded in summary procedure) or order the accused to be detained in hospital if he is found to be insane and unfit for trial or insane at the time of the offence.
(i) Impose a compensation order requiring the offender to compensate the victim of his crime for any resulting injury, loss or damage. The scope of the compensation is not limited to cases where a civil court could award damages, thus convictions obtained under consumer protection legislation, *e.g.* the Trades Description Act 1968 can now be of more tangible benefit to consumers. See P. Duff, "Compensation Orders in the Sheriff Court," 1982 S.L.T. (News) 171. On the use of Compensation Orders in practice see G. Maher and C. Docherty, *Compensation Orders in the Scottish Courts* (CRU: 1989).
(j) Impose a drug treatment and testing order instead of sentencing an offender where the offender is over 16 and is dependent on or has a propensity to abuse drugs which requires and is susceptible to treatment and is a suitable person and is willing to be made subject to an order—the order will last for not less than 6 months nor more than 3 years.
(k) Impose a restriction of liberty order on a person over 16 for up to 12 months restricting the person's movements to such an extent as it thinks fit, requiring the offender either to be in specified places at certain times or not to be in specified places or classes of places at specified times.
(l) Impose a suspended forfeiture order in relation to any property used in committing crime, the sale of which could be used to pay a compensation order to the victim—not available in the district court.
(m) Impose a supervised attendance order instead of a term of imprisonment in fine default cases, with the consent of the offender, requiring him or her to undertake between ten and 60 hours supervised attendance either of the community service type of activity or attendance at courses on topics such as on money management, first aid, alcohol or drugs (see P. Morran, "Supervised Attendance Orders" (1992) 192 SCOLAG 137).
(n) Where the accused has been convicted on indictment or summarily but the available penalty exceeds the normal statutory maximum impose a confiscation order requiring the offender to pay a penalty equal to the benefit derived from the crime.

On sentencing powers, see generally the Criminal Procedure (Scotland) Act 1995, Part XI (as amended by the Crime and Punishment (Scotland) Act 1997) and the Proceeds of Crime (Scotland) Act 1995.

TABLE 5.8

Court Disposals in 1996

Main penalty	Total	Males	Females	Companies	Sex unknown
Total	153,087	130,961	21,308	812	6
Prison	12,134	11,369	765	–	–
Young offenders institution	4,744	4,639	105	–	–
Detention of child	45	40	5	–	–
Insane or hospital order	159	142	17	–	–
Community service order	5,711	5,252	459	–	–
Probation	6,435	5,398	1,037	–	–
Fine	105,384	90,222	14,423	734	5
Compensation order	1,415	1,183	230	2	–
Admonition or caution	15,859	11,705	4,078	75	1
Remit to children's hearing	193	169	24	–	–
Absolute discharge	1,008	842	165	1	–

[Source: Scottish Office Statistical Bulletin Criminal Justice Series, *Criminal Proceedings in the Scottish Courts 1996*, March 1998.]

As Table 5.8 shows much the most common outcome in cases which are taken to trial is a fine. This is particularly true in the district court where 90% of penalties imposed are fines—the comparative figure for the sheriff court being 71%.

It is worth stressing, however, that in Scotland in contrast to the position in England and Wales, courts (except in private prosecutions) cannot make an award of expenses either against an accused who has been convicted or in favour of an accused who has been acquitted. The Thomson Committee (Chapter 61) recommended that this should continue to be the case.

B. A TOUGHER APPROACH TO SENTENCING

Aside from the increase in levels of penalties available in the sheriff court, there is now an increased range of offences that attract an automatic life sentence. For a lengthy period, the only automatic statutory life sentence was for murder (Criminal Procedure (Scotland) Act 1995, s.205). However, following consultation (see *Crime and Punishment*, Cm.3302, 1996, ch.8) the Crime and Punishment (Scotland) Act 1997 inserted a new s.205A and Schedule 5A into the Criminal Procedure (Scotland) Act 1995 requiring the High Court to impose automatic life sentences on persons over 21 who have previously committed a qualifying offence specified in Schedule 5A (including culpable homicide, attempted murder, rape, robbery with a firearm) and have again been convicted of a qualifying offence. However, if it is not in the interests of justice to impose such a sentence, (s.205A(3)) the High Court may decline to pass it, and pass any other sentence which it has the power to pass. This appears to render the life sentence discretionary rather than "automatic" and may indicate that the measure is designed to be more of a public relations exercise than a genuine move towards automatic life sentencing. However, the Lord Advocate has also been given a right to appeal against a decision not to impose an automatic life sentence (Criminal Procedure (Scotland) Act 1995, s.108A as inserted by the Crime and Punishment (Scotland) Act 1997).

Concerns about the imposition of unduly lenient sentences led the then government to give the Lord Advocate the power to appeal against such sentences in the Prisoners and Criminal Proceedings (Scotland) Act 1993 (see *Crime and Punishment*, Cm.3302, 1996, paras. 8.20–8.23). These powers may now be found in ss.108 (solemn proceedings) and 175 (summary proceedings) of the Criminal Procedure (Scotland) Act 1995.

C. CONSISTENCY

Following consultation in *Sentencing and Appeals* (1993, ch.4) the then government announced in its White Paper, *Firm and Fair* (Cm.2600, June 1994) that it proposed the introduction of a specific statutory power which would allow the appeal court to issue judgments establishing general guidelines for similar cases (see paras. 4.6–4.7). The intention of these reforms was to improve consistency in sentencing as well as contributing to a more logical and transparent approach to sentencing. Accordingly ss.118(7) and 189(7) of the Criminal Procedure (Scotland) Act 1995 permit the appeal court in disposing of any appeal in solemn and summary appeals respectively to pronounce an opinion on what sentence or other disposal order would be appropriate in similar cases. Section 197 of the 1995 Act requires a court passing a sentence to have regard to any relevant opinions pronounced under ss.118(7) or 189(7).

Another method of trying to improve consistency of sentencing is by ensuring that judges have access to detailed information on sentences passed in similar cases. Although the Scottish Executive (formerly the Scottish Office) now publishes statistical information on sentencing and passes this information to all summary courts, there is a lack of more detailed information about sentencing (see *Crime and Punishment* (Cm.3302, 1996, paras. 8.9–8.11). The High Court has set up a Sentencing Information System (SIS) for cases tried in that court and is funding a feasibility study of the system. In its White Paper *Firm and Fair* (Cm.2600, June 1994) the then government indicated that if the SIS proved workable and successful it saw "considerable attractions in assessing the feasibility of a similar system for the sheriff and district courts" (para.4.8).

The idea of a sentencing commission which would review the objectives of sentence and the basic principles to be followed in sentencing was also canvassed in *Sentencing and Appeals* (1993, para.4.36). However, in *Firm and Fair* (Cm.2600, June 1994) the government rejected the idea of establishing a sentencing commission although indicated that it would keep the case for such a commission under review (para. 4.9). Nonetheless the then government did note that the new group, Judicial Studies in Scotland, which would co-ordinate the provision of training for judges in Scotland, would wish to consider future training needs in relation to sentencing (para.4.9—see also Chapter 8).

Consistency and transparency in the approach to sentencing may be an important factor in reducing the number of appeals against sentence as many appeals may proceed because of uncertainty about what is the normal or fair sentence for a particular crime (*Sentencing and Appeals*, para.5.7).

VI. APPEALS

A. INTRODUCTION

A person convicted under summary or solemn procedure may appeal with leave against the conviction or the sentence or both. The prosecutor can only appeal against an acquittal or the sentence imposed in summary cases, and even then only on a point of law. All appeals in criminal cases go to the High Court of Justiciary sitting as an appeal court.

B. DEALING WITH THE GROWING NUMBER OF APPEALS

There has been considerable concern at the growing numbers of appeals and their impact on the workload of the High Court. Between 1981 and 1992 there was nearly a threefold increase in the number of appeals with 3,510 appeals being lodged in 1992. As a result the then government consulted on a number of changes to reduce the burden on the High Court in *Sentencing and Appeals* (1993, ch.5). These included (1) devolution of appeals from the district court to the sheriff principal; (2) introduction of a requirement to obtain leave to appeal from a single judge; and (3) reducing the quorum of the High Court to hear certain appeals. In the White Paper, *Firm and Fair* (Cm.2600, 1994) the then government rejected the devolution of appeals to the sheriff principal on the basis that only about 7% of the High Court's appeal work would be diverted away while there would be significant workload and organisation implications for the sheriff court. However, *Firm and Fair* indicated the government's intention to proceed with the other two reforms.

C. QUORUM OF THE HIGH COURT SITTING AS AN APPEAL COURT

Appeals were traditionally heard by a quorum of at least three Lords Commissioners of Justiciary. See also, *e.g. H.M. Advocate v. Kirkwood*, 1939 S.L.T. 209 and *Docherty v. H.M. Advocate*, 1987 S.L.T. 784 where 11 and 9 judges sat respectively. However, because of the concerns expressed above about the volume of appeals, the Government indicated in the 1994 White Paper, *Firm and Fair*, that it proposed reducing the quorum in appeals against sentence in both solemn and summary proceedings to two judges (para.5.11). Appeals against conviction would continue to be heard by a quorum of three judges. These proposals were implemented by the Criminal Justice (Scotland) Act 1995 and may now be found in ss. 103 and 173 of the Criminal Procedure (Scotland) Act 1995. This should result in better use of judicial time.

D. REQUIREMENT TO OBTAIN LEAVE TO APPEAL

A radical measure to address the growing burden on the High Court has been the ending of the automatic right of appeal. Support for the introduction of a requirement to obtain leave to appeal was canvassed in the consultation paper *Sentencing and Appeals* 1993. The 1994 White Paper, *Firm and Fair*, indicated that the then government was going to introduce legislation to implement its proposal (para.5.7). Applications for leave would be heard by a single judge. Where leave was refused, the application for leave could be renewed to the full court (para.5.8). Thus, there is now no automatic right of appeal and, in both solemn and summary appeals, leave must be obtained from a single judge (Criminal Procedure (Scotland) Act 1995, ss. 107 and 180). Where leave is refused, the application may be renewed to the full court within 14 days (ss.107(4) and 180(4)).

Unfortunately, two decisions of the European Court of Human Rights may have contributed to the withdrawal of the automatic right of appeal. In *Boner v United Kingdom* (1994) 19 E.H.R.R. 246 and *Maxwell v United Kingdom* (1994) 19 E.H.R.R. 97, both of which involved Scottish criminal appeals in which legal aid was denied and the appellants had to present their appeals personally, the European Court held that in circumstances where the appellant was facing a heavy sentence and was left without legal assistance before the appeal court, there was a breach of article 6 of the E.C.H.R. in relation to the right to a fair trial and to legal assistance see also pp. 130–131 above). Although *Firm and Fair* (Cm.2600, June 1994) noted that up to 40% of appeals are abandoned (para.5.3), with legal aid required by virtue of the decisions in *Boner* and *Maxwell* they might not be, which would put still more pressure on the High Court. In this context the then government made it clear to the European Court of Human Rights during the *Boner* and *Maxwell* proceedings that if a finding was made against the United Kingdom, the government might then consider ending the automatic right of appeal which is exactly what has occurred. Although the Seventh Protocol to the E.C.H.R. does require an automatic right of appeal, the United Kingdom is not a party to that Protocol and hence in so far as the UK is a party to the E.C.H.R., no automatic right of appeal is required. Yet, interestingly, it has been suggested that the introduction of the requirement to seek leave would not in fact be a cost effective response to the decisions in *Boner* and *Maxwell*:

W. Finnie, "The European Court of Human Rights and Criminal Legal Aid in Scotland" 1995 S.L.T. (News) 271 at p. 274

> "A moment's thought will show that it would not be cost effective, however, since a requirement of leave to appeal merely adds another stage to appeals which would at present go to a hearing, without removing a hearing from those which, prior to *Boner* and *Maxwell*, would have been denied legal aid; and the logic of *Boner* and *Maxwell* is that potential appellants seeking leave would require legal aid in the leave hearings."

The government proposed that legal aid would not be available to those refused leave by the single judge or by the full court if the application is renewed (*Firm and Fair*, para.5.9).

E. SUMMARY APPEALS

1. Appeal by Stated Case

Criminal Procedure (Scotland) Act 1995, s. 175

(1) . . .

(2) Any person convicted, or found to have committed an offence, in summary proceedings may, with leave granted in accordance with section 180 or, as the case may be, 187 of this Act, appeal under this section to the High Court—

(a) against such conviction, or finding;
(b) against the sentence passed on such conviction;
(c) against his absolute discharge or admonition or any probation order or any community service order or any order deferring sentence; or
(d) against both such conviction and such sentence or disposal or order.

(3) The prosecutor in summary proceedings may appeal under this section to the High Court on a point of law—

(a) against an acquittal in such proceedings; or
(b) against a sentence passed on conviction in such proceedings.

(4) The prosecutor in such proceedings, in any class of case specified by order by the Secretary of State under this subsection, may appeal to the High Court against the sentence passed on such conviction or, whether the person has been convicted or not, against any probation order or any community service order or against the person's absolute discharge or admonition or against any order deferring sentence if it appears to the prosecutor that, as the case may be—

(a) the sentence is unduly lenient;
(b) the making of the probation order or community service order is unduly lenient or its terms are unduly lenient;
(c) to dismiss with an admonition or to discharge absolutely is unduly lenient; or
(d) the deferment of sentence is inappropriate or on unduly lenient conditions.

(5) By an appeal under subsection (2) above or, as the case may be, against acquittal under subsection (3) above, an appellant may bring under review of the High Court any alleged miscarriage of justice in the proceedings, including, in the case of an appeal under the said subsection (2), any alleged miscarriage of justice on the basis of the existence and significance of additional evidence which was not heard at the trial and which was not available and could not reasonably have been made available at the trial."

In a stated case the judge in the inferior court prepares a statement of the facts found proved by him and formulates the questions of law (if any) which the accused or the prosecutor wishes to have answered. There is now provision for objections by the accused and his advisers to the form of the statement to be noted. For the first time, and contrary to the proposals of the Thomson Committee, the High Court has been given the power to authorise a new prosecution as an alternative to upholding or dismissing an appeal (Criminal Procedure (Scotland) Act 1995, ss.183(1)(d) and 185). The court may in certain circumstances increase the sentence imposed on the accused—but only if the accused has appealed against the sentence.

2. Appeal by Bill of Suspension or Advocation

If an appeal by stated case would be inappropriate or incompetent the accused may appeal by bill of suspension against conviction or sentence and the prosecutor can appeal against acquittal by bill of advocation, on the ground of an alleged miscarriage of justice in the proceedings (Criminal Procedure (Scotland) Act 1995, s. 191). Despite the efforts of the Thomson Committee and the passing of the Criminal Justice (Scotland) Act 1980 and the Criminal Procedure (Scotland) Act 1995 it is still not exactly clear when a bill of suspension should be used as opposed to a stated case. The best view seems to be that a bill of suspension is for reviewing procedural irregularities. Advocation is also used for review of irregularities usually in the preliminary stages of a case. Hitherto advocations have been rare and there is no reason to think that they are likely to increase in criminal proceedings. For an example of an appeal by bill of advocation, see *Wilson v Transorganics Ltd* [1996] E.L.M. 93.

3. Note of Appeal Procedure

Appeal against sentence by a convicted person is now normally dealt with by an accelerated "note of appeal" procedure (Criminal Procedure (Scotland) Act 1995, s. 186). The court may increase the length of the sentence (Criminal Procedure (Scotland) Act 1995, s.189). Sentences in summary cases are rarely increased but see *Briggs v Guild* 1987 S.C.C.R. 141.

4. Expenses

In appeals from summary cases the High Court can award such expenses both in the High Court and in the inferior court as it may think fit. This seems to be intended as a sanction against frivolous appeals, although successful applicants can also benefit from the provision. See *Hamilton v Friel*, 1992 S.L.T. 819.

F. SOLEMN APPEALS

As in summary cases there is now only one ground of appeal—miscarriage of justice. *The Sutherland Committee Report on Appeals Criteria and Alleged*

Miscarriages of Justice (Cm.3265, 1996) recently confirmed that this should remain the sole ground of appeal and should not be limited or qualified and this was accepted by the government (see *Crime and Punishment*, Cm.3302, para.15.7). However, as a result of the Sutherland Committee's recommendations the ground of appeal has been clarified (see *Crime and Punishment*, ch.15):

Criminal Procedure (Scotland) Act 1995, s.106 (as amended by the Crime and Punishment (Scotland) Act 1997)

> "106.–(1) Any person convicted on indictment may, with leave granted in accordance with section 107 of this Act, appeal in accordance with this Part of the Act, to the High Court— . . .
>
> (3) By an appeal under subsection (1) above a person may bring under review of the High Court any alleged miscarriage of justice, which may include such a miscarriage based on—
>
> (a) subject to subsections (3A) to (3D) below, the existence and significant of evidence which was not heard at the original proceedings; and
>
> (b) the jury's having returned a verdict which no reasonable jury, properly directed, could have returned.

For a discussion of these amendments, see Scott, "New Criminal Appeal Provisions" 1997 S.L.T.(News) 249.

The accused (but not the prosecutor) can appeal against conviction on indictment, or sentence or both. He cannot appeal against any sentence fixed by law, *e.g.* life imprisonment for a conviction of murder (Criminal Procedure (Scotland) Act 1995, s. 106(2)). The Lord Advocate may now appeal against sentences which he considers unduly lenient (Criminal Procedure (Scotland) Act 1995, s.108 and see *H.M.Advocate v McPhee* 1994 S.L.T. 1292) and against a decision not to impose an automatic life sentence (Criminal Procedure (Scotland) Act 1995, s.108A as inserted by the Crime and Punishment (Scotland) Act 1997) and see above p. 145). As discussed above, leave to appeal from the trial judge is now required (Criminal Procedure (Scotland) Act 1995, s.107), and fresh evidence can, as in summary appeals, be heard. Again, as in summary appeals, the High Court can authorise a new prosecution for the same or any similar offence arising out of the same facts (Criminal Procedure (Scotland) Act 1995, ss. 118(1)(c) and 119). See *Mackenzie v. H.M. Advocate*, 1983 S.L.T. 220 and *Cunningham v. H.M. Advocate*, 1984 S.C.C.R. 40. It is up to the Crown to decide whether or not a fresh prosecution (a re-trial) will take place. For a trenchant critique of the prosecutor's right to seek a re-trial see "Criminal Appeals, Retrials and Acquittals", 1984 S.L.T. (News) 341. The Appeal Court has used its re-trial powers sparingly—on only five occasions up to 1992 and only in one of them was a conviction attained.

Where the appeal is against sentence an accelerated, "note of appeal" procedure is used. The court may only increase the sentence if there has been an appeal against sentence. Expenses cannot be awarded in solemn appeals.

As a result of the Criminal Justice (Scotland) Act 1980, s. 35, advocation was extended to appeals from all solemn cases (see now Criminal Procedure

(Scotland) Act 1995, s. 131). Such appeals by the prosecutor in respect of alleged irregularities in the proceedings are unlikely to be very frequent. For an example, see *H.M.A. v Sinclair* 1987 S.L.T. 161.

G. LORD ADVOCATE'S REFERENCE

Where a person tried on indictment is acquitted or convicted of a charge the Lord Advocate may refer a point of law which has arisen in relation to that charge to the High Court for their opinion (Criminal Procedure (Scotland) Act 1995, s. 123). This is like an appeal on a point of law but has no effect on the acquittal in the trial. Prior to the enactment of the 1995 Act the Lord Advocate could only exercise this power where the accused had been acquitted but in the White Paper, *Firm and Fair*, (Cm.2600, 1994) the Government noted that it was anomalous that the power was only available where a person was acquitted as the Crown might still wish to seek clarification of the law even where the accused was convicted (paras.6.10–6.11). It was not thought that such references would occur frequently, and so it has transpired. Up to the end of 1998 there had only been six Lord Advocate's references. See *Lord Advocate's Reference No.1 of 1983* 1984 S.C.C.R. 62, *Lord Advocate's Reference No.1 of 1985* 1986 J.C. 137; *Lord Advocate's Reference No.1 of 1992* 1992 S.L.T. 1010; *Lord Advocate's Reference No.2 of 1992* 1992 S.C.C.R. 960; *Lord Advocate's Reference No.1 of 1994* 1995 S.L.T. 248; and *Lord Advocate's Reference No.1 of 1996* 1996 S.L.T. 740.

H. CRIMINAL CASES REVIEW COMMISSION

In the wake of several miscarriages of justice in England and Wales a Royal Commission on Criminal Justice was set up in 1991. One of its main recommendations was that an independent review authority should be established in England and Wales to take over the Home Secretary's role of deciding whether cases should be referred back to the Court of Appeal once the normal appeal process was exhausted. Although the Royal Commission's remit did not extend to Scotland, the Secretary of State for Scotland undertook to consider the implications of the report in a Scottish context.

Formerly, in Scotland the position was that if there was an allegation that a miscarriage of justice had occurred and the appeal process was exhausted the Secretary of State for Scotland had the power to refer the case back to the High Court to be heard as though it were an appeal (Criminal Procedure (Scotland) Act 1995, s.124).

In November 1994 the Government established the Committee on Appeals Criteria and Alleged Miscarriages of Justice under the chairmanship of Sir Stewart Sutherland. The Committee's report (Cm.3245) was published in June 1996. The Committee was of the view that the Secretary of State's role was incompatible with the constitutional doctrine of separation of powers between the executive and the courts and recommended the establishment of an independent body to consider and refer miscarriages of justice. However, the then government rejected its recommendations (see *Crime and Punishment*, 1996, para.15.6). Yet during the passage of the Crime and Punishment (Scotland) Bill through Parliament, the legislative timetable forced a government concession and a new provision setting up such a body to consider miscarriages of justice was added to the Bill, becoming s.25 of the Crime and Punishment (Scotland) Act 1997.

Section 25 of the 1997 Act inserted a new Part XA into the Criminal Procedure (Scotland) Act 1995 establishing a Scottish Criminal Cases Review Commission to take over the Secretary of State's functions in this regard. The Commission is independent of the Crown. The Queen on the recommendation of the Scottish Ministers appoints its members. At least one third of the members must be either solicitors or advocates of at least 10 years standing and at least two thirds must be persons who have experience of any aspect of the criminal justice system including the investigation of offences and the treatment of offenders. The first chairperson of the Commission is Professor Sheila McLean. The Commission may refer cases to the High Court if they believe that a miscarriage of justice has occurred and that it is in the interests of justice that a reference should be made. The Commission has been given extensive powers to assist it in carrying out its functions, for example to request precognitions on oath and to obtain documents. The Scottish Ministers are empowered to extend the Commission's remit to considering convictions and sentences in summary proceedings in addition to solemn proceedings. For a discussion of the workings of the Commission and the philosophy that will inform its working, see S. McLean, "Reshaping the criminal justice system" (1999) 44 J.L.S. 23.

CHAPTER 6

TRIBUNALS

Tribunals are an important element in the legal system of Scotland. Many, but not all, tribunals are kept under review by a statutory body, the Council on Tribunals. In 1997, the last year for which reasonably complete figures are available, the tribunals under the specific supervision of the Council's Scottish Committee disposed of over 41,000 cases. In the same year, the tribunals under the general supervision of the Council disposed of approximately 800,000 cases, a significant proportion of which would be cases in Scotland.

I. THE DEVELOPMENT AND RATIONALE OF TRIBUNALS

There is a wide range of tribunals in Scotland with different functions, composition and procedure. This diversity is a product of the history of their development.

Wraith and Hutcheson, *Administrative Tribunals*, pp. 29–33

> "Scottish legal history points to a much closer relationship between the administration of justice and the conduct of government than a superficial understanding of the separation of powers doctrine would admit. As in England, there was a period before the modern differentiation of legislative, executive and judicial institutions and functions had developed. Distinct judicial institutions appeared later in Scotland than in England, and the separation of functions occurred later still; indeed the differentiation of functions was probably never complete so long as Scotland was an independent kingdom. Three or four centuries ago, both at national and local levels, the same governmental organs exercised administrative, legislative and judicial functions. The growth of separate arrangements for judicial work during the sixteenth century was as much for reasons of practical convenience as for reasons of principle. The College of Justice was formally constituted in 1532 to give a firm and continuing basis to the Court of Session and the High Court of Justiciary with criminal jurisdiction was established in 1672. Yet the King's Council continued to exercise both civil and criminal jurisdiction and today it is difficult to see why certain cases came to the Council rather than to the Court of Session or the High Court of Justiciary.
>
> Since its inception, the Court of Session had been able to exercise some control over the jurisdiction of subordinate and inferior courts, a task which during the sixteenth and seventeenth centuries was itself subject to intervention from the Council. After the Union of 1707, the abolition of the separate

Privy Council for Scotland had repercussions for the role of the central civil court similar to those arising from the disappearance of conciliar jurisdiction in England: it was thereafter the duty of the Court of Session to provide redress for citizens' grievances which formerly had gone properly to the Privy Council. By comparison with the common law courts in England, the supervisory control of the Court of Session was marked by a greater flexibility that must in part have been due to the fact that no separate court of equity developed in Scotland. Through the exercise of the 'nobile officium', the Court of Session had an ultimate right to provide an extraordinary equitable remedy in a situation in which the strict law provided none. The eighteenth-century Scottish law reports provide numerous examples of an extensive supervisory jurisdiction being exercised by the Court of Session over inferior courts and tribunals, and this jurisdiction was not ignored in legal scholarship.

For certain purposes, the Court of Session itself could take on a different form to exercise a specialized jurisdiction. By what the late Lord President Cooper called 'a remarkable anticipation of the modern ad hoc tribunal' the multifarious ecclesiastical business arising after the reformation and associated with parish churches, manses, stipends and teinds (or tithes) was vested first in statutory commissions and then transferred to the Court of Session itself, sitting as the 'Commission for the Plantation of Kirks and the Valuation of Teinds'. In this capacity between 1707 and 1925, the Court of Session performed a wide variety of administrative and judicial functions for the church, during a period when the church itself had major public responsibilities in the government of Scotland, for example in the poor law and in education. (Since 1925, what remains of this jurisdiction is undertaken by a judge sitting as Lord Ordinary on Teinds.) In a similar way today, Senators of the College of Justice may sit to exercise a specialized statutory jurisdiction as the Lands Valuation Appeal Court, hearing appeals against rating assessments made by local Valuation Appeal Committees, and, less frequently, as the Registration of Voters Appeal Court and the Election Petition Court. In 1708, a Court of Exchequer for Scotland was reconstituted and equipped with procedures similar to those in the English Court of Exchequer but in 1856 its jurisdiction was transferred to the Court of Session, which still deals with revenue cases by procedures derived from English revenue practice . . . Many other inferior courts and tribunals, often exercising administrative functions, have existed in Scotland . . .

During the nineteenth century many specialized organs of central and local government were established, often with power to settle disputes arising out of the exercise of their administrative functions. [They were] superseded by government departments and local authorities."

From the early part of the twentieth century the development of the Welfare State in particular led to the establishment of many tribunals. The use of tribunals was considered by the Donoughmore Committee on Ministers' Powers which reported in 1932 (Cmd. 4060) and was fully examined by the Franks Committee on Administrative Tribunals and Enquiries which reported in 1957.

Franks Committee, paras 35–37

"At the time of the Donoughmore Committee (1929–32) there were few kinds of tribunal (although some of them, for example the Courts of Referees under the Unemployment Insurance Acts, dealt with important issues affecting large numbers of the population), and the Committee was able to regard tribunals as somewhat exceptional, to be resorted to only in special circumstances and requiring strict safeguards. The position today is different. The continuing extension of governmental activity and responsibility for the general well-being of the community has greatly multiplied the occasions on which an individual may be at issue with the administration, or with another citizen or body, as to his rights, and the post-war years have seen a substantial growth in the importance and activities of tribunals. In some cases new policies or regulating legislation have meant new tribunals . . . in other cases an earlier system has been adapted to wider purposes . . . in other cases tribunals now perform functions previously carried out by the courts . . .

Tribunals today vary widely in constitution, function and procedure . . . Most tribunals deal with cases in which an individual citizen is at issue with a Government Department or other public body concerning his rights or obligations under a statutory scheme. But a few . . . are concerned with disputes between citizens. Still others . . . have regulatory functions and are therefore just as much administrative bodies as they are adjudicating tribunals. Some tribunals, like the courts, have a detailed code of procedure, with testimony on oath and strict rules of evidence. Most have a simple procedure, usually without the oath and sometimes with a ban on legal representation. Finally, there are differences regarding appeals. Sometimes there is no appeal, and further redress can only be had by seeking a court order to set aside the decision. But in most cases there is an appeal—either to an appellate tribunal, a Minister or the courts.

Reflection on the general social and economic changes of recent decades convinces us that tribunals as a system for adjudication have come to stay. The tendency for issues arising from legislative schemes to be referred to special tribunals is likely to grow rather than to diminish . . .".

Tribunals are concerned with an immense spectrum of administrative activity, ranging from some of the functions of the Director General of Fair Trading to the Crofters Commission, from industrial tribunals to children's hearings, from the Immigration Appeal Tribunal to the Value Added Tax Tribunal for Scotland. The membership of tribunals, although commonly a chairman and two members, varies greatly. A civil servant may be classified as a tribunal for certain statutory purposes: National Insurance Commissioner's decision no. R(G)1/80; on the other hand, the Employment Appeal Tribunal, despite its name, is a superior court of record, which normally sits with a judge of the Court of Session and two or four lay members: Employment Tribunals Act 1996, ss. 20 and 28. The jurisdiction of tribunals varies. Some, such as the Immigration Appeal Tribunal, have a U.K. jurisdiction; some have a Scottish jurisdiction, although paralleled by other tribunals elsewhere in the United Kingdom; some are peculiar to Scotland, for example the Crofters Commission and children's hearings. Although there is a degree of central monitoring, tribunal procedure also varies. Some are more formal than others; some, such as Unified Appeal Tribunals under the Social Security Act 1998, are inquisitorial and some, such as Immigration Adjudicators and Employment Tribunals, are essentially adversarial in their procedure.

Their range and diversity have made tribunals difficult to classify and evaluate. Traditionally, they have been evaluated in institutional terms and in comparison with courts.

Franks Committee, paras 38–45

> "We agree with the Donoughmore Committee that tribunals have certain characteristics which often give them advantages over the courts. These are cheapness, accessibility, freedom from technicality, expedition and expert knowledge of their particular subject. It is no doubt because of these advantages that Parliament, once it has decided that certain decisions ought not to be made by normal executive or departmental processes, often entrusts them to tribunals rather than to the ordinary courts . . .
>
> Moreover, if all decisions arising from new legislation were automatically vested in the ordinary courts the judiciary would by now have been grossly overburdened . . .
>
> Tribunals are not ordinary courts, but neither are they appendages of Government Departments. Much of the official evidence, including that of the Joint Permanent Secretary to the Treasury, appeared to reflect the view that tribunals should properly be regarded as part of the machinery of administration, for which the Government must retain a close and continuing responsibility. Thus, for example, tribunals in the social service field would be regarded as adjuncts to the administration of the services themselves. We do not accept this view. We consider that tribunals should properly be regarded as machinery provided by Parliament for adjudication rather than as part of the machinery of administration. The essential point is that in all these cases Parliament has deliberately provided for a decision outside and independent of the Department concerned, either at first instance . . . or on appeal from a decision of a Minister or of an official in a special statutory position . . . . Although the relevant statutes do not in all cases expressly enact that tribunals are to consist entirely of persons outside the Government service, the use of the term 'tribunal' in legislation undoubtedly bears this connotation, and the intention of Parliament to provide for the independence of tribunals is clear and unmistakable.
>
> We have already expressed our belief that Parliament in deciding that certain decisions should be reached only after a special procedure must have intended that they should manifest three basic characteristics: openness, fairness and impartiality. The choice of a tribunal rather than a Minister as the deciding authority is itself a considerable step towards the realisation of these objectives, particularly the third . . .
>
> In the field of tribunals openness appears to us to require the publicity of proceedings and knowledge of the essential reasoning underlying the decisions; fairness to require the adoption of a clear procedure which

enables parties to know their rights, to present their case fully and to know the case which they have to meet; and impartiality to require the freedom of tribunals from the influence, real or apparent, of Departments concerned with the subject matter of their decisions . . .

. . . This is particularly so when a Government Department is a frequent party to proceedings before a tribunal".

Describing tribunals by reference to the ideals adopted by the Franks Committee has increasingly been considered, both in factual and policy terms, as inadequate. So, for instance, it is difficult to attribute to tribunals both the advantage of being better able than courts to adjudicate in areas of law with a high policy content, which in any event implies an assessment of the judiciary which is perhaps less true than it once was, and the advantage of having a high degree of independence from Government departments which effectively determine the policy.

Again, the cheapness of tribunals may be a limited economic evaluation. There is contemporary criticism of the inadequate level of Departmental resources devoted to initial assessment of social security benefit claimants. If the resources devoted to assessment are low this contributes to the volume of appeals to Unified (formerly Social Security) Appeal Tribunals and, therefore, no doubt, to the trend of their increasing delays in adjudicating appeals.

It may be true that as compared with courts many tribunals avoid procedural technicality, but the law with which they are concerned is frequently both technical and complex. This is certainly the case with, say, employment law, social security law and immigration law.

One response to this is to assert the value of courts within the legal system, as the Franks Committee did, or even to propose the institutional merger of tribunals and courts. Indeed, the supervision of the tribunal decision-making may be indirectly contributing to such a result.

Hughes Commission, p. 204

"We have had evidence, particularly from the Scottish Legal Action Group, suggesting that because of the expense, delay and formality of court procedures, there has been a 'flight' from the courts into alternative tribunals—statutory tribunals, statutory arbitrations or voluntary arbitrations. We think that there is an element of truth in this, though it can be exaggerated. It is not always the case that these alternatives are either quicker or cheaper (to the litigant or the State) than the civil courts; but cheapness, speed and informality are certainly characteristic of some of them. What we are not disposed to accept is the implication of some of the evidence that the civil courts have incurable defects and must always be looked upon as places of last resort; and accordingly that, wherever practicable, alternative tribunals should be made available. We certainly do not want to discourage arbitration or specialist tribunals for types of cases for which they are, for one reason or another, particularly suitable. We firmly believe, however, that the civil courts are, and should remain, the principal means for resolving civil disputes. We are anxious lest undue resort to remedies outwith the court may lead to the needed reform of court procedures being delayed and neglected. The aim should be to develop in the civil courts themselves those same qualities of cheapness, speed and informality in so far as these are compatible with fair and respected judicial procedures."

Abel-Smith and Stevens, *In Search of Justice*, p. 227–228

"Courts are said to be administering rules of law while tribunals are thought to be administering both law and policy. We would maintain that no such clear line can or should be drawn. Indeed it was the evolution of this myth which helped establish the tribunal system by convincing the judges of the ordinary courts that they were concerned with legal but not with policy questions. But continued insistence on this unsatisfactory distinction makes it increasingly difficult to entrust new matters to the courts or to merge courts and tribunals. Properly understood, tribunals are a more modern form of court. In some cases they may have more discretion than the courts, and this is particularly true of the policy oriented tribunals . . . Conversely the court-substitute tribunals are often as precedent-conscious as, and may even exercise a much narrower discretion than, the ordinary courts.

But we would reaffirm our position that there is no fundamental difference between courts and tribunals. We would argue, therefore, that every effort should be made to merge the two".

However, one of the considerations which make tribunals an appropriate form of adjudication is that they can be an ideal mechanism for decentralised determination of legal issues raised by large numbers of people. They only become an ideal mechanism where the tribunals provide consistent and accurate adjudication. This is an issue which faces many jurisdictions and its general aspects have been influentially explored in J. Mashaw, *Bureaucratic Justice* (Yale University Press, 1983).

In a Scottish and U.K. context there has been an increased awareness that the objective of providing consistent and accurate adjudication is paramount and that this objective may only with difficulty be reconciled with some of the attributes of tribunals identified by the Franks Committee, such as cheapness and lack of procedural technicality.

Sometimes the reconciliation may be attempted by reforming the structure and operation of tribunals, as was done with social security tribunals and again in the 1990s.

Sainsbury, "Social Security Appeals: in Need of Review?", p. 336–338

"Prior to the HASSASSA [Health and Social Services and Social Security Adjudication Act 1983] reforms there was a clear distinction between the administration and adjudication of supplementary benefit on the one hand and of national insurance benefits on the other. Decisions under the national insurance scheme lay with the statutorily independent insurance officer in the first instance, and with the National Insurance Local Tribunal (NILT) on appeal. Thence, there was a further right of appeal to the Social Security Commissioner. In contrast, initial decisions on the main means-tested benefit, supplementary benefit, were made by DHSS officials on behalf of the Supplementary Benefits Commission. Appeals were possible to Supplementary Benefit Appeals Tribunals (SBATs) but there was no right of appeal to the Social Security Commissioner. Under the industrial injuries scheme, 'disablement questions' were (until 1983) decided by a medical board of two doctors, from which an appeal was possible to a Medical Appeal Tribunal. Medical boards also heard appeals on mobility allowance on medical questions. Further appeal was allowed to the MAT, comprising a legally-qualified chairman and two doctors of consultant status.

Although NILTs were generally regarded as working satisfactorily, SBATs were subject to repeated criticisms in the 1970s. The strong current of dissatisfaction with SBATs led the DHSS to commission research by Professor Kathleen Bell of Newcastle University into their operation. Bell's research revealed numerous shortcomings in the SBAT system; tribunal chairmen, most of whom were not legally qualified, were found to have a limited knowledge and understanding of supplementary benefits; proceedings were unsystematic; there was an over-reliance on the clerk (an official seconded from the DHSS); decisions were not recorded satisfactorily; and discretion was not exercised in a disciplined or systematic way. Bell concluded that a comprehensive review was required as a matter of urgency and proposed a number of reforms to be achieved in three stages. Immediate improvements could be secured by providing training for chairmen and members; other changes would take longer to implement (such as the introduction of legally-qualified chairmen); whilst other changes were structural in nature, such as the provision of a further stage of appeal after the SBAT, and the merging of SBATs with NILTs.

Changes within the existing SBAT structure began to be implemented in 1977. More legally-qualified chairmen were appointed, training was instigated, a procedure manual produced, and a right of appeal from SBATs to the High Court in England and the Court of Session in Scotland was provided. Later, in the Social Security Act 1979, full-time senior chairmen were introduced, to have some responsibility for organising tribunals in addition to hearing cases.

Bell's structural reforms took longer to achieve. In 1980 the supplementary benefits scheme, which until then had been based largely on administrative discretion, was replaced by a scheme conferring legal entitlement to benefits. The case for merging SBATs and NILTs therefore became stronger, and the desirability of change was accepted by the government.

The culmination of the reforms which had begun in the late 1970s was HASSASSA, which in 1983 introduced a unified three-tier adjudication system comprised of adjudication officers (replacing insurance officers and supplementary benefit officers), a unified Social Security Appeal Tribunal (replacing SBATs and NILTs), and the Social Security Commissioner (whose jurisdiction now extended to supplementary benefit). Furthermore, the posts of Chief Insurance Officer and Chief Supplementary Benefits Officer (DHSS officials who had previously issued guidance to insurance officers and supplementary benefit officers respectively) were replaced by

> the statutorily independent Chief Adjudication Officer (whose primary tasks were to advise adjudication officers and to monitor the standards of their decision-making). Finally, the SSAT system was brought within a presidential organisation similar to that of other tribunals. The President is a barrister, advocate or solicitor of not less than ten years' standing appointed by the Lord Chancellor. As well as being responsible for the management of SSATs and MATs, the President also has a responsibility for training tribunal chairmen and members, and for ensuring that they have access to appropriate social security texts. To assist him, the President has seven Regional Chairmen of Tribunals to whom he can delegate appropriate duties. The rationale behind the presidential system is to remove any direct and obvious link between social security tribunals and the Department, and to concentrate experience and expertise relevant to both types of tribunal."

(Disability Appeal Tribunals and Child Support Appeal Tribunals were subsequently added to the presidential system. The system, now known as the United Appeal Tribunals, also serves the vaccine damage tribunals.)

However, policy considerations may persuade the Government to pursue other alternatives. Sometimes it is necessary to recognise the autonomy of local authorities when providing a national social security benefit; housing benefit is a case in point. There it was eventually decided that allowing appeals to be determined by a national tribunal structure would undermine local authority autonomy because the decisions of such tribunals would have the capacity to overturn the decisions of publicly accountable local authorities. The statutory solution adopted was a system of initial internal administrative review by local authority officers, with the possibility of a further hearing before a review board of local authority councillors which would be subject to judicial review by the courts. (See Social Security and Housing Benefits Act 1982 and Social Security Administration Act 1992; Housing Benefit (General) Regulations 1987 (S.I. 1987 No. 1971) (as amended); M. Partington and H. Bolderson, *Housing Benefit Review Procedures: A Preliminary Analysis* (Brunel University, 1984).)

On occasion, the Government has turned away from tribunals in areas where the number of claimants and the need for speedy determination of appeals would seem to make their continued use appropriate. One instance was the replacement of single payments under the supplementary benefit scheme by the social fund in 1988: see now Social Security Administration Act 1992, ss. 12, 64–66, 78, 167 and 168. Despite institutional appearances to the contrary, the revised scheme for exercising and reviewing the discretionary decisions appears, on both official and academic assessment, to be providing speedy and independent determinations: *Annual Report of the Social Fund Commissioner for 1988–89* (HMSO, 1990); R. Drabble and T. Lynes, "Decision-making in Social Security: the Social Fund—Discretion or Control?" [1989] P.L. 317.

Sainsbury, "Social Security Appeals: in Need of Review?", p. 339

> "The social fund replaced single payments under the supplementary benefit scheme in April 1988. The entitlement to payments for items such as furniture, cookers and refrigerators under regulations was replaced with a

discretionary scheme of loans and grants which would be administered not by the statutory authorities, (*i.e.* the adjudication officer in the local office) but by social fund officers acting within the directions and guidance of the Secretary of State. Applicants dissatisfied with the decision of a social fund officer can obtain a review of the decision if they apply in writing giving the grounds for their request. The social fund officer who made the original decision will either grant the appeal in full or invite the claimant for an interview, at which the decision will be discussed. If the social fund officer is not prepared to change the decision, the case is passed on to a senior member of the local office management, who will again review the original decision. Claimants who are still dissatisfied may then request a further review by a social fund inspector. The inspectors have three possible courses of action. They can substitute their own decision, uphold the original decision or refer the decision back to the social fund officer. There is no right of appeal to the Social Security Commissioner. The quality of decision-making by social fund inspectors is monitored by the Social Fund Commissioner who has a statutory responsibility to report annually to the Secretary of State. Reminiscent of the genesis of housing benefit review boards, the provision of a right of appeal to a social fund inspector was added to review by local office management only following the considerable opposition that the original proposals provoked."

A range of appeal tribunals, including the Social Security Appeal Tribunals, have been further rationalised with a composition which, significantly, effectively removes lay members: Social Security Act 1998, s. 4.

In general terms, tribunals occupy a place within the legal system between (a) intra-departmental determination and review, and (b) the courts. To maintain that place tribunals must offer decentralised, cheap and speedy adjudication, which is also consistent and fair, and must be capable of offering it to large numbers of people. This, in turn, depends on such factors as the selection, appointment and training of tribunal members, the procedures which tribunals adopt, the availability of representation and legal aid for those appearing before tribunals, and the nature and extent of judicial and non-judicial supervision and control of tribunals.

II. THE COMPOSITION OF TRIBUNALS

Wraith and Hutcheson, *Administrative Tribunals*, p. 93

"There are four distinguishable patterns [in the composition of tribunals]—first, where the tribunal is an individual sitting alone; second, where all members are entitled to be present, with provision for a quorum; third, where there is a single panel from which are normally selected a chairman and one or two other members; and fourth, where there is a chairman sitting with members of 'representative' panels."

Members of tribunals may be appointed by a variety of authorities. The Social Security Commissioners are appointed by the Crown; members of panels for children's hearings are appointed by the Secretary of State, to whom names of suitable applicants are submitted by a children's panel advisory committee in each Scottish local authority (Children (Scotland) Act 1995, Sched 1, para. 6);

the panel of members of local valuation appeal committees is appointed by the sheriff principal (Local Government etc. (Scotland) Act 1994, s. 29).

A common pattern is for members of a tribunal to be appointed directly by a government Minister but for the chairman to be appointed by the Lord President of the Court of Session either directly or to a panel from which the selection is made by a government Minister or by a president of tribunals. For example, the chairmen of industrial tribunals are selected by the President of Industrial Tribunals (Scotland), or a Regional Chairman, nominee, from a panel of chairmen appointed by the Lord President (The Employment Tribunals (Constitution and Rules of Procedure) (Scotland) Regulations 1993 (regs 5 and 7 (S.I. 1993 No. 2688); for text see below). The chairmen of a limited number of other tribunals in Scotland are selected from a panel appointed by the Lord President: Tribunals and Inquiries Act 1992, s. 6.

Frequently, statutory requirements may seek to ensure that members of a tribunal are conversant with the circumstances of those who are likely to appear before them but there has been some drift away from this in the late 1990s.

Social Security Act 1998, ss. 6 and 7

> **6.**—(1) The Lord Chancellor shall constitute a panel of persons to act as members of appeal tribunals.
> (2) Subject to subsection (3) below, the panel shall be composed of such persons as the Lord Chancellor thinks fit to appoint after consultation, in the case of medical practitioners, with the Chief Medical Officer.
> (3) The panel shall include persons possessing such qualifications as may be prescribed by regulations made with the concurrence of the Lord Chancellor.
> (4) The numbers of persons appointed to the panel, and the terms and conditions of their appointments, shall be determined by the Lord Chancellor with the consent of the Secretary of State.
> (5) A person may be removed from the panel by the Lord Chancellor on the ground of incapacity or misbehaviour.
> (6) In this section "the Chief Medical Officer" means—. . . .
> (c) in relation to Scotland, the Chief Medical Officer of the Scottish Office.
> **7.**—(1) Subject to subsection (2) below, an appeal tribunal shall consist of one, two or three members drawn by the President from the panel constituted under section 6 above.
> (2) The member, or (as the case may be) at least one member, of an appeal tribunal must—
> (a) have a general qualification (construed in accordance with section 71 of the Courts and Legal Services Act 1990); or
> (b) be an advocate or solicitor in Scotland.
> (3) Where an appeal tribunal has more than one member—
> (a) the President shall nominate one of the members as chairman;
> (b) decisions shall be taken by a majority of votes; and
> (c) unless regulations otherwise provide, the chairman shall have any casting vote.

(4) Where it appears to an appeal tribunal that a matter before it involves a question of fact of special difficulty, then, unless regulations otherwise provide, the tribunal may require one or more experts to provide assistance to it in dealing with the question.

(5) In subsection (4) above "expert" means a member of the panel constituted under section 6 above who appears to the appeal tribunal concerned to have knowledge or experience which would be relevant in determining the question of fact of special difficulty. . . ."

[The "President" is the President of appeal tribunals: s. 5. Regulations, effectively excluding lay members, were made under under s. 7(6): see S.I. 1999 No. 991.

It should be noted that, with respect to tribunals in Scotland, following devolution the function of the Lord Chancellor is to be formally transferred to a Minister of the Scottish Executive.]

The Employment Tribunals (Constitution and Rules of Procedure) (Scotland) Regulations 1993, regs 5 and 7

"**5.**—(1) There shall be three panels of members of the Industrial Tribunals (Scotland), namely—

(a) a panel of persons, being advocates or solicitors of not less than seven years' standing, appointed by the Lord President;
(b) a panel of persons appointed by the Secretary of State after consultation with such organisations or associations of organisations representative of employees as he sees fit; and
(c) a panel of persons appointed by the Secretary of State after consultation with such organisations or associations of organisations representative of employers as he sees fit.

(2) Members of the panels constituted under these regulations shall hold and vacate office under the terms of the instrument under which they are appointed but may resign their office by notice in writing, in the case of a member of the panel of chairmen, to the Lord President and, in any other case, to the Secretary of State; and any such member who ceases to hold office shall be eligible for reappointment.

7.—(1) For each hearing of any matter before a tribunal the President or the Regional Chairman shall, subject to paragraph 5, select a chairman, who shall be the President or a member of the panel of chairmen, and the President or the Regional Chairman may select himself.

(2) In any proceedings which are to be determined by a tribunal comprising a chairman (selected in accordance with paragraph (1) above) and two other members, those other members shall be selected by the President or by the Regional Chairman, as to one member from the panel of persons appointed by the Secretary of State under regulation 5(1)(b) and as to the other from the panel of persons appointed under regulation 5(1)(c).

(3) In any proceedings which are to be determined by a tribunal whose composition is described in paragraph (2), those proceedings may, with the consent of the parties, be heard and determined in the absence of any one

member other than the chairman, and in that event the tribunal shall be properly constituted.

(4) The President or the Regional Chairman may at any time select from the appropriate panel another person in substitution for the chairman or other member of the tribunal previously selected to hear any proceedings before a tribunal.

(5) Paragraph (1) does not apply where a Minister of the Crown has issued a direction in accordance with section 128(6) of the 1978 Act (direction on grounds of national security that proceedings be heard and determined by the President)."

["The 1978 Act" meant the Employment Protection (Consolidation) Act 1978 (reg. 2(1)) but see now Employment Tribunals Act 1996, s. 4(7). See also Employment Rights (Dispute Resolution) Act 1998, ss. 3 and 4.]

Children (Scotland) Act 1995, s. 35(5)

"A children's hearing shall consist of three members, one of whom shall act as chairman; and shall not consist solely of male, or solely of female, members."

Statutory requirements may create their own difficulties.

Cavenagh and Newton, "Administration tribunals: how people become members", p. 210

"Ambiguity about what lay members are supposed to contribute seems to have been the cause of practical problems in the Industrial Tribunal, where some lay members, particularly on the workers' side, appear to come on with the idea that they are there to 'represent' their own 'side' of industry; yet this conflicts fundamentally with the view of the previous Lord Chancellor [Lord Gardiner] as expressed in 1968 in a speech circulated to all members:

'One sometimes hears the members erroneously referred to as "the employers' representative" or "the employees' representative". They are not. They represent no one, except the interests of justice. Each is an entirely independent judicial officer, who decides a case upon its merits, upon the evidence and law applicable'.

But despite these words the problem persists and the misconception still seems quite widespread."

There is also the more general problem that, despite statutory requirements and informal arrangements, the membership of tribunals is not representative of society as a whole and may not provide a reasonable range of age and experience. These were, for example, legitimate criticisms of the former SBATs, as Flockhart's research demonstrates, and Wikeley and Young suggest that the rather different structure of the former SSATs attracts similar criticism.

Flockhart, "Some Aspects of Tribunal Membership", p. 99–100

"In the summer of 1971, a study of the membership of Supplementary Benefits Appeal Tribunals was carried out in Scotland . . . [at that time SBAT members were drawn from three panels]:

(1) chairmen; . . .
(2) persons appointed by the Secretary of State from among persons appearing to him to represent work-people. In practice they are selected from lists of names submitted by local Trades Councils. They are referred to here as Trades Council members (TCMs); and
(3) other persons appointed by the Secretary of State, here referred to as Other members (OMs).
In terms of the Registrar General's Classification 78% of the chairmen and Other members, taken together, were from Social Classes I and II. The social class breakdown of [the tribunal members who responded to a questionnaire] is summarised in the table below:

Social Class	Chairmen	OM	TCM	All Members
I	4	4	0	8
II	15	35	14	64
III (Non-manual)	2	4	9	15
III (Manual)	1	0	38	39
IV	0	1	10	11
V	0	0	1	1
Unknown	4	4	2	10
Total	26	48	74	148

There is a case for arguing that a welfare tribunal should be composed of three 'ordinary people' drawn from the local community, sitting together as lay persons to assess the extent of social need. If so, it might be thought that these three lay persons should represent in themselves a reasonably varied and wide social experience. The membership of the tribunals in this study reflects a narrowing grouping of social class and age amongst the chairmen and Other members but is significantly less narrow in terms of social class among the Trades Council members. In addition, of the 148 members only sixteen were women, *i.e.* 11%. When asked to rate the importance of having at least one woman member on a tribunal 60% said it was unimportant."

Wikeley and Young, "The Marginalisation of Lay Members in Social Security Appeal Tribunals", p. 131–133

"Chairmen were generally rather younger than lay members. Nearly half of the chairmen we interviewed were in their fifties; a quarter were under 50 and a further quarter aged 60 or more. By contrast the great majority of members (63%) were over 60 years old. One quarter of the chairmen were female, indicating that there has been some success in appointing a larger number of women to such posts (in 1982 the proportion was only 17% . . .).

Earlier studies were critical of the unrepresentative nature of those appointed to serve as lay members on tribunals . . . . The two lay members on each social security appeal tribunal, who receive expenses but no fee, are now drawn from a single list of people "appearing to the President to have knowledge or experience of conditions in the area and to be representative of persons living or working in the area" (Social Security Act 1975, Sched. 10, para. 1(2)). Formerly both of the old tribunals had employed a two panel system. In national insurance local tribunals there were separate lists for employees and employers, with the members nominated by Trades Councils and business interests respectively to reflect the role of both sides of industry in contributing to the national insurance fund. Supplementary benefit appeal tribunals were constituted rather differently. One member, called the Secretary of State's member, was meant to have knowledge or experience of conditions in the area concerned and of the problems of people living on low incomes. The other, the Trades Council member, was drawn from a panel representing work people.

The Government's plan to abolish the two panel system, and with it the automatic presence of at least one trade unionist on each tribunal, proved to be so politically controversial that it was dropped to ensure the passage of the HASSASSA Act 1983, before that year's General Election. The proposal was subsequently reintroduced and enacted in the Health and Social Security Act 1984. The rationale for the change, according to Government spokesmen, was the need to provide a more broadly representative base for tribunal membership. Critics feared that the middle class bias in the tribunals' composition would only become more pronounced . . . .

In practice it seems that the creation of a single panel has made little difference as yet to the make-up of tribunals. In our sample by far the largest single group of members, some 37%, had been nominated by trade unions, almost twice as many as fell into the next largest category, those nominated by somebody within the tribunal system itself. These trade union nominees were also amongst the longest serving members of the tribunals, two thirds of them having been members for between five and 15 years. As indicated above, members were on average older than chairmen, although the proportion of women (38%) was higher than amongst chairmen. Notwithstanding the continuing role of trade union nominees, our findings suggest that the tribunal system has failed to build up a broader base of lay membership to reflect in some measure the range of people that appear as appellants. Only one of the 97 members we interviewed described himself as unemployed. It is still the case that most appellants find themselves facing a row of white, rather elderly faces across the tribunal table."

(The figures are drawn from a study of 28 SSATs throughout Great Britain conducted in 1989–90; the full report of the research has been published: J. Baldwin, N. Wikeley and R. Young, *Judging Social Security* (OUP, 1992).)

Research suggests another problem is that in some tribunals, as compared with the chairmen, the other members (sometimes referred to as the "wing members") play a rather passive role. One reason for this can be the training and experience of the chairmen. In tribunals where the chairman or a member is required to be legally qualified, many of the issues to be considered may involve legal technicality, it might be expected that the legally qualified person would play a dominant role. In any event, tribunal chairmen are likely to be more experienced than the other members and thus may be expected to be more influential.

The relative passivity of the members of tribunals is a concern. The appointment of members of tribunals is presumably intended to guard against bias in chairmen and to inject lay experience which may be relevant in considering certain aspects of claimants' cases. To some extent, the passivity of tribunal members may be corrected by training, but such training can be limited and, in the view of some, is inadequate: C. Jones and M. Adler, *Can Anyone Get on These? A study of the systems of appointment and training of justices of the peace and members of social security appeal tribunals and children's panels in Scotland* (Scottish Consumer Council, Glasgow, 1990).

Wikeley and Young, "The Marginalisation of Lay Members in Social Security Appeal Tribunals", p. 137–139

> "Our observations of tribunal proceedings, based on a national sample, tend to confirm the view that the legalisation of the benefit system has made it more difficult for lay members to contribute (for a similar perspective on industrial tribunals, see Dickens et al., 1985, p. 83). In the tribunal hearings which we observed few of the members played a major role. In part this is attributable to the widespread (but questionable) view amongst members that, in those cases where the appellant is not present at the hearing (around half of the total), there is nothing they can do other than rely on the submission of the presenting officer. Sometimes this is due to a sense of powerlessness in the face of tight statutory provisions which seem to admit of no exceptions. As one member commented:
>
> > 'I'm a bit depressed on that score. It was far more interesting and our role was of far more value a few years ago, when there was an area of discretion. One was able to alter the result to fit the individual case. Now it is very rigid and sometimes I feel we are just rubber stamping a bad law.' (Member, North Wales, Interview 121.)
>
> Even when appellants attend their appeal hearings, members generally fail to make their presence felt. In all, we found that less than a fifth of the members made anything more than a limited contribution to the proceedings that we observed. One of our most striking findings was that almost a half were entirely silent throughout the appeal hearing. These members did not ask a single question or make a single comment. By way of contrast, Jackson, Stewart and Bland (1987) found that members made no contribution at all in the public part of the hearing in something over one fifth of hearings. Even allowing for methodological differences, this suggests a marked diminution in the potential for members to play a positive part in hearings over the course of the last five years. The phasing out of lay chairmen, the growing experience of lawyer chairmen, the replacement of supplementary benefit by a much simpler system of income support, and the loss of discretion represented by the abolition of single payments, are all significant factors in this development. The issues raised in many social security appeals are too legal, too technical, and too complex to allow the average lay member much scope to make a significant contribution. This is not to imply that there was once a golden age of lay member participation—the Bell report (1975) on supplementary benefit appeal tribunals noted that it was only in a minority of hearings that both members played an active

role. The problem of passive members seems, however, to have worsened considerably since Bell reported.

It is true that members may play a positive part in putting appellants at their ease even though they may not say a word—for example, by smiling, nodding or demonstrably paying close attention to the case. Yet about two thirds of those members who remained silent were entirely passive, and a few behaved in a distinctly off putting manner—such as by yawning or looking bored. One actually fell asleep during the hearing. Many of them can be said to have given the appearance of being seriously out of their depth.

It must be conceded that, with a few exceptions, we were only able to observe the public part of the tribunal proceedings. It should be noted that in terms of putting the appellant at ease and assisting in developing his or her case, this is the important stage of the hearing. Nevertheless, it might be argued that members who play only a limited role in the hearing may be more animated in the subsequent deliberations. A number of reasons lead us to doubt that this is the case. First, our interviews with chairmen and members themselves suggested that members often fail to participate actively in the deliberations following a hearing. Secondly, it was noteworthy that in 58% of the appeals observed, the deliberations took five minutes or less (in 21% of the cases in our sample there were no formal deliberations because the tribunal reached its decision in the course of the hearing). Thirdly, members rarely dissent from the decision considered correct by the chairman. In 331 cases out of our sample of 337, the decision was unanimous, and, in the six cases where there was disagreement, the chairman was in the majority. In other words, there was not a single case in which the chairman was outvoted by the lay members."

[See also S. McPhee, *Lay Representation in Courts and Tribunals* (Citizens Advice Scotland, 1998).]

III. TRIBUNAL PROCEDURE

A. PROCEDURAL RULES

Wraith and Hutcheson, *Administrative Tribunals*, p. 131

"Given the diversity and range of formal and informal procedures, the dilemma is two-fold: on the one hand procedure should not be so technical and formal as to discourage legitimate applications, and on the other even the most informal of tribunals will need some guidelines if the proceedings are to be fair to both parties. This is a tightrope which not all tribunals have managed to walk successfully.

The point was put with great clarity by Lord Gardiner (then Lord Chancellor) in a speech at the opening of the Central Office of the Industrial Tribunals:

'Tribunals try to be free from technicality. A tribunal must have a framework of procedure within which to operate. Experience has shown that informality of atmosphere in hearings before tribunals can be positively inimical to orderly procedure. Within that framework of procedure, it is essential that there should be sufficient informality of atmosphere to put the lay litigant at his ease. Lawyers sometimes forget what an ordeal it is for the ordinary citizen to go to law. 80% of the cases coming before the Industrial Tribunals are claims for redundancy payments. Many of the applicants, and a number of the respondents, are unsophisticated people caught up in a vast machine which they do not understand. They are frightened of what they imagine a court to be, and it is a major part of a tribunal's function to put them at their ease so that they present cases as well as possible. A tribunal must be tolerant and patient with the litigants before it, who are usually unrepresented, are often incapable of expressing themselves adequately, and are nearly always overwhelmed by the occasion. It is therefore essential that the proceedings should be kept as simple and as informal as possible within the framework of the procedure laid down by law.'"

Justice–All Souls Review, paras 51–56

"The procedure of most tribunals differs markedly from that of the courts of law. Whereas the procedure in court is strongly adversarial that of many tribunals combines the adversarial and the investigative. Thus, most tribunals can obtain their own evidence by calling witnesses, conduct examinations and inspect sites, and commission experts' reports. Even where there are no formal powers for these things tribunals often achieve them as a matter of practice.

There is a wide variety of procedures though, in the main, the order of proceedings in court is adopted but with much more latitude allowed to the applicant/appellant . . .

(a) Openness

With few exceptions the courts perform in public. In the case of tribunals there is much variation but private sessions are common (though this is scarcely noticed as in practice very few tribunal hearings are attended by members of the public or the press). Likewise judges have all the papers read to them in open court. Tribunal members, in order to save time, prepare for the hearings by reading the entire dossier in private.

(b) Evidence

Tribunals may rely on evidence that would be inadmissible in a court of law. The extent to which they do so varies according to the nature of the tribunal, and the nature of the case. Evidence is admitted if logically probative. Thus, hearsay is admissible. 'No doubt in admitting it, the tribunal must observe the rules of natural justice, but this does not mean that it must be tested by cross-examination. It only means that the . . . other side [must have] a fair opportunity of commenting on it and contradicting it', Lord Denning observed in *T.A. Miller Ltd v Minister of Housing and Local Government*

[1968] 1 W.L.R. 992. Naturally tribunal members make considerable use of their own expertise in the subject matter.

(c) Standard of proof

The usual standard of proof, as in the civil courts, is the balance of probabilities, but there are some instances where the criminal standard ('beyond reasonable doubt') is adopted. The burden of proof is, as in the courts, on he who asserts, but there are a number of presumptions prescribed by statute that favour applicants/appellants in some tribunals.

(d) Rules of procedure.

Most tribunals have a general power to regulate their own proceedings, and they may adopt quite different rules. Franks found that there was 'general agreement on the broad essentials which the procedure (of tribunals) in this wider sense (of before and after as well as during the hearing) should contain'. They included the provision of notice of the right to apply to a tribunal, knowledge of the case to be met, a reasoned decision by the tribunal, and notice of any further right of appeal. Franks was not in favour either of a standard code of procedure or of a small number of codes (para. 63) but did envisage that the Council on Tribunals would have a statutory power to formulate rules of procedure. Neither this nor the . . . proposal that [there] should [be] a central supervisory drafting department was adopted. Regulations containing rules of procedure are drafted in the legal sections of the various departments. This accounts for much of their variety. The Council on Tribunals try to achieve a unifying effect through the process of consultation. Sometimes their advice is ignored."

(On the obligation to consult the Council on Tribunals on tribunal procedural rules, see the Tribunals and Inquiries Act 1992, s. 8.)

Some aspects of tribunal procedure are governed by general statutory provisions. One of the most important is contained in the Tribunals and Inquiries Act 1992.

Tribunals and Inquiries Act 1992, s. 10(1)–(3), (6)

"**10.**—(1) Subject to the provisions of this section . . . , where—

(a) any tribunal specified in Schedule 1 gives any decision

. . . it shall be the duty of the tribunal . . . to furnish a statement, either written or oral, of the reasons for the decision if requested, on or before the giving or notification of the decision, to state the reasons.

(2) The statement referred to in subsection (1) may be refused, or the specification of the reasons restricted, on grounds of national security.

(3) A tribunal . . . may refuse to furnish a statement under subsection (1) to a person not primarily concerned with the decision if of the opinion that to furnish it would be contrary to the interests of any person primarily concerned . . .

(6) Any statement of the reasons for a decision referred to in paragraph (a) . . . of subsection (1), whether given in pursuance of that subsection or of any other statutory provision, shall be taken to form part of the decision and accordingly to be incorporated in the record."

(Section 10 applies to all tribunals under the jurisdiction of the Council on Tribunals. See also: *Crake v. Supplementary Benefits Commission; Butterworth v. Supplementary Benefits Commission* [1982] 1 All E.R. 498; *Save Britain's Heritage v. Number 1 Poultry Ltd* [1991] 1 W.L.R. 153, 167, *per* Lord Bridge of Harwich; *Curtis v. London Rent Assessment Committee and others* [1997] 4 All E.R. 842.)

B. APPEALS

From many tribunals an appeal lies to another tribunal on questions of law, or sometimes on questions of fact and law. In some cases there is no provision for further appeal, although tribunal decisions may be reviewed by the courts. So, for example, the Immigration Appeal Tribunal hears appeals from immigration adjudicators, but there is no provision for further appeal. In other cases, there is provision for appeal to the courts. For example, the Social Security Commissioners hear appeals from social security appeal tribunals (Social Security Act 1998, s. 14) and there is a further appeal to the Court of Session (*ibid.*, s. 15).

Social Security Act 1992, ss. 14 and 15

"**14.**—(1) Subject to the provisions of this section, an appeal lies to a Commissioner from any decision of an appeal tribunal under section 12 or 13 above on the ground that the decision of the tribunal was erroneous in point of law. . . .

15.—(1) Subject to subsections (2) and (3) below, an appeal on a question of law shall lie to the appropriate court from any decision of a Commissioner. . . ."

(See *Bland v. Chief Supplementary Benefit Officer* [1983] 1 All E.R. 557; see also *Burns v. Secretary of State for Social Services* 1985 S.L.T. 351. Where the premises in which a tribunal normally exercises its functions are in Scotland, the appropriate court is the Court of Session.)

In the case of certain tribunals there is provision for judicial review by the Court of Session by way of appeal or stated case. For example, the Tribunals and Inquiries Act 1992, s. 11, entitles any party to proceedings before specified tribunals who is dissatisfied in point of law with the decision of the tribunal to use these procedures. However, whether a person is a party to the proceedings may itself be a legal issue: *Fairpo v. Humberside C.C.* [1997] 1 All E.R. 183.

C. PRECEDENT

Justice–All Souls Review, para. 60

"Tribunals follow the precedents of the superior courts and, where appropriate, their own appellate tribunals. But they are not obliged to follow their own precedents and, indeed, are sometimes discouraged from doing so (*e.g. Merchandise Transport Ltd v. British Transport Commission* [1962] 2 Q.B. 173). It is fundamental to any system of precedent that the existence of the precedents should be known, and the chairmen and clerks of tribunals bear the chief responsibility for keeping abreast of them. The Franks Committee recommended that all final appellate tribunals should publish selected decisions and circulate them to any lower tribunals. It is plainly desirable that the precedents followed by tribunals should be made public but the extent to which they can be published is subject to limitations of cost."

The following decisions by National Insurance Commissioners (now Social Security Commissioners) demonstrate the use of precedent and reporting within a tribunal system.

R(I) 12/75

(Chief Commissioner) R.J.A. TEMPLE;
(Commissioners) J.S. WATSON, J.G. MONROE

"There have been nearly 60,000 Commissioners' decisions since 1948, and they fall into the following categories (a) unnumbered decisions (b) numbered decisions and (c) reported decisions.

(a) Unnumbered decisions which represent the vast majority of decided cases comprise those in which well established principles of law have been applied to the facts as found or in which the sole issues have been of fact. They were not thought by their authors to reflect any unusual circumstances or to contribute to the development of the law, save in some cases to reinforce accepted lines of authority.
(b) Numbered decisions are those to which the Commissioner concerned has had a number allocated . . . This ensures a limited distribution of the decision as being of interest.
(c) Reported decisions are those selected for reporting. They are so selected by the Chief Commissioner from numbered decisions and are primarily so selected if he is satisfied that they deal with questions of legal principle and that they command the assent of at least a majority of the Commissioners . . .

In addition to single Commissioner's decisions, decisions may be given by a Tribunal of three Commissioners nominated in accordance with what is now section 116 of the Social Security Act 1975 to decide a question of law of special difficulty. Such decisions are almost invariably reported.

Commissioners speak with equal authority. All their decisions whether unnumbered, numbered or reported may be cited to Commissioners, local tribunals and insurance officers. Where they decide questions of legal principle they must be followed by insurance officers and local tribunals in cases involving the application of that principle, unless they can be distinguished . . .

If confronted with decisions which conflict, insurance officers and local tribunals must prefer the decision of a Tribunal of Commissioners (whether a unanimous or majority decision) to that of a single Commissioner. A reported decision, for the reasons given in paragraph 17(c), should prima facie be given more weight than an unreported decision. Subject to the foregoing insurance officers and local tribunals must choose between conflicting decisions and there is no obligation on them to prefer the earlier to the later or vice versa.

In so far as the Commissioners are concerned, on questions of legal principle, a single Commissioner follows a decision of a Tribunal of Commissioners unless there are compelling reasons why he should not, as, for instance, a decision of superior Courts affecting the legal principles involved. A single Commissioner in the interests of comity and to secure certainty and avoid confusion on questions of legal principle normally follows the decisions of other single Commissioners . . .

It is recognised however that a slavish adherence to this could lead to the perpetuation of error and he is not bound to do so.

The insurance officer, local tribunals and Commissioners on questions of legal principle are all bound to follow the decisions of the High Court and Superior Courts."

(This decision was itself a decision of a Tribunal of three Commissioners. The procedure indicated in this decision was revised by a Practice Direction of the Chief Social Security Commissioner of October 28, 1982. Commissioners now star decisions which they consider may merit reporting and the Chief Commissioner selects the decisions to be reported from these starred decisions, after consulting the Commissioners and hearing any representations from those associated with particular cases.)

R(U) 8/80

(Commissioner) I.O. GRIFFITHS

"In Decision *R(1) 12/75* a Tribunal of Commissioners held in relation to the Law of England that a Commissioner on questions of legal principle is bound to follow decisions of the High Court and Superior Courts, meaning the Court of Appeal and the House of Lords. So far as I can discover there is no decision as to binding (as opposed to persuasive) effect of Scottish decisions upon the question of legal principle. In cases such as this where the same legislation applies to both England and Scotland it is clearly desirable that the laws of both England and Scotland should be uniform. So far as the High Court is concerned there is a well settled practice in revenue and taxation matters where the same statutes apply that courts of first instance keep in line with the courts of Scotland. An English court follows a unanimous judgment of a higher Scottish court where the question involved is one which turns upon the construction of a statute which extends to Scotland, leaving it to be reviewed if thought fit by the Appeal Court: see *Re Hartland; Banks v. Hartland* [1911] 1 Ch. 459 at page 466. The reason for this is the need to avoid interpretations which result in one meaning in one country and another in the other; *Commissioners for General Purposes of Income Tax for City of London v. Gibbs* [1942] A.C. 402 at 414. The position of a National Insurance Commissioner is different from that of a High Court Judge. All Commissioners are Commissioners for Great Britain. Commissioners who sit in Scotland are sometimes wrongly referred to as Scottish Commissioners. They are not—they are Commissioners sitting in Scotland. Moreover, the cases dealt with by Commissioners have no territorial connection. Cases occurring in Scotland are sometimes decided in London. Cases from the north of England are sometimes dealt with in Scotland particularly when oral hearings are concerned when it is easier for a claimant and his witnesses to travel to Edinburgh. It is quite obviously highly desirable that the same interpretation be applied on each side of the border.

In my judgment, I would apply to this case the same practice as is applied in the courts of first instance in the High Court in revenue and taxation cases, that is to say, I would follow the decision of a higher Scottish Court on a question of construction of the Social Security Act 1975."

IV. ADVICE, REPRESENTATION AND LEGAL AID IN TRIBUNALS

A. ADVICE AND REPRESENTATION

The importance of claimants and appellants seeking advice at an early stage is as great in areas of law which are largely subject to tribunal adjudication as it is to those primarily subject to judicial determination. The 1989 Genn Report to the Lord Chancellor (which considered SSATs, industrial tribunals, immigration adjudicators and mental health review tribunals in England and Wales) emphasises the importance of such advice not only for individuals directly concerned but also for the working of the tribunals.

H. Genn and Y. Genn, *The Effectiveness of Representation at Tribunals*, p. 157

"The evidence presented in this chapter has established that the availability of advice about social security claims and immigration requests at an early stage, can improve the quality of claimants' applications to Departments. This may avoid adverse decisions which are incorrect, and thus reduce the number of occasions on which the appeals process is mobilised to perform an expensive, information-gathering function.

Advice following an adverse departmental decision or employment problem can filter out of the tribunal process unmeritorious cases, and contribute to the acceptability of that outcome by providing a comprehensive explanation of the legal basis for the Department's decision or employer's action.

Representatives can also reduce the number of tribunal hearings by conducting direct negotiations with Departments and employers in order to achieve the satisfactory resolution of claims before a tribunal hearing takes place.

Case preparation and the provision of evidence is fundamental to the outcome of hearings. Unrepresented appellants and applicants have difficulty in identifying the facts which are relevant to their case. They therefore have difficulty in producing the evidence necessary to prove the case. In these situations, it becomes the responsibility of the tribunal to elicit relevant information from those who appear at tribunal hearings, and even when this can be accomplished to the satisfaction of the tribunal, the necessary evidence may not be immediately available. This may lead to adjournments or decisions taken on inadequate evidence.

In all tribunals the average delay between the lodging of an appeal or application and the tribunal hearing was greatest in those cases that were ultimately successful. Advice and representation tends to increase the average delay in all tribunals, although in immigration hearings and industrial tribunal cases it can reduce average delay. The effect of representation on delay was greatest where solicitors represented social security appeals."

A consistent feature of some tribunals is how few of those appearing before them are represented. Previous research in Scotland has revealed such a pattern. In a 1974 survey of Edinburgh and East Fife, 41 per cent were represented before NILTs and 30 per cent before SBATs: M. Adler and A.W. Bradley, *Justice, Discretion and Poverty* (Professional Books Ltd, 1976), p. 109–127. A 1983 study of 80 appellants throughout Scotland revealed even lower percentages of representation before NILTs and SBATs: D. Kay, *Tackling Tribunals* (Scottish Consumer Council, 1984).

A low percentage of representation was also a finding of the 1989 Genn Report, which was based on a broader survey of tribunals in England and Wales. That report confirmed earlier findings, both in Scotland and elsewhere in the United Kingdom, on the significance of representation on the outcome of tribunal adjudication, and again demonstrated that lawyers were not necessarily more successful than some other categories of representative when appearing before tribunals.

H. Genn and Y. Genn, *The Effectiveness of Representation at Tribunals*, p. 77–78, 86–87, and 99 and selected tables

"Social Security Appeal Tribunals

Outcome of Social Security Appeal Tribunal Hearings by Presence of Appellant or Representative

	% Dismissed	% Allowed	% Total	% of Sample
Appellant not present	88	12	100	44
Appellant present alone	58	42	100	29
Appellant present with friend	53	47	100	7
Appellant present with representative	47	53	100	11
Total Weighted Cases = 1115				

Significant P.<.00000

Social Security Appeals Tribunals Outcome of Hearing by Type of Representative

	% Dismissed	% Allowed	% Total	% of Sample
Welfare rights centre	33	67	100%	1
Law centre	34	66	100	*
Solicitor	44	56	100	1
Trade Union	46	54	100	1
CAB	48	52	100	4
Soc.Serv/Probation	49	51	100	1
Tribunal unit	53	47	100	1
Appellant unrepresented	56	44	100	37
Family/Friends	59	41	100	4
Other advice centre	65	35	100	2
Appellant absent	86	14	100	47
				100%

Total Weighted Cases = 1115 heard cases

Significant P. < 00001

Summary of Main Findings on Outcome of Hearings at Social Security Appeals Tribunals

1. Elderly appellants were less likely to succeed with appeals. Single parents were more likely to succeed with appeals.
2. Overpayment cases and disqualification from unemployment benefit cases were the most likely to succeed. Disqualification from supplementary benefit cases were the least likely to succeed.
3. Appeals decided in the absence of the appellant were the least likely to succeed.
4. Unrepresented appellants who attended their hearings were more likely to succeed if they had received some advice about their appeal.
5. All types of representation increased the likelihood of success. The overall success rate in social security appeals was 30%. Where the appellant was not present it was 12%. Where the appellant was present but unrepresented the success rate was 42%. Where the appellant was represented by someone other than a friend or relative it was 53%. Specialist advice and representation units had the most significant effect on success rates.
6. The presence of witnesses for the appellant increased the likelihood of success.
7. There were regional differences in success rates and large differences in success rates within regions between central urban hearing centres and outlying hearing centres.
8. There were significant differences in the rates at which appellants succeeded before different chairmen. Those chairmen who had the lowest success rates tended to sit at hearing centres with low representation rates.

9. A multiple regression analysis indicated that the identity of the chairman could reduce the chance of winning from 30% to 5%. It could also increase it to a maximum of 55%.
10. The multiple regression analysis indicated that holding constant factors such as characteristics of appellant, type of case, geographical location, type of chairman, etc., represented appellants are more likely to succeed with their appeals than unrepresented appellants. Specialist representation increases the probability that appellants will succeed with their appeal from about 30% to 48%.
11. The multiple regression analysis indicated that the main determinant of representation is advice, which is itself related to geographical location, and type of case. Those who live in urban areas are more likely, irrespective of case type and other factors, to obtain advice and representation at their hearing.

Hearings Before Immigration Adjudicators

Representation and Outcome of Hearings

Type of Representation	% Allowed or in Part	% of Representative Type in Sample
No representative	16%	8
UKIAS	31	49
Barrister	32	18
Solicitor	37	12
Specialist advice centre	40	2
Other advice centre	26	1
Law centre	24	4
JCWI	41	2
Relative/Friend	9	2
Total % Allowed All Cases	30	100
Total Weighted Heard Cases = 728 (Based on 770 unweighted cases)		

Summary of Main Findings on Outcome of Hearings Before Immigration Adjudicators

1. Overall 22% of cases were allowed or allowed in part. Of those that went to a full hearing 30% were allowed or allowed in part. Where cases were decided on the papers 2% were allowed. There was regional variation in the rates at which appeals resulted in a full hearing. Leeds had the lowest rate of full appeals. This is related to the low advice rate . . .
2. There were regional variations in success rate. Harmondsworth had the lowest success rate. Leeds the highest. There are, however, regional differences in type of appeal which might account for this.
3. Personal characteristics of appellants appeared to have little effect on success, although younger appellants were more likely to succeed and those with a previous immigration history were less likely to succeed with their appeals.

4. Political asylum, deportation cases, and visitors' extension cases were the least likely cases to succeed.
5. Unrepresented appellants were less likely to succeed with their appeals than represented appellants. All representatives, except friends and relatives, increased the likelihood of success.
6. A multiple regression analysis indicated that, holding other factors constant, the likelihood of success varied before certain adjudicators. The identity of the adjudicator could reduce the probability of success to 5% or increase it to 50% after controlling for other factors.
7. The multiple-regression analysis indicated that, holding all other factors constant, UKIAS has the highest rate of success among representatives, followed by solicitors and then other representatives. Over the sample as a whole, representation by counsel did not increase the likelihood of success more than representation by a solicitor or UKIAS. Representation by UKIAS would increase the probability of success from say 20% to approximately 38% after controlling for other factors.

Industrial Tribunals

Outcome of Industrial Tribunals in Relation to Applicants' Representation

	% Dismissed/ withdrawn	% Allowed	% Settled	% Total	% in Sample
Not represented	62	33	5	100	36
Solicitor	49	38	13	100	16
Barrister	47	30	22	100	12
Law centre	51	39	10	100	5
Trade Union	56	38	6	100	16
CAB/Other agency	67	27	5	100	7
Friend/Relative	67	29	4	100	

Total Weighted Heard Cases = 339 (Based on 550 cases)

Summary of Main Findings Relating to Outcome of Industrial Tribunal Hearings

1. Almost half of the applications to industrial tribunals were settled before a hearing. Applications were more likely to be settled where the applicant had obtained advice about his application.
2. The average amount of compensation received by applicants was, in general, higher if it was an award or settlement agreed after a hearing had commenced, than if it was agreed before a hearing.
3. Of the cases that resulted in a tribunal hearing, the applicants succeeded in 34% of cases. In 9% of cases a settlement was agreed after the hearing had commenced and a further 2% of applicants withdrew their applications after the hearing had commenced.
4. There was evidence that, as in social security appeals and immigration hearings, the identity of the tribunal chairman had an independent effect on the outcome of appeals.

5. The presence of witnesses for the applicant increased the likelihood that the applicant would succeed.
6. As far as representation is concerned, applicants can only improve their chances of success through representation when the respondent is not represented Where the applicant is legally represented and the respondent is not represented the probability of the applicant succeeding is increased from 30% to 48%. Where the applicant has no representation and the respondent is legally represented the applicant's probability of success is reduced to 10%. Where the applicant is represented by a non-lawyer, and the respondent is represented by a lawyer the probability of the applicant succeeding is 18%. . . . "

B. LEGAL AID

The legal advice and assistance scheme extends to tribunal proceedings and there is also provision for making assistance by way of representation (Legal Aid (Scotland) Act 1986, Pt II). (See Chapter 11.)

With the exceptions of the Lands Tribunal for Scotland and the Employment Appeal Tribunal, legal aid is not available in proceedings before tribunals in Scotland (*ibid.* Sched. 1, para. 1; S.I. 1987 No. 381). However, it would be available in further court proceedings on a tribunal decision, and it is also available in certain court proceedings arising out of children's hearings (see further, C.N. Stoddart and H.S. Neilson, *The Law and Practice of Legal Aid in Scotland* (4th ed., T. & T. Clark, 1994).

There are persuasive arguments, outlined in the extracts below, for a greater extension of the legal aid scheme to tribunals. An additional argument is that in rural areas, where there is limited access to advice and representation, solicitors may be the only available source of it. However, the financial implications of extending the legal aid scheme to tribunals would be considerable. There are those who view with caution such a development but would favour the financial encouragement of the provision of advice and representation by others.

Justice–All Souls Review, paras 68–70

"The Lord Chancellor's Advisory Committee on Legal Aid considered the question of legal aid for tribunals in its Annual Report published in 1974 (H.C. 20 (1974–75)) and concluded that it was essential for applicants (a term it used to include appellants, claimants and, where appropriate, respondents) to have (i) access to competent advice as to their rights, the advisability of appealing and the consequences of doing so; (ii) frequently, assistance in gathering information and preparing the case; and (iii), in a limited number of cases, representation at the hearing (para. 31). 'There is a wide spectrum of need on the part of tribunal applicants, ranging from moral support and encouragement at one extreme to experienced legal advocacy on difficult issues of law at the other' (para. 33). The Committee found that there were many types of case that were too complex for the applicant to handle in which welfare organisations and trade unions had developed skills and expertise. It rejected the suggestion made to it that there should be a specialised body, decentralised in its administration throughout the country, for providing non-legal representation wherever that was needed, and preferred a system of financial support to those existing agencies that were providing non-legal help as part of their general service of advice and assistance (para. 34). The Committee did not consider that a tribunal could itself provide a satisfactory substitute for effective representation, especially where the other side was represented (para. 37).

The Committee recognised that the extension of legal aid to all tribunals did involve some risk of formalisation of the proceedings. It concluded that the issue to be considered was whether the advantages of informality outweighed those of representation: 'if they do, the right course, we suggest, will be to ban legal representation altogether; what cannot be justifiable is to restrict its benefits to those wealthy enough to afford it for themselves' (para. 38). The Committee also recognised that an extension of legal aid carried with it the danger of lengthening proceedings.

Having considered all the evidence it had received in response to a Working Paper it had published on the subject, the Committee, in 1974, concluded that legal aid should be extended to all statutory tribunals then within the supervision of the Council on Tribunals in which representation was permitted. However, since 1974 the Committee have modified their views somewhat in the face of limited resources."

Hughes Commission, p. 72–73 and 91–93

"We recommend in Chapter 8 an extension of legal aid to enable claimants to be represented before tribunals by a solicitor—but only in limited circumstances. We believe that the best way to meet the needs of claimants before many tribunals is to encourage the development of lay representation at tribunals. Although a number of organisations such as Citizens Advice Bureaux, trade unions and claimants rights groups do excellent work in representing tribunal claimants, there is considerable variation in the help and advice available to claimants appearing before tribunals. The availability of representation also varies with the subject matter of the particular tribunal. Most claimants making an application to a tribunal both lodge the application and appear before the tribunal without the benefit of any informed and independent advice. This is unsatisfactory.

We know that a number of projects to try to build up lay representation before tribunals have been encouraged in England. From our observations such projects have helped both to extend the amount of representation and advice before tribunals, and also to improve the quality of such representation and advice. There have, however, only been a few projects of this nature. Some projects have concentrated on the training of lay representatives while others have built up teams who could provide representation before particular tribunals. Yet another scheme was aimed at providing a 'duty representative' at National Insurance Tribunals, who could advise all claimants and appear on their behalf if necessary. The source of funding of the different projects varies and is often only guaranteed for a short period. The future of the existing tribunal representation units, given the present funding basis, appears to be very insecure. While the inquisitorial approach of a tribunal may mean that the quality of presentation of a claimant's case is less critical to the outcome of his case, there is considerable scope for developing the system of lay representation before tribunals, and we are strongly of the opinion that finance should be made available for this purpose. While we recognise that there are a variety of kinds of tribunal, we recommend that encouragement should be given to developing the provision of lay advice and representation before those tribunals in which lay participation is appropriate, and that adequate training should be provided for lay representatives . . .

Those who appear before tribunals do so to assert or protect rights and should, therefore, qualify for legal aid in terms of the principle we have enunciated. In support of this view, it can also be argued that where legal representation is allowed and one side can afford to use it, it is wrong to refuse legal aid to the other party. However, there is a difference between most tribunals and courts. Our courts traditionally rely on the adversarial procedure which generally demands a degree of skill and knowledge of the law on the part of the pleader. Tribunals of the kind we have in mind, such as the Industrial Tribunal, are accustomed to proceed by a more inquisitorial approach, which makes the quality of presentation less crucial to the outcome. We think that this form of procedure is well suited for tribunals of this type and should be encouraged. We had this in mind in recommending in Chapter 7 that lay representation at such tribunals should be developed by generalist advice agencies. We certainly would not prohibit the employment of lawyers for this purpose. No doubt there are cases where difficult questions of law arise in which the assistance of lawyers appearing for the parties is valuable to the tribunal in question, but we think that the use of lawyers ought not to be encouraged in the general run of these cases since they tend to introduce adversarial formality to which the proceedings are not well suited.

The Scottish Committee of the Council on Tribunals recommended to us that legal aid should only be available at tribunals in the absence of suitable lay representation. We endorse that approach, though we consider that a solicitor should be entitled to claim from the legal aid fund for undertaking representation if the tribunal certify that a substantial point of law was at issue. So that it might be widely known whether there is 'suitable lay representation' locally available, each tribunal should publish a list of agencies providing what is, in the view of the particular tribunal, suitable representation. However, though it is important to provide representation where needed, tribunal proceedings are intended to enable citizens to appear without a legal representative to conduct their case; and we do not wish to encourage representation where the person himself could, after receiving advice as to what was involved, adequately present his own case. Legal aid should, therefore, be made available for representation at tribunals only if the client would otherwise be unable to follow the proceedings, and then only where there is no lay representation locally available which is recognised by the tribunal as suitable.

Tribunal hearings can involve substantial points of law. In addition, therefore, where the chairman of the tribunal, on an application made before the hearing, considers that a substantial point of law is likely to arise it should be competent for the tribunal to grant legal aid. If a substantial point of law arises during the course of a hearing, the tribunal should be able to authorise legal aid and to adjourn the hearing to allow legal representation to be obtained. In many such cases, the individual may already be represented by a full-time trade union official or by a lay representative, and although persons with such alternative means of representation should not be granted legal aid in straightforward cases, in cases where a substantial question of law is likely to arise they should be treated as regards legal aid in the same way as others using the tribunal system. We do not expect that such cases will arise frequently, and experienced chairmen and clerks of tribunals will readily recognise the cases where substantial questions of law are likely to arise. In practice, this extension of legal aid to tribunals will best be made tribunal by tribunal. The Legal Aid Act 1979 makes provision for legal aid to be extended to tribunals by regulation. It is clear that such regulations will need to be preceded by an examination of tribunals individually to see which require (or allow) legal representation and before which the exclusion of legal aid might cause inequity. An examination should be undertaken to identify those tribunals at which a substantial point of law is most likely to arise. All such tribunals should include a legally qualified member.

To sum up as regards tribunals, we recommend that legal aid should be available for representation at a tribunal, but only if the client would otherwise be unable to follow the proceedings and if there is no lay representation available locally which is recognised by the tribunal as suitable. We recommend in addition that a tribunal should have power to grant legal aid where it considers that the matter before it gives rise, or is likely to give rise, to a substantial point of law."

V. A TRIBUNAL IN PRACTICE: THE CHILDREN'S HEARING

The reporter and the children's hearing are the most significant elements in the Scottish system of juvenile justice.

Reporters are employed by the Scottish Children's Reporter Administration with an appeal against dismissal to the Secretary of State: see Local Government etc. (Scotland) Act 1994, ss. 128 and 129. The Secretary of State is empowered to prescribe their qualifications, but has not, as yet, done so. The reporters come from a variety of professional backgrounds; some are qualified in social work and some in law.

As indicated above, each children's hearing is constituted from panels appointed by the Secretary of State in each of the 32 local government areas in Scotland; the Secretary of State also appoints a chairman and deputy chairman of each panel. The appointments are made on the advice of a Children's Panel Advisory Committee formed by each local authority, which refers the names of potential panel members to the Secretary of State. Members of Children's Panels are appointed for a specified period although they can be removed at any time by the Secretary of State, but only with the consent of the Lord President.

Three members of the Panel—a chairman and two others—are chosen by the chairman or deputy chairman for children's hearings to consider the cases of individual children. There must be both a man and a woman panel member sitting at each hearing.

Anyone, including a local authority, may inform a reporter that there is reasonable cause to believe that, on one of a number of statutory grounds, "compulsory measures of supervision are necessary in respect of a child". In practice, the vast majority of information received by reporters is from the police. Having received information, it is for the reporter to decide on whether or not to refer the case to a children's hearing.

(For an analysis of the grounds of referral and the associated caselaw see K. McK. Norrie, *Children's Hearings in Scotland* (W Green, 1997), Chap. 3.)

Before a reference to a hearing, the reporter arranges for social background reports and other appropriate reports, such as school and psychiatric reports, on the child.

Normally, the child, his parents, the reporter and a representative of the social work department attend the hearing. The child and his parents may also be represented; in addition the children's hearing or the sheriff may appoint a person to safeguard the interests of the child: Children (Scotland) Act 1995, s. 41. If the grounds of the referral are not accepted by the child or his parents, the children's hearing is required to instruct the reporter to make an application to the sheriff for a finding on whether the grounds are established, unless it is intended to discharge the case. Once the grounds are agreed or established, the children's hearing after considering the case may make a supervision requirement, which may include the child living in a residential establishment. An important element of the hearing process is that where a child is placed under a supervision requirement the case is kept under review.

Although a children's hearing is informal in many respects, it has powers which may affect the rights of children and their parents and is, therefore, subject to a range of procedural rules. The child or his parents may appeal against a decision of a children's hearing to the sheriff and a further appeal lies to the Court of Session on a point of law or procedural irregularity. In 1996, 27,427 cases were decided by children's hearings.

Martin *et al.*, *Children out of Court*, pp. 102–107 and 256

"Frequency of compliance with certain procedural requirements

	Per cent of hearings
Formal rules	
Child identified by name and age	94
Purpose of hearing explained	63
Social background report referred to	35
School report referred to	60
Reasons for decision stated	58
Right to receive written reasons indicated	44
Right to appeal indicated	74

'Good practices'	
Right to legal aid indicated	6
Child asked if agrees/understands decision	37
Parent asked if agrees/understands decision	31
(N = 100%)	301

In 94 per cent of all cases, the child was identified by name and age (Act, s. 55) . . .

Surprisingly however there was a failure to explain the purpose of the hearing in slightly more than one-third of all the cases observed (rules 17(1) and 19(2)). 'Failure' in this sense does not mean that an attempt to explain the purpose was judged to have been unsuccessful, but that no attempt was made. An explanation of the purpose of the hearing was given marginally less frequently when the case had been continued for reports (43 per cent) and when the child had been referred to a hearing on some previous occasion (41 per cent); but fully one-third of the children who were appearing before a hearing for the first time in their lives were offered no explanation of the hearing's purpose. Explanations were more often overlooked in truancy referrals and least often when the ground of referral was a fairly serious offence, but variations of this kind were not very striking . . .

The grounds of referral were put to the child and parent in exactly one quarter of the hearings observed (Act, s. 42). What appears to be a quite serious level of omission is however attributable to the inclusion in the sample of 58 hearings that had been continued from a previous occasion, for reports or for some other reason, and 42 hearings that had previously been adjourned to go for proof. The grounds of referral were put in only a small minority of these cases (19 per cent and 29 per cent respectively of the two groups), but in those instances where the child was making his first appearance there was no failure to put the grounds of referral . . .

The chairman of the hearing is expected to disclose the essential features of any reports that have been made available to the panel members present unless he has reason to believe that disclosure would be detrimental to the interests of the child (rules 17(3) and 19(4)). On the face of it, this obligation is overlooked fairly frequently. Social background reports were available in all but three of the hearings studied, and school reports in all but 34, yet there was no explicit reference to the former in two-thirds of all hearings and no explicit mention of the latter in two hearings in every five. No report was ever shown to the family, and a formal summary of the contents of a school report was given at only one hearing. A partial account of the contents of the social background report was given to the family at slightly more than 5 per cent of hearings, while an extract from the school report was conveyed about three times as frequently. Most of the references that were made to reports were in the nature of allusions: 'I can see the social worker says you're more settled at home'. The social background report was referred to in the same way at three hearings in every ten, and the school report at four in every ten hearings. Social background reports were mentioned more frequently in initial than in continued or adjourned hearings, more often in cases where the child had never previously appeared before a hearing, but in no category did the frequency of mention exceed 40 per cent. A similar pattern is found in the frequency with which school reports were mentioned, the proportion reaching as high as 70 per cent in the case of initial appearances . . .

When a hearing reaches a decision, the chairman has a duty to announce the nature of the decision, to give the family orally reasons for that decision, and to advise the family that they have a right to receive a written statement of reasons (rule 17(4)). The obligation to formulate reasons at the conclusion of the hearing was overlooked in 42 per cent of the cases observed . . . Parents were notified of their right to receive a written statement of reasons at slightly less than one-half of all hearings . . . ; the more serious types of offence referral tended more often to elicit an indication that written reasons would be provided.

Appeals against the decisions of children's hearings are rare—perhaps twenty are raised every year—but it is essential for all families to be notified of their right to appeal. There was however a failure to adhere to this requirement at one hearing in every four . . . Even if a more lenient view is taken of this procedural failure when discharge was the outcome of the hearing, it is impossible to respond with any complacency to the neglect of rule 17(4) in cases where a supervision order was imposed. Fortunately, these omissions occurred in only about one-seventh of such hearings, but anything that falls short of 100 per cent compliance must be taken extremely seriously.

ASPECTS OF AN IDEAL HEARING

	PERCENTAGE SELECTING GIVEN ATTRIBUTE	
	Panel members	Social workers
The full participation of the child and parents in the discussion.	85	94
The parents' and the child's understanding of *all* that takes place at hearings.	86	89
The hearing's impact on the child and parents as a serious event.	43	40
An atmosphere of communality and equality between family and other hearing members.	38	30
The difference between the hearing and the court.	19	22
The hearing as a body of authority with powers over the family.	13	9
The observance of all procedural requirements.	6	4
Conveying legal and technical information to the family	4	9
(N = 100%)"		

(This study was based on a representative sample of 3 per cent of children's hearings in 1978–79 throughout Scotland (excluding Orkney, Shetland and the Western Isles). Questionnaires were sent to all children's panel members and to 300 Scottish local authority social workers. The extract refers to the Social Work

(Scotland) Act 1968 and the Children's Hearings (Scotland) Rules (S.I. 1971 No. 492), but see now the Children (Scotland) Act 1995, Pt II and the Children's (Scotland) Rules 1996 (S.I. 1996 No. 3261).)

Norrie, *Children's Hearings in Scotland*, pp. 4–5

"Though the children's hearing system in Scotland has many admirable qualities and is, it is submitted, hugely preferable to a court-based system of child care and protection and juvenile justice, our system is not perfect. It is operated by real men and women, who necessarily have the flaws of humanity. It also operates in the real world, where political and financial considerations play a large role in determining what resources are to be made available for the provision of services which can be called upon by the children's hearing. At the micro level, many panel members would be happier in requiring, say, an individual child to live in a residential establishment if that establishment had more resources than are, practically, available. The physical condition of many children's homes in Scotland is not impressive. At the macro level, hearings are frequently faced with having to make a decision as to what is the best resource available rather than the best resource for the child; and that often means that they have no effective choice at all.

As well as that practical flaw, which is unlikely ever to be resolved, there are at least two legal flaws which, given the appropriate political will, could be resolved quite readily. First, the unmarried father is not recognised as having a legal relationship with his child in Scots law: Within the context of the children's hearing system, this means that he (unlike the unmarried mother) has no automatic right (nor duty) to attend a children's hearing, nor to appeal against their decisions, nor to call for a review of any supervision requirement they impose. A high percentage of the children who appear before a children's hearing have parents who are not married to each other, and the exclusion of the unmarried father discourages men from playing a full role in the upbringing of their children. This is contrary both to the European Convention on Human Rights and to the UN Convention on the Rights of the Child. Article 14 of the European Convention prohibits unjustifiable discrimination based on sex; Article 18 of the UN Convention requires that both parents are placed under common responsibilities for the upbringing and development of the child.

Secondly, while the child and his or her parents are entitled to bring a representative to the hearing, there is no provision for paid legal representation at hearings. This is entirely unjustifiable. Children's hearings have huge, even draconian, powers over a child and his or her family and can exercise these powers (which might, for example, include removing the child from his or her parents or authorising the locking up of the child in a secure unit) in the complete absence of legal representation. It is no answer to say that legal representation is permitted at appeal or at the sheriff court when the reporter seeks to establish the grounds of referral. Neither the appeal court nor the grounds of referral court determines what disposal is appropriate, and it is at the disposal stage that children are expected to speak for themselves, to present their own cases (as it were) in as favourable a light as they can. It is, of course, right that the child should be encouraged to speak at his or her own children's hearing, but few children have the confidence or the articulateness to argue why their welfare demands an approach different from that which the hearing are inclined to favour. The failure to allow paid legal representation amounts, it is submitted, to a breach of Article 40 of the UN Convention. This article provides that children who arc accused of a crime are to have legal assistance in preparing and presenting his or her defence. 'Defence' means more than a denial of involvement and includes an explanation of that involvement. The children's hearing system encourages the child to give an explanation, but denies the child legal help in presenting that explanation. Yet, many who appear before the hearing have suffered from a lack of educational provision and are all the more in need of such assistance.

It is often argued that to allow lawyers into the hearing room would change the atmosphere, make it more adversarial, and discourage children from expressing their own views. To which it may be replied that the hearing members are masters of the proceedings and it is for them to set the atmosphere and, if necessary, to explain to attending lawyers that the adversarial manner which they may be more used to adopting is not appropriate at a children's hearing. A more substantial criticism is that a legal representative may see his or her role as protecting the parent's interests — to which the hearing members must reply, that is irrelevant to their consideration except insofar as it affects the child's interests.

The safeguarder does not fulfil the role of child-advocate, but rather the role of child protector, of trying to identify where the real interests of the child lie. But a child may have an entirely different perception of his or her own interests, and that perception is worthy of consideration by the hearing. The child's lack of articulateness will often prevent that perception from being presented for consideration, and the failure of the system to provide a mouthpiece (rather than a protector) is an unjustifiable and possibly even fundamental flaw in an otherwise admirable system."

VI. CONTROL OF TRIBUNALS

As tribunals determine the legal rights of the citizen, it is important that they apply the law correctly and act with procedural propriety. In the case of some tribunals this may be ensured by appellate tribunals or by an appeal system which provides for the reference of a question of law to the ordinary courts. In addition to this, the ordinary courts may in certain circumstances exercise a more general supervision over tribunals, and the Council on Tribunals keeps under review the constitution and working of tribunals under its jurisdiction.

A. THE COURTS

The ordinary courts may review the decision of tribunals which have acted outside their jurisdiction and may quash decisions arrived at in breach of natural justice. Even following *West v. Scottish Prison Service* 1992 S.C. 385, there is, however, doubt whether Scottish courts have a general power to review the decision of a tribunal which is within its jurisdiction but wrong in law. These matters raise questions of law which are somewhat outside the scope of this book (see further, *Remedies in Administrative Law* (Scottish Law Commission Memorandum No. 14, 1971); Court of Session Rules, r. 260B (application for judicial review); W.J. Wolffe, "The Scope of Judicial Review in Scots Law" [1992] P.L. 625; V. R. Smith, "Scope of Judicial Review Determined" 1997 J.R. 122) but some of the issues are explored in the following extracts.

***Watt v. Lord Advocate* 1979 S.C. 120**

Lord President (Emslie): "This case is not one in which the commissioner misconstrued certain statutory provisions in the course of attempting to answer the right question remitted for his decision. He misconstrued that very question itself and answered a different question as the result of his error. For these reasons I am persuaded that the pursuer is well founded in his contention that the decision of the commissioner was ultra vires . . . I feel bound to say that if, as I have held, the commissioner's decision proceeded upon an error of law, and if that error did not render his decision a nullity, I have the gravest doubt whether this court would have had power to review it . . . It seems clear that, however much of this is to be regretted, the Court of Session has never had power to correct an intra vires error of law made by a statutory tribunal or authority exercising statutory jurisdiction. As Lord Justice Clerk Moncreiff said in *Lord Advocate v. Police Commissioners of Perth*, at p. 245: 'In the ordinary case it would now, I think, be held that where statutory powers are given, and a statutory jurisdiction is set up, all other jurisdictions are excluded . . . '. There is no indication in any subsequent authority that this view has been doubted or even questioned . . .

I cannot leave this case without expressing my regret that whereas it appears that the High Court in England still has, in spite of the provisions of s. 75(1) of the National Insurance Act 1965, jurisdiction in procedure by way of the prerogative writ of certiorari to correct errors of law by National Insurance Commissioners which appear on the face of the record, the Court of Session has no such power. It can hardly be suggested that it is in the best interests of statutory tribunals themselves that recourse to the appellate courts of the United Kingdom to determine difficult questions of law authoritatively should not be available in both of the great jurisdictions."

Reed, "Judicial Review of Errors of Law", pp. 241–244

> "A distinction has traditionally been drawn between errors of law which go to jurisdiction and those which do not. In England, the latter have been reviewable only by way of certiorari and only if the error appears on the face of the record. In Scotland, errors of law within jurisdiction have not been reviewable at all, but it may be that the line between jurisdictional and non-jurisdictional errors would be so drawn as to permit review of decisions reviewable in England. In both jurisdictions it has become increasingly difficult to draw the line with much confidence, especially since the decision in *Anisminic v. Foreign Compensation Commission* [1969] 2 A.C. 147; . . .

The traditional distinction was well expressed by Lord Reid: 'If a magistrate or any other tribunal has jurisdiction to enter on the inquiry and to decide a particular issue, and there is no irregularity in the procedure, he does not destroy his jurisdiction by reaching a wrong decision. If he has jurisdiction to go right, he has jurisdiction to go wrong. Neither an error in fact nor an error in law will destroy his jurisdiction' (*R. v. Brixton Prison Governor, ex parte Armah* [1968] A.C. 192). However, as Lord Reid himself observed in *Anisminic*, this is true only if 'jurisdiction' is used in the narrow sense of the tribunal being entitled to enter on the inquiry in question. But 'jurisdiction' may also bear the wider sense of vires, as explained by Lord Pearce in *Anisminic*: 'Lack of jurisdiction may arise in various ways. There may be an absence of those formalities or things which are conditions precedent to the tribunal having any jurisdiction to embark on an inquiry. Or the tribunal may at the end make an order that it has no jurisdiction to make. Or in the intervening stage, while engaged on a proper inquiry, the tribunal may depart from the rules of natural justice; or it may ask itself the wrong questions; or it may take into account matters which it was not directed to take into account.'

The tribunal's jurisdiction is settled by the statute; so if it steps outside the statute at any stage in any of the ways listed by Lord Pearce, it exceeds its jurisdiction and its purported decision is a nullity. Lord Diplock has said extra-judicially that *Anisminic* 'renders obsolete the technical distinction between errors of law which go to "jurisdiction" and errors of law which do not' (33 C.L.J. 233, 243). However, all the judges in the House of Lords reaffirmed the traditional distinction. The clearest guidance was given by Lord Wilberforce: 'The extent of the interpretatory power conferred upon the tribunal may sometimes be difficult to ascertain . . . Sometimes it will be possible to form a conclusion from the form and subject-matter of the legislation. In one case it may be seen that the legislature, while stating general objectives, is prepared to concede a wide area to the authority it establishes: this will often be the case where the decision involves a degree of policy-making rather than fact-finding, especially if the authority is a department of government or the Minister at its head. I think that we have reached a stage in our administrative law when we can view this question quite objectively, without any necessary predisposition towards one that questions of law, or questions of construction, are necessarily for the courts.'

Thus the extent to which the courts will review errors of law—or, to put it another way, will substitute their interpretation of the statute for that of the tribunal—will vary according to the nature of the tribunal. Some are more or less judicial: the tribunal in *Anisminic*, for example, was charged with determining entitlement to compensation for sequestrated property, its decision turning on the interpretation of legal terms such as 'successor in title' and 'British national'. Other tribunals may be set up to determine a great number of small claims requiring expertise and speed, or claims involving political or economic judgment rather than the application of fixed rules to facts discovered through the hearing of evidence.

Thus, although the English courts can intervene to correct even non jurisdictional errors on the face of the record, this power has been sparingly exercised in respect of specialised tribunals such as those concerned with social security . . .

In Scots law the courts have no power to review a decision made *intra vires*, even if it involves an error of law. This is clearly established by the authorities (*e.g. Don Brothers, Buist & Co. Ltd v. Scottish National Insurance Commissioners*, 1913 1 S.L.T. 221; *Smeaton v. Commissioners of Police of St Andrews* (1865) 3 M. 816), despite speculative arguments based on *Pryde v. Heritors and Kirk-Session of Ceres* (1843) 5 D. 552 (a decision whose *ratio* depends on the special nature of parochial boards, as explained by Lord Fullerton in *Edinburgh & Glasgow Railway Co. v. Meek* (1849) 12 D. 153).

Some examples of intervention may be given. In *Caledonian Railway Co. v. Glasgow Corporation* (1905) 7 F. 1020 the corporation was empowered to enter the width of streets on a register. Planning permission would not be granted without special consent where the building would reduce the width of the street. The corporation entered target widths greater than the actual widths. It was held to be doing something quite different from what the statute directed. In *Bennett v. Scottish Board of Health* 1921 S.C. 772 the court was willing to determine whether a committee set up to hear complaints about 'medical attendance and treatment' could hear a complaint about a doctor's abusive language during a visit: the committee's jurisdiction depended on the meaning of the statutory phrase. Finally, in *Hayman v. Lord Advocate* 1952 S.L.T. 209 the approval of opticians depended (a) on their holding prescribed diplomas or being on an older approved list, and (b) on a finding by a committee that they had 'adequate, including recent experience'. Lord Cooper said that if the committee had investigated the pursuer's professional rectitude and the nature of his premises, instead of investigating whether he had recently utilised the prescribed qualifications so as to be a sufficiently experienced practitioner, then they had 'acted illegally by applying their minds to the wrong question and thus in effect acting *ultra fines compromissi*'. In these three cases the misinterpretation of the statutory language would have led the tribunal to do something quite different from what it was directed to do: to compile a quite different register from the one it was directed to compile, to hear a complaint it had no authority to hear, to make an inquiry into quite different matters from those it was supposed to investigate . . . [In the *Watt* case] Lord Emslie reaffirmed that the Court of Session had no power to correct an error of law within jurisdiction, and distinguished between cases in which the commissioner misconstrued statutory provisions in the course of answering the question remitted to him and cases where the question itself had been miscontrued so that a different question had been answered . . . any error of law, it appears, can be treated as jurisdictional by manipulating phraseology. In practice a distinction will be drawn; and one returns to Lord Wilberforce's dictum that it will be a functional distinction grounded in the nature of the tribunal's task."

Apart from the scope of judicial review, there are questions of the effect of judicial review on the tribunal system. Vigorous judicial assertion of the power to review may serve to undermine the tribunal system. So, *e.g.* the Court of Appeal in England, in *Chief Adjudication Officer v. Foster* [1991] 3 All E.R. 846, overruling previous decisions to the contrary, held that it was outside the jurisdiction of the Social Security Commissioners and of Social Security Appeal Tribunals to consider arguments that regulations were *ultra vires*. One consequence of the decision, although not in the instant case, may be that a claimant is obliged to raise some arguments by judicial review and others before a tribunal.

The relationship between the tribunal system and judicial review may also have more fundamental aspects. Despite the contemporary vigour of the remedy, judicial review is not well placed to provide the same degree of supervision over, often decentralised, administration as is a tribunal system. Certainly, as the following extract argues, it is undesirable to allow judicial review to compensate for a lack of a tribunal appellate structure (see also the address by the Rt Hon. Lord Woolf on "Tribunals and the Courts" in the *Annual Report of the Council on Tribunals 1991–92*, App. E).

***Annual Report of the Council on Tribunals 1991–92*, paras 2.2–2.5**

> "**2.2** In accordance with the recommendations of the Franks Report, we have always held the view that there should be a right of appeal on a point of law from tribunals to the courts. In some recent proposals for legislation we have noted a tendency to regard the machinery of judicial review as an adequate substitute. . . . In our view, judicial review is not apt for the purpose of providing a route of appeal from tribunal decisions. Still less does the existence of the machinery of judicial review relieve the policy maker from the need to consider the establishment of a new tribunal system or other form of appeal machinery to consider appeals against administrative decisions . . . .
>
> **2.3** Given the tendency to which we have referred, we think it right to emphasise here the distinction between a right of appeal and judicial review. The judicial review jurisdiction is fundamentally different from an appellate jurisdiction, not least in its discretionary element. An appeals procedure is a means by which a public body may be brought within the control of the courts when an issue of substantive law is at stake, whereas judicial review is a supervisory jurisdiction by which the courts may find the decision-making process of a variety of public bodies to be unlawful. Although it is true that an error of law may found both a successful appeal and a successful application for judicial review, the latter is not concerned with the question whether a decision was 'right' or 'wrong', it is concerned rather with the question whether something has gone so badly wrong with the decision-making process as to make it unlawful or an abuse of power.
>
> **2.4** In this connection, we draw attention to the comments of the House of Lords in *Regina v. Independent Television Commission, ex parte TSW Broadcasting Ltd* (*The Times*, 30th March 1992) [1996] E.M.L.R. 291]. Lord Templeman said in that case:
>
> > 'Parliament may by statute confer powers and discretions and impose duties on a decision-maker who may be an individual, a body of persons or a corporation. Parliament may or may not provide machinery for an appeal against a decision. The appeal machinery may be concerned with

fact or law or both. The appeal machinery may or may not involve the courts of law. For example, Parliament has provided that an appeal on fact or law shall lie from an Immigration Officer to an Immigration Tribunal. Parliament has provided that an appeal on law only shall lie from the General or Special Commissioners of Income Tax to the High Court. Where Parliament has not provided for an appeal from a decision-maker the courts must not invent an appeal machinery. In the present case, Parliament has conferred powers and discretions and has imposed duties on the ITC. Parliament has not provided any appeal machinery. Even if the ITC makes mistakes of fact or of law, there is no appeal from their decision. The courts have invented the remedy of judicial review not to provide an appeal machinery but to ensure that the decision-maker does not exceed or abuse his powers'.

2.5 We trust that for the future departments will observe the distinction between a right of appeal and the discretionary remedy of judicial review, and not seek to rely on the existence of the latter in order to ignore the need for the former in appropriate cases."

B. THE COUNCIL ON TRIBUNALS

Following recommendations by the Franks Committee, a Council on Tribunals was established by the Tribunals and Inquiries Act 1958. The constitution of the Council and its powers are now embodied in the Tribunals and Inquiries Act 1992. Its principal powers with respect to tribunals are to keep under review the constitution and working of the tribunals listed in Schedule 1 to the Act, and to consider and report on matters referred to the Council by the Lord Chancellor and the Lord Advocate, concerning any tribunal other than an ordinary court of law, whether or not it is a scheduled tribunal (Tribunals and Inquiries Act 1992, s. 1). The Council also has powers to consider and report on the administrative procedures of statutory inquiries.

The Council has a statutory Scottish Committee which supervises certain specified tribunals in Scotland (*ibid.* s. 2(2), Sched. 1, Pt II). Before the Council reports on any of these tribunals, or on any matter referred to it by the Lord Advocate, it must consult the Scottish Committee (*ibid.* s. 4). The Scottish Committee can also, in certain circumstances, report directly to the Lord Advocate, but it has not used this power. Some of the tribunals in Scotland, such as SSATs and the immigration adjudicators, are under the general supervision of the Council; others, such as industrial tribunals, rent tribunals and children's hearings, are under the particular supervision of the Scottish Committee. The Council makes an annual report to the Lord Chancellor and the Lord Advocate (*ibid.* s. 4); these reports are laid before Parliament.

In addition to broader policy matters (see, for example, the extract above and Report of the Council on Tribunals, *Tribunals their Organisation and Independence* (August 1997)), much of the work of the Council on Tribunals involves (a) consultation with Government departments on primary legislation and on draft rules of procedure for tribunals and inquiries, and (b) monitoring the practice of tribunals within its supervisory jurisdiction.

The manner in which the Council is consulted on draft procedural rules for tribunals has, in the past, been a source of friction. In 1985, the Council indicated that it had received draft regulations from the DHSS only a week before the regulations were laid before Parliament and declared "such consultation verges on the farcical" (*Annual Report 1984–85*, H.C. 54, para. 2.4).

A code of practice on Government consultation with the Council was drawn up by the Council and circulated in 1982 by the Lord Chancellor and the Lord Advocate; revised codes of practice were circulated in 1986 and 1992 (for the text of the 1992 code, see *Annual Report of the Council on Tribunals 1991–92,* H.C. 316, App. I).

In the year ending July 31, 1997, members of the Council and its Scottish Committee (and, in a few instances, their staff) paid 147 visits to over 40 different types of tribunal. By means of such visits, the Council has the ability to provide long-term independent supervision of the work of a tribunal; so, for example, its annual reports reveal that every year since their inception, members of the Council or its Scottish Committee have visited a children's hearing. The extract below reflects other examples of the Scottish dimension of the supervisory role of the Council and some of the implications of devolution to Scotland as perceived by its Scottish Committee.

Not all the activities of the Council have a statutory basis. There is, for example, no statutory requirement for Government departments to consult the Council on primary legislation which may be within its terms of reference, and the Council has no specific statutory powers to investigate complaints concerning procedure at tribunals within its jurisdiction.

Annual Report of the Scottish Committee of the Council on Tribunals 1996–97, paras 1.2–1.6 and 1.45–1.52

Constitutional Change

1.2 Towards the end of the reporting year, the Committee was able to consider the outline proposals for constitutional change set out in the White Paper "Scotland's Parliament" and to make its initial thoughts available to Scottish Courts Administration. We arranged a special meeting of the Committee in July for this purpose.

1.3 There are many details yet to be resolved, and at this stage we have not been able to evaluate all of the implications which devolution proposals have for our area of responsibility. Our overriding recommendation, however, is that there will be a continuing need for an independent organisation responsible for overseeing tribunals in Scotland. This is in keeping with the principles outlined in the 1957 Report of the Committee on Administrative Tribunals and Enquiries (The Franks Report), the conclusions of which remain as valid now as they were then when the establishment of a Council on Tribunals was first proposed. The Franks Report dismissed the view that tribunals were part of the ordinary machinery of administration for which the Government must retain a close and continuing responsibility; rather, tribunals were properly to be regarded as independent organs, provided by Parliament for adjudication outside and independent of the Department concerned. The Franks Report acknowledged that there was a great variety, not only in tribunals themselves, but in their rules and procedures. In order to allow the application of general and consistent principles, Franks recommended that there should be a standing body whose advice would be sought on the establishment of new tribunals and which would keep under review the constitution and procedures of existing tribunals. Thus the Council on Tribunals and its Scottish Committee came into being, reporting not to the Prime Minister, as is the case with other arms of the machinery of Government, but to the Lord Chancellor and the Lord Advocate with their particular responsibilities for the oversight of the judiciary and other matters of adjudication. We believe that the continuation of such an independent "watch dog" organisation is particularly important if, as is suggested in the White Paper, a large measure of responsibility for the tribunal system in Scotland would be transferred to a Scottish Parliament.

1.4 In making the foregoing recommendation, however, we felt obliged to point out that in terms of our constitutive Act, the Tribunals and Inquiries Act 1992, we enjoyed extensive autonomous powers with regard to our supervision of the working of tribunals in Scotland. We drew attention to the existing harmonious relationship between the Committee and the Council on Tribunals and the two-way interflow of ideas engendered by the present arrangement whereby our Chairman and two other members are appointed to membership of the Council.

1.5 We also recommended that consideration be given to renaming the Committee "The Scottish Council on Tribunals" to give the public a truer perspective of our *de facto* position. Subsidiary recommendations were that we should report to the Scottish Parliament and that the schedule in the Act which lists the tribunals under the direct supervision of the Scottish Committee should be revised to take account of devolved legislative competence.

1.6 The Committee will be considering the terms of any Bill to be introduced to give effect to constitutional change and we will report our conclusions next year. . . .

Sex Offenders—A Ban On Working With Children

1.45 Towards the end of March 1997, the Committee was invited to offer comment on a consultation paper which was produced jointly by The Home Office and The Scottish Office Home Department entitled "Sex Offenders: A Ban on Working with Children". The proposal contained in the document envisaged enacting UK legislation in order to create a new offence where anyone who had convictions for certain sex offences sought to work with, or provide services to, children.

1.46 The Committee's interest lay in the proposals relating to the individual's appeal rights. The Council's Annual Report covers the issues relating to this topic in finer detail, but suffice it to say that the Committee believes that, in the fundamental interest of justice, it would clearly be appropriate for the offender to have a right of appeal against any ban being placed on him. The Committee is fully supportive of the view that all such appeals should be handled within the criminal court system, rather than through any other forum such as a tribunal or The Parole Board. These views have been conveyed to the Departments.

NHS Discipline Committees

1.47 In last year's Report, we expressed some concern in relation to the new Regulations which would see the abolition of NHS Service Committees and their replacement by newly established NHS Discipline Committees. The NHS (Service Committees and Tribunal) (Scotland) Regulations which invoked this change came into effect on 1 April 1996.

1.48 Throughout the course of the reporting period. our Secretariat has continued to liaise with the Scottish Health Boards and The Scottish Office Health Department in order to monitor the progress of the change. We formed the view that, whilst cases were continuing to be heard under the old procedures in respect of complaints made prior to the enactment of the new Regulations, there was little action taking place under the new Regulations. Although we appreciated that there would be a residue of cases to be dealt with under the old Regulations, we had expected a flow of cases under the new procedures. We wondered whether, in line with the general thrust of the new procedures, complaints made by, or on behalf of, patients were now being dealt with at a local level without the need for recourse to a disciplinary hearing.

1.49 However in March and June 1997, we were made aware of the first two Discipline Committee hearings to take place in Scotland under the new Regulations and we made arrangements to visit both hearings which concerned complaints against dental practitioners.

1.50 We have to report that our initial impressions are not wholly favourable. In the first case, the tribunal judged that the referral did not meet the criteria set out in the Regulations and would have to be abandoned as out of time. In the second case, the tribunal members had obvious difficulty in interpreting the complexity of the Regulations. The Committee accepts that the procedure is novel and that the lack of cases has not yet permitted Discipline Committees to become familiar with the new Regulations. We appreciate that the new system will take time to bed down properly. We shall make further visits when possible to the new NHS Discipline Committees.

Immigration Appeals

1.51 In earlier years' Reports, we have expressed our concerns that the second stage appeal, from an Immigration Adjudicator to the Immigration Tribunal, could only be heard in London. This was an obvious burden of expense and inconvenience to appellants living in Scotland.

1.52 Last year we were pleased to note that hearings of the second stage appeal would commence in Glasgow. Arrangements were made for a Committee member to attend one of the first hearings of the Tribunal in order to observe the proceedings. Whilst the Committee recognised the professional manner in which the Tribunal operated, some disappointment has to be expressed at the apparent lack of training which is provided to the lay wing members, particularly in the complicated area of immigration law of which they are expected to have some knowledge.

The Council on Tribunals and its Scottish Committee have been specified as cross-border public authorities for the purposes of the Scotland Act 1998: see S.I. 1999 No. 1319.

CHAPTER 7

THE EUROPEAN DIMENSION

European Community law and the European Convention on Human Rights create legal rights which are enforceable by Scottish litigants. These two distinct bodies of law each have a quite different status in Scotland. However, they have an important common feature. Their authoritative interpretation, and in some instances their enforcement, fall within the jurisdiction of bodies outside the United Kingdom. This is the European dimension of the Scottish legal system, which is considered below.

I. EUROPEAN COMMUNITY LAW

A. INTRODUCTION

The United Kingdom is a member of the European Union. The European Union was established by the Maastricht Treaty on European Union with effect from November 1, 1993, and its structure is maintained and further developed by the Treaty of Amsterdam 1997. The European Union has three bases. The first is the three European Communities, each previously established by a separate Treaty: the Steel Community (ECSC), which came into operation in 1952, the European Economic Community (EEC) and the European Atomic Energy Community (EURATOM), both of which came into operation in 1958. Since then the Treaties establishing the three Communities have been amended by later treaties, including the Treaty of Amsterdam which renumbers Articles of the E.C. Treaty (the revised numbering is given in square brackets below). The United Kingdom became a member of the three Communities in 1973. The second basis is the provisions in the Maastricht Treaty on a common foreign and security policy; the third basis is the provisions in the same Treaty on police and judicial co-operation in the fields of criminal matters. So, the European Union encompasses the original three Communities and a wider degree of co-operation between the governments of the Member States for which the second and third bases provide. In addition to the United Kingdom there are, at present, 14 other Member States: France, Germany, Italy, Belgium, the Netherlands, Luxembourg, Denmark, Ireland, Greece, Spain, Portugal, Austria, Sweden and Finland. Norway, Iceland and Lichtenstein are members of the European Economic Area; in consequence, they are participants in the single market of the European Community for the free movement of goods, persons, services and capital, and most of the economic and social legislation of the European Community applies to them. However, these countries do not participate directly in the institutions of the European Community.

There are four principal institutions of the European Union. These institutions, and certain others, have functions with respect to the three European Communities and also the other functions of the European Union. The functions and powers differ between the three European Communities and between the European Communities and the other functions of the European Union. The functions and powers of these European institutions described here are essentially those that are applicable to the European Community.

The Council of Ministers—now designated the Council of the European Union (Council Decision 93/591 [1993] O.J. L281/18)—is the principal political organ of the Communities; in many cases it acts by qualified majority with weighted voting. Supported by working parties of Commission officials and civil servants from the Member States, it makes the final decisions on Community policies and formally adopts most Community legislation of general application. Representatives of the governments of each Member State—normally government Ministers—sit on the Council; each Member State in turn takes the Presidency of the Council for a period of six months.

The Commission has a range of administrative functions. It formulates Community policies and, once they have been adopted, supervises their implementation. After extensive consultation, it initiates and drafts most Community legislative proposals and has a direct treaty and also delegated competence to enact some legislation. It also has important duties, with corresponding powers, in monitoring compliance with, and enforcement of, Community law.

The Commission consists of 20 Commissioners, who, subject to their approval by the European Parliament (E.C. Treaty, Art. 158), are appointed by the governments of Member States for renewable five-year terms. Commissioners must be nationals of Member States, with at least one but no more than two being nationals of each Member State. Commissioners do not act as representatives of their states, but are required to carry out their functions independently and in the general interest of the Communities. Each Commissioner is given responsibility for specific areas of Community activity, but the Commission takes its decisions collectively. In addition, the Heads of State and Government of the Member States meet regularly as the European Council, with the President of the Commission of the Communities in attendance. Technically, the European Council is not a Community institution, but in some circumstances its meetings may be recognised as meetings of the Council of Ministers (Single European Act 1986 (Cm. 372), Art. 2; Maastricht Treaty on European Union, Art. D; E.C. Treaty, Art. 109(j)(4)).

The European Parliament has 626 members who are directly elected from the Member States, although not by a uniform electoral method. The members form groups based on political stance and not national origin. The European Parliament sits in Strasbourg and Brussels in plenary session but much of its work is done in committees. When first established it was primarily an advisory body, but it has acquired an increasingly important role in the Community legislative and policy process (see E.C. Treaty, Arts 138 and 189).

The Court of Justice interprets, and ensures compliance with, Community law. Its composition, jurisdiction and procedure are considered below.

Other important Community institutions include the European Council, the Economic and Social Committee, which serves both the E.C. and EURATOM and has an advisory role in the Community legislative process, and the Court of Auditors, which was established in 1977 to examine the finances and financial management of the Community, the European Central Bank and the Committee of the Regions.

The principal sources of the law of the European Communities are (a) the treaties establishing the Communities and other related treaties, (b) legislation adopted by the Community institutions in the form of regulations, directives and decisions, (c) the case law of the Court of Justice. Community law has important characteristics. It prevails over inconsistent national law of the Member States (*e.g.* Case 6/64, *Costa v. ENEL* [1964] E.C.R. 585), and much of it is directly effective, that is, it creates rights and duties which may be enforced in the courts and tribunals of Member States; and, even where it is not directly effective, an individual who is adversely affected by the failure of a Member State to implement Community legislation may be entitled to claim compensation from that state (Cases C-6 and 9/90 *Francovich and Bonifaci v. Italy* [1991] E.C.R. 1–5357).

The status of European Community law in Scotland was established by the European Communities Act, which was passed by the U.K. Parliament in 1972. By virtue of that legislation, directly effective Community law was recognised as law in the United Kingdom and became enforceable before U.K. courts and tribunals (s. 2; for some of the difficulties which may arise from the provision see *Garden Cottage Foods Ltd v. Milk Marketing Board* [1984] A.C. 130). The Act also recognised the jurisdiction of the Court of Justice of the Communities to interpret and enforce Community law, and its decisions became binding on U.K. courts and tribunals (ss. 2 and 3).

B. THE COURT OF JUSTICE OF THE COMMUNITIES

1. Composition

The membership of the Court of Justice consists of 15 judges and a permanent establishment of eight Advocates General (E.C. Treaty, Art. 166 [222]). The judges and Advocates General are appointed by common accord of the governments of Member States from "persons whose independence is beyond doubt and who possess the qualifications required for appointment to the highest judicial offices in their respective countries or who are jurisconsults of recognised competence" (Art. 167 [223]). These qualifications have allowed not only judges and private practitioners to be appointed, but also lawyers who have pursued academic and political careers.

In practice, there is a judge appointed from each Member State. The appointments are for renewable six-year terms and there is no retirement age. The judges elect a President of the Court from amongst their number for a three-year renewable term.

While they are members of the Court of Justice its judges are not permitted to hold any political or governmental appointments. They are not allowed to take any other employment unless an exemption is granted by the Council of

Ministers, and after they cease to be members of the Court they must "behave with discretion" in accepting appointments (Art. 4, Statute of the Court). A judge may be dismissed if, in the unanimous opinion of the other judges and Advocates General, "he no longer fulfils the requisite conditions or meets the obligations arising from his office" (*ibid.* Art. 6). No judge has been dismissed.

The Advocates General enjoy the same status as the judges, and the same provisions regarding appointment, qualifications, tenure and removal from office apply to them. The role of the Advocate General is to assist the Court by delivering impartial, independent and reasoned opinions on the cases coming before it. The opinion of the Advocate General is not binding on the Court, but it is carefully considered before the judgment is delivered and it is published with the judgment in the official report of the case.

A Court of First Instance, attached to the Court of Justice, was established in 1989, to address the volume of cases coming before the Court of Justice (E.C. Treaty, Art. 168a [225]; Council Decision (ECSC, EEC, Euratom) 88/591; for the 1998 statistics of cases before the Court of Justice and the Court of First Instance, see below).

The Court of First Instance has 15 judges who are appointed for renewable six-year terms by common accord of the governments of the Member States from "persons whose independence is beyond doubt and who possess the ability required for appointment to judicial office" (E.C. Treaty, Art. 168a(3) [225(3)]; the Statute of the Court of Justice is applied to the appointments). The judges elect a President of the Court from their number for a renewable three-year term. The Court of First Instance sits in Chambers of three or five judges, but may sit as a full court. No Advocates General are permanently allocated to the Court, but the duties of Advocate General are performed, in a limited number of cases, by one of the judges.

The jurisdiction of the Court of First Instance was initially limited to staff cases arising under the E.C. and Euratom Treaties, actions brought under the ECSC Treaty against the Commission by undertakings in respect of levies, production, prices and competition (ECSC Treaty, Arts 33 and 35), and actions under E.C. Treaty, Arts 173 [230], 175 [232] (in respect of competition rules) and 178 [235] (these Articles are considered below) (Council Decision 88/591, Art. 3); from 1993, its jurisdiction was extended to all direct actions (see below). Questions referred for a preliminary ruling under E.C. Treaty, Art. 177 [234] (see below) are expressly excluded from the jurisdiction of the Court of First Instance (E.C. Treaty, Art. 168a(1) [225]). There is a right of appeal, on points of law only, from the Court of First Instance to the Court of Justice (*ibid.*).

2. Jurisdiction

The jurisdiction of the Court of Justice rests primarily on the treaties establishing the three Communities. Most cases arise under the E.C. Treaty and the Court's jurisdiction under the treaty may be divided into: (a) references for preliminary rulings on questions of Community law from the courts and tribunals of Member States, and (b) direct actions.

(A) Preliminary Rulings

E.C. Treaty, Art. 177 [234]

> "177—(1) The Court of Justice shall have jurisdiction to give preliminary rulings concerning:
> (a) the interpretation of this Treaty;
> (b) the validity and interpretation of acts of the institutions of the Community [and of the ECB];
> (c) the interpretation of the statutes of bodies established by an act of the Council, where those statutes so provide.
>
> (2) Where such a question is raised before any court or tribunal of a Member State, that court or tribunal may, if it considers that a decision on the question is necessary to enable it to give judgment, request the Court of Justice to give a ruling thereon.
> (3) Where any such question is raised in a case pending before a court or tribunal of a Member State, against whose decisions there is no judicial remedy under national law, that court or tribunal shall bring the matter before the Court of Justice."

Many rights and duties in Community law are determined by the courts and tribunals of Member States. Article 177 [234] provides a mechanism for ensuring that Community law is interpreted in a uniform manner throughout the Community. It has also been used by the Court of Justice to develop important Community law principles such as the supremacy of Community law over national law, the direct effect of Community law and the liability of Member States for breach of Community law, for example a failure in certain circumstances to implement a directive.

In theory, and to a large extent in practice, the Court of Justice and the national court or tribunal have distinct roles under Article 177 [234]. The national court or tribunal refers a question of Community law to the Court of Justice for a preliminary ruling; the Court of Justice gives the preliminary ruling which, subject to any subsequent ruling it may give, is binding on the national court or tribunal making the reference, and on other national courts or tribunals which have jurisdiction in the case (*e.g.* Case 29/68 *Milchkontor v. Hauptzollamt Saarbrucken* [1969] E.C.R. 165); the national court or tribunal then decides the case, applying the preliminary ruling on the question of Community law, to the extent that the question of Community law remains applicable to its determination. These distinct roles permeate the jurisprudence of the Court of Justice on Article 177 [234]. The Court determines the scope of Article 177 [234] and the limits of the discretion within it for national courts and tribunals, but largely avoids regulating the exercise of that discretion.

Article 177(1) [234(1)] sets out the instruments in respect of which the Court of Justice has jurisdiction to give rulings. Article 177(1)(b) [234(1)(b)] clearly encompasses regulations, directives and decisions, but it has been liberally interpreted by the Court to include Association agreements between the Community and non-Member States (Case 181/73 *Haegeman v. Belgium* [1974] E.C.R. 449) and GATT (*e.g.* Cases 267–9/81 *SPI* [1983] E.C.R. 801), although other instruments have been excluded (Case 44/84 *Hurd v. Jones* [1986] E.C.R. 29).

The jurisdiction of the Court under Article 177(1)(b) [234(1)(b)] extends to rulings on both the validity and interpretation of instruments. The Court has held that, while a national court or tribunal may seek a preliminary ruling on the validity of a Community instrument, the Court has exclusive jurisdiction over questions of validity and it is not competent for national courts or tribunals to hold Community instruments to be invalid: Case 314/85 *Firma Foto-Frost v. Hauptzollamt Lubeck-Ost* [1988] 3 C.M.L.R. 57. On questions of interpretation, the Court will normally avoid giving preliminary rulings on questions of national law or the compatibility of national law with Community law (*e.g.* Case 93/75 *Alderblum* [1975] E.C.R. 2147; Case 34/79 *R. v. Henn and Darby* [1979] E.C.R. 3795; *cf.* Case 244178 *Union Laitiere Normande v. French Dairy Farmers Ltd* [1979] E.C.R. 2663). If the question referred to the Court would involve the interpretation of national law or a ruling on whether a national law or administrative act is contrary to Community law, the Court may well reformulate the question as an abstract question of Community law and give its preliminary ruling on the reformulated question (*e.g.* Case 28/70 *Otto Witt* [1970] E.C.R. 1021; Case 14/86 *Pretore di Salo v. X* [1987] E.C.R. 2545).

Article 177(2) [234(2)] empowers any national court or tribunal to refer questions of Community law for a preliminary ruling. Whether a body is a court or tribunal for the purposes of Article 177(2) [234(2)] is a matter of Community law, and the fact that it is not recognised as a court or tribunal in national law is not decisive (*e.g.* Case 61/65 *Vaasen* [1966] E.C.R. 261). For a body to be competent to refer a question under Article 177(2) [234(2)] the Court of Justice requires it to be one which exercises judicial functions, although these have not been closely defined (*e.g.* Case 36173 *Nederlandse Spoorwegen* [1973] E.C.R. 1299; Case 65/77 *Razanatsimba* [1977] E.C.R. 2229; Case 246/80 *Broekmeulen v. Huisarts Registratie Commissie* [1981] E.C.R. 2311; *cf.* Case 138/80 *Borker* [1980] E.C.R. 1975).

Before a national court or tribunal makes a reference it must consider that a preliminary ruling on the question of Community law is "necessary to enable it to give judgment" (Art. 177(2) [234(2)] and, by implication, Art. 177(3) [234(3)]). This is a matter for the national court or tribunal and is not reviewable by the Court of Justice (*e.g.* Case 6/64 *Costa v. ENEL* [1964] E.C.R. 585; Case 13/68 *Salgoil SpA v. Italy* [1968] E.C.R. 453; Case 98/85 *Bertini v. Regione Lazio* [1986] E.C.R. 1885). However, the Court of Justice has refused to give preliminary rulings on questions which are manifestly irrelevant or hypothetical (*e.g.* Case 244/80 *Foglia v. Novello (No. 2)* [1981] E.C.R. 3045; *cf.* Case 232/82 *Baccini v. Office National De L'Emploi* [1983] E.C.R. 583), or which seek abstract advisory opinions (Case 149/82 *Robards v. Insurance Officer* [1983] E.C.R. 171).

Even where a national court or tribunal within Article 177(2) [234(2)] considers that a decision on a question of Community law is necessary to enable it to give judgment, it still has a discretion as to whether to refer the question to the Court of Justice for a preliminary ruling. However, here the distinction between the operation of the Community and national legal systems is less clearly defined. In Community law any court or tribunal may refer a question to the Court of Justice, but national law may impose constraints on its power to do so. So, in Scots law an Article 177 [234] ruling is binding not only on the national court or tribunal which made the reference and other courts and tribunals with jurisdiction in the case, but on all courts and tribunals (European Communities Act 1972, s. 3) (but see further below). Again, a decision to refer may be the subject of an appeal to a superior national court or tribunal. A Scottish illustration is *Wither v. Cowie* 1990 S.C.C.R. 741 where there was an appeal to the High Court of Justiciary against the decision of a sheriff to seek an Article 177 [234] preliminary ruling (see further [1992] 2 C.M.L.R. 493; 1994 S.L.T. 363). In such circumstances, the Court of Justice may suspend consideration of the reference pending the outcome of the appeal (*e.g.* Case 31/68 *Chanel v. Cepeha* [1970] E.C.R. 403). However, the Court will give a ruling on the reference unless it is withdrawn by the court or tribunal which made it, or it is quashed on appeal by another national court or tribunal (Case 106/77 *Simmenthal* [1978] E.C.R. 629).

The operation of precedent is another area where national law may impose constraints on the discretion of a court or tribunal to refer a question of Community law for a preliminary ruling (see *Rheinmuhlen–Dusseldorf*, below).

Despite these various considerations, Article 177 [234] is widely used by national courts and tribunals falling within Article 177(2) [234(2)]. In Scotland, there have been references for preliminary rulings from the Court of Session (Case 197/86 *Brown v. Secretary of State for Scotland* [1988] E.C.R. 5445) and the sheriff court (*Wither v. Cowie* 1990 S.C.C.R. 741; [1992] 2 C.M.L.R. 493). There have been many judgments on references to the European Court from English courts within Article 177(2) [234(2)], ranging from the Court of Appeal to VAT tribunals and magistrates' courts.

National courts and tribunals falling within Article 177(3) [234(3)], unlike those within Article 177(2) [234(2)], are obliged to refer questions of Community law for a preliminary ruling by the Court of Justice. However, the obligation does not arise if the Community law question is not relevant to the case before the national court, or it involves a provision which has already been interpreted by the Court of Justice, or the correct application of Community law is obvious (Case 238/81 *C.I.L.F.I.T. Srl v. Ministro della Santina* [1982] E.C.R. 3415). Within the Scottish legal system, the courts obliged to make a reference under Article 177(3) would include both the House of Lords and the High Court of Justiciary. For examples of Article 177 [234] references by the High Court see Case 241/83 *Mehlich and Gewiese v. Mackenzie* [1984] E.C.R. 817; 1984 S.L.T. 449 (and 1985 S.L.T. (News) 53) and Case C-370/88 *Walkingshaw v. Marshall* [1990] 1 E.C.R. 4071.

To some extent the obligation to refer depends on the nature of the judicial remedy available and the nature of the action itself. There may be an obligation to refer a question of Community law which arises before a court or tribunal where the remedy against its decision is merely discretionary. On the other hand, the Court of Justice has held that where a question of Community law arises in interlocutory proceedings, in which the decision of the court is final, there is no obligation to refer if the point can be raised again in the main action (Case 107/76 *Hoffmann-La Roche v. Centrafarm* [1977] E.C.R. 957; Cases 35–36/82

Elestina Morson & Sewradjie Jhanjan v. Netherlands [1983] 2 C.M.L.R. 221; *cf. Portsmouth City Council v. Richards* [1989] 1 C.M.L.R. 673, CA).

Finally, a national court or tribunal may refer a question of Community law to the Court of Justice again where it has difficulty in understanding the initial preliminary ruling, or in applying it (*e.g.* Case 28167 *Molkerei-Zentrale* [1968] E.C.R. 143), or when a new question of law arises or new factors have been submitted which might lead to a different ruling, but not merely for the purpose of challenging the initial ruling (Case 69/85 *Wunsche v. Germany* [1986] E.C.R. 947). The possibility of making a second reference would avoid most of the difficulties which might be created by the European Communities Act 1972, s. 3.

The importance of Article 177 [234] for the uniform application of Community law is frequently emphasised by the Court of Justice. The Court did so in *Rheinmuhlen–Dusseldorf*, where it also examined the effect of precedent on the capacity of a court or tribunal to make a reference.

***Rheinmuhlen–Dusseldorf* Cases 146 & 166/73 [1974] E.C.R. 33, 139**

> [Judgment of the Court of Justice] "Article 177 is essential for the preservation of the Community character of the law established by the Treaty and has the object of ensuring that in all circumstances this law is the same in all States of the Community.
>
> Whilst it thus aims to avoid divergences in the interpretation of Community law which the national courts have to apply, it likewise tends to ensure this application by making available to the national judge a means of eliminating difficulties which may be occasioned by the requirement of giving Community law its full effect within the framework of the judicial systems of the Member States.
>
> Consequently any gap in the system so organised could undermine the effectiveness of the provisions of the Treaty and of the secondary Community law.
>
> The provisions of Article 177, which enable every national court or tribunal without distinction to refer a case to the Court for a preliminary ruling when it considers that a decision on the question is necessary to enable it to give judgment, must be seen in this light.
>
> The provisions of Article 177 are absolutely binding on the national judge and, in so far as the second paragraph is concerned, enable him to refer a case to the Court of Justice for a preliminary ruling on interpretation or validity.
>
> This Article gives national courts the power and, where appropriate, imposes on them the obligation to refer a case for a preliminary ruling, as soon as the judge perceives either of his own motion or at the request of the parties that the litigation depends on a point referred to in the first paragraph of Article 177.
>
> It follows that national courts have the widest discretion in referring matters to the Court of Justice if they consider that a case pending before them raises questions involving interpretation, or consideration of the validity, of provisions of Community law, necessitating a decision on their part.

It follows from these factors that a rule of national law whereby a court is bound on points of law by the rulings of a superior court cannot deprive the inferior courts of their power to refer to the Court questions of interpretation of Community law involving such rulings.

It would be otherwise if the questions put by the inferior court were substantially the same as questions already put by the superior court.

On the other hand the inferior court must be free, if it considers that the ruling on law made by the superior court could lead it to give a judgment contrary to Community law, to refer to the Court questions which concern it.

If inferior courts were bound without being able to refer matters to the Court, the jurisdiction of the latter to give preliminary rulings and the application of Community law at all levels of the judicial systems of the Member States would be compromised.

The reply must therefore be that the existence of a rule of domestic law whereby a court is bound on points of law by the rulings of the court superior to it cannot of itself take away the power provided for by Article 177 of referring cases to the Court."

Before a national court or tribunal makes a reference, it must consider that a ruling on the question of Community law is "necessary to enable it to give judgment", and unless Article 177(3) [234(3)] applies, it must also decide whether to exercise its discretion to refer the question. In *Bulmer v. Bollinger*, Lord Denning offered "guidelines" on these matters to English courts and tribunals; but see also *R. v. Stock Exchange, ex p. Else* [1993] 1 All E.R. 420.

***H.P. Bulmer Ltd v. J. Bollinger S.A.* [1974] Ch. 401**

Lord Denning, M.R.:

"*(1) Guidelines as to whether a decision is necessary*

(i) *The point must be conclusive*. The English court has to consider whether 'a decision of the question is necessary to enable it to give judgment'. That means judgment in the very case which is before the court. The judge must have got to the stage when he says to himself: 'This clause of the treaty is capable of two or more meanings. If it means this, I give judgment for the plaintiff. If it means that, I give judgment for the defendant.' In short, the point must be such that, whichever way the point is decided, it is conclusive of the case. Nothing more remains but to give judgment . . .

(ii) *Previous ruling*. In some cases, however, it may be found that the same point—or substantially the same point—has already been decided by the European Court in a previous case. In that event it is not necessary for the English court to decide it. It can follow the previous decision without troubling the European Court. But, as I have said, the European Court is not bound by its previous decisions. So if the English court thinks that a previous decision of the European Court may have been wrong—or if there are new factors which ought to be brought to the notice of the European Court—the English court may consider it necessary to re-submit the point to the European Court. In that event, the European Court will consider the point again . . .

(iii) *Acte claire*. In other cases the English court may consider the point is reasonably clear and free from doubt. In that event there is no need to interpret the treaty but only to apply it, and that is the task of the English court . . .

(iv) *Decide the facts first*. It is to be noticed, too, that the word is 'necessary'. This is much stronger than 'desirable' or 'convenient'. There are some cases where the point, if decided one way, would shorten the trial greatly. But, if decided the other way, it would mean that the trial would have to go its full length. In such a case it might be 'convenient' or 'desirable' to take it as a preliminary point because it might save much time and expense. But it would not be 'necessary' at that stage. When the facts were investigated, it might turn out to have been quite unnecessary. The case would be determined on another ground altogether. As a rule you cannot tell whether it is necessary to decide a point until all the facts are ascertained. So in general it is best to decide the facts first.

(2) Guidelines as to the exercise of discretion

Assuming that the condition about 'necessary' is fulfilled, there remains the matter of discretion . . . The English court has a discretion either to decide the point itself or to refer it to the European Court. The national courts of the various member countries have had to consider how to exercise this discretion. The cases show that they have taken into account such matters as the following.

(i) *The time to get a ruling*. The length of time which may elapse before a ruling can be obtained from the European Court. This may take months and months. The lawyers have to prepare their briefs; the advocate general has to prepare his submissions; the case has to be argued; the court has to give its decision. The average length of time at present seems to be between six and nine months. Meanwhile, the whole action in the English court is stayed until the ruling is obtained. This may be very unfortunate, especially in a case where an injunction is sought or there are other reasons for expedition. This was very much in the mind of the German Court of Appeal in Frankfurt in *Re Export of Oat Flakes*. It is said that it was important 'to prevent undue protraction of both the proceedings before the European Court and trial before the national courts'. On that ground it decided a point of interpretation itself, rather than submit it to the European Court.

(ii) *Do not overload the Court*. The importance of not overwhelming the European Court by reference to it. If it were overloaded, it could not get through its work . . .

(iii) *Formulate the question clearly*. It must be a question of interpretation only of the treaty. It must not be mixed up with the facts. It is the task of the national courts to find the facts and apply the treaty. The European Court must not take that task on themselves. In fairness to them, it is desirable to find the facts and state them clearly before referring the question . . . In any case, the task of interpretation is better done with the facts in mind rather than in ignorance of them.

(iv) *Difficulty and importance*. Unless the point is really difficult and important, it would seem better for the English judge to decide it himself.

For in so doing, much delay and expense will be saved. So far the English judges have not shirked their responsibilities . . .

(v) *Expense*. The expense to the parties of getting a ruling from the European Court . . . On a request for interpretation, the European Court does not as a rule award costs, and for a simple reason. It does not decide the case. It only gives advice on the meaning of the treaty. If either party wishes to get the costs of the reference, he must get it from the English court, when it eventually decides the case.

(vi) *Wishes of the parties*. If both parties want the point to be referred to the European Court, the English court should have regard to their wishes, but it should not give them undue weight. The English court should hesitate before making a reference against the wishes of one of the parties, seeing the expense and delay which it involves."

In a separate judgment, with which Stamp L.J. concurred, Stephenson L.J. refrained from adopting the detailed guidelines in Lord Denning's judgment. In any event, as we have seen, in Community law such guidelines are not binding on inferior courts and tribunals.

In the main, Lord Denning's guidelines tend to discourage Article 177 [234] references. The House of Lords has adopted a more circumspect approach by indicating that courts and tribunals should be cautious in assuming no question of interpretation is raised by a Community legislative text and that a reference should not be made (*Henn and Darby v. DPP* [1981] A.C. 850; see also the observation of Bingham J. in *Customs and Excise Commissioners v. ApS Samex* [1983] 1 All E.R. 1042, 1055). Certainly, English courts, including the Court of Appeal, have made substantial errors in assuming that a point of Community law is free from doubt (*e.g. Schorsch Meier v. Hennin* [1975] Q.B. 416; *cf. Miliangos v. George Frank (Textiles) Ltd* [1976] A.C. 443, 465; *R. v. Secchi* [1975] 1 C.M.L.R. 383).

On the other hand, the delay in obtaining preliminary rulings from the Court of Justice is an important consideration. In criminal cases it should normally, amongst other factors, discourage the making of a reference before the facts have been ascertained, so that the court is satisfied that the accused will not be acquitted on the facts or that the question of Community law is still relevant once the facts have been established (*Henn and Darby v. DPP*, above; *R. v. Plymouth Justices, ex p. Rogers* [1982] Q.B. 863). On the other hand, where there is no serious dispute over the facts, particularly in large commercial cases, time and expense may be saved by making a reference at an early stage in the proceedings, and the same may be true when there is a challenge to the validity of a Community legislative instrument on which the proceedings will turn (see, *e.g.*, *Polydor Ltd v. Harlequin Records Shops Ltd* [1980] 2 C.M.L.R. 413, CA, Case 270/80 [1982] E.C.R. 329; *Lord Bethell v. Sabena* [1983] 3 C.M.L.R. 1).

The risk of overloading the Court of Justice is not, though, a factor which should greatly influence a court or tribunal in deciding whether to make a reference. Pennycuick V.-C. commented: "I doubt whether that is a legitimate consideration" (*Van Duyn v. Home Office* [1974] 1 W.L.R. 1107, 1116).

Although Lord Denning's guidelines may be criticised, some of them were adopted by Lord Cameron in the Court of Session.

***Prince v. Secretary of State for Scotland* 1985 S.L.T. 74**

Lord Cameron:

"I have no difficulty in appreciating the force of [the] argument that a reference to the European Court can competently be made when it appears that it may be necessary to do so at any appropriate stage of a litigation. Having regard however to our Scottish system of pleading, I would not normally be persuaded that such a necessity, with whatever degree of urgency that word be interpreted, should be held to arise until the pleadings have been adjusted and the real questions in dispute focused on the pleadings. I am fortified in this view of the matter by reference to the judgment of Lord Denning in the case of *Bulmer v. Bollinger* . . .

In particular, I should find it difficult to make such a reference where preliminary issues of title, competency and relevancy remained unresolved. Neither this Court nor the European Court exists for the purpose of determining academic questions and, as both counsel pointed out, as the work-load of the European Court is both heavy and increasing, it is the more desirable that the Court should not be subjected to additions to its heavy burdens unless such addition is necessary. In the present case [counsel] for the defenders . . . indicated that he proposed to support all his preliminary pleas: I am in no position at this stage in the proceedings to assess the value or effect of these pleas when the arguments thereon have been fully deployed on adjusted pleadings. Thus, it may well be that neither occasion nor necessity for a reference will in this case ever arise. I certainly cannot prejudge the argument on these pleas. It is perhaps only right that I should add that in any event I would not accept or approve either of the questions proposed for reference as suitably drafted to raise the precise questions which the pursuers appear to wish to present."

In *Wither v. Cowie* 1990 S.C.C.R. 741, the sheriff adopted Lord Denning's guidelines in deciding to make an Article 177 [234] reference, and in the appeal against the decision to refer this approach was accepted by the High Court. In *Watt v. Secretary of State for Scotland* [1991] 3 C.M.L.R. 429, a decision by Lord Weir not to make an Article 177 [234] reference also appears to have been derived from the guidelines. Lord Weir observed: "In my view when a challenge is made to the lawfulness of a matter of this kind based as it is on legislation by the Parliament of the United Kingdom, the grounds should appear to be cogent. In this case I am not satisfied that this test has been passed and indeed having regard to the decisions of the European Court to which I have been referred, I consider that the law of this subject is tolerably clear".

Aspects of Denning guidelines have also been adopted in other Scottish cases (*e.g. Orru v H.M. Advocate*, 1998 S.C.C.R. 59; *Walter Stevenson v. Lord Advocate* (unreported) OH July 24, 1997; *Westwater v. Thomson*, 1992 S.C.C.R. 624).

(B) Direct Actions

The four major categories of action which may be brought directly before the Court of Justice are (a) actions against Member States, (b) actions against Community institutions, (c) actions relating to the non-contractual liability of the

Communities, and (d) staff cases. The volume of cases in some of these categories, particularly staff cases, coming before the Court of Justice has been significantly reduced as a result of the establishment of the Court of First Instance (see above).

The Commission (Art. 169 [226]) or another Member State (Art. 170 [227]) may bring a direct action against a Member State which fails to comply with Community law. Individuals and companies have no *locus standi* to bring such an action before the Court of Justice but, if the state is in breach of directly effective Community law, they would have a remedy before a national court. Before one Member State brings an action against another, the issue must first be referred to the Commission. Virtually all direct actions against Member States are brought by the Commission. Where the Commission considers there has been a breach of Community law it initially indicates this to the Member States and invites the State to submit its observations. If necessary, the Commission then delivers a reasoned opinion on the breach of Community law and requires the Member State to comply within a specified period. If the Member State fails to do so, the Commission may proceed to the Court of Justice. There the case is decided on the terms of the Commission's reasoned opinion and on the facts as they were at the time it was issued. Most of them do not proceed to judgment because the respondent state normally either complies with Community law or reaches a compromise with the Commission. Where the Court finds against a Member State, the State must take the necessary measures to comply with the judgment (Art. 171 [228]). Most states do comply, but there are instances where they have been extremely dilatory in doing so; the Court may impose financial penalties on non-compliant states.

Direct actions may be brought to challenge the legality of certain acts of the Council of Ministers and of the Commission (Art. 173 [230]); they are subject to a two-month limitation period. Any act which has legal effect may be challenged (*e.g.* Case 22/70 *Commission v. Council* [1971] E.C.R. 263), but on four grounds only: lack of competence, infringement of an essential procedural requirement, infringement of the E.C. Treaty or of any rule of law relating to its application, or misuse of powers. Where, contrary to the E.C. Treaty, the Council or Commission fail to act, this can also be challenged (Art. 175 [232]).

A Member State, the Council, the Commission and, for the purpose of protecting their powers, the European Parliament and the Court of Auditors may proceed under Article 173 [230]; a Member State or any Community institution may bring an action under Article 175 [232]. Individuals and companies may also bring actions under these Articles 173 and 175 [230 and 232], but only in very limited circumstances which tend to be restrictively interpreted by the Court (*e.g.* Case 246/81 *Lord Bethell v. E.C. Commission* [1982] 3 C.M.L.R. 300). The legality of regulations adopted by the Council or the Commission may also be challenged indirectly. Any party, including an individual or a company, may challenge the applicability of a regulation which is in issue in proceedings before the Court (Art. 184 [241]). The regulation may only be challenged on the grounds specified in Article 173 [230], but the limitation period laid down in that Article does not apply.

The Court also has jurisdiction in actions concerning the non-contractual liability of the Communities (*e.g.* E.C. Treaty, Art. 178 [235]). Relatively few such actions are brought and they are rarely successful. The Court imposes procedural requirements which tend to inhibit these actions. For example, before proceeding in the Court of Justice, a litigant may first have to seek a remedy in the courts of a Member State. The Court frequently requires this where the alleged liability arises out of a Community scheme which is jointly administered by a Community institution and a Member State (*e.g.* Cases 67–85/75 *Cotelle v. Commission* [1976] E.C.R. 391). The Court also adopts a restrictive approach to "the general principles common to the laws of Member States" (Art. 215 [288]) which is the basis of the law governing the non-contractual liability of the Communities. It has, for example, construed rather narrowly the liability of the Communities for the acts and omissions of its servants (*e.g.* Case 9/69 *Sayag v. Leduc* [1969] E.C.R. 329).

Finally, the Court has jurisdiction to hear actions brought against Community institutions by their employees in respect of their rights and status as laid down in staff regulations (*e.g.* E.C. Treaty, Art. 179 [236]). These "staff cases" represent a large proportion of the direct actions coming before the Court.

Table 7.1

Statistics of cases before the Court of Justice and the Court of First Instance, 1998

Proceedings of the Court of Justice General proceedings		
Completed cases	374	(420)
New cases	485	
Cases pending	664	(748)
Nature of proceedings in completed cases		
References for a preliminary ruling	204	(246)
Direct actions	132	(136)
Appeals	36	(36)
Opinions	—	—
Special forms of procedure	2	(2)
Total	374	(420)
Proceedings of the Court of First Instance General proceedings		
Completed cases	279	(348)
New cases	238	
Cases pending	569	(1007)
Nature of proceedings in completed cases		
Article 173 of the E.C. Treaty	99	(120)
Article 175 of the E.C. Treaty	8	(8)
Article 178 of the E.C. Treaty	29	(64)
Article 33 of the ECSC Treaty	2	(2)
Article 35 of the ECSC Treaty	1	(1)
Staff regulations	109	(119)
Special forms of procedure	27	(29)
Total	279	(349)

(Figures in brackets are the total number of cases, disregarding joined cases; "special forms of procedure" include procedural actions.)
(Source: Court of Justice website.)

3. Procedure

The Court of Justice sits either as a full court, for which the quorum is nine, or in chambers of three, five or seven judges. References for a preliminary ruling and the less difficult cases instituted by private litigants may be assigned to a chamber of the Court. The full Court hears all actions brought by a Member State or a Community institution, and also certain other actions where the state or institution requests it to do so. A state or Community institution may, for example, request the full Court to hear a reference for a preliminary ruling where it has made a written submission on the reference.

Normally, parties must be legally represented before the Court (Statute of the Court, Art. 17). However, in a reference for a preliminary ruling, a party may appear in person if he is permitted to do so before the court or tribunal which made the reference. Community institutions and Member States are represented by an agent. On occasion they brief outside counsel as their agents, but often a member of the legal service of the institution or state is appointed. A lawyer representing an individual or company must be entitled to practise before a court of a Member State. In the case of Scotland, this would allow both solicitors and advocates to appear before the Court. In England, the Law Society and the Bar entered into an agreement in 1971 which restricted the right of solicitors to practise before the Court of Justice. The Law Society rescinded the agreement in 1981 and English solicitors can now appear in any direct action and have done so (*e.g.* Case 175/80 *Tither v. Commission* [1981] E.C.R. 2345). There has been no such agreement in Scotland.

Once proceedings are initiated before the Court, an Advocate General is assigned to the case and a judge is appointed as rapporteur. Both play an important role in the determination of the case. At this time, one of the 11 official Community languages is designated as "the language of the case" (see Rules of Procedure of the Court, Art. 29). French is the working language of the Court and facilities for translation and interpretation into other Community languages are available, but the language of the case is authoritative for all purposes in the proceedings. Thus, strictly speaking, the authoritative judgment of the Court will be that in the language of the case, though the judgment will also be published in the other working languages of the Communities.

The principal stages in the conduct of a case before the Court are (a) the written proceedings, (b) the preliminary inquiry, (c) the oral proceedings, and (d) the judgment. The written proceedings are an extremely important element of the case. In preliminary rulings, proceedings are initiated by the reference from the national court or tribunal. The parties to the action in the national court, Member States, the Commission and, in some cases, the Council of Ministers, are all entitled to make written submissions on the reference. In direct actions proceedings are initiated by a written application to the Registrar of the Court. A defence is lodged, and this is usually followed by a written reply and a rejoinder. It is also normally at the stage of the written proceedings that questions of admissibility are considered by the Court.

In direct actions, the judge-rapporteur prepares a preliminary report after the written proceedings. On the basis of that report and the views of the Advocate General, the Court decides whether further evidence is required. The Court may obtain such evidence by conducting a preliminary inquiry. The inquiry, which may include the examination of witnesses, is inquisitorial rather than adversarial.

Before the oral proceedings the judge-rapporteur produces a report on the case which summarises the facts and the arguments in the written pleadings. This is made available to those making oral submissions. In a direct action, the parties may address the Court; in a reference for a preliminary ruling, those who have made written submissions may also make oral observations. The oral pleadings are not used to rehearse all the arguments in the written pleadings, but rather to emphasise the principal submissions and to comment on the report of the judge-rapporteur. Usually some two or three weeks after the oral submissions, the Advocate General presents his opinion on the case to the Court.

The judgment of the Court is always reserved, and a single judgment is delivered. The deliberations of the Court are based on a draft judgment prepared by the judge-rapporteur. This is considered in detail and where there is disagreement a vote is taken. Votes are cast in reverse order of seniority, to avoid, it is said, the votes of senior and more experienced judges influencing their junior and less experienced colleagues. The deliberation of the judges takes place in private without the assistance of interpreters, and the working language is normally French. Some of the implications of this are considered in the extract below.

Hartley, *The Foundations of European Community Law*, pp. 71–72

> "The choice of French as the working language of the Court means that the judges speak French when they discuss their judgment. All drafting is done in French and the final version approved by the Court is in French even if this is not the language of the case. The French text of the judgment is then translated into the language of the case and this text is signed by the judges and delivered in open Court. The result is that the text signed by the judges may be in a language which many of them do not understand. This throws a great deal of responsibility on those judges who are fluent in the language of the case to ensure that the translation truly reflects what was agreed on.
>
> One drawback of the unilingual mode of operation of the Court is that it puts judges whose mother tongue is not French at a disadvantage. Most people feel less confident giving their opinions in a group discussion if they are not fully at home in the language spoken. French-speaking judges must therefore enjoy a subtle psychological advantage over their colleagues. The use of French in the deliberation room must, moreover, work to some extent in favour of French legal thinking: it is hard to draft a judgment in French without using French legal terminology, while concepts peculiar to other systems might be ignored simply because they cannot easily be expressed in French.
>
> Another difficulty is that, although the official version of the judgment is in the language of the case, the French language version is the one actually agreed on by the Court and therefore might be said to represent the opinion

of the Court more accurately than the former. One can imagine that if there is a discussion in the deliberation room as to exactly what was decided in a previous case, it is the French text which will be examined."

4. Legal Aid

The Court of Justice may grant legal aid to parties in cases before it (Rules of Procedure of the Court, Art. 76; see also T. Kennedy, "Costs and Legal Aid Before the E.C.J." (1991) 36 J.L.S.S. 139). In direct actions, a decision on granting legal aid is taken by a Chamber of the Court during the initial stages of the written proceedings. In references for a preliminary ruling, the Court is also empowered to provide funds, in special circumstances, to assist the representation and attendance of a party.

Legal aid granted by the Court is in the form of a cash grant, which, in the case of direct actions, a recipient who loses may be ordered to repay in whole or part. Legal aid granted for preliminary rulings is not repayable.

Civil legal aid (Legal Aid (Scotland) Act 1986, s. 13, Sched. 2, Pt I) and criminal legal aid (*ibid.* s. 21(1)) are available for references from Scottish courts for a preliminary ruling under Article 177 [234] of the E.C. Treaty; no legal aid appears to be available for direct actions. Legal advice and assistance is available in Scotland on questions of Scots law (see Chap. 11). However, although European Community law is law in Scotland it is not, on one view, Scots law. In 1978, the Legal Aid Central Committee of the Law Society of Scotland took the view that the legal advice and assistance scheme is available in connection with proceedings in the Court of Justice "to a very limited extent, that is advising on jurisdiction and procedure" ((1978) 23 J.L.S.S. 143).

II. THE EUROPEAN CONVENTION FOR THE PROTECTION OF HUMAN RIGHTS AND FUNDAMENTAL FREEDOMS

A. INTRODUCTION

The European Convention on Human Rights is a treaty which provides for the protection and enforcement of certain basic rights of individuals. The United Kingdom was the first state to ratify the Convention; it came into force in 1953 and, by 1998, it had been ratified by 40 states.

The ratifying states undertake to secure the rights in the Convention for everyone within their jurisdiction without discrimination (Arts 1 and 14). Where the rights are violated, they must provide an effective remedy before a national authority (Art. 13). In addition to this, the Convention established international enforcement procedures. An important feature of these procedures is that they are not only available to states party to the Convention but also to individuals.

The rights protected by the Convention include: the right to life (Art. 2); freedom from torture or inhuman or degrading treatment or punishment (Art. 3); freedom from slavery or forced labour (Art. 4); the right to liberty and security of the person, including procedural safeguards on arrest and detention (Art. 5); the right to a fair trial both when charged with a criminal offence and for the determination of civil law rights and obligations (Art. 6); the prohibition of retrospective criminal law (Art. 7); the right to respect for private and family life, home and correspondence (Art. 8); freedom of thought, conscience and religion (Art. 9); freedom of expression (Art. 10); freedom of peaceful assembly and association with others, including the right to join and form a trade union (Art. 11); and the right to marry and found a family (Art. 12).

The range of rights protected has been extended by a series of protocols to the Convention. Protocol No. 1 provides that everyone is entitled to the peaceful enjoyment of their possessions (Art. 1); that no one shall be denied the right to education, and that states, in providing or controlling education, shall respect the right of parents to ensure that such education is in conformity with their religious and philosophical beliefs (Art. 2); it also requires states to hold free elections by secret ballot at reasonable intervals (Art. 3). Protocol No. 1 entered into force in 1954 and has been ratified by the United Kingdom. However, the United Kingdom has not ratified Protocols Nos 4, 6 and 7 which add further substantive rights. Protocol No. 4, *inter alia*, precludes a state from refusing to admit its own nationals, and under U.K. law not all citizens have the right to enter the United Kingdom. The Sixth Protocol requires the abolition of the death penalty, except in respect of acts, specified in domestic law, which are committed in time of war or imminent threat of war; the U.K. Government considers that the statutory imposition of the death penalty should be a matter for judgment and conscience of M.P.s. Protocol No. 7 provides, *inter alia*, for equality of certain rights between spouses, but as interpreted these rights would be inconsistent with some existing U.K. statutory property rights of spouses.

Many of the rights in the Convention are subject to qualifications and exceptions. When ratifying the Convention states may also limit their obligations by making reservations to specific provisions (Art. 64). The United Kingdom, for example, accepted the obligation to respect the right of parents under Article 2 of the first protocol "only so far as it is compatible with the provision of efficient instruction and training, and the avoidance of unreasonable public expenditure". Where it would not be inconsistent with their other international law obligations, states may also take measures derogating from their obligations under the Convention "in time of war or other public emergency threatening the life of the nation", but only "to the extent strictly required by the exigencies of the situation" (Art. 15). The United Kingdom has availed itself of this provision in respect of civil disturbances in Northern Ireland at various times since 1957, and most recently following the 1988 judgment in *Brogan v. U.K.* (11 E.H.R.R. 117; 13 E.H.R.R. 439). Although states are allowed a degree of discretion, the enforcement bodies established by the Convention are the final arbiters of whether there is an emergency within the meaning of Article 15 (*Lawless v. Ireland*, 1 E.H.R.R. 13; *Ireland v. U.K.*, 3 E.H.R.R. 25).

While the United Kingdom is required to secure and enforce the rights in the Convention within its jurisdiction, prior to the Human Rights Act 1998 the Convention had not been incorporated into U.K. domestic law. Consequently, the rights in the Convention were not enforceable before courts in the United

Kingdom. In England, some judges were prepared to take provisions of the Convention into account, for example in the construction of statutes (*e.g. R. v. Home Secretary, ex p. Bhajan Singh* [1976] Q.B. 198; *R. v. Home Secretary, ex p. Phansophar* [1976] Q.B. 606; *Garland v. British Rail Engineering Ltd* [1983] 2 A.C. 751; *R. v. Secretary of State for the Home Department, ex p. Brind* [1991] 1 A.C. 696; *cf. Malone v. Metropolitan Police Commissioner* [1979] Ch. 344). However, until 1996, on constitutional grounds, this approach had not been accepted in Scotland (*Re AMT (known as AC)* 1996 S.C.L.R. 897, 910–911, *per* Lord President Hope; *T, Petitioner* 1996 S.C.L.R. 897, and see J.L. Murdoch [1991] P.L. 40, A. Brown 1996 S.L.T. (News) 267; *cf. Surjit Kaur v. Lord Advocate* [1980] 3 C.M.L.R. 79; *Moore v. Secretary of State for Scotland* 1985 S.L.T. 38, 41; *Martin v. City of Edinburgh District Council* 1988 S.L.T. 329, 330; *Ralston v. H.M. Advocate*, 1989 S.L.T. 474, 478).

Although, prior to the Human Rights Act 1998, Convention rights were not enforceable as a matter of domestic law before U.K. courts, the European Court of Justice has held that the principles on which the European Convention is based must be taken into consideration in Community law. Thus, the European Convention effectively represents general principles of law which the European Court of Justice will protect in enforcing Community law (*e.g.* Case 11/70 *Internationale Handelsgesellschaft* [1970] E.C.R. 1125; Case 4173 *Nold* [1974] E.C.R. 491; Case 36/75 *Rutili* [1975] E.C.R. 1219; Case 63/83 *R. v. Kirk* [1984] E.C.R. 2689; Case 222184 *Johnson v. Chief Constable, R.U.C.* [1986] E.C.R. 1651; Case C-159/90 *Society for the Protection of Unborn Children (Ireland) Ltd v. Stephen Grogan and others* [1990] 1 C.M.L.R. 689 *Ebony Maritime SA v. Prefetto della Provincia di Brindisi* [1997] 2 C.M.L.R. 24; see generally H.G. Schermers, "The E.C. Bound by Fundamental Human Rights" [1990] C.M.L.R. 249; A. Clapham, "A Human Rights Policy for the E.C." [1990] E.L. 309; R.M. Dallen, "An Overview of the E.C. Protection of Human Rights" [1990] C.M.L.R. 761; see also Single European Act 1986, preamble). However, the Court of Justice has not held that the European Convention is part of Community law (*cf.* Case 98179 *Pecastaing v. Belgian State* [1980] E.C.R. 691, 716) and has declined to consider the compatibility of national legislation with the Convention (Cases 60 & 61/84 *Cinetheque S.A. v. F.N.C.F.* [1985] E.C.R. 2604; Case 12/86 *Demirel v. Stadt Schwabisch Gmund* [1987] E.C.R. 3719). As we have seen, decisions of the European Court of Justice on questions of Community law are binding on courts in Scotland; see further N. Grief, "The Domestic Impact of the European Convention on Human Rights as Mediated through Community Law" [1991] P.L. 555.

The Human Rights Act 1998 incorporated into domestic law the rights contained in Articles 2–12, 14, and Protocol 1, Articles 1–3, of the European Convention, as read with Articles 16–18 of the Convention (set out in Schedule 1, and U.K. reservations to, and derogations from, the Convention (set out in Schedule 2) (s. 1). These are referred to in the Act as "Convention rights". The 1998 Act provides that "so far as it is possible to do so" domestic U.K. legislation, both primary and subordinate, must be read and given effect in a way which is compatible with convention rights, but this does not affect the validity, continuing operation or enforcement of any incompatible domestic legislation (s. 3). Where there is such incompatible domestic legislation, in Scotland the High Court of Justiciary sitting as a court of criminal appeal or the Court of Session may make "a declaration of incompatibility" (s. 4). Where there has been such a declaration of incompatibility by a court, or where the Government considers, having regard to a finding of the European Court of Human Rights, that a provision of domestic legislation is incompatible with the obligations of the United Kingdom arising from the Convention, a Minister may make an Order amending the relevant primary or subordinate legislation to make it compatible with the Convention (ss. 10 and 11). Such an Order can be made only after a draft of the Order has been approved by resolution of each House of Parliament, unless the Minister declares that the urgency of the matter is such that it is necessary to make the Order without a draft being approved and in such a case the Order must be approved by each House within 40 days from being made or it ceases to have effect (s. 12). The Act also provides that a Minister in charge of a Bill must publish a written statement that the Bill is compatible with the "Convention rights" before the second reading of the Bill in either House, or publish a written statement that, while unable to make a statement of compatibility, the Government nevertheless wishes the House to proceed with the Bill (s. 19). The Act also makes provision for reservations to, and derogations from, "Convention rights" (ss. 14–17).

A further important element of the Human Rights Act is that it provides that it is unlawful for a public authority (which includes a court or tribunal) to act in a way which is incompatible with a "Convention right". This includes a failure to act, but not a failure to introduce in, or lay before, Parliament a proposal for legislation or to make any primary legislation or an Order to amend legislation incompatible with Convention rights (s. 6; see also ss. 7 and 8). The Human Rights Act 1998 seeks to incorporate many of the rights in the European Convention. The Lord Chancellor, Lord Irvine of Lairg, observed in opening the second reading debate on the Bill in the House of Lords, it does so by accommodating the notion of parliamentary sovereignty: 582 House of Lords Debates cols 1228–1229 (November 3, 1997).

Under the Scotland Act 1998, the Scottish Parliament does not have competence to enact legislation which is incompatible with a "Convention right" (as defined in the Human Rights Act 1998), although it has been argued that the Scottish Parliament could incorporate the European Convention in the domestic law of Scotland in a manner different from that in the Human Rights Act (C.M.G. Himsworth, "Devolving Rights", *Scotland Forum*, March 1998).

Scotland Act 1998, s. 28

"**28.** (1) Subject to section 29, the Parliament may make laws, to be known as Acts of the Scottish Parliament.

(2) Proposed Acts of the Scottish Parliament shall be known as Bills; and a Bill shall become an Act of the Scottish Parliament when it has been passed by the Parliament and has received Royal Assent.

(3) A Bill receives Royal Assent at the beginning of the day on which Letters Patent under the Scottish Seal signed with Her Majesty's own hand signifying Her Assent are recorded in the Register of the Great Seal.

(4) The date of Royal Assent shall be written on the Act of the Scottish Parliament by the Clerk, and shall form part of the Act.

(5) The validity of an Act of the Scottish Parliament is not affected by any invalidity in the proceedings of the Parliament leading to its enactment.

(6) Every Act of the Scottish Parliament shall be judicially noticed.

(7) This section does not affect the power of the Parliament of the United Kingdom to make laws for Scotland."

No doubt U.K. domestic law will now significantly reduce the need for individuals and non-governmental organisations in the United Kingdom to seek the enforcement of Convention rights through the enforcement procedure provided by the Convention itself. However, the Convention enforcement procedure will still remain an important procedure of last resort in the protection of Convention rights.

B. ENFORCEMENT UNDER THE CONVENTION

1. The European Court of Human Rights

With effect from November 1998 the procedure for enforcing rights under the European Convention was radically altered by Protocol No. 11, which substantially amended the Convention. Under the revised procedures the enforcement of rights is entirely a matter for the European Court of Human Rights.

The European Court of Human Rights consists of a number of judges equal to the number of states which are party to the Convention (Art. 20). The judges are elected, on a majority vote, by the Parliamentary Assembly of the Council of Europe from a list of three candidates nominated by each state party to the Convention (Art. 22). They are required to be "of high moral character" and must "either possess the qualifications required for appointment to high judicial office or be jurisconsults of recognised competence" (Art. 21(1)). They are elected for renewable terms of six years (Art. 23(1)) and once elected sit as individuals rather than as representatives of the states which nominated them (Art. 21(2)). However, half of the first group of judges elected will initially serve a three-year term (Art. 23).

The European Court of Human Rights sits in committees of three judges, in chambers of seven judges and in a grand chamber of 17 judges.

2. Determination of Admissibility

European Convention, Arts 33 and 34

"Article 33—Inter-state cases

Any High Contracting Party may refer to the Court any alleged breach of the provisions of the Convention and the protocols thereto by another High Contracting Party.

Article 34—Individual applications

The Court may receive applications from any person, non-governmental organisation or group of individuals claiming to be the victim of a violation by one of the High Contracting Parties of the rights set forth in the Convention or the protocols thereto. The High Contracting Parties undertake not to hinder in any way the effective exercise of this right."

A state which is a party to the Convention (a "High Contracting Party") may bring an alleged breach of its provisions before the Court. Individuals and others may only make application when "claiming to be a victim of a violation . . . of the rights" in the Convention (*e.g.* Case 436/58 *X v. Germany* 2 Y.B. 386; *cf.* Case 4185/69 *X v. Germany* 35 Coll. 140) but this has been broadly construed by the European Court of Human Rights (*e.g. Klass* 2 E.H.R.R. 214; *Marckx* 2 E.H.R.R. 330; *de Jong, Baljet and van den Brink* 8 E.H.R.R. 20).

European Convention, Art. 35—Admissibility criteria

"1. The Court may only deal with the matter after all domestic remedies have been exhausted, according to the generally recognised rules of international law, and within a period of six months from the date on which the final decision was taken.

2. The Court shall not deal with any individual application submitted under Article 34 that

(a) is anonymous; or
(b) is substantially the same as a matter that has already been examined by the Court or has already been submitted to another procedure of international investigation or settlement and contains no relevant new information.

3. The Court shall declare inadmissible any individual application submitted under Article 34 which it considers incompatible with the provisions of the Convention or the protocols thereto, manifestly ill-founded, or an abuse of the right of application.

4. The Court shall reject any application which it considers inadmissible under this Article. It may do so at any stage of the proceedings."

To be admissible, a reference by a state must satisfy Article 35(1) (*e.g.* Case 788/60 *Austria v. Italy* 6 Y.B. 796); an individual petition must satisfy Article 35(1)–(3).

The admissibility of inter-state cases under Article 33 is determined by a chamber of the Court and is taken separately from consideration of the merits of the case unless the Court, in exceptional cases, decides otherwise (Art. 29(2) and (3); *cf.* Art. 30).

The admissibility of applications from individuals or organisations under Article 34 may be taken by a committee of the Court. If the committee declares, by unanimous vote, the application inadmissible the decision is final (Art. 28), but in the absence of such a decision the admissibility of such applications is determined by a chamber of the Court (Art. 29(1)), and again admissibility decisions will be taken separately from decisions on the merits unless the Court, in exceptional cases, decides otherwise (Art. 29(3)). In all cases reasons must be given for declaring applications admissible or inadmissible (Art. 45(1)).

Under previous arrangements applications from individuals and organisations could attract free legal aid from the European Commission on Human Rights and it is likely that similar arrangements will apply to applications to the

European Court of Human Rights. In some instances, this grant of legal aid was subject to a means test. The legal aid schemes in Scotland have not been available for an individual wishing to petition the European Commission on Human Rights, but the legal advice and assistance scheme could be available where Scots law was applicable to the petition, for example, where advice was sought on whether local remedies had been exhausted (see (1978) 23 J.L.S.S. 256, 259). It is assumed that these arrangements will continue under the post-November 1998 procedures.

Under the pre-November 1998 procedures the vast majority of applications from individuals and organisations were rejected as inadmissible (see Table 2).

They were most commonly rejected because either they were not submitted within the specified six-month period, or all domestic remedies had not been exhausted, or the petition was incompatible with the Convention. This was hardly surprising, for to satisfy these requirements the petitioner and his legal advisers must be thoroughly familiar with the jurisprudence of the Convention institutions and, in the case of Article 26 (now 35), with the national law and legal system of the respondent state.

To satisfy the requirements of this Article the complaint must, for example, have been pursued before all appropriate judicial and administrative authorities in the respondent state, to the highest instance available. However, previously the European Commission of Human Rights had to be satisfied by the respondent state that a remedy was indeed available (*Alam and Khan* 10 Y.B. 478), where a remedy was available it was sometimes considered sufficient for the petitioner to have pursued the substance of the complaint (*Gazzardi* E.C.H.R., Ser. A., No. 39). Thus, the Commission decided that domestic remedies were not exhausted where a U.K. applicant, alleging unlawful arrest, had failed to bring a civil action against the police (Case 5197/71 *X v. U.K.* 42 C.D. 138), nor where a prisoner in England, alleging ill-treatment while in prison, failed to appeal to the competent prison authorities, including the Home Secretary (Case 5282/71 *X v. U.K.* 42 C.D. 99). However, the Commission did not require domestic remedies to be exhausted where they would have been likely to have been ineffective or to have provided insufficient redress. This on occasion involved detailed consideration of the national law of the respondent state and an assessment of the reasonable likelihood of success if the petitioner had pursued a particular domestic remedy (*e.g.* Case 3505/68 *X v. U.K.* 12 Y.B. 298; *Reed v. U.K.* 3 E.H.R.R. 136). It sometimes also involved an appreciation of the prevailing military or political circumstances in the respondent state (*e.g.* Case 8007/77 *Cyprus v. Turkey* 21 Y.B. 100; *cf.* Case 5577–83/72 *Donnelly et al. v. U.K.* 19 Y.B. 84).

TABLE 7.2
Petitions from Individuals to the Commission 1955–1997

Petitions registered		39,047
Decisions on admissibility taken		33,123
(i) petitions declared admissible	4,161	
(ii) petitions declared inadmissible	28,959	
Admissible petitions later rejected during examination of merits		12

(Source: E.Comm. H.R. Survey of Activities and Statistics 1997; procedural factors create apparent statistical discrepancies.)

3. Friendly Settlement Proceedings

Once an application has been declared admissible, the European Court of Human Rights examines and investigates the case and makes itself available to secure, on a confidential basis, a friendly settlement of the matter, but only "on the basis of respect for human rights as defined in the Convention and the protocols".

Article 38—Examination of the case and friendly settlement proceedings

"1. If the Court declares the application admissible, it shall

(a) pursue the examination of the case, together with the representatives of the parties, and if need be, undertake an investigation, for the effective conduct of which the States concerned shall furnish all necessary facilities;

(b) place itself at the disposal of the parties concerned with a view to securing a friendly settlement of the matter on the basis of respect for human rights as defined in the Convention and the protocols thereto.

2. Proceedings conducted under paragraph 1(b) shall be confidential."

Article 39—Finding of a friendly settlement

"If a friendly settlement is effected, the Court shall strike the case out of its list by means of a decision which shall be confined to a brief statement of the facts and of the solution reached."

Where a friendly settlement cannot be secured, the Court proceeds to a formal determination of the merits of the case.

4. Determination of the Merits

A chamber of the Court determines the merits of admissible cases (Art. 29), although where the case raises a serious question affecting the interpretation of the Convention or its protocols or the resolution of a question before the chamber may result in a decision inconsistent with a previous judgment of the Court, the chamber may relinquish jurisdiction in favour of the grand chamber of the Court, unless one of the parties to the case objects to this (Art. 30). Within three months from the date of the judgment of the chamber, any party to the case may, in exceptional circumstances, request that the case be referred to the grand chamber. A panel of five judges of the grand chamber must accept this request if the case raises a serious question affecting the interpretation or application of the Convention or its protocols, or raises a serious issue of general importance. If the request for referral is accepted by the panel, the grand chamber judges the case (Art. 43).

The judgments of the chambers and the grand chamber may include a reparation award (Art. 41), and must be reasoned (Art. 45(1)); there is a capacity for individual judges to deliver a separate opinion (Art. 45(2)). The judgments of chambers and the grand chambers, subject to referral to the grand chamber, are final (Art. 44). The states party to the Convention undertake to abide by the final judgment of the Court in any case to which they are parties (Art. 46(1)), and the final judgment of the Court is transmitted to the Committee of Ministers of the Council of Europe, which is placed under an obligation to supervise the execution of the judgment (Art. 46(2)).

5. Advisory Jurisdiction of the Court

The Committee of Ministers of the Council of Europe may request advisory opinions from the European Court of Human Rights on the interpretation of the Convention (Art. 47) and it is for the Court to decide whether such a request is within its competence (Art. 48). Advisory opinions, which must be reasoned, are communicated to the Council of Ministers; here too there is a capacity for individual judges to deliver a separate opinion (Art. 49).

Article 47—Advisory Opinions

> "1. The Court may, at the request of the Committee of Ministers, give advisory opinions on legal questions concerning the interpretation of the Convention and the protocols thereto.
> 2. Such opinions shall not deal with any question relating to the content or scope of the rights or freedoms defined in Section I of the Convention and the protocols thereto, or with any other question which the Court or the Committee of Ministers might have to consider in consequence of any such proceedings as could be instituted in accordance with the Convention.
> 3. Decisions of the Committee of Ministers to request an advisory opinion of the Court shall require a majority vote of the representatives entitled to sit on the Committee."

Article 48—Advisory Jurisdiction of the Court

> "The Court shall decide whether a request for an advisory opinion submitted by the Committee of Ministers is within its competence as defined in Article 47."

6. An Effective Procedure?

The enforcement procedure under the Convention has resulted in changes in the domestic law and practice in ratifying states. In the United Kingdom, for example, petitions by individuals eventually resulted in the introduction of immigration appeal tribunals and revised prison rules on access to lawyers. (See further, A.W. Bradley, "The United Kingdom before the Strasbourg Court" in Finnie, Himsworth and Walker (eds), *Edinburgh Essays in Public Law* (1991)).

However, the procedure, at least in the past, has been too elaborate and lengthy to provide an adequate remedy to the individual whose rights have been violated. This is well illustrated by the case of *Campbell and Cosans*, E.C.H.R.

Ser. A., No. 48, the first case from Scotland to reach the European Court of Human Rights.

Gordon Campbell attended a local authority primary school in Strathclyde, where corporal punishment was used for disciplinary purposes. The local education authority refused to give his mother an undertaking that her son would not be subjected to such punishment while at the school. Jeffrey Cosans was suspended from a local authority secondary school in Fife, after refusing, on his father's advice, to accept corporal punishment for attempting to take a prohibited short-cut through a cemetery on his way home from school. Although the local education authority was later willing to lift the suspension, the boy's parents would not allow him to return to school unless they received an undertaking that he would never be subjected to corporal punishment. The local education authority refused to give the undertaking and Jeffrey Cosans did not attend school from his suspension in September 1976 until he ceased to be of compulsory school age in May 1977.

Mrs Campbell and Mrs Cosans, using the then existing procedure, petitioned the European Commission of Human Rights in, respectively, March and October 1976, alleging (a) that the use of corporal punishment in Scottish local authority schools constituted torture or inhuman or degrading treatment or punishment contrary to Article 3 of the Convention, and (b) that the United Kingdom had failed to respect their rights as parents to ensure that the education and teaching of their children was in conformity with their religious and philosophical convictions, contrary to Article 2 of the First Protocol to the Convention. Mrs Cosans also argued that, contrary to the same provision, the suspension of her son from school denied him the right to education.

The two petitions, which were joined by the Commission, were declared admissible in December 1977. In May 1978, the Commission reported to the Committee of Ministers. The case was referred to the Court both by the Commission and the United Kingdom Government. In January 1982, the Court held unanimously that there had been no violation of Article 3 of the Convention; but, by six votes to one, it held that the United Kingdom had violated Article 2 of the First Protocol, as alleged. The judgment of the Court on the question of reparation was not delivered until March 1983; the claim for fees of Mrs Cosans' counsel was reduced by more than £3,000. Unlike many individual petitions, few of the facts in this case were in dispute and the exhaustion of domestic remedies was not really in issue. Nevertheless, the case was before the Commission and the Court for seven years. Furthermore, although the individual petitioners' cases were resolved, it was still necessary for the United Kingdom to bring its law and practice into conformity with the Convention. A number of education authorities altered their regulations to conform with Article 2 of the First Protocol and the U.K. Government eventually enacted legislation for the same purpose (the Education (No. 2) Act 1986, s. 48) which was brought into force in August 1987 (S.I. 1987 No. 344)—some 11 years after Mrs Campbell and Mrs Cosans petitioned the Commission.

Changes in both domestic law and the enforcement procedure under the Convention should serve to reduce the number of cases which will be referred to the European Court of Human Rights and the delay in the disposal of cases which do reach the court.

CHAPTER 8

THE JUDICIARY

While the Scottish judiciary numbers both legally qualified and lay individuals in its ranks, the bulk of criminal cases and all civil cases which proceed to an adjudication in Scotland are handled by legally qualified judges. (In England, by contrast, 98 per cent of all criminal cases are dealt with by lay magistrates.) Nevertheless, all Scottish judges, lay and legal, possess considerable power—including the authority to deprive unsuccessful litigants of their funds, and in some cases, their liberty. The higher judiciary, moreover, can make, develop and restate the law (see Chaps 13 and 14). In the light of these powers and of the virtual irremovability of the higher judiciary once appointed, it is clear that judicial selection is a matter of major public importance.

I. JUDICIAL SELECTION

Abraham, *The Judicial Process*, p. 23

> "What principles should govern the selection of the men and women who dispense justice? To raise this question brings us face to face with moral, as well as political, questions of the greatest importance. However awe inspiring their functions may be, our judges are still human beings. As such they make the ultimate decisions in the judicial process. In essence, there are just two basic methods of selection: appointment and election—no matter who does the actual appointing or electing—although . . . compromises between the two modes [have] been devised and [are] practised on certain levels of the judiciary in a good many jurisdictions. A collateral question is whether judges should be members of a career service as in France, chosen from a special group of lawyers as in England, or selected through appointments from the legal profession generally as in the United States. Practices of selection differ in large measure in accordance with the traditions and needs of the country concerned."

A. THE SUPERIOR COURTS

The nomination and appointment of Scottish judges in the superior courts is an inherent prerogative of the Crown. By constitutional convention Scottish appointments to the House of Lords and the offices of Lord President and Lord Justice-Clerk are by the Sovereign on the recommendation of the Prime Minister. Appointments to the Court of Session and the High Court of Justiciary are by the Sovereign on the recommendation of the Secretary of State for Scotland. Traditionally the Lord Advocate has been consulted before any recommendations are made and in the past half century his advice has almost invariably been accepted.

The appointments system for Court of Session judges was enshrined in statute by the Scotland Act 1998. Section 95 of the Bill provides that Court of Session judges, sheriffs principal and sheriffs shall be appointed by the monarch on the advice of the First Minister. While the Prime Minister shall continue to recommend appointments to the offices of Lord President or Lord Justice-Clerk, he may only recommend persons who have already been nominated by the First Minister. What remains unclear is the future role of the Lord Advocate. However, as the office of Lord Advocate remains after the Parliament is established, it is possible that these provisions will not greatly alter the established practice. It seems probable that the Lord Advocate will continue to perform a key role in the appointments process by recommending candidates to the First Minister.

The criteria for appointment to the House of Lords are set out in section 6 of the Appellate Jurisdiction Act 1876 (on such appointments, see Chap. 3 above) and for appointments to the Court of Session and the High Court of Justiciary, in the Treaty of Union.

Treaty of Union 1707, Art. XIX

> "Hereafter none shall be named by Her Majesty or Her Royal Successors to be ordinary Lords of Session but such who have served in the Colledge of Justice as Advocates or Principal Clerks of Session for the Space of Five years or as Writers to the Signet for the Space of ten years with this provision that no Writer to the Signet be capable to be admitted a Lord of the Session unless he undergo a private and publick Tryal on the Civil Law before the Faculty of Advocates and be found by them qualified for the said Office two years before he be named to be a Lord of the Session yet so as the Qualifications made or to be made for capacitating persons to be named ordinary Lords of Session may be altered by the Parliament of Great Britain."

This provision has recently been extended through sections 35(1), 35(3) of and Schedule 4(1) to the Law Reform (Miscellaneous Provisions) (Scotland) Act 1990.

Schedule 4, Judicial Appointments

"Appointments of sheriffs principal, sheriffs and solicitors as judges of the Court of Session

> 1. The following categories of person shall, in accordance with this paragraph . . . be eligible to be appointed as judges of the Court of Session—
>
> (a) sheriffs principal and sheriffs who have held office as such for a continuous period of not less than five years; and
>
> (b) solicitors who, by virtue of section 25A (rights of audience) of the Solicitors (Scotland) Act 1980, have for a continuous period of not less than five years had a right of audience in both the Court of Session and the High Court of Justiciary."

Section 35(3) provides that any person qualified to become a judge of the Court of Session may be appointed by the Secretary of State (after consulting the Lord President) to act as temporary judges of the Court of Session. At first blush the 1990 Act seems to have reduced the qualifying period for solicitors to become judges of the Court of Session from 10 years to five. In practice, however, no Writer to the Signet (solicitor) or Principal Clerk of Session has been appointed to sit in the Court of Session or the High Court of Justiciary in the past two centuries. The Lord Advocate, moreover, made it clear as the Bill proceeded through Parliament that the five-year period was selected simply to create a symmetry between the time period for advocates and solicitors. Judicial appointments to the higher courts in Scotland in modern times have invariably come from the senior ranks of the Scottish Bar (Queen's Counsel). In the same way it is highly unlikely that anyone will be appointed permanently under the new provisions until they have had many years of relevant experience.

The Scottish appointees to the House of Lords since 1876 include four Lords Presidents, four Lords Advocates, six former Lords Advocates, three from the Inner House and five from the Outer House. With the exceptions of Lords Mackay and Hope, all the Lords Presidents, Lords Advocates and former Lords Advocates were appointed before 1950, while those from the Inner and Outer Houses were appointed after that date. As the importance of political experience as an attribute has declined, so other factors have come into the reckoning. Thus of the nine Deans of the Faculty of Advocates or former Deans to be appointed, seven were appointed after 1948. (See further on the Scottish Lords of Appeal, A. Paterson, "Scottish Lords of Appeal 1876–1988" (1988) J.R. 235.)

Turning to the supreme courts in Scotland, of the 71 permanent higher judicial appointments in the last 46 years, all were Q.C.s, only 11 were of less than 10 years' standing as Queen's Counsel, while 17 had more than 15 years' standing. (The average standing was 14 years. The actual range of appointments was from three years' standing to 19 years' standing.) Of the 12 temporary judges appointed to the supreme courts by 1998, four were practising seniors, eight were sheriffs, and the other was the Chairman of the Scottish Land Court and President of the Lands Tribunal for Scotland. All of them were already Q.C.s or acquired that status immediately following on their appointment as temporary judges.

Paths to the Bench

As Ian Willock argued in "Scottish judges scrutinised" (1969) 14 J.R. 193, Queen's Counsel in the past whose careers have followed certain identifiable paths seem to have had an advantage in the pursuit of appointment to the higher judicial bench.

Since higher judicial appointments are made by the Executive there has always been a possibility that politics or party politics could play a part in such appointments. In its most obvious form this influence consisted of appointments as a reward for service to a political party (usually as an M.P.). Secondly, as in the case of appointments to the Federal judiciary in the United States, it has been manifested in attempts to place "right-thinking" appointees on the bench. In its weakest form it has led to candidates with political experience being favoured (irrespective of party) because of a belief that such experience is a useful attribute in a judge. In England, political factors, except occasionally in the last sense, now play little part in higher judicial appointments (less than 10 per cent of the higher judiciary in England have had political experience). In Scotland the position now is broadly similar. Although a rather higher percentage of the supreme court judiciary has been active in politics (17 per cent) the importance of political experience as a route to the bench is much less than it was only 20 years ago.

Thus in the 100 years prior to 1972, whenever the office of Lord President or Lord Justice-Clerk fell vacant it was filled by the Lord Advocate of the day or one of his predecessors. Lord Emslie's appointment as Lord President in 1972 was the first occasion in over 250 years when a vacancy in a chair of the Court of Session had not been filled by the appointment of a Lord Advocate or former Lord Advocate. The break in tradition was maintained in 1989 when the Dean of Faculty, David Hope Q.C., replaced Lord Emslie as Lord President and Lord Justice-General. However, upon his elevation to the House of Lords in 1997, Lord Hope was succeeded by the former Lord Advocate, Lord Rodger, a move which led to some criticism of the appointments mechanism. When the office of Lord Justice-Clerk subsequently fell vacant, it was filled by Lord Cullen, an apolitical Court of Session judge of 10 years' standing. Nevertheless, 12 of the last 15 Lords Advocate to hold office have been elevated to the supreme courts—sometimes on their own recommendation. Of the 71 appointments to these courts in the last 45 years, 22 were advocates who had been active in politics. However, the political influence is clearly on the wane. Law officers hold office for longer than in the past and the political climate is less sympathetic to lawyer M.P.s becoming judges than once it was. Thus of the 27 Senators of the College of Justice in the autumn of 1999, only five were known to have had an involvement with politics and four of them were in the Inner House. Moreover it is now not uncommon for an appointee with political experience to come from another political party to that of the Lord Advocate. (See, further, on politics and judicial appointment, A. Paterson, "Judges: a political elite?" (1974) 1 *British Journal of Law and Society* 118, S.C. Styles, "The Scottish Judiciary 1919–1986" (1988) J.R. 41; and I. Hamilton, "Simply Judge for Yourself" 1996 S.L.G. 164.)

The second route to the Court of Session bench is by attaining the leadership of the Bar. The Scottish Bar (the Faculty of Advocates) elects its leader (the Dean) on merit, from the ranks of the successful Queen's Counsel. Excluding the Dean and the Lord Advocate of the present day, only four of the 27 holders of the office of Dean since 1900 have not been elevated to the higher court Bench. (Two of the four were thought to have disqualified themselves from judicial office by their handling of their business or private affairs.)

Appointment as a part-time sheriff principal was the third route. Since the office of sheriff principal became a full-time appointment in 1975, this route seems to have disappeared. However, other routes have sprung up to replace it. Senior advocates who have accepted appointment to the Presidency of Industrial Tribunals or to the Scottish Law Commission in recent years are thought to have been informed that acceptance of these posts would be likely to improve their chances of higher judicial appointment. Being chairman of a Medical Appeal Tribunal is also seen as useful experience. Again, with the expansion of criminal work in the High Court in the past 15 years, counsel with aspirations to higher judicial office (but with little in the way of a criminal practice), have been led to believe that a period as advocate depute will do their chances of eventual selection no harm.

It would appear that appointment as a temporary judge is becoming an important stepping stone en route to a permanent post. Of the five temporary judges who have so far ceased to hold appointment, four did so on permanent appointment to the Court of Session, and the other on appointment as a sheriff principal. Most noteworthy of all, one of them, Sheriff Hazel Aronson, thus became the first woman to be permanently appointed to the supreme court bench, taking the judicial title of Lady Cosgrove. Temporary judges may therefore become the modern successors of Lords Probationer, the title given to Court of Session appointees in the eighteenth century during their mandatory trial period.

B. THE SHERIFF COURT

Scotland Act 1998, s. 94(4)(b)

> 94. "It is for the First Minister, after consulting the Lord President, to recommend to Her Majesty the appointment of a person as— . . . (b) a sheriff principal or a sheriff."

Sheriff Courts (Scotland) Act 1971, s. 5

> "5. Qualification for offices of sheriff principal and sheriff.—(1) A person shall not be appointed to the office of sheriff principal or sheriff unless he is, and has been for at least ten years, legally qualified. For the purposes of this subsection, a person shall be legally qualified if he is an advocate or a solicitor."

Although solicitors have long been eligible for appointment to the shrieval bench, until the 1970s such appointments were largely restricted to former advocates. In 1967 there were 58 sheriffs, of whom all but seven were former advocates. Following the Grant Report (which came out in favour of more solicitor appointments to the shrieval bench) the appointing authorities have been much more sympathetic to solicitors. Of the 151 permanent sheriffs appointed since 1967, 85 have been counsel and 66 solicitors (11 of whom were procurators fiscal). In the last 15 years there has been a rough parity between the numbers of former advocates and solicitors appointed as sheriffs. Some indication of the change can be seen from the fact that in 1967 12 per cent of sheriffs were former solicitors, in 1985 the figure was 29 per cent and by 1999 44 per cent were former solicitors. In fact, in summer 1999 there were 109 permanent sheriffs of whom 61 were advocates and 48 were solicitors. Of the six sheriffs principal at that date, five were originally advocates but one had been a solicitor who was appointed first to be a sheriff and subsequently as sheriff principal. Amongst those holding the post of temporary sheriff, however, the balance is reversed. Thus in summer 1999, of the 126 temporary sheriffs, 43 were advocates and 83 were solicitors. In fairness it should be stated that in general, advocates have tended to be appointed at a markedly younger age than solicitors and to the most sought-after shrieval posts. While several sheriffs have been promoted to sheriff principal, only one (Lord Caplan) has subsequently been elevated to the supreme court bench, and only one (Lady Cosgrove) has been elevated directly from the shrieval bench.

C. REFORM

The Scottish system of appointment to higher judicial office has been criticised for a number of reasons.

Campbell, "Judicial Selection", pp. 278–279

> "First the Scottish system is open to attack in so far as it relies on executive appointment rather than on an independent committee. There is room for abuse and for political appointments . . .
>
> Secondly the Scottish system is open to attack for its reliance on the knowledge and judgment of one man in selecting judges. Informal consultation and advising no doubt takes place—but is not visible or open . . .
>
> Thirdly in relying almost exclusively on such a small 'pool' (the Faculty of Advocates) for judicial appointments, the Scottish system is open to attack on grounds of patronage, social class bias and narrowness of experience . . .
>
> Fourthly in not regularly affording formal training to newly appointed judges the Scottish system is open to attack in so far as it does not fulfil its function of ensuring the judges are of the highest technical competence and that common standards are maintained.
>
> In making each of these points, which together amount to total criticism of the Scottish system, the phrase 'open to attack' is used. Most of the attacks have been made by one critic or another. It is not necessary to agree or disagree with the criticisms, it is only necessary to recall that if the point at issue is credibility and ostentatious impartiality the Scottish system must be adjudged a failure. It fails to meet the rational requirements of a system that the public, the profession, legal scholars and other commentators may accept with any confidence."

[It is now 20 years since this critique was penned. At least in relation to the appointments to the supreme courts, its message is just as pertinent today as it was then.]

1. The Appointive Mechanism

As we have seen, the Scottish system is primarily appointive, although when Deans of the Faculty are elevated to the Bench or local authority councillors sit *ex officio* in the district court, elective elements have a part to play. David Pannick once argued ("Election of the judiciary" (1979) 129 New L.J. 1064) that judges in the House of Lords should be popularly elected from a short list of legally qualified candidates selected on merit (a proposal akin to "the Missouri plan" which operates with some success in about half of the United States in relation to state judicial appointments). This proposal attracted little support. Most other commentators favour an improved appointive system. Unlike the Lord Chancellor in England or the President of the United States (when appointing Federal judges), the Lord Advocate does not go through an elaborate semi-formal consultation process prior to making a nomination. (See G. Stott, *Lord Advocate's Diary* (Aberdeen University Press, 1991), for example, at pp. 167, 172–173, 181, 184 and 188. On the procedures adopted by the Lord Chancellor, see A. Paterson, "Becoming a Judge" in R. Dingwall and P. Lewis (eds), *The Sociology of the Professions* (Macmillan, 1983) and *The Judiciary* (Justice, 1992).) For some years there has been a considerable body of opinion and commentary (particularly in England and Wales) to the effect that what is needed is an independent Judicial Commission of judges, lawyers and laypersons. Such judicial commissions have been experimented with in some Commonwealth countries, though it has been said that they tend to make "safe", unimaginative nominations. Nevertheless, as the pool for judicial selection broadens on both sides of the border, so the pressure is mounting to abandon the "old boy network" with its reliance on secret (and potentially prejudiced) references in favour of a more transparent process of selection on merit. It had been thought that the present Labour Government would establish a Judicial Appointments Commission, and Lord Irvine of Lairg L.C. stated in June 1997 that consultation was planned for later in that year on the feasibility of establishing a Commission for England and Wales. However, in October 1997, Lord Irvine stated that he would not proceed with the consultations and instead introduced a series of lesser reforms which he considered to be most urgent, most notably the advertising of High Court judgeships in the national and legal press. It was subsequently announced that the decision as to whether there should be a Judicial Appointments Commission for Scotland would be left to the Scottish Parliament.

In recent years, efforts have been made in the case of shrieval appointments to improve the transparency of the process. In particular, vacancies are now advertised in the *Scots Law Times*, the *Journal of the Law Society of Scotland* and within the Faculty of Advocates. Applicants are required to fill in application forms, and, if not currently serving as temporary sheriffs, to provide the names of referees. This is followed by a consultation process, interviews, and results in a recommendation to the Lord Advocate as to the suitability of their application.

[See, *e.g.*, Editorial "Shaking the Foundations" (1990) 160 SCOLAG 2; D. Pannick, *Judges* (Oxford University Press, 1987), p. 68; *The Judiciary* (Justice, 1992). *Cf.*; S. Nelson, "The Scottish Judiciary: A Case for Reform" (1992) 188 SCOLAG 71. Thomas and Malleson, *Judicial Appointments Commissions: The European and North American Experience and Possible Implications for the UK*, LCD Research Series No. 6/97 and R. Black, "The Scottish Parliament and the Scottish Judiciary", 1998 S.L.T. (News) 321].

2. Qualifications for Judicial Appointment

The Law Reform (Miscellaneous Provisions) (Scotland) Act 1990, at least on paper, considerably broadened the pool from which appointments are made to the supreme courts. The previous *de facto* stipulation that all appointees must be Queen's Counsel of sufficient standing had restricted selection to a pool of less than 10 serious candidates (including the Law Officers and the Dean of Faculty). Allowing sheriffs principal and sheriffs to be considered more than doubled the pool. In practice, it now seems unlikely that we shall see sheriffs principal or sheriffs promoted to the higher courts with any regularity, even if they are appointed as temporary judges. As for solicitors with rights of audience, the first appointment from their ranks is likely to be more than a decade away.

Although 1996 saw the appointment of Lady Cosgrove as the first female appointment to the Court of Session bench, there remains considerable pressure for more female judges to be appointed. In the summer of 1999, women made up 14 of the 109 permanent sheriffs in post and 13 of the 126 temporary sheriffs. Two of the temporary sheriffs were drawn from an ethnic minority group.

At one time the qualities required of a Court of Session judge were set out explicitly by statute. Thus an Act passed in 1592 stipulated that appointees must be God-fearing, well-read, practical in judgment, versed in the law, expeditious in the dispatch of business and possessed of independent means. Except perhaps in Northern Ireland, the first requirement is no longer seen as a relevant factor (nor are divorcees denied promotion to the Bench as once they were). Curiously, the long line of candidates who have refused judicial appointment on the grounds that they could not afford the drop in salary involved in leaving the Bar seems to indicate that the last requirement is not as irrelevant in modern times as might have been thought.

3. Trials and Training

A common criticism of the British system of judicial appointment (as opposed to the Continental preference for a career judiciary) is that the qualities which make a successful advocate or court practitioner may not be those required to make a successful judge. Although little discussed in the literature, appointing authorities in Scotland and England have long sought to overcome this problem by appointing would-be judges on a part-time basis to see if they possess judicial qualities. English Q.C.s are encouraged to serve as recorders (part-time judges) and Scottish Q.C.s became part-time sheriffs principal until 1975 for the same reasons. Similarly, as we saw earlier, there are presently 126 temporary (part-time) sheriffs, of whom 22 are Q.C.s. This partly makes up for the loss of part time sheriffs principal as a way of giving Q.C.s a "trial run" as superior judges. It is beginning to look as though appointment as a temporary judge in the supreme courts is being used in the same way. The problem is clearly a perennial one. In 1579 an Act was passed giving the Court of Session power to test the suitability of royal nominees to the Bench. Each nominee had to sit three days in the Outer House and one day in the Inner House and then be assessed on his handling of the cases he had heard. At least one nominee failed the test but in 1724 a further statute made it clear that the Crown could override the court's veto. These judicial examinations were only abolished in 1933, although they had become a formality many years earlier.

A closely related criticism is that British judges receive insufficient training before their appointment. Although in England there have for many years been one-day and one-week conferences for judges on damages, family law and sentencing, the Bridge Report on "Judicial Studies and Information" (HMSO, 1978) concluded that much more could and should be done. Following the report a Judicial Studies Board was established which is now chaired by a Lord Justice and its members include High Court and Circuit judges. In addition to introductory seminars for new judges appointed to the Crown Court it arranges visits to penal establishments, conducts sentencing exercises and runs refresher courses (every five years) for experienced judges sitting in the Crown Court. It also provides ethnicity and gender awareness training for judges. Due to a lack of resources it took almost 20 years for the Scots to follow suit. In 1997, the Scottish Office announced the establishment of a Judicial Studies Committee under the chairmanship of Lord Ross, formerly Lord Justice-Clerk, to promote the training of Supreme Court judges and sheriffs. This may mean that, in future, all judges in Scotland will receive formal training devised by their peers. Until now, judicial training has been conducted on an informal, *ad hoc* basis. The Sheriffs' Association has organised training events and conferences for sheriffs, while the Lord President oversaw training provided for Court of Session judges. [See Lord President Hope, "Judicial Business", 1991 J.L.S.S. 266, and Jessica Burns, "Judicial Education" (1989) 158 SCOLAG 171.]

D. THE DISTRICT COURT

District Courts (Scotland) Act 1975, ss. 9, 11 and 14

Justices of the peace

> "**9.**—(1) Subject to the provisions of this section, there shall, in Scotland, be a commission of the peace for each commission area; and the commission for any commission area shall be a commission under the Great Seal addressed generally, and not by name, to all such persons as may from time to time hold office as justices of the peace for the commission area.
>
> (2) Justices of the peace for any commission area, other than stipendiary magistrates and ex officio justices, shall be appointed by name on behalf and in the name of Her Majesty by instrument under the hand of the Secretary of State, and a justice so appointed shall only be removed from office in like manner.
>
> . . .
>
> **11.**—(2) Each local authority may nominate up to one quarter of their members to serve as *ex officio* justices for their area, and any person so nominated shall hold office as *ex officio* justice from the date on which the local authority intimate their nomination to the Secretary of State and shall continue as such for the period during which he remains a member of the authority and continues to retain the authority's nomination.
>
> . . .
>
> **14**. The Secretary of State may make schemes and provide courses for the instruction of justices of the peace, and it shall be the duty of the justices'

> committee of a commission area to implement and administer any such schemes in accordance with arrangements approved by the Secretary of State."

In addition to *ex officio* justices, justices are appointed by the Secretary of State on the advice of the J.P. advisory committees appointed by him in each district and islands area. The committees advise both on the need for new appointments and as to the suitability of candidates for appointment. The Secretary of State (like the Lord Chancellor when considering appointments to the magistracy) takes the view that "commissions of the peace should be drawn from all social classes and be broadly representative of the community which they serve" (100 H.C. Deb., col. 435 (W.A.), March 13, 1981). Attempts are also made to attain a political balance between the main political parties on each commission, though not a religious balance, except in areas likely to be sensitive on the matter.

There are several thousand justices in Scotland, over two-thirds of whom are male. Justices aged over 70 are ineligible to sit, and of those eligible to sit on the Bench, only a minority of around 1,000 actually do so in any given year.

The low percentage of female justices suggests that the Secretary of State's efforts to appoint commissions which are "broadly representative of the community" have been only partially successful. It is likely that (as in England) the professional and managerial groups in the community are over-represented and that ethnic minorities as well as women are under-represented.

The existence of lay judges in Scotland (and *ex officio* justices in particular) has long been a source of discontent in legal circles. When local government was being reorganised in the 1970s there were strenuous efforts (not least by the legal profession) to abolish the lay judiciary altogether. Just when the battle seemed to have been won there was a change of government and lay justices were reprieved. The controversy was revived with a Scottish Office study in 1984 (published as Z. Bankowski, N. Hutton and J. McManus, *Lay Justice* (T. & T. Clark, 1987)) concluding that the lay system works adequately and produces similar results to those which a professionalised system would. This study was fiercely criticised by the Law Society ("Professional Justice" (1985) 30 J.L.S.S. 13) who again called for the replacement of the lay justices by stipendiary magistrates' courts. Failing this the Society considered that a centralised training programme should be established to ensure the maintenance of standards throughout the country with compulsory refresher courses. Certainly, at present, although local training courses are run for justices on legal aid, procedure, evidence and sentencing (with visits to penal institutions) it is not entirely clear what their purpose is (presumably it is not to make them superficial lawyers) nor how effective they have been.

II. JUDICIAL INDEPENDENCE

A. JUDICIAL TENURE

The strongest safeguard of judicial independence in the United Kingdom is the security of tenure which judges possess. Tenure of high judicial office in Scotland is by custom and by Article 13 of the Claim of Right 1689, *ad vitam aut culpam*, *i.e.* during good behaviour. In the case of Law Lords, section 6 of the Appellate Jurisdiction Act 1876, as amended, provides that:

> "Every Lord of Appeal in Ordinary shall hold his office during good behaviour, . . . but he may be removed from such office on the address of both Houses of Parliament."

But the procedure for removing a judge from the Court of Session or the High Court has long been uncertain. (For an interesting historical account of attempts at judicial removal, see Esson, "Ad vitam aut culpam" 1972 J.R. 50.)

The lack of a formal procedure for removing supreme court judges was graphically highlighted in 1990 with the resignation of a Court of Session judge. Even if the allegations concerning the judge had been established (which they were not) and even if they were inconsistent with holding high judicial office (again a moot point), it is far from clear what the authorities could have done if he had chosen not to resign.

Several statutes have imposed restrictions on the tenure of high judicial office. Amongst the earliest (and now, possibly, in desuetude) was the Land Purchase Act 1594, in terms of which Lords of Session who purchase land or property which is the subject of litigation risk forfeiture of their judicial office. Much later came section 2 of the Judicial Pensions Act 1959 under which all judges in the House of Lords and Senators of the College of Justice appointed since 1959 must retire on attaining the age of 75. Sheriffs principal and sheriffs, on the other hand, had to retire at 72 (Sheriffs' Pensions (Scotland) Act 1961, ss. 6, 9). Following the passage of the Judicial Pensions and Retirement Act 1993 all Scottish judges appointed in the future will be required to retire at 70.

Section 95 of the 1998 Scotland Act at long last provides a clear mechanism for the removal of a Court of Session judge. The Bill allowed the monarch to remove a judge from office on the recommendation of the First Minister, although such a recommendation could only be made by a resolution of the Scottish Parliament where two-thirds of the total membership had voted in favour. These proposals were vigorously attacked by Lord McCluskey and a number of other Scots judges in the Lords as being open to abuse, undermining judicial independence and making us akin to a banana republic. As a result the Bill was amended to permit removal by the monarch on the recommendation of the First Minister following a majority resolution only of the Scottish Parliament. This apparent watering down of the protection was in fact a response to the introduction of several further safeguards, namely that (1) such a resolution could only go to the Parliament if the judge had first been deemed to be unfit for office "by reason of inability, neglect of duty or misbehaviour" (2) in a written report produced by (3) a tribunal set up by the First Minister or at the request of the Lord President. The three-person tribunal would have to be chaired by a member of the Judicial Committee of the Privy Council. (The details of this reform and its history are set out in Himsworth, "Securing the tenure of Scottish judges" [1999] *Public Law* 14). It also leaves unchanged the provisions for the removal of sheriffs. The mechanism for terminating the appointment of a sheriff is contained in the Sheriff Courts (Scotland) Act 1971, s. 12(1): "The Lord President of the Court of

Session and the Lord Justice Clerk may of their own accord and shall, if they are requested so to do by the Secretary of State, undertake jointly an investigation into the fitness for office of any sheriff principal or sheriff and, as soon as practicable after completing that investigation, shall report in writing to the Secretary of State either (a) that the sheriff principal or sheriff is fit for office, or (b) that the sheriff principal or sheriff is unfit for office by reason of inability, neglect of duty or misbehaviour."

Under section 15 of the District Courts (Scotland) Act 1975 justices of the peace can no longer sit after attaining the age of 70 and can be prevented from sitting by the Secretary of State on the grounds of infirmity, neglect of duty or failure to attend training courses.

Although temporary sheriffs may sometimes fail to have their appointment renewed (*e.g.* the one whose remarks in an under-age sex case had incensed the Asian community in 1982), only two permanent sheriffs have ever been removed through the use of the statutory procedure. The first occasion, in 1977, involved Sheriff Peter Thomson who was removed for "political activities incompatible with the holding of a judicial office". His offence consisted of associating himself (in his judicial capacity) too closely with a campaign for a Scottish plebiscite as a precursor to Scottish self-government. After a heated debate in the House of Commons, an attempt to annul the Secretary of State's order was defeated by 170 votes to 52. (See 940 H.C. Deb., cols 1288–1331, December 6, 1977.) The second, in 1992, involved Sheriff Ewen Stewart who was found by the Lord President and the Lord Justice-Clerk to be "unfit for office by reason of inability to perform the judicial functions which are expected of a sheriff . . . ". Sheriff Stewart's downfall stemmed from one case too many in which he had interrupted incessantly (over 100 times) or made ill-advised and tactless remarks. Curiously, the senior judges did not make a finding of misbehaviour but one of inability. Sheriff Stewart claimed that inability was synonymous with physical and mental incapacity and raised an action of judicial review against the investigating team. He took exception on natural justice grounds to aspects of the removal procedure, for example, to not being shown the case against him, to the lack of a public hearing or an opportunity to cross-examine the witnesses on whose testimony the judges had relied. The action was rejected by the Court of Session and the House of Lords (*Stewart v. Secretary of State for Scotland* 1998 S.L.T. 385).

Although there are no other occasions upon which a sheriff has been removed from office, several sheriffs have been the subject of extensive media coverage and public controversy as a result of their conduct on the Bench. Recent examples include a sheriff singing "The Sash" in court, subsequently described by the High Court as "deplorable in the highest degree"; and the refusal of a temporary sheriff to disqualify a drunk-driver as he would then be unable to pay school fees, a decision which was reversed on appeal.

Several commentators, for example, David Pannick in *Judges* (OUP, 1987) at pp. 96 *et seq*., the Chairman of the English Bar in 1992 and the recent report of Justice on *The Judiciary* (Justice, 1992) have called for the introduction of a Judicial Commission to set standards of conduct for judges and to monitor their performance through the provision of a complaints procedure and a disciplinary tribunal. As the original Justice sub-committee pointed out in 1972 in its report on *The Judiciary* (Stevens, 1972) the term "good behaviour" is imprecise and inadequate. Lord Hailsham endeavoured to define it in an article entitled "The Lord Chancellor and Judicial Independence", 1980 *Cambrian Law Review* 40:

> "It goes without saying that the misbehaviour complained of should be specified in the resolution and should be conduct of a culpable misuse of the judicial office or conduct calculated to bring the judicial office into disrepute. It would be contrary to every conception of fair play that it should not be specified (as was the case in a recent Commons resolution attacking Lord Denning) and it would be contrary to the terms of the judge's appointment . . . if conduct short of misbehaviour were relied on. At least in my view, misbehaviour means something much worse than a tendency to arrive at erroneous decisions or to make undesirable or ill considered remarks, and, so far as I know, the power of removal has seldom, if ever, been exercised."

The alleged inadequacy of the test stems from the fact that "good behaviour" does not expressly include the question of incapacity and incompetence. In England the Supreme Court Act 1981, s. 11, provides a mechanism for the removal of a judge of the Supreme Court who is "disabled by a permanent infirmity from the performance of the duties of his office and is for the time being incapacitated from resigning his office". There is no equivalent provision in Scotland and in neither country is there any machinery for tackling the, fortunately, unusual problem of judges who are unfit, as a result of physical or mental impairment, to carry out their duties but who are unwilling to resign. The Justice sub-committee concluded that judges should be removed for proven incapacity, mental or physical.

In practice the reforms in the grounds and mechanism for the removal of the higher judiciary while desirable are likely to have little practical effect. No Scottish or English judge holding high judicial office has been removed by the formal address procedure since before 1707. This is not because there have not been any unfit or incapable judges during that time. The perceived importance of the separation of powers and the independence of the judiciary has been such that successive Lord Chancellors and Lords President have preferred to put pressure—sometimes very strong pressure—on judges to resign rather than to invoke more formal measures. Since 1890 there have been at least 15 instances where judges of the superior courts in the United Kingdom have been the subject of strong pressures or inducements to resign, usually on the grounds of ill-health which they were reluctant to face up to or were incapable of recognising.

The problem with such an approach is not just the secrecy with which it is pursued, but that it provides no overt support for the democratic principle that public officials who are entrusted with considerable powers should be held accountable for the exercise of these powers. It may be that what is required is more effective intermediate sanctions. At present if a judge abuses his or her power to convict of contempt of court (*Macara v. Macfarlane* 1980 S.L.T. (Notes) 26), oppressively refuses an adjournment (*Tudhope v. Lawrie* 1979 S.L.T. (Notes) 13; *McNaughton v. McPherson* 1980 S.L.T. (Notes) 97), imposes his personal views on a jury (*McMillan v. H.M. Advocate* 1979 S.L.T. (Notes) 68), appears to fall asleep on the bench (*R. v. Weston-super-Mare Justices, ex p. Taylor* [1981] Crim. L.R. 179), fails to give proper consideration to an application (*Rae, Petitioner* 1982 S.L.T. 233), refuses to disqualify himself from presiding at a trial because of views he had previously expressed (the striking miners' case, *Bradford v. McLeod* 1986 S.L.T. 244), fails to disqualify himself in a case in which the judge has been a dismissed employee of the accused (*Harper of Oban Ltd v. Iain Henderson* 1988 S.C.C.R. 351), appears to indicate a belief in the veracity of the Crown witnesses before the defence has been heard (*Hogg v. Normand* 1992 S.C.C.R. 27) or interrupts, interrogates and criticises witnesses (*Harper v. Heywood* 1998 G.W.D. 3–110), he or she can be publicly rebuked and/or reversed on appeal. [On disqualification generally, see I. Dickinson, "Disqualification of Judges on Account of Interest" (1984) 29 J.L.S.S. 446.] But an appeal is not always available (for example, the case where a rapist was merely fined because the judge held that the victim had been contributorily negligent in hitch-hiking), financially practicable or satisfactory (see, *e.g.*, *R. v. Langham and Langham* [1972] Crim. L.R. 457—another case where a judge appeared to be asleep). In these situations Scotland is potentially in a stronger position than England since it already possesses two intermediate mechanisms which are capable of development.

Justice, *The Judiciary*, pp. 50–51

> "90. In Scotland, the Dean of Faculty has a duty to protect the interest of the Bar and all its members. In the past it was not unknown for him, if counsel were not being given a fair hearing, to intervene personally in order to remind the judge or judges of the rights and privileges of an advocate, and thereafter to remain in court seated beside the counsel appearing in the case, to make sure that the warning was heeded. Nowadays however such a complaint would be dealt with privately and after the event. The Dean investigates the complaint and, if he thinks it justified, he will have a word with the judge in question or possibly with the Lord President (who is expected to take it up with the judge). This procedure appears not to work as well as it should.
>
> 91. However, a more useful remedy is provided by the power of the Lord Advocate to investigate any matter connected with the administration of the law and law courts in Scotland. This is regularly invoked with reference to alleged misbehaviour by the lower judiciary, e.g. the sheriffs. In each sheriff court district the Lord Advocate has a local official, the procurator-fiscal, who is responsible only to him and is independent of both police and judiciary. If anyone (lawyer, M.P., private citizen) complains to the Lord Advocate about a sheriff, his complaint will be remitted to the local procurator-fiscal for inquiry. The latter will interview any witness and investigate the complaint privately, and finally report back to the Crown Office (the Lord Advocate's department in Scotland). After considering the report the Lord Advocate may write personally to the sheriff about it, he may ask him to come to the Crown Office to discuss it or in an extreme case he may set in motion the machinery for removal of the sheriff.

92. The Lord Advocate's powers are not statutory but arise from his inherent common law right to inquire into anything which concerns the rights and interests of the public of Scotland . . . There is in principle no reason (even though it might give rise to a delicate situation) why this power should not be exercised in relation to a judge of the Court of Session; so far, however, this has never happened."

If the latter mechanism were to be extended to the Court of Session Bench and if a power of reprimand or censure were invested in the Lord President or a judicial commission, genuine grievances could be remedied without exposing the judiciary to a flood of unfounded and damaging accusations.

The media could have a constructive role to play in this area, as they do in some parts of the USA, by publishing peer review polls on the local judiciary. A U.K. version of these is the periodic survey by the magazine *Legal Business*, which invites over 100 litigators to nominate their best and worst three judges on the High Court Bench. In the most recent surveys, Harman J. was identified as one of the worst, and shortly afterwards was heavily criticised by the Court of Appeal, for a 20-month delay in delivering a verdict (*Goose v. Wilson Sandford & Co*, *The Times*, February 19, 1998). He subsequently resigned.

B. SALARIES

As a further protection to the independence of the judiciary the salaries of Senators of the College of Justice, sheriffs principal and sheriffs are paid out of the Consolidated Fund. (Administration of Justice Act 1973, s. 9; Sheriff Courts (Scotland) Act 1907, s. 14.) The salaries are therefore not subject to direct parliamentary control. Further, while the size of the salaries can be increased by statutory order, they cannot be reduced.

C. JUDICIAL IMMUNITIES

1. Parliamentary

The immunity from criticism of the judiciary in Parliament, except where a substantive motion has been tabled, is a custom of both Houses which has occasionally in recent times been honoured more in the breach than in the acceptance. Nevertheless, the following extract accurately summarises the general position.

Shetreet, *Judges on Trial*, p. 163

"The general rule is that the conduct of judges cannot be discussed in Parliament unless upon a substantive motion which admits of a distinct vote of the House. Likewise, matters awaiting adjudication or pending before the courts cannot be brought before Parliament. As to motions for an inquiry into the conduct of a judge, the principle has been established that unless the prima facie case against the judge is strong and unless the charges, if

> proved, would justify an address for his removal, Parliament will not interfere. Given these principles, it seems that Parliament does not exercise any disciplinary function over judges short of removal by an address, and that it cannot pursue a course with the final aim not of an address for removal but of censure, criticism or condemnation of judicial conduct."

(See, however, the Speaker's ruling at 34 H.C. Deb., col. 285, December 15, 1982.)

2. Immunity From Suit

Judges of the Court of Session and the High Court are absolutely immune from civil suit in respect of acts done and statements made in their judicial capacity, whether or not they are within their jurisdiction and irrespective of malice or improper motive (*M'Creadie v. Thomson* 1907 S.C. 1176). The United States Supreme Court has ruled that the same rule holds true for judges of superior or general jurisdiction in America (*Stump v. Sparkman* (1978) 435 U.S. 349). In England it seems that the immunity ceases if the act done is outwith jurisdiction and motivated by malice (*Sirros v. Moore* [1975] Q.B. 118).

The position in relation to sheriffs was considered in the Court of Session in 1997, when a sheriff was sued on the basis of his conduct of the pursuer's trial for road traffic offences. (*Russell v. Dickson* 1997 S.C. 269). Despite the sheriff's conduct being described by the court as "manifestly unreasonable and incompetent" (at 277G), he was held to be immune and the action was dismissed as irrelevant. The issue of malice was said to be of no assistance whether proved or not. Although the temporary judge expressed considerable unease at the outcome, which he described as "against all equity and reason", he considered himself bound by existing lines of authority. Until such authorities are reconsidered, it is now clear that sheriffs enjoy a wide degree of immunity from suit covering almost all aspects of their judicial work.

Whatever the scope of a judge's immunity, commentators are agreed that some immunity is necessary to preserve the independence of the judiciary and to safeguard the administration of justice. (For further discussions of judicial immunities see D.L. Carey Miller, "Defamation by a judge? Fixing the limits?" 1980 J.R. 88 and M. Brazier, "Judicial immunity and the independence of the judiciary" [1976] P.L. 397.)

The problem with judicial independence is that almost every attempt to immunise the judiciary from undue pressure and influence has simultaneously the effect of making them less accountable to the society which they were appointed to serve. It is not clear how this impasse can be overcome. The best course seems to lie in trying to strike an appropriate balance between independence and accountability. This would extend from the procedures for judicial appointment to the setting and monitoring of standards for judicial conduct. Thus, for example, in relation to immunity from suit there may be a case, as Carey Miller has argued, for restricting immunity from defamation suits to statements which are reasonably relevant to the matters before the court.

CHAPTER 9

THE FACULTY OF ADVOCATES

Monopolies and Mergers Commission, "Advocates' Services", p. 3

> "In essence and in origin the Faculty is an independent corporation consisting of those who have been admitted to practice as advocates before the Court of Session (the supreme civil court of Scotland). It has long been a common feature of courts in Western Europe that there is a defined and recognised group of lawyers admitted to practice as advocates before those courts and having sole right of audience apart (in some but not all cases) from party litigants. From a very early stage, those who were admitted to practice before particular courts formed themselves into independent corporations, which came to administer their own affairs and to regulate matters of professional discipline and conduct. The Faculty became a separate and identifiable corporate body during the late sixteenth or early seventeenth century.
>
> Despite superficial resemblances, the Faculty is in certain basic respects unlike the Bar of England and Wales. Advocates form part of the College of Justice under a legal system which came into existence when Scotland was an independent nation and had close links with the continent. The Faculty has no written constitution but in origin, traditions and structure it can be compared with the Bars of most continental countries and their former colonies."

Faculty Evidence to the Hughes Commission, pp. 4–5

> "It is a common feature of these independent corporations of advocates including the Faculty that they elect their own leader, known in some countries as the Dean and in others as the Batonnier. An important aspect of his function is to assert the rights of the corporation and its members vis-à-vis the court and government, to maintain high standards on the part of the members and to adjudicate upon questions of discipline and conduct. Other office-bearers are elected from amongst the general body of members, who have an equal right to speak and vote at meetings. Apart from the office-bearers there is usually a Council whose functions may be executive or merely consultative."

In 1992 the Faculty decided to constitute an elected Council to exercise most of the powers previously exercised by the whole Faculty in general meeting. These include the formulation of policy, making provision for the maintenance of the Library, regulating admission and professional conduct. The Council consists of the Faculty office-bearers and three members each from the ranks of senior counsel, senior juniors and junior juniors together with one elected from the ranks of non-practising members.

[On the history of the Faculty, see J.M. Pinkerton's "Introduction" to *The Minute Book of the Faculty of Advocates*, Vol. I (The Stair Society, 1976), the essays contributed by G. Donaldson and N.T. Phillipson to N. MacCormick (ed.), *Lawyers in their Social Setting* (W. Green & Son, 1976) and paras 499–1301 of Vol. 13 of the *Stair Memorial Encyclopaedia of the Laws of Scotland*.]

I. RECRUITMENT

Entry to the Faculty is regulated by the Faculty, not by legislation. Intrants are also required to pass professional examinations (though exemption from most of them can be obtained by taking the relevant subjects in a Scottish law degree) and hold a pass in the Diploma in Legal Practice. They must also undergo a period of practical training (at least 12 months in a solicitor's office as a trainee followed by about nine months' pupillage or "devilling" to a practising member of Faculty). Special provisions exist for the admission of candidates who are already barristers from England and Wales and Northern Ireland or legal practitioners from another member state of the European Community.

In 1995 the Faculty radically revamped its training programme for intrants following the appointment of its first Director of Education and Training. Although the traditional period of "devilling" remains, all intrants are now required to commence their training in October with a six-week classroom-based training course. Subsequent training courses also occur during the devilling period, all of which focus on "learning by doing" and seek to develop specialist advocacy skills such as drafting pleadings, case preparation, negotiation, ethics and appearing in specialist tribunals and courts. The training has been widely praised within the profession and the Faculty of Advocates was awarded the "Best Use of Training" award in *The Lawyer's* annual awards for 1996. [See Sturrock, "Training Advocates", 1996 J.L.S.S. 30.]

Faculty Evidence to the Hughes Commission, p. 5

> "While it is the Court of Session which admits an Intrant to the public office of advocate, the Court since the latter part of the seventeenth century has left it to the Faculty to determine the conditions for admission and to determine whether an Intrant satisfies those conditions . . . The Court will not decline to admit to the Roll of Advocates a person who has been found duly qualified and admitted to membership of the Faculty."

The Hughes Commission, p. 263

> "16.61 At present, the content of the devil's training is a matter entirely between him and his master. In practice, the content is constrained by the range of work the master does and many trainees will inevitably find that their work is unrepresentative of the work of the Bar as a whole. On the other hand, since many newly-qualified advocates may receive some of their work through late instructions when more senior advocates have had to call off in particular cases, we have had to consider whether there should be a

> minimum range of experience which each devil should acquire before he can be considered qualified. It would certainly seem desirable that all devils should gain experience in both civil and criminal work. We recognise, however, that the small size of the Faculty might make it impossible for all devils to acquire such a range of experience within the necessarily short period of devilling. Without imposing an absolute requirement, therefore, we recommend that the Faculty should strongly encourage all devils to obtain a wide range of experience. If necessary, this could be facilitated by changing devil masters during the period of devilling."

Pupils, even if they are experienced solicitor pleaders, are not permitted to speak in court. In an innovative move to overcome this problem and to provide free assistance to CAB clients the Faculty reached an agreement with Citizens' Advice Scotland in 1990 that a rota of pupils would be established to provide representation before tribunals for clients of individual bureaux with complex cases. The travelling expenses of the pupils are met by the Faculty. Although the number of clients assisted in any given year is relatively small, the scheme has otherwise been very successful.

[Since 1991, pupil masters have been required to complete a report at the end of the period of pupillage confirming that the pupil has displayed sufficient diligence, competence and trustworthiness during his or her pupillage to make them suitable for admission to the Faculty.]

A. ADMISSION

Ultimately admission is determined by a resolution of the Faculty members gathered in public meeting, followed by the declaration of the oath of allegiance to the Sovereign, in open court.

[For an account of the pre-1966 procedure which involved the defence of a thesis in Latin (supposedly authored by the intrant) at public examination, see Pinkerton, "Introduction" (above) and N. Wilson, "The Faculty of Advocates Today" (1966) *Acta Juridica* 227. For a fuller account of admission and pupillage today see paras 1304–1314, Vol. 13, *Stair Memorial Encyclopaedia of the Laws of Scotland*.]

Professional qualifications aside, the Faculty imposes no formal restrictions on the numbers of candidates seeking admission to the Bar. Nor are Scottish intrants hampered, as English intrants are, by the need to obtain tenancies in chambers, which are in short supply. Nevertheless the cost of entry can still be high. The major outlay is simply living expenses to cover the two-year period from the start of pupillage, when fees are not coming in. But there are many other items—the matriculation fee, entry money (payable in instalments), Faculty rates, Widows' and Orphans' Fund dues, indemnity insurance premiums, journal subscriptions, books, travelling expenses and the cost of wig, gown and other items of formal dress. The aspiring advocate requires either savings (over a quarter of recent intrants have practised as solicitors for a period for this reason), a working spouse, an understanding bank manager or private means. While some take the view that the initial outlays are merely the counterpart to the capital required to set up a business, others have expressed concern at the practical barriers which are imposed by the high cost of entry.

Table 9.1 Admission to the Faculty

Year	*Male*	*Female*	*All*	*Year*	*Male*	*Female*	*All*
1975	15	2	17	**1987**	21	9	30
1976	11	2	13	**1988**	15	4	19
1977	8	2	10	**1989**	15	4	19
1978	15	–	15	**1990**	25	5	30
1979	17	–	17	**1991**	10	5	15
1980	13	2	15	**1992**	27	5	32
1981	9	4	13	**1993**	25	10	35
1982	10	2	12	**1994**	22	9	31
1983	9	4	13	**1995**	21	8	29
1984	9	–	9	**1996**	16	4	20
1985	14	1	15	**1997**	10	4	14
1986	14	2	16	**1998**	11	7	18

The Hughes Commission, p. 265

"16.66 The period of unremunerated devilling is one of severe financial hardship, particularly as advocates frequently take a year to recover their fees and can thus have no effective income for about a year following their admission to the Bar. Even then, given that they are unlikely to receive a great deal of work in their first years, the total fees they receive are likely to be small. The financial barriers to entry to the advocate branch of the profession . . . undoubtedly affect the flow of intrants to the Bar, and it has been suggested that this leads to a bias in the class composition of the Bar in favour of those who can support themselves from private means during their period of devilling and for the first years after admission. For these reasons, and because supreme court judges and many sheriffs are recruited from the ranks of practising advocates, we think that the remuneration of devils is a matter of public interest, and [that consideration should be given to] the possibility of making grants available to devils from public funds . . . A further possibility would be for the Faculty to establish an arrangement with a financial institution to provide loans for devils. The Dean of Faculty already has a small loans fund at his disposal to help intrants who require assistance, but this is not sufficiently large to accommodate those who may at present be discouraged from becoming advocates by the financial difficulties that exist at the outset of a career at the Bar. We recommend, therefore, that the Faculty should consider the possibility of arranging a wider loan scheme for devils than is at present available, in view of the importance of maintaining a representative flow of intrants to the Bar."

(In 1983 a scholarship fund was established from a bequest left by Lord Reid which has provided about two scholarships a year. In 1992 the Faculty established its own scholarship programme, worth in total £20,000 a year.)

B. TAKING SILK

Scotland, like England, has a two-tier Bar divided between junior and senior counsel. Elevation to the rank of senior or Queen's Counsel is self-initiated, but premature application is discouraged by the requirement that applicants must give notice of their intention to apply for the right to wear a silk gown to all juniors who were admitted to the Bar before them.

Monopolies and Mergers Commission, "Advocates' Services", p. 5

"The method of appointing Senior Counsel is as follows. When an advocate feels that the time has come for him to take silk, he approaches the Dean. If the Dean considers that the application is for any reason undesirable he will say so. If the Dean approves, or if the applicant insists, the Dean will discuss it with the Lord Justice General. The applicant will then be told whether or not his application is likely to be granted and, if not, why not. The formal application for silk is made by letter to the Lord Justice General asking him to recommend the applicant to Her Majesty, through the Secretary of State for Scotland, for appointment as one of Her Majesty's Counsel. In practice formal applications are seldom made unless it is clear that they will be granted. A point to which the Lord Justice General and the Dean have regard is that the number of applications for silk granted should not be such as to result in excessive depletion of the junior Bar. At present juniors are being given silk at about age 40 after 10 to 15 years in junior practice. The number of Senior Counsel is dictated by the needs of the work of the Bar."

[For further details on the status and function of senior counsel and their historical origin in the late nineteenth century, see para. 1317 of Vol. 13 of the *Stair Memorial Encyclopaedia of the Laws of Scotland*.]

II. COMPOSITION

At any given time around half of the Faculty will be in active practice as advocates. This is because a member of the Faculty, once admitted, remains a member even when he or she has ceased to practice or has taken up an appointment that is incompatible with practice at the Bar. Thus in 1998 the Faculty included 113 serving or retired judges, 11 academic lawyers, 11 working in central government or in industry, four Members of Parliament, 34 working furth of Scotland and over 360 practising advocates. In the past 30 years, between a third and a quarter of practising advocates have been Queen's Counsel—a considerably higher proportion than has been the case in England. In recent years, however, the substantial growth in the numbers of practising advocates has reduced the proportion of Q.C.s.

Table 9.2 Size of the Faculty

Year	*Nominal*	*Practising*	*Q.C.s*	*Year*	*Nominal*	*Practising*	*Q.C.s*
1710	250	170		**1984**	407	195	50
1832	442	?		**1985**	417	202	50
1860	300	115		**1987**	455	230	49
1876	337	130		**1990**	490	250	60
1962	281	106		**1992**	510	290	75
1967	285	114		**1995**	606	364	77
1975	322	128	32	**1997**	625	381	78
1979	361	148	36	**1998**	655	404	80
1982	387	173	44				

Table 3 Female Advocates in Practice

Year	*Total*	*Year*	*Total*
1974	3	**1987**	28
1975	4	**1988**	32
1976	5	**1989**	36
1977	6	**1990**	40
1978	8	**1991**	45
1979	8	**1992**	47
1980	8	**1993**	56
1981	13	**1994**	64
1982	13	**1995**	70
1983	16	**1996**	75
1984	16	**1997**	76
1985	17	**1998**	83
1986	19		

In the 20 years following the end of the Second World War the practising Bar remained in the range of 100–115 advocates. As Tables 1, 2 and 3 reveal, there has been a very considerable increase since then, particularly in the past 10 years. The same decade has witnessed the advent (for the first time in the Faculty's history) of women advocates practising at the Bar in sizeable numbers. A pilot study by Paxton as late as 1982 revealed that female advocates, although accepted by their male colleagues, were viewed by some with condescension. By 1999 only 117 women had been admitted to the Faculty and only 16 had gone on to become Q.C.s., (eight of whom were practising in 1999). Paxton found evidence of continuing sex discrimination in two related areas—in the attitude of some instructing solicitors and their clients, and in the range of work which came to female advocates. One advocate reported how, when acting as junior counsel at a consultation, she was taken for a secretary by the client who said: "Now I want the wee lassie to tak' this down." Equally startling was another suggestion that: "Is it cos' I'm on legal aid that I've got to tak' a lassie?" Certainly, in 1982 there were some solicitors who would never instruct a woman. Times have changed in the last decade and any residual discrimination against female advocates is dying out as their numbers grow. Nevertheless, female advocates in Scotland have been fortunate that they have not had to overcome discrimination against them in the granting of tenancies in chambers, a problem which their English sisters have had to endure for many years. Moreover, a survey of both branches of the legal profession for *The Lawyer* in 1992 found that 52 per cent of the female respondents complained of encountering discrimination in their work. (See H. Kennedy, "Women at the Bar" in R. Hazell (ed.), *The Bar on Trial* [Quartet Books, 1978), H. Kennedy, *Eve was Framed* (Chatto and Windus, 1992) and *The Lawyer* December 8, 1992, p. 6.]

III. ADVOCATES' SERVICES

Monopolies and Mergers Commission, "Advocates' Services", p. 4

"Advocates do not offer their services directly to the public; they accept

> instructions from solicitors. The professional services supplied by advocates . . . consist of services in relation to litigation, civil and criminal, in courts, tribunals and inquiries of all kinds, and of the giving of advice (including the drafting of documents) on legal matters."

[Since 1990 it has been competent for an advocate to accept instructions from a member of a recognised professional body without the need to use a solicitor. Over 20 such bodies have been recognised, including associations of accountants, architects, actuaries, auctioneers, engineers and surveyors. For further details see para. 1348, Vol. 13, *Stair Memorial Encyclopaedia of the Laws of Scotland*.]

A. MONOPOLIES

For centuries advocates had the sole right of audience in the Court of Session and the High Court of Justiciary (if we exclude party litigants), a right they shared with other United Kingdom barristers before the House of Lords. These monopolies have been slightly eroded in recent years. Solicitors can appear to present unopposed motions in the Court of Session during the vacations. Secondly, European Community lawyers now have certain rights of audience.

The European Communities (Services of Lawyers) Order 1978 (S.I. 1978 No. 1910), art. 5

"Representation in legal proceedings

> 5. No enactment or rule of law practice shall prevent an EEC lawyer from providing any service in relation to any proceedings, whether civil or criminal, before any court, tribunal or public authority (including appearing before and addressing the court, tribunal or public authority) by reason only that he is not an advocate, barrister or solicitor; provided that throughout he is instructed with, and acts in conjunction with, an advocate, barrister or solicitor who is entitled to practise before the court, tribunal or public authority concerned and who could properly provide the service in question."

(This Order implemented E.C. Council Directive No. 77/249 For the definition of an EEC lawyer, see art. 2 of the Order.)

This order will shortly be overtaken by the EU Lawyers Establishment Directive (98/5). The Directive, when implemented, will enable lawyers qualified in one Member State to practise under their home title permanently in another EU Member State. Lawyers who have been practising and registered for at least three years in another Member State will be entitled to integrate with the legal profession of the host state. In addition rights of audience in the supreme courts have been extended to certain solicitors following the passing of sections 24–27 of the Law Reform (Miscellaneous Provisions) (Scotland) Act 1990 (see "Reform", below).

B. CONCURRENT RIGHTS

Practising advocates have concurrent rights of audience with solicitors before all the inferior courts and tribunals in which legal representation is permitted. In recent years they have frequently been instructed to appear at public inquiries. Advocates also share with solicitors the right to prepare writs for gain which relate to legal proceedings but in practice it is the advocates who normally draft written pleadings in proceedings before the superior courts.

C. SENIOR AND JUNIOR COUNSEL

The division of labour between junior and senior counsel is now less clear cut than once was the case. In general, junior counsel are responsible for the written pleadings and the less onerous oral advocacy and advisory work. Senior counsel are usually instructed to conduct the more important types of litigation (usually with the assistance of junior counsel) and receive the more responsible advisory work.

The Hughes Commission, p. 227

> "15.39 Following the report of the Monopolies and Mergers Commission on the supply of services by senior counsel, the so called 'two counsel rule' was suspended in 1977. The two counsel rule was a requirement in most civil proceedings that junior counsel had to be instructed whenever a senior was engaged; in criminal proceedings, on the other hand, it was possible for a senior counsel to be engaged on his own. Since 1977 there has no longer been any requirement to engage junior counsel when a senior counsel is instructed, although the senior has a right to insist that a junior must be instructed if he considers the case warrants it. The client has the reciprocal right to decline to instruct any particular advocate who so insists; and so far as we can judge from the relatively limited period of operation of the new arrangements they appear to be operating satisfactorily."

D. WORKING ARRANGEMENTS

Each advocate has a box in the main corridor of Parliament House in which instructions are placed and papers kept. His or her "place of work" during court hours is the Advocates' Library. For reasons of convenience and expense over two-thirds of the Bar now practise exclusively from Parliament House although some counsel (mainly seniors) retain chambers in Edinburgh's New Town for consultations with solicitors and clients after court hours.

In 1971 the Faculty set up a non-profitmaking company entitled Faculty Services Ltd which employs the advocates' clerks, provides secretarial facilities and is responsible for the invoicing and collection of fees due to counsel. The 11 clerks each handle the work of a number of advocates colloquially known as their "stables". Each clerk is responsible for arranging his or her counsels' diaries, fixing consultations, suggesting replacement counsel and negotiating counsel's fees.

Monopolies and Mergers Commission, "Advocates' Services", p. 6

> "25. Throughout his professional life, every advocate operates entirely on his own. The Faculty, or Faculty Services Limited, provides most facilities

needed and any other sharing of facilities is purely in the nature of an ad hoc 'overhead-sharing' arrangement. There is no 'chambers' system such as exists in England. If an advocate cannot perform an item of work for which he has been instructed, he must (unless the matter is urgent) return the instructions to his clerk. The latter must seek fresh instructions from the solicitor before passing the work to another advocate, unless the matter is urgent or the clerk has a special arrangement with the solicitor. If the matter is urgent, the advocate passes the instructions to another advocate either directly or through the clerk. An advocate cannot employ another to help him nor is there any form of partnership."

It was suggested to the Hughes Commission that the ban on partnerships for advocates works against the interests of new advocates trying to get established or advocates who fall ill. The Faculty argued against any change stating that it would reduce the choice of counsel available to parties. The Hughes Commission concluded that the ban should continue.

Despite the Commission's conclusion on this point, the Government in pursuit of its policy on deregulation and the elimination of restrictive practices included a provision in the Law Reform (Miscellaneous Provisions) (Scotland) Act 1990 on partnerships between advocates and between advocates and other professionals. Section 31 of the Act requires that any rule prohibiting such partnerships has to be approved by the Lord President and the Secretary of State (after consultation with the Director-General of Fair Trading). The Director-General's Report on the Faculty of Advocates' proposed rule which continued to outlaw such partnerships was published in June 1992. He concluded that a ban on partnerships between advocates or between advocates and other professionals would not significantly restrict or distort competition and would preserve a pool of independent advocates as well as maximising the range of choice for clients. The Director-General, perhaps influenced by media reports of substantial fees alleged to have been charged by counsel in the Orkney and Piper Alpha inquiries, nevertheless expressed concern as to the breadth of the choice available to clients in terms of advocates' fees.

One factor which contributes to the public's freedom of choice of counsel is the "cab-rank rule".

The Hughes Commission, pp. 227–228

"15.40 The 'cab-rank rule' is a professional rule applying to advocates and it is incorporated in a rule of court which states that: 'No advocate, without very good cause, shall refuse to act for any person tendering a reasonable fee, under pain of deprivation of his office of advocate.'

In practice, what this rule means is that an advocate cannot refuse to accept a case on the grounds that he does not like a client or his cause . . .

There are, of course, recognised circumstances which justify an advocate declining a case, the main ones being that he is already acting for a party with a conflicting interest; ill health; or that he has already been instructed in a case which would be likely to be called in court at or about the same time. We understand that one of the main benefits of the cab rank rule so

> far as the public interest is concerned is that there cannot be any occasion when a litigant would find himself without representation. If the advocate of the client's choice is for a good reason unable to take the case, the cab-rank rule normally ensures that another suitable advocate is available."

As the Faculty pointed out in its evidence to the Hughes Commission, the cab-rank rule prevents formal specialisation at the Scottish Bar, although individual advocates do come to acquire specialised practices to a greater or lesser extent.

E. REFORM

From time to time in the last 100 years, whenever litigation has decreased or concern over the cost of litigation has increased, dissident voices have been heard in Scotland as to the merits of the divided profession. The separation between counsel and solicitors, it is said, involves unnecessary expense and duplication of effort—in short it acts as a restrictive practice which is not in the public interest. Inevitably this was a topic on which the Hughes Commission received considerable evidence—the bulk of it favouring the status quo.

The Hughes Commission, p. 231

> "15.50 Our feeling after weighing the evidence is that we should be very hesitant to make any recommendation which could result in a diminution or restriction of the legal services which are available at the present time; and we are, on balance, more impressed by the arguments in favour of, than those against, the present divided profession. In particular, we see great value in having an independent advocate service which is available to all solicitors and, therefore, to all clients in Scotland. One of the strengths of the independent Faculty of Advocates based in Edinburgh is the concentration of facilities in the Advocates Library, in Parliament House, Edinburgh. This is a significant factor in keeping advocates' costs low and in making available to them adequate opportunities for research. While we appreciate that modern technological developments will in due course allow lawyers outwith Edinburgh to have equally good access to legal texts stored on electronic retrieval systems, we feel that the concentration of the Faculty in Edinburgh also allows opportunities for informal exchange of information and opinion which would not be as easy if the advocate branch of the profession were distributed up and down the country. Another benefit of the location of the separate advocates branch of the profession in Edinburgh is that it strengthens the control of discipline and the maintaining of high ethical standards and we have no doubt that for these reasons alone it is in the public interest. We recommend, therefore, that the legal profession in Scotland should continue to consist of two branches, namely solicitors and advocates."

[For further arguments on the unification of the profession, see Hughes, paras 15.44–15.49 and S.S. Robertson, "Divided We Fall?" (1970) 15 J.L.S.S. 219.]

For a while in the late 1980s the topic of fusion attracted more serious consideration from both branches of the English legal profession. However, many members of both branches of the profession continued to be fiercely opposed to fusion. Interest began to shift to less radical options. Michael Zander suggested that the restrictive practices relating to litigation practice should be removed, but that fusion should be a matter for individual practitioners to decide.

Zander, *Legal Services for the Community*, pp. 173–174

> "The ideal would seem to be a situation where the rules permit the profession to organise itself in whatever way seems beneficial to individual practitioners in the light of their inclinations and the needs of their clients. There should, therefore, be no rule preventing lawyers from taking instructions only from other lawyers—but equally, legislation should prohibit any rule requiring it. Whilst most lawyers would . . . continue as before, some might experiment with new forms of organisation. Some solicitors would take cases in the higher courts . . . some barristers would take instructions from clients such as accountants, surveyors, banks and insurance companies, whilst others would be prepared to act directly for clients generally. (Barristers who held clients' moneys would, of course, have to be made subject to the same strict rules as now apply to solicitors.) Given the deep conservatism of the legal profession the probability is that change, if there were any, would be extremely slow. It would move at the speed at which lawyers themselves wanted to go. This at least should be permitted."

Zander's proposal is somewhat akin to the position favoured by the Law Society of Scotland known as the "New Zealand option". In New Zealand, every intrant to the profession is admitted as both a barrister and a solicitor. The intrant then obtains a practising certificate to practise as a barrister, or a solicitor, or as a barrister and solicitor. In all three of these categories full rights of audience are enjoyed. However, those practising as barristers only, may not do so in partnership. This has ensured the survival of a separate Bar while offering full rights of audience to solicitors and barristers alike. However, the publication of the Scottish Office consultation paper, "The Practice of the Solicitor Profession in Scotland" (1987) contained only the proposals that rights of audience in the supreme courts be extended to suitably qualified solicitors and rights of audience generally should be extended to non-lawyers. The Law Society responded enthusiastically to the first whilst rejecting the second. The Faculty of Advocates rejected both.

In the event the Law Reform (Miscellaneous Provisions) (Scotland) Act 1990 contains both provisions. Section 24 (enacting a new section 25A to the Solicitors (Scotland) Act 1980) creates a framework by which solicitors can obtain the requisite extended rights of audience. It provides that solicitors seeking rights of audience in the Court of Session or House of Lords or the Judicial Committee of the Privy Council on the one hand or the High Court of Justiciary on the other must undergo a course of training in evidence and pleading in the supreme courts and demonstrate an adequate knowledge of relevant aspects of practice, procedure and issues of professional conduct. The Practice Rules relating to extended rights of audience for solicitors (Admission as a Solicitor with Extended Rights (Scotland) Rules 1992) were drawn up by the Law Society with the approval of the Lord President and the Secretary of State. They provide for a period of induction training covering the procedures and practices of the supreme courts, sitting-in in either the Court of Session or the High Court of Justiciary in Edinburgh, and examinations covering evidence, pleading, practice, procedure and professional conduct. While suitably experienced solicitors can be exempted from most of these requirements, they cannot be exempted from the examinations.

The Faculty of Advocates argued that solicitor advocates should be subject to the cab rank rule. This was opposed by the Law Society. Section 25A(6) contains a compromise. Solicitor advocates must give priority to their supreme court work and the Society has a collective obligation to find a solicitor advocate to represent any client with a case before the supreme courts who wishes representation by a solicitor advocate. Solicitor advocates, however, are not required to take every case that comes to them in their own field even if it is accompanied by a reasonable fee.

The opportunity to become a solicitor advocate has only been taken up by a relatively small number of practitioners. In 1999, there were 112 solicitor advocates, 63 of whom were qualified for criminal matters and 51 of whom were qualified for civil matters with two being qualified for both. This represents just over 1 per cent of the total number of practising solicitors. There are various reasons for this, but the crucial factor seems to relate to levels of remuneration. Advocates require little in the way of offices and back-up staff. As a result, their overheads run at below 20 per cent of their gross fees. Solicitors in even the most efficient firms are fortunate if only 60 per cent of their gross fees go to overheads. Many firms operate with more adverse proportions than this. It follows that if solicitor advocates are paid the same rates as advocates they will not find it cost-effective to practise as solicitor advocates. While it appears fair that a solicitor advocate should be able to claim a fee for the solicitor's aspect of the work as well as the advocacy aspects, legal aid will only pay both sets of fees where two separate lawyers are involved (thus destroying most of the point of the reform). Even in private work the solicitor advocate will be at a disadvantage because of the overheads problem.

These issues affect the type of work handled by solicitor advocates. A recent study found that much of the work handled by solicitor advocates was of a short and straightforward nature, notably bail appeals on the criminal side. The difficulties faced by solicitor advocates in practising appear to exclude many of them from the more protracted, and complex litigation work which remains the province of Faculty members.

Section 25 of the Law Reform (Miscellaneous Provisions) (Scotland) Act 1990 confers rights of audience on members of professional or other bodies whose applications have been accepted by the Lord President and the Secretary of State. This highly controversial provision only survived the Committee stage in the Commons by the casting vote of the chairman. Although applauded by the consumer bodies in Scotland as a move designed to increase client choice, the provision is strongly opposed by both branches of the legal profession. As yet there have been no moves to implement this part of the legislation.

IV. PROFESSIONAL PRACTICE, CONDUCT AND DISCIPLINE

A. COMPLAINTS AND DISCIPLINE

In contrast to the solicitors' branch of the profession, ultimate authority in determining what constitutes professional misconduct in an advocate lies in the Faculty and its elected office bearers, particularly the Dean. Unwritten standards of conduct governing the professional and private life of the advocate have existed for centuries, supplemented in specific areas by rulings issued from time to time by particular Deans. (The rulings of former Deans can be abrogated or modified by the current Dean.) The current Disciplinary Rules for the Faculty date from 1992. Any complaints against the conduct of advocates are addressed to the Dean, who will either investigate them himself or arrange for their investigation. In determining the sanction to be imposed, if any, the Dean will frequently consult his Council. In 1998 a Disciplinary Tribunal for the Faculty was established which can both adjudicate on complaints and serve as a sentencing body. However, any determination or disposal by the Tribunal is subject to review by the Dean who may modify or rescind it. To date the Tribunal has had very little to do, although a Q.C. was disciplined by the Tribunal in 1993 for breaching client confidentiality and another Q.C. was disqualified for criticising a jury in 1999. Following the passing of the Law Reform (Miscellaneous Provisions) (Scotland) Act 1990, advocates can be found to have delivered inadequate professional services. As with solicitors, where complainants are dissatisfied with the way in which their complaint has been handled by the relevant professional body, they may write to the Scottish Legal Services Ombudsman (see p. 273 below). In fact, only two or three such complaints a year reach the Ombudsman.

The Hughes Commission commented adversely on the lack of a formal written code of conduct for advocates and recommended that one should be promulgated. Perhaps spurred on by the need to provide something for lawyers from E.C. countries, the Faculty published a Guide to the Professional Conduct of Advocates in 1988. In 1997 the Dean of Faculty announced a review of the Faculty's complaints procedures. This followed repeated suggestions from the Scottish Legal Services Ombudsman that the Faculty's complaints procedures be revamped by the establishment of a Complaints Committee with at least two lay members (see the Ombudsman's Annual Reports of 1994 and 1996). The review was still ongoing in 1999.

B. PROFESSIONAL NEGLIGENCE

The scope of an advocate's liability for negligence is unclear. A century ago it was thought that an advocate could not be held liable for professional negligence. This was because he had no contract with his client, because of the discretion entrusted to and the judgment expected of counsel in the conduct of litigation and because at that time the law of delict provided no remedy for professional negligence.

***Batchelor v. Pattison and Mackersy* (1876) 3 R. 914**

Lord President (Inglis): "An advocate in undertaking the conduct of a cause in the Court enters into no contract with his client, but takes on himself an office in the performance of which he owes a duty, not to his client only, but also to the Court, to the members of his own profession, and to the public. From this it follows that he is not at liberty to decline, except in very special circumstances, to act for any litigant who applies for his advice and aid, and that he is bound in any cause that comes into Court to take the retainer of the party who first applies to him. It follows, also, that he cannot demand or recover by action any remuneration for his services, though in practice he receives honoraria in consideration of these services. Another result is, that while the client may get rid of his counsel whenever he pleases, and employ another, it is by no means easy for a counsel to get rid of his client. On the other hand, the nature of the advocate's office makes it clear that in the performance of his duty he must be entirely independent, and act according to his own discretion and judgment in the conduct of the cause for his client. His legal right is to conduct the cause without any regard to the wishes of his client, so long as his mandate is unrecalled, and what he does bona fide according to his own judgment will bind his client, and will not expose him to any action for what he has done, even if the client's interests are thereby prejudiced."

When the House of Lords ruled in *Hedley Byrne v. Heller* [1964] A.C. 465 that negligent advice could give rise to delictual liability even where there was no contractual relationship between the parties, one of the principal bases for counsel's immunity disappeared. This was confirmed by the House in *Rondel v. Worsley* [1969] 1 A.C. 191 but the House also concluded that sufficient public policy grounds existed to justify the continuation of counsel's immunity. These were (1) counsel's duties to the court (which he should not be inhibited from fulfilling by the fear of an action from his client), (2) the cab-rank rule, (3) the general immunity from civil liability which attaches to all persons participating in proceedings before a court of justice and (4) the undesirability of litigating again between counsel and client what has already been litigated between the client and the opponent.

Nevertheless it was established in *Rondel v. Worsley* that counsel's immunity was not a blanket one and that it only applied to such cases as fell within the area of public policy. This entailed that henceforth counsel must be treated as liable for professional negligence except in certain specified situations—but there was no consensus amongst the Law Lords as to exactly what these situations were. In *Saif Ali v. Sydney Mitchell & Co.* [1980] A.C. 198 the Law Lords had to decide more precisely where the dividing line between liability and immunity was to be drawn. The majority held that counsel's immunity from suit extended only to his conduct of a case in court and those matters of pre-trial work which were so intimately connected with the conduct of the case in court that they could fairly be said to be preliminary decisions affecting the way that case was conducted when it came to a hearing. The majority also held (*obiter*) that a solicitor acting as an advocate in court enjoys the same immunity as counsel. (Yet see *Murray v. Reilly* 1963 S.L.T. (Notes) 49.)

Gamble, "Advocates' Liability", pp. 5–6

"The result of *Ali* is that counsel are now potentially liable (in addition to pure opinion cases) in all decisions connected with litigation, except the actual court-room appearances and other work necessarily and intimately connected with these, where they will continue to enjoy immunity. This latter category seems to include decisions on which witnesses are to be called or other evidence used, *e.g.* notes on the line or specifications of documents in Scots practice. It seems not to cover written pleadings or settlements or tendering in cases and advice thereon. The majority speeches do not seek to particularise the test for immunity too much and there is certainly force in the minority view that its application will be difficult and may lead to uncertainty. It is submitted in general that it can be easily inferred from the thrust of the majority speeches that the test of intimate connection will be interpreted restrictively . . .

Now that the areas of liability and immunity have been delimited more precisely than formerly, what is important is to consider the circumstances where counsel can be liable for professional negligence in the post-*Ali* situation. It must be emphasised that removal of the former wide immunity does not mean automatic liability in every case of mistake or error of judgment. Counsel are now, over a large area of their work, subject to the same liability as other professional persons, no less but also no more. This liability is not excessively exacting. It is generally stated to be that no member of the relevant profession would have taken the course under attack or scrutiny if he had been acting with ordinary care and skill. This is familiar law as regards medical negligence, but it seems to represent a more general principle. In its application to counsel, it must be stressed that attacks on decisions involving judgment and discretion are unlikely to succeed and most matters where counsel are instructed include these very elements. This point is made in all the majority speeches in *Ali*. Thus the elements of discretion used in the nineteenth century cases to justify immunity for counsel reappear in *Ali* as the basic defences open to him. The practical result may well be the same in that it is submitted that the likelihood of an action succeeding against an advocate is relatively slight . . .

An important point requiring brief mention is whether *Ali* necessarily represents the law of Scotland. As an English decision, it is not strictly binding in Scotland, but as it is on a point of so-called "general jurisprudence" it is entitled to the highest respect and may be seen as perhaps almost binding. In particular, if the liability of counsel were to be litigated upon in Scotland, the Court of Session would, it seems, standing *Ali*, at least be entitled to over-rule earlier inconsistent Scots authorities."

Rodger, "At Risk", p. 465

"It seems unlikely that, if dealing with a Scottish appeal on the same point, the House of Lords would feel that they should not follow *Saif Ali* merely because it was an English case . . . None the less, the fact remains that *Saif Ali* is strictly speaking only highly persuasive and that the leading Scottish case is *Batchelor v. Pattison and Mackersy*, and that the reasoning at least in *Batchelor* is largely inconsistent with the approach in *Saif Ali* . . . It would not, it is submitted, be sufficient under current notions of negligence, for an advocate to say that, however negligent his actings, they were done bona fide according to his judgment. If the exercise of judgment were shown to be negligent, then he would be liable. So one is forced to the conclusion that the reasoning in *Batchelor* no longer affords a safe guide to the reasoning which would be likely to find ultimate acceptance in a Scottish case today . . .

So the Scots law position is rather unsatisfactory. We are left with a binding Inner House decision which looks unlikely to survive serious challenge either by reference to a larger court or by appeal to the House of Lords, but which still technically binds all courts lower than these . . . It seems likely that lawyers and insurers will accept that *Saif Ali* represents the real position. There will scarcely be a rush on the part of the lawyers to clarify the position by means of litigation, so that *Batchelor* could well have a long, if sickly, life ahead of it."

[See further on the advocate's liability for negligence, para. 1380, Vol. 13, *Stair Memorial Encyclopaedia of the Laws of Scotland*.]

The Faculty of Advocates certainly considers that the English cases might be followed in Scotland and since 1976 it has had a Compulsory Indemnity Insurance scheme. All practising advocates are required to have cover of at least £100,000. To date there have been no claims against advocates under indemnity policies.

With the recent retreat by the House of Lords in the field of liability for negligent acts, it seems unlikely that we shall see much judicial threat to the advocate's (or solicitor advocate's) singular immunity from liability for professional negligence in the near future. Indeed, the Law Reform (Miscellaneous Provisions) (Scotland) Act 1990, s. 27 makes it clear that the immunity for liability for negligence will extend to non-lawyers who exercise rights of audience under the Act. This is unlikely to satisfy the critics of the immunity.

Wilson, "Carte Blanche for Counsel", pp. 211–212

"If advocates are held to be immune from liability for [negligence it leads to] the paradox . . . that lawyers . . . apply the rule 'ignorance of the law is no excuse' to all except the legal elite. Naturally no system which imposes liability for negligence on lawyers does so except in very clear cases—cases where no advocate of ordinary skill acting with ordinary care would have conducted himself as did the defender . . . The idea that the courts would be flooded with actions against advocates seems unrealistic. If they were, paradoxically the Bar as a whole would not lose. The professional solidarity which protects the medical man when sued would be even stronger if the defender was an advocate. As with the artist or the actor the difficulties of proving that an advocate was incompetent are formidable. Alleged negligence in cross-examination, for example, would seem to be no easier and no more difficult to prove than the surgeon's negligent handling of a scalpel in a very delicate operation or negligent treatment by a psychiatrist . . . If an advocate has been careless in the preparation and production of his case, or has failed in his duty to court and client and also perhaps to the public who finance legal aid, why should it be concluded that public policy must be invoked to protect him?

> The surgeon and physician have not been spared the prospect of possible litigation by a vexatious and disgruntled patient . . . Other professions have comparable problems—yet the courts do not shield them from harassing actions on grounds of public policy. Professions other than the Bar may well enviously conclude that counsel . . . 'with the connivance of the judges, built for themselves an ivory tower and have lived in it ever since at the expense of their clients'."

The rationale for the immunity has been undermined by the judiciary itself. The argument from contract was abandoned in *Rondel* and that from the existence of the cab-rank rule had disappeared by the time of *Saif Ali*. Of the three remaining bases for the now limited immunity, the view that the immunity is required to encourage counsel to fulfil their obligations to the court seems suspect as Lord Diplock recognised in *Saif Ali* (at p. 220). In fact, as the Faculty of Advocates accepted in their evidence to the Hughes Commission the strongest argument for the retention of the immunity is because it is necessary that litigation should have a cut-off point.

Faculty Evidence to the Hughes Commission, pp. 24–25

> "In a claim based upon alleged negligence in the conduct of a case in Court, there could be no way of investigating the question whether that negligence was the cause of any alleged loss without examining the whole facts and circumstances of the case . . . [*i.e.*] retrying the previous action . . . The fundamental reason why the conduct of a case in Court should not be scrutinised in later proceedings has nothing to do with the particular status requirements or deserts of Advocates as such or advocacy as a profession, but is an aspect of the public policy requirement that cases concluded by judicial decisions should not be reopened."

The obvious reply to this argument is why should the cut-off point be drawn where it is? If our legal system recognises the need for appeals (and it is not a ground for appeal that one's counsel has been negligent) and the occasional need for a retrial in civil and criminal cases, why should any investigation of professional negligence by a lawyer in a courtroom be prohibited? As the extracts from Gamble and Wilson suggest, there is no likelihood that if the immunity were removed it would lead to a flood of litigation. The Scottish Legal Aid Board scrutinises professional negligence applications carefully and would not support frivolous actions.

In the last analysis the question is, can the immunity from professional negligence for those conducting advocacy in court be justified when brain surgeons or heart transplant consultants are not so privileged? Do we really believe that litigation is more important than life?

CHAPTER 10

SOLICITORS

The changes which have taken place in relation to the solicitor's branch of the profession in the past 20 years have been greater than those that took place in the previous 100 years. Deregulation, exponential growth, feminisation, rampant competition, restructuring, specialisation and higher standards are but the main hallmarks of the transformation. Together they have brought about a major change in the traditional concept of professionalism as it was understood by solicitors. During half a century from the early 1930s the bulk of the profession behaved as if there were a tacit contract between them and the state/society. In return for high status, reasonable rewards, constraints on competition and self-regulation they offered competence, access to the legal system, a service ethic and public protection. This implicit contractualism reflected the enduring tension between service orientation and self-interest which marks all professions. However, by the early 1980s it was becoming increasingly clear that the state and the consumer movement had serious reservations as to the fairness of this "bargain". Almost every element in the tacit concordat came under scrutiny and became a topic for debate. What we have witnessed then in the past 20 years is the wholesale renegotiation of the traditional concept of professionalism. Both the state and consumers have been insisting that the appropriate balance between the two sides of the bargain must be determined by the public interest. More radical still has been their assertion that the determination of the public interest in relation to the profession is a matter that is as much for them to determine as the profession itself. (See A. Paterson, "Professionalism and the Legal Services Market" (1996) 3 *International Journal of the Legal Profession* 137.)

Solicitors (formerly known also as writers or law agents) constitute by far the larger sector of the legal profession in Scotland. The bulk of practising solicitors work in private practice (either on their own or in partnership), but in recent years an increasing proportion have been attracted into industry, public bodies and local or central government (see Table 10.7 below). Traditionally solicitors in private practice in Scotland have been seen as, and have seen themselves as general persons of business. However, in recent years it has become commonplace for solicitors (and those in larger firms in particular) to specialise. The professional body of Scottish solicitors is the Law Society of Scotland.

I. RECRUITMENT

Solicitors (Scotland) Act 1980, ss. 4, 5

"**4.** No person shall be qualified to practise as a solicitor unless—

(a) he has been admitted as a solicitor; and
(b) his name is on the roll; and
(c) . . . he has in force a certificate issued by the Council of the Law society in accordance with the provisions of this [Act] authorising him to practise as a solicitor (referred to in this Act as a 'practising certificate').

5. (1) The Council may, with the concurrence of the Lord President, make regulations for—

(a) practical training;
(b) attendance at a course of legal education;
(c) the passing of examinations . . . "

A. EDUCATION AND TRAINING

Table 10.1 Undergraduate Students in Law in Scotland

	1965–66	**1970–71**	**1975–76**	**1980–81**	**1990–91**	**1997–98**
Aberdeen	124	212	352	380	450	593
Dundee	123	192	243	287	400	445
Edinburgh	430	443	508	512	560	625
Glasgow	357	299	391	447	510	696
Strathclyde	—	114	206	224	256	390
TOTAL	**1,034**	**1,260**	**1,700**	**1,850**	**2,176**	**2,749**

(Sources: Report of the Royal Commission on Legal Services in Scotland (Cmnd 7846) (1980) (the Hughes Report); The Law Schools.)

Table 10.2 University Graduates

Year	**Law Graduates**	**Diploma Graduates**
1970	312	—
1971	352	—
1972	329	—
1973	350	—
1974	371	—
1975	406	—
1976	433	—
1977	487	—
1978	503	—
1979	545	—
1980	529	—
1981	542	230
1982	483	407
1983	486	425
1984	529	454
1985	468	464
1986	464	415
1987	468	400
1988	511	383
1989	536	415
1990	509	408
1991	669	483
1992	623	439

1993	638	485
1994	675	504
1995	640	496
1996	648	446
1997	74	434

(Source: The Law Schools.)

The Social Background of Law Students

Such evidence as we have suggests that law students in Scotland form a relatively homogeneous population. The social background of the students (judged by parental occupation) does not vary greatly between the law schools. In each, students from social classes I and II are heavily over-represented. Thus in Glasgow 77 per cent of law students admitted from 1971–79 and in Edinburgh 70 per cent of law students admitted from 1976–80 were from social classes I and II. The survey of students and apprentices carried out in 1978–79 on behalf of the Hughes Commission revealed a similar picture.

Table 10.3 Socio-economic group of fathers of law students and apprentices

	Students				
	Total	Intend solicitor training on graduation	Others	Appren-tices	Male household heads (GB 1976)
Sample (unweighted)	595	350	245	419	
Socio-economic group of father	%	%	%	%	%
Professional	31	27	37	27	5
Employer/manager	30	32	27	25	17
Intermediate and junior non-manual	18	19	16	17	17
Skilled manual and own accounts workers	15	15	16	20	40
Semi-skilled and unskilled manual	2	3	1	4	21
Armed forces/ unclassifiable	3	3	3	7	*

(Source: Hughes Commission, Appendix 6, Table 1.3.)

In the Hughes survey 15 per cent of students and 21 per cent of apprentices stated that they had close relatives who were or had been lawyers in Scotland. Surveys carried out by the Law Society of Scotland (the latest in 1980) have shown that under 15 per cent of intrants in the last five years prior to the survey had existing family connections with the profession. There is some evidence to suggest that the largest single parental occupational group from which law students are drawn is the teaching profession. There is also evidence that the intake of female students to Scottish law faculties has been increasing steadily. In 1970 less than 20 per cent of law students in Scotland were female. Within 20 years they had reached parity with the males, a position which they retain.

The Hughes Commission, pp. 244–245

Admission of law students

"16.8 In selecting among the candidates who present themselves, the universities rely to a very large extent on academic attainment at school. We have reviewed this practice because there is no guarantee that those with the best school results will make either the best law students or the best lawyers. Scottish Certificate of Education Higher and Ordinary grade marks have been criticised as being measures of a student's ability to learn and regurgitate material, rather than affording a measure of intellectual potential. Further, we think that a selection procedure which depends so heavily on good school examination results is liable to produce a very homogeneous group of students, and thus limit the scope for a fruitful exchange of experience amongst them. An important unintended consequence of selecting those with the best school marks can often be the rejection of a disproportionate number of candidates from working class backgrounds and from the newer six-year secondary schools. Indeed, it has been alleged that this factor has contributed to the slowness of the profession to respond to people's need for legal assistance in the areas of personal rights, particularly those created by housing, social welfare and employment statutes in recent years.

16.9 We agree with the Ormrod Committee when they say 'the demands which the legal profession has to meet, and the roles which professional lawyers are called upon to play in society, are so varied, and require such different qualities, that the profession will always need to recruit men and women widely of different character, temperament and intellectual attainments'. We do not believe that any form of quota system for university admissions would be desirable; nor do we think that any explicit discrimination in favour of particular groups who are at present disadvantaged ('positive discrimination') would be practicable or acceptable. Nevertheless, we think that the present criteria for admission to university law faculties call for some adjustment, and we recommend that universities should use wider criteria than academic attainment at school when selecting law students for admission. In particular, we wish to see more account taken of the following considerations: firstly, each applicant's aptitude for, and interest in, the study of law; secondly, the need for a student population more varied in age and socio-economic background so as to create a better educational environment; and thirdly, the need to ensure that all pupils of ability and potential, from whatever school background, have a real opportunity to study law at university if they so wish. To achieve this, the universities should continue to set a realistic minimum entry qualification based on academic attainment at school; that is a minimum level which indicates a high probability that the student will be able to fulfil the degree requirements. The three criteria outlined above should, however, come into play when the universities are deciding which candidates to admit of those who have the necessary minimum qualifications. We wish to emphasise that the minimum qualification should not be lowered for particular candidates; rather, once the minimum has been set, the selection should not favour exclusively those who have the best school marks."

[The Ormrod Committee reported on legal education in England and Wales in 1971; Cmnd. 4595.]

Ultimately, it is a matter for debate whether the Hughes Commission's argument that a social imbalance in the population of law students is not in the interests of the public or the profession, has been made out. Nor is it clear whether the reform which the Commission favoured in this field can be achieved. What would happen if two applicants existed with similar academic records but one had a higher aptitude score than the other while the other ranked above the first in terms of social background desirability? Could such conflicts be resolved without in effect introducing a quota system or positive discrimination in some shape or form?

B. PRACTICAL TRAINING

Prior to 1980 intrants to the profession received their practical training by becoming indentured apprentices. Growing dissatisfaction in the 1970s with the apprenticeship as a form of training led to discussions between the Law Society, the Faculty of Advocates and the university law faculties. The outcome of the discussions was a proposal that a compulsory, one-year, full-time university-based postgraduate Diploma in Legal Practice should be introduced. The Diploma would provide the all-round practical training with a prescribed minimum standard of competence which was becoming increasingly difficult to attain in apprenticeships. The proposal was implemented and since October 1980, subject to transitional arrangements, all intrants to the profession must have obtained the Diploma. The Diploma is followed by a two-year "contract of training" with a solicitor.

Table 10.4 Apprenticeships 1935–1979 & Traineeships 1982–1998

Year	*Apprentices/Trainees*
1935	170
1950	174
1955	83
1959	105
1962	35
1964	113
1969	215
1972	278
1974	314
1975	328
1978	390

1979	430
1982	392
1985	420
1988	384
1989	453
1990	431
1991	403
1992	395
1993	373
1994	350
1995	392
1996	370
1997	392
1998	418

(Source: The Law Society of Scotland.)

Table 10.4 shows that following a decline in apprenticeships during the early 1960s the demand for apprenticeships—fuelled by the ever increasing stream of LL.B. graduates (the full-time LL.B. degree was introduced in 1961)—grew steadily from 1964 to 1979 before levelling out in the 1980s at levels which broadly remain today. The figures suggest that approximately 80 per cent of law graduates in the late 1970s were going on to the profession. One unexpected consequence of the introduction of the Diploma and traineeships was that the perennial student desire "to keep one's options open" led to 90 per cent of graduates in the early 1980s wanting to take the Diploma. A quota for Diploma grants was introduced by the Government in 1985, which was lowered to 390 per annum in 1987 and subsequently to 300 in the early 1990s—well below the demand for Diploma places (see Table 10.2). In 1998/99, around one-third of Diploma places were self-financed. Perhaps because of this, by the early 1990s only 80 per cent of law graduates were entering the Diploma and by the late 1990s the figure had fallen to 68 per cent of law graduates. Nevertheless, in the mid-1990s, the recession and a cut back in traineeship places available in the profession meant that the demand for traineeships and assistantships in the profession began increasingly to exceed the supply. However, reductions in financial support coupled with an increasing awareness of the position among law students has helped to redress the balance slightly and in 1998 there were training places for around 85 per cent of Diploma graduates. Proposed student numbers for the revised Diploma (to be introduced in session 2000/2001) are broadly in line with the current number of traineeships available in the profession, although while there may be enough training places for Diploma graduates each year, entry to the Diploma itself is likely to become more demanding academically and financially in the next few years.

C. ADMISSION

Solicitors (Scotland) Act 1980, s. 6(1)

"Subject to the provisions of this section, no person shall be admitted as a solicitor in Scotland unless—

(a) he is aged 21 years or over; and

(b) he has satisfied the Council—

(i) that he has complied with the provisions of any regulations made under section 5 that apply to him; and

(ii) that he is a fit and proper person to be solicitor, and has obtained from the Council a certificate to that effect; and

(c) he has paid such sum in respect of his admission as has been fixed by the Council with the approval of the Lord President."

Table 10.5 Solicitors admitted to the profession 1949–1998

Year	*Male*	*Female*	*All*	*% Female*
1949	182	9	191	5
1952	113	12	125	10
1955	118	16	134	12
1958	74	7	81	9
1961	86	8	94	9
1964	65	4	69	6
1967	117	24	141	17
1970	102	10	112	9
1973	206	35	241	15
1976	224	59	283	21
1978	239	69	308	22
1980	265	132	397	33
1982	242	139	381	36
1984	256	171	427	40
1985	233	182	415	44
1986	223	186	409	45
1987	197	190	387	49
1988	207	175	382	46
1989	195	185	380	49
1990	203	194	397	49
1991	241	243	484	50
1992	143	205	348	59
1993	201	223	424	53
1994	163	193	356	54
1995	219	197	416	47
1996	197	197	394	50
1997	184	188	372	51
1998	172	208	380	55

(Source: The Law Society of Scotland.)

II. COMPOSITION

The trends in Tables 10.4 and 10.5 have had an effect on the composition of the profession. In the mid-1960s only 33 per cent of the profession were aged under 40, by 1985 60 per cent of the profession were under 40 and 27 per cent under 30. However, more recent figures suggest that the average age of the profession has begun to increase again—in 1998, 51 per cent of the profession were under 40, and only 16 per cent were under 30. Again in 1975 only 9 per cent of enrolled solicitors were female. By 1985 the figure had risen to 21 per cent and in 1998 it was 36 per cent. This does not necessarily mean that discrimination against women in the profession has been eliminated. A survey conducted by the Law Society of Scotland (at the suggestion of its Future of the Profession Committee) of its women members in 1984 revealed that many female solicitors considered that the profession had not yet adapted to the needs of the increasing numbers of women entering the profession.

Law Society Report on Women in the Profession, pp. 2–3

> "It is clear from the responses that the women members believe there is a need for change and do consider that they are discriminated against in many ways, both conscious and unconscious. The principal complaint is that the general attitude of men towards their women colleagues has not changed to meet the modern situation. In the view of many, there should be a much more general understanding by men of women's professional abilities and an acceptance that women can combine families and work and can and should be accepted as partners and in positions of responsibility. More effort should be made to overcome the disadvantages to women solicitors of male camaraderie arising out of social activities and business relationships and more encouragement given to women to take part in the work of the Society whose Council is at present dominated by men.
>
> The one major practical step which the participants considered should be taken by the Society was to set up regular refresher courses. These would allow both men and women who had ceased practising for any reason to be brought up to date before returning to practice. It was suggested that such courses should be compulsory if anyone had been absent from practice for more than two years.
>
> Coupled with a change in attitude towards women, the responses showed a need to alter working practices in order to utilise to the full the talents and skills of the women members and at the same time to meet their domestic commitments. . . . It was suggested that the introduction of part-time partnerships and assistantships, associate status and more flexible hours of working, holidays etc. should be considered and the view was strongly expressed that these changes should apply to both men and women to prevent those women enjoying these benefits from being categorised as second-class lawyers."

[See also W. Millar, "The Role of Women in the Profession" (1985) 30 J.L.S. 86.]

More than 10 years on, the available statistics afford some continuing empirical support for the survey results. Women are only gradually becoming principals (partners or sole practitioners) in any significant numbers. In 1961, of the 1,209 principals in Edinburgh and Glasgow, a mere five were women. In 1985 there were 1,530 principals in Scotland's two main cities, of whom 86 (6 per cent) were women despite the fact that 19 per cent of all practising solicitors in the two cities were then women. In 1998, although women accounted for 36 per cent of the profession as a whole, they comprised merely 17 per cent of principals. It is also disappointing to note the results of a 1997 study of the 10 largest Scottish offices, where 52 per cent of qualified lawyers but only 14 per cent of partners were female.

Table 10.6 Solicitors in practice as principals

Age	*Men*	*Women*
Under 30	6%	2%
30–39	56%	26%
40–49	71%	35%
50–59	72%	38%
60–69	52%	55%
AVERAGE	**55%**	**21%**

(Source: Law Society of Scotland.)

The small number of female partners cannot solely be explained by the fact that the average age of female solicitors is lower—as Table 10.6 shows, female practitioners are less likely than men to be principals across all age groups.

Table 10.7 Practising Solicitors

	1954	**% of Total**	**1998**	**% of Total**
Private Practice (Partners/ Consultants)	2,420	73	3,765	45
Private Practice (Qualified Assistants)	445	13	2,471	30
Local Authorities	253	8	634	8
Central Government and Public Bodies	106	3	577	7
Industry/Commerce	48	1	286	3
Miscellaneous	34	1	627	7
Total	**3,306**	—	**8,362**	—

(Source: Law Society Annual Reports.)

Table 10.7 reveals the large growth in solicitor numbers since the 1950s. Although all work areas have increased substantially over the period, the numbers of partners and consultants in private practice has grown much more slowly—at only 58 per cent compared to overall growth of the profession by 146 per cent. Thus while almost three-quarters of solicitors practising in 1954 were partners, in 1998 the figure was less than half, while at the same time there has been a huge increase in the number of qualified assistants, in accordance with the modern business practices of law firms.

A. DISTRIBUTION

In 1999 there were 1,257 solicitors' firms in Scotland with a total of 1,925 offices. (In England and Wales the comparative figures were 10,120 and 13,900.) Table 10.8 reveals the geographical distribution of solicitors in Scotland in 1997 at sheriff court district level. It is clear that the great majority of solicitors in Scotland are to be found in the urban conurbations. Indeed a 1989 survey commissioned by the Scottish Office indicated that 72 per cent of solicitor's offices were in districts defined as urban (the remaining 28 per cent being in rural districts). However, the table also shows that there are very significant variations between rural areas which at first blush might seem to be quite similar, *e.g.* Cupar and Stonehaven/Peterhead.

Table 10.8 Geographical distribution of solicitors by Sheriff Court district

Sheriff Court District	*Solicitors (1996)*	*Population (1991)*	*Population per solicitor*
Edinburgh/Midlothian	2,168	497,759	230
Glasgow/Strathkelvin	1,962	731,641	373
Aberdeen	695	281,527	405
Dundee	303	149,751	494
Perth/Kinross	201	128,757	641
Cupar	96	66,888	697
Elgin/Inverness/Dingwall/Tain	293	218,857	747
Argyll & Bute	82	65,140	794
Dumfries & Galloway	175	147,805	845
Ayr	176	155,252	882
Greenock	99	90,103	910
Kirkcaldy	148	147,053	994
Stirling/Falkirk/Alloa	262	267,657	1022
Borders/East Lothian	181	187,995	1039
Arbroath/Forfar	99	105,340	1064
Dunfermline	118	127,258	1078
Hamilton	297	328,994	1108
Dumbarton	143	163,502	1143
Paisley	226	258,556	1144
Wick/Ft William/Dornoch etc.	114	138,874	1218
Kilmarnock	164	216,736	1322
Stonehaven/Peterhead/Banff	100	138,745	1387
West Lothian	93	143,972	1548
Airdrie/Lanark	152	238,782	1571
TOTAL	8,347	4,996,944	—

(Source: Law Society of Scotland)

Although the highest concentrations of solicitors are to be found in the major population centres, this table masks the important fact that the overall ratio is one that has changed substantially in the last two decades. Thus, where in the 1970s there were 1,800 people per private practitioner in Scotland, by 1996 this figure had reduced to under 600. The change can be attributed to a slight fall in the population coinciding with the significant expansion of the profession noted in Table 10.7.

Table 10.9 Private practitioners in the principal cities

City	*% of Scottish Population*			*Solicitors*			*% of Total Solicitors*			*People per Solicitor*		
	1911	*1984*	*1996*	*1911*	*1984*	*1996*	*1911*	*1984*	*1996*	*1911*	*1984*	*1996*
Aberdeen	3.4	3.7	5.5	181	303	695	5	6.3	8.3	905	628	405
Dundee	3.5	3.4	2.9	122	135	303	3.4	2.8	3.6	1,352	1,294	494
Edinburgh	9	8.1	9.7	952	874	2,168	27	18.8	26	445	480	229
Glasgow	16	15	14.3	733	1,032	1,962	21	21	23.5	1,070	739	373

(Source: Law Society of Scotland)

Until the mid-1970s legal offices in Scotland were more concentrated in the urban areas and in the centre of cities than they are now. At that time all but nine of the 141 firms in Edinburgh, all but 11 of the 198 firms in Glasgow and all but three of the firms in Dundee were located in the city centres. Less than 10 per cent of firms had branch offices and even fewer had branch offices in the suburbs. A pilot study, conducted in 1980 (Keatinge), however, revealed that solicitors' firms had been moving into industrial areas and in particular into new and developing towns in the previous 10 to 15 years. The survey also revealed that there was an exponential growth in branch offices between 1975 and 1980. In that period 90 branch offices were opened in Scotland. Although the majority of them were located in the central belt, they were not, in the initial stages, situated in Glasgow or Edinburgh. Only three of the 29 opened between 1974 and 1976 as opposed to 22 of the 65 opened between 1977 and 1980 were located in Scotland's two principal cities. In fact, the spread of branch offices in the last 15 years has followed two paths.

First, there has been a growth of linked offices across the country. Ten firms based in Edinburgh or Glasgow now have offices in London. Twenty-two firms now have branches in Glasgow and Edinburgh—half of which have opened up within the last 5 years. In addition, over 70 firms in the two cities also have offices in towns and cities in other parts of Scotland.

Secondly, there has been a considerable increase in the number of branch offices in the suburbs. In 1970 there were only seven suburban branch offices in Glasgow and Edinburgh together, by 1980 there were over 40 and by 1985 Glasgow alone had 77 and Edinburgh 42—a seventeenfold increase in 15 years. The corresponding figures in Aberdeen were six and 15. In Edinburgh approximately half of the new offices have followed the pattern demonstrated in Birmingham by Bridges *et al.* (*Legal Services in Birmingham* (1975, Inst. of Judicial Administration, University of Birmingham)), by being located in major district shopping centres and presumably designed to attract property work. But the other half have been situated in local authority housing areas, usually at the instance of court firms in an endeavour to attract civil and criminal legal aid work. In Glasgow, court firms have been even more active. In marked contrast to the picture in the early 1970s, by the end of 1998 there were over 200 head and branch offices in the suburbs of Glasgow and Edinburgh.

B. SIZE OF SOLICITORS' FIRMS

Table 10.10 Size of solicitors' firms

	Scotland			*England*		
	1977	*1991*	*1999*	*1979*	*1991*	*1997*
Sole practice firms	32%	38%	44%	34%	38%	42%
2–4 partners	48%	42%	41%	48%	43%	41%
5–9 partners	17%	15%	11%	14%	14%	10%
10 or more partner firms	3%	5%	5%	4%	5%	6%

(Sources: Hughes Commission, Vol. I, p. 317; Law Society; Benson Commission, Vol. I, p. 187; Law Society.)

Table 10.10 reveals how similar the distribution of firms in terms of size has been in Scotland and England over the past 20 years. However, the somewhat static picture which emerges from the table conceals the growth in large firm practice both in Scotland and in England in recent years. Thus in 1976 only two Scottish firms had more than 20 partners. By 1998, 17 firms had more than 20 partners and three had more than 30 partners. Five had 100 or more fee-earners. As might be expected there are many more large law firms in England and Wales. There, 150 or so firms had more than 20 partners in 1997, including 89 with more than 100 fee-earners. (The largest law firms in England and Wales are much larger than their Scottish counterparts. The largest of all—Clifford Chance—had 1,795 fee earners and 178 UK-based partners in 1998, making it more than eight times larger than its Scots equivalent.) Even these figures are misleading. The 5 per cent of firms with more than 10 partners in England account for 43 per cent of all solicitors in private practice, and account for 57 per cent of the fees earned by the English profession. In Scotland the concentration, though not quite so high, is still startling. Thus in 1998 the 63 Scots firms with 10 or more partners account for around one-third of the private profession. This indicates that the importance of the large firms in the legal economy far exceeds its lowly status judged in terms of absolute numbers.

Large firm practice (sometimes known as "mega-lawyering") is even better established in the United States, where several firms have topped the 1,000–lawyer mark and over 60 firms have more than 300 lawyers. Nonetheless, mega-lawyering is far from the norm even in America, where less than 10 per cent of attorneys in private practice work in firms with more than 50 lawyers.

One contributing factor to the growth in large firm practice in Scotland has been that, in part as a response to the competitive pressure of the market, amalgamations between practices have become commonplace in Scotland over the past 30 years. This permits firms to offer a wide range of services and individual lawyers within these firms to specialise. Thus Campbell and Wilson found that nearly half the private practitioners in Scotland and 75 per cent of those in large firms considered themselves to be specialists [C.M. Campbell and R.J. Wilson, *Public Attitudes to the Legal Profession in Scotland* (1972, Law Society of Scotland), pp. 105–106].

Along with the trend towards practice in larger units there has been over the past 50 years a substantial decline in the proportion of the profession who are in sole practice. In 1936, 36 per cent of English solicitors were sole practitioners; by 1996 only 9 per cent of them were. Comparable data are not available in Scotland but Campbell and Wilson's study found that in 1971, 13 per cent of Scottish solicitors were in sole practice—a figure which had dropped to 10 per cent in 1977 (Hughes, p. 317). In 1998 the number of sole practitioners had declined further to 7 per cent. Certainly, in the United States (where there are now more than 600,000 lawyers) 49 per cent of those in private practice in 1980 were sole practitioners—a drop of only 1 per cent since 1970.

Podmore, "The Sole Practitioner—A Declining Species", p. 356

"The causes of the decline in the proportion and number of sole practitioner solicitors are fairly obvious and involve both economic and administrative factors, including the rapidly increasing overheads which afflict all businesses in modern society but hit small firms particularly hard, the 'economies of scale' which only large units can enjoy, the problem of administration in the sole practice (for the sole practitioner is usually his own office manager) and, above all, the intense pressure of legal work on the 'man on his own.' The point is, of course, that in all matters 'the buck stops here' as far as the sole practitioner is concerned. In addition the sole practitioner faces the dilemma that he must choose between depth and breadth in the range of legal services which he performs. The ever-more complex nature of the law puts a premium on specialisation, but it is dangerous for all a solicitor's eggs to be in one basket. The successful practice in the modern world needs to offer both a degree of specialisation and a variety of services to clients, but the sole practitioner is not well suited to meet these apparently paradoxical demands. The advantages of the larger practice are manifest not only in areas such as specialist company and commercial work, but also in the more general work of the family solicitor . . .

Whether or not The Law Society by its policies encourages the growth of large practices, it seems inevitable that the sole practitioner solicitor will continue to be a declining species. Any 'man on his own' in modern society is something of an anomaly, existing in defiance of prevailing social and economic forces. Just as hypermarkets displace 'corner shop' grocers and large brewers devour small, so sole practitioner solicitors are likely to amalgamate and form larger, more viable, practices or perhaps cease to practise altogether. The disadvantages to the consumer of a situation where the number of firms is shrinking and those which remain are becoming larger lie in the restricted choice of solicitors' firms available, in the possible lack of easy access to a solicitor's office, and in the inevitable accompanying decline in the highly personal relationship which used to characterise (both in stereotype and, very often, in fact) the solicitor-client relationship. Several of the solicitors interviewed regretted this last trend. One observed, 'More and more one must be business-like. I regret this, because business efficiency can lead to a decline in professionalism. Business efficiency often means you must be ruthless, *e.g.* with a client who wastes your time . . .'"

The stereotype of sole practice which has emerged from American research is of a graduate from a less prestigious law school whose work tends to be of a routine non-repeating nature for "one-shot" clients, *e.g.* criminal, family and personal injury work. As such, considerable disparities exist between the average income of sole practitioners and partners in the larger firms. Remuneration surveys in England and Wales have suggested that the latter, at least, also holds true on this side of the Atlantic. However, Hughes discovered relatively little discrepancy between the earnings of practitioners in different sizes of firm in Scotland.

In relation to Scotland, the American stereotype seems rather wide of the mark. Sole practitioners do as much conveyancing work as other private practitioners, significantly less company work than those in large firms and rather more court work. (Hughes also found that sole practitioners on average earn 18 per cent of their gross fees from legal aid—twice the average figure for other firms.) In fact, a pilot study conducted by Miller in 1981 suggested that sole practitioners in Scotland form neither a homogeneous nor a stable population.

Miller, "Sole Practice in Scotland", pp. 13–14

"Taking into account how long the practice has existed and how many employees it has, one may tentatively and rather impressionistically sketch in a typology of sole practitioners. Firstly, there are those who have been in sole practice for a long period, perhaps 15 years or more. They tend to have 2 or 3 employees. Their practice has stabilised at a level of moderate success. They work in only a very few fields of law . . .

Secondly, there are those who have been in sole practice for a period of 8 to 15 years or so. These may be subclassified into those whose practice is still gradually expanding towards a point where expansion is possible or necessary (a group which largely consists of practitioners who concentrate on conveyancing and wills, trusts and executries); those whose practice has already stabilised at a moderate level of success; and those who are still hanging on in very small practices against both the odds and the balance sheet.

Thirdly, there are those who have only been in sole practice for 6 or 7 years or less. Amongst these are many who will sooner or later move out of sole practice. Some practices expand rapidly, and quickly cease to be 'sole.' These solicitors perhaps receive their greatest reward from ambition-fulfilment rather than remuneration or pleasure at giving a good service. Of the rest of this group, a large number will be general practitioners who do a fair amount of legally-aided work. They have the greatest personal satisfaction from their work, but seem rarely to survive beyond 5 or 6 years as sole practitioners: either because the lure of mammon becomes too enticing, or because they, too, expand beyond sole practice."

C. THE WORK OF THE PROFESSION

Although we have no up-to-date information on the breakdown of fee income as between sole practitioners and others, the distribution of gross fee income in the profession as a whole and how it has changed in the last 15 years or so is set out in Table 11. While the growth in court work during this period is striking, as is the decline in corporate and executry work it is equally noteworthy that domestic conveyancing is still the largest single source of income for the profession.

Table 10.11 Distribution of Gross Fee Income of the Profession

Field	*1976*	*1996*
Domestic Conveyancing	34	36
Court (Civil and Criminal)	16	33
Corporate (inc. Commerical Conveyancing)	12	8
Trust/Executry	21	11
Miscellaneous	17	12

(Sources: The Hughes Commission, Table 19.6; The Law Society.)

III. MONOPOLIES

Contrary to popular mythology (and the position in many other western democracies) solicitors in Scotland possess very few pure monopolies. Their rights of audience before the courts are shared with advocates and party litigants. Their monopoly in relation to applications for the confirmation of executors only extends to the making of such applications for gain. Even their conveyancing monopoly (which was not established until 1891: see A. Rodger, "Marching to an Alien Tune?" (1991) J.R. 1) is, strictly speaking, a misnomer, since it is shared with advocates and unqualified persons provided they do not draw or prepare the writ for gain (see the Solicitors (Scotland) Act 1980, s. 32).

The Hughes Commission, pp. 130–131

> "9.22 Firstly, there is nothing in the monopoly which prevents a person doing his or her own conveyancing . . . Secondly . . . the statutory provisions prohibit a person who is not a solicitor or an advocate from preparing a writ relating to heritable or moveable property (with certain specific exceptions) only where such a writ is prepared for a fee, gain or reward, or the expectation of some reward. Thirdly, the monopoly has regard only to the drawing or preparing of a writ relating to heritable or moveable property . . . There is no monopoly with regard to negotiating the sale or purchase of a property, the exchange of missives, the making of searches in the Register of Sasines or the various other steps involved in the purchase or sale of a house. Having said this, however, we should say that it appears that solicitors have a virtual monopoly in all conveyancing work after the completion of the missives. The Keeper of the Registers has told us that it is very rare indeed for a writ to be presented for recording by anyone other than a solicitor. The difficulties and complexities of the legal procedures . . . and the requirement for personal undertakings to be given in letters of obligation, have all helped to maintain a monopoly for solicitors in conveyancing work which is in practice more extensive than that conferred by statute."

The Law Society in its evidence to the Hughes Commission argued that the conveyancing monopoly was in the public interest because (1) solicitors have to meet high standards of competence and discipline and (2) the guarantee fund and indemnity insurance (see below) protect the public in the event of fraud or negligence by solicitors. Hughes accepted the importance of competence, discipline and the protection of clients' financial interests but concluded that these could also be attained by other professional bodies.

Following the Hughes Report Mr Austin Mitchell, M.P., introduced a private member's Bill in 1983 designed to end the solicitors' monopoly of conveyancing. The support he received persuaded the Government to undertake to introduce their own legislation in this field. The Government threat was sufficient to persuade both the Scottish and English Law Societies to relax their rules against the advertising of solicitors' services in 1985 (see Chapter 10 below). In Scotland the profession was also persuaded to abolish its recommended Table of Fees for conveyancing and executries. These developments have led to a more competitive market for legal services and reduced fees for conveyancing in certain parts of Scotland. (See Paterson and Stephen, *The Market for Conveyancing in Scotland* (CRU, 1990).)

Despite this it looked for several years as if the Law Society's efforts to persuade the Government to ignore the Hughes recommendation were bearing fruit. Thus when "licensed conveyancers" were created in England and the Building Societies Act 1986 was passed with provisions permitting institutional conveyancing south of the border, nothing was introduced in Scotland. The publication of two Scottish Office consultation papers, *The Practice of the Solicitor Profession in Scotland* (1987) and *The Legal Profession in Scotland* (1989) and a White Paper, *The Scottish Legal Profession* (1989), however, contained a rude shock for the profession. The Government in its continuing efforts to remove what it regarded as anti-competitive restrictions on the supply of legal services had determined to abolish the solicitors' conveyancing and executry monopolies. Banks, building societies and insurance companies were to be given the opportunity to offer conveyancing and executry services. These provisions were included in the Bill but a rebellion by the Government's backbenchers forced the Scottish Office to withdraw its proposals for institutional conveyancing. The Scottish Conveyancing and Executry Services Board was established under the Law Reform (Miscellaneous Provisions) (Scotland) Act 1990, ss. 16–23 to regulate the training, admission and conduct of individual "qualified conveyancers" and "executry practitioners". However, in the light of the recession, the Board, and therefore the limited breaches to the conveyancing and executry monopolies contained in the Act, were suspended in 1992. The respite was only temporary. Three years later the Scottish Office were faced with the threat of judicial review by a group of disgruntled students from Abertay University who claimed that they had had their hopes of becoming Qualified Conveyancers or Executry Practitioners dashed by the suspension. Rather to the surprise of disinterested observers, the Scottish Office gave way, having concluded that the action might succeed. In November 1995 the suspension was brought to an end and the Board re-established under the chairmanship of a former President of the Law Society of Scotland. In a short conspectus the Board produced the Registration rules and Complaints procedures for the new breed of practitioners, set up a Compensation Fund and arranged Professional Indemnity Insurance. All that remained was for the Scottish Office to bring its Conduct and Practice Rules for Independent Qualified Conveyancers and Executry Practitioners into force, on March 1, 1997. The response has hardly been dramatic. The Board's Corporate Plan anticipated that 12 practitioners would be registered by April 1998, rising to 60 by April 2001. The actual figure in 1998 was one practitioner, which had risen to six practitioners by September 1999. The evidence to date suggests the new practitioners are not going to pose a serious threat to the conveyancing and executry monopolies of the solicitor's profession.

IV. THE LAW SOCIETY OF SCOTLAND

The Law Society of Scotland was established by statute in 1949. Its objects are now set out in the Solicitors (Scotland) Act 1980.

Solicitors (Scotland) Act 1980, s. 1(2)

"The objects of the Society shall include the promotion of—

(a) the interests of the solicitors' profession in Scotland; and
(b) the interests of the public in relation to that profession."

All practising solicitors are required to be members of the Society and to obtain from the Society an annual practising certificate.

The business of the Society is carried out by the Council and by a large number of standing, *ad hoc*, and statutory committees, though the day-to-day work of the Society is done by the Society's full-time staff. The Society sets the educational, training and admission requirements for those wishing to enter the profession (see above). It is the Society which is responsible for the regulation of non-court work fees and which negotiates with the Lord President and the Scottish Office over court fees and legal aid remuneration rates respectively. In recent years it has come to play a valuable role in co-ordinating, recording and providing support services to groups of solicitors involved in multi-party court cases ranging from transport disasters to drug dependency suits. The Society safeguards the interests of the profession in relation to proposals for law reform both domestically and in Europe. (The Society established an outpost in Brussels in 1991.) It is also responsible for the regulation of professional standards, the investigation of complaints and the enforcement of professional discipline.

A. PROFESSIONAL PRACTICE, CONDUCT AND DISCIPLINE OF SOLICITORS

There are at least three different groups of standards governing the behaviour of Scottish solicitors. First, those relating to professional conduct. Second, those relating to the level of competence attained by the solicitor in performing legal tasks and thirdly the law of negligence. Analytically, each set of standards is independent of the other and thus a solicitor can be guilty of misconduct without demonstrating a lack of competence or being negligent. On the other hand the standards are not mutually exclusive. Thus, the same conduct by a lawyer may constitute misconduct and negligence and provide an indication of deficiencies in competence.

In fact, improper professional conduct itself falls into three categories of seriousness. First, professional misconduct. Next unprofessional conduct, which is conduct which falls just short of misconduct but which may be punished by censure and/or an award of costs. Finally, there are breaches of etiquette or professional good manners. Until the last few years there was no formal code of ethics in Scotland, although the American legal profession has had one since the early part of the twentieth century. Partly as a result of the activities of the CCBE (Conseil des Barreaux de la Communauté Européenne), the Law Society of Scotland promulgated a brief Code of Conduct for Scottish Solicitors in 1989. (The Faculty of Advocates published its Guide to the Professional Conduct of Advocates in 1988.) The Society also regularly introduces Practice Rules (which have been approved by the Lord President) under its delegated statutory powers.

Turning to standards of competence it seems clear that the services provided by solicitors range on a continuum of performance:

EXCELLENCE

COMPETENCE PLUS

THRESHOLD COMPETENCE

INADEQUATE PROFESSIONAL SERVICES

NON-PERFORMANCE

Increasingly, in the modern era, attention has begun to be placed on the quality of the service delivered to the client. With this has come the recognition that sometimes the performance of solicitors can fall below the standard of basic or threshold competence. Following the Solicitors (Scotland) Act 1988, the Law Society and the Scottish Solicitors Discipline Tribunal have been given powers to order the rectification of poor work and to compensate clients in instances where inadequate professional services (IPS) have been delivered. Initially the Law Society took the view that the actings of solicitors could not be both IPS and professional misconduct or both IPS and negligence. Conceptually this was difficult to justify and it has now been recognised that a finding of IPS does not preclude a finding of misconduct or negligence.

1. The Complaints Procedure

The Law Society has the principal responsibility for investigating complaints against solicitors. When a complaint is received the secretariat endeavour to identify the gravamen of the problem and then write to the solicitor seeking his or her comments on the problem. If it is clear that the client has not spoken to his or her solicitor, the Society will send a copy of the client's letter to the solicitor and ask that the firm's complaints partner or senior partner meet with the client to discuss the complaint. If a meeting would not be useful or the meeting fails to bring agreement the Society will investigate the complaint. The complaints secretariat may handle the complaint administratively either by resolving to take no action on an unjustified claim or negotiating with both parties to see if a mutually acceptable reduction in fee or some other remedial action taken by the solicitor is possible. The great majority of complaints relate to delay or a failure to communicate with the client although "conduct unbecoming a solicitor" or "failure to adequately advise or to follow instructions" are also relatively frequent grounds. As such it is often possible to identify elements of IPS which the Society can persuade solicitors to remedy or compensate for after discussion with the client. Whilst such "service" complaints can also constitute conduct complaints which in the past frequently led to a finding of unprofessional conduct, there is evidence that findings of IPS are beginning to replace findings of unprofessional conduct in the Society's armoury. The secretariat, however, will not investigate complaints in respect of which the complainer has a legal remedy such as an action for professional negligence. If there are separable elements which relate to IPS or misconduct then action will be taken— otherwise the Society will limit itself to offering to put the complainer in touch with one of a panel of solicitors (colloquially known as "troubleshooters") recruited by the Society who are willing to act for complainants in cases of alleged solicitor negligence.

In recent years, there has been a marked change of approach in the attitude of the Law Society towards complaints:

"Conciliating Complaints", (1997) J.L.S.S. 151

> "Since 1993 the philosophy of the Society in relation to complaints has gradually evolved to embrace the concept of conciliation. The 'Complaints Department' is now the 'Client Relations Office' and we have even stopped using 'the red-headed letter'!
>
> Last year there was a change in the deployment of staff in the Client Relations Office to allow one of the Deputy Secretaries to deal with conciliation full-time by mediating directly between the parties and by assisting client relations partners who are endeavouring to resolve matters themselves. The figure of 609 for complaints resolved by conciliation in 1996 was almost double that of the previous year, and, in order to maintain this impetus, a series of Roadshows is currently being undertaken throughout the country in conjunction with local faculties.
>
> The vast majority of complaints about the services provided by solicitors are relatively simple, and involved two specific areas: delay and failure to communicate—often a failure to communicate *effectively*. In the past such complaints would have been dealt with by correspondence only. For the profession, the time spent on that correspondence was unremunerative because, even if the complaint was not justified, the solicitor is not entitled to make a charge for it. For the Society it is time consuming and therefore expensive.
>
> In many instances the written complaints procedure has the effect of polarising attitudes when, in reality, both the dissatisfied client and the solicitor wish to try to resolve the problem. From the solicitors' point of view, in most instances, they do not wish to lose what they consider to be a valuable client. Indeed, a number of client relations partners have commented that one of the main attractions of the conciliation system is the fact that they are able to deal with the matter themselves rather than having the Society's involvement. It is true that the majority of complaints received by the Society have not previously been the subject of discussion between the dissatisfied client and the firm."

Complaints which the secretariat consider merit more detailed examination will be referred to one of the Society's three Client Relations Committees. A separate committee exists for complaints relating to Legal Aid. The number of lay members of the Client Relations Committees has recently increased from three to 15, giving them a substantially greater say (if not a majority) in the handling of complaints. The Committees can dismiss the case or censure the solicitor, but in a significant minority of cases (between a quarter and a fifth) they reach a finding of misconduct which leads to a reprimand, the imposition of IPS sanctions or a prosecution before the Scottish Solicitors' Discipline Tribunal.

2. The Discipline Tribunal

The Scottish Solicitors' Discipline Tribunal consists of 10 to 14 solicitors recommended by the Council of the Law Society and appointed by the Lord President, and four lay members appointed by the Lord President. Complaints can be brought before the Tribunal by a wide variety of individuals including the Lord Advocate, the Dean of the Faculty of Advocates, judges, court auditors and the Scottish Legal Aid Board However, the great bulk of prosecutions are initiated by the Law Society who appoint a solicitor to act as fiscal in the case. The Tribunal has extensive powers and may strike solicitors off the roll, suspend them from practice for specified periods, fine them up to £10,000, censure them or suspend or revoke their rights of audience or investment business certificates. In the past the Tribunal had a discretion as to whether named publicity should be permitted in individual cases where a finding of professional misconduct was established. As a result of the Law Reform (Miscellaneous Provisions) (Scotland) Act 1990 decisions in all cases coming before the Tribunal must now be published (even those in which the prosecution fails).

The Tribunal also has wide powers in relation to inadequate professional services and where such provision has been established can vary the fees and outlays charged by the solicitor to nil, can direct the solicitor to secure rectification of any error or omission at his or her own expense and direct the solicitor to pay compensation to the client of up to £1,000. (Appeals lie to the Court of Session—Solicitors (Scotland) Act 1980, s. 54.)

Table 10.12 The Disposal of Complaints

Year	*Complaints*	*Taken to Discipline Tribunal*	*Referred to trouble-shooters*
1992	1,189	30	32
1993	1,294	30	27
1994	1,424	53	33
1995	1,321	74	32
1996	1,294	34	25
1997	1,481	27	26
1998	1,427	25	23

(Sources: Law Society of Scotland Annual Reports, the Journal of the Law Society of Scotland.)

3. The Scottish Legal Services Ombudsman

In 1976 the office of the Lay Observer was created to examine allegations by members of the public that the Law Society had mishandled their complaints concerning the conduct of their solicitors. As such the Lay Observer could only act once the Society had completed its investigations into the original complaint. The Lay Observer could require the Law Society to produce their files on relevant cases and frequently submitted observations to the Society on the handling of the case. The Law Society, however, were not bound to follow any of the suggestions made by the Lay Observer.

In 1990 the remit of the Lay Observer was extended to cover complaints handled by the Faculty of Advocates and the Scottish Conveyancing and Executry

Services Board. To mark the expanded role, the title of the office was changed to the Scottish Legal Services Ombudsman. Perhaps the most significant power of the Ombudsman lies in his ability to take cases directly to the Scottish Solicitors' Discipline Tribunal—as yet this power has never been used. The Ombudsman's caseload has been running at about 250 complaints per year, of which about a third are ineligible for investigation. Since 1991, the Ombudsman has submitted an Annual Report to the Secretary of State.

In practice, the Ombudsman influences the handling of complaints by recommending improvements to the Law Society and the Faculty of Advocates. Recently the Ombudsman successfully urged the Law Society to increase lay representation on its Client Relations Committees. In 1997, further statutory reform expressly empowered the Ombudsman to make recommendations that compensation be paid to complainers by either professional body, and all five such recommendations were implemented by the Law Society in 1997, resulting in payments of between £100 and £250. Not all recommendations are implemented, however. For several years the Society has declined to implement a recommendation that solicitors in Scotland should be required (as their English counterparts are) to write "letters of engagement" to new clients. Such letters confirm the nature of the work to be done and the firm's terms of business, including the firm's basis of fee charging. In 1999 the Society (who agree that the use of such letters constitutes "good practice") relented to the extent of issuing a Professional Practice Guideline advocating their use and strengthening the code of conduct in relation to this issue. What the Society did not do is make their use mandatory.

The Ombudsman has also proposed that the Secretary of State take powers to direct professional bodies with regard to their complaints procedures. This was vigorously opposed by the Law Society, who saw it as a threat to the principle of self-regulation, but it will nonetheless be considered by the Secretary of State.

A significant proportion of the Ombudsman's caseload are referrals from the Law Society.

4. Professional Misconduct

Despite the promulgation of the Code of Conduct in 1989, the Practice Rules introduced by the Society at regular intervals and the publication (in recent times) of the decisions of the Discipline Tribunal it is not always easy to establish what does and does not constitute professional misconduct. There are some clear cases—misappropriation of clients' funds, submitting false legal aid claims, abuse of trust, breach of confidentiality or the breach of one of the Law Society's rules of professional practice, *e.g.* attracting business unfairly, sharing fees with unqualified persons or failing to keep proper accounts. In other areas the definition of professional misconduct is left very much to the Discipline Tribunal. If the Tribunal thinks a solicitor's behaviour constitutes misconduct, then it is misconduct. The Inner House has continually refused to offer clearer guidance in this area.

E. v. T. 1949 S.L.T. 411

Lord President (Cooper): "I shall not attempt to define professional misconduct. But if the statutory tribunal, composed as it always is of professional men of the highest repute and competence, stigmatise a course of professional conduct as misconduct, it seems to me that only strong grounds would justify this Court in condoning as innocent that which the Committee have condemned as guilty."

***Sharp v. Council of the Law Society* 1984 S.L.T. 313**

"There are certain standards of conduct to be expected of competent and reputable solicitors. A departure from these standards which would be regarded by competent and reputable solicitors as serious and reprehensible may properly be categorised as professional misconduct. Whether or not the conduct complained of is a breach of rules or some other actings or omissions the same question falls to be asked and answered and in every case it will be essential to consider the whole circumstances and the degree of culpability which ought properly to be attached to the individual against whom the complaint is made."

[It was established in *Council of the Law Society v. J.* 1991 S.L.T. 662 that "the circumstances" could never include the fact that the solicitor was ignorant of a new practice rule which had only recently come into force. Somewhat surprisingly, however, the Court also ruled that the fact that the solicitor's breach of the practice rule involved no prejudice to the client might be relevant to establishing misconduct and not just a point which went to mitigation of sentence. This ruling seems at odds with the decisions of the Discipline Tribunal to the effect that ill health or substance addiction only go to mitigation and not to culpability.]

Report of the Clerk to the Discipline Tribunal 1979/80

"In considering any Complaint, the question is always whether there has been 'professional misconduct'. The phrase is not statutorily defined but in an early English case it was observed that 'if it is shown that a solicitor, in pursuit of his profession, has done something with regard to it which would reasonably be regarded as disgraceful or dishonourable by his professional brethren of good repute and competency, then it is open to the Disciplinary Committee to say that he had been guilty of professional misconduct'. This definition is not exhaustive but it is generally accepted as illustrating the required standard of proof."

Not only was it established in *E. v. T.* that professional negligence could amount to professional misconduct, since then the Tribunal has held in several decisions that gross carelessness, *e.g.* in the preparation of a case, in delaying the payment of an expert witness, or in carrying out a conveyancing transaction can also be misconduct. More often it will amount to IPS. Finally, it has also become clear from recent cases that the Tribunal and the Court will be prepared to find professional misconduct even in relation to behaviour which is entirely confined to the private life of the solicitor. (See, *e.g. United Bank of Kuwait v. Hammoud and Others* [1988] 3 All E.R. 418 at p. 430.)

5. The Guarantee Fund

In addition to the protection given to clients by the Accounts Rules (which, *inter alia*, require solicitors to have at all times a sum at credit of their client bank account or client accounts not less than the total of the clients' money held by the solicitors) the solicitors' profession in Scotland and England maintain at their own expense funds (financed by annual or special levies on their members) which are used to recompense clients who have "suffered pecuniary loss by reason of dishonesty on the part of any solicitor." Although it is no longer unusual for an occupational group to underwrite its clients in this way against the defalcations of individual practitioners and although the funds do not cover loss due to professional negligence, they nevertheless afford protection to clients in the United Kingdom which lawyers' clients in many other countries have good reason to envy.

6. Professional Negligence

The scope of professional negligence is not much clearer than that of professional misconduct. It is established that solicitors are liable for lack of due care and skill, judged by the standard of the reasonably competent practitioner. Thus a solicitor who, due to a conveyancing error, leaves his client with a defective title, or who delays so long that his client's action becomes time-barred or who fails to alert his client to the availability of legal aid will be liable for loss sustained by his client. But it is not clear whether this liability arises merely from contract, or from contract and delict. It has been argued that the basis of liability of a solicitor to his own clients is contractual only and that he owes no duty in delict to his clients or to third parties, *Robertson v. Fleming* (1861) 4 Macq. 167.

In the light of radical developments in the law of delict in the past century, it is likely that the Inner House would no longer accept this statement of the law. Nevertheless, the liability of Scottish solicitors to third parties remains uncertain, as does their liability for errors of judgment or when acting as advocates in the lower courts.

[For the position in England, see *Ross v. Caunters* [1980] Ch. 297, *Saif Ali v. Sydney Mitchell & Co.* [1980] A.C. 198, *Whitehouse v. Jordan* [1981] 1 W.L.R. 246 and *White v. Jones* [1995] A.C. 207. For a useful discussion of Scots law in this area, see R. Rennie, *Solicitors' Negligence* (Butterworths, 1997) and A. Gamble, "Solicitors and Claims by Third Parties" (1980) 25 J.L.S. 236.)

7. The Troubleshooters

"Complaints against solicitors", p. 179

> "At one time a complainer . . . would be advised [that the Society has no powers to award financial compensation for any loss suffered through negligence] . . . and in some instances would be put in touch with a solicitor who was prepared to take on the case, or would be given a list of firms from which to select someone to act. Judging from the response from members of the public, this was totally inadequate and many complained that it was impossible to find a solicitor prepared to raise an action against a fellow-practitioner. With a view to combating this, the Society decided to set up a panel of solicitors in various parts of the country who would be prepared to

advise complainers who felt they had grounds for a complaint based on negligence against their present solicitors.

The scheme has now been further refined into a two-tier process. First, a member of the public who approaches the Law Society with concerns as to whether a solicitor who has acted for them has been negligent will be given the names of solicitors in their locality who are thought to be willing to advise on negligence cases. If this fails to solve the problem the Society, if approached, will consider whether an appointment of a Troubleshooter is appropriate. These are senior solicitors spread throughout Scotland who have agreed to be on a Law Society panel to act as a last resort if no other solicitor can be found to act for a client in solicitor negligence cases.

If, having perused the client's papers, the Society considers a Troubleshooter appointment might be appropriate the papers are passed to a Troubleshooter. Where the Troubleshooter is prepared to advise the client, the latter will be told to fix an appointment with the Troubleshooter. The Law Society will pay for the cost of two meetings with the Troubleshooter and any other preparatory work required to establish whether a prima facie case exists. Any further help from the Troubleshooter has to be paid for on a normal agent and client basis, assuming both parties wish to continue with the case. In recent years the average number of Troubleshooters appointed in any one year has been 25."

8. Compulsory Professional Indemnity Insurance

In 1977 the Law Society's Council after consulting the profession and several leading insurance brokers, resolved to invoke its powers under the Solicitors (Scotland) Act 1976 (now contained in the Solicitors (Scotland) Act 1980, s. 44) to introduce mandatory professional indemnity insurance through a single master policy held in the name of the Society. The step was taken because, following the withdrawal of several insurance companies from the market, solicitors were encountering increasing difficulties in obtaining indemnity insurance cover; a quarter of the profession were thought to have no indemnity insurance. With a master policy the Society could bargain from a position of strength with the insurance companies over premiums and cover. From November 1, 1978, Scottish solicitors have been covered in terms of the policy for acts of professional negligence and for fraud or dishonesty on the part of their partners or staff. The limit for each and every claim by 1993 was £1 million irrespective of the size of the firm, although additional cover can be purchased. There is an excess of £2,000 per principal up to a maximum of £20,000 on each and every claim. Fidelity claims (relating to the fraud or dishonesty of a partner or member of staff) have an excess which is double that of ordinary claims. Premiums can be weighted up to 250 per cent in the event of a poor claims record. The premiums currently reflect a per capita charge for each principal in the firm and includes weightings for practices with higher ratios of staff to partners and adjustments to reflect the firm's individual claims record.

B. REFORM PROPOSALS

In recent years not a few of the reforms sought by consumer bodies and the Government in relation to the regulation of professional conduct and discipline have been implemented. IPS appears to be operating successfully and there is less overt criticism of the Law Society's complaints procedures. On the other hand, the need for an authoritative Guide to the Professional Conduct of Solicitors, along the lines of that produced by the Law Society for England, is still strong. Furthermore, there are still those, *e.g.* the Scottish Consumer Council, who are on record as favouring the establishment of an independent complaints body for lawyers (Complaints About Solicitors (SCC, 1999)). Despite this, and the fact that issues of competence are now being raised in relation to complaints and discipline, it must be doubted whether improved complaints procedure would do much to improve the competence of solicitors.

Zander, *Legal Services for the Community*, pp. 136–138

> "But improved procedures for handling complaints and better remedies for aggrieved clients are unlikely to make any real impact on the quality of work done by lawyers. There are three main reasons. One is that hardly any clients have the energy or inclination to complain even if they feel there is something to complain about . . .
>
> Secondly, the failure to complain is often because the client is unaware of the fact that the work has been badly done. It is of the nature of many professional services that the client cannot evaluate what has been done for him and therefore cannot know its quality . . .
>
> A third reason for reviewing complaints and disciplinary procedures as marginal to the problem of maintaining professional standards is that instances that are penalised are regarded by all concerned as exceptional. The presumption is that they are deviations from the norm, and the ordinary practitioner is, therefore, unlikely to be much influenced by reading or hearing that his colleague has been criticised for such failure . . .
>
> The only way to meet this difficulty is to have some mechanism for conducting research into the way in which legal services of different kinds are normally provided."

Zander's solution is similar to a proposal of the Hughes Commission on competence—that the quality of professional work should be monitored (R. 16.35). This is now beginning to happen as firms come to recognise the importance of pursuing quality in order to gain an advantage over the competition. Firms that have registered for BS 5750 or begun to toy with Total Quality Management are already committed to "file inspections" on a regular basis by internal or external audit staff. Client satisfaction surveys are also becoming recognised as valuable marketing and client retention devices. In England the Law Society introduced a "client care" rule in 1991 requiring every firm to have an internal complaints procedure, to advise clients as to its existence and to keep them properly informed of the action being taken on their behalf. Scotland is still contemplating its reforms in this area but firms with three or more partners have been asked to appoint a complaints partner and to identify the same to the Society.

One reform which sought to improve professional standards was the introduction of mandatory continuing professional development by the Law Society in

1993. This requires each member of the profession to complete 20 hours of further education/training every year, partly through self-study and partly through seminars, group training and conferences. A significant section of the curriculum is devoted to management and skills training.

Finally, improved quality and efficiency may come from the increasing competition within the profession which has been engendered in recent years by the Government and to a lesser extent by the consumer movement. As we have seen, several of the changes contained within the Law Reform (Miscellaneous Provisions) (Scotland) Act 1990 were designed to increase competition within the profession. After a slow start, the impact of the 1990 Act is beginning to be felt. The Conveyancing and Executry Services Board was finally established in 1996, and higher education courses leading to qualification as a qualified conveyancer or executry practitioner have been up and running for some time.

The emergence of multi-disciplinary partnerships could also lead to increased competition within the profession. The Government has already expressed its intention to permit such practices, which would require the abolition of the rule against fee-sharing with unqualified persons. Although MDPs may develop in different ways across the profession—*e.g.* personal injury specialists could enter partnership with medical practitioners, litigation firms could assume advocates as partners—the initial growth of MDPs is likely to be through the assimilation of large, corporate firms, into large accountancy practices which already dwarf their legal counterparts. For example, the largest of the then "Big Six" firms, Andersen Worldwide, received global fees of around $10 bn in the year 1996–97, employing 100,000 professional staff. (This will soon be overtaken by PriceWaterhouseCoopers). Baker & McKenzie, the world's largest law firm, employs around 2,000 lawyers. The first steps towards the emergence of MDPs in Scotland occurred when Andersen's took over the 14–partner Glasgow firm, Dorman Jeffrey. However, the news in 1997 that an agreement had been reached between Andersen's and Dundas & Wilson, one of Scotland's largest and most prestigious firms, surprised many within the profession, who expected the pace of change to be more gradual.

The accountancy giants are motivated to move into the field of legal services for a variety of reasons. Audit work, traditionally the "bread and butter" of accounting, has gradually become less profitable as costs are driven down by clients, while remaining high-risk, and firms have diversified to provide a range of professional services to meet the demands of, initially at least, existing clients. The facility to provide legal services would allow the Big Five to offer a global "one-stop shop" to clients operating on a similar level, whereby all their professional services can be obtained from the one provider.

Critics of this trend question whether there is a genuine demand for such service provision from companies who are becoming increasingly sophisticated and discerning buyers of legal services—it is common, nowadays, for even medium-sized business entities to employ more than one firm of lawyers to handle different areas of work in specialised areas (*e.g.* licensing law). Certainly it is unlikely that clients would unquestioningly transfer their business from one firm to another simply on the basis of a recommendation from their auditors. Also, some of the Big Five have found that the increasing diversification of work within the organisation has led to factionalism developing among the partners, particularly where one area of the business is substantially more profitable or growing more rapidly than the others. There are also important ethical questions where the theoretically independent roles of auditor and legal adviser to a client are part of the same MDP.

The impact of MDPs on the Scottish legal services market remains to be seen—the European Court of Justice has already upheld their prohibition by the Netherlands Bar Association, while they have taken off rapidly in France and Spain.

CHAPTER 11

UNMET LEGAL NEEDS

Since the 1960s "the unmet need for legal services" has been the subject of much discussion and research. It is argued that many people, through ignorance of the law or lack of financial resources, have an "unmet legal need". Those who are ignorant of the law do not enforce their legal rights, which simply go by default. This is said to be particularly so in areas such as consumer, housing, employment and social security law, where legislation has proliferated. Again, people with legal problems who cannot afford a lawyer may also be described as having an "unmet legal need". Egalitarian principles suggest that in such cases lawyers should be provided from public funds, if more affluent persons would employ a lawyer when faced with a similar legal problem. Such assertions are premised on a number of assumptions, for example as to the nature of legal problems, as to the assessment of legal needs and in relation to who should meet those needs.

I. THE NATURE OF LEGAL PROBLEMS

Zander, *Legal Services for the Community*, p. 273

> "A legal problem may be defined to include any difficulty which can be solved by reference to law. Alternatively, it might be defined much more restrictively to mean problems that are in fact taken to lawyers. By this standard a social security problem would not qualify as a legal problem. Again, it may mean those matters that lawyers, or at least some lawyers, at any given time think ought to be taken to them for solution. Some lawyers would identify the social security problem as 'legal', others might not."

Lewis, "Unmet Legal Needs", pp. 78–79

> "People often speak as if to say that someone has a legal problem is to make a statement of fact about his situation; once one has appreciated that situation, one can realize that it falls within the class of situations which raise a legal problem, and any lawyer can say what situations are contained in that class, just as he can say what the statute book has to say on some given point. A closely related way of speaking is to treat the judgment that someone has a legal problem as a judgment which is typically a clear one, admitting of no doubt; people either do or do not have a legal problem. It is this clarity which makes it possible to come to the judgment that people with a legal problem 'need' a lawyer, just as no one would suppose that an engineering problem could be solved by anyone else than an engineer.
>
> This way of speaking should be suspect. Usually if we say simply that a person has a problem we mean that there is a difficulty about deciding what

he should do or what should be done for him: that is what makes it a problem, not merely the presence of the circumstances which have to be coped with. If we define what kind of problem the person has or the circumstances present, if, say, we refer to an arithmetic problem, we are defining the kinds of solution seen as appropriate. Thus, to tell someone that the problem of measuring the height of a building is a trigonometrical problem is to suggest the methods that should be used to find out the answer . . .

It seems likely then that when someone says that a person has a legal problem or says that a particular problem under discussion is a legal one he is offering a suggestion about the action that the person should take or the method which should be adopted to solve the problem. The typical suggestion is that action should be taken before some court or similar institution or that the services of a lawyer should be employed. Very broadly, the point I should like to make in this paper is that if certain problems are spoken of as legal ones, and official support is given to legal methods of solving them, that is to take a particular attitude to problems of that kind, problems which may be capable of solution in some other way, and which may be seen by those most closely concerned as best solved in that other way. For instance, if a tenant in a flat has a leaking roof he may be regarded as having a legal problem; does his lease provide that the landlord should do the repairs, and is the mechanism of the courts adequate to ensure quick action? But he may choose to get a ladder and not a lawyer, and we can argue whether it is better that people should be made to fulfil their legal duties or that they should be encouraged to take practical steps to avoid material damage regardless of their legal responsibilities."

Arguments such as Lewis's have led some scholars to assert that there are no specifically legal problems only social ones which can be tackled by a variety of approaches only one or two of which may be specifically legal.

II. THE ASSESSMENT OF LEGAL NEED

Zander, *Legal Services for the Community*, pp. 274–275

"The need of the rich man to redress a legal wrong may be less than that of a poor man afflicted by the same problem. Perception of need will be influenced by the availability of resources . . . The more legal services are provided, the more the community may perceive the need for lawyers. (It has been found that if the number of hospital beds is increased, the average length of stay in hospital increases too.) Moreover, the concept of need presumably ought to include some sense of a hierarchy of values. The need for a lawyer of a man who faces a charge carrying the death penalty is different from that of another whose kettle proves to be defective. Both can validly be said to need a lawyer, but the disparity between the extent of their needs is so gross as to require some stratification of levels of need. At the extremes this can be done without difficulty. But how is one to reach agreement as to the relative need of one man for reinstatement of his job, against another's claim for compensation for loss of the sense of smell, or a third man's protection against eviction?

One tenant faced with a notice to quit may throw it into the fire, believing (rightly) that he is fully protected by the Rent Acts. Another does so because he believes (wrongly) that he is legally protected, but comes to no harm because the landlord fails to follow through with proceedings for possession when the tenant sits tight. Did either have a 'need' for legal services? Or what of the tenant who leaves on receipt of the notice to quit because he believes (rightly) that he is not protected and he prefers to take the opportunity of reasonable alternative accommodation which has just presented itself rather than stay to fight a costly, losing battle? Should he first have seen a lawyer? From a certain point of view it would, of course, be reasonable to say that in any of these situations the tenant would have benefited from the additional peace of mind of having legal advice. Yet, there is room for differing views as to whether there was or was not a need for legal advice. The answer may be influenced both by one's capacity for empathy and by the value one places on the intervention of lawyers."

III. MEETING UNMET NEED

Zander, *Legal Services for the Community*, p. 275

"It cannot be assumed that a person with a legal problem has any need for legal services if by that is meant the services of lawyers. He may be best advised to take his problem, at no cost, to the local citizens' advice bureau, his trade union official, or a well-informed friend or relative. He may indeed be best served by doing nothing at all and allowing the problem to go unresolved, or to solve it by quite different means."

Lewis, "Unmet Legal Needs", pp. 87 and 95

"Discussions should not proceed on the basis of whether it would be generally agreed that a person should use a lawyer, but on whether his interests and temperament require an adviser, a negotiator, or a champion, and who in his particular situation can best fulfil this role. The answer might then be someone like his M.P., or one might want to set up new organizations or professions. [Alternatively] it might turn out on inquiry that the interests of individuals with problems might be best served by referring them to solicitors, since to some extent they profess flexibility of role . . . It is said that if we give people rights we are acting in vain unless we give them the ability to enforce them. I sympathize with this, but representation by lawyers may not be the best way of doing it. If, for instance, we want to make consumers' rights against the sellers of unmerchantable goods effective, the best way may be to set up some kind of consumers' representative, or a small claims court where no lawyers are allowed. It may not be so; I only want to point out that giving legal aid for litigation is not the only possibility to be considered."

Paterson and Goriely, "Introduction to Resourcing Civil Justice", p. 2

> "Traditionally, legal services have been thought of as services provided by lawyers. There is a growing understanding, however, that legal services can be provided by a much wider range of people . . . Providers include advice centres such as Citizens' Advice Bureaux, trade unions, motoring organizations, or social workers."

IV. STUDYING UNMET NEED

Despite the problems outlined above, a number of surveys have been conducted in an endeavour to establish the existence of an "unmet legal need" in a particular geographical or legal area. Two strategies are used to get over the semantic hurdles. First, to study situations or areas where the "need" for legal assistance is so gross that the value judgment involved in asserting that there is a need for lawyers in that situation or area is one which would be widely accepted; *e.g.* studies of the number of accused persons who are unrepresented, of the number and success rate of unrepresented applicants appearing before tribunals or of the uneven distribution of solicitors in the country and the shortage of solicitors who are welfare specialists. The second strategy has been to go into the community to ask individuals about their "legal problems".

Zander, *Legal Services for the Community*, p. 277

> "The most common technique of such studies is to take a check-list of 'legal problems' and ask members of the community which, if any, they have experienced, and, if so, what they did about them. It is obviously important in conducting such research not to alert the respondent to the fact that he is being asked about his response to legal problems. If he knew this it might slant his replies. He is, therefore, asked simply whether he has had, say, an accident, or has divorced his spouse, or has ever been threatened with eviction. It is then possible to evaluate the extent to which different members of the community do have problems that by one or another definition may be said to be 'legal'." [Zander goes on to discuss a number of these studies.]

The difficulty in such research is in balancing the subjective and objective elements. Where the individual's subjective perception of need alone is relied on the researcher is not measuring unmet need for legal services but perceived unmet need for legal services which may depend on a number of factors including the individual's state of knowledge and even his psychological needs. Adopting such an approach makes it impossible for the researcher to say that an individual's perception that he has a need for legal services (no matter how trivial the problem) is erroneous, or for him to say that an individual has an unmet need for legal services but does not realise it. On the other hand, where the researcher introduces objectivising factors, *e.g.* by stipulating the criteria which make a problem "serious", he risks substituting his own subjectivity and value judgments for those of the individuals whom he is studying.

Griffiths, "The Distribution of Legal Services in the Netherlands", p. 281

> "The trouble is that legal services are a scarce good, in competition with other scarce goods, and it is a matter of personal judgment whether one's legal problems are, in relation to other things one could spend one's money for, 'serious' enough to justify such an expenditure. The question is never, is it 'serious'? but always, is it 'serious enough'?, and there is therefore no empirical criterion by which to measure the amount of legal services that anyone 'needs'. You want a divorce for £200, I prefer a colour T.V. Do I lack 'access' because I can't have both? Of course not—I decided I 'needed' a lawyer less than someone else might have: my legal problem was less 'serious' for me than yours was for you."

The question of what makes a civil dispute "serious" was considered in a recent study by the Scottish Consumer Council (*Civil Disputes in Scotland* (1997)). Respondents were asked what factors they considered made a civil dispute "serious". The most important factors were: money (41%), principles (24%), personal well-being (21%), concerns for children/relationships (16%) and poor service (13%).

V. UNMET NEED: THE HUGHES APPROACH

The Hughes Commission, pp. 19–21

"Legal services

> 2.1 It is tempting to say that 'legal services are services provided by lawyers', but we reject this for two reasons. Firstly, not all work done by lawyers falls into the category of a legal service . . . Secondly, not all legal services are provided by lawyers. There are many sources of legal services outwith the legal profession. Other professional people, whether they be architects, accountants or social workers, give advice to their clients on the legal aspects of their services. Much of the work of organisations such as Citizens Advice Bureaux, consumer advice centres, trade unions and motoring organisations, consists of giving information and advice about the law. Such provision is as much a legal service as the same information and advice given by a lawyer . . . We also regard as a form of legal service the dissemination of information through notices, leaflets, advertisements and booklets which give the citizen information about his legal rights and responsibilities and how he may exercise or carry them out.
>
> 2.2 Accordingly, when we speak of legal services we mean advice, information or assistance involving a knowledge of rights and obligations conferred by law and of legal procedures, whether provided by a lawyer or otherwise. These services may include action taken on behalf of a client, or facilities used by a client (whether the client is an individual, a group or an organisation) . . .

Unmet Need

> 2.7 Ideally, the use made of legal services would express the total need for legal services. However, not all need results in use of legal services and in

some cases the service provided may, by its inadequate quality or supply, fail to meet the whole need. The total need for legal services with which we must be concerned is the sum of actual use plus unmet needs. In broad terms the meaning of need for legal services and the nature of unmet need are clear enough. Certain causes of unmet need are clearly recognisable—shortages of lawyers in particular geographical localities and areas of the law, for example. There is, however, more to legal need than simply people having a legal problem and not being able to secure the services of an adviser. It is impossible to estimate how many legal problems there are, other than perhaps for research purposes in a small group under study. Many problems which could be resolved by legal means do not necessarily have to be. There are other non-legal solutions . . .

2.9 Where a citizen finds a non-legal solution which satisfies him, we would not be justified in claiming that he is deprived of legal services. That would depend on his awareness of his legal rights. In assessing the need for legal services we must therefore think in terms of two stages—firstly enabling the client to identify and, if he judges it appropriate, to choose a legal solution; and, secondly, enabling the client to pursue a chosen legal solution.

2.10 Accordingly, when we speak of a need for legal services in our Report we are speaking of a need for services—facilities, advice, assistance, information or action—to enable a citizen with a problem to assert or protect his rights in law by identifying and, if he so chooses, pursuing a legal solution, that is a solution which involves a knowledge of rights and obligations or of legal procedures. When we speak of 'unmet need' we are concerned about instances where a citizen is unaware that he has a legal right, or where he would prefer to assert or defend a right but fails to do so for want of legal services of adequate quality or supply."

Hughes recognised that "need", as in the "need for legal services", was a relative concept. In answer to the question, "when can an unmet need for legal services be said to exist?" Hughes resorted to stipulative definition—starting from the standpoint of the client and the client's perception of need. The implicit, if not explicit, assumption was that a need for legal services existed if a legal solution was available to a problem facing a person or group of persons, and that person or group of persons perceived that the legal solution was more convenient or satisfactory than the various non-legal solutions available.

Such an assumption is open to two challenges. First, because the subjectively based concept of need which it enshrines posits a model of individuals as rational beings capable of making informed choices, when some litigants are anything but rational. This objection has little merit; indeed the model both avoids the trap of paternalism and accords with democratic theory. The second objection perhaps carries more credibility, namely, that the model ignores questions of cost. At a time when financial constraints on legal aid expenditure look like being with us for the foreseeable future, it seems that the model should be adjusted to take account of issues such as value for money.

Hughes commissioned a public survey to discover how people attempted to solve problems of a relatively serious nature and to identify the extent of unmet need amongst them (as defined by Hughes). The Commission concluded (at pp. 51–52):

> "5.16 Our evidence suggests that the unmet need for legal services in Scotland is not the result of people's dissatisfaction with the services they have obtained from lawyers. Those of our respondents who had consulted a solicitor were generally satisfied with the help they received. The problem is rather a considerable unwillingness on the part of the public to consult a solicitor in the first place—61 per cent of our respondents had never done so, although the proportion is smaller among younger people. It appears in particular that many people fail to take independent advice when faced with a comparatively worrying problem such as an accident or injury, a consumer complaint or a landlord/tenant dispute. Most judged these problems not appropriate for a solicitor. There are undoubtedly cases where the sum at issue is so small that it would be out of all proportion to incur the expense of employing a solicitor to recover it. If, as a result, people fail to assert their rights, this suggests that an alternative form of legal service may be needed. The small numbers taking legal advice . . . coupled with the level of dissatisfaction at the outcome . . . suggest strongly to us that significant numbers of people make decisions as to the value of legal advice on the basis of inadequate information.
>
> 5.18 From this analysis we can identify three major causes of unmet need for legal services. The first barrier the citizen has to overcome is one of information—he must know that he has a legal right. A further aspect of this barrier is that the citizen must know what sources of help are available to him, what order of costs might be involved, what financial assistance could be available, and in particular whether he is eligible for legal aid . . .
>
> 5.19 A second barrier between the citizen and legal services is ease of access. Not only must legal advisers be available in a convenient place at a convenient time, they must be seen as approachable . . .
>
> 5.20 A third barrier to use of legal services is cost."

A. THE INFORMATION PROBLEM

The first stage in the Hughes approach to unmet legal need centred on the "need" of the citizen for information as to his legal rights, as to the legal and non-legal remedies available to him and as to the relative cost and viability of these remedies.

Kelly and Lorber, "The Medway: Unmet Need for Legal Services", p. 10

> "To a lawyer a specific situation may appear to be a legal problem, especially where apparent legal rights have been breached and legal remedies are available. However, an individual who actually experiences such situations may not perceive them as problem situations of a legal nature, or even problems at all. He may not apply the lawyer's definition of a social situation, and therefore will not bother to consult him. Although he may seek some social solution to his problem, he is effectively denied a legal

> solution, as he does not see the law as relevant to his circumstances. In many areas of the law, individuals with problems are completely ignorant of their legal rights and remedies."

Although the complexity and ever-changing nature of consumer, employment, housing and welfare legislation is such that it is highly unlikely that the average citizen has an accurate awareness of his legal rights in these areas, few studies have actually been carried out to test the legal awareness of the public.

The Hughes survey did not research this area either, though it did look into the public awareness of legal services. Table 1 summarises their findings.

Table 11.1 Proportion of respondents with no or very inaccurate information about various schemes

	%
Legal aid	39
Legal aid symbol	48
Tribunal system	50
Small estates procedure	86
Legal advice and assistance	91
Summary cause procedure	99

N = 1,658 for each scheme

(Source: Hughes Commission, Appendix 4, Table 65.) (See also the National Audit Office Report on The Administration of Legal Aid in England and Wales (HMSO, London: 1992) at p. 50.)

Moreover the survey revealed that the lack of information amongst the public about legal services was not randomly distributed. Lack of knowledge was greatest amongst those in the lower socio-economic categories. This was particularly so in relation to knowledge of the legal aid system, with those categories of respondent who would be most likely to qualify for legal aid being least knowledgeable about it, *i.e.* manual workers or those over 65.

Table 11.2
Knowledge of legal aid and legal aid symbol, by socio-economic status

	Proportion (%) of respondents in each group having no or very inaccurate knowledge about:	
Socio-economic status	Legal Aid	Legal Aid Symbol
Higher professional/managerial	19	47
Lower professional/managerial	24	42
Other non-manual	31	40
Skilled manual	39	48
Semi-skilled and unskilled manual	47	53
Other	55	64
All non-manual	28	41
All manual	43	50

(Source: Hughes Commission, Appendix 4, Table 66.)

[This last finding has been replicated in several Scottish studies. See, *e.g.* Myers, "CABx and Knowledge of Legal Services" (1976) 4 SCOLAG Bul. 46; S.C.C. Evidence to the Royal Commission on Legal Services in Scotland; "Awareness of Legal Services in Aberdeen" (1979) 31 SCOLAG Bul. 62; and Lindley, "Access to Legal Advice", *Consumer Policy Review*, Vol. 7, No. 4.]

Hughes' strategy in relation to the problem of public ignorance of legal rights and remedies was to tackle it at source—at the level of the citizen. Accordingly the Hughes' recommendations included:

(1) the provision of teaching on law and legal services at school (R. 6.1);
(2) the advertisement by the Government of major changes in the law in the media (R. 6.4);
(3) the use of the media for the provision of public information on legal rights and legal services (Para. 6.13);
(4) the encouragement of CABx and law centres to devote a significant portion of their energies to community education (R. 6.6);
(5) the creation of a network of generalist advice agencies as information providers, for example as to the potential cost or viability of a legal solution to a client's problem (R. 7.1). (This recommendation, of course, was also relevant to the problem of access.)

Nearly 20 years later the Scottish Office Consultation document, "Access to Justice beyond the Year 2000" (1998) again focused on information as the first of its three key themes. The paper asserts that communities need information about the best way of resolving the types of disputes and legal problems they experience and information as to the sources of help available. By introducing the concept of community legal services with an emphasis on the need for local intake and referral services, the Scottish Office were confirming the far-sightedness of Hughes' proposals.

B. THE PROBLEM OF ACCESS TO LEGAL SERVICES

The Royal Commission on Legal Services in England and Wales (Benson) laid less emphasis on the value of attempting to raise the general legal awareness of the public. Benson treated the problem of ignorance as a variant of the problem of access—defined by Benson as the problem of getting the potential client to the professional adviser who has the knowledge and expertise. Accordingly the Benson recommendations are designed to encourage direct access to solicitors, *e.g.* by permitting solicitors to advertise their specialisms, by subsidising private practitioners to move into deprived areas and by introducing a half-hour interview free of charge for all clients, irrespective of their means, when they consult a solicitor who undertakes legal aid work, paid for from the legal aid fund.

Hughes' definition of the problem of access was different. Hughes recognised the need for "initial advice to allow a citizen to identify and, if he judges it appropriate, to choose a legal solution to his problem" but was impressed by the record of lay advice agencies in this field.

The Hughes Commission, p. 39

> "To recognise a potential legal solution to a problem, the citizen must have some knowledge of the legal rights and responsibilities involved. In many cases, people are aware only of the problem and have little awareness of its relationship to the complex and ever-increasing volume of legislation surrounding their daily lives. Further, many problems are not, at least to the person who suffers from them, clear-cut single issues. Before seeking any solution it is helpful, indeed often necessary, to discuss the problem in order to identify its various aspects and discover what is really at issue. The potential client therefore requires initial advice which will help to clarify the problem and to identify the possible solutions, including potential legal solutions. Many people are reluctant to enter a solicitor's office unless they are sure they have a real and important legal problem; but they are less reluctant to approach more informal advice agencies."

Some evidence of the reluctance of individuals to consult solicitors emerged from a pilot study in Aberdeen ("Awareness of Legal Services in Aberdeen" (1979) 31 SCOLAG Bul. 62). When confronted with hypothetical consumer, housing, employment and social security problems and asked whom they would go to for help in relation to them, few respondents mentioned solicitors. The respondents' explanations for this included: "But it would be more bother than it was worth"; "But he'd just refer me to someone else"; "The advice people have their own solicitors"; "I've got through life without needing solicitors" (from a retired Post Office worker); "The small fee might not be all that small"; "Solicitors wouldn't be bothered with things like that"; "The Citizens' Advice Bureau do a better job—they handle more cases like that"; "It's better if you can sort things out for yourself"; "The CAB people put one on to a solicitor"; "I've never needed anything like that"; "They would be too busy"; "It's simpler to go to the CAB"; "But that would just confuse me further"; "But they're not really questions for a solicitor."

VI. CITIZENS' ADVICE BUREAUX SERVICES IN SCOTLAND

Allen, "CABx and Legal Services in Scotland", pp. 41–42

> "A Citizens' Advice Bureau is an information and advice centre which depends largely on local authority funding but remains firmly outside the statutory set-up. A bureau is run by an independent management committee drawn from local people. Its members may also include one or two councillors, and representatives of Social Work, Consumer Protection, and Housing Departments as well as perhaps a lawyer, teacher, community workers and others active in the community.
>
> The bureau staff in Scotland are almost entirely volunteers, but a bureau aims by careful recruitment, selection and training policies to ensure a high standard of service combined with commitment and local knowledge. Administratively the key figure in a bureau is the organiser, who is now

increasingly salaried, though improvements in the provision of salaries by local authorities have been hit by local government's financial problems.

A bureau has to satisfy certain conditions in its methods of operation and premises before it can register as a member of Citizens' Advice Scotland. In exchange for registration, it receives regular updated information from CAS's Edinburgh offices and other back-up services such as training advice.

A Citizens' Advice Bureau aims to provide a service of information and advice which is both geographically accessible and does not inhibit anyone who needs help. It steers away from formal reception desks or other trappings that might associate it with the official aspects of statutory departments and imposes no restrictions on the types of problems or enquiries that can be brought to it. One of the misgivings we have about the proliferation of advice-giving services is that the man-in-the-street is not always clear as to which, if any, single category his problem belongs to.

The Citizens' Advice Bureau aspires to be the well-informed general practitioner of advice services, 'combining the roles of prevention, diagnosis and referral to the specialist consultant'. A bureau is therefore not a mere signpost. Many people, of course, come for simple information or to get the address of another agency and others are identified by the bureau as needing help from a lawyer or social worker. But the key criterion when deciding whether to advise a client to go elsewhere for help or to seek to help him at least initially within the bureau is what is felt to be in the client's interests. Increasingly clients come to bureaux with problems, rather than enquiries. They bring them to the bureau either because they have not liked to go to more official services or because other offices have not had the time to sort out their problems or have felt that they were not within their remit. They may be tired of being shunted from one office to another or they may have had to summon extra resources of courage to consult anyone at all about their problem. To take the easy way out, and give these people another address to go to, may not be what they are needing, nor will the information necessarily be used.

There is a growing consciousness amongst bureaux too that even in giving simple information, they are also passing on advice and that there is no easily defined point beyond which a bureau can say it does not act. If there is no boundary between information and advice, so there is none between advice and speaking on behalf of the client and even acting on his behalf. If there is someone else more able to do this job and acceptable to the client, then of course the bureau will refer. Most bureaux err on the side of diffidence rather than taking on too much, almost overwilling to defer to the 'professionals', whether they are lawyers, social workers or local government officials."

In 1997–98, the 56 CABx in Scotland operating through 150 service points, handled around 501,253 initial and repeat inquiries. The most common inquiries concerned consumer, debt or benefit matters. CAB clients are more likely to be unemployed, living in rented accommodation and aged between 25 and 59 than the Scottish population generally. CABx also see proportionately more people with disabilities and from ethnic groups. (Source, *Statistics of CAB in Scotland 1997/98*.)

Table 11.3 - Inquiries handled by CABx

Category	1983–84 No.	%	1997–98 No.	%	Overall Change %
Family and personal	34,362	9.6	29,136	5.7	−15.2
Housing	45,007	12.5	48,125	8.7	+7.1
Employment	44,911	12.5	58,323	10.6	+29.9
Goods and services	56,086	15.6	32,862	6.4	−41.4
Money	93,203	26.0	212,159	40.5	+127.6
Compensation for injury/damage	8,996	2.5	2,986	0.6	−66.8
Foreign Travel/ Nationality	2,221	0.6	2,346	0.4	+5.6
Administration of Justice	4,529	1.3	13,008	2.4	+187.2
Miscellaneous	69,338	19.3	102,218	24.8	+47.4
Total	356,653	100	501,253	100	+40.5

(Source: CAS Annual Reports.)

VII. CABx AS A PART OF LEGAL SERVICES

S.A.C.A.B. Annual Report 1981/82

"Much of the work of Citizens' Advice Bureaux consists of giving information and advice about the law and more than [50%] of the enquiries made to bureaux have a legal dimension. The CAB service is a necessary and valuable complement to the legal profession. It attracts people who may need but would otherwise not seek legal advice. It provides the basic advice which can help a client to make an informed approach to the legal profession. It deals with areas of the law that the profession does not adequately cover and it acts as a sieve identifying cases which require the professional attention of solicitors . . ."

Allen, "CABx and Legal Services in Scotland", pp. 43–44

"1. Whilst bureaux handle many enquiries which have a legal element within them they are not setting themselves up to be lawyers and for the most part are most careful to refer a client to a lawyer as soon as it becomes apparent that he requires professional help. Skill at referring is increased the more dialogue there is between local lawyers and the CAB. It also depends on there being lawyers available to send the client to and on the client being willing to keep his appointment . . .

2. A matter of deep concern to us therefore is the uneven spread of the profession in Scotland. It is all too often the same areas which have neither a Citizens' Advice Bureau nor a local lawyer. The two extreme situations for particular concern are the vast, sparsely-populated areas of the north of Scotland and the high-density, low-amenity housing estates of Edinburgh and Glasgow.

3. Lawyers need to be both better dispersed and more accessible to people. They need to be willing and interested in handling the less popular areas of law such as housing, consumer and welfare rights.

Legal sessions in the bureau

1. A better spread of lawyers' firms and more information about what work they will do will only help the client who has identified or had identified his problem as needing a lawyer. There are still those who do not want to go to a lawyer's office, at least initially. And there are those who have a problem with several facets, of which only one requires legal advice. Traditionally bureaux have relied on informal contact with a lawyer over the phone. This is not really as satisfactory as the client seeing a lawyer, and a standard development for bureaux is to invite local lawyers to run legal clinics on a voluntary basis within the bureau, usually one evening a week or fortnight.
2. [In 1997–98, 15 bureaux were operating legal sessions in Scotland.] . . . There is a steady flow of clients who visit the bureau during the day and return in the evening to seek the lawyer's advice (few fail to keep their appointments, which have the benefit of being in familiar surroundings). The standard type of problem is the more complicated case of consumer redress, some aspect of a matrimonial problem, or a landlord or tenant seeking information about his rights. The system of sifting cases through the bureau ensures that the lawyer's time is used to the best advantage. Bureaux staff tend also to save up queries they have had themselves over the past week on aspects of the law. Solicitors seem also to enjoy the work; they often find it an interesting and challenging change from the normal run of business in a legal firm. There is no doubt too that in towns where the CAB runs legal sessions, there is a closer relationship between the legal profession and the CAB: each has a better understanding of the work of the other."

One problem with legal sessions in the past was that the volunteer lawyers were not permitted by the ethical rules of the profession to take clients back to their office if they required further professional legal help. To overcome this it was agreed between the CAB service and the Law Societies in the United Kingdom that solicitors would be permitted to take any case requiring further professional help back to their own office, if this is what the client wishes, provided a rota scheme has been established. Under the scheme every solicitor in the area served by a particular bureau must be invited to participate in the legal sessions on a rota basis. There is now no requirement to have a rota system due to the lifting of the previous restrictions. It is left up to each Bureau to decide whether to operate a rota system or select firms and solicitors. In either event the solicitor advisers are free to take clients back to their office.

VIII. OTHER ADVICE CENTRES

Although CAS is undoubtedly the largest network of linked advice centres in Scotland there are two other networks of Scots advice agencies—local authority run agencies and those affiliated to the Federation of Independent Advice Centres (FIAC). According to a research report by Carole Millar for the Scottish Office, in 1997 there were 302 agencies in Scotland including CABx, money advice centres, neighbourhood information centres, consumer advice centres, citizens' rights offices, unemployed workers' centres, Women's Aid, Shelter, housing advice centres, planning aid services, legal advice centres and many more. Almost all will be called on routinely to offer advice on legal matters to their clients. While some centres will write letters for clients and even represent them at tribunals, others refer clients requiring legal assistance to law centres, specialist agencies or to private solicitors. [See C. Millar, *Referral Between Advice Agencies and Solicitors* (Scottish Office Central Research Unit, 1999).]

IX. HUGHES AND THE PROBLEM OF ACCESS

The Hughes Commission, p. 69

> "7.3 . . . an important part of the demand for legal services can be effectively and economically met by agencies providing general advice, initially through laymen, but with suitable back-up facilities (including referral to legal firms) to provide necessary further advice and assistance. These agencies can be particularly effective in helping clients to define the nature of their problems, which will often be complex and without a clearly identifiable 'legal' component; in providing a service in a convenient and familiar location; in assisting those with misgivings about the costs of legal help; and in reassuring clients who may not know their legal rights, or may have inhibitions about consulting solicitors."

Accordingly Hughes' primary solution to the problem of access was the introduction of a network of generalist advice agencies (R. 7.1). Hughes implicitly rejected the introduction of measures designed to encourage clients to go directly to the profession. They did not propose that clients should have a free, half-hour, diagnostic interview. Hughes considered it "wasteful to use a solicitor's skill to carry out tasks which a trained layman can perform effectively" (para. 7.4). Instead, Hughes recommended that improved access to legal services should be promoted by the development of a network of generalist advice agencies which could "in appropriate cases provide the first access point to the machinery of legal services." These advice agencies would be based very much on the CAB model and would, the Commission hastened to add, be complementary to the services provided by solicitors. They would normally be staffed by trained volunteers and a paid organiser but with ready access to a range of specialist advisers. Such specialists would include lawyers who would normally be volunteer helpers or those taking part in a rota scheme or acting on a referral, although some salaried lawyers would be employed. While Benson was opposed to CABx building up teams of lawyers on their staff to act as legal advisers to clients (Benson had no objection to their being used as an information source for the staff of a CAB or a group of CABx), Hughes did not consider that salaried lawyers attached to generalist advice agencies should be limited in this way. The Scots consultation Paper "Access to Justice beyond the

Year 2000" (1998) backs the Hughes approach. Unfortunately Hughes devoted less than a quarter of a page to the problem of the link between the generalist advice agencies and the private practitioner—an area which has caused many problems in the past. As we saw earlier, when examining the information problem, a central element in the concept of Community Legal Services (see chapters 12 and 13 below), at least as perceived by the consumer bodies and the Scottish Legal Aid Board, is an intake and referral service somewhat akin to Hughes' general advice centres. However, the needs for information and advice are many and varied—flexibility will have to be the hallmark of the response. The success of the "in-court adviser" project in Edinburgh sheriff court which has provided invaluable assistance to unrepresented parties who arrive bewildered in court, needs to be replicated in other courts. Telephone help lines, conferencing telephone kiosks, intelligent kiosks on the internet will all have a place in the information era of the new millennium. [See R. Susskind, *The Future of Law*, OUP, 1994.]

X. SOLICITOR ACCESSIBILITY

Advice centres, law centres or even information technology are not intended to be, and, indeed, fall far short of being, the complete answer to the problem of access. Many clients will choose to employ a solicitor in private practice to solve their problems. Such clients face the problem of solicitor accessibility. Thus, a would-be client wishes to find a solicitor whose office is within a reasonable distance of the client's home or work and who is willing and competent to handle and, if possible, expert in handling his type of case. He should also be willing to do it at a reasonable price. There is reason to believe that solicitors with experience and expertise in legal aid work, or in social security, employment, education, consumer and local authority housing matters are in short supply and even less well-distributed than solicitors in general (see A.Paterson and M.Turner Kerr, *The Distribution of the Supply of Legal Aid in Scotland* (Scottish Legal Aid Board, 1993) and A.Paterson, "Unmet Legal Needs in Strathclyde Region" unpublished report for Strathclyde Region, 1984). This is particularly the case in rural areas (see A. Paterson, "Access, Legal Aid and Rural Scotland" 1995 *Juridical Review* 266.) Part of the explanation appears to lie in demographic differences but also important is the significant variation in the availability of specialist suppliers and niche practices, who are committed to the provision of social welfare law (see A. Paterson and P. Montgomery, *Access to and Demand for Welfare Legal Services in Rural Scotland* (SLAB, 1997)). Even if the problems of distribution can be eased, for example by grants or interest-free loans to encourage solicitors to set up offices in deprived or under-provided areas (Benson R. 16.5, Hughes R. 7.10), that is only the first hurdle. How are the other elements in the problem of solicitor accessibility to be overcome?

A number of surveys have been published which suggest that at present individuals choose their solicitors in the same ways as they select their doctors or dentists—mainly through acquaintances or on the recommendation of a relative or friend. These methods only overcome some of the problems of access. In the first place, many individuals, particularly those from the lower income sector of the population, do not have a "family solicitor" or a friend who is a solicitor. Secondly, assessing the competence of a solicitor is perhaps more difficult for a layman than assessing a doctor or dentist. Various solutions to the information needs of would-be clients have been put forward, ranging from individual advertising and solicitor directories to the certification of competence or expertise.

One recent initiative by the Law Society of Scotland to improve solicitor accessibility has been the development of the "Dial-a-Law" service. This allows members of the public to call the service (on 0990–455–554) and access a range of pre-recorded messages relating to specific legal problems, including family law, criminal law, consumer law, employment law and wills and executries. The facility also offers advice on how to choose a solicitor and prepare for an initial interview. There is also a referral service which will provide callers with the names and contact details of local solicitors.

A. INDIVIDUAL ADVERTISING

The "Salisbury and Winchester Journal", December 6, 1779

CONVEYANCES made as cheap as by London Attornies by JAMES MOXHAM, of Fordingbridge, affifted by an eminent practitioner of the Law in London.

The "Daily Record and Mail", August 14, 1909

LAW, &c.

LAW Advice, 1s. Wills. Courts attended. Experienced Law Agents.—William Jarvie Co., Writers, 50 Wellington Street, off Argyle Street. 9–8.30.

MARRIAGES Privately Completed, 10s; particulars sent free; experienced Law Agents.—William Jarvie & Co., Writers, 50 Wellington Street, off Argyle Street (convenient to all Stations). 9–8.30.

LAW Advice; Courts Attended; Marriages Privately Completed, 10s; particulars sent free.—John Younger, Writer, 19 Howard Street, off Jamaica St. 9 till 8.

As these advertisements show, the prohibition on advertising by individual practitioners, which many have regarded as one of the hallmarks of a profession, is of comparatively recent origin, dating back only to the early twentieth century. When, in the 1970s, it was suggested that advertising should once more be permitted, proponents of the prohibition argued that individual advertising would undermine the relationship of trust between solicitor and client; it would be incompatible with the solicitor's duty to the wider community; it would be inherently misleading to the layman; and it would entail expenses which would have to be passed on to clients. Further, it was said that it would give larger firms an advantage in the market as compared with small firms which could not afford to advertise. Lastly, if price advertising was to be permitted it was alleged that it might encourage some solicitors to cut corners and thus lead to a reduction in the quality of legal services. Lying behind these objections seemed to be the feeling that advertising and competition were undignified and commercial, incompatible with the status of a profession.

Those who favoured the relaxation in the rule restricting individual advertising riposted that advertising would increase demand, innovation and competition; it would lower the price for routine legal services as a result of increased competition; it would enable consumers to make more informed choices as to which lawyer to approach with their problems; and it would make it easier for new lawyers to establish viable practices.

In *Bates v. State Bar of Arizona* (1976) 433 U.S. 350, the U.S. Supreme Court held, by a majority, that it was unconstitutional to prevent lawyers advertising the availability and cost of routine legal services, and in the succeeding years the Law Societies in Scotland and England came under considerable pressure to relax the prohibition in advertising. In 1976 the Monopolies and Mergers Commission pronounced itself in favour of individual advertising by solicitors in Scotland and England.

Monopolies and Mergers Commission, *Services of Solicitors in Scotland*, pp. 31–33

> "We [consider] . . . that the existing restrictions on the advertising of solicitors' services (i) prevent the public and potential new entrants to the profession being given information about the services offered by individual solicitors or firms of solicitors . . . (ii) are likely to have disadvantageous effects on the competitiveness and efficiency of the profession generally, on the introduction of innovatory methods and services and on the setting up of new practices . . .
>
> 125. We consider that . . . [the] general prohibition on advertising and soliciting business, should be terminated and replaced by a rule which would permit any solicitor in Scotland to use, whenever he thinks fit, such methods of publicity as he thinks fit, provided that:
>
> (1) No advertisement, circular or other form of publicity used by a solicitor should claim for his practice superiority in any respect over any or all other solicitors' practices.
> (2) Such publicity should not contain any inaccuracies or misleading statements.
> (3) While advertisements, circulars and other publicity or methods of soliciting may make clear the intention of the solicitor to seek custom, they should not be of a character that could reasonably be regarded as likely to bring the profession into disrepute."

(For a further discussion of the competing arguments relating to solicitor advertising, see Paterson, "Advertising by Lawyers; The American Experience" (1984) 29 J.L.S. 125, Macaulay, "Lawyer Advertising: 'Yes, but . . .'" (Paper on Price Information and Public Controls, Consumer and Market Performance, presented to the Fourth European Workshop on Consumer Law, Brussels 1985).)

Despite the fact that both the Benson and Hughes Commissions endorsed the proposals of the Monopolies Commission, the profession continued to drag its feet. However, in 1983 the Government accepted that the practice rules of the profession required to be relaxed in an effort to permit more competition within the profession. Under Government pressure the English and Scottish Law Societies introduced revised practice rules permitting more individual advertising by solicitors (from October 1, 1984 and March 1, 1985 respectively).

The Scots adopted a minimalist approach. The only advertising that would be permitted was that specifically allowed under the Practice Rules. While relatively liberal in relation to the permitted media (television was allowed, cinema and bus posters were not) the provisions as to content were highly restrictive. The only significant advance on the pre-existing rule was the ability of a solicitor to advertise "any services provided by him in areas of practice in which he has experience". Yet this was strictly construed, thus excluding reference to specialisms or expertise, work done for particular clients, line drawings, photographs, chatty dialogue, blurb or offers to give a free or fixed fee interview to new clients. Advertisements which encouraged readers to telephone a solicitor were struck at as solicitation. Once it became clear that advertising did not herald the end of the profession or even professionalism, as some critics had feared, a much less restrictive set of rules were introduced in 1987.

Thereafter solicitor advertising in Scotland became commonplace. A survey conducted in 1989 found that 57 per cent of Scots firms had advertised in the previous six months—a higher figure than in the United States. (In fairness, however, the number of repeat or frequent advertisers was lower, perhaps much lower, than in the United States.) Predictably, radio, television and cinematic advertising were pursued by less than 4 per cent of firms but over 40 per cent had experimented with an advertisement in a newspaper or freesheet. Price advertising, however, was very rare (less than 0.5 per cent). As in the United States, Yellow Pages were seen by solicitors as a particularly effective form of advertising and over 40 per cent of firms had advertised in them. Other promotional devices such as novelties, brochures and sponsorship had been used by about 25 per cent of firms. Perhaps ominously, only 23 per cent of firms reported that their promotional activities were part of a long-term plan. (This confirms the impression of observers that the majority of Scottish solicitor advertising to date has been tactical and *ad hoc* rather than strategic in nature.) [For fuller details on the survey, see Paterson and Stephen, *The Market for Conveyancing in Scotland* (Scottish Office, 1990), pp. 16–21.] The popularity of solicitor advertising and its non-problematic nature led in 1995 to the introduction of an even less restrictive set of rules on advertising.

Solicitors (Scotland) (Advertising and Promotion) Practice Rules 1995, rr. 4–8, 2(1)

> "4. Subject to rules 5 and 8 hereof a solicitor shall be entitled to promote his services in any way he thinks fit.
>
> 5. A solicitor shall not make a direct or indirect approach whether verbal or written to any person whom he knows or ought reasonably to know to be the client of another solicitor with the intention to solicit business from that person.
>
> 6. Rule 5 shall not preclude the general circulation by a solicitor of material promoting that solicitor's services whether or not the persons to whom it is directed are established clients.

7. A solicitor shall not be in breach of these rules by reason only of his claim to be a *specialist in any particular field of law or legal practice; provided that:—

(a) the onus of proof that any such claim is justified shall be on the solicitor making it; and
(b) an advertisement of or by a solicitor or other material issued by or on behalf of a solicitor making any such claim shall conform otherwise to the requirements of rule 8.

8. An advertisement of or by a solicitor or promotional material issued by or on behalf of a solicitor or any promotional activity by or on behalf of a solicitor shall be decent and shall not:—

(1) claim superiority for his services or practice over those of or offered by another solicitor; or
(2) compare his fees with those of any other solicitor; or
(3) contain any inaccuracy or misleading statement; or
(4) be of such nature or character or be issued or done by such means as may reasonably be regarded as bringing the profession of solicitors into disrepute; or
(5) identify any client or item of his business without the prior written consent of the client; or
(6) be defamatory or illegal.

2.—(1)
*'specialist' means an individual solicitor who possesses knowledge of and expertise in a particular branch or area of law or legal practice significantly greater than that which might reasonably be expected to be possessed by a solicitor who is not a specialist in that branch or area of law or legal practice."

As can be seen, the new rules are very close to the proposals of the Monopolies and Mergers Commission. Almost all restrictions on the media in which advertising can appear have been removed. As for content, anything can be published which is not specifically banned. A solicitor can even claim to be a specialist provided he or she can justify such a claim. Since being a "specialist" might mean only having experience in a particular field, as opposed to expertise, the rules stipulate that a specialist must have knowledge and expertise in a particular area of law which is significantly greater than might be expected of a non-specialist. Finally, solicitors can now issue general mail-shots promoting their services, provided they do not target specific recipients for the circular (unless they know that the recipient has no existing solicitor or could not reasonably be expected to know that the recipient had a solicitor.) This is a bizarre restriction, requiring as it does that mail-shots be used inefficiently rather than aimed at those who are known to require the services of a solicitor. Targeted advertisements, on the other hand, are permitted as can be seen from the following advertisement which appeared in the *Shetland Times* following the oil tanker disaster in January 1993.

THE TANKER BRAER

- When faced with a disaster like this it is vital to be able to rely on professional, skilled advice.
- This is what solicitors LEVY & McRAE can offer.
- LEVY & McRAE have a considerable breadth of experience having been directly involved in the legal aftermath of the Piper Alpha and Lockerbie disasters.
- Our Head of Litigation, Mr Peter Watson, handled international claims both in this country and the U.S.A.
- In a statement Mr Watson said: "Shetlanders who believe they may have a claim must not rush to settle without consulting a solicitor. Bearing in mind the operating country of origin of the tanker *Braer* is the USA these claims may be best pursued in the American courts."
- Whether you have suffered loss directly or indirectly as a result of this tragedy or are simply unsure of your position contact us for our expert advice.
- LEVY & McRAE can assist you by handling all your claims whether relating to agriculture, fishing, crofting, tourism, retail or personal. These claims may include:—

1 LOSS OF PROFITS

2 LOSS OF OR DAMAGE TO STOCK

3 DERELICTION OF LAND

4 PROPERTY DAMAGE

- If you are interested please contact us by telephone, letter or fax. Alternatively why not meet Peter Watson free of charge at The Shetland Hotel, Lerwick any time today (Friday) January 8 or tomorrow Saturday before 12 noon.

LEVY & McRAE
266 St Vincent St
Glasgow
G2 5RL
Phone: 041 307 2311
Fax: 041 307 6857/6858

There are also signs that the Law Society is prepared to adopt a less restrictive approach towards rule 5, which aims to prevent touting for business among the clients of other solicitors. A few years ago it was accepted that a solicitor "ought reasonably to know [that someone was] the client of another solicitor" if they owned a house or ran a business. However, the Professional Practice Committee now takes the view that, while such persons may have had a solicitor in the past, this does not necessarily mean that they still do, and mere ownership of a house or business is not sufficient to require a solicitor to conclude that such a person still has an existing solicitor.

B. ALTERNATIVES TO INDIVIDUAL ADVERTISING

The Law Society's preferred alternatives to individual advertising were institutional advertising of the services offered by the profession (which meets even fewer of the information needs of potential clients) and solicitor directories. It is not without irony that it was only in 1990, well after individual advertising had become successfully established, that the Law Society launched its largest and most sustained institutional advertising campaign, "It's never too early to consult a solicitor".

For a while the Law Society published a Directory of General Services provided by solicitors. As its title implied, it contained lists of law firms and their solicitors setting out the areas of work which they generally handled. By providing standardised information on the bulk of the profession the Directory offered an advantage over even yellow page advertising. However, it suffered from a number of weaknesses which were in the end of the day sufficient to bring about the Directory's demise. The entries were paid for by the firms and as a result it contained only about two-thirds of the profession. The entries were based on self-report tick-box forms and some firms simply ticked every box—suggesting that they normally handled everything from crofting law to management buy-outs. This reduced its value to the public, as did the absence of any information on the firms' normal charging rates. To cap it all the Directory was time-consuming and expensive to compile, so after a while it was simply abandoned by the Law Society, although such directories still exist in England and Wales. Subsequently, basic information about firms and categories of work in which they claim to have a particular expertise, has been included in the *White Book*—one of the two main commercially produced directories of the Scots profession. However, this also suffers from the "self-report problem" and accordingly falls short of a quality assured solution to the problem of helping the public identify solicitors who are specialists—in the sense of experts.

This problem was considered by the Royal Commissions. Benson concluded that some system of certification of specialisms should be introduced in England and Wales. In California, such a system, based on examinations and peer review, has been in operation since 1971.

The Benson Commission, p. 366

"Eligibility for designation as a specialist

27.21 We suggest that the following criteria should be satisfied.

(a) Designation should be granted to an individual and not to a firm. The solicitor concerned should have held a full practising certificate for at least five years immediately preceding his application.
(b) The solicitor should have devoted at least one-quarter of his time to the subject in question during each of the last five years.
(c) No solicitor should be designated as a specialist in more than two subjects at any one time.
(d) The claim to be designated as a specialist should be by written application to the Law Society which should satisfy itself that the work carried out by the applicant has been such as to justify the designation of specialist. The names of referees should be provided if requested by the Law Society.
(e) The applicant should be interviewed by a panel of three experienced practitioners who should investigate in confidence the professional record and work of the applicant in order to determine whether the designation of specialist would be justified.

27.22 Applicants satisfying these criteria would be entitled to describe themselves as specialists in the appropriate category of work on their firm's writing paper, in the Solicitors' Directory, in the legal aid solicitors lists and other referral lists and in advertisements. A solicitor who has been recognised as a specialist should certify on every successive application for an annual practising certificate that he has devoted at least one quarter of his normal working time to his specialism. A solicitor who ceases to meet this requirement should no longer be entitled to claim to specialise in it. In the event of a complaint being upheld against a solicitor's conduct or competence in his specialism, his designation as a specialist should be reviewed."

[See further, A.A. Paterson, "Specialisation and the Profession: Lessons from the United States" (1986) 31 J.L.S. 8.]

Hughes, on the other hand, was not convinced that such a system was worthwhile, preferring instead the introduction of a semi-formal system for monitoring the competence of the profession with reports from the Keeper of the Registers, court officials, judges and clients. Nevertheless, the extent of *de facto* specialisation (more than 70 per cent of the profession in Scotland and England regard themselves as specialists) led the Scots and the English Law Societies in the 1980s to establish groups to investigate specialisation. As in the United States the choice lay between self-designation schemes and objective certification. In England, panels for mental health review tribunals, child care and insolvency practitioners were established on the basis of interviews, course attendance and objective work experience tests in 1984 and 1985. The pressure grew on the profession to proceed with more panels fuelled by the endorsement of formal certification by the Civil Justice Review. Both Societies came out in favour of objective certification for panels using peer review and oral examination/interviews. But even as these proposals emerged, a majority of the English Council of the Law Society in 1990, perhaps fearing a fragmentation of the profession into different sub-professions, forced through a change in the publicity code for solicitors. The reform allowed any solicitor to design themselves as a specialist provided they could justify their claim if challenged. This, of course, was simply self-designation in its crudest form. The Scots performed a similar *volte face*, leaving the United Kingdom with a laxer approach to the publication of specialisation than any other country in the western world.

More recently, the relevant groups within the Societies have revived the cause of certified specialists. In England, the Law Society has established specialist panels in the areas of personal injury, medical negligence, child law, mental health, planning and insolvency. The personal injury panel had the largest membership, around 2,500 in mid-1998. In Scotland the first specialist panel (Employment Law) was established in 1991, and there are now 14 specialist panels. Certification is based on peer review, considerable experience in the field and references. However, in nearly eight years fewer than 200 specialists have become registered, suggesting that the best vehicle for identifying specialist solicitors for Scottish clients has yet to be developed. One innovation which may improve things is the Law Society of Scotland's website, set up in 1998, which allows members of the public to search for accredited specialists by area of expertise and geographical location (www.lawscot.org.uk/accredited), as well as the name and details of all firms and solicitors in Scotland.
(Source: Law Society of Scotland (Website).)

CHAPTER 12

PAYING FOR LEGAL SERVICES

The third barrier between citizens and legal services identified by Hughes was cost. Hughes did not fall into the error of asserting that the poor use lawyers less often than other sectors of the community. Modern studies in the United States and in Australia and indeed the Benson Commission's user survey all show that, save in property-related matters, the public consults lawyers infrequently and that their use of lawyers is largely unrelated to class or income. However, the costs of professional services and of litigation in particular are now of such an order that all sectors of the community, except perhaps the most wealthy or those in commercial circles, are inhibited (though in varying degrees) from resorting to law. In response to the problem of cost a system of legal aid has evolved.

I. THE BACKGROUND TO LEGAL AID

The Hughes Commission, pp. 83–84

> "8.2 Civil legal aid in more or less its present form was introduced in Scotland in 1950. Prior to that date, however, the Scottish legal profession had long accepted the representation of the poor without fee as a professional duty. An Act of 1424 made provision for the court to appoint an 'advocate' in civil cases for 'onie pure creature, for faulte of cunning, or expenses, that cannot, nor may not follow his cause'. In 1535, two advocates for the poor were appointed and received a stipend from the Treasury; but the system was probably rudimentary until the seventeenth century when there developed the practice of appointing members of the Society of Writers to the Signet as agents for the poor in the Court of Session. An Act of Sederunt of 10 August 1784, which probably for the first time formalised the procedure for admission to the poor's roll, required the Faculty of Advocates to appoint six advocates and the Writers to the Signet and the other agents practising in the Court of Session each to nominate four of their members to act for the poor in civil cases in the Court of Session. The applicant was required to produce a certificate of indigence from the minister and two elders of his parish and a report on the merits of the case by lawyers appointed for this purpose. This was, accordingly, the beginning of a system where the means of an applicant and the merits of his case are first examined before legal aid may be granted. From at least the 16th century, the legal profession accepted as a public duty the defence of poor persons on criminal charges. The statutory basis is uncertain, but two Acts of the Scottish Parliament in 1587 are thought to have regulated the provision of this service. Formal provision for the appointment of poor's agents in civil

and criminal cases in the sheriff courts was made by the Act of Sederunt of 12 November 1825. Local schemes for providing representation for the poor were modified from time to time in the years after 1825, but the 'Poor's Roll' remained substantially in the same form until 1950. At an earlier stage, however, there had been recognition that radical reform was necessary, and a committee under the chairmanship of Sheriff Morton was appointed in 1936 to review the facilities available to poor persons as parties before the civil courts and as accused persons before the criminal courts. Before action could be taken on the Morton Report, the second world war intervened. In 1945, the Cameron Committee reviewed the need for legal aid in Scotland following a report on this subject which had been made by the Rushcliffe Committee relative to England and Wales. After considerable debate there emerged the Legal Aid (Scotland) Act 1949, which envisaged a system whereby persons of limited means could receive civil and criminal legal aid and advice. However, because of economic considerations at the time, civil legal aid alone was introduced in 1950. It was not until 1964 that criminal legal aid was introduced following a further review, this time by the Guthrie Committee. In 1972, legal advice and assistance (providing for limited advice and assistance short of representation in court) was added to the system."

II. LEGAL AID TODAY

A. ADMINISTRATION

There was always a latent conflict of interest between the Law Society acting as the governing body of solicitors and as the supervisor of the payment of substantial sums of public money to its members. For this reason the Hughes Commission (para. 8.73) recommended that legal aid in Scotland should be administered by an independent authority (a Legal Services Commission) to continuously review the scheme, to scrutinise accounts for payment and to experiment with new forms of delivering legal aid. In part in response to this recommendation the Government in the Legal Aid (Scotland) Act 1986 vested the administration of legal aid in the hands of a new non-departmental public body, the Scottish Legal Aid Board. (It consists of 11 individuals appointed by the Secretary of State, of which at least four must be lawyers.) However, the remit of the Board is considerably narrower than that suggested for the Legal Services Commission. Thus its general functions are almost entirely reactive and tactical rather than pro-active and strategic, consisting as they do of administering the legal aid fund and securing that legal aid and advice and assistance are available in accordance with the 1986 Act. Unlike its predecessor, the Board was also given the responsibility for the assessment of applicants' resources in civil legal aid and for the granting of criminal legal aid in summary cases.

B. LEGAL AID IN CIVIL COURT PROCEEDINGS

Legal aid as it operates in Scotland and England today consists of three main schemes: Legal Aid in Civil Proceedings, Advice and Assistance and Criminal

Legal Aid. (For further details on Criminal Legal Aid, see chapter 5 above.) Civil Legal Aid, which is governed by section 13 of the Legal Aid (Scotland) Act 1986 provides legal representation in virtually all proceedings before the more important and the most commonly used Scottish courts.

The proceedings in which legal aid is not available (described as the "excepted proceedings" in the Act) are those in respect of defamation or verbal injury (except in respect of certain counterclaims: Schedule 2, Part II, para. 2 to the Act); simplified divorce applications; election petitions; small claims at first instance; and proceedings under the Debtors (Scotland) Act 1987 other than proceedings under section 1(1) or 3(1). It would appear that any doubts as to whether legal aid was available for summary causes or proceedings for summary removing in which the liability for the debt and its amount were admitted have been removed by the passing of the 1986 Act (Stoddart, *Legal Aid in Scotland* (3rd ed., W. Green, 1990), paras 7–18 and 7–19.) Legal aid is not available for any proceedings in the Court of the Lord Lyon, the Court of Teinds, the Registration of Voters Appeal Court, the Election Petition Court, the courts of the Church of Scotland and the military courts-martial. Perhaps most significant of all, legal aid is not available for proceedings before tribunals, with the exception of the Lands Tribunal for Scotland (Schedule 2, Part 1, para. 1 to the 1986 Act) and the Employment Appeal Tribunal (Schedule 2, Part 1, para. 1 to the 1986 Act), which is a superior court of record.

To qualify for civil legal aid the applicant must satisfy the Board as to the merits of his or her case, as well as being financially eligible.

1. Legal Criteria

Legal Aid (Scotland) Act 1986, s.14(1)

> " . . . civil legal aid shall be available to a person if, on an application made to the Board—
> (a) the Board is satisfied that he has a *probabilis causa litigandi*; and
> (b) it appears to the Board that it is reasonable in the particular circumstances of the case that he should receive legal aid."

This twofold legal eligibility test is commonplace in the western world, although in some jurisdictions the two are subsumed under a single "reasonableness" test. (The latter is an option which appeals to the Board). Only the Netherlands is significantly out of line, by merely requiring that the action be not "wholly unfounded" or unjustified in terms of the likely cost of the action.

2. Financial Criteria

Legal aid is available in civil cases to all persons:

(a) who do not have rights or facilities making it unnecessary for them to have legal aid (*e.g.* when a trade union will pay for the case as one of the benefits of membership or where the applicant is covered by a legal expenses insurance policy);

(b) whose "disposable" income (*i.e.* net wage under deduction of allowances for expenditure such as rent, hire purchase commitment and allowances for dependants) does not exceed the limit from time to time prescribed by the Secretary of State. The current upper limit is £8,751. Where the applicant's "disposable" income lies between the upper limit and £2,680 (the non-contributory limit) he or she will have to make a contribution towards the cost of the case. This will not exceed one third of the excess of the disposable income over £2,680;

(c) where the applicant has "disposable" capital (*i.e.* capital under certain deductions and disregarding the value of any house, furniture, personal clothing and tools of his trade) of more than £8,560, he or she may be refused legal aid if it appears that they can afford to proceed without it. Where the disposable capital lies between these upper limits and £3,000 (the non-contributory limit) then applicants are required to contribute towards the cost of their litigation. This will be not more than the amount by which the applicant's disposable capital exceeds £3,000.

The Board calculates the maximum contribution of applicants by the simple process of totalling their capital and income contributions. However, if the likely cost of the action is below this sum, an "actual" contribution will be fixed based on the Board's estimate of what the case will cost. Contributions from capital are usually paid in a lump sum but income contributions are normally payable by instalments over ten months. Where the assisted party is successful in his or her action but the expenses of the litigation are not recovered in full from the other side the Board will look to the assisted party to meet any shortfall from their contributions or any property recovered as a result of the action (section 17(5) Legal Aid (Scotland) Act 1986). This is known as the "statutory clawback".

3. Liability for Expenses

Mellick, "Legal Aid in Scotland", p. 188

"In the event of the legally assisted person failing in his action or defence and/or having an award of expenses made against him, then it is the duty of the solicitor to ask the court to modify the award or the sum payable thereunder to the opponent having regard to the means of the legally assisted person. Unless there has been any change in circumstances since the application for Legal Aid was made, this information is usually obtained from the Legal Aid application and from the Legal Aid Certificate . . . Alternatively up to date information must be supplied to the court. It is not uncommon for the court to limit any award of expenses against a legally assisted person to payment of an amount equal to the legally assisted person's original contribution: but the matter is entirely in the discretion of the court. A legally assisted person is very seldom ordered to pay the full amount of any award of expenses made against him. This is a safeguard to the legally assisted person against the possibility of insolvency or bankruptcy in the event of his otherwise engaging in litigation . . .

Provision is also made for the case where a legally aided person sues a non-legally aided person and fails in his action and has an award of expenses made against him. Presumably on the theory that public funds having financed the litigation of the legally assisted person, the court can where hardship can be shown on the part of the non-legal aid defender through his inability to recover expenses from the legally assisted person, make an order that the expenses of the non-legal aid defender be paid out of the Legal Aid Fund."

C. ADVICE AND ASSISTANCE

Advice and Assistance is a form of legal aid which enables persons of limited means to obtain advice on practically any matter involving an issue of Scots law. The main exclusion relates to steps in the institution or conduct of any proceedings before a court or tribunal. Even this restriction has been modified in recent times by the introduction of ABWOR (assistance by way of representation) as part of Advice and Assistance to cover representation in certain criminal proceedings and appeals under the Mental Health (Scotland) Act 1984. Unlike civil legal aid there are no merits tests. Advice and Assistance has the additional advantage of flexibility in that:

(1) The person seeking the advice need not go to the solicitor, provided that there is a good reason for not doing so. The advice may be obtained by telephone or mail or even through an adult intermediary who attends on the applicant's behalf.
(2) The solicitor need not give the advice and assistance at his or her office. It may be given outside the office, *e.g.* in the home of a disabled or infirm client, in hospital, in prison, in a police station or in the precincts of a court.

The statutory clawback operates in relation to Advice and Assistance as well, although, contrary to the position in civil legal aid actions, the Board has a discretion to allow the whole sum recovered to be paid over to the client without deduction of expenses where to do otherwise would cause grave hardship to the client or could only be effected with unreasonable difficulty.

D. STRENGTHS AND WEAKNESSES

A study of other legal systems reveals that legal aid can be provided in a wide variety of different forms. (See Paterson, "Legal Aid at the Crossroads" (1991) 11 *Civil Justice Quarterly* 124.) Principally these consist of the charitable model (provided by volunteer members of the profession on a gratuitous basis), judicare (provided by the private profession funded by the state), the salaried model (provided by state salaried lawyers) and the mixed model (provided by a mixture of private practitioners and state salaried lawyers). Legal aid in Scotland today (as in the rest of the United Kingdom) primarily takes the form of the judicare model.

It is generally considered that its principal strengths relate to the fact that it is state funded, independently administered, broad in its scope, provides a wide choice of lawyer and risk protection if the action is lost. In all these respects the Scots model is superior to the charitable model. Although, as we shall see, eligibility for legal aid is declining in Scotland, the proportion of the population covered is still greater than in most other countries except the Netherlands. Indeed the per capita expenditure on all forms of legal aid in the United Kingdom exceeds that in any other country. (See E. Blankenburg, "Comparing Legal Aid Schemes in Europe" (1992) 12 *Civil Justice Quarterly* 106 and Legal Action Group, *A Strategy for Justice* (LAG, London, 1982).) Similarly, although there are significant omissions in the coverage of legal aid in Scotland, the overall breadth of potential cover bears comparison with that in most other countries. In the eyes of the profession and perhaps also of the public, the fact that any qualified lawyer can provide legal aid is seen as a significant advantage, in that it maximises access. However, legal aid policy makers and others have begun to question whether this feature is always as beneficial as it appears, since it fails to address issues such as economies of scale, the benefits of specialisation and the cost-effectiveness of state salaried lawyers. Such doubts are strengthened by the fact that it appears that about 25 per cent of solicitors in the United Kingdom do 75 per cent of legal aid work. (In Quebec, by contrast, less than 20 per cent of the private profession undertakes any legal aid at all.) Certainly, the thrust of the franchising programme for legal aid lawyers in England has been to begin to reward those who specialise in legal aid work and offer quality assurance measures as a result. A possible step on from this would be exclusive contracts to specialist suppliers. Finally, under the United Kingdom model of legal aid, the Legal Aid Fund bears the bulk of the risk of loss if assisted parties are unsuccessful in their actions, since losing assisted parties will usually have their liability to pay the other sides' expenses severely modified by the court. In most European jurisdictions there is no such protection for assisted parties who are unsuccessful in their litigation.

Despite these advantages, the Scottish judicare model shares the drawbacks of its English counterpart. Indeed, viewed from the perspective of the state, of the profession and the consumer there are a number of weaknesses in the model.

1. The State's Perspective

The principal concern of western governments is that the cost of providing legal aid through the private profession is rising exponentionally—frequently well in excess of inflation. Thus in Scotland between 1987/88 and 1997/98 payments from the Legal Aid Fund rose from £48 million to £145 million. [In real terms, taking into account inflation, legal aid expenditure in Scotland in 1996/97 was 71 per cent higher than in 1990/91 — F. Stephen, *Legal Aid Expenditure in Scotland* (The Law Society of Scotland, 1998).] Similarly, in England and Wales between 1985/86 and 1990/91 average legal aid bills were rising at more than twice the rate in increase in the retail price index (NAO Report on *The Administration of Legal Aid in England and Wales* (HMSO, London, 1992) at p. 12.) Indeed, over the 10 years between 1987/88 and 1997/98 the average legal aid bill rose 90 per cent faster than retail prices (Legal Aid Board Annual Report 1997/98 (HMSO) at p. 5). There has been considerable debate amongst scholars (especially economists) and policy-makers as to the causes of these dramatic rises. Some crudely assert that the root cause is supplier-induced demand, in other words that lawyers are profit-maximising through putting in more hours (and thereby boosting their fees) than their cases actually warrant. In truth, the reality is much more complex than that. The factors which influence the growth in expenditure are many and varied, ranging from new legislation, *e.g.* the Children's Act, to increased court fees and from a greater throughput of cases to procedural reforms. [See Goriely and Paterson, "Introduction: Resourcing Civil Justice" in *Resourcing Civil Justice* (Oxford University Press, 1996) at pp. 18–20.]

2. The Profession's Perspective

To the profession, the deficiencies of the United Kingdom model of judicare are threefold. First, that bureaucratic hurdles are increasing, necessitating delays, abandonment or the option of doing work for nothing. Secondly, that there is no effective payment mechanism which supplies the necessary working capital to support firms through cash-flow problems. (Cases may take months or years to complete before a legal aid account can be rendered by the lawyers, who in the meantime may be out of pocket for considerable levels of incidental expenses, not to mention fees. In the Netherlands, by contrast, lawyers can receive lump sum payments in advance which reflect the level of legal aid work undertaken by them in the previous year.) Thirdly, the profession considers that the level of remuneration for legal aid work is inadequate since legal aid rates are now significantly below the private rates set by the profession and the courts.

3. The Consumer's Perspective

Consumers, on the other hand, are more concerned that legal aid has still not been extended to cover proceedings before most tribunals, despite the fact that tribunals now deal with many issues that are vital to the welfare of the ordinary citizen (see chapter 6 above). Equally, the repeated failure to permit pursuers in defamation actions to obtain legal aid effectively denies the bulk of the population the opportunity to defend their reputations against public vilification. The exclusion of small claims cases has been justified on the basis that the procedure is designed to be used without the assistance of qualified lawyers. While this may be acceptable where small sums are concerned, critics point to proposals that the financial limit for small claims be raised substantially as posing a threat to inarticulate litigants who would no longer be eligible for legal aid. (See D. O'Carroll and P. Brown, "Small Claims" (1991) 181 SCOLAG 154.) The strength of this critique, however, must be tempered by the fact that for many consumers with small claims or personal injury actions the operation of the statutory clawback can deprive them of much of the benefit of legal aid if they win their cases but are unable to recover costs from their opponent.

There is also concern that a declining proportion of the population is now eligible for legal aid. When civil legal aid was introduced in 1950, 80 per cent of the population was eligible on income grounds. By 1978 the figure had fallen to 40 per cent. Measures were introduced to bring the coverage up to 70 per cent (in terms of income) but again the failure to keep pace with inflation meant that only about half the population were eligible by 1990. The position was not improved in 1993 when the Government introduced swingeing cuts in eligibility for civil legal aid. (See M. Murphy, "Civil Legal Aid Eligibility" 1989 *Legal Action* October, p. 7 and LAG, *A Strategy for Justice* (Appendix 1) 1992.)

A third problem for consumers comes from the fact that the structure of legal aid in the United Kingdom presupposes that the problems of applicants are best tackled on an individual basis. Bodies of persons are ineligible for legal aid.

Myers, "The future of Legal Aid in Scotland", p. 316

> "Legal aid—as is the case with legal practice—has always emphasised the protection of individual rights. In modern society, more and more disputes affect groups. These disputes have been particularly significant in planning and development matters . . . [Yet] there has been an almost complete lack of legal assistance available for poorer communities faced with large-scale redevelopment or a loss of basic amenities.
>
> The legal aid scheme provides a 'curative' service, offering legal assistance to pursue legal rights. It ought to be devoting more time and money to the provision of a 'preventive' service, educating groups in the community about law and legal rights."

Of course, one member of a group could raise an action as a test case and be granted legal aid, as Mrs McColl was in her action against Strathclyde Region's plans to add fluoride to the water supply. However, unless the Board consider that the applicant's individual interest is significant, it may well decide that it would not "be reasonable in the particular circumstances" to grant the application. This is all the more likely to be the case after the remarks by Lord Jauncey in *McColl v. Strathclyde Regional Council* 1983 S.L.T. 616 criticising the award of legal aid to Mrs McColl. The considerable growth in disaster or multi-party litigation in Scotland in the last 10 years, however, has led the Board to adopt a collective approach (dovetailing with a parallel approach of the Law Society which endeavours to bring together solicitors in multi-party cases). The Board's strategy is for applicants in such cases to be covered by generous advice and assistance extensions (in some cases in excess of £2,000) and/or given a legal aid certificate limited to raising the action and then sisting it until one case—the "test" or lead case—is determined in the courts. In England the Board has introduced a form of tendering by firms wishing to undertake multi-party litigation funded by legal aid.

4. Conclusion

Whatever the strengths and weaknesses of legal aid in Scotland it is clear that here, as in most jurisdictions with advanced legal aid programmes, the government has had enough. Legal aid expenditure cannot continue to rise exponentially.

T. Goriely and A. Paterson, "Introduction: Resourcing Civil Justice" p. 17

" 'Legal Aid in crisis' has a journalistic ring, but it is hard to deny that schemes are now facing serious problems. Over the last decade almost every government with a developed programme has come to the conclusion: legal aid is too expensive. Expenditure has risen faster than the rate of inflation, despite declining eligibility, higher contributions and reduced scope. 'A worse service at a higher price' is how the Social Market Foundation pithily described it. 'Stagflation' is the Legal Action Group's more prosaic description . . .

In the United Kingdom the Government has made a clear commitment towards curbing the rise in expenditure, even if this means striking at the basis of the scheme. In 1992 the Lord Chancellor, Lord Mackay, told the Annual Conference of the Law Society that legal aid could not continue to take an ever-increasing share of public expenditure: 'what is certain, is that the overall cost of legal aid must be made more affordable. It must also be better targeted.' "

In sum, it is an uncomfortable truth in advanced western societies that individual demand for access to law is infinite, while resources are all too finite. There is no escaping it. Priorities will have to be set.

III. HOW LEGAL AID IS USED

Any rational examination of prioritisation/rationing of legal aid expenditure has to start with how legal aid is currently used.

Table 12.1 Civil legal aid certificates issued in Scotland 1997/98

Family/Matrimonial	13,233	76%
Debt	536	3%
Reparation	1,719	10%
Judicial Review	101	1%
Other	1,816	10%

(Source: Annual Report Scottish Legal Aid Board 1997/98)

Table 12.2 Number of Advice and Assistance Bills paid 1997/98

	Scotland	England
Family/Matrimonial	20%	25%
Criminal	51%	26%
Debt/HP	5%	5%
Housing, Landlord & Tenant	3%	7.5%
Employment	1%	1%
Welfare Benefit	2%	12%
Mental Health	0.25%	0.7%
Immigration	—	5%
Reparation	5%	5%
Consumer	—	2%
Other	13%	10.5%

(Source: Annual Reports Scottish and English Legal Aid Boards 1997/98.)

The picture of legal aid usage revealed in Table 1 is one that has remained relatively constant over the past 20 years. Civil Legal Aid in Scotland is overwhelmingly used to support litigation between husbands and wives. As Table 12.2 shows, the over-emphasis on traditional areas of law remains depressingly true of applications for Advice and Assistance. Yet, 60 per cent of the workload of the publicly funded law centres in England and Wales concerns housing, welfare, employment and immigration law. Legal advice centres in Scotland and England in addition handle many consumer cases. In part such discrepancies between the public and private sectors can be attributed to the distinctive role of law centres in tackling unmet need (see chapter 11) but probably more significant is the operation of the statutory clawback and the lack of publicity given to the Legal Aid schemes.

IV. LEGAL AID: THE WAY FORWARD

1. The Purpose of Legal Aid

Prioritisation also requires that we be sure of the basis upon which state provision of legal services for its citizens rests. The traditional rationale, that subsidised legal services are necessary to provide "equal access to justice", remains true today, although some policy-makers would like to see it restricted to the very poor, leaving those with a modest income completely exposed.

Paterson, "The Purpose of Legal Aid", pp. 232–234

"The rationale for legal aid

> There is no universally accepted rationale or justification for the provision of state subsidised legal services . . . Although it has occasionally been argued that legal aid is a form of wealth redistribution or that the redistribution of legal services can lead to desirable social change, neither argument has attracted many supporters. The two principal justifications for legal aid which are put forward today are: (1) a utilitarian argument that more widespread use of legal services is a public good and that in a time of scarce resources the development of legal services should follow lines which would generate the greatest benefit for the greatest number of recipients; and (2) an argument that more widespread use of legal services is required in the interests of justice. Under this view the integrity of the adversary system (particularly where prosecutors are publicly funded) requires an equality in the distribution of legal services since its efficacy is predicated on both sides being competently represented.
>
> One of the best expositions of this second line of thought is contained in the 25th Legal Aid Annual Report of the English Law Society (1975, para. 1): 'Legal aid is increasingly being thought of as a social service and part of the welfare ideal; its fundamental importance however, has not been

sufficiently recognised in that its function is to ensure that justice—the first of all social services—is made available to all and is not confined to those able to bear the cost of protecting their lawful rights. The help afforded to those of limited means and the disadvantaged must be seen in the broad context of the role of the law itself, which provides the only foundation upon which the whole edifice of social welfare depends. In so far as the law is not made effective in the lives of all citizens it must fail in its social purpose and weaken all other social measures. Only through a truly comprehensive legal aid scheme can laws enacted to benefit those in need fully serve their intention. Legal aid is not an independent social instrument; it is an essential ingredient in the administration of justice without which the law must remain partial and socially discriminative.' Some exponents of this view have been prepared to go further and to argue that the receipt of legal services is a 'civil right' (34th Legal Aid Annual Report, para. 58). Such an assertion has problematic elements in the United Kingdom context since the entitlement to legal aid is hedged around with discretionary judgments . . .

Civil legal aid

The [legal aid] consultation paper [issued by the Scottish Home and Health Department in 1985], however, asserted that: 'There are many misconceptions about the purpose of legal aid. In civil cases the aim is that legal aid should permit those of insufficient means that same opportunity to pursue their rights as is available to those of moderate rather than abundant means. It should in general not be available in a case which would not be pursued by a person of moderate means' (para. 4)."

If this statement is an assertion that persons of moderate means are and have always been ineligible for legal aid then it is incorrect, as we have seen. If it means that legal aid is designed to put a poor person in the same position as a person of moderate means then not only is it historically inaccurate but it also represents a major erosion in the availability of legal aid. The aim of legal aid has not been to put poor persons in the position of those of moderate means who are ineligible for legal aid. Its aim has been to enable persons of low or moderate income who meet the legal and financial tests for legal aid to raise or defend an action unhampered by their lack of resources or a fear of having to pay crippling expenses should they lose.

2. The Scope of Legal Aid

Proposals for rationing or prioritisation frequently involve reducing the scope for legal aid.

Paterson, "Legal Services for All?", p. 327

"In relation to legal aid [the Hughes Commission] looked first at the proposal of the Scottish Legal Action Group (which coincided with a proposal of the English LAG) that the constraints on available funds are such that we should readjust our priorities in legal aid. In the first place certain services should be regarded as so essential, for example legal procedures relating to (a) the deprivation of liberty by custodial sentence or (b) the preservation of jobs, homes or welfare benefits, that they should normally be provided to everyone free of charge—at least up to the point of the first judgment of disposal. Secondly, SLAG proposed that certain desirable but non-essential legal services, for example help in making a will, obtaining a divorce, adoptions, minor criminal proceedings and the like, should be obtainable on payment of a flat rate contribution. Thirdly, services which would produce some gain for clients, for example house purchase and sale or forming companies or trusts, should be charged at a fair fee."

The Hughes Commission, pp. 90–91

"The scope of legal aid

8.16 The Scottish Legal Action Group proposal contains a number of points. For example, it does away with the principle of contribution on the basis of means. We know that many people find means testing abhorrent; but we believe that it is only fair that those who are able should make some contribution to the cost of the legal services they use. Some form of assessment of means will thus continue to be essential . . .

8.17 The Scottish Legal Action Group proposal also involves what might be called 'needs testing': a categorisation of kinds of case some of which would attract free legal aid; some of which would attract legal aid subject to a flat rate contribution; and some of which would attract no legal aid at all. In the way in which this was presented to us we were not convinced that the proposal was sound; and we thought it could lead to injustice. As regards civil matters we do not think it desirable for us, the legislature, or anyone else, to attempt to define in general terms for others what types of case are 'important' to them. Unless the category for which unlimited or generous legal aid is to be available were drawn so widely as to make this proposal meaningless, we think it inevitable that the proposal would result in legal aid being granted in cases of relative triviality and being withheld in cases where hardship cries out for it to be available. Nevertheless, we believe that there should be a limit, in principle, to the scope of legal aid. In civil matters, as we have already said, we believe it is right that the State should help a citizen to take legal action to assert or protect his rights; but we do not think it justifiable that public funds should be expended to assist individuals in arranging their affairs for the benefit of themselves or for others."

34th Legal Aid Annual Report 1983–84

"290. The Hughes Report . . . argument has some force, but it does not in our view constitute the decisive objection of principle to the ['needs testing'] proposal. In the context of legal aid, there is no reason why taxpayers generally should provide a 100% subsidy for people who can afford to contribute substantially towards the cost of their cases, however important are the particular rights those people wish to defend. We would not welcome a situation in which people of considerable means were able to litigate entirely at public expense. We adhere to the general principle that people should pay towards the cost of the legal services they require what they can reasonably afford. Insofar as it is necessary to ensure that people are not deterred from defending their fundamental rights, that objective can best be attained by maintaining the value of the legal aid limits generally.

291. Even were it to be agreed that there were areas of law involving fundamental civil rights, it is doubtful how far agreement would be reached over precisely what those areas were. And even if there were a consensus as to the types of cases that should be singled out, it is doubtful whether they would be easily defined in terms of categories of proceedings."

The Hughes proposal that legal aid should only be available to help citizens to assert or protect their rights, and not to assist them in arranging their affairs for the benefit of themselves or others, is based on a value judgment no less questionable than that contained in the proposals of the Scottish and English Legal Action Groups. In the intervening years since the Report it is increasingly been recognised that preventative or proactive lawyering, *e.g.* making a will, can prevent more expensive and painful legal intervention, *e.g.* a litigation between dependents over their succession rights because the deceased did not leave a will. Hughes's proposals would have funded the latter but not the former. In its 1998 White Paper *Modernising Justice* (para. 3.7), the Lord Chancellor's Department outlined its priorities for spending, namely, social welfare cases, other cases of fundamental importance to the people effected (*e.g.* major issues in children's lives or protecting people from violence) and cases involving the wider public interest (*e.g.* those that may produce benefits for a significant number of people or those challenging the actions of public bodies—including human rights cases).

3. Eligibility

The Hughes Commission and the Legal Aid Eligibility Review (SOHHD, *Review of Financial Conditions for Legal Aid: Eligibility for Civil Legal Aid in Scotland*, 1992) both floated the additional possibility of removing the upper eligibility limit of disposable income coupled with a sharply rising scale of contributions (ensuring that better off assisted parties would in effect pay near to 100 per cent of the cost of their litigation). This proposal would remove the current anomaly whereby applicants just within the financial limits can afford to litigate and those with a few more pounds of disposable income, cannot. Although the fiscal implications of such a step are, perhaps surprisingly, not significant, it seems unlikely that in times of economic restraint the Government will go down this path.

Ostensibly, the Eligibility Review was an attempt to tackle anomalies caused by fixed eligibility limits. However, its principal proposal, the "safety net", appeared to be as much focused on the growing Treasury concern with the spiralling cost of legal aid—particularly in England and Wales.

Paterson, "Financing Legal Services", p. 160

"In brief, the review proposed that contributions should be increased and made to last throughout a case while assessment of means should be made

> less expensive by adopting a more broad brush, not to say crude, approach. In a purported attempt to tackle the problems of those outwith the legal eligibility limits it was suggested that a safety-net should be introduced. Under this system the applicant would spend up to £2,500 of his or her own money (the spending limit) before becoming eligible for legal aid. While this proposal offered assistance to some better off litigants, the paper hinted that the scheme might also be applied to poorer applicants currently eligible for legal aid but with a contribution (*i.e.* those above the free legal aid threshold). For them the safety net would be more akin to a tripwire. The Government claimed that the proposal would encourage responsible litigation and settlements. In reality, however, there is no evidence of assisted parties behaving irresponsibly by pursuing their actions. Even those who fall below the free legal aid limit have an interest to be prudent in litigating because of the mechanism of the statutory charge. To suggest that the spending limit would encourage litigants to exercise greater control over their lawyers overlooks the fact that it is very difficult for lay clients to assess the quality of the work being done for them by their lawyer."

The Eligibility Review was heavily criticised by almost all of the respondents, but worse was to follow. The Treasury, alarmed by the spiralling costs of legal aid in England and Wales which were being further driven up by the recession, called a halt, forcing the Lord Chancellor and his Scottish counterpart to introduce Draconian cuts in civil legal aid in early 1993. These included the reduction of the free limit for civil legal aid from £3,060 to £2,293 per annum, freezing the upper eligibility limit, reducing dependants' allowances and increasing the contributions paid by assisted parties (from a quarter of the sum by which their disposable income exceeds the free limit, to a third).

The cuts were particularly unpalatable in Scotland for a number of reasons. First, they represented a fundamental departure from the purpose of legal aid as it has operated to date. Instead of access to justice being a citizenship right for a majority of the population, it was being transformed into a welfare benefit. Secondly, the cuts only effectively restricted expenditure in relation to civil legal aid. Yet the real problem area of growth in recent years has been criminal legal aid which has increased by over 100 per cent in real terms since 1987/88 and is taking over a greater and greater share of Advice and Assistance (51 per cent in 1997/98) and of the total legal aid bill (70 per cent of the total in 1997/98). The cuts have done nothing to remedy this situation, indeed they may have exacerbated it, since criminal legal aid is non-contributory. Even the Scottish Legal Aid Board in its response to the "Access to Justice beyond the Year 2000" consultation paper called for a reduction in legal aid contributions to the pre-1993 levels in order to encourage a greater uptake of offers of legal aid.

4. Value for Money

It is now clear that the United Kingdom, like most other jurisdictions with highly developed legal aid programmes, is determined to rein in rampant expenditure growths and to improve the cost-effectiveness and quality of the services provided under legal aid. In these countries, *e.g.* the United Kingdom, Australia, Canada, Norway, and the Netherlands, very similar proposals are being considered. These include fixed fees, vouchers, contracts and quality assurance. Germany and the Netherlands have long had fixed fees and found them to be an invaluable instrument in keeping expenditure in check. The initial attempt to introduce fixed fees in criminal cases in England and Wales was a mixed success, because the architects of the reform failed to prevent case-splitting by practitioners. However, this experience has not prevented the Scottish Office from introducing fixed fees in summary criminal cases in Scotland from 1999. The Law Society of Scotland have been quick to point to the English research that suggests that "the introduction of standard fees creates a set of incentives for solicitors which could result in a less than optimal supply of inputs in legally aided cases", *i.e.* they encourage solicitors to avoid complex and difficult cases and to undersupply legal services in the cases that they do take (F. Stephen, *Legal Aid Expenditure in Scotland*, 1998). This, of course, is just the reverse of the incentives under the pre-1999 era when solicitors were paid according to how much work they had done. Proposals that eligible applicants for legal aid should be supplied with a voucher providing legal aid which could be cashed in with either salaried or private practitioners have been floated in the United States and Australia. There is no evidence to date that such schemes can provide effective quality controls.

Contracting out legal aid work to private lawyers on a bulk basis is an idea which has been examined in several countries, *e.g.* Norway, the Netherlands, Australia, the United States and England and Wales. In relation to duty lawyer schemes, contracts are thought to have had some success in Australia and Canada but not in the United States. Part V of the Crime and Punishment (Scotland) Act 1997 permits the introduction of exclusive contracts to suppliers in criminal cases. The *Access to Justice beyond the Year 2000* consultation paper suggests contracts might be introduced for civil legal aid or, more likely, advice and assistance. In the case of the latter contracts, advice agencies and other "not for profit" suppliers, *e.g.* law centres, would be eligible to be awarded contracts, *e.g.* to supply social welfare law advice in particular geographic areas. Indeed, in England and Wales the Lord Chancellor instructed the English Legal Aid Board to introduce contracts for advice and assistance in 1999 without waiting for the results of the Board's research into pilot contracting projects to see which was the optimum form of contract (LAB, *Reforming the Civil Advice and Assistance Scheme: Exclusive Contracting—the Way Forward*, 1998). Initially, therefore, contracts will be based as before 1999 on payment for time. In future, however, the Board hopes to move to payment at fixed prices for units of work (fixed fees). The English interest in value for money from legal aid suppliers through the use of contracts is a logical extension of the English Legal Aid Board's supplier development strategy as evidenced in the Franchising project.

Paterson, "Financing Legal Services", pp. 163–164

"The [Franchising] project is confined to firms and advice agencies in parts of Birmingham who are prepared to implement certain quality systems. In return for putting these systems in place and operating them franchise firms receive certain advantages from the Legal Aid Board. Originally it was proposed that all decisions on advice and assistance, ABWOR and emergency applications would be delegated to the franchisees and that in addition firms would receive monthly payments in advance representing a twelfth of the firm's earnings from all types of legal aid over the past twelve months. After last minute negotiations with the Law Society it was agreed that the firms would get four new early payment systems: up to £250 on account for each self-granted emergency certificate, up to £150 on account of each self-certified ABWOR case, the right to be paid at least two hours' worth of costs each time an advice and assistance extension is granted in-house and 75% on account of costs incurred once a civil legal aid certificate has run for nine months.

The concept of franchising was chosen in preference to tendering or contracting-out since it offered more access to the public with a better guarantee of quality. Originally the Board wanted to pursue economies of scale and suggested that franchise firms should have a turnover of £40,000 a year in legal aid fees and employ supervisors who would not be permitted to supervise more than three categories of work or seven people doing that work. After extensive discussions with the profession and the consumer bodies these requirements were dropped for the purposes of the experiment. However it is probable that both the Board and the Lord Chancellor's Department presently envisage that the supplier development strategy which is emerging from the franchising experiment will hinge around firms prepared to specialise in and to undertake substantial amounts of legal aid work ('preferred suppliers'). If this line is pursued it may produce considerable problems of access, particularly in the rural areas.

Largely for these reasons the case for franchising in Scotland has hitherto seemed to be less attractive to Scottish policy makers. It may be therefore that the current proposals of the Ministry of Justice in the Netherlands on this issue will prove more attractive. These include the registration of legal aid practitioners. Registration would be subject to a number of conditions:

- — a minimum (about ten) and a maximum number of cases that a lawyer can accept during one year;
- — specialisation, restricting registration to a limited number of legal areas;
- — good office procedures with adequate back-up cover;
- — annual reports to the legal aid authorities.

Exceptionally, where there is good reason clients will be permitted to instruct private practitioners who are not registered. Registration will be refused if the conditions cannot be met, if the lawyer is over 70 or if the lawyer works much less efficiently than other members of the profession (judged by a series of performance indicators)."

Franchising has moved on considerably from the Birmingham pilot. As at June 1998 there were 2,382 franchised solicitors' offices, advice agencies or law centres spread around the country. Since exclusive contracts for advice and assistance will only be awarded to franchised suppliers in the future the Board has set up 13 Regional Legal Services Committees throughout England and Wales, inter alia, to identify areas where there are insufficient suppliers/franchise holders. It is envisaged that these Committees will play a central role in the evolution of Community Legal Services in England and Wales. In particular they will be expected to estimate the need for different types of legal advices and assistance in their regions, and thus the number and range of contracts that will be required there. For similar reasons, if contracting is introduced for Scotland, it will be necessary to set up similar regional committees throughout Scotland to build on the work of Paterson and Montgomery in estimating the need for advice and assistance in different locales [A.Paterson and P. Montgomery, *Access to and Demand for Welfare Legal Services in Rural Scotland* (SLAB, 1997)].

As at the date of publication of this book, the Scottish Executive has yet to issue its White Paper [equivalent to the English *Modernising Justice* (LCD, 1998) following its consultation paper, *Access to Justice* (SOHD, 1998).

V. ALTERNATIVES TO LEGAL AID

The ever-increasing cost of legal aid to the Treasury has already prompted numerous proposals for curbing legal aid expenditure, as we have seen. It has also led reformers to consider alternatives to legal aid which might address the problem of the cost of legal services.

A. CONTINGENT OR CONDITIONAL FEES

Paterson, "Paying for Legal Services", pp. 237–238

"There are several variants on this theme. Straightforward contingent fees (arrangements whereby a lawyer takes a case on the basis that if he loses there will be no fee and if he wins he will obtain a percentage of the court's award) are unlawful and contrary to professional ethics in England, and prohibited at common law as *pacta de quota litis* in Scotland. Under the Land Purchase Act 1594 *c*. 220 it is also unlawful for any member of the College of Justice or any inferior court (including advocates, solicitors and clerks) to purchase pleas where litigation is pending. (The penalty under the Act is not nullity but deprivation of office for the offender!) It is not, however, illegal for debt collection agencies or claims assessors to purchase pleas or to undertake litigation for a fee which is a percentage of the sum in dispute or the sum recovered. On the other hand, solicitors who take a percentage fee on claims which they are instructed to litigate, might well be acting unlawfully if they habitually waive fees where no recovery is made.

It is not the taking of a proportion of the subject of the litigation on its own which is objectionable. It is always open for clients to enter into a special charging agreement with their lawyers. Moreover, the fees for extra-judicial settlements of claims for damages or reparation in cases where no proceedings in court have been initiated are calculated as a percentage of the sum settled for. Nor is it the agreement to act on the speculative basis that no fees will be payable unless the action is successful, which is objectionable. In *X Insurance Co. v. A and B* [1936 S.C. 225, 239] Lord President Normand remarked:

> 'It has long been recognised by our Courts that this is a perfectly legitimate basis on which to carry on litigation and a reasonable indulgence to people who . . . are . . . unable to finance a costly litigation.'

It is only where the percentage fee is combined with a speculative action that the agreement is struck at as a contingent fee. Yet, where a solicitor in Scotland has undertaken a speculative action for damages and subsequently settles it extrajudicially he is in effect receiving a contingent fee which is very unlikely to be declared *pactum de quota litis*."

(The acceptability of speculative fees was endorsed in the Law Reform (Miscellaneous Provisions) (Scotland) Act 1990, s. 36 which provides that solicitors and advocates can not only charge speculative fees but a percentage increase in the fee to a limit laid down by the court.)

Paterson, "Contingent Fees and their Rivals", pp. 81–83

"In the United States of America, contingent fees are most frequently used in personal injury actions, though they are by no means confined to such cases. Indeed their usage ranges from product liability to debt collection cases and from employment discrimination to anti-trust actions. In certain areas of law, however, the courts and ethical codes prohibit the use of contingent fees on public policy grounds. These are criminal cases, family cases and in some states, legislative lobbying. Contingent fees may be calculated as a percentage rate, as a fixed fee, or on an hourly basis. In practice, percentage rates are the most common: a typical contingent fee agreement in the United States of America may provide that the lawyer's reward will be 25 per cent of any settlement prior to a writ being issued, a third of any settlement or award made after the writ is issued, and 40 per cent or more if either side appeals. For this, the expenses of the case (such as court dues, experts' reports and witness fees) are usually advanced by the lawyer.

The first, and strongest, argument in favour of contingent fees is that they permit poor clients who are unable to pay lawyers' fees to bring their cases to court. 'One shot' litigants, who engage in litigation very rarely, are often in a poor position to bear the financial risks of going to court. The American system allows these risks to be shifted to the lawyers, who can spread the risks over many cases, and are therefore in a better position to bear them. Again, contingent fees can be viewed as 'productivity bonuses' or as an unusual form of venture capitalism which encourages the commitment of the lawyer to the client's case.

On the other hand, contingent fees are frequently blamed for two ills which are said to beset the legal system in the United States: excessive awards and a litigation explosion. Critics point to the rise in the number of substantial jury awards in civil cases: in 1984, for example, there were 401 awards of over $1 million, compared with 27 in 1975. This is attributed to the juries' wish to ensure that the victim remains fully compensated after the contingent fee has been met. Nevertheless, it should be remembered that most damages awards are for small amounts. There are many other reasons why civil juries may make an occasional very large award—to show public indignation against the tortfeasor, for example, or as a result of inadequate directions from the judge, and it has not been proved that contingent fees are to blame.

The existence and extent of a litigation explosion is the subject of some debate amongst academics in the United States. Even if there has been a substantial increase in litigation, it is by no means established that this is undesirable or that contingent fees are responsible for it. Contingent fees have been used in the United States of America for over 80 years, and it is unlikely that they alone have effected an increase in litigation in the last 10 or 20 years.

The second, and more telling, argument against contingent fees is that they create a conflict of interest between the lawyer and the client. It is argued that lawyers will wish to avoid the heavy expense of preparing for trial and of the trial itself, when this will not add proportionately to the award. Thus they may encourage settlements when this is not in the client's best interests. For example, a lawyer may decide that the true worth of the claim is $33,000, but this will require 100 hours of work to obtain. At an early stage, after just five hours work, the insurance company offers $15,000. The lawyer who successfully urges acceptance gains an hourly rate of $3,000, compared with a rate of $330 if the case goes the full distance.

There have been two research studies to test whether this occurs in practice. The first, based on a non-random sample of 59 personal injury cases in New York found some evidence to support the theory that contingent fee lawyers invest less time than hourly paid lawyers in a given case (D. Rosenthal, *Lawyer and Client*, 1974). The second, more recent, study had a considerably larger sample drawn from 12 courts around the United States of America (Kritzer *et al.*, 'The Impact of Fee Arrangements on Lawyer Effort' 19 *Law and Society Review* 251, 1985). The authors found that in comparison with hourly paid lawyers, contingent fee lawyers invested 20 per cent less time in the cases involving sums of around $6,000. But they devoted more time than their hourly paid counterparts to cases worth over $10,000. There was no clear evidence that the difference in hours allocated made any systematic difference to the damages awarded. As the authors themselves state, the results are not easy to interpret and it may be that the effects of fee arrangements on lawyers' behaviour are indirect rather than direct. In short, the case against contingent fees on the grounds of conflict of interest is not proven. All fee arrangements have their problems. Fixed fees are if anything more likely to cause lawyers to settle early, while hourly fees can encourage lawyers to 'run up the meter' by over preparing.

Thirdly, it is argued that contingent fees lead to excessive fees since lawyers have superior knowledge of the risks and costs involved, and they can use their superior knowledge to charge an unreasonable percentage. On the other hand many American states have taken action to control excessive fees and at least 17 states have enacted laws limiting the size of contingent fees. While controls can be placed on fees which are clearly excessive, it is much more difficult to ensure that fees are fair in every case. In practice, American lawyers tend to charge very similar contingent rates. This means that it is difficult for clients to shop around. Although a third may be fair in some cases, it will be very high in other cases where damages are high and the risk of failure is low. These clients are effectively subsidising those with weaker cases.

The final argument against contingent fees is that they encourage lawyers to use unethical tactics in the way they conduct cases. This argument carried considerable weight with both the Benson commission (1979) and the Hughes commission (1980), but there is little hard evidence to support it. Moreover, it appears to take an exceedingly pessimistic view of the ethical probity of the profession. Lawyers have a natural desire to win their cases, and it is not clear that a different basis for charging will by itself transform an honest lawyer into a dishonest one.

Should contingent fees be introduced in the United Kingdom?

The evidence suggests that in principle the arguments against contingent fees are not insurmountable provided certain safeguards are introduced, for example, maximum fee limits, judicial supervision, taxation and fee arrangements in writing. This does not necessarily mean that contingent fees are the best way forward in the United Kingdom. In the first place, the existence of the 'costs with the event rule' reduces the attractiveness of such fees to United Kingdom litigants since they are only protected from paying their own lawyers' costs if they lose—they will still have to pay the other side's costs. Moreover the practices of tendering or payments into court (which do not exist in the United States) may well encourage insurance companies to tender a poor settlement early in order to drive a wedge between the lawyer and the client. Alternatively, as Dr Carey Miller has argued ('A Case for Considering the Contingent Fee' (1987) 32 J.L.S.S. 461) the costs rule might be an advantage viewed from an objective perspective since it might inject 'a desirable restraint upon legal action where the merit of the claim was questionable'. Unfortunately, in those situations where the costs with the event rule does not apply, for example, small claims and tribunals hearings, the level of award is usually too small to leave much over to pay the contingent fee.

Secondly, while they might be attractive to claimants with a substantial legal aid contribution, those outwith the legal aid limits, or those ineligible for legal aid, they would seem to offer little to the 80 per cent to 90 per cent of assisted parties who have no contribution to pay (unless there was a strong risk of the statutory clawback eating up much of the award). Thirdly, contingent fees would provide no assistance in cases where no financial claim was being made, for example, interdicts, declarators or petitions for judicial review. Even in personal injury cases their use could be limited since several studies have shown that 85 per cent to 90 per cent of English personal injury cases result in a payment to the plaintiff. Where the risk of loss is as small as this, the need for contingent fees is not evident. Nevertheless, there is abundant evidence that many, possibly a majority, of individuals with valid personal injury claims take no action because of the fear of costs. For them, contingent fees might be beneficial."

Contingent fees continue to attract the attention of reformers and regularly appear in consultation papers or responses thereto. Nevertheless, despite being used by several non-lawyer organisations specialising in personal injury claims work, they are still distrusted in many quarters. A Law Society of Scotland working party considered and rejected their introduction in Scotland as recently as 1996. However, a closely related concept, conditional fees, may well play a considerable role in the provision of legal services in the future. Conditional fees are the English term for speculative fees. Introduced by the Courts and Legal Services Act 1990 they entitle lawyers to an uplift of up to 100 per cent on their normal fee when successful and nothing if the case is lost. The real attraction of the fee, however, came when the English Law Society negotiated with an insurance company to provide cover (at a very modest premium) for conditional fee litigants against the risk of having to pay the other side's expenses if the case was lost. Preliminary research on the first two years experience with conditional fees in England found that, in practice, in three quarters of the cases studied the uplift or success fee had been 50 per cent or less. Moreover, in 90 per cent of the cases solicitors had kept their success fee to below the Law Society's recommended but voluntary level of 25 per cent of the client's winnings. Nonetheless, the research also found that solicitors appeared to overestimate the risk associated with conditional fee cases, thus justifying a heightened uplift in their fees.(S.Yarrow, *The Price of Success: Lawyers, Clients and Conditional Fees* (Policy Studies Institute, 1997)). There has been no comparable research on the impact of the success uplift on speculative fees in Scotland, even although the Scots Law Society have launched their Compensure scheme with the same low premium insurance cover against the risk of paying the other side's expenses. The real importance of conditional fees, however, is that the policy-makers in the Lord Chancellor's Department see it as a way of replacing legal aid in a wide range of money related actions. As they observed in their consultation paper *Access to Justice with Conditional Fees* (LCD, 1998), this would allow legal aid to be targeted to priority needs through concentrating "publicly funded support on legal services towards helping people secure their basic rights such as a decent home, appropriate social security benefits and challenging officialdom through judicial review, and towards assisting cases that raise issues of wider public interest". The LCD have accepted, however, that before civil legal aid is totally withdrawn in favour of conditional fees, further research will be required.

A proposal that conditional fees should replace legal aid in personal injury cases is contained in the Scots consultation paper, *Access to Justice beyond the Year 2000* (Scottish Office, 1998). However, it is thought that there is less enthusiasm amongst policy-makers here for the proposal than in England. Certainly, the idea has not been well received by the profession or the consumer movement and the Government are well aware that the Scottish Legal Aid Board recover at least 80 per cent of the cost of supporting personal injury actions with legal aid.

B. A CONTINGENT LEGAL AID FUND

Paterson, "Financing Legal Services", pp. 167–169

"In 1966 (and again in 1978 and 1992) Justice put forward a proposal, which has since attracted considerable support, that a Contingency Legal Aid Fund

(CLAF) be set up to underwrite the litigation costs of persons who fall outwith the ambit of the legal aid schemes. This proposal has now been floated by the Lord Chancellor's Department and the Scottish Office Home and Health in their consultation papers on eligibility for civil legal aid. The CLAF would initially be funded from a government grant, but subsequently from a proportion of the winnings of claimants whose cases had been supported by CLAF. Where claimants were unsuccessful, their costs and those of their opponents would be met by the Fund. The administrative costs of the Fund would be met from a non-returnable registration fee. This scheme, it is argued, would overcome the main disadvantages of contingent fees without losing many of their advantages. (Because the claimants' lawyers would be paid a normal fee, win or lose, there would be no conflict of interest and no possibility of excessive fees.)

Successful claimants would also pay less than under a normal contingent fee arrangement (20% was Justice's suggested figure, however the LCD suggest that 25–30% of a damages award would be needed for the Fund to be self-financing). While claimants would not be subject to a means test (though large corporations would be excluded) they would have to show (as in legal aid cases) that their claims had a reasonable prospect of success. Justice thought that the scheme should not be available to defendants nor would it apply where a reasonable sum of money was not at issue (the figure proposed was £500) since otherwise the returns to the Fund would be inadequate. However the LCD considers that a combination of high non-returnable fixed fees and subsidisation from reparation actions would enable the CLAF to be used even where damages were not in issue. The attraction of such a scheme to governments is that it is, in effect, an insurance which spreads the risk of loss to other litigants rather than the legal aid fund. The attraction to clients would be that it would cover areas, as well as people, presently excluded from legal aid.

To date only one jurisdiction has any substantial experience of a CLAF—Hong Kong. In 1984 Hong Kong introduced such a scheme as an adjunct to their legal aid scheme for those whose means were just outwith the legal aid limits but who were nonetheless unable to afford the services of private practitioners. The Supplementary Legal Aid Scheme (SLAS) is restricted to substantial (over $60,000) claims for death or personal injury. The scheme is administered by the Legal Aid Department, the usual merits test is applied and a more generous means test. Instead of legal aid contributions the applicants are required to pay fees of $1000 (about £80) which are returnable if they are successful. They must also agree to a deduction of between 10% and 12% of any damages recovered (though the deductions can be reduced by up to 50% if the claim is settled at an early stage). Up to November 1990 there had been 297 successful applications to the scheme, representing 67% of all decided applications. It was three or four years before income under the scheme consistently exceeded expenditure. In Hong Kong the start-up costs were met by an interest free loan of up to $1,000,000 from the State Lotteries Fund. This has now been repaid.

Similar proposals in Western Australia (also backed by the Lotteries Commission) led to the setting up of a 'Litigation Assistance Fund' in 1991.

New South Wales and South Australia are also considering such Funds. The English Law Society is optimistic that taking advantage of the lessons to be learned from the Hong Kong experience it will be possible for a CLAF to become self-financing in a shorter period in the United Kingdom. One way to achieve this would be to make speedier cases eligible. The National Consumer Council is also supportive of such a development especially in class actions or test cases.

Nevertheless, the critics remain unconvinced. Carey Miller argues that a CLAF scheme involves unnecessary bureaucratic controls and administrative costs. The Benson Commission in a critique subsequently endorsed by the Legal Action Group argued that a CLAF scheme would be inequitable because poor successful claimants might be subsidising unsuccessful individuals or even companies. Furthermore, those who have suffered most in personal injury cases—and therefore have the largest claims, would have to pay the most, despite the fact that such claimants tend to be undercompensated as it is. The critics have also claimed that a CLAF would be vulnerable to adverse selection. Thus the success of the scheme would depend on a reasonable take-up. Yet claimants with good chances of success, it is said, would be reluctant to take part in the scheme and those who would be attracted to the scheme would have the weaker cases. Since litigants are rarely so claims conscious as to know the strength of their own cases, and risk-averse claimants would be attracted by the immunity from paying costs offered by a CLAF, it is likely that this argument is overstated. Nevertheless, as we have seen, most personal injury pursuers/plaintiffs obtain an award of some sort and frequently solicitors will advise clients with strong cases to bypass legal aid in order to avoid delays. If CLAFs are to be set up in different parts of the world, lawyers will be torn between advising clients with strong cases to proceed without cover from the CLAF or legal aid on the one hand or suggesting that they apply to the CLAF because they know that the success of the scheme depends on a reasonable take-up by claimants."

The possibility of a Contingent Legal Aid Fund appears in the Scottish Office "Access to Justice beyond the Year 2000" paper (1998), but it is not anticipated that it will receive much support. The option of using a CLAF to fund multi-party actions was considered by the Scottish Law Commission in 1996 and rejected: *Multi-Party Actions* (Edinburgh: HMSO) at para. 5.50.

C. GROUP LEGAL SERVICES

Paterson, "Paying for Legal Services", pp. 238–239

"One feature of contingent fees is that they spread the risk of loss among all pursuers. Prepaid legal services endeavour to reduce further the expense of going to law by spreading the risk of loss among an even larger sector of the community. There are two principal forms—group legal services and legal expenses insurance—which are in theory analytically discrete, even if in practice most prepaid legal service schemes are hybrids lying at different intervals on a continuum between the two polar forms.

Group legal services are joint ventures between the legal profession and the public designed to provide routine and non-routine legal services for the individual members of a group at reduced or subsidised rates. The exponential growth of such schemes in the United States in recent years is partly attributable to their appeal to certain sectors of the profession because they provide a constant supply of legal work . . . and their appeal to group members because they usually offer easy access to specialist lawyers at a cheaper price than that available on the open market. Groups who have sponsored such schemes include, inter alia, trade unions, employers' organisations, trade associations, professional associations, social clubs, automobile clubs and consumer groups.

The services offered under these schemes vary quite considerably, but the majority place a stress on preventive law. Most of them seem designed to encourage subscribers to undergo routine legal check-ups although few, if any, have specifically provided for this in the terms of the scheme. Consultations to cover routine legal services, *e.g.* house purchase, leases, preparation of wills, the completion of tax returns and company returns are comparatively inexpensive and efficient uses of legal expertise, and as such are strongly favoured by the schemes. Representation in court is highly expensive and accordingly less freely available. Typically, in return for an annual fee (which may be included in one's professional dues or as a fringe benefit offered by an employer) the group member and his family will be entitled to a stipulated number of hours of advice or back up or representation work from a lawyer, either free or at a reduced rate of charge . . . Claims which are considered by the lawyer to be frivolous, spiteful or very unlikely to be successful [will] usually be excluded . . . The schemes may be 'open' or 'closed' or somewhere in between. 'Open' schemes are those where the member may select any lawyer he chooses to provide the legal services offered in the scheme. 'Closed' schemes are those where the claimant is given little or no choice in the selection of the lawyer who will provide the services. Most group schemes are of the closed variety because by insisting that the legal services be provided by the staff lawyers of the group or by a restricted panel of private lawyers, the scheme organisers can take advantage of the economies of scale. The volume of cases enables greater specialisation and expertise to be built up among the lawyers and improved research facilities and machinery to be provided, while at the same time enabling fees to be kept down and the quality of the work monitored. It has been estimated that the average cost of a divorce in America under a closed scheme is approximately one-sixth the average cost of one under an open scheme. On the other hand, closed schemes largely remove the clients' freedom to choose their own lawyers and are liable to provoke accusations of unfair attraction of business from lawyers excluded from the schemes. Nor are they of assistance where the client's dispute is against the organisers of the scheme, *e.g.* a worker's dispute with his trade union.

In the United Kingdom group legal services are a well-established, although little discussed, phenomenon. Some employers offer legal services to their management staff as fringe benefits. The Automobile Association organises and funds certain legal services for its members as do the Medical Defence Union and the Medical Protection Society. But it is trade unions who have really developed such schemes on a large scale . . . Trade unions view legal services for their members as an important service and it is one of the strong 'selling' points of union membership. Unlike legal aid, the pursuer has no contribution to pay and if the case is lost the union pays all the expenses. Indeed, there is some evidence that in an attempt to boost the attractions of union membership, certain unions apply only a minimal merit test and will fund litigation which would have very little chance of success in court and which would be refused legal aid for lack of *probabilis causa*. It is clear that a considerable proportion of personal injuries cases in the United Kingdom are funded by trade unions and the structure of the legal aid schemes contributes to this, for applicants can be refused legal aid if they have access to other facilities or sources of financial assistance. The most common alternative sources of such assistance are trade unions. Although most group schemes in the United Kingdom are closed ones, both the Law Societies have declared that such schemes do not involve any unfair attraction of business. However, clients who resent the curtailment of their freedom of choice of lawyer under such schemes have to convince a legal aid committee that their objection is a reasonable one if they wish to avail themselves of the greater freedom of choice afforded by our legal aid schemes.

Unlike the United States, most group schemes in the United Kingdom restrict the legal services offered to areas relevant to the activities of the group and the emphasis is put on meeting the clients' non-routine and more serious legal needs, *e.g.* for representation in court. As such, 'the schemes are in many ways equivalent to legal expenses insurance.'"

D. LEGAL EXPENSES INSURANCE

Paterson, "Financing Legal Services", pp. 171–172

"Legal Expenses Insurance policies for individuals first appeared in mainland Europe in the 1920s but their significance in the legal services market dates from the 1960s. It is the dominant form of LEI in Europe (although in Sweden and in Italy trade unions are important providers of legal aid). It is estimated that at least 50% of all households in Germany have some kind of LEI and 80% in Sweden, though the figure is lower in other European countries. Predictably, the available evidence suggests that higher income individuals are disproportionately likely to take out LEI. In contrast to the evolution of group legal services in the USA, individual LEI in Europe has developed along commercial lines. Its aim, like other forms of insurance is to spread the risk of loss consequent on the happening of an uncertain event. As a result the typical coverage of individual policies in Europe is restricted in a variety of ways—not least in excluding many of the routine legal expenses which are the primary focus of group legal services. Thus in Germany the drafting of wills and other documents, negotiations, representation in divorce and succession actions are usually excluded. Similar exceptions exist in Sweden. In fact, in most European countries the coverage of individual policies is closely aligned to more general areas of insurance. There is, however, little evidence available as to types of claims experienced by LEI companies. One of the few studies in this area was conducted in Germany and found that 39% of claims related to traffic violations, another 30% to other car related matters, and 31% to other areas (principally, consumer, labour law, and landlord and tenant cases).

The United Kingdom

In the United Kingdom individual LEI policies, whether free standing or 'add-ons' to car or home contents insurance policies, have only been available since 1974. Most policies provide a free legal advice telephone line, a free choice of lawyer and, most important in this context, they usually offer European-wide coverage. For individuals or firms ineligible for legal aid LEI clearly has much to offer, but there are a number of drawbacks. The policies tend to be expensive for the cover offered and the cover offered is limited—most have a financial ceiling on cover and most exclude matrimonial disputes, defamation, tax matters, building disputes and defence of criminal prosecutions involving violence. However, the importance of LEI as a factor for UK based litigants deciding to litigate abroad is most severely limited by its very restricted penetration of the market. Most people in the UK simply do not have an LEI policy. (A 1991 survey by the Consumers' Association and the Law Society, *Legal Expenses Insurance in the UK* (London: Consumer's Association/The Law Society) suggested that only 7% of respondents had any form of LEI.) Moreover, its relatively low penetration makes it at risk of 'adverse selection' thus undermining the viability of the market. For these reasons even the Eligibility Review felt unable to recommend it as a replacement for legal aid in the UK—at least for the time being."

While legal expenses insurance undoubtedly has its attractions for business organisations (who are ineligible for legal aid), a number of problems remain. First, marketing private schemes through lawyers in private practice has proved ineffective both in the United Kingdom and the United States. As in the case of health insurance, it may be easier to reach individuals by selling the package to employers or trade unions. Secondly, should the scheme be open or closed? Thirdly, legal expenses insurance, unlike group legal services, is not suitable for routine legal expenses. Indeed it has been argued that to introduce comprehensive cover for legal expenses would be to contradict the basic philosophy behind insurance, *viz*. spreading the risk of an uncertain loss. Many legal needs are just the reverse—routine, foreseeable and within the control of the client. Comprehensive cover would encourage frequent use of the benefit and increase the possibility of adverse selection thus creating a situation where the great majority of subscribers would be high-risk individuals. Where all subscribers claim benefit, the premiums become uneconomic for there are no non-beneficiaries among whom to spread the loss. The beneficiaries would in effect have to bear the full cost of the legal services and the administrative costs of the middle man—the insurance company. Despite the hopes of some reformers in America, it would appear, therefore, that legal insurance cannot meet the routine unmet legal needs of the public and remain economically viable. It may provide a useful service for those ineligible for legal aid, but it is group legal services which in the long run are likely to make the greater impression on both the profession and the public.

(See on LEI, M.Bell, "Legal Expenses Insurance" 1997 J.L.S.S. 501.)

E. CLASS ACTIONS

Reducing cost by spreading the risk of loss could also be achieved by introducing a form of action which aggregates claims, namely, the class action. This procedural innovation would enable a group of individuals who have similar complaints against a common defender (for example, a multiple accident claim, persons affected by a common pollutant, or consumers with the same defective product), to join together in one action to pursue their claims. A working party of the Scottish Consumer Council recommended in 1982 that class actions should be introduced in Scotland. One major obstacle to such a reform is the problem of financing class actions if contingency fees are not permitted. Both these issues were investigated by the Scottish Law Commission and a report favouring the introduction of procedure for multi-party actions funded by legal aid was published in 1996, *Multi-Party Actions* (Edinburgh: HMSO). As yet their proposals have not been acted on.

F. SELF-HELP

Another way to reduce the expense of going to law is to do without legal representation. Following the Litigants in Person (Costs and Expenses) Act 1975 and the Acts of Sederunt (Expenses of Party Litigants) (S.I. 1976 No. 1606; S.I. 1983 No. 1438), party litigants can now recover expenses and outlays reasonably incurred (if awarded), though the remuneration rates are well below those of solicitors. The simplified "do-it-yourself" divorce procedure has proved popular. However, self-representation has made less progress in relation to the new small claims procedure. As we saw in Chapter 2, less than a third of individual or small business parties in a small claim chose to represent themselves. (See CRU/ Strathclyde and Dundee Universities, *Small Claims in the Sheriff Court* (Scottish Office, Edinburgh, 1991) at p. 23.) In the non-litigation spheres of conveyancing, wills and executries the "do-it-yourself" movement has again progressed further in England than in Scotland, although Scotland has a "small estates procedure" which makes it easier for laymen to handle small executries without the aid of a solicitor.

G. LAY REPRESENTATION AND ASSISTANCE

It was established by the Court of Appeal in *McKenzie v. McKenzie* [1971] p. 33 (and by implication by the House of Lords in the Scottish appeal of *Malloch v. Aberdeen Corporation (No. 2)* 1973 S.L.T. (Notes) 5) that a lay person or a solicitor can attend court proceedings and sit beside a party litigant in order to assist him or her by prompting, taking notes and quietly giving advice. Such "McKenzie friends" have enjoyed some currency in squatting cases and latterly cases relating to the poll tax. Attempts to extend the tactic to lay advocacy before the courts have not always been well received. (See *Mercy v. Persons Unknown*, *The Times*, June 5, 1974; *E.M.A. v. A.C.A.S. (No. 1)* [1979] 3 All E.R. 223 and *R. v. Leicester City Justices* [1991] 3 W.L.R. 368.) [It is worthy of note that sections 25–29 of the Law Reform (Miscellaneous Provisions) (Scotland) Act 1990 and sections 27 and 28 of the Courts and Legal Services Act 1990 contain provisions for non-lawyers to be given rights of audience by the courts.]

The status of the "McKenzie friend" came under attack in *R. v. Leicester City Justices* [1991] 2 Q.B. 260. In the event, the right of party litigants in civil cases to have the assistance of a "McKenzie friend" to give advice and to take notes was reaffirmed, on appeal, by the Court of Appeal. The Court of Appeal indicated that the title and status should be abandoned but seems to have relented. It is still clearly concerned at the continuing development of the device—particularly at the emergence of "professional" McKenzie friends: *R. v. Bow County Court, ex p. Pelling*, Times Law Report, August 18, 1999.

In Scotland "McKenzie friends" have been even less common, and the right to lay representation before the Scottish courts is procedurally and practically limited (see, *e.g.* Sheriff Courts (Scotland) Act 1971, s. 36(1) (as amended) and Small Claims Rules 1988, r. 30). However, lay representation before tribunals is commonplace.

H. IN-COURT ADVISERS

One final avenue for the layperson is the emergence in Scotland of in-court advisers. These have existed in England and Wales for more than 15 years but have taken a long time to arrive in Scotland due to a shortage of funds. The first pilot was introduced in Edinburgh Sheriff Court in April 1997, managed by Citizens Advice Scotland and by the Scottish Consumer Council. The remit of the in-court adviser was to offer information and advice (including legal advice) to unassisted litigants in small claims, summary cause, heritage and ordinary cause cases and to refer them, where appropriate, to relevant agencies for further help. The aim of the advice was to provide clients with the necessary tools to construct a legal argument in their case. Court representation was only rarely provided, and then only in exceptional circumstances. The pilot was a resounding success with 893 consultations being undertaken with 674 clients in the first nine months. The great bulk of cases related to small claims (37%) or heritage cases (51%). It is thought that the most likely way to continue the project would be through the implementation of Part V of the 1986 Legal Aid (Scotland) Act. [A research report on the operation of the Edinburgh pilot was published in 1999, *Supporting Court Users* (The Scottish Office Central Research Unit).]

CHAPTER 13

THE FUTURE OF LEGAL SERVICES

The future of poverty legal services in Scotland is as difficult to predict now as at any time in the last decade. The Government appears committed to "capping" legal aid expenditure one way or another and the proposed introduction of Community Legal Services still looks a bit like a policy "black hole". Undoubtedly, the most significant development in the last 25 years was the emergence and development of neighbourhood law centres. Yet, in the face of continuing financial stringency and the uncertainties associated with the Community Legal Services concept, it is far from clear what the future holds for the law centre movement.

I. LAW CENTRES

There is no universally accepted definition of such centres but the Scottish Association of Law Centres defines them as projects which:

(1) are democratically controlled;
(2) provide free or low cost legal services to tackle unmet legal need;
(3) work in a defined catchment area or field of specialisation;
(4) are independent;
(5) are non-profit making;
(6) have adequate quality control arrangements;
(7) adhere to all professional practice requirements.

In 1998 there were 10 such centres in Scotland, with several other bodies closely resembling them in most particulars. Law centres are defined slightly differently by the Law Centres' Federation (the association of English, Welsh and Northern Irish law centres), which numbers 52 centres in its membership. The proliferation of law centres in Scotland is a fairly new phenomenon, only Castlemilk Law Centre existing prior to 1990. The Scottish law centres employ around 60 people, including 30 solicitors, and also make use of volunteers, commonly law students and local residents. The focus of law centres is generally on meeting unmet legal need either within a community (*e.g.* Govan Law Centre, East End Community Law Centre) or to deal with particular types of legal problem across a wide area, such as the Scottish Child Law Centre or Enable.

Zander, *Legal Services for the Community*, pp. 78–80

"Law centres are different in a variety of ways from private firms of solicitors. On the most obvious level, they look different. Instead of the formality and staid dignity of the typical solicitor's office, law centres go out of their way to present an informal, casual atmosphere. They are normally at street level in main shopping centres. Instead of the usual discreet name-plate, they have a large sign in the window, 'LAW CENTRE'. Their shop fronts and interiors are plastered with posters and notices about legal rights, campaigns for racial equality, meetings of the local tenants' association, and information as to what to do about bad housing, wife-battering, or harassment from landlords. They have large, open-plan offices with desks in every corner . . . Volunteer workers mill about. In several centres lawyers take their share of filing, receptionist and telephone-operator work and even typing. Law centres commonly have evening and Saturday sessions. Many have a 24–hour telephone emergency service, used mainly in criminal and harassment cases. Their services are free and they are permitted to advertise.

But the centres are different not only in the way they will provide their services, but also in the services they actually provide. One difference is the nature of the work they do. Most private firms of solicitors depend for the bulk of their income on conveyancing and probate work. Law centres typically devote the largest proportion of their time to landlord–tenant disputes and other housing problems. In a survey of the first fifteen law centres, housing problems accounted for 40 per cent or more of the total work-load in ten of the centres. Employment, social security and consumer problems played a larger part in the work of the centres than for most firms of solicitors.

Another difference is the type of client. Solicitors in private practice tend naturally to work for individual clients who instruct and pay them. Law centres place great emphasis on the value of helping groups and the community more generally. By concentrating on problems that affect large numbers of people rather than just individuals the law centres believe they are getting the best value out of their own scarce and over stretched resources. Group and community work are increasingly the dominant mode of service provided by law centres. There are innumerable examples: forming and servicing tenants' associations; running campaigns on how to get rents or rates reduced; writing and distribution of leaflets, posters, pamphlets and even newspapers about aspects of the law; lecturing in schools, old people's homes, prisons, hostels; running surveys; performing in street theatre entertainment on legal rights.

Many centres have concentrated on particular local problems—bad landlords, breaches of the fire regulations, redevelopment plans of the local authority, relations between the police and the coloured community. Law centres commonly identify a problem and then go out of their way to try to cope with it. A centre may swamp the local county court with cases of illegal evictions as a means of sensitising the judge to the problem, and of alerting bad local landlords that evictions will be effectively resisted. In another area the centre may decide that too many elderly people are failing to get their heating allowance, or that immigrant workers are being exploited by a particular employer or that the harassment office of the local authority requires to be pressured to prosecute landlords who harass their tenants.

One centre became aware that the fuel allowance in supplementary benefit payments was inadequate to meet the costs of tenants on a particular estate. It conducted a number of successful appeals, but a report it commissioned under the Legal Advice scheme from a consulting engineer showed the problem to be common to the estate generally. As a result, it started negotiations with the Supplementary Benefits Commission to get the rate of benefit raised for everyone living on the estate.

Law centres have used test cases in the traditional sense of cases that seek to establish a point of law in the courts. But they interpret the concept more broadly to include any form of legal action that involves community gain. It may be conducted purely at the local level and achieve no more publicity than is available from the local press. Yet if the conduct of one landlord, or employer, or builder, or local authority, is altered as a result, the action may have had its desired effect. Sometimes it is not necessary to achieve any publicity. The fact that the action has been started may be enough to achieve a settlement not merely for one person but for a whole group similarly situated. A law centre provides expertise in the special legal problems of the poor. It can take a long view and set priorities for action. It has a means of keeping the community informed of developments and of receiving the views of the community through its management committee and its network of local contacts."

The work of the first three law centres in Scotland is described in the following article:

Smith, "North of the Border", p. 11

"Castlemilk Law Centre

Castlemilk is one of four major estates on Glasgow's periphery, housing about 25,000 people. The law centre occupies the ground floor of a small block of flats. Right opposite there is a run-down shopping centre, where Castlemilk Advice Centre, with which the law centre shared premises from its start in 1978 until 1984, is to be found. Two firms of solicitors also have offices in shop premises in the centre, with one—Ross Harper and Murphy—providing the smartest frontage in the complex. Most of the surrounding housing consists of low-rise blocks of flats, their uniform drabness relieved only by a small section of more colourful, recently rehabilitated stock . . .

The law centre's largest area of work—about 40 per cent of its cases and 50 per cent in terms of time expended—concerns housing. Until recently, almost all the surrounding housing was owned by the local authority. (About a tenth of the Castlemilk estate has now been transferred to Scottish Homes, the equivalent of the English Housing Corporation. In addition, four housing associations have acquired houses.) Most of the housing work has involved repair claims—mainly relating to damp and condensation—against the local authority. The law centre has pursued a number of related cases of claims both for compensation while repairs were being done and for home loss payments.

During its many years as Scotland's only law centre, Castlemilk regarded disseminating its experience as a central task and, from early on, became involved in training, conferences and publications. Recent training sessions have covered fuel debts, cohabitation, sex discrimination and court debt orders, while over 150 people attended a conference on how to deal with dampness. The law centre's range of leaflets covers housing, police, family, drugs and debt . . .

Legal Services Agency

The Legal Services Agency (LSA) is an interesting variant on the law centre concept. Reflecting the changing nature of the times, it describes itself as a 'community business', albeit within a charitable framework. It was developed by Glasgow's Technical Services Agency, a community controlled architectural aid centre which has been very involved with dampness and condensation.

Unlike Castlemilk Law Centre, the LSA aims to serve the whole of the city and beyond into the Strathclyde region. Initial funding has come from the Federation of Strathclyde Community Business and Glasgow district council, though the aim is to raise core funding from fees for training and legal aid work. Its management committee is made up of representatives of its funders and community organisations throughout Strathclyde, which are among its 100 or so members.

Senior solicitor Paul Brown says that the idea is to be 'more research and developmentally minded than Castlemilk, which is a local law centre with the strong populist element of being orientated towards its community. Its approach is not possible for an agency based in a city centre.' Much of the LSA's early work has been related to housing—this, says Paul Brown, has been in response to demand. Now the LSA is getting to the stage where it can begin to choose priorities.

In common with all three law centres, the LSA has a creditable list of leaflets and booklets. These include rights guides like *Right to a Decent House* (co-published with Shelter) and an action pack on backdating benefits.

It has also published material on aspects of personal injuries, such as an introduction to post-traumatic stress disorder and a study of quantification of damages in head injury cases, based on papers produced for its courses.

Scottish Child Law Centre

The Scottish Child Law Centre is the one avowedly national law centre of the three. In 1988/89, for instance, it undertook training in all but one of the nine regions into which mainland Scotland is divided—from Inverness in the north to Dumfries in the south. Its location in Glasgow means, however, that most of its work is concentrated in the Strathclyde region, in recognition of which it receives a limited amount of funding—£9,000 in 1990/91—from the regional council.

The centre is the equivalent of the Children's Legal Centre in London and, like it, grew out of the International Year of the Child in 1979. A group

> of professionals formed themselves the following year into the Scottish Child Law Group and began campaigning for more resources. A particular problem was the simple fact that no commercial publisher would produce a textbook equivalent to H.K. Bevan's *Child Law* for the small Scottish market. So, there was no definitive collation of Scottish law on the subject. Funding was eventually obtained from the Scottish Office—first for a collection of legal material and then for the law centre . . . .
>
> The centre has focused particularly on the need for information—to the extent that it has not yet undertaken any continuing casework. It has embarked on an ambitious project, in conjunction with the Highland regional council, to bring together relevant child law cases in a database which will then be regularly updated. The plan is to produce the information on disc, hence the project's name—ChilDBase. Two of the centre's management committee members have worked on this project which will, when complete, have about 850 entries.
>
> In addition, the centre has produced a number of publications, ranging from a single page of notes on leaving children unattended to a booklet on compensation for abused children under the Criminal Injuries Compensation Scheme (all three law centres collaborated on its content). The centre has organised a number of conferences, aimed largely at a professional audience, on subjects like child sexual abuse and access. It is also working on a pilot scheme, likely to start soon in the Lothian region, for lay spokespeople for children involved in children's hearings. Kathleen Marshall [the Director] says: 'We have an important function in being a voice for children and in letting professionals know what can be done to link children with the law.'"

Since its inception, the law centre movement in the United Kingdom has been dogged by three principal problems: independence, management and control; work style; and funding.

A. INDEPENDENCE, MANAGEMENT AND CONTROL

1. Independence

In order to offer free legal services and to advertise their existence law centres have needed a waiver from the Law Society of the ethical rule against the unfair attraction of business. In 1977 an agreed basis for waivers was reached in England:

> "(i) Apart from initial advice and assistance . . . salaried solicitors will not normally act in cases where the professional business of the client involves: (I) conveyancing; (II) commercial matters; (III) divorce proceedings; (IV) probate matters (save for personal applications in small estate(s)); (V) personal injury claims where the damages, as initially and approximately quantified exceed scale 2 of the county court costs band, or (VI) in criminal matters where the accused is aged 21 or over."

Like its English counterpart, the Law Society of Scotland saw its power to grant waivers as a way of controlling the work which law centres should be permitted to undertake. The Hughes Commission, recognising the difficulties that this had caused in relation to the setting up of Scotland's first law centre in Castlemilk, Glasgow, recommended (para. 7.15) that in future:

> "Law Centres should concentrate their work on whatever areas of law are not adequately catered for locally by solicitors. There should be no prohibition on their doing other work, however, as long as they do not neglect the areas of need."

The Castlemilk management committee following this proposal renegotiated the scope of their centre's "statement of intent".

Castlemilk Law Centre's Statement of Intent, 1981

> "The purpose of the Neighbourhood Law Centre is to provide advice, assistance and representation to clients from the Castlemilk area. Apart from initial advice and assistance and except in cases of emergency, the Centre's solicitors will not normally undertake (but will refer to private practitioners in accordance with the principles laid down in the guidelines on the use of referral lists) conveyancing, commercial matters, reparation, (other than non-personal injury cases not exceeding the maximum financial limit permissible under the Summary Cause procedure in the Sheriff Court and in respect of personal injury cases where the award would not exceed £400), matrimonial proceedings (and proceedings relating to the custody of children), testate and intestate succession (other than the preparation of wills and the administration of Small Estates as defined in the Confirmation of Small Estates (Scotland) Act 1979), and criminal matters (except in a court of summary jurisdiction for the purposes of offering pleas in mitigation, in cases where the accused is already a client of the centre, and the Director considers that legal aid is unlikely to be granted for the plea in mitigation and the accused cannot afford to instruct a solicitor in private practice). The Centre's activities will be directed primarily to Community Matters, Representation at Children's Panels and Appeals therefrom, Adoptions, Welfare Law, Housing, Consumer Protection, Immigration and Representation at Boards and Tribunals not covered by Legal Aid. Although the Centre will operate both the Legal Advice and Assistance and the Civil Legal Aid Scheme in appropriate cases, it will not take part in the Criminal Legal Aid Scheme. Only in cases where the Director alone considers there would be hardship will the Centre represent in any court a client who is outwith the financial limits of the Legal Aid Scheme subject to the foregoing."

In the early days the interpretation of this statement caused considerable friction between the Law Society and the Castlemilk management committee. So too did the Law Society's threat to put at risk the practising certificates of centre solicitors who stepped outside the Society's interpretation of the statement. (In England the Law Society has always accepted that the appropriate penalty for such "offenders" is withdrawal of the centre's waiver, rather than action against the individual solicitors involved.) However, today such differences have long since disappeared. Moreover, the *locus* for the Law Society to insist on adherence to statement of intent has largely been removed by the relaxation in the rules against advertising by solicitors and the reform of the practice rule against fee-sharing with unqualified persons. It follows that the main constraints on the type of work a law centre can now undertake are those imposed by resources or the policy of the management committee. This, of course is the position that the Hughes Commission had recommended. This raises the possibility that law centres in Scotland could begin to emulate their counterparts in Sweden, Quebec and the Netherlands by competing with the private profession for staple legal aid work such as criminal or family law. However, given the paucity of publicly funded salaried legal services in Scotland, serious questions must be raised as to the value to the wider society of such a development—particularly in areas which are adequately catered for by the private profession.

Law centres may also find that their independence is under threat owing to their limited sources of funding. In October 1997, Stockwell & Clapham Law Centre obtained leave to judicially review Lambeth Council's decision to withdraw all its funding. The law centre claimed that it was victimised by the council because it had acted for clients pursuing court actions against it.

2. Management and Control

Law Centres' Federation, "The role of management committees"

> "One of the fundamental principles of Law Centres is that they should be independently managed by representatives of their local community who are committed to the work of the Law Centre. It is only by having an active management committee of local people controlling the policy and organisation of the Law Centre that it can ensure that the service which is provided is appropriate and that the Law Centre is accessible to the people it is serving . . . Experience has shown that it is not easy to reflect in a management committee the various elements of a community. Clearly there will be limitations on how comprehensively it is able to represent the consumers of a service as a whole but a successful management committee will be composed of a majority of representatives of organisations which actually use and benefit from the centre and which reflect as far as possible the main areas of work of the law centre—tenants' associations, trades councils, women's groups and youth groups."

Law Centres' Working Group, "Evidence to the Benson Commission", pp. 46–47

> "The most common shorthand description of the role of the Management Committee is that they decide the policy of Law Centres. Policy means choosing the most effective application of the resources in the community. That means the determination of priorities and, consequently, the selection of the appropriate combination of work-methods, which is to say how much

effort will be put into each task. In order to perform this central function, the Management Committee must be wholly free from any interference which will prevent the execution of that task from being one that is performed exclusively by way of representation of the community. [There is] the possibility of conflict of interest between funding agency and Law Centre but such external influences could also come from other sources: Law Society, other professional representation, central or local government if one or other is not the actual funding agent . . . The truly effective Management Committee serves as a constant check that the Law Centre is remaining responsive to local need and not getting bogged down in rigid work-structures as professionals left to their own devices have an inclination to do. By imposing upon the lawyers a demand for constant explanation in terms that are comprehensible by a lay Management Committee, they fulfil the additional valuable function of preventing the lawyer from drifting back into a professional distance from the community and hiding in the shadows of professional or technical language and ideas. Again, only the truly local community representative is in a position to judge the extent to which the Law Centre is remaining properly accessible."

Cooper, "Structure and Management of Law Centres", p. 194

"In Brent, the management committee structure is carefully organised, in such a way that it is democratically representative of certain selected groups of the community. In Manchester, it is predominantly reflective of statutory and professional agencies. In Adamsdown, . . . management tends to be interested, local individuals from the community.

It is clearly important to establish the extent to which the management committee members really direct policy rather than follow the policy suggested by the staff. Random conversations with law centre staff in centres in the United Kingdom throw up very different attitudes to the problem. The theory of 'community control' is supported by all. But many individuals acknowledge that this really means selective control by those groups whose . . . perspective on the role of the centre is in line with their own."

As Cooper's extract suggests the concept of community control remains highly problematic. This is due to a number of factors. There may, for example, be no single community but a multiplicity of minority groupings whose interests clash, in the geographic area which is a centre's catchment area. Secondly, even if a definable community exists, how can representative members of it be identified? Can a committee composed largely of statutory representatives, *i.e.* representatives of the region, the district, the local law society, the national law society, the funding agency, be fairly described as community control? How can the demand of law centres for independence be reconciled with the argument that they ought to be accountable for their use of public funds? Do management committees actually control the work of the centre's staff?

These problems are not confined to the United Kingdom, as the following extract about the work of the Redfern Legal Centre in Sydney reveals.

Smith, "Redfern Legal Centre", p. 9

"The district of Redfern has been subject to the problems usual in an inner area and the centre has been active in a variety of campaigns. It has, for

> instance, undertaken rent surveys and helped to establish a domestic violence project.
>
> The centre works with some discrimination in relation to the 'community' which it serves: 'We recognise that there are many different groups of people within the geographical area often referred to as "our community". The interests of these groups can conflict. A recent example is the conflict between residents (and business people) who support the gentrification of the area, and the aboriginal community over proposals to create alcohol-free zones within the municipality. These happened to coincide with locations frequented by aboriginal people. The centre consulted the aboriginal community on this issue and prepared a submission.' This argued that the proposals would not stop public drunkenness but would exacerbate race relations.
>
> Its management structure allows the centre to take an independent view of a local situation, as in this case. It is not under even notional community control. Issues are effectively decided by a management committee with an unashamedly volunteer and staff bias. Of its 15 members, five are staff, two are volunteer lawyers and four are volunteer students. Only one of the four other members must be from a local community organisation.
>
> This management structure would render Redfern ineligible for membership of our Law Centres Federation. The lack of community control and domination of workers has attracted internal criticism."

The Benson Commission's solution to these problems was to argue that a central agency should be set up independent of central and local government which would be responsible both for financing and managing law centres, though local committees would remain to act in an advisory capacity and to sensitise the law centres to local circumstances (paras 8.25–8.27). The Law Centres' Federation was aghast at this proposal which rejected community control out of hand. The Federation was far more sympathetic to the Hughes Commission proposal that law centres should be centrally funded (by a Legal Services Commission) but locally managed (para. 7.15):

> "Law Centres should be managed by local committees representing the community on the widest possible non-partisan basis. Their independence of special interests should be written into their constitution, which will need to be approved and monitored by the Legal Services Commission from which their funds should come."

Law centres have moved some way towards this recently, since they are now generally formed as companies limited by guarantee. The management committee then takes on the role as the board of directors, hiring a specially formed firm of solicitors to undertake work for them exclusively. The principal solicitor will normally be the sole or senior partner of that firm. Thus, there is a clear division between the control of policy and the legal services provided.

B. WORK STYLE

Typically, law centres concentrate their efforts on casework, groupwork, community education and, to a lesser extent, law reform and test cases. The following extract illustrates the type of community education work undertaken by law centres.

East End Community Law Centre Newsletter No. 2, p. 3

> "Our solicitor provides seminars in situ to the older children at Kennyhill School giving them advice on housing law, benefits, their rights in relation to the Police and an overview of constitutional and administrative law so that they can attain a better understanding of their society. The environment of Kennyhill School is a very close knit one and our solicitor hopes to extend her service later this year to the parents of the children thereby strengthening the community ethos of Kennyhill. She recently commented that:
>
> > "Students in the post-16 group have participated in legal education classes over a 6 week period. Topics included: the police and your rights, housing and your rights, family law and social security. These issues are of direct relevance to Kennyhill students and their families. Many of the students advised me that they hoped to obtain their own tenancy when they left school. However they had little knowledge of the problems they might encounter. For example, they were unclear as to how they could get help with their rent or what type of help was available. I also explained what might happen if they fell behind with their rent and how they should deal with it . . . With regards to the police the students were more knowledgeable. However explaining that it is important to cooperate with the police was useful information and could help prevent future problems . . .
> >
> > In addition to the classes the Law Centre has provided work experience for several Kennyhill pupils over the last year. Senior teaching staff have advised that this opportunity has helped develop the confidence of students. It is hoped that the work can continue next year expanding to provide access to the Law Centre's services to Kennyhill parents . . ."

Although the balance of work varies between centres and over time, the overall trend is for centres to move away from individual casework towards groupwork and community education.

Campbell, *Law Centres and Legal Services*, pp. 45–46

> "6.2 The initial law centres . . . were of the open door variety. Briefly this meant that the centres sought to be as accessible as possible to their 'public client body', and they catered, without discrimination, to supplicant clients provided they were of moderate means. The primary tasks of the law centre staff were to provide advice and assistance on legal issues. In time deficiencies and weaknesses in such an orientation were noticed. Typically the law centres became submerged with work and could not cope with their backlog of cases. Some law centres in London indeed simply shut their doors (regularly or sporadically) for the days needed to allow staff to catch up on outstanding matters. Apart from pressure of business, however, the repetitive nature of much of the work came to be regarded as a striking feature. An analogy used was that law centre staff were behaving like doctors in

setting and splinting a series of broken legs incurred when clients had fallen over an uncovered manhole . . . when a more constructive contribution to the community at large might have been to ensure the manhole was covered and safe. Surely it was wasteful to use professional skills treating problems on an entirely repetitive basis if the cause of the problem was not tackled? Thus if it became known that the unlawful practices of large landlords were the source of the stream of clients seeking advice about tenancy agreements, might it not be better to seek to persuade the landlord to alter or modify his practices? On this basis the undiscriminating policy of maintaining an open door was questioned, and the desirability of law centres selecting cases that deserved particular attention was appreciated."

Stephens, "Law Centres and Citizenship: The Way Forward", pp. 108–109, 116

"Reactivity and proactivity may be viewed as opposite ends of a continuum, and individual law centres may be identified as exhibiting an operational philosophy tending towards one pole or the other. A reactive tendency or orientation within a law centre is based largely on a system of self-referral by clients of referrals from outside agencies. Once the client has decided to seek advice at the law centre the relationship with the lawyer is likely to be passive, the lawyer typically taking important decisions about the legal viability, processing, and eventual disposition of the case. Informed consent is low and many problems are handled or referred routinely, thus not allowing clients to develop their own legal and civil competencies. The emphasis in such centres is on law and legal strategies, with few resources effectively devoted towards group work and educational projects in the community . . .

A more proactive approach seeks ways to transcend the individualizing process of the traditional lawyer–client relationship. It demands that law centres reach out into their respective communities in order to encourage collective and concerted action by neighbourhood groups. This requires that law centres act as a resource for such groups and that lawyers and non-lawyers within the centres co-operate to promote legal and non-legal solutions to commonly experienced problems. Expertise is shared with local people under a proactive orientation, and clients are encouraged to take an active role in the disposition of their case. The attempt is made to develop competence and to strengthen the capacity of clients to realize their rights through group formation. Despite difficulties in overcoming some of the problems caused by the adoption of an overly reactive approach, in the majority of British law centres the operational trend is towards proactivity.

Processing individual grievances in reactive law centres is unlikely to make any impact on the wider problems of poor housing standards, meagre welfare entitlements or rising unemployment. While it is true that proactive law centre policies will not provide 'ultimate' solutions, nonetheless more significant inroads can be made in respect of local solutions to such problems with the adoption of a proactive approach. The adoption of particular examples of groupwork and community campaigns in pursuit of solutions to commonly experienced local problems is the expression of community needs and demands; it is not the result of decisions unilaterally taken by law centre staff and imposed on the community."

Groupwork involves a number of strategies ranging from providing legal advice to local groups and associations (for example, tenants' associations, claimants' unions, environmental groups, women's groups, pensioners and single-parent groups) to under taking broadly defined test cases. Nevertheless, successful group work not infrequently leads to an increased demand for law centres to take on individual cases. The experience of Castlemilk law centre is but one illustration of this phenomenon.

Castlemilk Law Centre

"In Castlemilk during the past few years the emphasis has been towards taking legal services to the community in forms of groups. The undernoted are some examples of the provision of that type of service:—

— The Law Centre acting as Legal Advisors to the Glasgow Tenants' Associations in their negotiations with Glasgow District Council on the drafting of the new Lease to be sent to all tenants under the Tenants' Rights, etc. (Scotland) Act 1980;
— arising from that the preparation of materials to explain the contents of the substantially amended Lease;
— preparation of materials on particular issues, *e.g.* eviction, dampness, flooding, employment and criminal injury to increase awareness of legal rights, such materials being distributed through community groups within Castlemilk;
— progressing test cases in Employment, Housing and Welfare Law;
— involvement with and speaking to community groups and schools to increase awareness of legal rights;
— assisting specific campaign groups, *e.g.* dampness action groups on the Law in relation to that subject.

This type of involvement which is very important and essential in the operations of a Law Centre, nevertheless creates a demand for legal representation on an individual basis. Where a solicitor from a Law Centre is involved in such community legal activities there does arise a demand by individuals for assistance with particular problems as a consequence of that involvement. Individuals who might otherwise have been reluctant to mention their own problems having seen a solicitor with whom they can identify and with whom they are familiar will then seek assistance. The assistance may be on any number of issues and in many instances will be unrelated to the matter which was the subject of the community legal process. This is in addition to those who will approach the Law Centre either through the knowledge of its existence or by recommendation from other clients who have been satisfied with the service received. The essential point being made is that any legal representation provision must embrace facilities for representing individuals in addition to acting for community groups or merely taking cases arising from the groups' activities."

Groupwork and educational work highlight the importance of having informed members of the community on the management committees of law centres in order to decide the priorities in the allocation of the centres' resources. Critics who object to the selectivity involved in such decisions ignore the fact that every reactive open-door law centre to date has sooner or later been forced into selectivity in relation to its clients because demand comes to outstrip resources. In the words of S. Wexler, "Practicing Law for Poor People" (1969–70) Yale L.R. 1049, 1055:

> "A seemingly neutral policy of 'first-come, first served' cuts against the least informed, the least mobile and the most oppressed. Some sieve is inevitably applied to the work a poverty lawyer does; that sieve can be one he chooses consciously in order to serve a particular end, or it can be one he chooses without thinking, and with no aim at all."

The Benson Commission expressed disquiet at some of the group and community work (particularly local campaigns) undertaken by law centres, considering such activities to be too political or partisan in nature. Law centres, it thought, should confine themselves to providing legal advice to individuals and groups. Again, the Hughes Commission seemed more aware of the value of group and educational work. It argued that (para. 7.15) "law centres should play an active educational role in the community, ensuring that groups and individuals know the legal resources available to them." Hughes recognised the danger of law centres getting involved in community politics but believed that groups should continue to receive advice and representation from law centres.

Specialism is also becoming more important. The growth of centres such as Enable and the Scottish Child Law Centre which cater for a particular client group or legal problem are indicative of this trend. Other centres too are adopting a more specific approach to their work. The Legal Services Agency has a mental health unit, Drumchapel Law and Money Advice Centre has projects on money advice and on children's rights and the East End Community Law Centre operates a drop-in service at a prostitute support group.

C. FUNDING

Law centres in the United Kingdom have been funded from three main sources: central government (Community Development Projects, the Urban Aid Programme, the Lord Chancellor's Fund—now replaced by the Legal Aid Board—and Legal Aid), local government and charitable foundations. Today there is a growing tendency for centres to receive funding from a mix of these sources. Even the centres which are directly funded by the Legal Aid Board are gradually being moved over to joint funding with local authorities (Legal Aid Board Annual Reports 1991–92, para. 6.28). This seems a wiser policy than the proposal from the Benson and Hughes Commissions—also endorsed by the Society of Conservative Lawyers (Prior, *Law Centres* (1984), p. 6)—that there should be a central funding agency with a long-term commitment to law centres. The vulnerability of such agencies has been graphically demonstrated by the repeated attacks on the budget of the U.S. Legal Services Commission by the Reagan and

Bush administrations and by the Republican-dominated Congress in the Clinton administration.

However, fiscal constraints on local authority spending have put law centres under increasing financial pressure. One solution would be to expand the amount of legal aid work that such centres can undertake, unhampered by statements of intent. Since the statement of intent was predicated on two ethical rules which have largely disappeared (the ban on touting and fee-sharing with unqualified persons), this proposal seems superficially attractive. The fact remains, however, that it is hardly a cost-effective use of public funds to finance law centres to undertake routine undefended divorces when there are many private firms which are perfectly capable of doing the work. Another solution—again favoured by the Royal Commissions—would be to permit law centres to charge clients for their services. This too would involve the removal of the restrictions on the work which law centres can undertake. It would also deprive law centres of much of their uniqueness and would be deeply unpopular with the law centre movement.

The final option is new sources of money such as the national lottery. Scots law centres have proved remarkably adept in developing new projects which appeal to external funders, *e.g.* Drumchapel Law and Money Advice Centre's success in obtaining a grant of nearly £132,000 from BBC Children in Need to set up a Children's Rights Project. However, as a long-term strategy this may be difficult to sustain given the recent growth of the law centre movement in Scotland. It may be that a redistribution of civil advice and assistance funds in the guise of contracts with the Scottish Legal Aid Board or Community Legal Services may prove a better long-term bet. Much will depend on the approach of the Scots Parliament to poverty legal services.

II. THE WAY FORWARD: PUBLIC OR PRIVATE?

A. WHAT IS NEEDED?

As the Lord Chancellor's Advisory Committee noted in their 34th Annual Report (1983–84) (at p. 341), law centres aim to fill gaps in legal service provision by the private profession. Fifteen years on these gaps remain unfilled. There is still a glaring shortage of private practitioners who are skilled in the fields of child law, consumer law, welfare law, employment law and housing law. These shortages cannot be made up by the heroic efforts of legal advice centre volunteer staff. Moreover, in many of these areas, advice without the possibility of representation is a worthless commodity. (On the advantages of being represented before tribunals, see Chapter 6.) In the absence of any Tribunal Assistance Units in Scotland the burden of representation falls on welfare rights workers, voluntary advice workers and on law centre staff.

The deficiencies of the private profession in welfare and consumer law areas have long led other jurisdictions with developed legal aid programmes to try to adjust the balance between their public and private programmes. In England and Wales the Legal Aid Board Annual Report for 1990/91 indicated that less than a third of 1 per cent of net expenditure on legal aid went to law centres. Research also suggests that advice agencies and law centres account for less than 2 per cent of advice and assistance work. However, in the Netherlands 15 per cent of legal aid expenditure goes to salaried lawyers in Buros, while in New South Wales and Quebec the comparable figures are 42 per cent and 71 per cent respectively. These figures clearly point to the fact that these countries have achieved significantly more success in introducing a mixed model of legal services provision than presently pertains in the United Kingdom.

B. COST EFFECTIVENESS

In the face of continued economic restraint and financial stringencies it is more imperative than ever that we should look at the relative cost effectiveness of various forms of publicly funded legal service. This is another reason why the balance between the public and private programmes of legal aid needs to be re-examined in the United Kingdom. From such a study a national policy could then emerge. Despite having a governing body in the shape of the Scottish Association of Law Centres, each law centre remains, very much, a separate entity. This strong decentralisation of the law centre movement entails that there is a lack of uniform standards as to staffing, work methods, management recruitment and the quality of legal services provided. This makes it exceedingly difficult to say if the public funding of law centres is being as well directed as it could be, or how such funds should be deployed in the future. The same problem exists even more acutely in relation to legal aid, which accounts for 98 per cent of the public funds expended on legal services in the United Kingdom. Do we get value for money from legal aid? The bulk of legal aid work is done by a relatively small number of firms in Scotland and England—is this more cost effective than all firms doing a little legal aid work? Would it be a more effective and economical strategy to develop more salaried legal services (such as law centres), rather than to continue to pay the private profession on a case-by-case basis under the present legal aid schemes? Questions such as these have hardly begun to be considered in the United Kingdom, although one pilot study has been completed in England which compared the delivery of legal services in private and public practice.

Sherr and Domberger, "Measuring Legal Work", pp. 80–82

> "We compared the work of one law centre lawyer and one private solicitor practitioner in their handling, on behalf of complainants, of some 30 unfair dismissal cases divided equally between them. The particular subject area of unfair dismissals was chosen because it is one of the few in which both law centres and private practitioners operate, and the lawyers' work involves a smaller degree of procedural choice so that differences in the handling of cases would be more likely to result from differences between the two modes of operation, or between the lawyers themselves, than extraneous reasons related to the particulars of individual cases or individual approaches . . .
>
> The lawyers' performance was assessed by measuring both inputs and outputs. On the input side measurement was in terms of hours spent by each lawyer over a case; . . .
>
> On the output side two measures were used, one quantitative and one qualitative. Figures on success/failure and on gross compensation received

are an obvious measure of output, but have to be treated with caution. This is because the award of compensation by the tribunal depends on a number of specific client characteristics, *i.e.* age, wage and length of employment, all of which must be taken into account when making comparisons . . . We . . . set out to identify any systematic differences in size of awards obtained by the private practitioner and the law centre, whilst being sure that these other factors did not obscure those differences by using a system of statistical analysis able to normalise for these different variables.

Some compensation figures alone leave out certain important qualitative aspects of legal performance. In order to capture these . . . we undertook a questionnaire survey of the clients in the sample in order to identify any marked differences in the degrees of clients' satisfaction with their cases. The clients were asked to rank their level of satisfaction in relation to questions such as the outcome of the case, the way in which it was handled, and the lawyer's explanation of the legal position and of the necessary legal steps to be taken.

Analysis and Summary of Results

In summary . . . the results of the study showed that on average the law centre devoted . . . less than a third of the time to its cases than was spent by the private practitioner. We would therefore have expected the latter to have better over-all results in terms of compensation obtained for the client. Although the size of award obtained by the private practitioner was slightly higher, this difference did not reach statistical significance and could have been due to chance.

The results are consistent with the law centre having to exercise tighter control over the legal resources allocated to each case than the private practitioner. What is surprising is that differences in input levels are not reflected in significantly greater financial benefits for the private practitioner's clients. It would appear that the law centre, more independent from its individual clients, is in a better position to restrict its own input to a reasonable level for expected outcome. The private practitioner, however, for reasons of image, personal satisfaction, or client pressure spends more time in an illusory attempt to obtain larger gross benefits for his clients. Our calculations do not take into account the private practitioner's cost to his client for the extra work put in, and the slightly larger compensation received by them may be easily dissipated in their extra outlay for solicitors' fees. On the other hand the perceived slightly larger gross benefits may well give the clients a satisfaction that will not be removed by the lawyer's bill.

As regards clients' satisfaction we did not find any significant differences between the two legal modes, although over-all the private practitioner's clients were a little more satisfied and he tended to provide them with more information concerning the legal position and the steps involved in the case than did the law centre. This tendency may well be a direct result of the pressure of caseload in a law centre, and the far less time spent on a case. It is an interesting counter-intuitive result since it is contrary to the image of the law centre, bringing law to the people by demystifying it for them with full explanations . . .

Conclusions

> It would be tempting to draw policy implications from these findings, that public funds should be allocated to what seems to be the more economically 'efficient' mode of provision of legal service, the law centre, rather than through legal aid to the private practitioner.
>
> Such temptation must be resisted, since the small size of the sample of cases and the fact that we only investigated one private practitioner and one law centre renders our findings suggestive at most."

As the authors rightly point out, it would be dangerous to draw firm conclusions from such a limited pilot study. At first blush it might appear that salaried programmes must inevitably prove more cost effective than the private sector, since they almost invariably pay lower salaries, take on a higher caseload, rely more on volunteers and para-legals and frequently undertake groupwork. Those with a high community education profile are arguably even more cost-effective because of their preventative approach. However, there are countervailing arguments. The start-up costs of salaried lawyers are usually higher since they cannot be defrayed from private earnings. Moreover, although salaried lawyers specialise in the poverty law areas they also tend to be younger and less experienced than judicare lawyers. The pressure of heavy caseloads tends to lead to staff "burnout" and salaried lawyers tend to move on after a few years. Moreover, most judicare programmes pay private practitioners considerably below the going rate for private work and increasingly judicare work is being delegated to less qualified and experienced staff. This may perhaps account for the fact that the surveys in North America and Australia comparing the relative cost-effectiveness of the private and salaried approaches have been somewhat inconclusive. [See National Legal Aid Advisory Committee, *Funding, Providing and Supplying Legal Aid Services* (Commonwealth of Australia, 1989) and NLAAC, *Legal Aid for the Australian Community* (Commonwealth of Australia, 1990) and A Currie, *Legal Aid Delivery Models in Canada* (1999) (http://faculty.law.ubc.ca/ilacl). The most comprehensive survey, The Legal Services Corporation's *Delivery Systems Study* (1980), found that there was little to choose between the judicare (legal aid) and staff attorney (law centres) models in terms of cost, quality and client satisfaction but that the staff-attorney programmes had a greater impact on the "poverty community". Most of the studies have concluded that it would be desirable to experiment with mixed models. This would shift the debate away from the somewhat sterile and stereotyped debate as to which model is better, to a more constructive inquiry as to the conditions under which each model can be deployed to its best advantage or as to the appropriate division of labour between the two models in any given environment. Such an approach would dovetail with the increasing emphasis on quality assurance and specialist providers of legal services for the poverty community by policymakers. (See the discussion of franchising in the previous chapter.)

There is clearly a need for research into these questions and for a central body to be responsible for long-term policy and for practical experiments in the provision of legal services, as the Hughes Commission recognised.

The Hughes Commission, pp. 353–354

"20.10 We [recommend] that a Legal Services Commission . . . should be responsible for:

— the provision of public information as to legal rights and services in Scotland (R6.7);
— developing lay advice and representation at tribunals and training for lay representatives (R7.3);
— studying and experimenting with the best use of Law Centres in Scotland (R7.4);
— grants to advice centres and Law Centres, the conduct of research, experimenting with ways to provide services, and the setting of standards (R7.7);
— providing financial assistance to firms of solicitors to establish themselves in under-provided areas (R7.10);
— administering legal aid (R8.27);
— developing money management counselling in Scotland (R12.1);
— publishing advice on how to leave one's affairs in good order (R13.8);

In exercising all of the foregoing responsibilities, we consider that the fundamental principle guiding the Legal Services Commission should be to secure in the provision of legal services the best possible value for money consistent with justice."

The Hughes Commission's call for a Legal Services Commission was reiterated by the Legal Action Group in a major policy report, *A Strategy for Justice* (LAG, 1992). This report was the product of a wide-ranging research study into legal aid programmes in Canada, Australia, the Netherlands and the United Kingdom. Its final chapter contains a detailed plan for the development of a genuinely planned and balanced model of legal services provision.

LAG, *A Strategy for Justice*, pp. 134–144

"LAG believes that services should be provided by the most effective and coherent means; but this must, of course, take existing provision into account. We envisage a mixed model of services, whereby private practitioners and other types of providers combine to ensure an overall pattern of comprehensive cover. This raises the controversial issue of salaried services.

The large-scale replacement of private practitioners by a salaried national legal service has been recently proposed by the Law Centres Federation. It argues that there should be 'a salaried service comprising independent generalist front-line advice and legal casework agencies, strategic services and specialist centres. All elements would be co-ordinated regionally and nationally.' The implications of the LCF proposal are unclear. Its salaried service could be seen as ultimately taking over the role of private practitioners, even in such traditional areas of legally aided practice as matrimonial law and crime; alternatively, it could remain as an additional and supplementary provision.

LAG considers that much more use could be made of salaried services—directly employed or indirectly resourced by the funding authority—which offer various advantages, including flexibility and cost effectiveness. However, we recognise certain pragmatic limitations to major change. First, current providers have their areas of expertise. Law centres and advice agencies have concentrated on social welfare law, while private practitioners have a wealth of experience in traditional legally aided work, particularly in the fields of crime, matrimonial and personal injury. Second, the fact that salaried services, by their very nature, offer an easy target for a government that wishes to restrict costs cannot be ignored. Their widespread introduction allows for the possibility of capping the legal services budget, moving away from the advantages, despite the present unsatisfactory eligibility levels, of the current demand-led system of legal aid expenditure. Advice agencies and law centres already face funding problems . . . .

LAG's proposals are, therefore, expressly tempered by a concern to be realistic. While wishing to maximise services, we do not intend to put forward plans which provide government with the opportunity for cuts in provision. This makes us cautious about supporting any major extension of salaried services. However some restructuring is necessary, with greater priority given to the funding of advice agencies and the 'community legal centres' . . .

Advice services

A national policy on advice agencies is long overdue . . . [Earlier we] . . . argued for changes in central government funding of the national organisations representing the advice sector. Although the initiative reflected in the diversity of existing advice agencies has been a positive by-product of local funding, another, less welcome, consequence has been patchy provision. There needs to be some way of combining national standards of provision with locally determined forms.

Accordingly, there should be a statutory responsibility on local authorities to provide an adequate level of independent advice for those living and working within their areas; how such advice is best provided should be determined locally. The legal services commission, taking over an expanded role from the Legal Aid Board, should advise on a minimum acceptable level of provision, based on objective indices of need (such as local housing conditions and numbers of people on benefit), to prevent national standards being set so low that some authorities act opportunistically to cut their own existing provision. Subsidy from central government should be forthcoming for this minimum level.

More secure funding and greater national involvement in local provision raises the question of identifying and maintaining performance criteria. Adherence to such criteria, which should be linked to the needs of a particular area, not just based on a crude count of enquiries, would be a condition of funding.

Community Legal Services

A planned national network of community legal centres should be phased in gradually. This would avoid too great an initial expenditure, while also ensuring that centres are established only where adequate preparatory work has been done . . .

Each community legal centre should employ at least three lawyers, two non-lawyer practitioners and two support staff. Volunteer legal advisers have played a vital role in assisting law centres, particularly in evening advice sessions. This tradition, which has not only provided a source of free labour but has also involved private practitioners in the voluntary sector, should continue, as should training and use of volunteer lay advisers. The exact range of services provided by each community legal centre, (which will depend, in part, on what is already available in the area) will have to be negotiated through the kind of local planning process that Belfast Law Centre has already experimented with in Northern Ireland. The overall objective is, however, quite clear: advice agencies and the community legal centre in an area should, between them, provide a comprehensive range of services within social welfare law.

The community legal centres should receive core funding to provide specified minimum levels of service, not only in relation to advice, assistance and representation, but also in the field of legal education and appropriate law reform activity. The presence of a central funding authority in the planning of this process would introduce a new dimension to the existing position, in which the majority of law centres are accountable only at a local level.

Core funding should be sufficient for the community legal centres to follow the voluntary advice sector tradition of acting without charge for all clients, thus providing the free element in essential legal services. Furthermore, the centres should be the vehicle by which representation is extended before tribunals. With a mix of lay and legally qualified practitioners, they will have the ability to provide the appropriate levels of representation in any case. Such a system would clearly be more economic than a wholesale extension of legal aid. However, at least one firm of private practitioners should also be encouraged, by franchise or other means, to provide a service in this area. As well as giving clients an element of choice, this would provide some measure of competition and comparison; it would also provide a safeguard against community legal centre staff becoming overworked, to the detriment of clients.

Community legal centre lawyers should be able to claim legal aid on a case-by-case basis for cases falling within their general areas of competence but outside the tribunal system, though they should be under a general injunction not to take such cases simply to raise finance.

Eventually, a network of community legal centres should cover the whole country. As a first step, a sufficient number should be established both to test and refine the idea. A reasonable target might be for the Legal Aid Board to fund 90 community legal centres, phased in over three years. A centre of the minimum size envisaged above would cost about £330,000 per year on current rates. So, in crude terms, establishing 30 in each of the next three years would require expenditure of £10 million in the first year, £20 million in the second and £30 million in the third. To start with, centres

> should be situated in poorer areas not currently covered by private practitioners doing social welfare law work. In some cases, rather than start a centre from scratch, an existing law centre may wish to transfer to the new regime. The law centre movement should not, however, be expected to transfer wholesale . . .
>
> Funding should also be made available for specialist law centres to provide back-up services such as information for advisers, nationally coordinated educational campaigns, law reform activity, specialist advice, and a resource for helping with, or taking over, the more complex and time-consuming cases. Such centres stimulate the quality of the work of all practitioners in their fields, as has been shown in Ontario and Australia, . . .
>
> Private practitioners should continue as the main providers of services in the field of matrimonial and family work, crime and personal injury, as well as having some involvement in other areas of law . . .
>
> . . . Services in some areas of the country may be improved if legal aid were channelled through a smaller number of higher quality providers: one example is criminal work in certain inner city areas. However, some mechanism must remain whereby new practices can break into the market.
>
> In looking for greater control over where and how legal services are provided, the [Legal Aid] Board's starting point should be to ask whether the existing pattern of services provides acceptable access to legal services. In support of its own definition of what is acceptable, it should draw up criteria setting minimum levels of provision . . .
>
> . . . If sufficient legal aid outlets do not exist, it must create them. It could do this through a range of measures, including grant aid towards the establishment costs of private practices, enhanced rates of legal aid remuneration or the setting up of a branch office with salaried lawyers or some form of mobile community legal centre."

Many of these ideas have yet to be implemented. The Labour Party's election manifesto in 1997 contained a commitment to introducing a community legal service and this has been followed by *Modernising Justice* (LCD, 1998), *The Community legal service* (LCD Consultation Paper, 1999) and the Access to Justice Act 1999. Although in some respects resembling the Cheshire cat, "the more she looked at it, the more it wasn't there", the Government thinking behind the concept is gradually being worked out. The English Legal Aid Board is to be replaced by a Legal Services Commission charged with developing (in conjunction with local funders) a comprehensive network of legal services providers of consistently good quality, reporting annually to the Lord Chancellor on the effectiveness of the overall poverty legal services delivery and on the management of the community legal service fund which will replace legal aid in civil and family cases. The Commission will be able to enter contracts with service providers, pioneer new ways of delivering information and services (*e.g.* the Internet, digital television, phone advice lines) and use a wide variety of providers including mediators and those from the not-for-profit sector. It is clear that law centres will have a key role to play in the community legal service. The Scots version of community legal services was rather sketchily spelled out in *Access to Justice—Beyond the Year 2000* (Consultation Paper, Scottish Office,

1998). Its suggestions included the employment of solicitors in advice agencies by the Scottish Legal Aid Board; legal aid funding for the provision of advice and assistance by non-legally qualified staff; a law centre run by the Scottish Legal Aid Board; and contracts with solicitors to provide social welfare law in geographic areas of need. As yet the Scottish Executive has yet to show its hand on the results of this consultative exercise.

CHAPTER 14

LEGISLATION

I. LEGISLATORS AND INTERPRETERS

Many activities and relationships are regulated by legislation, and the volume of legislation enacted is considerable. Each year, the Council of Ministers of the European Communities may adopt up to 5,000 regulations, directives and decisions: the figure for 1997 was 1,827 (H.C. Deb., col. 557). This legislation is drafted by lawyers in the Commission of the Communities. (On the Community legislative process, see T. St J. N. Bates, "The Drafting of Community Legislation" [1983] Stat.L.R. 24; D. Gordon-Smith, "The Drafting Process in the European Community" [1989] Stat.L.R. 56.) In addition to other legislation, the United Kingdom Parliament enacts public general statutes. Most of this type of legislation is introduced by the Government and the remainder, private members' Bills, is introduced by members of either House who are not in the Government. It was estimated that, in 1974, some 3,480 such statutes were still in force, in whole or in part (349 H.C. Deb., col. 940) and those in force in 1965 ran to some 33,000 pages (*The Preparation of Legislation*, Cmnd. 6053 (1975), para. 7.2).

The volume of primary legislation is steadily increasing. The public general acts passed in 1901 totalled 247 pages; those passed in 1991 covered 2,222 pages. These statistics only suggest general trends and have to be qualified by such factors as changes in page size; neither, of course, is the length of statute necessarily indicative of its social or legal significance. (See generally *Making the Law* (Hansard Society: 1993) App. 7.) Nevertheless, the increasing volume of legislation has remained a parliamentary concern: see, *e.g.* 514 H.L. Deb., col. 1157 (Jan 24, 1990); 515 H.L. Deb., col. 382 (Jan 31, 1990).

Public general Bills introduced by the Government are drafted, on the instructions of the relevant government department, usually by legally qualified parliamentary drafters employed by the Government in the Lord Advocate's Department, the Office of Parliamentary Counsel and in Northern Ireland, although there has been some attempt to contract out drafting (see T. St J. N. Bates, "Privatised Drafting and the Finance Bill" 1996 S.L.T. (News) 153). Private members' Bills are normally drafted outside Government, although the Government may extend the assistance of parliamentary drafters to their sponsors.

Delegated legislation is made, usually by government Ministers, under statutory authority; it is almost always drafted by lawyers in the appropriate government department (79 H.C. Deb., col. 313 (W.A.) (May 20, 1985); R. Brodie, "Drafting Subordinate Legislation" (1993) 38 J.L.S.S. 132); for the role of the departmental lawyer in respect of both primary and delegated legislation see A. Graham, "Well in on the Act—A Government Lawyer's View of Legislation" [1988] Stat.L.R. 4. Like primary legislation, and subject to the same qualifications, there has been a significant growth in the volume of delegated legislation. The number of general delegated instruments made in 1901 was 156; the number made in 1991 was 2,945 (*Making the Law* (Hansard Society, 1993), App. 7). A certain rationalisation of delegated legislation has been achieved under the Deregulation and Contracting Out Act 1994, but there still appears to be an upward trend in the volume of delegated legislation made. So, for example, the number of general statutory instruments (those "in the nature of a public general Act") registered was 1,168 in 1976, 1,359 in 1986 and 1,832 in 1996 (298 H.C. Deb., col. 165 (W.A.) (July 16, 1997)).

In addition, there are many rules of legal significance which are not contained in statutes or delegated legislation (*e.g.* immigration rules and codes of practice: see Immigration Act 1971, s. 3(2); *Alexander v. Immigration Appeal Tribunal* [1982] 2 All E.R. 768, 770; W. A. Wilson, "Knowing the Law and Other Things" (1982) J.R. 259; Lord Campbell of Alloway, "Codes of Practice as an Alternative to Legislation" [1985] Stat.L.R. 127; 469 H.L. Deb., cols 1075–1104, (January 15, 1986); A. Samuels, "Codes of Practice and Legislation" [1986] Stat.L.R. 29, T. St J. N. Bates, "Parliament, Policy and Delegated Power" *ibid.* at 114; W.A. Wilson, "Studying Statutes" (1992) J.R. 213, 218–219). Occasionally legislation may recognise a rule but not enact it (*Palatine Graphic Arts Co. Ltd v. Liverpool City Council* [1986] 1 Q.B. 335).

Inevitably, much of the time of courts is occupied by interpreting legislation. Lord Hailsham estimated that "nine cases out of ten which come before the House of Lords depend in the end upon the interpretation of a statute" (405 H.L. Deb., col. 302).

The importance of legislation as a source of law depends partly on the range of matters which it regulates, partly on its volume, and partly on the relationship between those who make it and those who apply and interpret it. It is with this relationship, and its uncertainties, that this chapter is primarily concerned. For a witty and erudite survey of such uncertainties, see W. A. Wilson, "Studying Statutes" (1992) J.R. 213.

U.K. legislation is sometimes criticised for its lack of general coherence; it is not codified, determining the current statute law may be difficult because repealed provisions are often not easy to establish, and provisions may be enacted but not brought into force. So, for example, in the period May 1979 to December 1992, 810 Bills received Royal Assent but 8.5 per cent of them still had provisions which had not been brought into force by March 1997 (see *Bringing Acts of Parliament into Force* (Cm. 3595)); 581 H.L. Deb., cols 290–296 (July 2, 1997).

It is also criticised for its style, its language and its typography. Such criticism may come from the judiciary. So, for example, in *Short's Trustee v. Keeper of the Registers of Scotland* 1996 S.C. (H.L.) 14, 26, Lord Jauncey of Tullichettle observed, of the Land Registration (Scotland) Act 1979, "nobody could accuse the Act of being well drafted but the more I look at sections 9 and 12 the more difficult do I find it to determine what was intended to be achieved by section

12(3)(b) and (c)". There has also, for example, been sustained judicial criticism of the drafting of the (English) Landlord and Tenant Act 1987: *e.g. Denetower Ltd v. Toop* [1991] 3 All E.R. 661, 668, *per* Sir Nicolas Browne-Wilkinson V.-C.; *Belvedere Management Ltd v. Frogmore Developments Ltd* [1996] 1 All E.R. 312, 330, 331 *per* Sir Thomas Bingham M.R. and Hobhouse L.J.

Certainly U.K. primary legislation, as compared with some continental European legislation, is detailed. However, some argue that even with legislation which is detailed, there could be stylistic improvements. So, for example, Sir William Dale, an experienced drafter, argues for a more relaxed style and shorter sentences.

Dale, "The European Legislative Scene", pp. 91–92

> "As an Anglo-Saxon I wish my conclusions to be practical. They will relate to the style of legislation. Roger Scruton, Professor of Aesthetics at London University, says, 'Style is the search for simplicity and naturalness, for the phrase which not only says what you mean but also embodies within itself all the nuances.' He was talking philosophically; but his words both give to the draftsman a definition of style, and set an ambition before him. Simplicity, naturalness, and nuances are what we want—and nuances are what we get from statements of principle rather than rules.
>
> I conclude with two specific points. First, we ought to relax the strenuousness, the laboriousness, the narrowness, of the United Kingdom style, and aim at something freer, easier, and broader. It should not be difficult to achieve this . . .
>
> Secondly, one of the cardinal differences between civil law and common law styles of drafting is the length of the section. I am in favour of the short section for two reasons. The first reason is that it can be an aid to drafting. I have previously given examples taken from copyright legislation. There the draftsman had various categories of work to be treated, the rules to be in some respects the same for all categories, in other respects different. He dealt with the categories separately, in long, cumbersome sections, and was forced to repeat material. If he had drafted in short sections, there would have been no difficulty, each section laying down the appropriate rule for the category or categories the section covered. Short sentences can of course be grouped together, under a cross-heading.
>
> The second reason is that to think in short sections and sentences will encourage more concise thoughts. We do not pay sufficient attention to the effect that form and verbal style may have on thought. To take an illustration so near the bone that it has appeared in these pages before. If Wordsworth had set out to describe what he saw from Westminster Bridge in a lyric or an epic poem rather than in a sonnet, he would have had thoughts greatly differing from those he expressed in his famous fourteen lines; thoughts not so telling, or so memorable."

Again, as Sir William Dale argues below, even complex legislation would be easier to interpret and apply if it contained statements of principle or "objects" sections, although this may not always be possible.

Dale, "Principles, Purposes and Rules", pp. 15, 24–26

"All legislation presumably has a purpose; it may, or it may not, state a principle; it will contain rules, if that is the right word. My chief object is to consider statements of principle, but all three topics are closely connected. I shall consider them separately, and then try to draw them together by suggesting a few practical conclusions . . .

What are the practical conclusions to be drawn from all this? I suggest the following:

1. Parliament wishes its legislation to be effective. Its impact will be the greater if some principle is stated at 'each new step in a statute.' An enunciation of principle gives to a statute a firm and intelligible structure. It helps to clear the mind of the legislator, provides guidance to the Executive, explains the legislation to the public, and assists the courts when in doubt about the application of some specific provision. But by a 'principle' we do not, on the one hand, mean a vague, jurisprudential generality, or maxim; nor, on the other hand, do we mean merely a particular provision broadly drafted: we mean a statement in general terms, showing on its face, so far as may be, the moral, social, or economic basis on which the statement itself, and the particular provisions which follow it, rest, and which is itself law-making.

2. But we should recognise that many statutes do not lend themselves to a statement of principle of that kind: minor amending Acts, for example, most penal statutes, Acts dealing with matters of administration, Consolidation Acts. I have particularly looked at chapters 1–40 of our Statute book for 1984 and see that the larger part of them fall within these four categories. We must find other ways of making the purport of a statute clear—an informative long title, for instance, or an objects clause. There is a trend in some Commonwealth countries to replace the long title by an objects clause. Looking again at chapters 1–40, we find long titles that are nicely informative to the Telecommunications Act, the Foreign Limitation Periods Act and the Rates Act. None of the Acts contains an objects clause, unless one counts section 1(1) of the Registered Homes Act, which almost manages an objects clause, a principle and 'rules' in one sentence—all the more meritorious in a Consolidation Act. But I have doubts about the indiscriminate use of objects clauses. I suggest they should be used if there is a particular legislative end to be achieved, as in the example from Barbados I have cited, or for some other specific purpose as recommended by the Renton Committee.

3. Yet that will still leave us with statutes that ought to signal their purport at the outset, and do not do so. Take the Prevention of Terrorism (Temporary Provisions) Act 1984 as an example. Of course one knows from the short title that the Act aims to prevent terrorism. But what sort of all the terrorism related in our newspapers is it directed to preventing? One has to go through the whole of the Act, which has five Parts, 19 sections and three Schedules, and runs to 20 pages, most meticulously, to find out. Stowed away in subsection (4) of section 1 and Schedule 1, subsection (6) of section 3, and subsection (5) of section 10 is the information that, so far, the Act is

concerned with Northern Ireland. But then in section 12(3) there suddenly comes:

'(3) The acts of terrorism to which this Part of this Act applies are—

(a) acts of terrorism connected with the affairs of Northern Ireland; and
(b) acts of terrorism of any other description except acts connected solely with the affairs of the United Kingdom or any part of the United Kingdom other than Northern Ireland.'

It is the sort of drafting that numbs the mind. But my point is to suggest that the Act might perhaps have begun with something like this:

> 'This Act is directed to preventing terrorism in relation to Northern Ireland by means of the proscribing of organisations (Part I), the making of exclusion orders (Part II), and the prescribing of various offences (Part III). Powers of arrest and other powers conferred by Part IV extend also to international terrorism.'

That is neither a statement of principle, nor is it an objects clause, though it resembles one. It is a descriptive clause. It might be given the marginal note 'Description of Act.'

4. The Prevention of Terrorism Act had been preceded by earlier Acts, and parts of it must have been difficult to draft. Still, it is a typical product of our legislative style, a true spider's web; and it is this legislative style that I maintain should be our main concern. The debate about principle versus detail, which has grown tiresome, deflects attention from the main problem of securing clarity of drafting throughout an Act. The two sides intend different things by 'principle,' and rarely does either side vouchsafe to us an example of what it does intend. Those arguing for drafting 'in terms of principle' really mean drafting the 'detail' in broader terms, whereas the other side attacks the concept as if its proponents mean drafting the 'detail' in terms of general statements of a jurisprudential nature. No conclusion is reached. Let us be clear that by a 'principle' we mean 'a first position'—first in place in the statute as well as in logic— 'from which others are deduced,' the 'others,' so far as they are not implied, being expressed in the remaining provisions of the statute, or the Part, as the case may be. The question we ought to be dwelling on is how to secure in these remaining provisions sufficiency of particularity without undue prolixity and complexity. This must be what the Prime Minister had in mind when, speaking of the 'thicket of detail,' she said that we ought to 'mount a rule of law, and not to make a multiplicity of regulations.' It is too easy to say that, as things stand, our Acts are much like regulations and our regulations much like Acts. We should be able to recognise a greater difference than that the Acts are bound in red, the Regulations in blue."

[On the application of purposive drafting to U.K. legislation, see *Tax Law Rewrite: A Purposive Approach to Rewriting Tax Legislation*, Technical Discussion Document No. 2 (Inland Revenue, February 1998); 584 H.L. Deb., cols 1583–1602, January 21, 1998.]

The need to express often complex matters with great precision may make it difficult for the parliamentary drafter to adopt a more relaxed style and to use, as is sometimes proposed, simpler language.

The Preparation of Legislation, paras 11.2–11.5

"11.2 The most important technique, if the least tangible, is simplicity of vocabulary and syntax. Varying degrees of emphasis have been placed by witnesses on the need for this. Lord Simon of Glaisdale formulated the ideal in the following terms: 'Desirably the language of legislation should be as near to ordinary speech as precision permits.' But he recognised that 'most ordinary terminology contains ambiguity'. Another formulation (by Mr Ian Percival Q.C. M.P.) is that 'wherever possible, what is intended should be set out in the simplest terms, in the language nearest to that which would be used by those affected by it'. The Statute Law Society suggest that 'clarity of expression, of grammar and construction should be a primary consideration'. According to the Faculty of Advocates 'The solution here must . . . lie in a compromise between the precision of technical language and the ready comprehensibility of the ordinary use of words . . . The words used should be reasonably simple . . . the sentences should be reasonably short'. A number of other witnesses have expressed a preference for simpler language than is to be found in most statutes at present. Many witnesses recognise, however, that it may be difficult or even impracticable to achieve it in some kinds of legislation, notably in fiscal statutes.

11.3 In paragraphs 6.3 and 6.4 we quoted criticisms of current drafting style by the Statute Law Society and other witnesses, and referred to the examples in Appendix B of particular statutory provisions that had caused difficulties of interpretation in the courts. On the other side of the scales should be placed the following tribute by Professor Driedger:

> 'With a new British statute, where I understand the subject matter and the social background, I really have no problems and no difficulty in reading and understanding the statute. Of course, if it is a statute dealing with your building societies, or your rent regulations, I would not understand it because I do not understand your practices, but an ordinary statute that deals with a familiar subject, or with a legal subject, I really have no difficulty in understanding. I think on the whole they are well written and well organised, and can be understood by anyone who is familiar with the subject matter of the statute and the circumstances that give rise to it.'

We would, moreover, mention here that Parliament does not always take kindly to the homely phrase. In a recent Bill the expression 'the owner has tried his best to let the building' was not well received in the House of Commons, which preferred the more orotund 'used his best endeavours'.

11.4 In the 1940s and 1950s, when those who are now senior draftsmen were learning the craft, there was still a general belief that the language, or rather the style, must be formalised, on mere grounds of decorum; and that the precision needed to attain immediate certainty overrode every other consideration. In both respects the belief has since weakened. Language is

> increasingly informal. As to certainty, the need for it remains amply recognised (as it must be); but certainty is obtainable at two different levels. One is where the draftsman deliberately words his clause so that at no point can it possibly be challenged for ambiguity, even by a reader (or legal practitioner) so perverse, or having such a professional interest in finding a way round the law, that he is resolved to find an ambiguity which to any ordinary reader is invisible. At this level of certainty, language becomes by gradations more and more convoluted, and the legislative proposition obscured. At the other level, sufficient certainty is obtained for a fair-minded and reasonable reader to be in no doubt what is intended, it being assumed that no one would take entirely perverse points against the draft, or that such points would be brushed aside by the court. Most of us are satisfied that there has been a substantial and desirable retreat from the first level, with resultant simplification and abbreviation of language.
>
> 11.5 On the other hand, the draftsman must never be forced to sacrifice certainty for simplicity, since the result may be to frustrate the legislative intention. An unfortunate subject may be driven to litigation because the meaning of an Act was obscure which could, by use of a few extra words, have been made plain. The courts may hold, or a Government department be driven to conclude, that the Act which was intended to mean one thing does not mean that thing, but something else. Where this occurs, the draftsman's discomfort is considerable, and he will instinctively guard against its happening to him a second time."

The Committee on the Preparation of Legislation, chaired by the Rt Hon. Sir David (now Lord) Renton, did not suggest that drafting in a simpler style and language was an unrealistic aspiration. Recommendations that, without sacrificing legal certainty, a simpler drafting style should be considered in the United Kingdom are to be found in the Hansard Society Commission on the Legislative Process, "Making the Law", (Hansard Society, 1993), Chap. 4. Success has been achieved in this regard in other Commonwealth countries: see, for example, I.M.L. Turnbull, "Clear Legislative Drafting: New Approaches in Australia" [1990] Stat.L.R. 161; P.E. Johnson, "Legislative Drafting Practices and other Factors affecting the Clarity of Canada's Laws" [1991] Stat.L.R. 1; W. Isles, "Legislative Drafting Practices in New Zealand" *ibid.* 16. And in the United Kingdom, the Inland Revenue, in collaboration with parliamentary counsel and private sector tax professionals, has embarked on a project, the *Tax Law Rewrite*, to redraft the bulk of the existing U.K. primary tax legislation to make it clearer and easier to use, without changing or making less certain its general effect. This has resulted in a number of consultative and discussion documents published from 1996 onwards (see *Tax Law Rewrite: Plans for 1998/99* (Inland Revenue, May 1998) and htpp://www.open.gov.uk/inrev/rewrite.htm; see also the Hon. Dame Mary Arden, "Modernising Legislation" [1998] P.L. 65).

However, maintaining legal certainty while adopting a simpler drafting style is not always easy. Martin Cutts redrafted the Timeshare Act 1992 in a simpler style and language with a modern layout and typography (the "Clearer Timeshare Act 1993"). The new layout and typography was a distinct improvement, but the simpler language sometimes resulted in a loss of legal clarity. This is illustrated by a brief extract of the 1992 Act and the parallel provision from the 1993 redraft, followed by an extract of a letter to Mr Cutts from Mr Euan Sutherland, who drafted the 1992 Act.

Cutts, "Unspeakable Acts?"

"Timeshare Act 1992, s. 12(4)

> 'This Act shall have effect in relation to any timeshare agreement or timeshare credit agreement notwithstanding any agreement or notice.'"
>
> *"Clearer Timeshare Act 1993, s. 1.3*
> 'The parties may not prevent this Act applying to an agreement.'"

Sutherland letter to Cutts

> " . . . The clarity for the lay reader at which your draft aims has led, I think, in certain places to the danger described in that recommendation [*i.e.* the recommendation at para. 11.5 of The Preparation of Legislation quoted above]. For example, section 12(4) of the Act says that the Act has effect 'in relation to any timeshare agreement or timeshare credit agreement notwithstanding any agreement or notice'. Your section 1.3 says 'the parties may not prevent this Act applying to an agreement'. Certainly your formulation seems more straightforward. But what does it mean?
>
> Imagine that an agreement is being made between a tourist and a British salesman abroad and the tourist asks that the contract be made subject to English law. If the salesman refuses, he is by doing so preventing the Act from applying to the agreement. Does section 1.3 prohibit that? Read simply, perhaps it does; and if it does, what is the effect of the prohibition? Does the Act apply anyway, or has the salesman merely committed a wrong for which no penalty is given? . . ."

[The words in square brackets have been added to clarify the context.]

Other factors, apart from statutory style and language, may contribute to the uncertainties which surround the relationship between the legislator and the interpreter. First, words are an imprecise way of conveying meaning and this may be accentuated in legislation. For example, legislation is normally drafted to regulate future events. As it is difficult to anticipate all such events, broad terms are often used, and they may raise questions of interpretation. So, what does "habitual residence" mean (E. M. Clive, "The Concept of Habitual Residence" 1997 J.R. 137)? When legislation prohibits "fishing", does it include the act of pumping fish from nets into a boat after the fish have been caught (*Alexander v. Tonkin* [1979] 1 W.L.R. 629)? Does keeping two fierce dogs so close to a footpath that pedestrians are frightened to use it amount to wilfully obstructing free passage along the footpath (*Kent C.C. v. Holland*, *The Times*, July 26, 1996)? Is a person "driving" a car when grabbing the steering wheel from the driver while sitting in the front passenger seat (*Jones v. Pratt* [1983] R.T.R. 54), or when pushing a car with one hand on the steering wheel (*McArthur v. Valentine* 1990 J.C. 146)? Does a co-driver "take over a vehicle" when he gets into it as a passenger with the intention of driving it on a subsequent leg of a journey (*Browne v. Anelay*, *The Times*, June 10, 1997)? Do the words "without reasonable excuse" apply to the child or to the parent, where the parent is charged with "failing without reasonable excuse to secure the regular attendance" of a child at school (*MacIntyre v. Annan* 1991 S.C.C.R. 465)? Is the cost of a headstone a reasonable expense incurred "in connection with the deceased's funeral" (*Prentice v. Chalmers* 1985 S.L.T. 168)? Is a shopping and leisure development isolated from residential property a "neighbourhood" (*R. v. Family Health Service Appeal Authority, ex p. Boots the Chemist Ltd*, *The Times*, June 28, 1996, 33 B.M.L.R.I.)? Is a building with an annexe 12 yards away which contains sleeping accommodation for travellers a "hotel" (*Chief Constable, Northern Constabulary v. Lochaber District Licensing Board* 1985 S.L.T. 410)? Is an electronic notepad a "document" (*Robb v. H.M. Advocate* 1997 J.C. 23)?

Secondly, the drafters may make mistakes. They may draft imprecisely. They may fail to provide for situations which the legislation would be presumed to encompass, or they may misunderstand the law on which the legislation is based. For example, the Official Secrets Act 1920 made it a specific offence to cause an obstruction "in the vicinity of" any prohibited place but not actually in it (*Adler v. George* [1964] 2 Q.B. 7), and in the Natal Ordinance No. 1 of 1856, the drafter misunderstood the relevant private international law (*Salmon v. Duncombe* (1886) 11 App. Cas. 627; see also A. Samuels, "Errors in Bills and Acts" [1982] Stat.L.R. 94). Defective drafting which creates immediate practical difficulties, for example, determining the release dates of prisoners, may be addressed by vigorous judicial interpretation, *e.g. R. v. Secretary of State for the Home Department, ex p. Naughton* [1997] 1 All E.R. 426; *R. v. Governor of Brockhill Prison, ex p. Evans* [1997] 1 All E.R. 439). Minor textual omissions which are judicially considered to be obvious may be rectified by the courts, particularly where a failure to do so would defeat the object of the legislation (*e.g. Gateshead Metropolitan B.C. v. L* [1996] 3 All E.R. 264), but the courts are unlikely to correct more substantial mistakes and omissions (*e.g. R. v. Horseferry Road Magistrates' Court, ex p. K* [1996] 3 All E.R. 719).

Thirdly, legislative ambiguity may arise out of political expediency. For instance, an important consideration for a Government is that a Bill should be drafted to attract as little opposition as possible during its passage through Parliament. Lord Thring, an early parliamentary drafter, wrote, "Bills are made to pass, as razors are made to sell" ((1874) 136 L.Q.R. 66). Mr Moran, of the Lord Advocate's Department, indicated that such political considerations still constrain the modern parliamentary drafter.

Moran, "The Parliamentary Draftsman", p. 36

> "It has often seemed to me, in more jaded moods, that many of the critics of the parliamentary draftsman—particularly (let me whisper it) on the Bench—are under the impression that the object of their censure inhabits some secure and peaceful haven—a haven where he can draft his Bills untroubled by the ebb and flow of tides and currents or by the squalls which disturb the sea outside—a haven, above all, where time stands still. Were this the case, the draftsman's lapses would indeed merit little leniency. And

is it true? It is not true. No such retreat exists for the draftsman. He is abroad on that sea—a political and parliamentary sea which is at best treacherous, and which can on occasion be cruel indeed. 'Oh, yes,' one is told, 'your clause is clear and accurate, but we can't have it presented that way: our back-benchers would vote against it.' Or: 'Yes, we accept that there is doubt here and we agree that the amendment which you have suggested would remove it. But if we put it down it will reopen the whole question of cruelty to animals (or gambling or police powers) and that will add at least two days to the Committee Stage, which the Whips say we can't afford.' Or, again: 'The Minister says the amendments must go down tonight. Yes, we know this is only a first draft of them and they're worth a week's thought anyway, but there it is.' There it is indeed. You might be surprised how many statutes owe much of their shape and content not to the conscious wish of the parliamentary draftsman but to political or parliamentary accident entirely outwith his control."

[See also D. Johnstone, "Role of the Administrator in the Preparation of United Kingdom Legislation" [1980] Stat.L.R. 67; G. Engle, "Bills are made to pass as razors are made to sell: practical constraints in the preparation of legislation" [1983] Stat.L.R. 7.]

Such political and parliamentary constraints have been particularly acute for those drafting Scottish legislation. (See J. Rankin, "Scottish Business at Westminster" (1988) 33 J.L.S.S. 423.) Governments are not generous in providing parliamentary time for purely Scottish legislation. As it is easier to find parliamentary time for one Bill rather than three or four, it is not uncommon for a Scottish statute to encompass a range of disparate provisions. So, for example the Law Reform (Miscellaneous Provisions) (Scotland) Act 1990 not only enacted a miscellany of law reform in Part IV but also provided for the supervision of charities in Scotland (Part I), made important reforms of the Scottish legal profession (Part II) and extensive amendment of the Licensing (Scotland) Act 1976 (Part III). Accommodating Scots law within a Bill which will apply to Great Britain or the United Kingdom, and which has been structured on the basis of English law, also creates a whole range of problems (see further, Lord Mackay of Clashfern, "The Drafting of Government Bills Affecting the Law of Scotland" [1983] Stat.L.R. 68). However, at least in areas of devolved legislative competence, these difficulties should be ameliorated by the Scottish Parliament and Executive.

Law reform and the rationalisation of existing legislation can be considered in a more detached and systematic manner. They may be considered by official bodies which are not as closely associated with the day-to-day concerns of Ministers and civil servants in Government departments and the parliamentary draftsmen they instruct. Two such bodies are the Law Commission (which has English law as its principal concern) and the Scottish Law Commission.

Law Commissions Act 1965, ss. 2, 3

"2.—(1) For the purpose of promoting the reform of the law of Scotland, there shall be constituted in accordance with this section a body of

Commissioners, to be known as the Scottish Law Commission, consisting of a Chairman and not more than four other Commissioners appointed by the Lord Advocate.

(2) The persons appointed to be Commissioners shall be persons appearing to the Lord Advocate to be suitably qualified by the holding of judicial office or by experience as an advocate or solicitor or as a teacher of law in a university . . . .

3.—(1) It shall be the duty of each of the Commissions to take and keep under review all the law with which they are respectively concerned with a view to its systematic development and reform, including in particular the codification of such law, the elimination of anomalies, the repeal of obsolete and unnecessary enactments, the reduction of the number of separate enactments and generally the simplification and modernisation of the law, and for that purpose—

(a) to receive and consider any proposals for the reform of the law which may be made or referred to them;

(b) to prepare and submit to the [Lord Advocate] from time to time programmes for the examination of different branches of the law with a view to reform, including recommendations as to the agency (whether the Commission or another body) by which any such examination should be carried out;

(c) to undertake, pursuant to any such recommendations approved by the [Lord Advocate], the examination of particular branches of the law and the formulation, by means of draft Bills or otherwise, of proposals for reform therein;

(d) to prepare from time to time at the request of the [Lord Advocate] comprehensive programmes of consolidation and statute law revision, and to undertake the preparation of draft Bills pursuant to any such programme approved by the [Lord Advocate];

(e) to provide advice and information to government departments and other authorities or bodies concerned at the instance of the Government with proposals for the reform or amendment of any branch of the law;

(f) to obtain such information as to the legal systems of other countries as appears to the Commissioners likely to facilitate the performance of any of their functions.

(2) The [Lord Advocate] shall lay before Parliament any programmes prepared by the Commission and approved by him and any proposals for reform formulated by the Commission pursuant to such programmes.

(3) Each of the Commissions shall make an annual report to the [Lord Advocate] on their proceedings, and the [Lord Advocate] shall lay the report before Parliament with such comments (if any) as he thinks fit.

(4) In the exercise of their functions under this Act the Commissions shall act in consultation with each other."

(As amended by S.I. 1972 No. 2002.)

The Chairman of the Scottish Law Commission, currently a part-time appointment, is a Senator of the College of Justice; of the other four members of the

Commission, two are full-time and two part-time. The Commission has a small legal staff. In 1998, it comprised two parliamentary counsel (who, working from the Lord Advocate's Department in London, prepared the draft legislation referred to in section 3 above), the Secretary of the Commission and five other lawyers seconded from the Scottish Office. There were also seven legal assistants employed on short-term contracts who were either recent law graduates, or had recently completed traineeships in the private sector. The work of this staff may be supported by consultants and advisory groups and, in addition, the Commission has for some years employed senior law students or recent graduates as research assistants during the summer; in 1997, two law graduates were so employed.

The most significant duties of the Scottish Law Commission and its English counterpart are proposing reforms in the law and preparing consolidation and statute law revision Bills (see Sir Michael Kerr, "Law Reform in Changing Times" (1980) L.Q.R. 515; Hon. Lord Davidson: "Law Reform—Who Cares"? (1992) 37 J.L.S.S. 130; Lord Simon of Glaisdale and J. Webb, "Consolidation and Statute Law Revision" [1975] P.L. 285). Opinions have differed on how successful the Scottish Law Commission has been in carrying out its statutory duties: see D.M. Walker, "The Scottish Law Commission under Review" [1987] Stat.L.R. 115; *cf.* Lord Hunter, "Law Reform: the Scottish Law Commission" (1988) J.R. 158.

The Scottish Law Commission draws up law reform programmes which are approved by the Lord Advocate (s. 3(1)(b), 3(2); its fifth programme of law reform will be completed in 1999 and the sixth will run for three to five years from 2000). Other law reform is undertaken at the request of government departments (s. 3(1)(e)). So, for example, in 1997 the Scottish Law Commission was requested by the Secretary of State for Scotland to consider the law on leasehold casualties, and the Department of Trade and Industry has asked the two Commissions to review the duties of directors and the law of partnership. Proposed areas of law reform may also be submitted to the Commission from other sources. So, for example, the Commission's Consultative Memorandum No. 60 on the law of mobbing and rioting was the product of a proposal from the Crown Agent, and the Commission considered computer crime at the instance of the Law Society of Scotland.

The Commission consults widely before recommending reforms of the law. This is done primarily by issuing consultative memoranda or, in recent years, discussion papers, on which comment is invited; other forms of consultation are also used, such as holding public meetings. Following consultation, the Commission publishes a report with its recommendations; the report often includes draft legislation based on the recommendations. In the year to June 1998, the Scottish Law Commission published six reports and discussion papers, and a further three jointly with the (English) Law Commission. They covered such diverse topics as interpretation in private law, shareholder remedies and boundary walls. However, not all the work of the Commission has related directly to domestic law. The Scottish Law Commission is sometimes specifically invited to consider European Community law and international treaties; in 1976 it was asked to consider a White Paper containing proposals for devolution to Scotland and Wales, and it published a memorandum on the subject.

However detached and carefully considered, whether Scottish Law Commission proposals for law reform are to be implemented is dependent on the availability of parliamentary time. (Accelerated parliamentary legislative procedures apply to consolidation and statute law revision bills, so there the issue is less acute.) Successive governments have been slow in introducing as government Bills those Commission law reform proposals which they have accepted; some Commission proposals have been introduced as private members' Bills. Various procedural solutions have been explored but the position may be ameliorated as many of the Bills incorporating Scottish Law Commission proposals will be within the competence of the Scottish Parliament to enact. In this context it should be noted that the Scottish Law Commission is a Scottish public authority with mixed functions (Scotland Act 1998, s. 12, Sched. 5, Part III, para. 1) and reports, through the Law Officers, to the Scottish Parliament in respect of devolved Scots law matters and to the U.K. Parliament on Scots law within reserved matters.

The role of the interpreter also contributes to the uncertain relationship between those who make law and those who apply and interpret it. At a fundamental level, legislation as a source of law depends on the recognition of the authority of the legislator. So, for example, judges in the United Kingdom recognise the supremacy of the U.K. Parliament as a legislative body (*e.g. Mortensen v. Peters* (1906) 8 F.(J.) 93), although in certain circumstances Community law (*e.g. Macarthys Ltd v. Smith* [1979] 3 All E.R. 325) and possibly the Treaty and Acts of Union 1707 (*e.g. MacCormick v. Lord Advocate* 1953 S.C. 396; *Murray v. Rogers* 1992 S.L.T. 221; and see N. Walker and C.M.G. Himsworth (1991) J.R. 45) may be recognised as prevailing over conflicting parliamentary legislation. To some extent interpretation is governed by statutory provisions and precedent, although the former may themselves be interpreted and the latter distinguished. Beyond that there is a wide measure of discretion left to the judiciary in the interpretation of legislation. There are, for example, a number of principles which judges may read into legislation unless the legislation expressly excludes them. Again, when faced with a legislative ambiguity, judges may choose to apply a variety of rules to resolve the ambiguity. The way in which this judicial discretion is exercised depends to some extent on the judge's perception of his constitutional role. Compare, for example, the views of Denning L.J., for which he was subsequently rebuked in the House of Lords ([1952] A.C. 189 at p. 191), with those of Lord Simon of Glaisdale.

Magor and St Mellons R.D.C. v. Newport Corporation [1950] 2 All E.R. 1226

> **Denning L.J.**: "I have no patience with an ultra-legalistic interpretation . . . We do not sit here to pull the language of Parliament and of Ministers to pieces and make nonsense of it. That is an easy thing to do, and it is a thing to which lawyers are too often prone. We sit here to find out the intention of Parliament and of Ministers and carry it out, and we do this better by filling in the gaps and making sense of the enactment than by opening it up to destructive analysis."

Stock v. Frank Jones (Tipton) Ltd **[1978] 1 W.L.R. 231**

Lord Simon of Glaisdale: "The final task of construction is still, as always, to ascertain the meaning of what the draftsman has said, rather than to ascertain what the draftsman meant to say. But if the draftmanship is correct these should coincide. So if the words are capable of more than one meaning it is a perfectly legitimate intermediate step in construction to choose between potential meanings by various tests (statutory, objective, anomaly, etc.) which throw light on what the draftsman meant to say.

It is idle to debate whether, in so acting, the court is making law. As has been cogently observed, it depends on what you mean by 'make' and 'law' in this context. What is incontestable is that the court is a mediating influence between the executive and the legislature, on the one hand, and the citizen on the other. Nevertheless, it is essential to the proper judicial function in the constitution to bear in mind: (1) modern legislation is a difficult and complicated process, in which, even before a bill is introduced in a House of Parliament, successive drafts are considered and their possible repercussions on all envisageable situations are weighed by people bringing to bear a very wide range of experience: the judge cannot match such experience or envisage all such repercussions, either by training or by specific forensic aid; (2) the bill is liable to be modified in a Parliament dominated by a House of Commons whose members are answerable to the citizens who will be affected by the legislation: an English judge is not so answerable; (3) in a society living under the rule of law citizens are entitled to regulate their conduct according to what a statute has said, rather than by what it was meant to say or by what it would have otherwise said if a newly considered situation had been envisaged; . . . (5) Parliament may well be prepared to tolerate some anomaly in the interest of an overriding objective; (6) what strikes the lawyer as an injustice may well have seemed to the legislature as no more than the correction of a now unjustifiable privilege or as a particular misfortune necessarily or acceptably involved in the vindication of some supervening general social benefit; (7) the parliamentary draftsman knows what objective the legislative promoter wishes to attain, and he will normally and desirably try to achieve that objective by using language of the appropriate register in its natural, ordinary and primary sense: to reject such an approach on the grounds that it gives rise to an anomaly is liable to encourage complication and anfractuosity in drafting; (8) Parliament is nowadays in continuous session, so that an unlooked-for and unsupportable injustice or anomaly can be readily rectified by legislation: this is far preferable to judicial contortion of the law to meet apparently hard cases with the result that ordinary citizens and their advisers hardly know where they stand.

All this is not to advocate judicial supineness: it is merely respectfully to commend a self-knowledge of judicial limitations, both personal and constitutional."

II. THE LAW OF INTERPRETATION

A. EUROPEAN COMMUNITY LAW

European Communities Act 1972, s. 3(1), (2)

> "3.—(1) For the purposes of all legal proceedings any question as to the meaning or effect of any of the Treaties, or as to the validity, meaning or effect of any Community instrument, shall be treated as a question of law (and, if not referred to the European Court, be for determination as such in accordance with the principles laid down by and any relevant decision of the European Court [or any court attached thereto].
>
> (2) Judicial notice shall be taken . . . of any decision of, or expression of opinion by the European Court [or any court attached thereto] on any such question as aforesaid."

(For the definitions of "Treaties" and "Community Instrument" see section 1 and Schedule 1; the "European Court" means the Court of Justice of the European Communities: *ibid.*; the words in square brackets were added by the European Communities (Amendment) Act 1986, s. 2, in anticipation of the establishment of the Court of First Instance.)

Section 3 of the European Communities Act 1972, which reflects the Community obligations of the United Kingdom as a Member State, provides that decisions of, and principles laid down by, the Court of Justice of the European Communities (the "Court of Justice"), or the Court of First Instance, on the interpretation and effect of Community treaties and Community legislation are binding on all courts in the United Kingdom. As indicated below, this status accorded to the jurisprudence of the Court of Justice has important implications for the manner in which U.K. courts interpret both Community law and domestic legislation.

However, before turning to those implications, there are complicating factors in establishing the principles of interpretation laid down by, and evaluating the decisions of, the Court of Justice and the Court of First Instance. The Court of Justice may sit as a full court, but it also sits for some purposes in chambers of three or five judges; the Court of First Instance, which has a limited jurisdiction, may also sit as a full court or in chambers of three or five judges. Thus it is possible that, in each court, one chamber may fail to follow the previous decision of another; this may be of somewhat less practical significance with respect to the Court of First Instance, which does not hear Article 177 references (see below and chapter 6). Secondly, Advocates General who, although not judges, are members of the European Court, submit opinions on cases before the Court; a similar arrangement exists in the Court of First Instance. The opinions of the Advocates General are commonly more fully argued than the judgments; they are frequently adopted in the judgments, but sometimes they are not: *e.g.* Cases C-6 and 9/90 *Francovich and Bonifaci v. Italian Republic* [1991] E.C.R. I-5357 (retrospectivity of a state's liability to an individual for breaches of Community law). Finally, the Court of Justice does not regard itself as bound by its previous decisions (*e.g.* Case 48172 *de Haecht (No. 2)* [1973] E.C.R. 77; *cf.* Case 43169 *Bilger v. Jehle* [1970] E.C.R. 127 and Case 10/69 *Portelange* [1969] E.C.R. 309), although it does prefer to follow them (*e.g.* Case 35/75 *Matisa* [1975] E.C.R. 1205, 1210).

Section 3(1) refers to principles laid down by the Court of Justice. Some of the more significant of these principles have obvious implications for the interpretation of national legislation which is implementing Community law, for example directives. They include such principles as the supremacy of Community law over inconsistent national law (*e.g.* Case 6/64 *Costa v. ENEL* [1964] E.C.R. 585; Case 11/70 *Internationale Handelsgesellschaft* [1970] E.C.R. 1125; Case 106/77 *Simmenthal* [1978] E.C.R. 629), and the circumstances in which Community legislation has direct effect and gives individuals rights which are enforceable in national courts (*e.g.* Case 149/77 *Defrenne v. Sabena* [1978] E.C.R. 1365; Case 93/71 *Leonesio* [1972] E.C.R. 287; Case 41/47 *Van Duyn* [1974] E.C.R. 1337; Case 148/78 *Ratti* [1979] E.C.R. 1629; Case 9/70 *Grad* [1970] E.C.R. 825).

In addition there are decisions of the Court of Justice which bear on the interpretation and effect to be given to national legislation in order to give effect to Community obligations. In *Von Colson* (Case 14/83 [1984] E.C.R. 1891), the Court of Justice held that a national court should interpret national legislation adopted to implement a directive in the light of the wording and purpose of the directive, so as to be in conformity with Community law (see also Case 222/84 *Johnston v. Chief Constable, RUC* [1986] E.C.R. 1651, 1690; [1987] Q.B. 129, 153). In *Marleasing* (Case C–106/89 [1990] E.C.R. I-4135), the Court of Justice developed the duty placed on national courts requiring them to interpret national legislation in the light of Community law, so that national law conforms "so far as possible" with Community law. *Marleasing* suggests that this is not limited to national legislation implementing a Community obligation, but extends to the construction of all national legislation. Sometimes essentially procedural decisions of the Court of Justice determine the effect which national courts give to national legislation. So, in a preliminary ruling on a reference from the House of Lords, the Court of Justice held that where interim relief in a case concerning Community law could not be granted solely because of national legislation, a national court should suspend operation of the national legislation, in this case the Merchant Shipping Act 1988: *R. v. Secretary of State for Transport, ex p. Factortame Ltd* [1990] 3 W.L.R. 818, ECJ. There are implications in this for the domestic legislative implementation of E.U. directives (see T. St J. N. Bates "United Kingdom Implementation of E.U. Directives" (1996) 17 Stat.L.R. 27).

The response of Scottish and other U.K. courts to this jurisprudence of the Court of Justice is tempered by aspects of public law which, in their detail, fall outside the scope of this book. U.K. courts have, for instance, held that Community law prevails over inconsistent domestic law, unless in the case of primary legislation that legislation clearly demonstrates an intention to prevail over a Community obligation: see European Communities Act 1972, s. 2; *Macarthys Ltd v. Smith* [1979] 3 All E.R. 325; *cf. Prince v. Secretary of State for Scotland* 1985 S.L.T. 74.

What appears to be the more specific contemporary response of the U.K. courts is illustrated by the House of Lords, on a Scottish appeal, in *Litster v. Forth Dry Dock and Engineering Co. Ltd.*

***Litster v. Forth Dry Dock and Engineering Co. Ltd* [1990] 1 A.C. 546**

The appellants were employees of Forth Dry Dock and Engineering Co. Ltd, which was one of a group of companies which became insolvent and went into receivership. The receiver agreed to sell the assets of the company to Forth Estuary Engineering Ltd. An hour before the assets were transferred, the receivers dismissed the employees with immediate effect.

Lord Keith of Kinkel: "My Lords, I agree with the speeches of my noble and learned friends Lord Oliver and Lord Templeman, which I have had the opportunity of reading in draft, and will add only a few observations of my own.

In *Pickstone v. Freemans plc* [1989] A.C. 66 there had been laid before Parliament under para. 2(2) of Sched. 2 to the European Communities Act 1972 the draft of certain regulations designed, and presented by the responsible ministers as designed, to fill a lacuna in the equal pay legislation of the United Kingdom which had been identified by a decision of the Court of Justice of the European Communities. On a literal reading the regulation particularly relevant did not succeed in completely filling the lacuna. Your Lordships' House, however, held that in order that the manifest purpose of the regulations might be achieved and effect given to the clear but inadequately expressed intention of Parliament certain words must be read in by necessary implication.

In the present case the Transfer of Undertakings (Protection of Employment) Regulations 1981, S.I. 1981/1794, were similarly laid before Parliament in draft and approved by resolutions of both Houses. They were so laid as designed to give effect to E.C. Council Directive 77/187 dated 14 February 1977. It is plain that if the words in reg. 5(3) of the 1981 Regulations 'a person so employed immediately before the transfer' are read literally, as contended for by the second respondents, Forth Estuary Engineering Ltd, the provisions of reg. 5(1) will be capable of ready evasion through the transferee arranging with the transferor for the latter to dismiss its employees a short time before the transfer becomes operative. In the event that the transferor is insolvent, a situation commonly forming the occasion for the transfer of an undertaking; the employees would be left with worthless claims for unfair dismissal against the transferor. In any event, whether or not the transferor is insolvent, the employees would be deprived of the remedy of reinstatement or re-engagement. The transferee would be under no liability towards the employees and a coach and four would have been driven through the provisions of reg. 5(1).

A number of decisions of the European Court, in particular *P. Bork International A/S (in liq.) v. Foreningen af Arbejdsledere i Danmark* Case 101/87 [1989] I.R.L.R. 41, have had the result that where employees have been dismissed by the transferor for a reason connected with the transfer, at a time before the transfer takes effect, then for purposes of art. 3(1) of E.C. Council Directive 77/187 (which corresponds to reg. 5(1)) the employees are to be treated as still employed by the undertaking at the time of the transfer.

In these circumstances it is the duty of the court to give to reg. 5 a construction which accords with the decisions of the European Court on the corresponding provisions of the directive to which the regulation was intended by Parliament to give effect. The precedent established by *Pickstone v. Freemans plc* indicates that this is to be done by implying the words necessary to achieve that result. So there must be implied in reg. 5(3) words indicating that where a person has been unfairly dismissed in the circumstances described in reg. 8(1) he is to be deemed to have been employed in the undertaking immediately before the transfer or any of a series of transactions whereby it was effected.

My Lords, I would allow the appeal."

Lord Templeman: ". . . In *von Colson v. Land Nordrhein-Westfalen* Case 14/83 [1984] E.C.R. 1891 at 1909 (para. 26) the European Court, dealing with E.C. Council Directive 76/207 forbidding discrimination on grounds of sex regarding access to employment, ruled:

> '. . . the Member States' obligation arising from a directive to achieve the result envisaged by the directive and their duty under Article 5 of the Treaty to take all appropriate measures, whether general or particular, to ensure the fulfilment of that obligation, is binding on all the authorities of Member States including, for matters within their jurisdiction, the courts. It follows that, in applying the national law and in particular the provisions of a national law specifically introduced in order to implement Directive No. 76/207, national courts are required to interpret their national law in the light of the wording and the purpose of the directive in order to achieve the result referred to in the third paragraph of Article 189.'

Thus the courts of the United Kingdom are under a duty to follow the practice of the European Court by giving a purposive construction to directives and to regulations issued for the purpose of complying with directives. In *Pickstone v. Freemans plc* [1989] A.C. 66 this House implied words in a regulation designed to give effect to E.C. Council Directive 75/117 dealing with equal pay for women doing work of equal value. If this House had not been able to make the necessary implication the Equal Pay (Amendment) Regulations 1983, S.I. 1983/1794, would have failed in their object and the United Kingdom would have been in breach of its treaty obligations to give effect to directives. In the present case, in the light of E.C. Council Directive 77/187 and in the light of the ruling of the European Court in *Bork's Case* [1989] I.R.L.R. 41, it seems to me, following the suggestion of my noble and learned friend Lord Keith, that reg. 5(3) of the 1981 Regulations was not intended and ought not to be construed so as to limit the operation of reg. 5 to persons employed immediately before the transfer in point of time. Regulation 5(3) must be construed on the footing that it applies to a person employed immediately before the transfer or who would have been so employed if he had not been unfairly dismissed before the transfer for a reason connected with the transfer . . ."

> **Lord Oliver**: ". . . It will be seen that, as is to be expected, the scope and purpose of both the directive and the regulations are the same, that is to ensure that on any transfer of an undertaking or part of an undertaking, the employment of the existing workers in the undertaking is preserved or, if their employment terminates solely by reason of the transfer, that their rights arising out of that determination are effectively safeguarded. It may, I think, be assumed that those who drafted both the directive and the regulations were sufficiently acquainted with the realities of life to appreciate that a frequent, indeed, possibly the most frequent, occasion on which a business or part of a business is transferred is when the original employer is insolvent, so that an employee whose employment is terminated on the transfer will have no effective remedy for unfair dismissal unless it is capable of being exerted against the transferee. It can hardly have been contemplated that, where the only reason for determination of the employment is the transfer of the undertaking or the relevant part of it, the parties to the transfer would be at liberty to avoid the manifest purpose of the directive by the simple expedient of wrongfully dismissing the workforce a few minutes before the completion of the transfer. The European Court has expressed, in the clearest terms, the opinion that so transparent a device would not avoid the operation of the directive, and if the effect of the regulations is that under the law of the United Kingdom it has that effect, then your Lordships are compelled to conclude that the regulations are gravely defective and the government of the United Kingdom has failed to comply with its mandatory obligations under the directive. If your Lordships are in fact compelled to that conclusion, so be it; but it is not, I venture to think, a conclusion which any of your Lordships would willingly embrace in the absence of the most compulsive context rendering any other conclusion impossible . . ."

(See also *Pickstone v. Freemans plc* [1989] A.C. 66; *cf. Duke v. GEC Reliance Ltd* [1988] A.C. 618, *Finnegan v. Clowney Youth Training Programme* [1990] 2 All E.R. 546, HL; *R. v. D.H.S.S., ex p. Organon Laboratories* [1990] 1 C.M.L.R. 49, CA; see further *Mediguard Services v. McVeigh*, 1997 S.L.T. (Sh. Ct 38), *Meecham v. Secretary of State for Scotland* 1997 S.L.T. 936, *Commissioners of Customs and Excise v. Robert Gordon's College* 1996 S.L.T. 98, HL; J.D.N. Bates, "The Impact of Directives on Statutory Interpretation: Using the Euro-meaning?" [1986] Stat.L.R. 174; P. Craig, "Directives, Direct Effect, Indirect Effect and the Construction of National Legislation" (1997) 22 E.L.Rev. 519.)

Litster shows that U.K. courts, following *von Colson*, are capable of taking a robust approach in interpreting domestic legislation, enacted to implement Community obligations, to ensure compliance with Community law. Reference may be made to the Community obligation, and to decisions of the Court of Justice which interpret it, to ensure the compliance of national legislation with Community law and not merely for the purpose of resolving an ambiguity in the national legislation, at least where the national legislation has been enacted for the purpose of implementing the Community obligation. Following *Marleasing*, the role of national courts in construing national legislation to comply with Community law may be further enlarged.

The decision of the Court of Justice in *Bork*, to which reference is made in the Opinions in *Litster*, demonstrates that in the interpretation of Community law the Court of Justice places greater emphasis on the purpose of the legislation, and on its underlying policy, than on literal interpretation. Placing emphasis on purpose and policy obviously has greater utility where, as in the case of articles of Community treaties and many directives, legislation is drafted in terms of economic and social objectives and words and phrases are not closely defined. Also, the value of literal interpretation is limited where there are authoritative texts of legislation in different languages (*e.g.* Case 9179 *Worsdorfer* [1979] E.C.R. 2717; Case 80/76 *N. Kerry Milk Products Ltd* [1977] E.C.R. 425; Case 150/80 *Elefanten Schuh v. Jacqmain* [1981] E.C.R. 1671; Case 13/83 *European Parliament v. European Council* [1986] 1 C.M.L.R. 138).

In considering the purpose and policy of legislation, the Court of Justice makes greater use of *travaux préparatoires* than U.K. courts. In Case 71/76 *Thieffry* [1977] E.C.R. 765, as an aid to interpretation the Court referred to a programme of proposals for eliminating discrimination which had been adopted by the Council of Ministers; and it frequently refers to explanatory notes of nomenclature in cases concerning the interpretation of the Community common customs tariff (*e.g.* Case 22/76 *Import Gadgets* [1976] E.C.R. 1371). However, the Court will not normally consider debates in the European Parliament as an aid to interpretation of Community legislation (Case 136/79 *National Panasonic (U.K.) Ltd v. E.C. Commission* [1980] E.C.R. 2033 at 2066 2067, *per* A.G. Warner; *cf.* Case 29169 *Stauder v. City of Ulm* [1969] E.C.R. 419), although it has referred to debates in the national parliaments of Member States when interpreting Community treaties (*e.g.* Case 6/60 *Humblet* [1960] E.C.R. 559). The Court has also refused to consider a subsequent legislative proposal from the European Commission in interpreting Community legislation (Case 113/83 *Re Road Haulage Licences: E. C. Commission v. Italy* [1985] 3 C.M.L.R. 407, 422). Nor for purposes of interpretation will it rely on minuted reservations of a Member State in its negotiations on a directive or domestic rules of interpretation in a Member State (Case 143/83 *Re Equal Pay Concepts: E.C. Commission v. Denmark* [1986] 1 C.M.L.R. 44). On the interpretation of Community legislation, see also T. Millett, "Rules of Interpretation of E.E.C. Legislation" [1989] Stat.L.R. 163.

Arguably on the basis of the European Communities Act 1972, s. 3, in the United Kingdom, the emphasis on schematic and teleological interpretation adopted by the Court of Justice must be adopted in the construction of Community legislation (*e.g. H.P. Bulmer Ltd v. J. Bollinger SA* [1974] Ch. 401; *R. v. Henn* [1981] A.C. 901; *Customs & Excise Commissioners v. Ap.S. Samex* [1983] 1 All E.R. 1042) and of domestic legislation implementing Community legislation (*e.g. Litster v. Forth Dry Dock and Engineering Co. Ltd* and *Pickstone v. Freemans plc*, both cited above), in preference to domestic rules of statutory interpretation. This may involve departure from accepted domestic rules on recourse to non-legislative materials in the interpretation of Community legislation. So, for example, in *O'Brien v. Sim-Chem Ltd* [1980] 1 W.L.R. 734, a background report issued by the Commission of the European Communities was considered in England to establish the legal effect of a directive.

B. EUROPEAN CONVENTION ON THE PROTECTION OF HUMAN RIGHTS AND FUNDAMENTAL FREEDOMS

The substantive provisions of the European Convention on Human Rights as they apply in the United Kingdom have effectively been incorporated into U.K. domestic law by the Human Rights Act 1998 (see Chapter 6). The Act requires U.K. primary and subordinate legislation to be read and given effect in a way which is compatible with these "Convention rights", "so far as it is possible to do so" (s. 3(1)), and in determining the scope of a "Convention right" U.K. courts and tribunals must take into account the jurisprudence of the European Court of Human Rights, opinions of the European Commission on Human Rights and decisions of the Committee of Ministers of the Council of Europe (s. 2).

Human Rights Act 1998, ss. 2, 3

"2.—(1) A court or tribunal determining a question which has arisen in connection with a Convention right must take into account any—

(a) judgment, decision, declaration or advisory opinion of the European Court of Human Rights,
(b) opinion of the Commission given in a report adopted under Article 31 of the Convention
(c) decision of the Commission in connection with Article 26 or 27(2) of the Convention, or
(d) decision of the Committee of Ministers taken under Article 46 of the Convention

whenever made or given, so far as, in the opinion of the court or tribunal, it is relevant to the proceedings in which that question has arisen.

(2) Evidence of any judgment, decision, declaration or opinion of which account may have to be taken under this section is to be given in proceedings before any court or tribunal in such manner as may be provided by rules.

(3) In this section "rules" means rules of court or, in the case of proceedings before a tribunal, rules made for the purposes of this section—

(a) by the Lord Chancellor or the Secretary of State, in relation to any proceedings outside Scotland; or
(b) by the Secretary of State, in relation to proceedings in Scotland. . . .

Interpretation of legislation

3.—(1) So far as it is possible to do so, primary legislation and subordinate legislation must be read and given effect in a way which is compatible with the Convention rights.

(2) This section—

(a) applies to primary legislation and subordinate legislation whenever enacted;
(b) does not affect the validity, continuing operation or enforcement of any incompatible legislation; and

(c) does not affect the validity, continuing operation or enforcement of any incompatible subordinate legislation if (disregarding any possibility of revocation) primary legislation prevents removal of the incompatability".

[The references in section 2(1) to Articles of the European Convention are to those Articles as they have effect before the entry into force of the 11th Protocol to the Convention and the references to reports and decisions of the Commission and the decisions of the Committee of Ministers include reports or decisions made under transitional provisions of the 11th Protocol: s. 21(2)–(4).]

C. LEGISLATION OF THE SCOTTISH PARLIAMENT AND SUBORDINATE LEGISLATION OF THE SCOTTISH EXECUTIVE

The Scotland Act 1998 prescribes the legislative competence of the Scottish Parliament (ss. 28, 29), although the grant of this legislative competence "does not affect the power of the Parliament of the United Kingdom to make laws for Scotland" (s. 28(7)). Reserved matters are specified in Schedule 5, but there are specified scheduled enactments which may not be modified by the Scottish Parliament (Schedule 4). Similarly, the devolved competence of the Scottish Executive includes the making, confirming and approving of subordinate legislation (ss. 53, 54). Whether such primary or subordinate legislation is within this legislative competence is a "devolution issue" which may fall to be determined by courts and tribunals in Scotland, in England and Wales, and in Northern Ireland. The procedures for such a determination are set out in Schedule 6 to the Act.

Of particular significance in the present context, such a primary and subordinate legislation is to be read and given effect, so far as possible, so as to be within the competence of the Scottish Parliament and the Scottish Executive (s. 101). This statutory provision would also apply to statements by a member of the Scottish Executive in charge of a Bill that it was within the legislative competence of the Parliament and decisions by the presiding officer of the Parliament that Bills were within its legislative competence (s. 31), pre-Royal Assent determination by the Judicial Committee of the Privy Council on whether a Bill was within the legislative competence of the Scottish Parliament (s. 33) and presumably determinations by the Secretary of State in respect of both primary and subordinate legislation (ss. 35, 38).

Scotland Act 1998, ss. 29–30, 53–54

"29.—(1) An Act of the Scottish Parliament is not law so far as any provision of the Act is outside the legislative competence of the Parliament.

(2) A provision is outside that competence so far as any of the following paragraphs apply—

(a) it would form part of the law of a country or territory other than Scotland, or confer or remove functions exercisable otherwise than in or as regards Scotland,

(b) it relates to reserved matters,

(c) it is in breach of the restrictions in Schedule 4,

(d) it is incompatible with any of the Convention rights or with Community law, or
(e) it would remove the Lord Advocate from his position as head of the systems of criminal prosecution and investigation of deaths in Scotland.

(3) For the purposes of this section, the question whether a provision of an Act of the Scottish Parliament relates to a reserved matter is to be determined, subject to subsection (4), by reference to the purpose of the provision, having regard (among other things) to its effect in all the circumstances.

(4) A provision which—
(a) would otherwise not relate to reserved matters, but
(b) makes modifications of Scots private law, or Scots criminal law, as it applies to reserved matters,

is to be treated as relating to reserved matters, unless the purpose of the provision is to make the law in question apply consistently to reserved matters and otherwise.

30.—(1) Schedule 5 (which defines reserved matters) shall have effect.

(2) Her Majesty may by Order in Council make any modifications of Schedule 4 or 5 which She considers necessary or expedient.

(3) Her Majesty may by Order in Council specify functions which are to be treated, for such purposes of this Act as may be specified, as being, or as not being, functions which are exercisable in or as regards Scotland.

(4) An Order in Council under this section may also make such modifications of—
(a) any enactment or prerogative instrument (including any enactment comprised in or made under this Act), or
(b) any other instrument or document,

as Her Majesty considers necessary or expedient in connection with other provision made by the Order.

. . .

53.—(1) The functions mentioned in subsection (2) shall, so far as they are exercisable within devolved competence, be exercisable by the Scottish Ministers instead of by a Minister of the Crown.

(2) Those functions are—
(a) those of Her Majesty's prerogative and other executive functions which are exercisable on behalf of Her Majesty by a Minister of the Crown,
(b) other functions conferred on a Minister of the Crown by a prerogative instrument, and
(c) functions conferred on a Minister of the Crown by any pre-commencement enactment,

but do not include any retained functions of the Lord Advocate.

(3) In this Act, 'pre-commencement enactment' means—
(a) an Act passed before or in the same session as this Act and any other enactment made before the passing of this Act,
(b) an enactment made, before the commencement of this section, under such an Act or such other enactment,
(c) subordinate legislation under section 106, to the extent that the legislation states that it is to be treated as a pre-commencement enactment.

(4) This section and section 54 are modified by Part III of Schedule 4.

54.—(1) References in this Act to the exercise of a function being within or outside devolved competence are to be read in accordance with this section.

(2) It is outside devolved competence—

(a) to make any provision by subordinate legislation which would be outside the legislative competence of the Parliament if it were included in an Act of the Scottish Parliament, or

(b) to confirm or approve any subordinate legislation containing such provision.

(3) In the case of any function other than a function of making, confirming or approving subordinate legislation, it is outside devolved competence to exercise the function (or exercise it in any way) so far as a provision of an Act of the Scottish Parliament conferring the function (or, as the case may be, conferring it so as to be exercisable in that way) would be outside the legislative competence of the Parliament."

D. GENERAL STATUTORY RULES OF INTERPRETATION

Interpretation Act 1978, ss. 6–11

"6. In any Act, unless the contrary intention appears,—

(a) words importing the masculine gender include the feminine;

(b) words importing the feminine gender include the masculine;

(c) words in the singular include the plural and words in the plural include the singular.

7. Where an Act authorises or requires any document to be served by post (whether the expression 'serve' or the expression 'give' or 'send' or any other expression is used) then, unless the contrary intention appears, the service is deemed to be effected by properly addressing, pre-paying and posting a letter containing the document and, unless the contrary is proved, to have been effected at the time at which the letter would be delivered in the ordinary course of post.

8. In the measurement of any distance for the purpose of an Act, that distance shall, unless the contrary intention appears, be measured in a straight line on a horizontal plane.

9. Subject to section 3 of the Summer Time Act 1972 (construction of reference to points of time during the period of summer time), whenever an expression of time occurs in an Act, the time referred to shall, unless it is otherwise specifically stated, be held to be Greenwich mean time.

10. In any Act a reference to the Sovereign reigning at the time of the passing of the Act is to be construed, unless the contrary intention appears, as a reference to the Sovereign for the time being.

11. Where an Act confers power to make subordinate legislation, expressions used in that legislation have, unless the contrary intention appears, the meaning which they bear in the Act."

(For examples of the use of these provisions see *Skinner v. Patience*, 1982 S.L.T. (Sh. Ct) 81, *Adam v. Secretary of State for Scotland* 300, 1988 S.L.T. OH. For their application to legislation enacted before the 1978 Act came into force, see Sched. 2, Pt I. The provisions also apply to the interpretation of subordinate legislation made after 1978 (s. 23(1)), except s. 9 which applies to subordinate legislation whenever made (Sched. 2).)

The Interpretation Act 1978 makes provision for the enactment and operation of legislation. As the extract illustrates, it also contains some general rules applicable in Great Britain for the interpretation of legislation enacted by the U.K. Parliament. However, these rules are not broad principles of statutory interpretation and the Act does not provide a comprehensive code for the interpretation of legislation.

In general, the rules that are in the Act only apply where no "contrary intention appears" in the legislation to be interpreted: *e.g. R. v. Brentwood Justices, ex p. Nicholls* [1992] 1 A.C. 1. A court may infer a contrary intention for a part of a definition only (*e.g. Starke and anor (executors of Brown (decd) v. IRC* [1996] 1 All E.R. 622) or in respect of the certain provisions of the Act in which the defined word is used (*e.g. Shimiza (U.K.) Ltd v. Westminster City Council* [1997] 1 All E.R. 481). The courts may, in practice, infer a contrary intention if the rules do not resolve the problem of interpretation. In *Prior v. Sovereign Chicken Ltd* [1984] 1 W.L.R. 921, 928, Oliver L.J. observed, "I cannot for my part make sense of the provisions of the two sections . . . if . . . the provisions of section 6 of the Interpretation Act 1978 are applied to them". See generally, H. M. Thornton "Contrary Intention" (1994) 15 Stat.L.R. 182.

The rules may also be too limited in scope to assist interpretation. Section 7 applies to service of documents by post, but has been held not to apply where a statute does not refer to posting documents: *House v. Emerson Electric Industrial Controls* [1980] I.C.R. 795. Sometimes the Act is ignored by courts when assistance might have been derived from the rules it contains, *e.g. Aikman v. White*, 1985 S.L.T. 535.

In 1969 the Law Commissions recommended a broad approach to interpretation, and included in their report draft legislation which, following the practice of some Commonwealth countries, would have put the major principles of interpretation on a statutory basis (Law Com. No. 21; Scot. Law Com. No. 11 (H.C. 256, 1968/69)). In 1975, the views of the Law Commissions received the support of the Renton Committee on the Preparation of Legislation (Cmnd. 6053). In 1980 and 1981, private members' Bills based on the Law Commissions' proposals were introduced by Lord Scarman but were not enacted. (See 405 H.L. Deb, cols 276–306 (February 13, 1980); 418 H.L. Deb, cols. 64–83, 1341–1347; 419 H.L. Deb, cols 518, 796–797 (March 9 and 26, April 7 and 13, 1981)).

E. STATUTORY DEFINITIONS

A word or phrase may be defined by statute (for an excellent survey, see W.A. Wilson, "The Complexity of Statutes" (1974) 37 M.L.R. 497). A statutory definition may extend the ordinary meaning of a word: "'horse' includes ass or mule" (Animal Health Act 1981, s. 89(1)). On the other hand, it may restrict ordinary meaning: "'animal' does not include bird or fish" (Food Act 1984, s. 132(1)). The definition may give a word or phrase a precise meaning or illustrate it by examples. It may be generally applicable or have a limited applicability.

Interpretation Act 1978, s. 5 and Sched. 1

"5. In any Act, unless the contrary intention appears, words and expressions listed in Schedule 1 to this Act are to be construed according to that Schedule.

SCHEDULE 1

'Month' means calendar month. [1850] . . .
'Registered medical practitioner' means a fully registered person within the meaning of the Medical Act 1983. [January 1, 1979] . . .
'Secretary of State' means one of Her Majesty's Principal Secretaries of State.
'Sheriff' in relation to Scotland, includes sheriff principal. [1889] . . .
'Writing' includes typing, printing, lithography, photography and other modes of representing or reproducing words in a visible form, and expressions referring to writing are construed accordingly."

[These definitions apply to statutes passed after the date or year specified and where no year or date is specified, to all statutes (Sched. 2, para. 4(1); in the absence of contrary intention, they also apply in the same way to subordinate legislation made after 1978 (s. 23(1)).]

Zoo Licensing Act 1981, ss. 1, 21

"1. . . . (2) In this Act 'zoo' means an establishment where wild animals (as defined by section 21) are kept for exhibition to the public otherwise than for purposes of a circus (as so defined) and otherwise than in a pet shop (as so defined); and this Act applies to any zoo to which members of the public have access, with or without charge for admission, on more than seven days in any period of 12 consecutive months . . .

21.—(1). In this Act—

'animals' means animals of the classes Mammalia, Aves, Reptilia, Amphibia, Pisces and Insecta and any other multicellular organism that is not a plant or a fungus and 'wild animals' means animals not normally domesticated in Great Britain;

'circus' means a place where animals are kept or introduced wholly or mainly for the purpose of performing tricks or manoeuvres at that place; . . .

'pet shop' means premises for whose keeping as a pet shop a licence is in force, or is required, under the Pet Animals Act 1951 . . ."

A statutory definition is normally binding, unless its application would be contrary to the purpose of the legislation (*Strathern v. Padden* 1926 J.C. 9; *cf. Savoy Hotel Co. v. L.C.C.* [1900] 1 Q.B. 665).

Definitions of limited application are usually contained in one or more interpretation sections, but they may be elsewhere in the statute (*e.g.* Zoo Licensing Act 1981), and authoritative definitions may be included in a glossary of expressions (*e.g.* Social Security Act 1975, s. 168(1), Sched. 20).

A word or phrase may sometimes be defined in different ways in different parts of the same statute: see, for example, the definitions of "intestate estate" in the Succession (Scotland) Act 1964, ss. 1(2), 9(6)(a), 36(1) and (2), 37(1)(a) and (b), and of "container" in the Weights and Measures Act 1985, ss. 68(1), 94(1). In the Child Abduction and Custody Act 1985 the word "convention" refers to two different treaties in different parts of the Act: ss. 1(1), 12(1). The definition of "disease" in the Animal Health Act 1981, s. 88, is disapplied for the purposes of s. 32.

A definition in one statute may be incorporated by reference into another (*e.g.* the definition of "pet shop", above).

In addition to authoritative definitions, legislation may also provide examples and non-authoritative descriptions, as an aid to the user, which are not binding on the courts in interpreting the legislation (*e.g.* Consumer Credit Act 1974, s. 188 and Sched. 2; Wildlife and Countryside Act 1981, Scheds 2–6).

F. PRECEDENT

The interpretation of a word or phrase in legislation enacted in the United Kingdom is governed by precedent (see Chapter 14), and generally courts are reluctant to overrule their own previous decisions on questions of interpretation.

Walker v. Dick Engineering Co. (Coatbridge) Ltd 1985 S.L.T. 465

The pursuer averred that while cutting a piece of metal on a lathe, sharp cuttings from the metal emerged at speed and injured his hand. The Factories Act 1961, s. 14(1), provides that "every dangerous part of any machinery . . . shall be securely fenced . . ."

> **Lord Davidson**: ". . . the pursuer has averred a contravention by the defenders of s. 14(1) of the Factories Act 1961 . . . Counsel for the defenders presented two main arguments. In the first place he noted that . . . [I]t was well settled by the decisions cited that s. 14(1) of the Factories Act 1961 requires a distinction to be observed between the dangerous parts of a machine and the materials which are worked in that machine. In the present case the defect in the pursuer's pleadings was elementary, because plainly he was injured not by any part of the machine but by cuttings given off from the material worked on.
>
> The second argument advanced by counsel for the defenders was that the dangers against which the fencing legislation was designed to protect the operator were limited. In particular, the decisions previously referred to laid down that there was no obligation to fence part of a machine in order to prevent material emerging or being ejected by it so as to cause injury. In the present case the pursuer did not aver that his body made contact with any part of the machine. His complaint was that he was injured by a piece of material which projected from the machine. Accordingly, on that separate ground, his case was irrelevant.
>
> In my opinion the submissions made by counsel for the defenders are well founded in law. In *Johnson v. F.E. Callow (Engineers) Ltd* [1971] A.C. at p. 343, after reviewing the main authorities relating to the protection afforded

by s. 14 of the Factories Act 1961, Lord Hailsham L.C. said this: 'No-one contemplating the situation set up by this series of decisions can wholly avoid the conclusion reached by Holroyd Pearce, L.J., . . . that the gap in the protection afforded by the statute is one "which neither logic nor common sense appears to justify". It is however too late for the courts to close the gap. The gap can only be closed by legislation or to some extent by the use of the regulatory powers of the minister. It has, however, to be said that I for one would be slow to enlarge the gap or to extend the ambit of the criticised decisions beyond the limits required by the fact of the cases concerned and the reasoning of the judgments in them.' Counsel for the pursuer maintained that the pursuer's pleadings in the present case fall on the right side of the gap. I do not agree."

[See also *R. v. National Insurance Commissioner, ex p. Hudson* [1972] A.C. 944; *Carter v. Bradbeer* [1975] 1 W.L.R. 1204, 1206–1207.]

Over a period of time, where a statutory provision is re-enacted on a number of occasions and may be interpreted by numerous courts, the operation of precedent may not be particularly helpful in clarifying the law. Lord Johnstone described precedents on the interpretation of the Employment Rights Act 1996, s. 123, and precursors of the provision over a 20–year period as "chaotic" (*Hoggie v. Uniroyal Englebert Tyres Ltd* (Edinburgh EAT, May 8, 1998).

However, a decision on interpretation in one statute is merely persuasive where the same word or phrase falls to be interpreted in another statute (*Carter v. Bradbeer, above; Royal Court Derby Porcelain Co. Ltd v. Raymond Russell* [1949] 2 K.B. 417). This is so even where a statute re-enacts a word or phrase which was judicially interpreted in earlier legislation (*Kelly v. MacKinnon* 1982 S.C.C.R. 205, 211–212; *R. v. Chard* [1984] A.C. 279, 291, 294, 295).

The operation of the doctrine of precedent in questions of interpretation depends on the jurisdiction of the court and on the nature of the legislation. Thus, a decision on a question of interpretation by the House of Lords in a Scottish appeal is binding on courts in Scotland. Such a decision in an English civil appeal is similarly binding where the legislation applies in both Scotland and England (*Dalgleish v. Glasgow Corporation* 1976 S.C. 32; see Chap. 14). However, other decisions by courts elsewhere in the United Kingdom, including decisions of the House of Lords in English criminal appeals, are only persuasive in Scotland (*Dalgleish v. Glasgow Corporation*, above). This is so even where the decisions concern the interpretation of legislation which also applies in Scotland or which is legislation parallel to that applying in Scotland (*cf. Viewpoint Housing Association v. Lothian Regional Council, The Scotsman*, November 6, 1991 OH and *Forest Hills Trossachs Club v. Assessor for Central Region* 1991 S.L.T. Lands Tr. 42; *cf. Ross v. Davy* 1996 S.C.L.R. 369, *Clydebank District Council v. Keeper of the Registers of Scotland* 1994 (Lands Tr.), S.L.T. 1, *Morgan Guaranty Trust Company of New York v. Lothian Regional Council* 1984 S.C.L.R. 213, *Armour v. Anderson* 1994 S.C.L.R. 642, *Bradley v. Motherwell District Council* 1994 S.L.T. 739, *Friel (Procurator Fiscal, Paisley) v. Contract Services Ltd* 1993 S.C.C.R. 675).

Criminal legislation applying to both Scotland and England may receive divergent interpretation in the two jurisdictions (*e.g. Kelly v. MacKinnon* 1982 S.C.C.R. 205; *cf. R. v. Freeman* [1970] 1 W.L.R. 788); this is clearly undesirable and, where it does arise, judges seek to rectify it (*e.g. Allan v. Patterson* 1980 J.C. 57; *R. v. Murphy* [1980] Q.B. 434; *R. v. Lawrence* [1982] A.C. 510; *Keane v. Gallacher* 1980 J.C. 77; *R. v. Carver* [1978] Q.B. 472; *R. v. Boyesen* [1982] A.C. 768; *Re B* 1996 S.C.L.R. 874).

Certainly, in both jurisdictions courts will seek to give uniform interpretation to fiscal legislation which applies throughout the United Kingdom.

***Lord Advocate v. Earl of Moray's Trustees* (1905) 7 F. 116, HL**

The case concerned the interpretation of the Finance Act 1894, on a Scottish appeal.

> **Lord MacNaghten**: "I am not at all insensible to the grave difficulties which have been pointed out so forcibly by the learned Judges in Scotland. But I cannot think that those difficulties are insuperable. It must be borne in mind that the Act which your Lordships are now called upon to construe in its application to Scotland applies equally to the whole of the United Kingdom. It is a taxing Act. It must be presumed to have been the intention of Parliament to make the incidence of the taxation the same in Scotland as in England and Ireland, and to extend the same measure of relief, such as it is, to limited owners called upon to discharge a burthen on the inheritance wherever the property burthened may be situated.
>
> Your Lordships may remember that much the same sort of question arose in *Lord Saltoun's Case* (1860) 3 Macq. 659, which was referred to in this House not long ago in *Special Commissioners for Income-Tax v. Pemsel* [1891] A.C. 531. In *Lord Saltoun's Case* the Succession-Duty Act, 1853, came under consideration, and it was held by this House, reversing the judgment of the Court of Session, that an extrinsic technicality—a technical rule of Scotch feudal conveyancing—must be disregarded when its effect would be to produce inequality."

[See also *Commissioners for General Purposes of Income Tax for City of London v. Gibbs* [1942] A.C. 402, 414; *Secretary of State for Employment and Productivity v. Clarke Chapman & Co. Ltd*. [1971] 1 W.L.R. 1094.]

III. JUDICIAL PRINCIPLES AND INTERPRETATION

In interpreting legislation, judges may apply a variety of principles to the legislation unless the legislation expressly excludes them. So, when faced with a textual ambiguity in U.K. legislation, a court will adopt an interpretation which is in accord with international law in preference to one which is not (*e.g. Mortensen v. Peters* (1906) 8 F.(J.) 93), and will often give a strict construction to penal legislation (*e.g. H.M. Advocate v. R.M.* 1969 J.C. 52). However, not all questions of interpretation concern textual ambiguity. A court may resolve such questions by applying principles which may affect the substance of the application of the legislation. Examples of the application of such principles are given below.

***Sweet v. Parsley* [1970] A.C. 132**

The Dangerous Drugs Act 1965, s. 5 provided:

"If a person—(a) being the occupier of any premises, permits those premises to be used for the purpose of smoking . . . cannabis resin . . . or (b) is concerned in the management of any premises used for such purpose as aforesaid; he shall be guilty of an offence . . . "

Miss Sweet let rooms in a farmhouse to tenants who, unbeknown to her, smoked cannabis. Cannabis was found in the farmhouse and she was charged and convicted under section 5(b) of the 1965 Act. On appeal, one question before the court was whether a section 5(b) offence could be committed by a person without some blameworthy state of mind, *mens rea*.

Lord Reid: "Our first duty is to consider the words of the Act; if they show a clear intention to create an absolute offence that is an end of the matter. But such cases are very rare. Sometimes the words of the section which creates a particular offence make it clear that *mens rea* is required in one form or another. Such cases are quite frequent. But in a very large number of cases there is no clear indication either way. In such cases there has for centuries been a presumption that Parliament did not intend to make criminals of persons who were in no way blameworthy in what they did. That means that whenever a section is silent as to *mens rea* there is a presumption that, in order to give effect to the will of Parliament, we must read in words appropriate to require *mens rea*."

(The presumption may be displaced by the subject matter of the statutory provision (see *Sherras v. De Rutzen* [1895] 1 Q.B. 918; *R. v. Bradish* [1990] 1 Q.B. 981 (possession of a weapon, a canister of CS gas); *Chichester DC. v. Silvester*, DC, *The Times*, May 6, 1992 (organisation and management of an "acid house" party)) and may not be applicable where the statutory provision does not create a criminal offence (*Customs and Excise Commissioners v. Air Canada* [1991] 2 Q.B. 446).)

***Malloch v. Aberdeen Corporation* 1971 S.C. 85, HL**

Lord Reid: "The right of a man to be heard in his own defence is the most elementary protection of all and, where a statutory form of protection would be less effective if it did not carry with it a right to be heard, I would not find it difficult to imply this right. Here it appears to me that there is a plain implication to that effect in the . . . Act. The terms of that Act have been altered by later legislation, but I can find nothing in any later Act which can reasonably be interpreted as taking away that elementary right."

***Brown v. Magistrates of Edinburgh* 1931 S.L.T. 456**

Lord Mackay: ". . . it is common ground that in [England] all statutes are enforceable, however antiquated, until repealed, and never fall into desuetude. It is also common that that is not true of the older Scots statutes, but it is true of all Acts passed for Scotland by the common Legislature after 1707.

> A few words are needed on what desuetude means and requires . . . I hold it clear in law that desuetude requires for its operation a very considerable period, not merely of neglect, but of contrary usage of such a character as practically to infer such completely established habit of the community as to set up a counter law or establish a quasi-repeal . . . Erskine treats it as 'a posterior custom repealing or derogating from a statute'; and assigns his reason, 'for the contrary immemorial custom sufficiently presumes the will of the community to alter the law in all its clauses.' . . . My own disposition would be to think that very rarely, if ever, could a statute be judicially held by mere judicial knowledge to be in desuetude without averment of, and, if disputed, proof of, contrary custom."

The Statute Law Revision (Scotland) Acts 1906 and 1964 repealed many obsolete Acts of the Parliament of Scotland. There is a strong, but rebuttable, presumption that Scots Acts which remain in force are not in desuetude. See further, J.R. Philip, "Some reflections on desuetude" (1931) 43 J.R. 260; *DB. Britton v. R. Johnstone* (July 24, 1992, OH unreported).

***Kerr v. Marquis of Ailsa* (1854) 1 Macq. 736**

> **Lord Cranworth L.C.**: "My Lords, unless there be something in the language, context, or objects of an Act of Parliament showing a contrary intention, the duty and the practice of Courts of Justice is to presume, in conformity with the adage of Lord Coke, that the legislature enacts prospectively and not retrospectively. There may, however, be enactments that are evidently on the face of them by their language and subject-matter intended to be retrospective; and when such is the case, the maxim of Lord Coke must give way."

(See also *Gardner v. Lucas* (1878) 5 R. 105, HL.)

In *Wilson v. Wilson*, 1939 S.C. 102, it was held that the Divorce (Scotland) Act 1938, which introduced cruelty as a new ground for divorce, was retrospective to the extent that cruelty could be established by conduct which took place before the Act came into force. (See also *Santa Fe International Corp. v. Napier Shipping SA* 1985 S.L.T. 481; *Forbes v. Forbes* 1991 S.C.L.R. 389; *L'Office Cherifien des Phosphates v. Yamashita-Shinnihon Steamship Co. Ltd* [1994] 1 All E.R. 20.)

The argument that the Drug Offences Act 1986, s. 1(2), which required the court to determine whether a convicted person had benefited from drug trafficking, should be construed as an inquisitorial process was rejected by Stoughton L.J. in *R. v. Redbourne* [1993] 2 All E.R. 753, 758, where he observed "such a process, although favoured by some other nations, would be so foreign to our law that we would expect Parliament to say so expressly if it were intended".

IV. JUDICIAL RULES OF INTERPRETATION

The law of interpretation leaves considerable discretion to the judiciary. The attitude of judges to textual interpretation, as we have seen, depends to some extent on their perception of their constitutional rule. The spectrum of attitudes has been traditionally characterised by the emphasis placed on various rules of interpretation. The principal rules are the literal rule, the golden rule and the mischief rule.

A. THE LITERAL RULE

***R. v. Judge of the City of London Court* [1892] 1 Q.B. 273**

> **Lord Esher M.R.**: "If the words of an Act are clear, you must follow them, even though they lead to a manifest absurdity. The Court has nothing to do with the question whether the legislature has committed an absurdity."

***Black-Clawson International Ltd v. Papierwerke Waldhof-Aschaffenburg AG* [1975] A.C. 591**

> **Lord Diplock**: "The acceptance of the rule of law as a constitutional principle requires that a citizen, before committing himself to any course of action, should be able to know in advance what are the legal consequences that will flow from it. Where those consequences are regulated by a statute the source of that knowledge is what the statute says. In construing it the court must give effect to what the words of the statute would be reasonably understood to mean by those whose conduct it regulates."

The literal rule, as expressed by Lord Esher and given a modern justification by Lord Diplock, emphasises the plain, ordinary or literal meaning of words. Perhaps, in practice, the literal rule creates a rebuttable presumption that words bear their most obvious meaning (see *Saul v. Norfolk C.C.* [1984] Q.B. 559). However, in some of the applications of the rule there is an assumption that words are unambiguous and this is not always so.

B. THE GOLDEN RULE

***River Wear Commissioners v. Adamson* (1877) 2 App. Cas. 743**

> **Lord Blackburn**: ". . . we are able to take the whole statute together, and construe it all together, giving the words their ordinary signification, unless when so applied they produce an inconsistency, or an absurdity or inconvenience so great as to convince the Court that the intention could not have been to use them in their ordinary signification, and to justify the Court in putting on them some other significance, which, though less proper, is one which the Court thinks the words will bear."

(See also *Manson v. Duke of Westminster* [1981] Q.B. 323.)
The golden rule is, in reality, a gloss on the literal rule. It lays somewhat less emphasis on the plain meaning of words, but it offers no guidance on either identifying those inconsistencies, absurdities or inconveniences which permit a

departure from a particular meaning of words, or on choosing an alternative meaning.

C. THE MISCHIEF RULE

Maunsell v. Olins **[1975] A.C. 373**

> **Lord Simon of Glaisdale**: ". . . in construing an Act of Parliament, you identify the 'mischief' which the statute seeks to remedy (*i.e.*, in modern parlance the statutory objective), and so construe the statute that it advances the remedy and suppresses the mischief (*i.e.*, in modern parlance, in construing the statute you bear its objective in mind). It is, in other words, a positive and not a negative canon of construction; it enjoins a liberal, and not a restrictive, approach. For a court of construction to constrain statutory language which has a primary natural meaning appropriate in its context so as to give it an artificial meaning which is appropriate only to remedy the mischief which is conceived to have occasioned the statutory provision is to proceed unsupported by principle, inconsonant with authority and oblivious of the actual practice of parliamentary draftsmen."

The mischief rule, or purposive approach, may be traced to *Heydon's Case* (1584) 3 Co. Rep. 7a. Its modern use, and its limitations, are well described by Lord Simon. It places greater emphasis on the intention of the legislature and depends less on words having a plain meaning.

Where the emphasis on legislative intention in the face of a literal meaning is too great, it has been judicially criticised as "over-purposive" interpretation (*R. v. Popular Coroner, ex p. Thomas* [1993] 2 All E.R. 381, 387, *per* Dillon L.J.). Sometimes the judge cannot identify the "mischief" at all (*Re K (a minor) (adoption: nationality)* [1994] 3 All E.R. 353, 557). Finally, the mischief rule offers little guidance as to when it is appropriate to depart from the legislative text and on how the intention of the legislature should be established. Where the "mischief" which the legislature intends to remedy is identified, there may still be difficult questions as to how, and to what extent, the legislature has remedied it (*e.g. Knowles v. Liverpool City Council* [1993] 4 All E.R. 321).

V. INTERPRETATION IN PRACTICE

The three rules described in the last section have much in common. They all place a primary emphasis on the legislative text and recognise the possibility of legislative inconsistency or absurdity. This has led some commentators to suggest that there is only one rule of interpretation, which is a conflation of the three rules (see E.A. Driedger, *The Construction of Statutes*, 1974, p. 67). The argument may be presented in more utilitarian form, by suggesting that exclusive reliance on any of the three rules is of limited value. Judges frequently resort to all three in interpretation or, having formed a view by using one rule, resort to other rules to confirm their view.

Using any of the three rules in an absolute manner also has a limited utility, because each leaves unresolved a range of practical problems. The use made of them depends on the nature of the question before the court. Judges may resolve questions of interpretation by examining a statutory word or phrase in its linguistic, grammatical and legal context. In doing so, they may turn to dictionaries, legal dictionaries and other reference works. So, for example, in *Reed International Ltd v. I.R.C.* [1976] A.C. 336, 359, Lord Wilberforce referred to *Palgrave's Dictionary of Political Economy* of 1896 to determine the meaning of "funded debt". And dictionaries have been consulted by the House of Lords for the scope of "inability" (*Stewart v. Secretary of State for Scotland* 1998 S.C.L.R. 332), by the High Court of Justiciary for a definition of "prostitute" (*White v. Allan*, 1985 S.L.T. 396), by the Inner House for the meaning of "reciprocal" (*Nicoll (Liquidator of RDM (Contracts) Ltd) v. Steelpress (Supplies) Ltd* 1992 S.C.L.R. 332), and by the Lands Tribunal for the meaning of "shopping mall" (*Sunblest Bakeries Ltd. v. Assessor for Strathclyde Region* 1990 S.L.T. Lands Tr 76). (See generally W.A. Wilson, *Introductory Essays on Scots Law* (2nd ed.), pp. 97–98.) Use may also be made of textbooks and of commentaries on the statute concerned (*e.g. Bastin v. Davies* [1950] 2 K.B. 579; *Allan v. Patterson* 1980 J.C. 57; *Hardy v. Robinson* 1985 S.L.T. (Sh. Ct) 40.

In interpreting in linguistic, grammatical or legal context the courts may be seen to be adopting a literal approach to interpretation, albeit in a modified form. However, in many instances, interpretation in context also involves consideration of the purpose of the legislation, in effect using the mischief rule. Where interpretation in context fails to resolve an ambiguity, more reliance may then be placed on establishing the purpose of the legislation. In recent years there has been an increasing emphasis on the purposive approach to interpretation in U.K. courts. This may be a consequence of the many multinational treaties which are now incorporated into domestic law by legislation, and also of membership of the European Communities. Certainly, the Court of Justice of the Communities places considerable emphasis on the purposive approach, and the same is true of courts in the United States and many European and Commonwealth countries.

A. LINGUISTIC CONTEXT

***Maunsell v. Olins* [1975] A.C. 373**

A landlord sought to recover possession of a farm cottage. The case turned on whether the farm fell within "premises" as defined in the Rent Act 1968, s. 18(5).

> **Lord Simon of Glaisdale**: "Statutory language, like all language is capable of an almost infinite gradation of 'register'—*i.e.*, it will be used at the semantic level appropriate to the subject matter and to the audience addressed (the man in the street, lawyers, merchants, etc.). It is the duty of a court of construction to tune in to such register and so to interpret the statutory language as to give to it the primary meaning which is appropriate in that register (unless it is clear that some other meaning must be given in order to

carry out the statutory purpose or to avoid injustice, anomaly, absurdity or contradiction). In other words, statutory language must always be given presumptively the most natural and ordinary meaning which is appropriate in the circumstances . . .

The subject matter of the legislation under your Lordships' instance considered provides an example of what we mean by language having various 'registers.' In popular parlance 'landlord' can mean 'innkeeper'—indeed, even 'lessee from a brewery.' But in ordinary legal parlance, which is, we think, the appropriate register of language in legislation dealing with rent restriction and security of leasehold tenure, 'landlord' presumptively means 'lessor', and it would take a good deal to displace the presumption. Similarly, in popular parlance 'premises' can mean 'building.' But in ordinary legal parlance 'premises' means 'the subject matter of a letting.' Or, even higher in the register, if the Rent Act 1968 is considered as dealing with legal technicalities, 'premises' presumptively bears its most ordinary meaning as a term of art—namely, the subject matter of the habendum clause of the relevant lease."

***Mills v. Cooper* [1967] 2 Q.B. 459**

Section 127 of the Highways Act 1959 provided, *inter alia*: "If, without lawful authority or excuse . . . (c) a hawker or other itinerant trader or a gipsy pitches a booth, a stall or stand, or encamps, on a highway, he shall be guilty of an offence . . ." The respondent was charged that, he, being a gipsy, did without lawful excuse or authority encamp on the highway contrary to section 127. The magistrates dismissed the charge on the ground that they were not satisfied that the respondent was a gipsy. On appeal the court had to consider the proper meaning to be given to the term "gipsy".

Diplock L.J.: "I agree that the word 'gipsy' as used in s. 127(c) the Highways Act, 1959, cannot bear its dictionary meaning of a member of a wandering race (by themselves called Romany) of Hindu origin. If it did, it would mean that Parliament in 1959 had amended the corresponding section of the Highway Act, 1835, (1) which referred to 'gipsy or other person' so as to discriminate against persons by reason of their racial origin alone. It would raise other difficulties too. How pure blooded a Romany must one be to fall into the definition? . . . As members of this race first appeared in England not later than the beginning of the sixteenth century, and have not in the intervening centuries been notorious for the abundance of their written records, it would be impossible to prove Romany origin even as far back as the sixteenth century, let alone through the earlier centuries of their peripatetic history from India to the shores of this island. The section, so far as it referred to 'gipsy', would be incapable in practice of having any application at all. Confronted by these difficulties, [counsel for the respondent] only faintly argues that the word 'gipsy' in the context of the section does not bear its popular meaning, which I would define as a person without fixed abode who leads nomadic life, dwelling in tents or other shelters, or in caravans or other vehicles. If this meaning is adopted, it follows that being a gipsy is not an unalterable status. It cannot be said 'once a gipsy always a gipsy'. By changing his way of life a modern Borrow may be a gipsy at one time and not a gipsy at another . . ."

(See also *Blankley v. Godley* [1952] 1 All E.R. 436.)

***Fisher v. Bell* [1961] 1 Q.B. 394**

The defendant displayed a flick-knife, with a price-ticket, in his shop-window. He appealed against a conviction under the Restriction of Offensive Weapons Act 1959, s. 1(1), which provided that any person "who manufactures, sells or hires or offers for sale or hire, or gives to any person" a flick-knife, commits an offence.

> **Lord Parker**: "The sole question is whether the exhibition of that knife in the window with the ticket constituted an offer for sale within the statute. I confess that I think most lay people and, indeed, I myself when I first read the papers, would be inclined to the view that to say that if a knife was displayed in a window like that with a price attached to it was not offering it for sale was just nonsense. In ordinary language it is there inviting people to buy it, and it is for sale; but any statute must of course be looked at in the light of the general law of the country. Parliament in its wisdom in passing an Act must be taken to know the general law. It is perfectly clear that according to the ordinary law of contract the display of an article with a price on it in a shop window is merely an invitation to treat. It is in no sense an offer for sale the acceptance of which constitutes a contract. That is clearly the general law of the country. Not only is that so, but it is to be observed that in many statutes and orders which prohibit selling and offering for sale of goods it is very common when it is so desired to insert the words 'offering or exposing for sale', 'exposing for sale' being clearly words which would cover the display of goods in a shop window. Not only that, but it appears that under several statutes—we have been referred in particular to the Prices of Goods Act, 1939, and the Goods and Services (Price Control) Act, 1941—Parliament, when it desires to enlarge the ordinary meaning of those words, includes a definition section enlarging the ordinary meaning of "offer for sale" to cover other matters including, be it observed, exposure of goods for sale with the price attached.
>
> In those circumstances I am driven to the conclusion, though I confess reluctantly, that no offence was here committed. At first sight it sounds absurd that knives of this sort cannot be manufactured, sold, hired, lent, or given, but apparently they can be displayed in shop windows; but even if this—and I am by no means saying it is—is a *casus omissus* it is not for this court to supply the omission."

Determining the linguistic context of a word or phrase has limitations as an aid to interpretation. By examining the linguistic context of the legislation, it was possible to prefer a non-technical meaning rather than a more precise technical meaning in *Mills v. Cooper*. However, as in *Fisher v. Bell* the linguistic context does not help to decide between an ordinary meaning and a technical legal meaning.

Another limitation is that a word or phrase may change its meaning over time. Interpretation may change with the change of meaning. For instance, the interpretation of "family" in the Rents Acts has been extended to include, in some instances, unmarried couples who live together (see chapter 14). However, in other cases, the courts have sought the meaning at the time of the enactment of legislation and applied that meaning in preference to a more modern meaning (*e.g. McKinlay v. McKinlay* (1851) 14 D. 162; *Scottish Cinema and Variety Theatres Ltd v. Ritchie* 1929 S.C. 350).

B. GRAMMATICAL CONTEXT

Judges may consider a word or phrase in its grammatical context as an aid to interpretation. In doing so, they can resort to a variety of maxims. So, they may apply the *ejusdem generis* rule: where general words follow more specific words with some common feature they will take their meaning from them. However, there may be uncertainty over whether there is a common feature (*e.g. Secretary of State for Social Security v. McSherry* 1995 S.L.T. 371). The maxim is often associated with the more general maxim *noscitur a sociis*—a thing is known from its associates. For example, in construing the Offences Against the Person Act 1828, which made it a felony in England to shoot at or to "stab, cut or wound" any person, the word "wound" was held to be restricted by the preceding words to injuries inflicted by an instrument, and not to include biting off a finger (*R. v. Harris* (1836) 7 C. & P. 446; *cf. Mortimer v. Samuel B. Allison Ltd* 1959 S.C. 1, HL).

Another maxim which is frequently applied is *expressio unius est exclusio alterius*—to mention one or more things of a particular class can be regarded as excluding other things in the same class. Consequently, where the Poor Relief Act 1601 in England imposed a poor rate on the occupiers of "lands", houses, tithes and "coal mines", it was held that as coal mines were expressly mentioned, "land" did not include other types of mine (*R. v. Inhabitants of Sedgley* (1831) 2 B. & Ad. 65). The maxim will not be applied, however, where the court considers something has been inadvertently omitted from the legislation (*e.g. Stevenson v. Hunter* (1903) 5 F. 761); or where its application conflicts with the purpose of the legislation (*e.g. Dean v. Wiesengrund* [1955] 2 Q.B. 120). See further, J.M. Keyes, "*Expressio Unius*: the Expression that Proves the Rule" [1989] Stat.L.R. 1.

However, the purpose of the statute may prevail over the normal grammatical context of a word. For example, "shall" normally has a mandatory connotation, but it may be interpreted as merely directory (*e.g. H.M. Advocate v. Graham* 1985 S.L.T. 498; *R. v. Sheer Metalcraft Ltd.* [1954] 1 Q.B. 586; *Petch v. Gurney (Inspector of Taxes)* [1994] 3 All E.R. 731). Similarly, "must" is usually mandatory and "may" directory, but "may" is sometimes interpreted as mandatory (*e.g. Baron Inchyra v. Jennings (Inspector of Taxes)* [1965] 2 All E.R. 714 at p. 723 *per* Pennycuick J.). Again "and" is normally interpreted as conjunctive and "or" as disjunctive (*e.g. Docherty v. Stakis Hotels* 1991 S.C.C.R. 6), but not where it conflicts with the purpose of the legislation (*e.g. John G. Stein & Co. Ltd v.*

O'Hanlon [1965] A.C. 890 at p. 904 *per* Lord Reid; *R. v. Oakes* [1959] 2 Q.B. 350; *Re H (a minor) (foreign custody order: enforcement)* [1994] 1 All E.R. 812).

C. LEGAL CONTEXT

The courts will interpret a statutory provision in its legal context. Lord MacFadyen, interpreting the Insolvency Act 1986, s. 60(1)(c), considered not only the general scope of the Act, but also the development of receivership in English law and the purpose of adopting it in Scots law (*Roger Lindop v. Stuart Noble & Sons* April 7, 1998, unreported).

Certainly, the legal context commonly includes considering the text of the legislation as a whole, other elements of the legislation and other legislation enacted both previously and subsequently.

1. The Whole Text

***Shepherd v. Pearson Engineering Services (Dundee) Ltd* 1980 S.C. 268**

The pursuer sustained injuries while he was employed replacing lights on the superstructure of a ship. He sued his employers and argued that they had failed to comply with the Construction (Working Places) Regulations 1966. The argument depended on his work being "work of engineering construction" as defined in the Factories Act 1961 and in regulations made in 1960. The definition included work on "any steel or reinforced concrete structure." One question before the court was whether a ship could be a "steel . . . structure."

> **Lord Cameron**: "The steel structure was a ship according to the pursuer's argument and this argument is crucial . . . Literally considered and even without reference to their context and the purposes the specific regulations are designed to serve, the words 'steel structure' could or might be construed as the pursuer would wish . . .
>
> But I do not think that this is a proper approach to the issue here. The question is not whether a ship can be properly described as a 'steel structure' in the abstract, but whether a ship is included within the meaning of 'work of engineering construction' as that is defined in the regulations founded upon and this required attention to be paid to the precise language of the relevant provisions as well as to the protective purposes of the legislation . . . Not only must the regulations founded upon be the lexicon from which the meaning of the words 'steel structure' is to be discovered but at the same time, as counsel for the defenders pointed out in the course of the debate, it is to be kept in view that the shipbuilding regulations of 1960 provide for the protection of workmen and place duties on employers of workmen in respect of access and plant in those circumstances in which it was reasonably to be expected that an employer could have some measure of control. Regulation 4 makes precise provision as to the various responsibilities of employers of workmen, dock operators, shipowners and shipmasters whose ships are

under construction, repair or refit in dock or harbour as docks and harbours are defined in the Merchant Shipping Act. Here is a code of conduct and obligation precisely defining duties of *inter alios* such persons as the defenders, in respect of matters which form the subject of the present proceedings. It appears to me that there was force in the defenders' arguments to the extent that here is a statutory code specifically referable to that type of operation which is in question, and that this fact is relevant when one has to consider the scope of definition in the regulation on which the pursuer founds. The definition of 'work of engineering construction' in s. 176(1) of the 1961 Act which contains no reference to 'steel structure' is detailed but certainly does not suggest that a ship under refit or repair would naturally fall within it unless it could be covered by regulations which so specified. When one turns to the regulation of 1960 and its Schedule—The Engineering Construction (Extension of Definition) Regulations 1960 (S.I. 1960 No. 421)—one finds it covered 'works to be included in the definition of the expression "work of engineering construction"' and opens with the words 'The construction, structural alteration or repair (including re-pointing and re painting) or the demolition of any of the following [other than in a defined factory or upon a railway or tramway]'. It goes on 'that is to say, any steel or reinforced concrete structure other than a building, any road, airfield, sea defence works or river works, and any other civil or constructional engineering works of a similar nature to any of the foregoing works.' In my opinion to deduce from this catalogue that ships are included *sub silentio* is an impossible task—the pursuer's argument to the contrary was only made plausible by ignoring the language of the Schedule itself and treating the words steel and structure as if the only structure covered by the Schedule were a steel structure. That however ignores the important words 'or reinforced concrete' which separate 'steel' from 'structure' in the Schedule. What therefore one has to interpret are the words 'steel or reinforced concrete structures' and not the simple words 'steel structure'. This in my view not only alters the sense, but gives a very clear indication of the meaning of the phrase and leads to the conclusion at which I arrive that a ship is not something which is buried within these words of extended definition of the phrase 'work of engineering construction'. I therefore reject the pursuer's construction of . . . the Construction (Working Places) Regulations 1966."

(See also *Parvin v. Morton Machine Co.* 1952 S.C. 9, HL; *MacPhail v. Tayside Regional Council* 1991 S.C.C.R. 370; *R. v. Crown Court at Knightsbridge, esp. Dunne* [1993] 4 All E.R. 491.)

Schedules to an Act, like sections, are enacted provisions; so substantive provisions in Schedules are interpreted in the same manner as other enacted provisions (see T. St J. N. Bates, "Schedules in Scotland" 1996 J.R. 77). The long title of a statute may be used as an aid to interpretation (*e.g. Ayr v. St Andrew's Ambulance Association* 1918 S.C. 158; *Black Clawson International Ltd v. Papierwerke Waldhof-Aschaffenburg A G* [1975] A.C. 591; *Manuel v. Att.-Gen.* [1983] Ch. 77; *S. v. Kennedy* 1996 S.C.L.R. 34; *cf. Re Boaler* [1915] 1 K.B. 21). However, a short title given to an Act by a Statute Law Revision Act will only be used with caution as an aid to interpretation, because it may be inaccurate (*Lockheed-Arabia Corp. v. Owen* [1993] 3 All E.R. 641, 643, *per* Mann L.J.; *cf. Sin Yin Kwan v. Eastern Insurance Co. Ltd* [1994], 1 All E.R. 213, 244). The preamble may also be used as an aid to interpretation, although it cannot prevail over the legislative text (*e.g. Att.-Gen. v. Prince Ernest Augustus of Hanover* [1957] A.C. 436; *Andrew Oliver & Son Ltd v. Douglas* 1981 S.C. 193; *Sin Yin Kwan v. Eastern Insurance Co. Ltd* (above); *Manuel v. Att.-Gen.*, above). Similarly, the preamble of a Community regulation or directive may be used as an aid to interpretation (*e.g. H.P. Bulmer Ltd v. J. Bollinger SA* [1974] 1 Ch. 401, Case 9/72 *Brunner* [1972] E.C.R. 961).

2. Other Elements of the Legislation

D.P.P. v. Schildkamp [1971] A.C. 1

Lord Reid: "The question which has arisen in this case is whether and to what extent it is permissible to give weight to punctuation, cross-headings and side-notes to sections in the Act. Taking a strict view, one can say that these should be disregarded because they are not the product of anything done in Parliament. I have never heard of an attempt to move that any of them should be altered or amended, and between the introduction of a Bill and the Royal Assent they can be and often are altered by officials of Parliament acting in conjunction with the draftsman.

But it may be more realistic to accept the Act as printed as being the product of the whole legislative process, and to give due weight to everything found in the printed Act. I say more realistic because in very many cases the provision before the court was never even mentioned in debate in either House, and it may be that its wording was never closely scrutinised by any members of either House. In such a case it is not very meaningful to say that the words of the Act represent the intention of Parliament but that punctuation, cross-headings and side-notes do not.

So, if the authorities are equivocal and one is free to deal with the whole matter, I would not object to taking all these matters into account, provided that we realise that they cannot have equal weight with the words of the Act. Punctuation can be of some assistance in construction. A cross-heading ought to indicate the scope of the sections which follow it but there is always a possibility that the scope of one of these sections may have been widened by amendment. But a side-note is a poor guide to the scope of a section, for it can do no more than indicate the main subject with which the section deals.

If we take these matters into consideration, then we are in effect searching for the intention of the draftsman rather than the intention of Parliament. And then it becomes very relevant to ask—could any competent draftsman have adopted this form of drafting if he had intended the result for which the appellant contends? If the answer is no, then there is such real doubt that it must be resolved in favour of the accused."

3. Previous Legislation

The courts may refer to previously enacted legislation, *in pari materia*, as an aid to interpretation.

***Kiely v. Lunn* 1982 S.C.C.R. 436**

The appellant's son had failed to attend school because he had been in ill-health as a result of glue-sniffing. At the appellant's trial for having committed an offence under the Education (Scotland) Act 1980, s. 35, it was proved that the son's addiction could be treated with his co-operation, but the boy would not co-operate. The appellant was convicted and appealed by stated case to the High Court of Justiciary.

The Education (Scotland) Act 1980, s. 35, provides that where a child fails to attend school without reasonable excuse his parent shall be guilty of an offence. Section 42(1)(b) of the same Act provides that it is a "reasonable excuse" if "the child has been prevented by sickness from attending school".

The previous legislation, the Education (Scotland) Act 1945, contained a similar provision. However, in its original statutory form, the Education (Scotland) Act 1883, s. 11, the provision read "the child has been prevented from attending school by sickness *or any other unavoidable cause*" (italics added).

> **Lord Justice-General (Emslie)**: "Looking at the terms of [the 1883 Act] it is perfectly clear from the words 'or any other unavoidable cause' that the word 'sickness' was not intended to include a state of mental or physical incapacity or disability induced or brought about by the deliberate actings of the person concerned . . . Although the words 'or any unavoidable cause' were dropped from the legislation in and after 1945 it cannot be supposed that the word 'sickness' used in 1945, and in the Act of 1980, was intended to bear a different meaning from that which it had borne from 1883 to 1945. 'Sickness' accordingly, in the legislation from and after 1945, must be understood to mean an unavoidable cause of absence, at least in the sense that it cannot be construed to include a state of ill-health brought about by the deliberate actings of the child concerned."

Reference may be made, as above, to legislation no longer in force and, in the same way, to the previous common law position (*e.g. E.T.U. v. Tarlo* [1964] Ch. 720); courts may also refer to previously enacted legislation which is still in force (*e.g. Hamilton v. N.C.B.* 1960 S.C. (H.L.) 1). In *Mackin v. Mackin*, 1990 S.C.L.R. 728 a statute was construed against the existing sheriff court procedure. *Kiely v. Lunn* is a somewhat vigorous use of previous legislation as an aid to interpretation; courts are usually more circumspect in its use: *e.g. R. v. Lawrence* [1982] A.C. 510, 522; *Gunning v. Mirror Group Newspapers Ltd* [1986] 1 All E.R. 385; *H.M. Advocate v. Muir* 1997 S.C.C.R. 677.

Sometimes the use of previous legislation is quite unhelpful. In *Manson v. Duke of Westminster* [1981] Q.B. 323, it was necessary to determine the meaning of the undefined term "letting value" in the Leasehold Reform Act 1967 and the court was referred to a definition of "lettable value" in a 1944 statute.

Stephenson L.J. (at p. 327) observed, "I derive no more help from the definition in the Act of 1944 than from the absence of any definition in the Act of 1967."

Previously enacted legislation will be used with caution to interpret legislation which codifies the law on a subject by subsuming and possibly amending statutory and common law rules (*e.g. Bank of England v. Vagliano Brothers* [1891] A.C. 107; *R. v. Fulling* [1987] QB 426; *R. v. Smurthwaite* [1994] 1 All E.R. 898, 902, *per* Lord Taylor C.J.). It is also used cautiously in the interpretation of consolidation statutes (*cf. MRS Environmental Services Ltd v. Marsh* [1997] 1 All E.R. 92, 102, *per* Phillips L.J.).

***R. v. Heron* [1982] 1 W.L.R. 451**

> **Lord Scarman**: "First, when construing a consolidating statute, it is particularly useful to have recourse to the legislative history if a real difficulty arises. Consolidation is, or is intended by Parliament to be, the re-enactment in a more convenient, lucid and economical form . . . of existing statute law. It is, in its 'pure' form neither amendment nor reform nor codification, but re-enactment. Strictly, as draftsmen have always recognised, a pure consolidation must incorporate the law as it stands, including its difficulties and ambiguities. The earlier statute law, therefore, and judicial decisions as to its meaning and purpose, are very relevant, if there be difficulty or ambiguity.
>
> Second, I would not think it correct to distinguish between the various types of consolidation. There are now three and more may be added in the future. They are: (1) 'pure' consolidation, *i.e.* re-enactment; (2) consolidation with 'corrections and minor improvements'; (3) consolidation with Law Commission amendments. I have discussed the first. The second was made possible by the Consolidation of Enactments (Procedure) Act 1949 which confines permissible amendment to very minor matters. Certainly that Act in no way changes the essential character of consolidation, which is re-enactment. It cannot make any less legitimate a reference to the legislative history where there is difficulty or ambiguity.
>
> The same observations apply to consolidation with Law Commission amendments. But here there is an added feature. The Law Commission publishes a report which specifies the particular mischief (or mischiefs) which its proposed amendments are intended to remove. It is, therefore, perfectly plain to what extent one may use legislative history in the interpretation of a Law Commission consolidation.
>
> For those reasons I would not go further than Lord Wilberforce did in *Farrell v. Alexander* [1977] A.C. 59 at 73, where he said:
>
> > '. . . recourse should only be had [to antecedents] when there is a real and substantial difficulty or ambiguity which classical methods of construction cannot resolve.'
>
> But, when there is such a difficulty, I believe the courts should not hesitate to refer to the legislative history. In some cases, as in the present, it will still doubt and resolve difficulty."

[*cf. Farrell v. Alexander* [1977] A.C. 59 at pp. 82–85 *per* Lord Simon of Glaisdale; *Prior v. Sovereign Chicken Ltd* [1984] 1 W.L.R. 921, 928–929 *per* Lawton L.J.; *Harvey v. MacTaggart & Mickel Ltd* 1998 S.L.T. 20, Land Court.]

4. Subsequent Legislation

***Kirkness v. John Hudson & Co. Ltd* [1955] A.C. 696**

> **Lord Reid**: "[Unless the earlier statute is obscure or ambiguous] in construing a provision of an earlier Act, the provisions of a later Act cannot be taken into account . . . and . . . that rule applies although the later Act contains a provision that it is to be read as one with the earlier Act. Of course, that does not apply where the later Act amends the earlier Act or purports to declare its meaning; in such cases the later Act operates directly by its own force."

(See also *Payne v. Bradley* [1962] A.C. 343 at p. 357 *per* Lord Denning.)

Lord Reid refers to a later statute amending an earlier one. This may be done expressly or it may arise by implication. Where a later Act is inconsistent with an earlier one, but does not expressly amend or repeal it, the courts will normally apply the later Act. The earlier legislation is considered to have been impliedly amended or repealed by the later legislation (*e.g. Vauxhall Estates Ltd v. Liverpool Corporation* [1932] 1 K.B. 733; *Ellen St Estates Ltd v. Minister of Health* [1934] 1 K.B. 590; *Manuel v. Att.-Gen.* [1983] Ch. 77). However, this is subject to the maxim, *generalia specialibus non derogant*—general provisions do not derogate from particular ones. So, the Housing Act 1925 which empowered local authorities to appropriate any land vested in them for building purposes did not abrogate by implication the obligation imposed on the London County Council by the London Open Spaces Act 1893 to maintain Hackney Marshes as an open space (*R. v. Minister of Health, ex p. Villiers* [1936] 2 K.B. 29; *cf. Aberdeen Suburban Tramways Co. v. Aberdeen Magistrates* 1927 S.C. 683). In such circumstances as these, reference will be made to subsequent legislation to resolve questions of the application, and possibly the interpretation, of an earlier Act.

In some cases a statute is interpreted by reference to delegated legislation made under it (*e.g. MacNeill v. Wilson*, 1981 J.C. 87; *Glasgow District Council v. Secretary of State for Scotland*, 1981 S.C. 188). This may be essential where delegated legislation may amend (*e.g.* International Conventions Act 1983, s. 8) or repeal (*e.g.* Transport Act 1985, s.46) the enabling statute. For the interpretation of an Act amended in this way and incorporated in amended form in delegated legislation, see *Re S-L* [1995] 4 All E.R. 159.

In *Jackson v. Hall* [1980] A.C. 854 at pp. 889–890, Lord Fraser of Tullybelton suggested that more general use of delegated legislation to interpret the enabling Act was only appropriate where the delegated legislation was subject to affirmative resolution (*cf. Hanlon v. Law Society* [1981] A.C. 124 at pp. 193–194, *per* Lord Lowry; in *Re NRG Victory Reinsurance Ltd* [1995] 1 All E.R. 533, 535, Lindsay J. suggested that "it may be inappropriate to construe an Act by reference to the secondary legislation made under it", although he did note that the drafter of the secondary legislation had apparently adopted the same construction of the primary legislation as he proposed, on different bases, to adopt). See also *Pharmaceutical Society of Great Britain v. Storkwain Ltd* [1986] 1

W.L.R. 903, 908–909 *per* Lord Goff of Chieveley; *British Amusement Catering Trades Association v. Westminster City Council* [1989] A.C. 147; *Drummond & Co., W.S. v. Scottish Legal Aid Board* 1992 S.L.T. (H.L.) 337; *Deposit Protection Board v. Dalia* [1994] 2 All E.R. 577; *R. v. Secretary of State for the Home Department, ex p. Mehair* [1994] 2 All E.R. 494; *cf. Fane v. Murray* 1995 S.L.T. 567 (where no assistance could be derived from reference to delegated legislation made under parallel English legislation which did not contain the same specific provisions as the Scottish legislation).

D. LEGISLATIVE PURPOSE

Faced with a legislative ambiguity, a court may try to establish the "mischief" which the legislation seeks to remedy. The process is also described as establishing the object or purpose of the legislation, or the intention of the legislator. This approach is adopted with primary (*e.g. Norris, Applicant* 1990 S.C.L.R. 628, Sh.Ct) and secondary (*e.g. MacMillan v. Wimpey Offshore Engineers & Constructors* 1991 S.L.T. 515) legislation. One important question is what material a court may appropriately consider to establish the purpose of U.K. legislation or the intention of the legislator.

1. Legislation Incorporating Treaties or Community Legislation

***Salomon v. Commissioners of Customs and Excise* [1967] 2 Q.B. 116**

> **Diplock L.J.**: "Where, by a treaty, Her Majesty's Government undertakes either to introduce domestic legislation to achieve a specified result in the United Kingdom or to secure a specified result which can only be achieved by legislation, the treaty, since in . . . law it is not self-operating, remains irrelevant to any issue in the . . . courts until Her Majesty's Government has taken steps by way of legislation to fulfil its treaty obligations. Once the Government has legislated, which it may do in anticipation of the coming into effect of the treaty, as it did in this case, the court must in the first instance construe the legislation, for that is what the court has to apply. If the terms of the legislation are clear and unambiguous, they must be given effect to, whether or not they carry out Her Majesty's treaty obligations, for the sovereign power of the Queen in Parliament extends to breaking treaties . . . and any remedy for such a breach of an international obligation lies in a forum other than Her Majesty's own courts. But if the terms of the legislation are not clear but are reasonably capable of more than one meaning, the treaty itself becomes relevant, for there is a prima facie presumption that Parliament does not intend to act in breach of international law, including therein specific treaty obligations; and if one of the meanings which can reasonably be ascribed to the legislation is consonant with the treaty obligations and another or others are not, the meaning which is consonant is to be preferred. Thus, in case of lack of clarity in the words used in the legislation the terms of the treaty are relevant to enable the

court to make its choice between the possible meaning of these words by applying this presumption.

It has been argued that the terms of an international convention cannot be consulted to resolve ambiguities or obscurities in a statute unless the statute itself contains either in the enacting part or the preamble an express reference to the international convention which it is the purpose of the statute to implement . . . I can see no reason in comity or common sense for imposing such a limitation upon the right and duty of the court to consult an international convention to resolve ambiguities and obscurities in a statutory enactment. If from extrinsic evidence it is plain that the enactment was intended to fulfil Her Majesty's Government's obligations under a particular convention, it matters not that there is no express reference to the convention in the statute. One must not presume that Parliament intends to break an international convention merely because it does not say expressly that it is intending to observe it. Of course the court must not merely guess that the statute was intended to give effect to a particular international convention. The extrinsic evidence of the connection must be cogent."

Diplock L.J. considered the interpretation of legislation which incorporated the provisions of a treaty, with or without express reference to it. Sometimes legislation incorporating treaty provisions may specifically require courts to refer to the Treaty (*e.g. James Buchanan & Co. Ltd v. Babco Forwarding and Shipping (U.K.) Ltd* [1978] A.C. 141; *Fothergill v. Monarch Airlines* [1981] A.C. 251).

In Scotland, a treaty which has not been incorporated into domestic law may nevertheless be used as an aid to statutory interpretation (*e.g. Re AMT (known as AC)* 1996 S.C.L.R., 897, 910–911, *per* Lord President Hope; *Advocate v. West End Construction*, 1990 S.C.L.R. 777, Sh.Ct). In England such treaties have also been used in interpretation (*e.g. Waddington v. Miah* [1974] 2 All E.R. 377; *R. v. Home Secretary, ex p. Bhajan Singh* [1976] Q.B. 198; *Ahmad v. I.L.E.A.* [1978] 1 Q.B 36; *Fothergill v. Monarch Airlines*, above, *cf. Malone v. Commissioner of Police for the Metropolis* [1979] Ch. 344); as have treaties to which the United Kingdom is not a party (*e.g. The Philippine Admiral* [1977] A.C. 373).

Where the provision of a treaty falls to be considered as an aid to statutory interpretation, it may itself be ambiguous and require interpretation. The court may then consider authoritative texts of the treaty in other languages (*e.g. Fothergill v. Monarch Airlines*, above), and it will certainly seek to interpret its provisions on broad principles of interpretation which are common to other states which are parties to the treaty rather than on narrower rules of statutory interpretation adopted in the United Kingdom (*e.g. Stag Line Ltd v. Foscolo Mango & Co. Ltd* [1932] A.C. 328; *James Buchanan & Co. Ltd v. Babco Forwarding & Shipping (U.K.) Ltd*, above; *Fothergill v. Monarch Airlines*, above; *ex p. Postlethwaite* [1988] A.C. 924). This may include resort to *travaux préparatoires*, including for example the records of a conference in which the treaty was drafted (*e.g. Gatoil International Inc. v. Arkwright-Boston Manufacturers Mutual Insurance Co.*, 1985 S.L.T. 68), the decisions of courts in other states on the interpretation of the treaty and academic commentaries on the treaty.

Similarly, European Union law must be interpreted in domestic courts by reference to E.U. law, and not domestic canons of construction (*Westminster v.*

Thomson 1992 S.C.C.R. 624; and see section IIA above). Also, in terms of legislative history, no assistance can be derived from earlier legislation where the statutory provision being interpreted, unlike the earlier legislation, implements an E.U. directive: *British Sugar plc v. James Robertson & Son Ltd* [1996] RPC 281, 298, *per* Jacob J.

2. Non-Governmental Material

Exceptionally, legislation may empower the courts to consider certain non-governmental material as an aid to interpretation (*e.g.* Civil Jurisdiction and Judgments Act 1982, s. 3(3)). Otherwise, public reports on the subject of the legislation, by bodies which have a degree of independence from the Government may be examined to establish the purpose of the legislation and in some cases as aid to construction. So, for example, a report of the Scottish Law Commission may be considered where a statutory provision is ambiguous, but not otherwise (*Monteith v. Cape Insulation Ltd* 1998 S.L.T. 456; *Redrow Homes Ltd v. Bett Brothers plc* 1997 S.C.L.R. 469; *Amour v. Anderson* 1994 S.C.L.R. 642; *Barratt Scotland Ltd v. Keith* 1993 S.C.L.R. 120; and see G. Maher, "Statutory Interpretation and Scottish Law Commission Reports" 1992 S.L.T. (News) 277). The dangers of using such material, as perceived by the judiciary, were emphasised in *Assam Railways & Trading Co. v. I.R.C.* [1935] A.C. 445 and restated in *Davis v. Johnson*, although there has been some judicial reassessment following *Pepper (Inspector of Taxes) v. Hart* (see below).

***Davis v. Johnson* [1979] A.C. 264**

> **Lord Diplock**: "Where legislation follows on a published report of [the law commissions and committees or commissions appointed by government or by either House of Parliament to consider reforming particular branches of the law] the report may be used as an aid to identify the mischief which the legislation is intended to remedy, but not for the purpose of construing the enacting words in such a way as to conform with recommendations made in the report as to the form the remedy should take . . . This does not mean, of course, that one must shut one's eyes to the recommendations, for a suggestion as to a remedy may throw light on what the mischief itself is thought to be; but it does not follow that Parliament when it legislates to remedy the mischief has adopted in their entirety or, indeed, at all the remedies recommended in the report. This is well illustrated in the instant case. The report on which the Domestic Violence and Matrimonial Proceedings Act 1976 was undoubtedly based is the Report from the Select Committee of the House of Commons on Violence in Marriage published in July 1975. It deals almost exclusively with the plight of married women exposed to violence by their husbands and the resulting homelessness for themselves and their children. In the single paragraph referring to unmarried couples described (regrettably I think) as 'co-habitees' the members of the committee disclaim any particular knowledge of the problem, on which

they had not taken evidence. Nevertheless they recommended that so far as the grant of injunctions against violence by their paramours was concerned mistresses should have the same procedural rights as married women. As regards homelessness of mistresses, however, all the committee recommended was that the Guardianship of Minors Acts should be amended to provide that, where there was a child of the illicit union of which paternity could be proved, the court should have power to make orders giving the mistress while she was caring for the children during their minority sole right of occupation of the premises which had been occupied by the unmarried couple as their home. Whatever s. 1(2) of the 1976 Act may do it does not do that."

[See also *Black-Clawson International Ltd. v. Papierwerke Waldhof-Aschaffenburg AG* [1975] A.C. 591; *Keith v. Texaco Ltd* 1977 S.L.T. (Lands Tr.) 16; *Re 1st Indian Cavalry Club* 1998 S.C. 126; *Kaur v. Singh* 1998 S.C. 232; *cf. Commission for the New Towns v. Cooper (GB) Ltd* [1995] 2 All E.R. 929, 952 *per* Stuart-Smith L. J.]

3. Governmental Material

The general rule, as reflected in *Inglis v. British Airports Authority* below, is that courts will not consider material issued by the Government as an aid to construction, or to establish the purpose of legislation. The danger in using such material is that it may not reflect what is enacted (in *R. v. Secretary of State for the Environment, ex p. Tower Hamlets LBC* [1993] 3 All E.R. 439, the court declared statutory guidelines to be wrong in law) and that it might come to be drafted with a view to influencing the interpretation of the legislation.

Inglis v. British Airports Authority 1978 S.L.T. (Lands Tr.) 30

W.A. Elliott, Q.C.; W M. Hall, F.R.I.C.S.: "The respondents referred in their pleadings to para. 5 of the Scottish Development Department memorandum no. 85/1973 and at the hearing urged that the tribunal should be guided in construing the 1973 Act by this memorandum, a copy of which was lodged in process. It was explained by their solicitor that the respondent authority had relied on para. 5 in other cases as indicating that a person like the claimant should register his or her claim before selling; and that a notice of claim should be served before the actual sale of the interest in question. As the respondents' solicitor appeared surprised by our refusal to use this memorandum to guide our construction of the Act it is necessary to state why we decline to do so.

The memorandum is purely an administrative circular designed to give guidance to public authorities on the scope of the new enactment. It cannot provide a gloss on the actual words used by Parliament nor can it be used by a judicial tribunal as an aid to construing the wording of a statute or as a guide to the intentions of Parliament. To use a departmental memorandum in this way would indeed tend to undermine the rule of law as enacted by

> Parliament; and we cannot conceive that its use in judicial proceedings was ever contemplated by the department itself when it issued this circular for the help of public authorities."

There are exceptions to the general rule. Government material, such as a White Paper, issued before enactment has been judicially considered to establish the legislative purpose (*Attorney-General's Reference (No. 1 of 1988)* [1989] A.C. 971), as has such material issued after enactment (*Government of Canada v. Aronson* [1990] 1 A.C. 579 (forms issued in respect of the administration of the Fugitive Offenders Act 1967); *cf. Jackson v. Hall* [1980] A.C. 854, 884, *per* Viscount Dilhorne). A further exception to the general rule is technical matter to which the legislation makes express reference (*e.g. Lord Advocate v. Reliant Tool Co.* [1968] 1 W.L.R. 205; *cf. MacCormick v. Lord Advocate*, 1953 S.C. 396, 410–411, *per* Lord President Cooper). An analogous exception is consideration given by the courts to advice issued by the Government, such as Inland Revenue circulars, on the construction and proposed administration of statutory provisions (see, for example, *Matrix-Securities Ltd v. I.R.C.* [1994] 1 All E.R. 769).

4. Parliamentary Materials

Prior to the judgment of the House of Lords in the English appeal of *Pepper v. Hart*, in both England and Scotland there had been a long-standing rule that reference to parliamentary material was not admitted as an aid to statutory construction, although reference might be made to such material for the more general purpose of establishing legislative intent. The rule was sometimes ignored (*e.g. Re Aeronautics in Canada* [1932] A.C. 952, 971) but the danger of doing so was illustrated in *Hadmore Productions Ltd v. Hamilton* [1983] A.C. 191. Sometimes it was avoided by judicial reference to articles and textbooks which contained quotations from parliamentary debates (*e.g. R. v. Local Commissioner for Administration for the North and East Area of England, ex p. Bradford Metropolitan City Council* [1979] Q.B. 287, 311 (Lord Denning)). However, *Pepper v. Hart* significantly, albeit cautiously, relaxed the exclusionary rule.

Pepper (Inspector of Taxes) v. Hart [1993] AC 593

> **Lord Browne-Wilkinson**: ". . . Under present law, there is a general rule that reference to Parliamentary material as an aid to statutory construction is not permissible ('the exclusionary rule'): *Davis v. Johnson* [1979] A.C. 264 and *Hadmor Productions Ltd v. Hamilton* [1983] 1 A.C. 191. This rule did not always apply but was judge-made. Thus, in *Ash v. Abdy* (1678) 3 Swans. 664 Lord Nottingham took judicial notice of his own experience when introducing the Bill in the House of Lords. The exclusionary rule was probably first stated by Willes J. in *Millar v. Taylor* (1769) 4 Burr. 2303, 2332. However, the case of *Re Mew and Thorne* (1862) 31 L.J.Bank. 87 shows that even in the middle of the last century the rule was not absolute: in that case Lord Westbury L.C. in construing an Act had regard to its Parliamentary history

and drew an inference as to Parliament's intention in passing the legislation from the making of an amendment striking out certain words.

The exclusionary rule was later extended so as to prohibit the court from looking even at reports made by commissioners on which legislation was based: *Salkeld v. Johnson* (1848) 2 Exch. 256, 273. This rule has now been relaxed so as to permit reports of commissioners, including law commissioners, and white papers to be looked at for the purpose solely of ascertaining the mischief which the statute is intended to cure but not for the purpose of discovering the meaning of the words used by Parliament to effect such cure: *Eastman Photographic Materials Co. Ltd v. Comptroller-General of Patents, Designs and Trademarks* [1898] A.C. 571 and *Assam Railways and Trading Co. Ltd v. Commissioners of Inland Revenue* [1935] A.C. 445, 457–458. Indeed, in *R. v. Secretary of State for Transport, ex p. Factortame Ltd* [1990] 2 A.C. 85 your Lordships' House went further than this and had regard to a Law Commission report not only for the purpose of ascertaining the mischief but also for the purpose of drawing an inference as to Parliamentary intention from the fact that Parliament had not expressly implemented one of the Law Commission's recommendations.

Although the courts' attitude to reports leading to legislation has varied, until recently there was no modern case in which the court had looked at parliamentary debates as an aid to construction. However, in *Pickstone v. Freemans Plc* [1989] A.C. 66 this House, in construing a statutory instrument, did have regard to what was said by the Minister who initiated the debate on the regulations. My noble and learned friend, Lord Keith of Kinkel, at p.112B, after pointing out that the draft Regulations were not capable of being amended when presented to Parliament, said that it was 'entirely legitimate for the purpose of ascertaining the intention of Parliament to take into account the terms in which the draft was presented by the responsible minister and which formed the basis of its acceptance.' My noble and learned friend, Lord Templeman, at pp. 121–122, also referred to the minister's speech, although possibly only by way of support for a conclusion he had reached on other grounds. My noble and learned friends, Lord Brandon of Oakbrook and Lord Jauncey of Tullichettle, agreed with both those speeches. This case therefore represents a major inroad on the exclusionary rule: see also *Owens Bank Ltd v. Bracco* [1992] 2 A.C. 443.

Mr. Lester, for the taxpayers, did not urge us to abandon the exclusionary rule completely. His submission was that where the words of a statute were ambiguous or obscure or were capable of giving rise to an absurd conclusion it should be legitimate to look at the Parliamentary history, including the debates in Parliament, for the purpose of identifying the intention of Parliament in using the words it did use. He accepted that the function of the court was to construe the actual words enacted by Parliament so that in no circumstances could the court attach to words a meaning that they were incapable of bearing. He further accepted that the court should only attach importance to clear statements showing the intention of the promoter of the Bill, whether a minister or private member: there could be no dredging through conflicting statements of intention with a view to discovering the true intention of Parliament in using the statutory words . . .

. . . [T]he reasons put forward for the present rule are first, that it preserves the constitutional proprieties leaving Parliament to legislate in words and the courts (not Parliamentary speakers), to construe the meaning of the words finally enacted; second, the practical difficulty of the expense of researching Parliamentary material which would arise if the material could be looked at; third, the need for the citizen to have access to a known defined text which regulates his legal rights, fourth, the improbability of finding helpful guidance from *Hansard* . . .

. . . I therefore reach the conclusion, subject to any question of Parliamentary privilege, that the exclusionary rule should be relaxed so as to permit reference to Parliamentary materials where (a) legislation is ambiguous or obscure, or leads to an absurdity; (b) the material relied upon consists of one or more statements by a minister or other promoter of the Bill together if necessary with such other Parliamentary material as is necessary to understand such statements and their effect; (c) the statements relied upon are clear. Further than this, I would not at present go."

In *Pepper v. Hart* the use of parliamentary materials as an aid to statutory construction was referred to an enlarged Appellate Committee of seven Lords of Appeal in Ordinary. Only Lord Mackay of Clashfern L.C. dissented from the Opinion of Lord Browne-Wilkinson and the dissent was primarily based on the increased costs of litigation which might flow from relaxing the previous exclusionary rule; *cf.* Lord Mackay of Clashfern, "Finishers, Refiners and Polishers: The Judicial Role in the Interpretation of Statutes" [1989] Stat.L.R. 151 and the views expressed by various Law Lords in a parliamentary debate on the subject: 503 H.L. Deb., col. 278 (January 18, 1989). In *Pepper v. Hart* their Lordships were unanimous in holding that the relaxation of the exclusionary rule did not amount to questioning or impeaching proceedings in Parliament contrary to Article 9 of the Bill of Rights 1688 and no other parliamentary privilege was identified in the pleadings which would be breached by the relaxation of the rule.

Admitting parliamentary materials where they were previously excluded has forensic implications both for the courts, practitioners and litigants. For the courts there is the danger that litigation may be prolonged by the citation of additional material of only marginal significance to the interpretation issue before the court. This was recognised by Lord Browne-Wilkinson in *Pepper v. Hart* where he observed that "attempts to introduce material which does not satisfy [the test for the admissibility of parliamentary material] should be met by orders for costs made against those who have improperly introduced the material" (at 637), a view which he reiterated subsequently (*Melluish (Inspector of Taxes) v. BMI (No 3) Ltd* [1995] 4 All E.R. 453, 468). It was perhaps further reinforced by the terms of the reported additions made on February 1, 1993 to the Practice Direction applicable to appeals to the House of Lords which read "supporting documents, *including extracts from Hansard*, will only be accepted in exceptional circumstances" ([1993] 1 W.L.R. 303; [1993] 1 All E.R. 573; however, both reports are incorrect in including the italicised words which were not included in the Practice Direction as issued by the Judicial Office of the House of Lords). For the litigant and practitioner, *Pepper v. Hart* may have implications of expense and time in that much legal research may be required to establish whether there are any relevant parliamentary materials which should be brought before the court or to determine whether objection should be made to such material being introduced by the other side (*e.g. Building Societies Commission v. Halifax Building Society* [1995] 3 All E.R. 193, 209, *per* Chadwick J.; *Denny v. Yeldon* [1995] 3 All E.R. 624, 632, *per* Jacob J.), and in some cases the court has proposed that parliamentary material be examined by counsel to determine whether there is any admissible material. Furthermore, the petitioner who fails to research the full parliamentary material in advising a client on the question of statutory interpretation may be liable for a breach of professional duty (see B. J. Davenport (1993) 109 L.Q.R. 149).

Given that counsel will seek to admit material advantageous to their cause, it is perhaps not surprising that Lord Browne-Wilkinson's three-fold test for the admissibility of parliamentary material has been somewhat generously, and sometimes inconsistently, interpreted and applied. So, for example, whether legislation is ambiguous for the purposes of *Pepper v. Hart* may turn on whether there is textual ambiguity, structural ambiguity (in the sense that there is ambiguity as the consequences of the relationship between words and phrases within a provision, or of the relationship between provision and others in the same or related legislation), ambiguity in the sense of the application of legislation to the case before the court, or even uncertainty of the consequences of the application of the legislation generally. It may also be sufficient to establish ambiguity that judges in lower courts took differing views over interpretation, rather than the legislation being considered ambiguous by the court considering it. Secondly, there may be doubt over what amounts to parliamentary material to satisfy the second of Lord Browne-Wilkinson's tests. Sometimes, surprising material has been admitted; indeed in *Pepper v. Hart* itself Lord Browne-Wilkinson referred to a press release issued contemporaneously with an admitted ministerial statement to a standing committee. Sometimes material has been somewhat surprisingly excluded; so, for example, in *Van Dyck v. Secretary of State for the Environment* [1993] P.L.R. 124, statements made by a Minister promoting a Bill were excluded, partly on the ground of a lack of clarity, but also because there were in part "finer remarks [which] were necessarily *extempore* responses to various points raised by [a member] during the debate".

Finally, there is the third test of admissibility, namely whether the statement is clear. Obviously there is some subjectivity in satisfying this test but there are also other problems. First, it is possible that a Minister may make a clear but legally inaccurate statement. Secondly, there is some danger that attempting to satisfy this test may involve interpreting a parliamentary statement rather than using a parliamentary statement to interpret ambiguous legislation. Finally, the notion that a clear statement implies that unlike some other jurisdictions only positive statements are admissible and may not be the case. In *Watson v. Fife Health Board* [1993] S.C.L.R. 534, the Inner House heard submissions on the parliamentary debates on the Damages (Scotland) Act 1976, s. 1, which did no more than reveal that nothing specific was said about the effect of the provision on the issue before the court. It may be that forensic pressures have seriously eroded the original test in *Pepper v. Hart*, and indeed there are cases which suggest that courts have essentially ignored the test and admitted parliamentary materials on the basis of judicial discretion (*e.g. Michaels v. Harley House (Marylebone) Ltd* [1997] 3 All E.R. 446, 465; *Fitzpatrick v. Stirling Housing Association Ltd* [1997] 4 All E.R. 991, 1014–1015).

See further, T. St J. N. Bates, "The Contemporary Use of Legislative History in the United Kingdom" (1995) 54 C.L.J. 127; T. St J. N. Bates, "Parliamentary Material and Statutory Construction: Aspects of the Practical Application of *Pepper v. Hart*" (1993) 15 Stat.L.R. 45; N. Walker, "Discovering the Intention of Parliament", 1993 S.L.T. (News) 121; T. St. J. N. Bates, "Judicial Application of *Pepper v. Hart*" (1993) 38 J.L.S.S. 251.

Finally, *Pepper v. Hart* again demonstrates that, in practice, the line between admitting material to establish the legislative purpose and as an aid to statutory construction is a fine one.

CHAPTER 15

CASE LAW AND THE DOCTRINE OF PRECEDENT

I. THE NATURE OF PRECEDENT

Twining and Miers, *How to do things with rules*, pp. 162–163

"In law, resort to precedent, that is to say the use of prior decisions to assist in the resolution of present disputes, has in general reached a considerable degree of refinement . . . [But] 'Precedent' and related notions are not unique to law. People who serve on committees, in administrative agencies and other decision-making bodies may often be faced with a problem which demands a solution but which, for instance, involves issues of conflicting values or competing interests in a borderline case. In such circumstances, in the process of reaching a decision, they may express their reluctance to resolve the conflict in one particular way in the phrase, 'Let's not create a precedent'. This phrase contains certain assumptions, about problem-solving both for the present and the future. Thus, it is implicit that future decision makers have some kind of obligation to come to the same conclusion should a similar case arise; that others who observe or rely upon the decisions of the particular body may expect that similar cases in the future will be similarly decided and thus may base their conduct upon such expectations; that the decision-making process is not constituted simply by the ad hoc resolution of particular cases, but involves the rational development of general policies of principles through these cases; and that the individual decisions themselves have status as expressions of policy or principle. Such factors provide a basis for demands that precedents be treated as having force or weight, and should not be ignored upon a whim but departed from only on the basis of rational argument and distinction. These four notions, of obligation, expectation of future behaviour, interstitial growth of policy and principle, and the authority of decisions form the basis of the common law's treatment of precedent.

Systems of law may be unique in their development of rules which relate to the operation of precedents. Whatever those rules may prescribe, they are cumulatively and generally known by the expression, 'a doctrine of precedent'. In a sense, nearly all legal systems have a doctrine of precedent, though its requirements may vary from system to system. Even a legal system which explicitly prohibits the citation of prior cases in court can be said to have a doctrine of precedent in that it has a rule which regulates the use of precedent."

A. THE ORIGINS OF PRECEDENT

1. THE RATIONALE OF PRECEDENT

A number of justifications and explanations for the emergence of legal doctrines of precedent have been put forward.

Llewellyn, "Case Law", p. 249

> "Toward its operative drive all those phases of human make-up which build habit in the individual and institutions in the group: laziness as to the reworking of a problem once solved, the time and energy saved by routine, especially under any pressure of business; the values of routine as a curb on arbitrariness and as a prop of weakness, inexperience and instability; the social venues of predictability; the power of whatever exists to produce expectations and the power of expectations to become normative. The force of precedent in the law is heightened by an additional factor: that curious, almost universal, sense of justice which urges that all men are properly to be treated alike in like circumstances. As the social system varies we meet infinite variations as to what men or treatments or circumstances are to be classed as 'like'; but the pressure to accept the views of the time and place remains."

In addition, precedent is said to provide or promote:

(1) Certainty and predictability in the law, enabling citizens to conduct themselves and to arrange their affairs in the light of decided cases in the knowledge that future judges will normally uphold these decisions. In turn, certainty and predictability minimise unnecessary litigation and expense for citizens.
(2) Guidance to judges lower down in the legal hierarchy, legal officials and lawyers.
(3) Uniformity and consistency of judicial decisions, reducing judicial error, bias or idiosyncrasy and thus promoting public respect for the judiciary and the administration of justice.
(4) Accountability.

Lord Devlin, "The Judge and Case Law", p. 181

> "[C]ase law, being made out of reasons which judges give in their judgments, necessarily contains the judiciary's account to the nation of the way in which they are using their vast powers. It makes possible criticism, amendment, or curtailment. It is more than an account; it is also, because of the doctrine of precedent, a broad description of the way in which, unless Parliament intervenes, the judges intend to continue using their powers. Respect for precedent is exacted, not only to keep the law in good shape, but primarily as a safeguard against arbitrary and autocratic decision-making."

2. THE EMERGENCE OF PRECEDENT IN SCOTLAND

The modern "strict" doctrine of precedent or *stare decisis* whereby a single decision in point can be binding on subsequent judges did not become established in Scotland or England before the nineteenth century. In the preceding 200 years precedents in both countries were cited merely as evidence of what the common law was or to prove the existence of an established policy or practice. Such precedents were not decisive of the point in question but more or less persuasive, depending in part on the rank and reputation of the judge(s) who decided them. The strict doctrine only took root once an established hierarchy of courts and appeals and an efficient system of law reporting came into existence. [For a useful historical account of the evolution of *stare decisis* in Scotland, see G. Maher and T.B. Smith, "Judicial Precedent" in Vol. 22 of the *Stair Memorial Encyclopaedia: The Laws of Scotland*, pp. 92–98.]

Erskine, *An Institute of the Law of Scotland*, I, 1, p. 47

> "Judgments ought not to be pronounced by examples or precedents. Decisions, therefore, though they bind the parties litigating create no obligation on the judges to follow in the same tract, if it shall appear to them contrary to law. It is, however, certain that they are frequently the occasion of establishing usages, which, after they have gathered force by a sufficient length of time, must, from the tacit assent of the state, make part of our unwritten law. What has been said of decisions of the Court of Session is also applicable to the judgments pronounced upon appeal by the House of Lords; for in these that august court acts as the character of judges, not of law givers; and consequently their judgments, though they are final as to the parties in the appeal cannot introduce any general rule which shall be binding either on themselves or inferior courts. Nevertheless, where a similar judgment is repeated in this court of the last resort, it ought to have the strongest influence on the determinations of inferior courts."

Smith, *The Doctrines of Judicial Precedent in Scots Law*, pp. 10–12

> "It may be suggested that several causes concurred in developing doctrines of strict precedent in the Scottish judicial process . . .
>
> The Court of Session was divided in 1808, and this, according to Lord Wark, was in part responsible for the growth of a strict doctrine of precedent, since it gave to the Senators of the College of Justice more time to formulate their opinions . . .
>
> It may be observed that soon after the court divided law reporting in Scotland was greatly improved and developed. One consequence of this was that it became no longer possible for the judges to disregard unwelcome decisions over which an official censorship was something exercised by excluding them from the reports. Thus Robertson, in the preface to his first volume of Scottish Appeals, notes that there had been occasions when the judgments of the Court of Session had been reversed in Parliament, yet the original decisions still remain as precedents in Scottish reports and works of authority. Nor were the judges of the Court of Session always anxious that a verbatim account of their opinions should be noted by the reporter . . . When Mr Bell announced that he intended to report the opinions of the judges without any official appointment, his proposal was met with threats

and obstruction, and it was some time before the publishing of full opinions was viewed favourably by the Bench. It is probable, therefore, that fuller and more accurate reporting from about 1825 gave an added incentive to the judges to prepare careful opinions which would bear close scrutiny. Associated with actual reporting, was the work devoted in the early years of the nineteenth century to compiling useful indexes to the decisions, so that they might be traced when required."

[Smith originally considered that the House of Lords (dominated as it was in the nineteenth century by English judges) was the single most important cause of a strict doctrine of precedent emerging in Scotland. However, he modified his position subsequently in his essay (co-authored with G. Maher) on Precedent in the *Stair Memorial Encyclopaedia of the Laws of Scotland*.]

Smith and Maher, "Precedent in the Nineteenth Century", para. 255

"255. The influence of the House of Lords in the nineteenth century. Various commentators have attributed much of the blame for the imposition of an alien doctrine of *stare decisis* into Scots law to the influence of the House of Lords as an appellate court. But it is necessary to make clear the ways in which the House of Lords could have, and did, influence Scottish courts on judicial precedent. Certainly after a period of hostility on the part of the Court of Session, decisions of the House came to be treated as binding precedents on the Court of Session, but this development can largely be explained by the idea of the role of appellate jurisdiction. Although it is arguable that decisions of the House of Lords in Scottish appeals imported into Scots law many doctrines of substantive law which were purely English in origin and inconsistent with Scottish legal principle, it is not so readily apparent how the House could have imposed the English approach to *stare decisis* on doctrines of precedent in the Court of Session. In any case, precedent in the nineteenth-century English legal system, although narrower than the Scottish conception of judicial practice, was itself in the process of developing towards *stare decisis*. This process was not finalised in the House of Lords until almost the beginning of the present century in the *London Tramways* case."

Some commentators have argued that historically Scots law has been deductive, rights-oriented and based on principle whereas English law is said to have been primarily inductive, remedy-oriented and based on precedent. Whatever may have been the truth in previous centuries, scholars are now agreed that in modern times principles play a significant part in English law and that in Scotland a strict doctrine of precedent has evolved.

[See Lord Cooper, "The Common and the Civil Law", pp. 470–471; I.D. Willock, in J.P. Grant (ed.) *Independence and Devolution* (1976); *Pioneer Shipping Ltd v. B.T.P. Tioxide Ltd* [1982] A.C. 724 at p. 751 and *Lambert v. Lewis* [1982] A.C. 225 at p. 274. For a recent striking case in which three English Law Lords decided an appeal in the Lords on grounds of basic principle and the two Scots Law Lords dissented on pragmatic grounds, see *Woolwich Building Society v. IRC (No. 2)* [1992] 3 All E.R. 737.]

B. WHEN MUST A PRECEDENT BE APPLIED?

The doctrines of binding precedent in Scotland and England do not require every court to follow the earlier decisions of itself and other courts. The doctrines only require a court to follow a previous decision which is (a) "in point" and (b) binding. Even then, only part of the earlier decision need be followed. A case is in point if it decided the same issue of law as arises in the instant case and no material, *i.e.* legally relevant distinction exists between the facts of the two cases. This is always a question of interpretation and as we shall see, the technique of distinguishing precedents on the grounds that they are not in point is one that is assiduously practised by judges who wish to retain their freedom for manoeuvre.

Precedents may be either binding or persuasive. While a case either is binding or is not, there are varying degrees of persuasiveness. Sometimes, even though the judge in the instant case is not technically bound to follow an earlier decision, it may be so strongly persuasive that he would find it difficult to justify not following the precedent. In other situations precedents, even though in point, may have little persuasive value. What determines whether a precedent is binding or merely persuasive (and if the latter, to what degree) is the level of the court which decided the case in the hierarchy of courts, the legal system from which the case emanated and the prestige of the judges who decided the case. The first of these, the place of the court in the hierarchy of courts, is the most significant factor.

The Hierarchy of Courts

The civil and criminal courts of Scotland (and England) each form separate hierarchies, which largely, though not entirely, coincide with their respective appeals structure.

Walker, *The Scottish Legal System*, p. 422

> "The general principle is that any court is bound by prior decisions in point pronounced by courts superior to it in its own vertical line of authority, normally treats as binding precedents in point pronounced by a prior court of its own rank in its own vertical line, and that prior decisions in point of courts of equal or higher rank in other vertical lines of authority are persuasive in varying degree. Decisions of courts of lower rank in any vertical line of authority may be ignored but may sometimes be of persuasive value."

In the light of the 1966 Practice Statement on Precedent in the House of Lords (see p. 425 below), it is clear that the House when sitting as the final court of appeal in Scottish civil cases is not bound by earlier decisions of the House. Its decisions in Scottish appeals are binding on all civil courts in Scotland.

***Dalgleish v. Glasgow Corporation* 1976 S.C. 32**

> **Lord Justice-Clerk (Wheatley)**: "The question whether a decision of the House of Lords in an English case is binding on the courts in Scotland is not

free from difficulty. In the seven Judge case of *Virtue v. Commissioners of Police of Alloa* (1874) 1 R. 285 the Judges were divided on the point as it arose in that case. Lord President Inglis, Lord Justice-Clerk Moncrieff, Lord Benholme and Lord Jerviswood thought that the English authority was binding, Lord Cowan, Lord Deas and Lord Neaves in varying degrees thought that it was not. Doubts were expressed by the minority Judges as to whether the legal point in issue in that case was the same as the legal point in the English case. Lord President Inglis said at p. 296: 'I think it is an error in constitutional law to represent the House of Lords as sitting at one time as a Scottish Court and at another time as an English Court. That House, I apprehend, sits always in one character, as the House of Lords of the United Kingdom, and as such the Imperial Court of Appeal for the whole three parts of the United Kingdom. It has occasion to administer at one time the law of Scotland, at another the law of England, and at another the law of Ireland. But in appeals coming from all three countries it has to deal with principles of law that are common to the whole three.' He went on to state that it was with such principles—the rules applicable to the construction of statutes of the Imperial legislature—that the House was dealing in the previous conflicting decisions of the House in appeals from the courts in Scotland and England. Lord Justice-Clerk Moncrieff said at p. 304 that he thought that the Scottish Courts were entitled to take as a precedent a House of Lords decision in an English case where on a question of general jurisprudence or of mercantile law the two systems concur. Lord Cowan on the other hand said at page 299: 'I cannot hold the judgment, even of the House of Lords—sitting as a Supreme Court of Appeal, and determining a purely English case under an English local statute—as a binding precedent on the courts of this country.'

In *Orr Ewing's Trustees v. Orr Ewing* (1886) 13 R. (H.L.) 1, Lord Chancellor Selborne said at p. 3: 'A decision of this House, in an English case, ought to be held conclusive in Scotland, as well as England, as to questions of English law and English jurisdiction which it determined. It cannot of course, conclude any question of Scottish law. So far as it may proceed upon principle of general jurisprudence, it ought to have weight in Scotland; as a similar judgment of this House on a Scottish appeal ought to have weight in England. If, however, it can be shown that by any positive law of Scotland, or according to authorities having the force of law in that country, a different view of the proper interpretation, extent or application of these principles prevails there, the opinions on those subjects, expressed by noble and learned Lords when giving judgment on an English appeal ought not to be held conclusive in Scotland.'

In *Glasgow Corporation v. Central Land Board* 1956 S.C. (H.L.) 1 Lord Normand stated at pp. 16 and 17 that a decision in the House of Lords in an English case wherein no question of Scots law fell to be decided is not binding on the Scottish courts nor in the House of Lords sitting as a court of ultimate appeal in a Scottish case.

The difficulty is not just one of deciding which of the conflicting views our courts should adopt. It is one of finding an all-embracing and definitive

> formula to regulate the case where a decision of the House of Lords in an English case should be regarded as a binding precedent in our courts. Manifestly, in my view, a decision on a U.K. statute which has equal or similar applicability in both countries, is one such case. (I note in parenthesis that this does not apply to appeals in criminal cases in Scotland, where the ultimate court of Appeal is the High Court of Justiciary or the Court of Criminal Appeal, and decisions of the House of Lords in criminal cases in England are not binding on these Scottish courts even in relation to the interpretation of U.K. statutes applicable equally to both countries.) How far beyond that can the principle extend? Here I find myself inclined to resort to what might be regarded as an age old cliche, but what is the practical answer to so many questions, namely, that each case must be determined on its own circumstances. I feel, however, that something more positive is required. Since we have in Scotland our own system of Law, then in my opinion no legal issue in Scots law should be held to be governed by a House of Lords decision in an English appeal, unless the point in issue is based on legislation which has equal applicability and force in both countries, or has been decided by an authoritative and binding court to be exactly the same and have the same legal significance in both countries."

Lord Wheatley's view has since been challenged when the Court of Session declined to follow a preceding English House of Lords case concerning the interpretation of a U.K. statute. The case considered whether interdict against the Crown was competent under section 21 of the Crown Proceedings Act 1947, which applies to England and Scotland. The House of Lords, in an English appeal, *Re M*, had held that an injunction could be granted against the Crown in similar circumstances. The Inner House demurred.

***McDonald v. Secretary of State for Scotland* 1994 S.L.T. 692**

> **Lord Justice-Clerk** (**Ross**): "I am therefore satisfied that what was stated in the House of Lords regarding the interpretation of this section for the purposes of English law is not binding upon this court. On the other hand, the views of Lord Woolf upon this matter are clearly of high persuasive value. Insofar as his decision is based on principles of general jurisprudence, it has great weight, but insofar as it is based on peculiarities of English law, it may have no real relevance in a Scottish court. In *Dalgleish v. Glasgow Corporation*, Lord Justice-Clerk Wheatley stated that a House of Lords decision in an English case should be regarded as a binding precedent in a Scottish civil court if the decision involved a United Kingdom statute which had equal or similar applicability in both countries. With all respect I feel that that statement is expressed too widely. Section 21 of the Act of 1947 applies to both England and Scotland but as there are differences between England and Scotland as to the procedure for suing the Crown, I am of opinion that a decision such as *Re M* is not binding in Scotland though it must be considered as having weight."

This case does not clearly address whether a decision of the House of Lords on a point of common law (sometimes called "a point of general jurisprudence") is binding on Scottish courts or only strongly persuasive—here, Lord Ross merely states that such a decision carries "great weight". In practical terms it may not make much difference except in a few cases and in these the answer may well depend on whether it is English Law Lords or Scottish Senators of the College of Justice who are considering the point.

Section 103 of the Scotland Act 1998 expressly provides that decisions of the Privy Council on "devolution matters" are to be binding in all legal proceedings other than Privy Council proceedings.

Normally, Divisions of the Inner House are regarded as bound by previous decisions of a Division. They are undoubtedly bound by decisions of seven or more judges of the Court of Session. Lords Ordinary are bound by decisions of seven or more judges or of the Divisions. One Lord Ordinary, however, does not bind another (see, *e.g. McFarlane v. Tayside Health Board* 1997 S.L.T. 211) nor, probably, are his decisions binding in the sheriff court—though they may be persuasive. The decisions of a sheriff principal will normally be followed by sheriffs in his sheriffdom, but it is not clear that this is an example of *stare decisis*. [Compare *Thomson's Trs v. Harrison* (1958) 74 Sh. Ct. Rep. 77 and *MacKays v. James Deas & Son Ltd* 1977 S.L.T. (Sh. Ct) 10.]

Smith, *The Doctrines of Judicial Precedent in Scots Law*, p. 105

> "With regard to the criminal courts, the decisions of single judges are not binding on each other, but the practice has grown for a quorum of the High Court of Justiciary to follow the previous decisions of a like quorum unless a fuller court be convened to overrule the earlier case. And of course, a single judge follows the law laid down by a bench of judges. There is no known precedent or reason which would restrict a full Court of Justiciary from reversing a precedent which it considered bad. The universal jurisdiction of the High Court of Justiciary implies that it is to concern itself with all that pertains to the furtherance of justice in criminal matters. Certainty and finality can be no real substitutes for justice. However, in the interests of consistency, precedent normally is followed, subject to the safeguards of review of the doctrine by a larger court."

Until 1988 it was universally assumed that decisions of a single judge in the High Court of Justiciary did not bind a sheriff (there being no line of appeal between them). However, in a startling decision by the Lord Justice-General (Emslie) with the concurrence of Lords Grieve and Kincraig, it was held in *Jessop v. Stevenson*, 1988 S.L.T. 223 that a "decision of a judge of the High Court of Justiciary is a decision of the High Court of Justiciary and unless it has been recalled on appeal, it is binding on all judges in the lower courts." This decision appears to be based on the principle that the High Court of Justiciary (like the Court of Session) is a collegiate court and single judges of the court exercise a delegated function on behalf of the whole court. While the historical logic of this argument seems beyond reproach it is very far from clear that it represented an accurate statement of the practice of the judiciary until that date. Yet precedent is not a set of legal rules. It is a set of normative practices, *i.e.* an amalgam of what the judges do and what they ought to do. As such, it is difficult to know what to make of the *Jessop* decision. It is clearly a statement of belief by eminent members of the High Court of Justiciary as to what they consider the normative practice of sheriffs and district justices ought to be. However, unlike the House of Lords Practice Statement in 1966 (see below, p. 425) it does not purport to be a statement on behalf of the whole of the court. In the end the impact of *Jessop* will depend on how it is viewed by the lower court judiciary. If it is adhered to, then irrespective of its correctness as a statement of the normative practice when it was decided, it will have become a self-fulfilling prophecy.

Jessop is also puzzling in that it offers no guidance as to whether a decision of one member of the High Court now binds any subsequent member of the Court sitting on his or her own. On the assumption that it does not, then which decision should the lower courts follow? Moreover, the same logic which underpins *Jessop* would also apply to Lords Ordinary in the Outer House binding sheriffs and sheriffs principal on civil cases. Until *Jessop* this was not the normative practice in civil cases. Since 1988 this question has arisen on several occasions. In *Cromarty Leasing Ltd. v. Turnbull*, 1988 S.L.T. (Sh. Ct) 62 and *Johnstone v. Hardie*, 1990 S.C.L.R. 387 Sheriff Wilkinson and Sheriff Principal Ireland respectively, concluded that *Jessop* had changed the normative practice for sheriffs in civil cases as well as criminal cases. However, in a persuasive judgment Sheriff Stoddart determined in *Farrell v. Farrell*, 1990 S.C.L.R. 717 that despite *Jessop* he was not bound by the decisions of the Outer House—particularly since the issue at stake involved divorce where sheriffs and Lords Ordinary share a wide concurrent jurisdiction. The question will have to await the verdict of history but, in reality, it may not make much difference in practice since even if the traditional position is restored sheriffs will continue to regard the decisions of the Outer House as being highly persuasive, if not absolutely binding. [See further on *Jessop*, T.B. Smith, "Precedent in the Sheriff Court" 1988 S.L.T. (News) 137 and G. Maher, "Precedent, the Sheriff Court and Colleges of Justice" 1988 S.L.T. (News) 209.]

It is still unsettled (at least in the minds of some commentators) whether Divisions of the Inner House are always bound by the previous decisions of a Division and whether the whole court is bound by its own decisions or those of a seven judge court. At first sight it may appear somewhat curious that there is any doubt about such matters. Part of the answer lies in the fact that precedent is a set of normative practices. In the case of whole court decisions the doubt arises because whole courts are never convened now and even when they were, they were not often asked to reconsider decisions of seven or more judges. The celebrated case where the issue did arise, *Yuill's Trs v. Thomson* (1902) 4 F. 815 is inconclusive because the judges split (largely on Divisional lines) over the question. The case is clear evidence that the judges in the Court of Session in 1902 had no settled practice on the matter and were heavily divided amongst themselves about what their practice ought to be. The issue was unresolved then and it remains so today.

On this analysis it may be asked why there is any doubt whether a Division is always bound by previous Divisional decisions. Surely situations must arise not infrequently when one Division has to consider a previous decision of the Inner House? In fact, in the bulk of reported cases where this has occurred the judges have regarded themselves as bound. But there have been a number of dissenting voices, particularly in older cases. This would seem to suggest that at one time (possibly even until as late as the 1930s) there was no settled practice on the question and no consensus amongst the judges. Nevertheless the practice of the judges for the last 50 years seems to have crystallised. Divisions nowadays do regard themselves as bound by previous Divisional decisions and a larger court is convened if it is felt that the earlier decision ought to be reconsidered. (See, *e.g.* *Grainger v. City of Edinburgh District Licensing Board* 1989 S.L.T. 633.)

These issues raise the larger question of whether courts ought to be bound by decisions of their own or of co-ordinate courts. Judges at the lower levels have always been free in this respect, even at the risk of producing conflicting decisions. [Compare, *e.g.* *Macrae v. Macrae* 1977 S.L.T. (Notes) 72; *McKay v. McKay* 1978 S.L.T. (Notes) 36; *Craig v. Craig* 1978 S.L.T. (Notes) 61; *Henderson v. Henderson*, 1981 S.L.T. (Notes) 25; *Lambert v. Lambert*, 1982 S.L.T. 144.] The House of Lords having resolved in 1966 that it should no longer be absolutely bound by its own decisions, the only courts that remain so bound are those at the intermediate level. The Divisions can resolve the problems by convening a larger court. The Court of Appeal in England, however, since it is not collegiate in origin cannot increase its powers by convening a larger court (see *Davis v. Johnson* [1979] A.C. 264). Lord Denning's solution was to assert that the Court of Appeal is and ought to be free to depart from its own decisions like Courts of Appeal in Australia and New Zealand. However, he signally failed to convince his colleagues that the Court should change its practice in this way.

[For a much fuller account of the hierarchical rules of *stare decisis* in both civil and criminal cases, see G. Maher and T.B. Smith, "Judicial Precedent", *op. cit.*]

C. RATIO DECIDENDI

Even where a precedent is in point and binding, judges and commentators are agreed that only part of it, the *ratio decidendi*, must be followed by the later court. Unfortunately, here the consensus ends. Agreement over the definition of *ratio decidendi* or how it is to be ascertained in actual cases, is conspicuous by its absence. Some restrict its meaning to the proposition of law to be found in the judge's opinion, which forms a necessary part of his reasoning in disposing of the case. On this view (let us call it R_1) every case has at least one *ratio* and that *ratio* does not vary, although later judges may interpret it in different ways. Others argue that the *ratio* of a case is the proposition of law for which the case will be held to be authority by later courts (we shall call this R_2). From this standpoint the *ratio* of a case may well change over time. A third group asserts (correctly in our view) that *ratio decidendi* is used in both senses, R_1 and R_2.

MacCormick, *Legal Reasoning*, p. 215

> "Professor Rupert Cross, the leading English authority on judicial precedent in English law has put forward the following as a 'tolerably accurate description of what lawyers mean by "*ratio decidendi*"': 'The *ratio decidendi* of a case is in any rule of law expressly or impliedly treated by a judge as a necessary step in reaching his conclusion, having regard to the line of reasoning adopted by him.'

By taking full account of the justificatory function and the general structure of the type of legal reasoning involved in judicial opinions, we can perhaps improve on that.

The *ratio decidendi* is the ruling expressly or impliedly given by a judge which is sufficient to settle a point of law put in issue by the parties' arguments in a case, being a point on which a ruling was necessary to his justification (or one of his alternative justifications) of the decision in the case. (The caveat must be repeated here that, on this view, by no means all cases—even 'leading' cases—have a single *ratio decidendi*.)"

Cross, *Precedent in English law*, pp. 76–77

"[It has been] suggested that the expression *ratio decidendi* is used in two senses: (i) 'The rule of law for which a case is binding authority', and (ii) 'The rule of law to be found in the actual opinion of the judge, forming the basis of his decision'. If our description of the *ratio decidendi* is correct, there is generally no distinction between these two senses of the phrase until a decision has been interpreted in subsequent cases. Up to that moment the rule of law for which the decision is binding authority is that which is to be found in the actual opinion of the judge, forming the basis of his decision. Very often there will continue to be no distinction between the two suggested senses of the phrase *ratio decidendi* even after the decision has been interpreted in subsequent cases."

Llewellyn, *The Bramble Bush*, p. 52

"There is a distinction between *ratio decidendi*, the court's own version of the rule of the case, and the true rule of the case, to wit what it will be made to stand for by another later court."

Twining and Miers, *How to do things with rules*, p. 176

"When we interpret cases we ask such questions as 'for what rule(s) of law is this case an authority?' or 'for what proposition(s) of law can this be made to stand?' Some have answered these questions by maintaining that it is possible to extract from any case, one proposition of law and that this constitutes its *ratio decidendi*. Although there are competing versions of this view, we may characterize it as the 'buried treasure' argument. In this view it is typically assumed (a) that every case had one pre-determined *ratio decidendi* (at least for each question of law) and (b) that the *ratio decidendi* can be found, by reading the case, without referring to other cases; and (c) that the *ratio decidendi* does not, indeed cannot, change over time. These assumptions do not accord with the realities of the practice of handling precedents in our system. Talk of finding the *ratio decidendi* of a case obscures the fact that the process of interpreting cases is not like a hunt for buried treasure, but typically involves an element of choice from a range of possibilities. How unfettered is the choice and how wide the range of possibilities will depend on a variety of factors. One such factor, of crucial importance, relates to (b). In reasoning on a point of law we are typically confronted not with a single isolated precedent, but a collection of potentially relevant precedents. Each case has to be read in the context of all the other potentially relevant cases and this is one factor which limits the range of possible interpretations which can be put on it. Any test for determining the ratio decidendi, which suggests, explicitly or implicitly, that a case can be interpreted in isolation, without reference to other cases, is unrealistic and misleading. As the courts hand down new decisions, so the range of plausible interpretations of an earlier case may change over time."

Harari, *Negligence in the Law of Torts*, pp. 16–17

"The *ratio decidendi* of a case is the proposition of law the case supports when it is co-ordinated with all other cases. Once it is conceded that the law is not static, but develops and changes, it must also be conceded that the *rationes decidendi* of the cases change. If this is not generally recognised it is only because the notion of a changing law is still a relatively new one.

The concept *ratio decidendi* emerged at a time when it was seriously thought that the judges merely 'discover' the law, when there seemed to be a valid distinction between 'the law as such' and 'our conception of the law'. With *ratio decidendi* as a vague concept meaning 'the principle of law applied by the decision', and with a refusal to recognise that the judges were constantly making law, a distinction between 'the *ratio decidendi* of the case' and 'our conception of its *ratio decidendi*' was inevitable. A case would be regarded as establishing a certain rule of law, which would be modified when additional cases further 'clarified' the law: the *ratio decidendi* of the old case obviously was not what it appeared to be—that has been conclusively shown by the new decisions. Since the judges were not regarded as making or changing law it was quite logical to regard as the true *ratio decidendi* of the old case the rule of law which the new case seemed to imply.

To-day, when we no longer believe in 'the law as such', and when it is recognised that the law is not static, there is no room for the old concept of *ratio decidendi*. When looking for the *ratio decidendi* of a case we are not trying to discover the pre-existing rule of law which was applied in the case. What we are trying to determine is the rule of law the decision will support when all other existing law-making decisions have been taken into account. As new law-making decisions are given and taken into account, a given decision may no longer support a given rule . . ."

In most cases R_1, is clear enough—though not always (see "Multiple *ratios*", p. 440 below). In most cases also, as Cross argues, where R_1 is clear, it will coincide with R_2. Yet there are many cases where R_2 will differ from R_1. This is because ascertaining the *ratio* of a case is an art and judicial artists have a measure of licence in pursuing their art.

Glanville Williams, *Learning the Law*, pp. 66–67

"What is really involved in finding the *ratio decidendi* of a case is a process of abstraction. Abstraction is the mental operation of picking out certain qualities and relations from the facts of experience. Imagine a baby in whose household there is a terrier called Caesar. The baby will be taught to call this dog 'bow-wow,' because 'bow-wow' is easier to say than 'Caesar'. If he sees another dog he will guess or be told that this other dog is to be called 'bow-wow' as well. This is an example of one of the baby's earliest feats of abstraction. Abstraction comes through the perception of similarities between individual facts, and all language and all thinking depend upon it.

The next point to be noticed is that this process of abstraction may be carried to progressively higher flights. The individual dog Caesar is, at a low level of abstraction, a terrier; at a higher level he is a dog; higher still, a mammal; and then an animal and a living thing. In the same way a man might say that he was born at the Piccaninny Nursery Home; in London; in England; in Europe. All these are 'facts,' but they are facts belonging to different levels of abstraction.

We are now in a better position to state the *ratio decidendi* of a case. The ascertainment of the *ratio decidendi* of a case depends upon a process of abstraction from the totality of facts that occurred in it. The higher the abstraction, the wider the *ratio decidendi* . . . How do we know when to stop with our abstraction? The answer is: primarily by reading what the judge says in his judgment, but partly also by our knowledge of the law in general, and by our common sense and our feeling for what the law ought to be."

Llewellyn, *The Bramble Bush*, pp. 42–43

"Our job [is] to crack the kernel from the nut, to find the true rule the case in fact decides: the rule of the case . . . Perhaps . . . we may find guidance in the facts the court assumes. Surely this much is certain: the actual dispute before the court is limited as straitly by the facts as by the form which the procedural issue has assumed. What is not in the facts cannot be present for decision. Rules which proceed an inch beyond the facts must be suspect.

But how far does that help us out? What are the facts? The plaintiff's name is Atkinson and the defendant's Walpole. The defendant, despite his name, is an Italian by extraction, but the plaintiff's ancestors came over with the Pilgrims. The defendant has a schnautzer-dog named Walter, red hair, and $30,000 worth of life assurance. All these are facts. The case, however, does not deal with life insurance. It is about an auto accident. The defendant's auto was a Buick painted pale magenta. He is married. His wife was in the back seat, an irritable, somewhat faded blonde. She was attempting back-seat driving when the accident occurred. He had turned round to make objection. In the process the car swerved and hit the plaintiff. The sun was shining; there was a rather lovely dappled sky low to the West. The time was late October on a Tuesday. The road was smooth, concrete. it had been put in by the McCarthy Road Work Company. How many of these facts are important to the decision? How many of these facts are, as we say, legally relevant? Is it relevant that the road was in the country or the city; that it was concrete or tarmac or of dirt; that it was a private or a public way? Is it relevant that the defendant was driving a Buick, or a motor car, or a vehicle? Is it important that he looked around as the car swerved? Is it crucial? Would it have been the same if he had been drunk, or had swerved for fun, to see how close he could run by the plaintiff, but had missed the guess?

Is it not obvious that as soon as you pick up this statement of the facts to find its legal bearings you must discard some of no interest whatsoever, discard others as dramatic but as legal nothings? And is it not clear, further, that when you pick up the facts which are left and which do seem relevant, you suddenly cease to deal with them in the concrete and deal with them instead in categories which you, for one reason or another, deem significant? It is not the road between Pottsville and Arlington; it is 'a highway'. It is not a particular pale magenta Buick eight, by number 732507, but 'a motor car', and perhaps even 'a vehicle'. It is not a turning around to look at Adoree Walpole, but a lapse from the supposedly proper procedure of careful drivers, with which you are concerned. Each concrete fact of the case arranges itself, I say, as the representative of a much wider abstract category of facts, and it is not in itself but as a member of the category that you attribute significance to it. But what is to tell you whether to make your category 'Buicks' or 'motor cars' or 'vehicles'? What is to tell you to make your category 'road' or 'public highway'? The court may tell you. But the precise point that you have up for study is how far it is safe to trust what the court says. The precise issue which you are attempting to solve is whether the court's language can be taken as it stands, or must be amplified, or must be whittled down.

This brings us at last to the case system. For the truth of the matter is a truth so obvious and trite that it is somewhat regularly overlooked by students. That no case can have a meaning by itself! Standing alone it gives you no guidance. It can give you no guidance as to how far it carries, as to how much of its language will hold water later. What counts, what gives you leads, what gives you sureness, that is the background of the other cases in relation to which you must read the one. They color the language, the technical terms used in the opinion. But above all they give you the wherewithal to find which of the facts are significant, and in what aspect they are significant, and how far the rules laid down are to be trusted."

It follows that every case contains not only (at least, in theory) an R_1 (or possibly more than one) but also a range of potential R_2s of increasing and decreasing levels of generality. Usually the later courts select an R_2 which coincides with or closely approximates to R_1. Yet if later judges feel that the R_1 of a case was too broadly stated, *i.e.* framed at too high a level of generality or abstraction, they can restrict it by reference to the facts of the case. This has been called "restrictive distinguishing" (see p. 431 below). If, on the other hand, they wish to apply the case analogically to a rather different set of facts, they will frame R_2 more broadly than R_1. Although the R_2 of a case can continue to contract or expand over time as it is considered in later cases, in general the R_2 of a case will tend to crystallise after it has been interpreted on a number of occasions by later courts.

Obiter Dicta

Any proposition of law contained in the original judgment which does not form part of the *ratio decidendi* is termed an *obiter dictum*. Since it is defined by exclusion the concept of *obiter* is as hard to pin down as ratio. It is clear, however, the *obiter dicta* may be persuasive to a greater or lesser degree. In some situations, *e.g.* where there is a considered dictum of the House of Lords, the proposition may be so highly persuasive as to be binding in all but name. (*Hedley Byrne & Co. v. Heller* [1964] A.C. 465 is one such case.) On other occasions dicta may be little more than off-the-cuff speculations. Since the R_2 of a case may vary, it follows that occasionally a proposition in the case which was initially considered to be obiter may subsequently become part of the *ratio*, and vice versa.

Glanville Williams, *Learning the Law*, p. 72

"In contrast with the *ratio decidendi* is the *obiter dictum*. The latter is a mere saying by the way, a chance remark, which is not binding upon future courts, though it may be respected according to the reputation of the judge, the eminence of the court, and the circumstances in which it came to be pronounced. An example would be a rule of law stated merely by way of analogy or illustration, or a suggested rule upon which the decision is not finally rested. The reason for not regarding an *obiter dictum* as binding is that it was probably made without a full consideration of the cases on the point, and that, if very broad in its terms, it was probably made without a full consideration of all the consequences that may follow from it; or the judge may not have expressed a concluded opinion."

***Saif Ali v. Sydney Mitchell & Co.* [1980] A.C. 198**

Lord Wilberforce: *Rondel v. Worsley* was concerned and only concerned with matters taking place in court which resulted in an outcome unfavourable to the client. But the speeches contain considered observations as to the extent of barristers' immunity for matters taking place outside court and in barristers' chambers. Since the case was not concerned with such matters, these observations have the status of *obiter dicta*. However, not all *obiter dicta* have the same weight, or lack of weight, in later cases. Of those then made in the House two things may be said. First, they were considered and deliberate observations after discussion of the same matters had taken place in the Court of Appeal and in the light of judgments in the Court of Appeal. It may be true that the counsel in the case did not present detailed arguments as to the position outside the courtroom—they had no interest in doing so—but I cannot agree that this invalidates or weakens judicial pronouncements. Judges are more than mere selectors between rival views; they are entitled to and do think for themselves. Secondly, it would have been impossible for their Lordships to have dealt with the extent of barristers' immunity for acts in court without relating this to their immunity for other acts. As I shall shortly show their Lordships attached the immunity to the conduct of litigation. But litigation takes some time to arrive in court for trial, so, unless they were prepared to confine the immunity to the part of litigation which occurs in the court room, it was not only appropriate but necessary to deal with such acts, in relation to litigation, as occur outside the courtroom. A statement of principle which stopped at the door of the court would have been truncated and irrational. These factors, in my opinion, tell in favour of giving considerably more weight to their Lordships' expressions than obiter dicta normally received. We may clarify them, but we should hesitate before disregarding them."

Lord Salmon: "When *Rondel v. Worsley* came to this House, this House faced a dilemma. The Law Lords did not agree with the majority of the Court of Appeal which had decided, *obiter*, that a barrister enjoyed a blanket immunity against any claim in negligence in respect of all paperwork. It was indubitably plain to this House that the obiter dictum of the majority of the Court of Appeal, although not binding, would carry great weight. Indeed it was extremely doubtful that any judge of first instance or any division of the Court of Appeal would depart from that obiter dictum unless this House disagreed with it. Accordingly, this House had no real choice but to deal with it. And this they did. By a majority of four to one the Law Lords rejected the proposition that the Bar enjoyed the blanket immunity proclaimed by the majority of the Court of Appeal."

[*Rondel v. Worsley* [1967] 1 Q.B. 443, CA; [1969] 1 A.C. 191, HL(E).]

D. THE DRAWBACKS OF PRECEDENT

The advantages conferred by a doctrine of precedent must be assessed in the light of that doctrine's attendant drawbacks. The doctrines of binding precedent which currently prevail in Scotland and England carry with them the risk that sometimes the certainty being pursued is the certainty of injustice. Justice demands not merely that like cases be treated alike but that different cases be treated differently. Where social conditions have greatly changed since the precedent was decided it may no longer be a "like" case. Similarly, uniformity and consistency may be purchased at the price of the perpetuation of error.

Lord Devlin, "Who is at fault when injustice occurs?", p. 71

"The object of a rule is to ensure that similar cases are similarly decided; if they were not, then there would not be justice at all . . . [yet] any rule, however well phrased, may occasionally interfere with judgment on the merits. Justice for all carries with it the possibility of something less than justice in the individual case."

Jackson, *The Struggle for Judicial Supremacy*, p. 295

"*Stare decisis* means that on the same point of law yesterday's decision shall govern today's decision. Like a coral reef, the common law becomes a structure of fossils. Precedents govern the conclusions and the reasoning of lawyers and judges . . . The judge who can take refuge in a precedent does not need to justify his decision by reason . . . He may reluctantly feel himself bound by a doctrine, supported by a respected historical name, that he would not be able to justify to contemporary opinion or under modern conditions."

Lord Devlin, "The Judge and Case Law", p. 184

> "Case law has to be very skilfully made and maintained if its great asset, its elasticity, is to be properly used. The danger is that a precedent, once created, will be treated as if it was as impregnable to a judge as is statute law. It gets forgotten that a judge-made rule should always be designed to fit the circumstances. The circumstances are general and not special; the latter must be left for the trial judge. They are expected to last for some time, else there would be no place for a general rule, but they are not expected to last for ever."

II. THE JUDICIAL ROOM FOR MANOEUVRE

Any doctrine of precedent should permit the judiciary to draw a balance between the need for stability and the need for flexibility in the common law.

Lord Reid, "The Judge as Law Maker", p. 26

> "People want two inconsistent things; that the law shall be certain, and that it shall be just and shall move with the times. It is our business to keep both objectives in view. Rigid adherence to precedent will not do. And paying lip service to precedent while admitting fine distinctions gives us the worst of both worlds. On the other hand too much flexibility leads to intolerable uncertainty."

Lord Edmund-Davies, "Judicial Activism", p. 13

> "[W]hatever a judge does, he will surely have his critics. If, in an effort to do justice, he appears to make new law, there will be cries that he is overweening and that he has rendered uncertain what had long been regarded as established legal principles. On the other hand, if he sticks to the old legal rules, an equally vocal body will charge him with being a reactionary, a slave to precedent, and of failing to mould the law to changing social needs. He cannot win and, if he is wise, he will not worry, even though at times he may ruefully reflect that those who should know better seem to have little appreciation of the difficulties of his vocation."

In practice the judges have developed a number of techniques for handling precedents within the limits of choice permitted by the respective doctrines of binding precedent which currently prevail in Scotland and England.

A. OVERRULING

Courts higher up in a hierarchy have the power to overrule or not to follow the decisions of courts lower down in that hierarchy, and in certain instances, precedents of their own or co-ordinate courts. In the Court of Session an Inner

House decision, which would normally be binding on a subsequent Division of the Inner House, may be overruled if a larger court is convened.

Even if a court considers that an earlier case was wrongly decided and it has the power to overrule it, it may hesitate to do so. This is in part because overruling a precedent involves the historical fiction that the precedent never represented the law—that is, overruling alters the law retrospectively. This is thought to be unfair to parties who have organised their affairs in the belief that the earlier case was good law.

For this reason some judges and commentators have called for the introduction of overruling with prospective effect only—a technique available in the Supreme Courts of India and the United States. See "Prospective Overruling" (below, p. 457).

Between 1898 and 1966 the House of Lords regarded itself as bound by its own decisions. However, in the latter year the Law Lords led by Lord Reid persuaded the Lord Chancellor (Lord Gardiner) to issue a Practice Statement on Precedent in the House of Lords announcing that the House would in future regard itself as free to depart from its own previous decisions. The choice of the phrase "depart from" rather than "overrule" undoubtedly reflected the Law Lords' awareness of the artificiality of the fiction that a previous decision never represented the law. The whole purpose of the Practice Statement was to permit them to change the development of the law openly rather than evading precedents by sleight of hand. Nevertheless, they did not embrace prospective overruling, retaining instead the traditional retrospective approach. This has led to continuing debates as to when the House should use its newly created power.

***Practice Statement (Judicial Precedent)* [1966] 1 W.L.R. 1234**

> "Their Lordships regard the use of precedent as an indispensible foundation upon which to decide what is the law and its application to individual cases. It provides at least some degree of certainty upon which individuals can rely in the conduct of their affairs, as well as a basis for orderly development of legal rules.
>
> Their Lordships nevertheless recognise that too rigid adherence to precedent may lead to injustice in a particular case and also unduly restrict the proper development of the law. They propose therefore to modify their present practice and, while treating former decisions of this House as normally binding, to depart from a previous decision when it appears right to do so.
>
> In this connection they will bear in mind the danger of disturbing retrospectively the basis on which contracts, settlements of property and fiscal arrangements have been entered into and also the especial need for certainty as to the criminal law.
>
> This announcement is not intended to affect the use of precedent elsewhere than in the House."

The statement was issued to the press with the following explanatory note:

> "Since the House of Lords decided the English case of *London Street Tramways v. London County Council* in 1898, the House have considered

themselves bound to follow their own decisions, except where a decision has been given *per incuriam* in disregard of a statutory provision or another decision binding on them.

The statement made is one of great importance, although it should not be supposed that there will frequently be cases in which the House thinks it right not to follow their own precedent. An example of a case in which the House might think it right to depart from a precedent is where they consider that the earlier decision was influenced by the existence of conditions which no longer prevail, and that in modern conditions the law ought to be different.

One consequence of this change is of major importance. The relaxation of the rule of judicial precedent will enable the House of Lords to pay greater attention to judicial decisions reached in the superior courts of the Commonwealth, where they differ from earlier decisions of the House of Lords. That could be of great help in the development of our law. The superior courts of many other countries are not rigidly bound by their own decisions and the change in the practice of the House of Lords will bring us more into line with them."

[*London Street Tramways Co. Ltd v. L.C.C.* [1898] A.C. 375.]

***Jones v. Secretary of State for Social Services* [1972] A.C. 944**

Lord Reid: "My understanding of the position when this resolution was adopted was and is that there were a comparatively small number of reported decisions of this House which were generally thought to be impeding the proper development of the law or to have led to results which were unjust or contrary to public policy and that such decisions should be reconsidered as opportunities arose. But this practice was not to be used to weaken existing certainty in the law. The old view was that any departure from rigid adherence to precedent would weaken that certainty. I did not and do not accept that view. It is notorious that where an existing decision is disapproved but cannot be overruled courts tend to distinguish it on inadequate grounds. I do not think that they act wrongly in so doing: they are adopting the less bad of the only alternatives open to them. But this is bound to lead to uncertainty for no one can say in advance whether in a particular case the court will or will not feel bound to follow the old unsatisfactory decision. On balance it seems to me that overruling such a decision will promote and not impair the certainty of the law.

But that certainty will be impaired unless this practice is used sparingly. I would not seek to categorise cases in which it should or cases in which it should not be used. As time passes experience will supply some guide. But I would venture the opinion that the typical case for reconsidering an old decision is where some broad issue [of justice or public policy] is involved, and that it should only be in rare cases that we should reconsider questions of construction of statutes or other documents. In very many cases it cannot be said positively that one construction is right and the other wrong.

Construction so often depends on weighing one consideration against another. Much may depend on one's approach."

***Fitzleet Estates Ltd v. Cherry* [1977] 1 W.L.R. 1345**

The appellant company contended that a 3:2 decision of the House of Lords in 1966 on a point of statutory construction was wrongly decided.

> **Lord Wilberforce**: "This contention means, when interpreted, that three or more of your Lordships ought to take the view which appealed then to the minority.
>
> My Lords, in my firm opinion, the 1966 Practice Statement was never intended to allow and should not be considered to allow such a course. Nothing could be more undesirable, in fact, than to permit litigants, after a decision has been given by this House with all appearance of finality, to return to this House in the hope that a differently constituted committee might be persuaded to take the view which its predecessors rejected. True that the earlier decision was by majority: I say nothing as to its correctness or as to the validity of the reasoning by which it was supported. That there were two eminently possible views is shown by the support for each by at any rate two members of the House. But doubtful issues have to be resolved and the law knows no better way of resolving them than by the considered majority opinion of the ultimate tribunal. It requires much more than doubts as to the correctness of such opinion to justify departing from it."

Maher, "Statutory Interpretation and Overruling in the House of Lords", pp. 88–89

> "In *Vestey v. I.R.C.* Lord Wilberforce spoke of the need to exercise discretion conferred by the 1966 Practice Statement 'sparingly and [to] try to keep it governed by stated principles.' The importance of the *Jones* case can be measured by the fact that the passage in Lord Reid's speech in that case concerning the general appropriateness of the use of the power has been cited in part or in full in a number of later cases, including *R. v. Knuller (Publishing etc.) Ltd*, *Fitzleet Estates Ltd v. Cherry (Inspector of Taxes)*, *R. v. Camplin*, and *Vestey v. I.R.C.*, and has also been referred to in a number of other cases by their Lordships and by counsel. Most of the cases where *Jones* has been cited are in the context of the general doctrine that the 1966 power is to be used sparingly, but the more specific point mentioned in *Jones* that matters of interpretation will rarely be suitable for use of the power to overrule has been expressly mentioned in *R. v. Knuller (Publishing, etc.) Ltd*, *Taylor v. Provan*, and *Vestey v. I.R.C.* . . . When we look at the cases involving the use of 1966 power, we find a whole range of standards, co-existing with and potentially conflicting with each other, that the House has regard to when contemplating use of the power to overrule. In those cases where the issue of statutory construction has been raised, three other principles have also been in issue, either competing with or adding support to that principle. These are the argument that the issue of injustice to the

particular litigants is involved, that Parliament has approved the precedent in question, and that the age of the precedent and the reliance placed upon it precludes use of the 1966 power."

[*Vestey v. I.R.C.* [1980] A.C. 1148; *R. v. Knuller (Publishing, etc.) Ltd* [1973] A.C. 435; *R. v. Camplin* [1978] A.C. 705; *Taylor v. Provan* [1975] A.C. 194.]

***R. v. Cunningham* [1982] A.C. 566**

Lord Edmund-Davies: "The cases are probably rare where your Lordships' House would think it right to invoke the Practice Statement (Judicial Precedent) . . . notwithstanding the conclusion that a relevant earlier decision had been correctly arrived at. But that such a power exists is recognised in the Practice Statement itself, and *Miliangos v. George Frank (Textiles) Ltd* [1976] A.C. 443 is an instance of this House, while not condemning as wrong a decision it had delivered 15 years earlier, declining to follow it on the ground that the instability which had meanwhile overtaken major currencies was such that, in the words of Lord Wilberforce, 'To change the rule would . . . avoid injustice in the present case' (at p. 467F).

Even where an earlier decision is not approved of, the Practice Statement stresses . . . 'the especial need for certainty as to the criminal law', and in *R. v. Knuller (Publishing, Printing and Promotions) Ltd* [1973] A.C. 435, 455 Lord Reid emphasised that ' . . . our change of practice in no longer regarding previous decisions of this House as absolutely binding does not mean that whenever we think that a previous decision was wrong we should reverse it.'"

Paterson, "Lord Reid's unnoticed legacy—A jurisprudence of Overruling", pp. 375–376, 380–382, 388–389

"Throughout his career in the Lords, Lord Reid endeavoured to spell out what he considered to be the limits of legitimate judicial lawmaking in the House. It was predictable, therefore, that once the Practice Statement had been made, Lord Reid's concern to demarcate between Parliament and the judiciary would lead him to formulate guidelines stipulating the typical situations in which the freedom asserted in the Statement should be exercised. This is precisely what occurred. Lord Reid, in a series of cases between 1966 and 1975 articulated at least seven criteria with respect to the new freedom. They were

1. The freedom granted by the 1966 Practice Statement ought to be exercised sparingly.
2. A decision ought not to be overruled if to do so would upset the legitimate expectations of people who have entered into contracts or settlements or otherwise regulated their affairs in reliance on the validity of that decision.
3. A decision concerning questions of construction of statutes or other documents ought not to be overruled except in rare and exceptional cases.

4. (a) A decision ought not to be overruled if it would be impracticable for the Lords to foresee the consequences of departing from it.
   (b) A decision ought not to be overruled if to do so would involve a change that ought to be part of a comprehensive reform of the law. Such changes are best done 'by legislation following on a wide survey of the whole field.'
5. In the interests of certainty, a decision ought not to be overruled merely because the Law Lords consider that it was wrongly decided. There must be some additional reasons to justify such a step.
6. A decision ought to be overruled if it causes such great uncertainty in practice that the parties' advisers are unable to give any clear indication as to what the courts will hold the law to be.
7. A decision ought to be overruled if in relation to some broad issue or principle it is no longer considered just or in keeping with contemporary social conditions or modern conceptions of public policy.

In setting out these criteria Lord Reid showed that like Lord Wilberforce, his successor as senior Law Lord, he believed that the discretion asserted in the 1966 Practice Statement ought to be exercised according to set principles or guidelines. It is also clear that in the pronouncements on this matter, particularly his seminal excursus on the purpose and parameters of the Practice Statement in the *Jones* case, he was consciously seeking to influence his colleagues . . .

It is clear . . . that whether it is fair to attribute it to his influence or not, Lord Reid's criteria reflected very accurately the dominant consensus amongst his fellow Law Lords . . . at the time . . . of his retirement (January 1975). So accurately that apart from the criteria already mentioned, only one further criterion not suggested by him (though he probably accepted it) had received much support from his colleagues by the date of his retirement. This eighth criterion was the expectation that a decision in criminal law ought to be overruled only in exceptional circumstances, in view of the especial need for certainty in criminal law.

Lord Reid's success in providing a lead for his colleagues or in encapsulating their views was all the more noteworthy in that it was not (so far as I could ascertain) the result of formal or informal discussions. Moreover, there has been no shortage of alternative criteria suggested by his colleagues which have failed to achieve widespread support. An attempt by Lord Hailsham to introduce as a criterion for overruling a precedent, that it involved a 'logical impossibility' has been rejected more than once by his brethren. The Law Lords have also been divided as to the importance to be attached to the age of the precedent under review. Lord Dilhorne's reluctance to interfere with longstanding precedents (voiced in the *Jones* case) was shared by Lord Kilbrandon (and possibly Lords Diplock and Edmund-Davies) in *Dick v. Burgh of Falkirk* [1976 S.C. (H.L.) 1]. In *The Albazero* [1977] A.C. 774, Lord Diplock (Lords Dilhorne, Simon and Fraser concurring), concluded that 'the almost complete absence of reliance' by litigants on a House of Lords case for over 120 years did not provide 'a sufficient reason for abolishing it entirely'. On the other hand Lord Simon (with the express concern of Lords Wilberforce, Cross and Fraser on this point) held in *Miliangos* that the maxim *cessante ratione cessat ipsa lex* was a relevant consideration in deciding whether to override a previous decision of the House. To add to the confusion, Lord Dilhorne's suggestion that it is easier to depart from a recent case than one that has stood for a long time was rejected by Lord Pearson in his interview, by Lord Diplock in the *Jones* case and by Lord Reid in *Conway v. Rimmer* [[1968] A.C. 910]. Yet in *D.D.P. v. Nock* [[1978] A.C. 979] Lord Scarman (Lords Diplock, Edmund-Davies, Russell and Keith concurring) gave as a reason for not overruling a decision of the House, the fact that it was 'very recent'. In point of fact, none of the arguments relating to the age of the precedent in question seem as yet to have acquired particularly widespread support amongst the Law Lords except to the extent to which they are really a restatement of Lord Reid's second criterion.

The disagreements extended to other criteria. Some Law Lords considered arguments based on 'parliamentary inactivity' to be accepted in this area—others did not; some relied on a 'floodgate' argument to justify inaction—others did not. One appellate committee argued that judicial unanimity in a precedent was a reason for it not being overthrown. Yet, another appellate committee the year before had held that the converse was not true, *i.e.* that the lack of unanimity in a precedent was not a reason for it being overthrown. Acceptance of a precedent in other common law jurisdictions had been used to justify retaining it; yet the rejection of a precedent in other common law jurisdictions, has not proved a strong argument for overruling it here. Similarly, acceptance of a precedent by textbook writers has been used to justify its retention; yet overwhelming criticism of a precedent by academics and textbook writers has not proved a strong argument for overruling it here . . .

We saw earlier that in addition to the better established criteria, certain other criteria relating to the exercise of the Practice Statement have been put forward and rejected. This may suggest that the 'established' guidelines are nothing more than a convenient shorthand for the existing consensus amongst the Law Lords in this field. Alternatively, it might be argued that they reflect not just the Law Lords' views, not just their practice, but also their perceptions as to how they ought to act. The evidence from the Law Lords' interviews and from the decided cases . . . shows that the Law Lords perceive the established criteria as prima facie valid reason for justifications for, or as presumptions in relation to, the exercise of their new freedom. The guidelines are not simply rules of practice. In the Law Lords' eyes they clearly possess a normative content. But they are not rules of law either. What then is their status? They are, I believe, best described in terms of the social science framework or role analysis. Viewed from this perspective the guidelines are normative expectations which form part of the role of a Law Lord.

But the role expectations (the guidelines) are of a flexible nature. They may conflict with one another and they are not always determinative of the outcome of a case. There are dissenting voices as to the scope and even the existence of some of the guidelines discussed in this article. The guidelines are open to different interpretations. In the words of Lord Scarman (with which Lord Reid would undoubtedly have agreed), 'Judicially indicated guidelines should not be treated as though they were a rule of law. They are to be followed unless the particular circumstances of a case . . . indicate that they would be inappropriate.'"

[Since 1981 the House has been asked to invoke the 1966 Practice Statement in one to two cases each year, the most significant being *Pirelli General Cable v. Oscar Faber* [1983] 2 A.C. 1, *Khawaja v. Secretary of State for the Home Dept.* [1984] A.C. 74, *Paal Wilson & Co. v. Blumenthal* [1983] 1 A.C. 854, *President of India v. La Pintada Cia Navegacion SA* [1985] A.C. 104, *Food Corporation of India v. Antclizo Shipping Corporation* [1988] 2 All E.R. 513, *R. v. Shivpuri* [1987] A.C. 1, *R. v. Howe* [1987] A.C. 417 and *Murphy v. Brentwood District Council* [1991] 1 A.C. 398. Arguably, none of these cases involved a departure from the criteria articulated by Lord Reid. Indeed, *Pirelli*, *Khawaja*, *Paal Wilson* and *The Antclizo* contain positive endorsements of Lord Reid's criteria. In only four, *Khawaja*, *Shivpuri*, *Howe* and *Murphy* was the Practice Statement successfully invoked. While it is true that two, *Khawaja* and *Shivpuri*, turned on points of statutory interpretation, in each case the House was able to argue, with some conviction, that the precedents involved errors of interpretation of constitutional or fundamental importance. Interestingly, both cases involved departing from relatively recent decisions—a point which seems to confirm the suggestion that arguments in relation to the age of the precedent are equivocal in the Law Lords' ears when considering the Practice Statement.

Some commentators have argued that the practical importance of the Practice Statement has been very limited. In fact, in the eyes of the Law Lords, they exercised their new freedom in about nine of the 36 cases between 1966 and 1983 in which the possibility of invoking the Practice Statement was raised. The Law Lords saw the Statement as a relaxation in their attitude to precedent, not a revolution. But the change was psychologically important. The commentators have been misled by the fact that the House (like the U.S. Supreme Court) in the early years after 1966 was wary of overturning decisions in explicit terms, preferring instead to distinguish them out of existence, even though they would not have felt able to evade the precedents had the Practice Statement not existed. In part, this could be attributed to understandable caution, lest overt overrulings should encourage a flood of requests for them to reverse earlier decisions. It was also due, however, to divisions amongst the Law Lords as to the wisdom of overt as opposed to covert, judicial law-making.

The power conferred by the Practice Statement has been used in one Scottish appeal, *Dick v. Burgh of Falkirk*, 1976 S.C. (H.L.) 1. See G. Maher, "Scots law and the 1966 Practice Statement" 1981 S.L.T. (News) 181. [See further on the House of Lords overruling its own decisions, J.W. Harris, "Towards Principles of Overruling" (1990) 10 O.J.L.S. 135.]

B. DISTINGUISHING

Any judge, irrespective of his or her location in the court hierarchy, may decline to follow a precedent which would otherwise be binding on them provided they can establish some material distinction between the facts of the instance and those in the earlier decisions which justifies them in departing from that decision. Since no two cases are ever identical, if the precedent is one which the later judges considers to be unjust or unsound, they may be tempted to draw illogical or specious distinctions between the cases.

Smith, *The Doctrines of Judicial Precedent in Scots Law*, p. 81

> "The process of evaluating and comparing material facts may result in the rejection of an alleged precedent. The techniques of 'distinguishing', 'not following', 'doubting', and relegation for 'reconsideration' may in some cases be compared with diplomatic illness. They can provide opportunities—which the initiated understood—for evading undesirable results without undermining the corporate prestige of the Bench, or giving offence to particular judges. The practice of 'distinguishing' precedents is familiar in Scotland. The technique applies to two broad classes of case—the one where there is distinction with a substantial difference in material fact (which needs no further discussion); and the other where the distinction is without a substantial difference at all."

We saw earlier that the *ratio(s)* intended to be laid down by the judge(s) in a case may differ from that or those which subsequent courts will be prepared to hold the case to be authority for. As Professor Glanville Williams argues in *Learning the Law* at pp. 75–77:

> "Courts do not accord to their predecessors an unlimited power of laying down wide rules. They are sometimes apt to say, in effect: 'Oh yes, we know that in that case the learned judge purported to lay down such and such a rule; but that rule was unnecessarily wide for the decision of the case before him because, you see, the rule makes no difference to fact A, which existed in the case, and which we regard as a material fact, and as a fact that ought to have been introduced into the *ratio decidendi*.' One circumstance that may induce a court to adopt this niggling attitude towards an earlier decision is the necessity of reconciling that decision with others. Or again, the court in the earlier case may have enunciated an unduly wide rule without considering all its possible consequences, some of which are unjust or inconvenient or otherwise objectionable. Yet another possibility is that the earlier decision is altogether unpalatable to the court in the later case, so that the latter court wishes to interpret it as narrowly as possible.
>
> This process of cutting down the expressed *ratio decidendi* of a case is one kind of 'distinguishing.' It may be called 'restrictive' distinguishing, to differentiate it from the other kind, genuine or non-restrictive distinguishing. Non-restrictive distinguishing occurs where a court accepts the expressed *ratio decidendi* of the earlier case, and does not seek to curtail it, but finds that the case before it does not fall within this *ratio decidendi* because of some material difference of fact. Restrictive distinguishing cuts down the expressed *ratio decidendi* of the earlier case by treating as material to the earlier decision some fact, present in the earlier case, which the earlier court regarded as immaterial . . .

Some precedents are continually left on the shelf in this way, as a wag observed, they become very 'distinguished.' The limit of the process is reached when a judge says that the precedent is an authority only 'on its actual facts.' For most practical purposes this is equivalent to announcing that it will never be followed. It is not suggested that this extreme form of distinguishing is a common occurrence, for generally judges defer to the decisions of their predecessors both in the letter and in the spirit, even though they dislike them. But restrictive distinguishing does happen, and the possibility of its happening makes it of great importance to the lawyer."

***Turner's Trustees v. Turner* 1961 S.L.T. 319**

The deceased left her house to her son in her will. In an addendum to the will (the codicil) she directed her trustees that in the event of her son predeceasing her daughter the house should go to the daughter and on her death to the deceased's grandson. The trustees sought guidance from the Inner House (by way of a Special Case) as to whether the codicil had restricted the son's interest in the house to living in it during his lifetime or whether it left him free to dispose of the house if he so wished.

Lord President (Clyde): "We were . . . referred to the case of *Jamieson's Trustees v. Jamieson* (1899) 2 F. 258, 7 S.L.T. 279, the facts in which it was contended were undistinguishable from the present and compelled us to reach an opposite conclusion to that which I have just indicated. But *Jamieson's Trustees* was decided on its own particular facts without reference in the opinions delivered by the Court to prior authorities, although these were quoted in the course of the argument. The case has, so far as I see, never been followed, it is not referred to in any of the text books and it is not a case that I would be prepared to follow unless the facts were completely identical. For it seems almost impossible to reconcile the case with principle, or with any of the other authorities. In my view, the facts in the present case although similar to those in *Jamieson's Trustees* are not the same. The basis as I understand it for the conclusion reached in *Jamieson's Trustees* was that stated by Lord McLaren, at page 263—'The conflict in the directions to the trustees which was to be found in the settlement and in the codicil were so direct as to constitute, in effect, a case of plain repugnancy between the two directions If that be the *ratio decidendi* in *Jamieson's Trustees*, it does not conclude the present case. Here there is no such plain repugnancy at all. *Jamieson's Trustees*, therefore, is not a case which compels us to decide that the codicil cuts down the right of the second party to a liferent."

[For further examples of distinguishing, see the cases set out below and the treatment given to *Manners v. Whitehead* (1898) 1 F. 171 in *Ferguson v. Mackay* 1985 S.L.T. 94.]

C. PER INCURIAM

Wesley-Smith, "The *Per Incuriam* Doctrine", pp. 58, 64

"For any judge impatient with the restrictions of *stare decisis* there is an obvious temptation to overcome his difficulties by a liberal application of the *per incuriam* label. But there are dangers in doing so, and the courts have defined the doctrine very narrowly . . . In summary, it can be said that, as a general rule, a decision can properly be labelled *per incuriam* only when these conditions are satisfied: (1) there was a binding rule of law (contained in a statute, subordinate legislation or judicial decision) which, if taken into account, would have affected the result of the case; (2) the court was unaware of the binding rule of law when it made its decision; and (3) the court's decision was therefore manifestly wrong. A case is not *per incuriam* merely because counsel's argument before the court was weak or inexpert; or only one party was before the court; or only one side of the argument was considered; or the reasoning upon which the decision was based was faulty (for some other reason than ignoring a material, binding and contrary rule of law); or the court was not aware of practical or policy objections to the decision made, or of a rule of statutory interpretation; or the court adopted a conclusion not suggested by counsel; or the court appeared to misunderstand a binding rule of law to which it had been referred. It may be, however, that a case can properly be labelled *per incuriam* when ignorance of a binding authority arises from use of a misleading law report or where there is a clear error in the interpretation of a statute. A court may only apply the doctrine, and therefore decline to follow a precedent, in regard to the decisions of itself, a court of co-ordinate jurisdiction, or of a court lower in the hierarchy.

Per incuriam can be seen, not as an exception to, but as a necessary component of the *stare decisis* doctrine. All courts are under a duty to apply the law, and in so doing they must comply with the ground rules of the system; the most important of these are legislative supremacy and the binding effect of higher courts' decisions. A case decided in ignorance of and contrary to 'the law' (as represented by a statute or a binding judicial decision) is not 'the law' but a corruption of it, and the principle upon which the case proceeded cannot be considered authoritative. The notion that there are other circumstances in which *per incuriam* may arise has not proved fruitful, and it is difficult to imagine any situation which would justify departing from an otherwise binding judicial decision on the ground of want and care."

Cassell & Co. Ltd v. Broome [1972] A.C. 1027

Lord Hailsham L.C.: " . . . I am driven to the conclusion that when the Court of Appeal decided the decision in *Rookes v. Barnard* as decided '*per incuriam*' or 'unworkable' they really only meant that they did not agree with it. But, in my view, even if this were not so, it is not open to the Court of Appeal to give gratuitous advice to judges of first instance to ignore decisions of the House of Lords in this way and, if it were open to the Court of Appeal to do so, it would be highly undesirable. The course taken would have put judges of first instance in an embarrassing position, as driving them to take sides in an unedifying dispute between the Court of Appeal or three members of it (for there is no guarantee that other Lords Justices would have followed them and no particular reason why they should) and the House of Lords. But, much worse than this, litigants would not have known where they stood. None could have reached finality short of the House of Lords, and, in the meantime, the task of their professional advisers of advising them either as to their rights, or as to the probable cost of obtaining or defending them, would have been, quite literally, impossible. Whatever the merits, chaos would have reigned until the dispute was settled, and, in legal matters, some degree of certainty is at least as valuable a part of justice as perfection.

The fact is, and I hope it will never be necessary to say so again, that, in the hierarchical system of courts which exists in this country, it is necessary for each lower tier, including the Court of Appeal, to accept loyally the decisions of the higher tiers."

The House of Lords made it clear that *per incuriam* cannot be used to avoid the binding decision of a higher court, for the reasons given in Lord Hailsham's speech. This cannot be an assertion of infallibility by the House but merely an indication that in the furtherance of judicial comity and discipline no court (other than the House itself) may declare that a House of Lords decision was made *per incuriam*, even if it was. (For a case where the House has described one of its own previous decisions as *per incuriam*, see *Re Poh* [1983] 1 All E.R. 287.) Since higher courts do not need to offend lower courts by labelling their decisions as *per incuriam* it follows that the doctrine is only likely to be invoked by a court which is bound by its own decisions or those of a court of co-ordinate jurisdiction. In Scotland, only the Divisions of the Inner House are so bound, and they may convene a larger court. This may explain why per incuriam is rarely invoked in Scotland.

***Re Probe Data Systems Ltd (No. 3)* 1992 B.C.C. 110**

Scott L.J.: "[T]here is a residual category of cases which, exceptionally, may be treated as decided *per incuriam*. But, in my opinion, they establish that in order to come within this category it must be shown not only that the decision involved some 'manifest slip or error', but also that to leave the decision standing would be likely to produce serious inconvenience in the administration of justice, or significant injustice to citizens, or some equally serious consequences."

[For a House of Lords Case which falls somewhere between *per incuriam* and overruling one of their precedents see *Moodie v. IRC* [1993] 2 All E.R. 49.]

D. CESSANTE RATIONE CESSAT IPSA LEX

Maher, "Cessante Ratione Cessat Ipsa Lex", p. 162

"Two contrasting interpretations . . . can be given to *cessante ratione*. In the strong sense, which accords more readily with the literal translation of the phrase, the maxim is to the effect that where a rule has lost its underlying rationale then the rule itself is no longer a valid rule and no effect is to be given to it. In the weak sense, on the other hand, it simply means that a rule may have less weight as a result of changed circumstances and it may thus prove desirable to distinguish the rule or seek some way round it. Nonetheless, a rule it remains until repealed by a competent authority. The former approach has the quite radical consequence that no matter the origin of the rule in question, then any court irrespective of its position in the judicial hierarchy would be able to disregard it given the existence of changed circumstances."

In England the maxim is applied in the weak sense.

***Miliangos v. George Frank (Textiles) Ltd* [1976] A.C. 443**

Lord Simon: "To sum up . . . (1) the maxim in the form '*cessante ratione cessat ipsa lex*' reflects one of the considerations which your Lordships will weigh in deciding whether to overrule, by virtue of the 1966 declaration, a previous decision of your Lordships' House; (2) in relation to courts bound by the rule of precedent the maxim '*cessante ratione cessat ipsa lex*,' in its literal and widest sense, is misleading and erroneous; (3) specifically, courts which are bound by the rule of precedent are not free to disregard an otherwise binding precedent on the grounds that the reason which led to the formulation of the rule embodied in such precedent seems to the court to have lost cogency; (4) the maxim in reality reflects the process of legal reasoning whereby a previous authority is judicially distinguished or an exception is made to a principal legal rule; (5) an otherwise binding precedent or rule may, on proper analysis, be held to have been impliedly overruled by a subsequent decision of a higher court or impliedly abrogated by an Act of Parliament . . . This has nothing to do with the maxim '*cessante ratione*': it arises from the legal rule of *stare decisis* together with the constitutional hierarchy of courts and the constitutional supremacy of Parliament over all courts."

In Scotland the scope of the maxim is a matter of academic debate.

Smith, *The Doctrines of Judicial Precedent in Scots Law*, pp. 100–101

"One does not need to go as far back as Morison's *Dictionary* before encountering decisions which any reasonable man would recognise as having now fallen into desuetude. There are many cases in Dunlop, Macpherson and Rettie which are so redolent of antiquated ideas that a Scottish court would, it is submitted, feel justified—as would a codifying commission—in ignoring them, even though it was impossible to distinguish them convincingly. If this is the correct view, then the maxim *cessante ratione legis cessat lex ipsa* can be invoked by a court in Scotland, not merely as in England to justify the overruling of obsolete decisions of inferior courts, but as warranty for refusing to follow the outmoded precedents of courts of equivalent jurisdiction. It is reasonably obvious, of course, that antiquity is not *per se* an objection to a precedent. In some chapters of the law, as for example those concerned with heritable rights, the tendency is more towards conservatism than is the case where personal rights of negligence in relation to moveables have to be considered. Again, judges clearly may differ as to what decisions have been superseded by events . . . the personal factor cannot be eliminated from the judicial process.

In *Beith's Trustees* 1950 S.C. 66 the Lord President, after quoting Lord Dunedin on precedent, continued, 'I propose to apply this authoritative guidance in considering the cases relied upon by the first parties, and to add this corollary that, if it is manifest that the *ratio decidendi* upon which a previous decision has rested has been superseded and invalidated by subsequent legislation or from other like cause, that *ratio decidendi* ceases to be binding'. In this case a wife's funds had been conveyed to marriage contract trustees for the wife in liferent, then for the issue of the marriage, whom failing for the wife's appointees or heirs in fee. The lady, having passed the age for child-bearing without issue, sought immediate payment of the fund to herself. When the case was argued before the First Division, counsel for the trustees cited three authorities, including a seven judge case decided in 1875, for the proposition that *stante matrimonio* the trust was irrevocable. These cases were swept aside by the Lord President with the concurrence of Lord Russell and Lord Carmont—the first two cases because in view of the diverse views expressed a *ratio* could not be spelled out without great difficulty; and the seven judge case because its *ratio* rested on the common law rules prevailing in 1875 as to the diminished capacity of a married woman—whereas the general law regarding the property and the rights of married women had been radically altered since that date. The Lord President observed, 'Nor do I see any need to convene a larger court for the purpose of reconsidering *Menzies v. Murray*. In 1875 and for some time after, the decision was unexceptionable and in harmony with the then existing general law. But the general law has passed *Menzies v. Murray* by, and under the fundamentally altered conditions which have prevailed for a generation the decision and its rationale have been as completely superseded as if they were based on a statute which has subsequently been repealed. There is no need to overrule *Menzies v. Murray* and no justification for so doing. The proper course is simply to cease to follow it.'"

Maher, "Cessante Ratione Cessat Ipsa Lex", pp. 163–165

"The basis of Lord Cooper's approach in *Beith's Trs* has often been characterised in terms of *cessante ratione*. If this is so, then it would be a case of applying the maxim in the strong sense, for Lord Cooper is evidently saying that due to changed circumstances one Division of the Court of Session can rightfully cease to follow a case decided by a court of seven judges, without there being any need to convene a larger court to reconsider *Menzies v. Murray*. But it is worthy of note that *cessante ratione* is used solely in commentators' accounts of *Beith's Trs* and not in the case itself. And this is no doubt for the very good reason that *Beith's Trs* has nothing at all to do with *cessante ratione*.

That this is so can easily be discovered if we look at what Lord Cooper actually said and did in *Beith's Trs*. For the relevant type of change which he held as justifying his course of action was not 'any substantial change in the social background' to *Menzies v. Murray* . . . or the changing social role or position of married women, but instead whatever alterations on the common law rules that had been brought about by statute. Lord Cooper was quite explicit about why he saw *Menzies v. Murray* as no longer constituting binding authority: 'We owe respect to previous decisions of superior or equal authority, but we also owe respect to Acts of Parliament; and if subsequent statutes have deprived a decision of its whole content, we have no duty to echo outmoded and superseded conceptions (1950 S.L.T. at p. 73). Thus *Menzies v. Murray* could be simply ignored by the court in *Beith's Trs*, not because of any rule about 'changed circumstances', but more straightforwardly by application of the standard doctrine of constitutional law that courts give effect to later statutes which abrogate previous common law rules. And such cases of repeal by statute, whether express or implied, as Lord Simon stressed in *Miliangos*, are only confusingly described in terms of *cessante ratione* . . .

In general, then, examination of actual practice does not bear out the traditional view, still urged by textbook writers, about the extent to which Scottish courts will disregard prior cases on the ground of substantial change in social or economic circumstances. In most cases the courts go no further than pursuing the necessary implications of statutory change. Admittedly, in England there is little scope for the application of *cessante ratione*, but at least the range of relevant 'changed circumstances' is fairly wide. In Scotland there must be countless cases in the reports where there has been some significant change in social and economic background (indeed many nineteenth century cases in areas of mercantile law, such as bankruptcy, are simply difficult to follow because of the different underlying commercial practices), yet these cases are still confidently cited as authoritative by practitioners and textbook writers alike."

Commerzbank Aktiengesellschaft v. Large 1977 S.C. 375

The pursuers were a bank incorporated, and carrying on business, in West Germany. The defender obtained a loan from the bank while he was stationed in West Germany on military service. The defender returned to Scotland and the pursuers raised an action against him for the repayment of the loan. The conclusion was in deutschmarks. The Lord Ordinary (Maxwell) reported to the Inner House as to the competency of a foreign pursuer seeking decree in the currency of a foreign country.

Lord President (Emslie): We have no hesitation in holding that the . . . conclusion in this action is competent in our law. This was the course recommended to us by the Lord Ordinary. As his report discloses, the only decision which might be thought to preclude us from taking this course is *Hyslops v. Gordon* (1824) 2 Shaw's Appeals 451. This was an action raised in respect of a sum due on a transaction the money of account of which was American dollars. The sum sued for was expressed in sterling but the Court of Session, for a reason which is not obvious, pronounced decree for a sum

> expressed in dollars. When the case came before the House of Lords on appeal Lord Gifford said that the judgment ought to have been for the sterling equivalent converted at the date of raising the action. The arguments are not reported and no other conversion date appears to have been considered. In *Miliangos v. George Frank (Textiles) Ltd* [1976] A.C. 443 Lord Fraser of Tullybelton at p.502 had this to say about *Hyslops*—'the reason for that part of the decision was the difficulty of ascertaining the rate of exchange at the date when the action was raised, but that reason is not applicable today, at least where dollars or other important currencies are concerned . . . The case should, I think, be treated as one decided in accordance with a practice that existed in circumstances which were very different from those existing today and therefore as one not necessarily to be followed now.' We agree with these observations and in our opinion the case of *Hyslops*, decided as it was in the context of conditions which no longer apply, does not now bind this Court. We are accordingly free to consider, in the context of the age of floating currencies and rapidly fluctuating exchange rates, the true objectives of our law . . . In our opinion justice requires that a foreign creditor who is entitled to payment of a debt due in the currency of his own country or the currency of a particular foreign country should not be bound to accept payment of the debt in the money of his debtor's country if any prejudice would be caused to him thereby."

Commerzbank failed to convince the doubters. Maher sees it simply as relating to a rule of practice. Nor is he convinced by the case of *Todd v. H.M. Advocate* 1984 S.L.T. 123 where a five judge High Court of Justiciary confirmed that the old common law rule that evidence adduced from a witness for one accused is not evidence against another accused where they have separate defences, had been abrogated by subsequent practice and by the impact of modern legislation. In support of Maher the Lords Ordinary in *Twomax v. Dickson, McFarlane and Robinson* 1983 S.L.T. 98 at pp. 102–103 and *Weir v. J.M. Hodge & Son* 1990 S.L.T. 266 at p. 270 concluded that the reported cases provided insufficient evidence for the existence of a strong doctrine of *cessante ratione* in Scots law.

***Weir v. J.M. Hodge & Son* 1990 S.L.T. 266**

> **Lord Weir**: "I do not consider that it is within my power to hold that the case of *Robertson v. Fleming* is no longer binding. In the case of *Beith's Trs*, the supervening event was legislation and it is easy to see how this can deprive prior decisions of content. I am not clear what Lord President Cooper had in mind when he referred to such decisions being superseded by subsequent legislation 'or from other like cause'. In the case of *Commerzbank*, the full court was considering a rule of practice which had become outmoded by changing commercial and economic conditions. So far, no court has held that it is free to depart from a rule of the common law laid down by a higher court on account of subsequent developments in that branch of the common law. It may be thought desirable that in such circumstances a court should feel free to hold a decision, even of the House

of Lords, to be no longer binding. On that question I express no opinion. However in the absence of clear authority that such a change of attitude towards the binding force of judicial precedent is permissible, I am not prepared to take this step."

[*Robertson v. Fleming* (1861) 4 Macq. 167; *Beith's Trs. v. Beith*, 1950 S.C. 66; *Commerzbank Atkiengesellschaft v. Large*, 1977 S.C. 375.]

However, in contradistinction it can be argued that *S. v. H.M. Advocate*, 1989 S.L.T. 469 in which the High Court abandoned the age old doctrine that a husband is legally incapable of raping his wife, is based on reasoning which is closely akin to the strong form of *cessante ratione*.

It seems, therefore, that the debate as to the status of the *cessante ratione* doctrine in Scots law today remains unresolved. Equally problematic is the question as to what the status of the doctrine ought to be in modern day Scotland. [For another critique of the Maher position, see Willock, "Judges at Work" 1982 J.Rev. 237 at pp. 240–243. Maher provides a lengthy reaffirmation of his position and of his co-author's (T. B. Smith) disagreement with him in paras 353–354 of Vol. 22 of the *Stair Memorial Encyclopaedia of the Laws of Scotland*.]

E. MULTIPLE RATIOS

***Behrens v. Bertram Mills Circus* [1957] 2 Q.B. 1**

Devlin J.: "It is well established that if a judge gives two reasons for his decision, both are binding. It is not permissible to pick out one as being supposedly the better reason and ignore the other one; nor does it matter for this purpose which comes first and which comes second. But the practice of making judicial observations obiter is also well established. A judge may often give additional reasons for his decision without wishing to make them part of the *ratio decidendi*; he may not be sufficiently convinced of their cogency as to want them to have the full authority of precedent, and yet may wish to state them so that those who later may have the duty of investigating the same point will start with some guidance. This is a matter which the judge himself is alone capable of deciding and any judge who comes after him must ascertain which course has been adopted from the language used and not by consulting his own preference."

[See also Lord Simonds, *Jacobs v. London County Council* [1950] A.C. 361 at p. 369.]

It does not follow, however, that each *ratio* is binding where in an appellate decision the judges have reached the same conclusion for different reasons, *i.e.* where each judge's opinion contains a different *ratio*. The *ratio* in an appellate decision is the highest common factor of the propositions which a majority of the court supports. If there is one or more dissent the *ratio* must be found in the majority opinions. Where the reasoning of a judge is so obscure that the *ratio* of his decision cannot be discerned, then his reasoning does not bind later judges. Similarly, if in an appellate decision there is no discernible majority support for any *ratio* then there is nothing to bind later courts except the decision of the specific facts of the earlier case. This leaves open the room for manoeuvre of later and lower courts. Thus, juggling with multiple *ratios* is one more technique which the wise judge acquires.

***Aitken's Trustees v. Aitken* 1927 S.C. 374**

A testator, who professed to be one of the last of a family which had been connected with a burgh for several centuries, and who had twice by the votes of his fellow citizens acted as champion at the riding of the marches, expressed in his will the desire that a monument should be erected in memory of his family and himself. He conveyed his estate to trustees, and directed them to erect a massive equestrian bronze statue of artistic merit of himself as champion on a site in one of the main streets of the burgh then occupied by shops and dwelling-houses of which he was the proprietor. The trustees sought guidance as to the validity of the directions, by way of a special case.

> **Lord Sands:** "A testator's intentions may be reasonable, but may nevertheless fall to be disregarded if he has provided a means for carrying them out which will clearly be ineffectual. The object of the testator I take to be that the memory of his family should be held in honour in Musselburgh, that his own name and memory should likewise be held in honour, and that interest and pride in ancient civic customs should be kept alive in his native town. Can the carrying out of the directions which he has given be reasonably regarded as calculated to effect these objects or any of them? . . . The municipality of Musselburgh, representative of the community, are strongly opposed to the carrying out of the testator's scheme, and they have passed a resolution to the effect that it is a 'fantastic proposition'. Eighteen years have been allowed to pass since the testator's death without any steps having been taken by anybody to stimulate the activity of the trustees. I conceive that, if there had been any minority or other movement counter to the opinion of the Town Council, it would have been the duty of the trustees to bring the matter before us. The attitude of the trustees, in upholding in argument the validity of the bequest, is correct, but it seemed clear in the course of the discussion that, so far as they are concerned, there is no conviction behind it.
>
> These considerations all point in the direction that the purpose of the testator would not be effected by the erection of the proposed statue, but that, on the contrary, its erection would cause the memory of the testator and his family to stink in the nostrils of the community of Musselburgh, as associated with a monument which tended to make their town and their ancient civic customs ridiculous.
>
> The citizens of Edinburgh regard the Scott Monument with pride as an imposing architectural memorial to a citizen whose name is held in honour throughout the world. But, if that monument had been erected, where it is and as it is, to the memory of an obscure tradesman who had happened to be captain of the orange colours, with a massive statue of the tradesman in the centre of it, would the citizens of Edinburgh have regarded this

monument with pride, would they have cherished the memory of that tradesman with affection, would their hearts have glowed with honest civic pride in the orange colours whenever their eyes rested upon the stately pile? I think not. I think that they would have regarded the monument and the statue with loathing as making the city ridiculous, and that, despite the artistic merits of the edifice and sculpture, they would have wished the monument and the statue and the orange colours with the memory of the deceased tradesman all at the bottom of the Forth.

One must not compare Musselburgh with Edinburgh, or High Street, Fisherrow, with Princes Street. But Musselburgh people as well as Edinburgh people may be credited with some local pride and sensitiveness, and with some sense of the ridiculous. It can hardly be suggested that this equestrian statue can be of interest to anybody outside of Musselburgh, except, perhaps, as a curious illustration of human vanity. It is in Musselburgh that the memory is to be cherished and civic pride stimulated. There is, in my view, every indication that the erection of this statue would not effect these purposes, but would militate against them . . . I am accordingly of opinion that the testamentary directions fail as being an irrational, futile, and self-destructive scheme to carry out not unreasonable purposes."

Lord Blackburn: "In my opinion the directions in the present cases are . . . unreasonable, extravagant, and useless, and they merit fully the epithet of 'fantastic' applied to them in the resolution of the Town Council . . . They are . . . objectionable from a public point of view . . . in respect that they involve the destruction of a valuable rent-producing property in the middle of a burgh without any conceivable benefit to the inhabitants of the burgh . . . I do not think we are entitled to hold that the direction in this case is other than invalid as contrary to public policy."

Lord Ashmore: "The adverse criticism of the Town Council seems to me to negative the suggestion of the testamentary trustees of the truster that the erection of the statue would be in the interest of the inhabitants of Musselburgh, or would confer a benefit of any kind on the community. Moreover, nothing is stated in the special case to show that the carrying out of the truster's directions would be helpful to the citizens of the burgh or beneficial in any way; nor was anything said to indicate that there is any desire on the part of the public, or any section of the public, for the erection of the statue . . . For the reasons which I have given, I am in favour of holding the truster's directions . . . invalid and ineffectual, in respect that if these directions were carried out they would confer no benefit or advantage of any kind on anyone."

[It is not clear what *ratio*, if any, can be derived from this case.]

For a case where a lower court has concluded that there is no discernible *ratio* in the majority opinions in a House of Lords decision, see *Harper v. National Coal Board* [1974] Q.B. 614. Because of the difficulties encountered in ascertaining the *ratio* of a decision in the House of Lords where there are several speeches, some judges and academics began to argue in the early 1970s that the House, particularly in criminal cases, should move towards the practice of the Privy Council of only issuing one majority judgment. Lord Reid was an inveterate opponent of single judgments in appellate courts except in special circumstances. His successors as presiding Law Lord (particularly Lord Diplock), led the House more in the direction of the Privy Council practice. (In 1975, when Lord Reid retired, 28 per cent of decisions in the House consisted of single judgments. By 1983 the figure had reached 68 per cent. In recent years there would seem to have been a swing back to Lord Reid's direction. See Bradney, "The Changing Face of the House of Lords" 1985 J.R. 178 and Lord Diplock in the case of *Re Prestige* [1984] I.R.L.R. 166.)

Cross, "The *Ratio Decidendi* and a Plurality of Speeches", pp. 379, 385

> "A case with a clear *ratio decidendi* may sink to the level of being authority for no more than it actually decides on account of the impact of subsequent decisions, but, when this lowly status has to be accorded to a case by the first court which considers it in a subsequent case, there has to some extent been a failure of judicial technique. This is because it is the function of courts to give judgment according to a principle or rule of law discernible to other courts. There are, however, several situations in which it is only too plain that this function has not been fulfilled. No reasons may be given for the judgment, something of a rarity these days, or, something of a rarity at any time, a judge may express himself so obscurely that it is impossible to say which facts he considered material and which immaterial; but the most frequent instances of cases which are only authority for what they actually decide are those in which five speeches are delivered in the House of Lords. There is of course no question of any want or obscurity of reasoning, there is simply nothing which can be described as the *ratio decidendi* of the House. The result is that the authority of the House of Lords as the body which finally declares what the law is is neither so extensive nor so coercive as is sometimes supposed, for, where there is no *ratio decidendi* of the House, lower courts are only bound by its decisions in cases in which the circumstances are not reasonably distinguishable from those which gave rise to the decisions. Everything said by any law lord in the course of his speech in any case is of course of great persuasive authority, but the persuasiveness loses much of its force when the observation is contradicted by that of another law lord in the same case; the result is that the lower courts have a wide choice in cases concerning matters on which there is a decision, but no *ratio decidendi*, of the House of Lords . . .
>
> Provided it was liberally construed by the presiding judge, I would welcome a provision under which criminal appeals to the House of Lords were normally disposed of in a single speech. I think there is all the difference in the world between the functions of the House of Lords in civil and criminal cases. The assistance of the development of the law by the formulation of principles is so much more appropriate in the former. In criminal cases one particular certified point has to be clarified. The common law is a dynamic force in tort and contract in a way that it is not in the case of the criminal law.

Even if we cannot have the norm of single speeches in criminal appeals to the House of Lords, might we not have, in civil and criminal cases alike, a greater co-ordination of the speeches?"

Lord Reid, "The Judge as Law Maker", pp. 28, 29

"We are often told that there should only be one judgment instead of, it may be, five speeches in the House of Lords. At first sight that seems good sense: the law will then be clear and judges and others who have to apply it will know where they are. The trouble is that it won't work and experience has shown that. As you know, until recently there could only be one judgment in the Privy Council and now if there is a dissent there can only be one judgment on each side. If you compare the quality of Privy Council judgments with speeches in the House of Lords for a long time back I think you will agree that from the point of view of developing the law Privy Council judgments have been much inferior. They are perfectly adequate to decide the particular case but not often of wide importance. Yet the same Law Lords have sat and they have taken just as much trouble. The reason is that a single judgment must get the agreement of at least all in the majority so it tends to be no more than the highest common factor in their views. So often in the House of Lords it is the second or third speech which now carries the greatest weight but we would not have had it at all if there had been only one judgment. Or take another example. For a time it was customary in the House of Lords to have only one speech in criminal appeals. But after the disaster of *Smith v. D.P.P.* we changed that: I don't believe that decision would have been so bad if there had been more than one speech. Differences would have been expressed which would have taken the edge off it.

The truth is that it is often not possible to reach a final solution of a difficult problem all at once. It is better to put up with some uncertainty—confusion if you like—for a time than to reach a final solution prematurely. The problem often looks rather different the second time you deal with it. Second thoughts are not always best but they generally are."

(*D.P.P. v. Smith* [1961] A.C. 290.)

Paterson, *The Law Lords*, pp. 184–185

"[Lord Reid commented], 'I take the view that when . . . you are breaking new ground, you don't know what your successors are going to do and you have got to leave a certain number of options open, and if you are going to try and define everything you'll do it wrong, it can't be done with one bite. You are far better, I think to put down your own views, having read the other man's . . . and then leave it to the next generation to pick out what they like best. The law develops very slowly you know, and we can't do it, not satisfactorily, by making a sort of final pronouncement on a new point. It would never do . . . and get us into far more trouble than the way we do it now.'

Even Lord Radcliffe who strongly disagreed with Lord Reid on the desirability of multiple opinions, was at one with him on this point. As he put it, 'I believe in the law as an inter-woven system and I do not believe in these great formative single decisions . . . It's the infinite number of cases which are influenced by a House of Lords case one way or the other that really makes the law'."

***Cassell and Co. Ltd v. Broome* [1972] A.C. 1027**

Lord Reid: "With the passage of time I have come more and more firmly to the conclusion that it is never wise to have only one speech in this House dealing with an important question of law. My main reason is that experience has shown that those who have to apply the decision to other cases, and still more those who wish to criticise it, seem to find it difficult to avoid treating sentences and phrases in a single speech as if they were provisions in an act of Parliament. They do not seem to realise that it is not the function of noble and learned lords or indeed of any judge, to frame definitions or to lay down hard and fast rules. It is their function to enunciate principles and much that they say is intended to be illustrative and explanatory and not to be definitive. When there are two or more speeches they must be read together and then it is generally much easier to see what are the principles involved and what are merely illustrations of it."

F. PRACTISING PRECEDENT

The following cases on the meaning of "family" in the Rent Acts illustrate that the techniques for handling precedent set out above are frequently employed in combination.

***Gammans v. Ekins* [1950] 2 K.B. 328**

For some 20 years a man had lived with the tenant of a dwelling house to which the Rent Restrictions Act applied. He had never married her, but he had adopted her name and posed as her husband. After her death in 1949 he remained in the house. In an action by the landlord for possession of the house, the defendant claimed the protection of the Rent Restrictions Acts on the ground that he was a "member of the tenant's family" within the meaning of the Acts.

Asquill L.J.: "It has been held that 'family' in the subsection should be given its popular meaning: see *Brock v. Wollams* [1949] 2 K.B. 388. Consanguinity is not a pre-requisite of membership of the same family. On the authorities not only are children members of their parents' family, but a husband is a member of his wife's family, an adopted child is a member of the adoptive parents' family, and a husband, on unusual facts, has been held to be a member of the same family as his wife's niece. Counsel for the landlord was right in saying that the material decisions limit membership of the same family to three relationships—first, that of children; secondly, those constituted by way of legitimate marriage between husband and wife, and, thirdly, relationships whereby one person becomes *in loco parentis* to another. Beyond that point the law has not gone. I do not think we should be justified in saying that the defendant was a member of Mrs Smith's family. If the relations between them had been platonic I can see no principle on which one could say that they were members of the same family which would not require the court to predicate the same of two old cronies of the same sex innocently sharing a flat. If, on the other hand, the relationship involves sexual relations it seems to me anomalous that a person can acquire a 'status of irremovability' by having lived in sin, even if the liaison has been, not a mere casual encounter, but one protracted in time and conclusive in character. I would, however, decide the case on a simpler view. To say of two people masquerading, as these two were, as husband and wife—there being no children to complicate the picture—that they were members of the same family, seems to me an abuse of the English language . . ."

Jenkins L.J.: "The defendant was not, in my view, a member of Mrs Smith's family in any reasonable sense whatever. The parties, for reasons of convenience, had chosen to live together, and the defendant had taken the name of Smith. The neighbours assumed that they were husband and wife and accepted them as such. I cannot regard this as giving the defendant the same claim to be considered a member of Mrs Smith's family as if they had been lawfully man and wife."

Sir Raymond Evershed M.R.: "It may not be a bad thing that it is shown by this decision that in the Christian society in which we live one, at any rate, of the privileges which may be derived from marriage is not equally enjoyed by those who are not married."

Dyson Holdings Ltd v. Fox **[1976] 1 Q.B. 503**

The defendant and Mr Wright lived together as man and wife for 40 years. She used his name but they were never married and they had no children. For the 21 years prior to his death in 1961 they lived in a house in which he was a statutory tenant. In 1973 the landlords discovered that the couple had never been married and sought to repossess the house on the grounds that the defendant was not "a member of the original tenant's family" within the meaning of the Rent Acts.

Lord Denning: "In the present case the lady is protected if she was a 'member of the tenant's family'; but not otherwise . . . The word 'family' in the . . . Act is not used in any technical sense, but in a popular sense. It is not used in the sense in which it would be used by a studious and unworldly lawyer, but in the sense in which it would be used by . . . the ordinary man in the street . . .

Applying this test, there are two cases in this court which are near to the present. The first is *Gammans v. Ekins*. The other case is *Hawes v. Evenden* [1953] 2 All E.R. 737. A dwelling-house was let to a Mr Randall. He lived there with a Miss Evenden. For 12 years they occupied the same house as man and wife, though they were not married, and two children had been born of the association. She kept her own name—Evenden—but the children used the name Randall. He died. She claimed to be a member of the tenant's family. The county court judge held that she was. The court upheld his decision. Somervell L.J. said ' . . . there the evidence justifies a finding that they all lived together as a family, and so . . . I think that the [mother] is a member of the family . . .'

If both these cases were rightly decided, it seems to follow that an unmarried woman (who has lived with a man as his wife for many years) is a 'member of the tenant's family' if she has children by him; but she is not a member of his family if she has no children. That means this: if the couple had a baby 19 years ago which died when a few days old, or as a young child, the woman would be a 'member of the tenant's family'; but if the baby had been still-born, or if the woman had had a miscarriage 19 years ago, she would not be a member of his family. Yet for the last 19 years they had lived together as man and wife. That seems to me a ridiculous distinction. So ridiculous, indeed that it should be rejected by this court; and that we should hold that a couple who live together as man and wife for 20 years are members of the same family, whether they have children or not.

But, is this court at liberty to reject the distinction? Are we bound by *Gammans v. Ekins*? That case can be distinguished on narrow grounds, such as that the woman was the tenant and not the man, or that their relationship might perhaps have been platonic. But I dislike the device of distinguishing a case on narrow grounds. I prefer to say, as I have often said, that this court is not absolutely bound by a previous decision when it is seen that it can no longer be supported. At any rate, it is not so bound when, owing to the lapse of time, and the change in social conditions, the previous decision is not in accord with modern thinking."

James L.J.: "In *Gammans v. Ekins* . . . the strongly expressed view was that as at 1949, the relevant date, the popular meaning of family did not include the male consort of a female tenant whose relationship had all the incidents of a marriage short of the birth of a child and all the outward appearances of marriage. Between 1950 and 1975 there have been many changes in the law effected by statute and decisions of the courts. Many changes have their foundation in the changed needs and views of society. Such changes have occurred in the field of family law and equitable interests in property. The popular meaning given to the word 'family' is not fixed once and for all time. I have no doubt that with the passage of years it has changed. The cases reveal that it is not restricted to blood relationships and those created by the marriage ceremony. It can include *de facto* as well as *de jure* relationships. The popular meaning of 'family' in 1975 would, according to the answer of the ordinary man, include the appellant as a member of Mr Wright's family. This is not to say that every mistress should be so regarded. Relationships of a casual or intermittent character and those bearing indications of impermanence would not come within the popular concept of a family unit.

It is not easy to decide whether in 1961 the ordinary man would have regarded the appellant as a member of Mr Wright's family. The changes of attitude which have taken place cannot be ascribed to any particular year. Had we to consider the position as at 1955 I would not be satisfied that the attitude reflected in the words of Asquith L.J. in *Gammans v. Ekins* had changed. I am confident that by 1970 the changes had taken place. There is no magic in the date 1961. I think that, having regard to the radical change which has by 1975 taken place, it would be a harsh and somewhat ossified approach to the present case to hold that in 1961 the appellant was not in the popular sense a member of the family.

I turn to the issue whether there is any rule of law which precludes the appellant being a member of the family for the purpose of the Rent Acts. If there is, it is to be found only in the decision of this court in *Gammans v. Ekins*. I confess that I have been troubled in the course of argument as to how far the decision of this court in that case is conclusive of the present appeal. The court in *Gammans v. Ekins* reversed the trial judge. They could not have done so unless the issue was a question of law. It is not a decision which can be explained on the basis of a question of fact. The cases which are said to be inconsistent with the decision are in my judgment not shown to be inconsistent. They are based on the added fact of birth of a child or children to the illicit union. All the members of the court in *Gammans v. Ekins* left that situation open for future consideration. The distinction between the mistress who is childless and the mistress who has a child by the tenant all forming a family unit is to my mind a vital distinction, I find it impossible to say that the decision in *Gammans v. Ekins* was *per incuriam*; all the judgments were carefully directed to the precise point. On its facts the case is distinguished from the present case because the tenant was a female who had taken a man into her house and the man claimed the statutory tenancy. But that factual difference to my mind does not affect the general principle. I cannot take the view that *Gammans v. Ekins* was wrongly decided. The decision is binding on the court, but it is binding only on the meaning to be given to 'family' at that time. The point decided was that applying the popular meaning of the word 'family' as it was used and understood in 1949 the evidence of relationship could not support a finding that the defendant was a member of the tenant's family. The decision is not authority for the proposition that at some later time a person in a similar position to Mr Ekins could not in law be a member of the tenant's family within the meaning of the [Rent Acts]. The word 'family' must be given its popular meaning at the time relevant to the decision in the particular case.

To hold that *Gammans v. Ekins* precludes the appellant from bringing herself within the Act would be to apply a precedent slavishly in circumstances to which it is not appropriate having regard to reality."

Bridge L.J.: "It is clear . . . that *Gammans v. Ekins* . . . proceeded on the basis that the question who is a 'member of the tenant's family' is to be answered according to the understanding of the ordinary man, and this test has been consistently applied in all the other cases decided on this provision.

> It is, I think, not putting it too high to say that between 1950 and 1975 there has been a complete revolution in society's attitude to unmarried partnerships of the kind under consideration. Such unions are far commoner than they used to be. The social stigma that once attached to them has almost, if not entirely, disappeared. The inaccurate but expressive phrases 'common law wife' and 'common law husband' have come into general use to describe them. The ordinary man in 1975 would, in my opinion, certainly say that the parties to such a union, provided it had the appropriate degree of apparent permanence and stability, were members of a single family whether they had children or not."

Leaving aside the question whether a word used in a statute can change its meaning over time the difficulty facing the Court of Appeal in *Dyson* was how to evade the precedent of *Gammans* which they regarded as out of touch with modern conditions. For Lord Denning the answer was straightforward. He continued with his one-man crusade to free the Court of Appeal from the rule that it is bound by its own decisions. It is not clear what techniques the other judges in *Dyson* used to evade the decision in *Gammans*. In Scotland, of course, in a similar situation all that would have been required would have been a five judge sitting of the Inner House.

In *Joram Developments Ltd v. Sharratt* [1979] 1 W.L.R. 3 the defendant, a young man, and the elderly childless widow of an English High Court judge (ironically one who many years previously had raised the question of what "family" meant in tenancy succession cases) had cohabited platonically together as "aunt" and "nephew" for 18 years. The widow was a statutory tenant of the flat in which they lived. Her family thoroughly approved of the relationship since the defendant looked after the widow and because he did so she did not have to enter a nursing home in her declining years. On her death the landlords sought to recover possession of the flat and the defendant claimed protection under the Rent Acts on the grounds that he was "a member of the original tenant's family". On appeal another division of the Court of Appeal distinguished *Dyson* on the grounds that no sexual cohabitation was involved, and applied *Gammans*.

The next case was *Helby v. Rafferty* [1979] 1 W.L.R. 13. Rafferty, the defendant, lived with a statutory tenant of a flat as her lover, for five years. The couple had no intention of getting married and did not hold themselves out to be married. The health of the tenant began to deteriorate and the defendant nursed her as a husband would have done. After the tenant's death the landlady sought to recover possession of the flat from the defendant. He claimed that he was "a member of the original tenant's family" and therefore protected under the Rent Acts. The case came before yet another division of the Court of Appeal. This time *Dyson* was acknowledged to be binding on the Court of Appeal but was distinguished once more on the facts because it was felt that in *Rafferty* the relationship was not of such permanence and stability that the ordinary man would say that the parties were "members of a single family". Then came *Watson v. Lucas*.

Watson v. Lucas [1980] 1 W.L.R. 1493

The defendant's wife left him after the first year of their marriage. He subsequently went to live with a widow who was a protected tenant of a flat. The couple slept together but had no children. For the most part they continued to use their own surnames. The relationship lasted for 19 years until the widow's death. The owner sought to recover possession of the flat and the defendant claimed to be "a member of the original tenant's family".

> **Stephenson L.J.**: "*Dyson Holdings Ltd v. Fox* . . . [was] distinguished by this court in *Helby v. Rafferty* . . . because during their five years' cohabitation the parties never pretended to be married and the tenant wished to remain independent, so that their relationship lacked the permanence and stability necessary to create a family unit. All three members of this court in *Helby v. Rafferty* regarded *Dyson Holdings Ltd v. Fox* as binding on them, and we must do the same. To go back to *Gammans v. Ekins* would be to introduce impermanence and instability into our own decision in this case. Only the House of Lords can reinstate *Gammans v. Ekins* and that they have so far declined to do . . . But can *Dyson Holdings Ltd v. Fox* be distinguished? The county court judge thought it could . . . As I read his judgment he denied Mr Lucas the protection of the statute because (1) usually he and Mrs Sullivan kept their own names and so remained independent of each other and (2) Mr Lucas deliberately chose not to get a divorce from his legal wife and so get into a position to marry Mrs Sullivan. The county court judge seems to have regarded his married status as an absolute bar to his being in fact a member of her family. He was there accepting the argument of counsel for the plaintiff, . . . that a man cannot have two families; Mr Lucas had a family in Ireland and not having legally rid himself of his wife and children in Ireland he could not be a member of another family here.
>
> That is, in my view, a plain error of law. The ordinary man often has two families, one by his first wife and another by his second, and often has, or at any rate knows, a man who has one by his wife and another by his mistress. I can see no legal impossibility in a man being a member of both families though he will have difficulty in fact in residing with more than one and it will be impossible in fact for him to reside with more than one, as required by the statute, if he is to succeed to a protected tenancy; and the question whether he is a member of his mistress' family cannot any longer be decided by any moral preference for the family to which his lawful wife belongs . . .
>
> I agree with the judge that Mr Lucas's remaining married is an important factor, as may be the retention of the couple's own names. But not in this case. For both factors are of importance, in my judgment, only as indications of independence and instability. The retention of the woman's name may indicate both, as I think it did in *Helby v. Rafferty*, but, if it does not indicate either, it has little relevance to the right answer to the ordinary man's question . . . .
>
> The ordinary man has to consider whether a man or a woman is a member of a family in the light of the facts, and whatever may have been held before *Dyson Holdings Ltd v. Fox* I do not think a judge, putting himself in the place of the ordinary man, can consider an association which has every outward appearance of marriage, except the false pretence of being married, as not constituting a family. If it looks like a marriage in the old

and perhaps obsolete sense of a lifelong union, with nothing casual or temporary about it, it is a family until the House of Lords declares . . . that *Dyson Holdings Ltd v. Fox* was wrongly decided because the reasoning of the majority was wrong. The time has gone by when the courts can hold such a union not to be 'familial' simply because the parties to it do not pretend to be married in due form of law."

Oliver L.J. (dissenting): "Essentially every case of this kind turns on its own facts and the impression that these facts make on the mind of the judge assuming for the purpose the mantle of the ordinary man. Speaking for myself I would regard the decision in the *Dyson* case as one which rested on its own peculiar facts and as standing at the very limit of an ordinarily accepted or acceptable definition of a family relationship. I would certainly not regard it as establishing a principle which is susceptible of further extension or which ought to be extended. The judge in the instant case had the difficult task of applying to the facts before him a test which, though neither an easy one nor a certain one, is certainly one which required him to consider all the available factors. The decision was essentially one which depended on the inferences to be drawn from all of the facts before him, which included the fact that the defendant was and remained by choice married to a lady who was living at the material time and who was the mother of his only child.

If and so far as the judge was of opinion that the continued existence of the defendant's marriage was, in itself, and by itself, an absolute answer in law to his claim. I respectfully disagree. I think, however, that it was one factor, and a not unimportant factor, to be taken into account, although I accept that a man may sometimes have two families. One possible inference to be drawn from it was that, however agreeable and convenient his relationship with Mrs Sullivan may have been, he was not prepared to make himself responsible for her maintenance and support indefinitely or to put himself in a position in which he might have become susceptible to convert the relationship into a permanent one by marrying her . . . I have concluded, not without hesitation, that I am not prepared to say that the judge, who saw and heard the witness, in making his assessment as a whole and in reaching the conclusion which he did reach on all the facts, was wrong to attribute weight to the factors which I have mentioned. They are, in my judgment, factors which do distinguish the instant case from the *Dyson* case, and I would dismiss the appeal."

Sir David Cairns: "I do not find the test of Cohen L.J. as helpful in this case it was in *Brock v. Wollams* . . . To the question 'Was Mr Lucas a member of Mrs Sullivan's family?', I have no idea what 'an ordinary man' would answer, Stephenson L.J. would answer Yes and Oliver L.J. would answer No.

I agree with both my brethren that we should proceed on the basis that *Dyson Holdings Ltd v. Fox* . . . was rightly decided, though I respectfully share the doubts that have been expressed about that decision and I recognise the force of the reasoning of Oliver L.J . . .

I have reached the conclusion that this case cannot sensibly be differentiated from *Dyson Holdings Ltd v. Fox*. I attach little or no importance to the continued use by Mr Lucas and Mrs Sullivan of different surnames. It is the relations between the man and the woman that are relevant rather than the appearance that they present to the public. In this case the permanence of the relationship is not in doubt.

That Mr Lucas had a wife in Ireland is to my mind, having regard to the brevity of cohabitation, the long separation and the refusal of Mr Lucas of reconcilation, neither an absolute bar to his being considered a member of Mrs Sullivan's family nor a weighty reason for finding as a fact that he should not be so considered. Even if he could be regarded as a member of his wife's family (which I doubt) I agree with Stephenson L.J. that it is perfectly possible for a man to be a member of more than one family."

Appeal allowed.

These cases illustrate not merely the techniques used by judges for avoiding precedents they dislike but also the problems that can be encountered where judges operate at the limits of these techniques. Following *Joram v. Sharratt* and *Helby v. Rafferty* it began to look as if the Court of Appeal had embarked on a campaign to distinguish restrictively the *ratio* of *Dyson v. Fox* in an effort to return to the law as it was stated in *Gammans v. Ekins*. The majority in *Watson v. Lucas* may have interrupted this trend but the central issues in the debate have yet to be ruled on by the House of Lords.

The *ratio* of *Dyson v. Fox* was narrowed still further by the decision of the Court of Appeal in *Harrogate B.C. v. Simpson* [1985] R.V.R. 10, from which it appears that neither a homosexual nor a lesbian couple could count as "family" for the purposes of the Rent Acts. However, *Dyson* received welcome support in *Chios Property Investment Co. Ltd v. Lopez*, *The Times*, November 3, 1987. In this case the Court of Appeal held that Ms Lopez who had moved into her cohabitee's flat with the intention of marrying him when their financial circumstances permitted had become a member of his family for the purposes of the Rent Acts by the time of his death two years later. *Chios* is significant, for the Court not only concluded that two years' cohabitation could constitute a sufficient state of permanence to establish a familial relationship, but also that children are not necessary for the constitution of a family and neither is a common surname (Ms Lopez had retained her maiden name).

If *Chios* marked a reversal in the gradual erosion of the *ratio* of *Dyson*, *Sefton Holdings Ltd v. Cairns*, *The Times*, November 3, 1987 reaffirmed the limitation to *Dyson* which was laid down in the *Sharratt* case. In *Sefton Holdings* the defendant in 1941 went to live with her friend's family when aged 23. Her parents were dead and her boyfriend had just been killed in the war. She was effectively adopted by the family and treated as a daughter of the family. (Because of her age she could not legally be adopted.) Her friend succeeded to the tenancy on her parents' death, but on her death the landlords served notice to quit on the defendant (now aged 70). The Court of Appeal held that although she had been a member of the household for 46 years, who was treated as a member of the family, she was not actually a member of the family. In the circumstances this seems a decision which accords neither with common sense, contemporary conceptions of "family", nor equity. It does, however, firmly underline that platonic relationships will not be considered by the courts as being capable of creating a familial nexus.

The most recent case revisited the question of whether homosexual or lesbian couples could be counted as "family". This time the court was much less sure.

***Fitzpatrick v. Sterling Housing Association Ltd* [1997] 4 All E.R. 991**

> **Waite L.J.**: " 'Member of the family' is in this instance undefined. Case law has held it to be a term of wide import capable of being interpreted flexibly by the courts according to the social perceptions of the time (*Dyson*) as reflected through the eyes of the ordinary man or woman . . . but the instances in which, following that interpretation, it has been applied outwith the strict family ties of marriage or kinship are limited to a child informally adopted (*Brock v. Wollams*) and persons of opposite sex living together as man and wife (*Dyson* and *Watson v. Lucas*). There has (until this present case) been no decision on the question whether a surviving lesbian or gay partner of a deceased statutory tenant qualifies for the status of 'member of the family'.
>
> . . . To adopt an interpretation of the statute that allowed all sexual partners, whether of the same or opposite sex, to enjoy the privilege of succession to tenancies protected by the Rent Acts would . . . be consistent not only with social justice but also with the respect accorded by modern society to those of the same sex who undertake a permanent shared life. The law in England regarding succession to statutory tenancies is firmly rooted in the concept of the family as an entity bound together by ties of kinship (including adoptive status) or marriage.
>
> The only relaxation, first by court decision and then by statute, has been a willingness to treat heterosexual cohabitants as if they were husband and wife. That was a restrictive extension, offensive to social justice and tolerance because it excludes lesbians and gays . . . The law of succession to Rent Act protected tenancies is, in short, arbitrary and discriminatory. No one today would attempt to defend the favour it accords outside the marriage tie, to heterosexual relationships over same-sex households . . . The judge was nevertheless right, in my view, to resist the temptation to change a bad law by giving it a new linguistic twist. He correctly acknowledged that such changes could only be made by Parliament . . . They are changes which will certainly need to be made."
>
> **Roch L.J.**: "The decision in *Dyson Holdings Ltd v. Fox* was considered by Lord Diplock to 'pose a difficult question' . . . [on the one hand, the approach in *Dyson*] can be said to prolong the life and usefulness of a statutory provision. On the other hand, it must inevitably increase the uncertainties which the imprecision of our language, even in the hands of skilled parliamentary draughtsmen, creates and cause the judiciary to run the risk of usurping the legislative function . . . The principle stated in *Dyson's* case allows the judge who can detect a change in the ordinary

popular meaning of a word used in a statute to escape from the doctrine of precedent . . . Having expressed my reservations with the decision in *Dyson*, I must, as have others in this court, follow it."

Ward L.J. (dissenting): "As I have already explained, the words of this Act must be given their contemporary meaning. Professor Ronald Dworkin expressed the point well in *Law's Empire* (1986) p.348 when he said: '[The judge] interprets not just the statute's text but its life, the process that begins before it becomes law and extends far beyond that moment, [the judge's] interpretation changes as the story develops.'

Since families are dynamic, the statutory interpretation must equally reflect the motive forces, physical or moral, affecting behaviour and change in domestic organisation. I realise, with some apprehension (but with some pleasure at the recollection of it) how close I am to a return to Celsus, *The Digest of Justinian* D 1, 3, 17, whose rule of interpretation was 'Scire leges non hoc est verba earum tenere, sed vim A.C. potestatem': to know the laws is not a matter of sticking to their words but of grasping their force and tendency.

. . . As the decided cases show, the meaning of family has been progressively extended. The movement has been away from the confines of relationship by blood and by marriage to the reality of family life, and from *de jure* to *de facto* relationships.

[Ward L.J. then referred to the earlier cases and continued] . . . If the law is as my Lords state it to be, then it discriminates against a not insignificant proportion of the population who will justly complain that they have been denied their constitutional right to equal treatment under the law . . . There being no remedy to cure such injustice, my approach will, therefore, be to say that if I find the statute ambiguous, or even if I am left in doubt as to its meaning, then I should err on the side of preventing that discrimination.

Waite and Roch L.J.J., for reasons with which I could well have agreed, believe us to be in year Y whereas I have been persuaded that the discrimination would be thought by the broad mass of the people to be so unsustainable that this must now be year Z. To conclude otherwise would be to stand like King Canute, ordering the tide to recede when the tide in favour of equality rolls relentlessly forward and shows no sign of ebbing. If I am to be criticised—and of course I will be—then I prefer to be criticised, on an issue like this, for being ahead of the times, rather than behind the times. My hope, to reflect the intent of this judgment, is that I am in step with the times."

G. CAVEAT

In distinguishing at such length the judicial room for manoeuvre which exists especially in the case of appellate judges—under the doctrines of binding precedent currently prevailing in Scotland and England, there is a risk of misleading the reader. Judicial law-making is inhibited by a number of factors quite apart from doctrines of precedent. A judge can only rule on points which are relevant to the cases brought before him. Thus even if the House of Lords is convinced that a particular case was wrongly decided, it may have to wait many years before the vagaries of litigation provide the court with the opportunity of reconsidering the case. Nor will Scottish courts normally rule on hypothetical or moot cases.

(See *Glasgow Navigation Co. Ltd v. Iron Ore Co. Ltd* 1910 S.C. (H.L.) 63 and "Pronouncing on Hypothetical Questions" (1980) 48 SCOLAG 126.)

Moreover, appellate judges, particularly those in the House of Lords, while they have become more open in the past 20 years in discussing their law-making role, have been careful to stress the limits within which their creative powers can be exercised.

Lord Reid, "The Judge as Law maker", p. 22

> "There was a time when it was thought almost indecent to suggest that judges make law—they only declare it. Those with a taste for fairy tales seem to have thought that in some Aladdin's cave there is hidden the Common Law in all its splendour and that on a judge's appointment there descends on him knowledge of the magic words. Open Sesame. Bad decisions are given when the judge has muddled the password and the wrong door opens. But we do not believe in fairy tales any more.
>
> So we must accept the fact that for better or for worse judges do make law, and tackle the question how do they approach their task and how should they approach it."

Lord Devlin, *The Judge*, pp. 5, 9

> "Let me repeat the distinction, since it may be one which I have freshly drawn, between activist and dynamic lawmaking. In activist lawmaking the idea is taken from the consensus and demands at most sympathy from the lawmaker. In dynamic lawmaking the idea is created outside the consensus and, before it is formulated, it has to be propagated. This needs more than sympathy: it needs enthusiasm. Enthusiasm is not and cannot be a judicial virtue. It means taking sides and, if a judge takes sides on such issues as homosexuality and capital punishment, he loses the appearance of impartiality and quite possibly impartiality itself . . . It is essential to the stability of society that those whom change hurts should be able to count on evenhanded justice calmly dispensed, not driven forward by the agents of change.
>
> It is this evenhandedness which is the chief characteristic of the British judiciary and it is almost beyond price. If it has to be paid for in impersonality and remoteness, the bargain is still a good one . . . The reputation of the judiciary for independence and impartiality is a national asset of such richness that one government after another tries to plunder it. This is a danger about which the judiciary itself has been too easy going. To break up the asset so as to ease the parturition of a judicial creativity, an embryo with a doubtful future, would be a calamity. The asset which I would deny to governments I would deny also to social reformers.

> I have now made it plain that I am firmly opposed to judicial creativity or dynamism as I have defined it, that is, of judicial operations in advance of the consensus. The limit of the consensus is not a line that is clearly marked, but I can make certain what would otherwise be uncertain by saying that a judge who is in any doubt about the support of the consensus should not advance at all. This however leaves open quite a large field for judicial activity. In determining its extent it is, I think, necessary to distinguish between common law and statute law. This is because the requirement of consensus affects differently the two types of law. The public is not interested in the common law as a whole. When it becomes interested in any particular section of it, it calls for a statute; the rest it leaves to the judges. The consensus is expressed in a greater warrant for judicial lawmaking. This warrant is an informal and rather negative one, amounting to a willingness to let the judges get on with their traditional work on two conditions—first, that they do it in the traditional way, *i.e.* in accordance with precedent, and second, that parliamentary interference should be regarded as unobjectionable. In relation to statute law, by contrast, there can be no general warrant authorising the judges to do anything except interpret and apply."

[See also *D.P.P. for Northern Ireland v. Lynch* [1975] A.C. 653 at p. 700, *per* Lord Kilbrandon; *Miliangos v. George Frank (Textiles) Ltd* [1976] A.C. 443 at pp. 481–482, *per* Lord Simon of Glaisdale; and A.A. Paterson, *The Law Lords*, pp. 170–173. Despite these avowals of judicial restraint there have been several powerful (and controversial) examples of judicial activism in the High Court of Justiciary in recent years. These have included: *H.M. Advocate v. Wilson* 1984 S.L.T. 117 (malicious mischief being held to cover pure economic loss caused by pressing the emergency stop button in a power station); *Khaliq v. H.M. Advocate* 1984 S.L.T. 137 (supplying "glue sniffing kits" being held to be a crime known to Scots law) and *H.M. Advocate v. Paxton* 1985 S.L.T. 96 (where it was held that a husband could be found guilty of raping his wife where the parties were living apart from each other); *Purcell Meats Ltd v. McLeod* 1987 S.L.T. 528 (in which it was held for the first time that a limited company could be guilty of a common law offence involving *mens rea*); *S. v. H.M. Advocate* 1989 S.L.T. 469 (holding that a husband could rape his wife if they were still living together). These cases have provoked a not inconsiderable body of academic comment, see *e.g.* I. Willock, "The Declaratory Power; an Untenable Position" (1989) 157 SCOLAG 152; T. Jones, "Common Law and Criminal Law" (1990) C.L.R. 292; L. Farmer, "The Genius of our Law" (1992) M.L.R. 25.]

III. REFORM

Proposals for the reform of precedent in Scotland in recent years have focused on two main points: introducing overruling with prospective effect and abolishing the doctrine of binding (as opposed to persuasive) precedent.

A. PROSPECTIVE OVERRULING

Lord Simon, "Some Judicial Processes in England", p. 17

"My own view is that there are two further desirable developments if the House of Lords is to make the most effective use of its newly vouchsafed power. First, I think that it should enjoy the power (already enjoyed by the United States Supreme Court) to overrule its previous decisions prospectively only, with a discretion even whether to apply the new rule to the parties before the court. This might well require legislation; since, according to our existing doctrine of precedent, a decision only constitutes binding law in so far as it is necessary for the determination of the issues before the court; and the decision I have envisaged would apply only to future situations, not that before the court. But such a power of prospective overruling would mean that desirable developments in the law could be made without anxiety that existing rights were being disturbed.

The second development that I venture to suggest is that, where the court is uncertain as to the social repercussion of any decision, it should be enabled to obtain from the Law Officers a balanced executive view. The great difference between forensic and executive (or, for that matter, legislative) decision-making is that it is only in the minor field of 'lawyers' law' that courts can adequately envisage the repercussions of their decisions, whereas, in an executive decision, repercussions in other fields than those immediately in question (often entirely unlooked for) are carefully assessed."

Tur, "Varieties of Overruling and Judicial Law-Making", pp. 33–34, 63–64

"Prospective overruling is a technique whereby courts can change the law without upsetting the reasonable expectations of those who relied upon it prior to the change. 'In the hands of skilled judicial craftsmen, acting under well-reasoned guidelines, it can be an instrument of justice that fosters public reason for law.' It is also a potential instrument of law reform by the judiciary. Whenever a court is of the opinion that a well established precedent is 'bad law' (which might simply mean that the social conditions have changed since the original decision) it may yet be unwilling or reluctant to change the law because doing so will redound not only upon the parties to the instant case, but also upon all parties to unexhausted transactions based upon the law as then understood, all of whom might reasonably be thought to have acted in reliance on the then known law. If it is a necessary consequence of overruling a precedent that a number of individuals are treated unfairly, judicial development of the law will be limited. Prospective overruling seeks to provide a solution to this predicament by insisting that there are no jurisprudential or constitutional obstacles to a court overruling for the future only, whilst deciding the instant case according to the law in force at the time the transaction was entered into. Prospective overruling implies a clear admission that the courts do make new law, and the very raising of the question, 'Prospective or retrospective?' indicates an awareness of this. Thus prospective overruling is antithetical to the Blackstonian doctrine, still accorded lip-service, that the courts do not pronounce new law but merely maintain and expound the old . . .

What is clear, however, is that overruling in Scotland tends to proceed by way of a public-warning-before-disqualification process whereby the judiciary satisfies itself that an overruling is not upsetting legitimate expectations. Thus judicial changes are presaged by 'rumblings for Olympus.' The destructive work is cleanly done, albeit in two stages. First, doubt is expressed, a precedent is questioned; secondly, it is overruled, though the second stage may only follow the first after a 'sufficient' span of time. Nor should it be too readily assumed that any and every expression of doubt gives warning that overruling is in the offing. Thus the public-warning-before-disqualification functions more as a justification for the judiciary once it has decided to overrule rather than a criterion whereby the lawyer can anticipate overrulings. The Scottish position differs to a considerable degree from the English situation where doubtings, etc., issue less frequently in subsequent overrulings but more often in increasingly restrictive distinguishings.

An advocate of prospective overruling would urge that his technique achieves everything that the public-warning-before-disqualification system achieves and, as a further bonus, permits instant overrulings without thwarted expectations. It provides a facility for judicial reform without upsetting those who reasonably relied upon the law. It would seem that prospective overruling could quite happily be added to the armoury of the Court of Session."

Lord Devlin, "Judges and Lawmakers", p. 11

"Courts in the United States have begun to circumvent retroactivity by the device of deciding the case before them according to the old law while declaring that in future the new law will prevail: or they may determine with what measure of retroactivity a new rule is to be enforced. This device has attracted the cautious attention of the House of Lords. I do not like it. It crosses the Rubicon that divides the judicial and the legislative powers. It turns judges into undisguised legislators. It is facile to think that it is always better to throw off disguises. The need for disguise hampers activity and so restricts the power. Paddling across the Rubicon by individuals in disguise who will be sent back if they proclaim themselves is very different from the bridging of the river by an army in uniform and with bands playing. If judges can make law otherwise than by a decision in the case at Bar, why do they wait for a case? Prevention is better than cure, so why should they not, when they see a troublesome point looming up, meet and decide how best to deal with it? Judicial lawmaking is at present, as Professor Jaffe phrases it, 'a by-product of an *ad hoc* decision or process.' That this is so is of course in itself one of the objections to judicial lawmaking. Dependent as it is upon the willingness of individuals to litigate, it is casual and spasmodic. But to remove the tie with the *ad hoc* process would be to make a profound constitutional change with incalculable consequences. What is the business of a court of law? To make law or to do justice according to law? This question should be given a clean answer. If the law and justice of the case require the court to give a decision which its members think will not make good law for the future, I think that the court should give the just decision and refer the future to a lawmaking body."

Would Lord Devlin's objections apply equally to overruling by the House of Lords in pursuance of the 1966 Practice Statement? Do you think the case for experimenting with prospective overruling has been sufficiently made out?

[See, further on prospective overruling, R. Traynor, "Quo Vadis, Prospective Overruling: A Question of Judicial Responsibility", 1975, University of Birmingham; A. Nicol, "Prospective Overruling—a new Device for English Courts?" (1976) 39 M.L.R. 542 and Lord MacKay, "Can Judges change the Law?", *The Times*, December 3, 1987.]

B. ABOLISHING BINDING PRECEDENT

Lord Cooper, "The Common and the Civil Law", pp. 206–207

"Everyone will freely admit that in judicial administration a very large measure of consistency must be secured in order that the law affecting any given situation may be reasonably predictable. The utmost respect will always be conceded to a tract of similar decisions, or the settled opinion of jurists of weight, or the accepted practice and understanding of the profession. But such principles are far from the superstitious fetish of ancestor worship which inspires the rigid rule of the individually binding precedent. For practical reasons, if for no other, the rule is bound to be abandoned soon, because the crushing weight of centuries of law reports, digests, and indices has become all but overwhelming, and it is fast increasing every year. But, practical considerations apart, is there any answer to the protest of Holmes that it is revolting to act in blind imitation of the past and to magnify consistency at the expense of common sense? Too often the imitation of the past is a 'blind' imitation, for the parallelism between cases is much less common than we lawyers pretend. Very slight differences in the facts—and these are not always recorded fully in the reports—may easily turn the scale; and even when the facts are to all appearances identical, the social, political, and economic background may be entirely different if the cases are separated, as often happens, by a long period of time . . . In the eyes of the civilian the common lawyer has tried to make his professional life too easy by excessive reliance upon precedent and the ascription of infallibility to hierarchies of judges down the ages. The attempt has failed, and its abandonment will be joyfully received in Scotland by those who are ashamed to have to decide cases upon grounds with which they disagree simply because their remote ancestors have decided another case long ago upon a rationale which it is impossible to distinguish. All legal systems require a cement to bind them into a coherent whole; and the question which the common law system will . . . have to face is whether a better cement than rigid precedent cannot be found in more codification and in methodized reasoning from clear principles in accordance with the civilian tradition. The judge should not be the parties' oracle, but he must be something more than an animated index to the law reports."

Walker, "Reform Restatement and the Law Commissions", pp. 256–259

"The principle of *stare decisis* is a natural and, on the whole, valuable development, making for continuity, uniformity, reasonable certainty and predictability of law. But the rules have become so complicated, and the task of searching out the precedents so onerous that it is self-defeating. Above all, too frequently the question is not, what is the proper principle to apply, and what is the reasonable course or the fair and just decision? but: has the precise issue arisen before, and what was done then? Deference to the authority of precedent, frequently the opinion of a long dead judge in a case arising in quite different social, political and economic circumstances, too frequently counts for more than the convincing of reason or the reference to some overriding principle.

It is thought that the most useful liberalisation of the principles, while not destroying the undoubted value of the system of judicial precedent, would be to provide by statute that from a stated date no court, tribunal, judge or arbiter should in any circumstances be bound to follow or apply the principle of the decision in any previous case merely because of the rank in the judicial hierarchy of the court pronouncing the precedent decision. In other words the doctrine of binding precedent should be abolished, leaving it quite open to a subsequent court to be influenced or persuaded by the *ratio* of, or *obiter dictum* in, any precedent case, having regard to such factors as the status of the court, the personal eminence and reputation of the judges, whether or not the precedent had been criticised in the journals, looked upon askance by the profession, or generally approved and acted upon, and regarded as embodying a sound statement of principle. Precedents, that is, should continue to be persuasive.

The only good ground for following precedent is that a particular precedent contains a statement of a legal principle or rule which satisfies the reason of the subsequent judge, as being just and fair and reasonable, consistent with settled and accepted principles in that general branch of law, and capable of generalisation and application to other similar instances without apparent absurdity or injustice. A precedent should commend itself to the reason and for its reason, not impose itself by any artificial rule of antiquity or authority. The modern doctrine of *stare decisis*, with its elaborate grading of courts in the judicial hierarchy, its deference in many cases to previous rulings of courts of equal authority, and casuistic distinctions when the court does not wish to be bound by a precedent, is as artificial as the Theodosian Law of Citations. It is also quite inconsistent with the older Scots law, and with the Romanistic tradition generally and the United States experience shows that some liberalisation is essential to avoid a breakdown.

Such a change would, it is thought, in fact have a valuable, but only marginal effect. The majority of precedents are accepted as sound and sensible and reasonable, but a few are not, and if pronounced by superior courts cannot easily, if at all, be circumvented . . .

It need not be thought that, if all precedents were reduced to merely persuasive authority, chaos would result. Precedents can be, and are, of different degrees of persuasiveness, and any court or judge will naturally treat a decision of a higher court or of more eminent judges or one long accepted and acted upon as much more highly persuasive than some other decisions. No doubt under a legal system in which no precedent is binding it would be open to a single judge to say that *Donoghue v. Stevenson* 1932 S.C. (H.L.) 31, was bad law and that he would not follow or apply it, but in practice is it conceivable that any judge would do so? What is important and valuable is that such a single judge could, if he considered [a] decision unreasonable and the criticisms convincing, refuse to follow or apply [it]. A superior court may have power to reverse, but it does not necessarily have a monopoly of judicial wisdom, particularly in the light of more mature consideration, academic criticism and changed conditions.

The change would undoubtedly introduce a slightly greater measure of uncertainty into the law in permitting rules at present 'settled by authority' to be challenged, but in the first place such a challenge is likely to be successful only where the precedent is really questionable, which applies to only a minority of cases, and in the second place, the law is in fact much less fixed and certain than the layman thinks and any increased uncertainty seems likely to be negligible in relation to the whole corpus of the law. It is not in anyone's interest frivolously, or merely for the sake of the argument, to challenge precedents, but only if there do seem substantial grounds for doing so, and in such a case it is very much in the interests of justice that the precedent should be challenged and the point reconsidered. Certainty of law is a merit, but certainly can be of bad law and irrational and unjust rules."

MacCormick, "Can *stare decisis* be abolished?", p. 213

"In the path of those who would like to see an end of strict *stare decisis*, the obstacle is this: even if it ceases to be necessary to justify a decision by reference to precedent, it may in effect remain sufficient to do so. Such is the warning of history. The needs for reasonable finality in litigation and for judicial impartiality tend also in the same direction. It is suggested with great diffidence that reform can only be meaningful if generally acceptable grounds for setting aside single precedents or even 'established usages' can be thoroughly worked out and perhaps actually included in the Act of Parliament envisaged."

While the words of Lord Cooper and Professors Walker and MacCormick have so far fallen on deaf ears, it remains to be seen what impact the advent of computerised legal information retrieval (and the greater accessibility to unreported cases which comes with this) will have on the Scots doctrine of precedent. In England the House of Lords acted swiftly in an attempt to forestall the excessive citation of unreported cases which it considered might follow from the arrival of legal databases. See 1983 S.L.T. (News) 56 and *Roberts Petroleum Ltd v. Bernard Kenny Ltd* [1983] 2 A.C. 192.

CHAPTER 16

AUTHORITATIVE WRITINGS, CUSTOM AND EQUITY

Three further formal sources of Scots law are recognised: authoritative writings, custom and equity. Although their theoretical status is secure, it is nevertheless debatable whether in practice any of them now constitute a significant source of new or hitherto unrecognised rules in Scotland.

I. AUTHORITATIVE WRITINGS

Writings, like judicial precedents, are more or less persuasive in character. Some, referred to as "institutional writings", are, or have been, very highly persuasive indeed, while others are cited by counsel at their peril. The institutional writings include Craig's *Jus Feudale* (1655), Stair's *Institutions of the Law of Scotland* (1681), Bankton's *Institute of the Laws of Scotland* (1751–3), Erskine's *Institute of the Law of Scotland* (1773) and Bell's *Commentaries on the Laws of Scotland* (1804) and *Principles of the Law of Scotland* (1829). In the criminal sphere Mackenzie's *Laws and Customs of Scotland in Matters Criminal* (1678) and Hume's *Commentaries on the Law of Scotland Respecting Crimes* (1797) are accorded institutional status. Some of these institutional works were written, and possibly available to practitioners in manuscript, long before publication: Craig's *Jus Feudale*, for example, was written in 1603, but only published in 1655. For the standard editions in modern use see D.M. Walker, *The Scottish Legal System* (7th ed., 1997), p. 486.

Like precedent, the authority of writings depends on the normative practice of the legal community. A century ago only institutional writings were regarded as authoritative sources of law. Other legal writings could usually not even be cited in court if their author was still alive. The practice of the legal community in the United Kingdom has now departed from this restrictive approach, although the House of Lords and English courts seem to be more receptive to the writings of living academics—particularly in the sphere of criminal law—than the Scottish judiciary.

Lord Reid, "The Judge as Law Maker", p. 22

> "I think we are making some progress . . . In the House of Lords at least we turn a blind eye to the old rule that an academic writer is not an authority until he is dead, because then he can no longer change his mind."

Lord Diplock, "A.L.G.: A Judge's View", p. 459

> "In contrast to the judicial attitude in my early days at the Bar, judges no longer think that the sources of judicial wisdom are confined to judgements

in decided cases and, exceptionally, some pronouncement of the illustrious dead. In appellate courts, at any rate, when confronted with a doubtful point of law we want to know what living academic jurists have said about it, and we consider that counsel have not done their homework unless they come equipped to tell us about it."

Willock, "Scottish Criminal Law—Does it Exist?", p. 226

"[Gordon's *Criminal Law*] in a manner pioneered by the founder of Scottish Criminal Law, David Hume, in 1797, seeks to reconcile the decisions of judges, to show their underlying reasoning and their implications. Yet while still paying lip-service to Hume's genius, the judges have either studiously ignored Gordon's work (see *e.g.* Cawthorne 1968 J.C. 32, Brennan 1977 J.C. 38, *Watt v. Annan* 1978 S.L.T. 198, *Allan v. Patterson* 1980 S.L.T. 77) or brusquely rejected his views. Thus in *Smart v. H.M.A.* 1975 S.L.T. 65 they rejected his suggestion that consent is a defence to a charge of assault, though not of murder, as 'wrong' . . . Things are very different in England, where the role of writers in helping to put order into the law is well recognised, at least at the highest level. For instance in *Lynch v. D.P.P.* [1975] A.C. 653 the views of Glanville Williams and of Smith and Hogan in their works on Criminal Law were repeatedly canvassed by their Lordships in exploring the scope of the defence of duress. So too in *D.P.P. v. Majewski* [1977] A.C. 443—on self-induced intoxication as a defence.

The Scottish judges have preferred the terse snippets of Macdonald's *Practical Treatise on the Criminal Law*, the last edition of which is more than 30 years old. But Macdonald was a High Court judge and so was one of his last editors, who became Lord Walker."

The persuasiveness of writings varies with the prestige of the writer (thus institutional writings edited by a later hand lose some of their authority), the respect accorded to the work by the legal community and the age of the writings (either because they have been repeatedly relied on or because they have become severely dated). The normative practice of a substantial body of specialists over an extended period of time is rarely uniform in all respects. Hence, it is not surprising that there have been differing views, both over time and within the legal community at any given time, as to the authority of institutional and other writings and as to whether certain writings have or have not attained institutional status.

Blackie, "Stair's later reputation as a Jurist", pp. 209 *et seq.*

"The title Institutions or Institutes [was not in the late seventeenth and the eighteenth centuries] . . . evidence that there was a recognised category of 'institutional' writing forming an authoritative and binding source of law. The word 'authoritative' was used in connection with this class of writing, but it meant no more than that this was appropriate material for a court to take into account in coming to a decision. That a work should be entitled Institutions or Institute indicated to contemporaries nothing in itself, other than that the author was adopting a recognised method in the treatment of his subject, namely that of systematic, ordered exposition . . . Notwithstanding that certain writers, including Stair, were in fact accorded particular respect, this was always subject to the view that an opinion reported by a number of writers was more entitled to respect than a single opinion. This approach was the counterpart, as it were, of the recognition that a tract of decisions was of weight rather than an individual decision . . .

From the early years of the 19th century a different attitude to Stair and other writers emerges. By the 1840s it had become a matter of considerable moment that an 'institutional' opinion was not followed. This is associated with an express unwillingness to depart from written authority, with a tendency to distribute badges of ability amongst the writers, and a resulting special place being accorded to Stair . . .

Present day views of Stair are grounded in the 19th century understanding of his work, which was itself an elaboration on the earlier understanding. Why did this come about? The answer to this question goes deep into the way Scots lawyers have thought about the law, and only a tentative answer can be given. Four factors, however, stand out. Firstly, having neither a code nor a wealth of case law, the institutional writers and particularly Stair filled the gap . . . Secondly, the end of the critical technique of the enlightenment resulted in a changed attitude to the value of opinions. Thirdly, the creation of a system of judicial precedent had as its counterpart the need to create an equivalent with the works of writers. Finally, romantic nationalism as it affected the 19th century almost certainly played an important role."

[For a more detailed account of what is meant by the term "institutional writing", the role which such writings played in the development of the law of Scotland in the seventeenth and eighteenth centuries and their modern significance, see John W. Cairns, "Institutional Writings in Scotland Reconsidered" (1983) 4 J.L.H. 76. See also "Sources of Law", *Stair Memorial Encyclopaedia*, Vol. 22, paras 433–441.]

***Drew v. Drew* (1870) 9 M. 163**

Lord Benholme: "When on any point of law I find Stair's opinion uncontradicted, I look upon that opinion as ascertaining the law of Scotland."

Lord Normand, "The Scottish Judicature and Legal Procedure", p. 40

"Stair, Erskine and Bell are cited daily in the courts, and the court will pay as much respect to them as to a judgment of the House of Lords, though it is bound to follow a judgment of the House of Lords whatever the institutional writers have said."

Smith, *A Short Commentary on the Law of Scotland*, p. 32

"The precise relative authority of an institutional opinion in comparison with a judicial decision is uncertain. An opinion from Stair, Erskine or Bell, for example, would never be rejected by a Scottish court without anxious consideration . . . The present writer would submit that the authority of an institutional writer is approximately equal to that of a decision by a Division of the Inner House of the Court of Session."

Walker, *Introduction to Stair's Institutions* (1981 ed.), p. 40

> "In the literature of Scots law the *Institutions* has always held a pre-eminent place, as the most authoritative and respected general treaties, and one of the few institutional works, statements in which, save where and when clearly overruled or rendered obsolete by later law, have an authority similar to that of decisions of the Court of Session and which settle the law."

It might seem from the foregoing that in the absence of statutory or higher judicial authority a Division of the Inner House, a Lord Ordinary or a sheriff is now bound to follow an institutional writing on a point before them and that if the writing is not brought to their attention then their decisions may be said to be *per incuriam*. While institutional writings—particularly where they are unanimous on a point—are still considered to be very highly persuasive it is far from clear that the judiciary regard themselves as absolutely bound in this way. This is perhaps supported by the fact that the Scottish judiciary have never felt the need for an equivalent to the Roman Law of Citations (A.D. 426) to rank jurists in the event of a contradiction between them. For an instance of such a contradiction see *Fortington v. Kinnaird* 1942 S.C. 239.

Irrespective of their present authority, institutional writings are not now relied on in the courts with the frequency that they were in the nineteenth century.

Smith, *The Doctrines of Judicial Precedent in Scots Law*, p. 70

> "Naturally in the course of the centuries many of the principles set out in the institutional writers . . . have been adopted by judicial reasoning and given additional warrant thereby. Moreover, citation from the institutional writers unsupported by other authority is now relatively rare. [It has been said that] during the present century there has been a noticeable trend from institutional law to case law. There have, however, been a number of important decisions in recent years depending . .. on the institutional writers. The fact that they are few does not affect the fundamental position that such citations are treated with great respect."

[Such decisions include *Wills' Trs v. Cairngorm etc. School Ltd* 1976 S.C. (H.L.) 30, *Sloans Dairies Ltd v. Glasgow Corporation* 1977 S.C. 223, *Spook Erection (Northern) Ltd v. Kaye* 1990 S.L.T. 676, *Spencer-Thomas of Buquhollie v. Newell* 1992 S.L.T. 973, *Stirling v. Bartlett* 1993 S.L.T. 763, *Kamperman v. MacIver* 1994 S.L.T. 763, *L v. Wilson* 1995 S.C.C.R. 71, *Rafique v. Amin* 1997 S.L.T. 1385, and *Clydesdale Bank plc v. Davidson* 1998 S.C. 51, HL.]

An example of a recent case in which institutional writings were disapproved is *Burns v. H.M. Advocate* 1995 S.C.C.R. 532. In this case, Hume and Macdonald were not followed when the High Court held that a plea of self-defence is available to a person who starts a fight under certain circumstances.

Black, Review of Stair's *Institutions* (1981 ed.), p. 284

> "[Lord Cameron] in his foreword to the volume under review, writes that Stair's *Institutions* 'are still the daily resort of the practising lawyers and their authority is still accorded the highest respect'.

> The reviewer respectfully and regretfully takes leave to doubt whether, in the past two decades at least, recourse to and citation of Stair by practitioners has been as frequent as these statements might suggest. Certainly during the present century practitioners have been in use to treat judicial decisions rather than institutional works as the first (and too often today, the only) source of authority to which resort will be made. Citation of the institutional writers, even in such areas as obligations, property and family law in which their authority would seem to be still most clearly of contemporary relevance, has become the exception and not the rule. The hunt is for decided cases with facts as similar as possible to those giving rise to the instant dispute rather than for an institutional statement of principle from which a solution to that dispute can be obtained by deduction."

II. CUSTOM

It seems curious to us now, but Stair considered custom to be the most important formal source of Scots law. Custom for Stair consisted not only of immemorial usages (which he sometimes termed "the common law or laws of the realm") but also recent custom (by which he principally meant judicial decisions). However, recent work by Scottish legal historians suggests that Stair's views on formal sources were not shared by the majority of institutional writers. In the mainstream of Scottish legal writing from the sixteenth century, written law (Acts of Parliament and Acts of Sederunt) was afforded primacy over unwritten or customary law. (A view which is epitomised in the writings of Sir George Mackenzie.) Moreover, precedent was not generally regarded as an authoritative source of law during the seventeenth and eighteenth centuries, although a uniform series of decisions could establish a usage which in time was accepted as part of the customary or unwritten law (Erskine, *Institute*, I, 1, 47).

Today custom is still recognised as a formal source—in at least three senses—but its significance has declined and it ranks behind statute and case law in authority.

A. ANCIENT AND IMMEMORIAL USAGE

Stair, *Institutions*, 1, 1, 16

> "Next unto equity [*i.e.* natural law], nations were ruled by consuetude [*i.e.* custom], which declareth equity and constituteth expediency . . . so that every nation, under the name of law, understand their ancient and uncontroverted customs time out of mind, as their fundamental law . . . In like manner we are ruled in the first place by our ancient and immemorial customs, which may be called our common law . . . By this law is our primogeniture, and all degrees of succession, our legitim portion of children, communion of goods between man and wife, and the division thereof at their death . . . which are anterior to any statute, and not comprehended in any, as being more solemn and sure than those are."

MacQueen, "Mackenzie's Institutions", p. 500

"Mackenzie's views were very different. He distinguished between the written and unwritten sources of law. Written law comprised statutes or Acts of Parliament, acts of sederunt and the books of *Regiam Majestatem* collected by Sir John Skene. Unwritten law was made up first of 'the constant tract of decisions past by the Lords of Session', second 'our ancient customs'. Roman law had 'great influence in Scotland, except where our own express laws or customs have receded from it', and, he went on, 'by the common law in our Acts of Parliament is meant the civil law'. For Mackenzie, it is clear, statute was the pre-eminent source of law. It is ranked first among the written sources and is used to justify the inclusion of the other examples of written law. So acts of sederunt are 'statutes made by the Lords of Session by virtue of a particular Act of Parliament', but 'are not properly laws, the legislative power being the King's prerogative'. Skene's collection, *Regiam Majestatem*, was 'called the old books of our law by many express acts of parliament'. Ancient custom was law because 'the tacite consent of king and people operates as much in these as their express concourse [*i.e.*, in Parliament] does in making laws'; so adverse custom could have the effect of repealing a statute. But the decisions of the Lords of Session could only be 'considered as law' because the lords, although entitled to do so, seldom actually departed from them. And finally . . . Roman law was a source because it was described in statute as the common law of Scotland (Institutions I, i)."

Not all of the immemorial customs were derived from the usages of the indigenous community. W.D.H. Sellar has argued in the *Stair Tercentenary Studies* (1981) that Stair's ancient customs, the common law of Scotland, were in great measure taken from the Anglo-Norman law of England. Other of our customs seem to have been derived from civil law. Nevertheless all of these immemorial customs have become part of our common law. As such they do not require to be proved in court. Custom used in this sense is no longer a source of new or unrecognised rules of law in Scotland.

B. PARTICULAR CUSTOMS

Since the eighteenth century particular customs, whether local or general, have not been recognised as rules of law unless it has been shown to the satisfaction of a court that the alleged customs possess certain identifying features. A custom must (1) be generally acquiesced in as having the force of law in the areas in which it is observed, for a substantial—though undefined—period of time; (2) it must be definite and certain and (3) fair and reasonable; (4) a custom cannot be inconsistent with legal principle. It will necessarily vary in some particular from the general rule of the common law—yet it must not conflict with a statutory provision or other fundamental rule of law. (*Walker Trs v. Lord Advocate* 1912 S.C. (H.L.) 12.) Clearly, custom used in this sense has a very limited potential as a source of new rules of law in modern times.

Erskine, *Institute*, I, 1, 44

"44. The most essential articles of our customary law are so interwoven with our constitution that they are notorious, and so require no evidence to prove them; . . . but where any later usage which has been gradually gathering strength is pleaded upon as law, the antiquity and universality of that usage must be proved to the judge as any other matter of fact; for all customary law is founded on long usage, which is fact. No precise time or number of facts is requisite for constituting custom; because some things require in their nature longer time, and a greater frequency of acts to establish them than others. Neither is it necessary for this purpose, as some writers have affirmed, that the custom be declared by the previous sentence of a judge; for no court of justice can constitute law; and therefore any sentence declaring the customary law is of itself a clear proof that the law was constituted before."

***Bruce* v. *Smith* (1890) 17 R. 1000**

Lord Justice-Clerk (MacDonald): "The pursuer in this case is the proprietor of lands in Shetland, who raises an action against certain fishermen and others for his alleged claim on the value obtained for a school of caaing whales which were captured on the sea-shore next to the property. He founds his action upon an alleged custom having the force of law by which the heritor where whales of this description are captured in this way has right to a certain proportion of their value . . .

Before going into the facts it is desirable to see what is the legal principle on which the matter is to be dealt with. There is no doubt that the customs of particular districts, though merely local, may have the force of law. But must not the custom, to have such force, commend itself as reasonable? Must it not be according to sound legal principle? Must the custom not conform to good reason and to justice? It may no doubt arise from the consent of the community in the locality, and in that case there is every presumption in favour of its reasonableness, and therefore in favour of its being in accordance with sound principle and justice. If a law-abiding community acquiesces in such a usage, it is not to be supposed that it is against principle and justice.

On the other hand, the custom may be the result of compulsion; it may be forced on an unwilling community. I question whether the mere existence of a custom is sufficient to establish its legality without regard to the circumstances in which it is found existing. The nature of the custom, the relations of those who benefit by the custom and suffer from it respectively, the position of power of the one party to enforce and the position of feebleness of the other party effectually to resist, may all have a most important bearing on the question whether the custom is truly the outcome of a social consensus, or is, on the other hand, truly of the nature of an impost,—the result of a law made by one part of the community as against the other,—which the other could not effectively resist. My opinion is that no local custom can be proved to have the force of law merely by proof of its existence, unless it be either in itself consonant with the principles of justice, and demonstratably based on reasonable grounds, or be so plainly the outcome of the consent of the local community, as that there is an absolute presumption that, in the circumstances of the locality, it was a custom based on just principles.

In this case I think there can be no doubt that a custom is established. But nothing more is established. I find nothing in the evidence to shew that there is any basis of principle or of justice for the custom . . .

I cannot hold that such a custom is established as local law by its inherent reasonableness, and upon the facts I hold that it has not become local law by consensus of the community."

Lord Young: "I am not prepared to . . . admit a particular or local custom to govern outwith . . . those considerations of utility and expediency and also of good sense upon which all the local customs or admissions of them hitherto by our Court have rested."

Lord Rutherford Clark: "That a custom may have the force of law is an obvious proposition . . . But it does not necessarily follow that every custom by the mere fact of its existence has legal force . . . [especially] where the custom is confined to a particular locality, and is different from, or it may be opposed to the general law . . . [W]e should not enforce a particular or local custom which consists neither with legal principle nor with reason, for if it do not it must be unjust."

(For a detailed consideration and critique of this case see "Sources of Law", *Stair Memorial Encyclopaedia*, Vol. 22, paras 385–388.)

C. CUSTOM AS COMMUNITY PRACTICE

Today custom is most commonly relied on as a source of law in a third sense, namely taking account of the practice of a trade or profession. In this sense custom is only a secondary source of law since the recognition of the usage depends on other common law rules. Typically such usages are founded on for assistance in the interpretation of a contract between individuals engaged in a particular trade. In such cases it is alleged by one party that the usage is so universally accepted in that trade, that in the absence of express words in the contract to the contrary, the contract and the usage should be read as one. As with particular customs such usages need not be known to the other party but must meet certain criteria. Thus, they must be (1) universally or widely accepted within the trade; (2) definite and certain; (3) reasonable; and (4) not inconsistent with the terms of the contract.

***Hogarth & Sons v. Leith Cotton Seed Oil Co.* 1909 S.C. 955**

The pursuers owned a ship which was carrying a mixed cargo from Bombay to Leith for delivery to a number of different consignees. On the ship's arrival at Leith the owners in order to save time and money delivered the cargo into shed rather than over the side to the individual consignees. The consignees refused to pay the extra charges necessitated by this mode of delivery. The shipowners then sued for the charges, asserting that it was the custom of all ships discharging mixed cargoes at Leith to deliver them into shed.

Lord Ardwall: "A custom of trade must have quite as much certainty as the written contract itself. The reason of this is evident; if the custom is not definite, it is not possible to say what is the term which is to be held to be incorporated in any individual contract. But in this case the uncertainty does not end with the description of the class of cargo to which the alleged custom is to apply. It also extends, according to the proof, to the amount or proportion of charges to be paid . . .

But in the second place, a usage or custom of trade will not be admitted to add to or explain a contract unless it can be shewn to be uniform and universal in the trade to which it relates, and so notorious that both parties to the contract must either have known or be held to have known of it. Now, I agree with the Lord Ordinary that this has not been made out by the pursuers with regard to the alleged custom . . . In the present case, it is noticeable that not a single Leith merchant is brought by the pursuers to say that he is aware of the alleged custom, while, on the other hand, the defenders adduce a number of well-known Leith merchants and manufacturers as witnesses who say that they never heard of the custom alleged by the pursuers . . .

Accordingly, I consider that on the evidence that has been led in this action it has not been proved that the practice alleged by the pursuer is either uniform, universal, or notorious.

In the third place, I am of opinion that the alleged custom is contrary to the contract between the parties, and therefore cannot be given effect to in the present case, even supposing it had been otherwise proved."

(The shipowners were unsuccessful in the action.)

***Wilkie v. Scottish Aviation Ltd* 1956 S.C. 198**

The pursuer, a chartered surveyor, was employed by the defenders under a contract which made no reference to his remuneration. His account was feed in accordance with the schedule of charges issued by his professional body but the defenders refused to pay for his services at these rates. The pursuer sued for his fees alleging that remuneration on the basis of the schedule was customary and should therefore be deemed to be an implied condition of the contract.

Lord President (Clyde): "To establish a custom . . . of this kind the evidence must show that it is reasonable, certain and notorious . . . To establish the custom it is not essential to prove that the defenders actually knew of it. It is enough if it was so well recognised that it ought to have been known to both parties . . . There is, after all, nothing inequitable in such a requirement. If a person employs a professional man to perform some service and makes no inquiry as to the basis upon which the professional man is to be remunerated for the service, it is not unreasonable that he should pay for the service on the usual and customary basis. It is not open to him to complain that he is unaware of it, if he has never even taken the trouble to ascertain it before engaging another to do work for him without specifying a precise fee."

In discussions of custom it is sometimes overlooked that the practice of a profession or a community can be taken account of in delict as well as contract. The standard of care required of a professional man in negligence cases is highly dependent on the practice of that profession provided it is generally followed, clear, reasonable and not illegal.

[For a recent case where a legally binding custom was upheld, see *Stirling Park & Co. v. Digby, Brown & Co.*, 1996 S.L.T. (Sh. Ct) 17. For a more comprehensive and perhaps controversial account of legal custom in Scotland see T.J. Cameron, "Custom as a Source of Law in Scotland" (1964) 27 M.L.R. 306 and "Sources of Law", *Stair Memorial Encyclopaedia*, Vol. 22, paras 355–393.]

III. EQUITY

Equity as a legal term has several meanings. In Scottish legal writings it has been used to denote two different aspects of justice, "justice as equality" and "justice as fairness".

Stair, *Institutions*, 1, 1, 6

> "6. [The] law of nature is also called Equity, from that equality it keeps amongst all persons, from that general moral principle . . . whereby just persons in their deliberations and resolutions state themselves in the case of their adversaries, and so change the scales of the balance; which holds most in commutative justice. So parents in the duties of children ought to consider, as if their children were their parents, and what in that case they would do to them: and children in their obedience ought to yield all to their parents that they would demand, if they were their children. But equity is also taken for the law of rational nature . . . whereby the common interest of mankind is preferred to the interest of any part of men; whereas vicious self-love preferreth the interest of a part to the interest of the whole."

Walker, "Equity in Scots Law", pp. 105–106

> "General rules of law take no account of the circumstances of individual cases where their generality may work injustice . . . Likewise human foresight cannot provide against all eventualities where a wrong may require a remedy, and in such cases it is sometimes necessary to go beyond the law or even contrary to the strict letter of the law, and to administer justice in accordance with the dictates of natural reason. So far as a tribunal can supplement or reject rules of law in special cases by admitting pleas founded on reason and justice it is a court of equity as opposed to a court of law and it is in this sense . . . that the Court of Session is a court of equity as well as of law."

Both these usages must be distinguished from the more specific use of the term in England to denote the body of legal rules and principles formerly administered by the Court of Chancery, as contrasted with the common law.

***Gibson's Trs* 1933 S.C. 190**

> **Lord President (Clyde)**: "Owing to its peculiar history the law of Scotland has never known either distinction or conflict between common law and the

principles of equity. It is often said, and truly said, that in the law of Scotland law is equity, and equity law; and when a Scots lawyer uses the expression common law, he uses it in contradistinction to laws made by Parliament."

[On the historical reasons why a separate equitable jurisdiction never arose in Scotland, see D.M. Walker, "Equity in Scots Law", 1954 J.R. 103.]

Walker, "Equity in Scots Law", pp. 145–147

"There is overwhelming evidence that the Court of Session has always been regarded as a court both of law and of equity. In numerous branches of Scots law the basis or justification of the rule in observance has been ascribed to 'equity', 'natural justice', 'substantial justice', 'reason and justice' and similar phrases, and . . . there are repeated acknowledgements of this fact in judgments and the most authoritative text-writers. There is not, and never has been, any separate jurisdiction in equity in Scotland, and consequently equity and the equitable do not refer almost exclusively, as in England, to the subjects which belonged to a particular jurisdiction. On the other hand it is equally manifest that equity and the equitable in Scottish practice do mean that which is fair, reasonable, and naturally just . . . Numerous subjects . . . are equitable in their nature and basis but are administered in and through and as part of the common law.

Of the subjects falling within the ordinary equitable jurisdiction . . . many have their roots in Roman law; one or two, such as the law of trusts, have derived something from the equity of the Chancery; in many, Chancery authority has been referred to with respect, and it is particularly noteworthy how many of the topics of Scottish equity have their counterparts in Chancery equity. Substantially every topic dealt with in a modern English textbook on equity not only has a Scottish counterpart, albeit under a different name, but a counterpart which has been considered to be founded on equity and natural justice.

Examination of the subject today gives strong support to Kames's contention that 'many actions, founded originally on equity, have, by long practice, obtained an establishment so firm as to be reckoned branches of the common law.' This is abundantly true today when every branch . . . is applied in accordance with fairly settled rules and takes account of precedent. The submergence of fundamentally equitable pleas in common law actions has contributed to the neglect by Scottish judges and text-writers of the existence of equity. So, too, many pleas, originally reserved to the equitable powers of the Court of Session, have been extended by statute to inferior courts.

With the increasing extent to which law is made and modified by legislation and the extent to which doctrines of law and equity have become settled, it rather appears that the creative function of equity in Scots law is ended. No substantial new doctrine or change in common law seems now possible, save by statute."

As Walker's essay shows, equity as a source of law in Scotland is a testimony to the perceived importance of "justice as fairness" in the eyes of the Scottish legal profession over the centuries. For this very reason Walker's pessimistic assessment that equity is now past the age of childbearing in Scotland, seems unjustified. Judicial attempts to evade the binding chains of precedent (see chapter 15 above) attest to the continuing force of equity today. Moreover, equity is an important secondary source of law, for in a number of fields judges are required by statute and the common law to pay heed to equitable considerations, or to pursue the lodestar of "just and equitable" or "fair and reasonable" solutions. [For an informed discussion of equity in Scots law, see "Sources of Law", *Stair Memorial Encyclopaedia*, Vol. 22, paras 394–425.]

THE NOBILE OFFICIUM

The precise historical relationship between the *nobile officium* of the Court of Session and the High Court of Justiciary and the ordinary equitable jurisdiction of the courts is obscure. Many of the matters referred to by Stair as pertaining to the *nobile officium* are now treated as part of the general equitable jurisdiction of the courts or of the common law. Some have even argued in the past that the two jurisdictions are not really separable. Nevertheless the modern view is that a clear distinction should be drawn between the special or extraordinary equitable jurisdiction of the Court of Session and the High Court of Justiciary (their *nobile officium*) and their general or ordinary equitable jurisdiction.

1. The Nobile Officium of the Court of Session

***The Royal Bank of Scotland v. Gillies* 1987 S.L.T. 54 at p. 55**

> **Lord Justice-Clerk (Ross)**: "The *nobile officium* has been defined as an extraordinary equitable jurisdiction of the Court of Session inherent in it as a supreme court; it enables it to exercise jurisdiction in certain circumstances which would not be justified except by the necessity of intervening in the interests of justice. Although the court tends to limit the exercise of its jurisdiction under the *nobile officium* to cases in which the power has already been exercised, it is neither possible nor desirable to define exhaustively or comprehensively all the circumstances in which resort may be had to the *nobile officium*."

(See also Maxwell, *The Practice of the Court of Session*, (S.C.A.: 1980) at p. 127.)

***London and Clydeside Estates v. Aberdeen D.C.* 1980 S.C. (H.L.) 1**

> **Lord Keith**: "It was suggested that recourse might be had to the *nobile officium* of the court. I regard that suggestion as entirely misplaced. The *nobile officium* does not exist to deal with matters of disputed right. Its chief object is to provide a means of rectifying obvious errors or omissions, principally of an administrative character, which cannot be dealt with in any other way."

The *nobile officium* has been exercised under three main heads:

1. Application by petitions not founded on statute, *e.g.* for the appointment of judicial factors or public officers *ad interim* where the incumbent official is ill or has died. New remedies where no other means are available can be granted under this head. Thus in *Solheim Petitioners* 1947 S.C. 243 the widows of three Norwegian seamen who had been buried in Scotland during the Second World War successfully petitioned the court for authority under its *nobile officium* to disinter the bodies and to transport them to Norway for reinterment in the family burial grounds.
2. Equitable jurisdiction with relation to charitable trusts particularly their variation through *cy-près* schemes.
3. Rectifying omissions in statutes or deeds, or curing procedural deficiencies which have arisen through inadvertance, and for which the statute provides no remedy. (The Bankruptcy and the Licensing Acts seem to be the worst culprits under this head.) If the omission is thought to have been deliberate the court will not exercise its *nobile officium*.

***R, Petitioner* 1993 S.L.T. 910**

Opinion of the Court (delivered by Lord President Hope): "The power may be exercised in highly special or unforeseen circumstances to prevent injustice and oppression. If the intention of a statute is clear but the necessary machinery for carrying out that intention in special or unforeseen circumstances is lacking, the power may be invoked to provide that machinery. In *Sloan, Petitioner* [1991 S.L.T. 527], for example, where there was no power either in the 1968 Act or in the Social Work (Sheriff Court Procedure) Rules 1971 to enable the sheriff to do what was considered to be appropriate in the exceptional circumstances of that case, a direction was made in the exercise of the *nobile officium* to enable the sheriff to do what was required. But the power cannot be exercised in such a way as to conflict with or defeat a statutory intention, express or implied. Nor may it be invoked to extend the provisions of an Act of Parliament, such as by supplementing the statutory procedure by what would, in effect, be an amendment of the statute . . ."

***Roberts, Petitioner* (1901) 3 F. 779**

The Bankruptcy (Scotland) Act 1856 required that before discharge a bankrupt should swear that he had made a full and fair disclosure and had not made any secret arrangements with his creditors. The petitioner having become of unsound mind was unable to make the declaration and without it the Act provided no other way for him to be discharged.

Lord President (Balfour): "This case is attended with some nicety, because it appears that the bankrupt has satisfied all the requirements of the statute, in so far as it is possible for a man mentally afflicted to do so. The sequestration was awarded as far back as 1894, and all the known estate has been got in and divided among the creditors, including certain estate which accrued to the bankrupt after the sequestration. In these circumstances the alternatives are either that the bankrupt shall never get his discharge, or that someone else shall make the declaration or oath required by . . . the Bankruptcy Act . . . in place of him, or that the Court should in the very special circumstances of the case dispense with that declaration or oath. It appears to me that the last-mentioned course is the proper one to follow."

[The court agreed to exercise its *nobile officium* to dispense with the oath.]

***Ferguson, Petitioners* 1965 S.C. 16**

The petitioners discovered that their names had been taken off the register of persons entitled to vote because the registrar had been told they were dead. No remedy for the deletion was contained in the regulations. The court was persuaded to exercise its *nobile officium* by restoring the petitioners' names to the register.

[On the use of the *nobile officium* in the Court of Session generally, see McBryde and Dowie, *Petition Procedure in the Court of Session* (W. Green & Son, 1987), chap. 18. and "Sources of Law", *Stair Memorial Encyclopaedia*, Vol. 22, paras 426–431.]

2. The Nobile Officium of the High Court of Justiciary

While the Court of Session is reluctant to exercise its *nobile officium* except in situations where there is a precedent for it, the High Court of Justiciary until relatively recently has been reluctant to exercise its *nobile officium* at all.

Stoddart, "The Nobile Officium", p. 37

"Until recently the *nobile officium* of the High Court of Justiciary seems rarely to have been invoked since the time of the institutional writers . . .

Many of the circumstances enumerated by Hume and Alison in which the court exercised its nobile officium to fill gaps in the law have either been dealt with by statute or have vanished with the passage of time . . . Hume was being over-optimistic when he envisaged that many other instances would occur with the development of the criminal law, for the power seems to have remained dormant for many years before Scottish criminal procedure became the creature of statute around the beginning of the present century. Even in modern times prior to 1966 only two cases on the *nobile officium* found their way into the law reports."

***Anderson v. H.M. Advocate* 1974 S.L.T. 239**

Lord Justice-General (Emslie):

"As it is stated by Alison, *Criminal Law of Scotland*, Vol. II, in the well-known passage beginning on p. 23: 'Akin to the well-known *nobile officium* of the Court of Session, is a similar power enjoyed by the Justiciary Court, of providing a remedy for any extraordinary or unforeseen occurrence in the course of criminal business in any part of the country. This is an unusual remedy, not to be called into operation when any of the ordinary courts are adequate to the matter; but still abundantly established wherever no other means of extricating it appears . . . In short, the principle is, that wherever the interposition of some authority is necessary to the administration of justice, and there exists no other judicature by whom it can competently be exercised, or which has been in use to exercise it, the Court of Justiciary is empowered and bound to exert its powers, on the application of a proper party, for the furtherance of justice.' To the same effect is Moncrieff in *Review in Criminal Cases*, p. 264, who says 'In addition to its power of reviewing, the High Court of Justiciary as the Supreme Court in criminal matters has in respect of its *nobile officium* the power of interfering in extraordinary circumstances for the purpose of preventing injustice or oppression although there may not be any judgment, conviction or warrant brought under review.' These classical descriptions of the power have been accepted by this court as authoritative in all cases in which the scope of its power under the *nobile officium* has been called in question, and as the cases show, have been interpreted to mean that the power will only be exercised where the circumstances are extraordinary or unforeseen, and where no other remedy or procedure is provided by the law . . . We have only to add that the *nobile officium* of this court, and for that matter of the Court of Session, may never be invoked when to do so would conflict with statutory intention, express or clearly implied."

[See also *Macpherson, Petitioner* 1989 S.C.C.R. 518 at p. 522.]

***Wan Ping Nam v. Federal German Republic* 1972 J.C. 43**

The petitioner was accused of murder by the German government, who sought his extradition under the provisions of the Extradition Act 1870. The Act provided the English remedy of habeas corpus where detention under the Act was challenged as illegal, but no Scottish remedy was provided.

Opinion of the Court: "The answer to this question depends essentially upon the intention of the Act. In our opinion the intention that relief shall be available to all persons committed under s. 10 is plain. This we discover from the express reference to habeas corpus procedure in s. 11. In any event, we cannot decern in the statute any indication of an intention that persons committed by a sheriff in Scotland should be in any less advantageous position than those committed by a police magistrate in England. In these circumstances we are in no doubt that, the statute having disclosed the intention, this court has ample power to provide what the statute has omitted to provide, namely, the means of giving effect to that intention . . . In our opinion, the circumstances of this case to which we have drawn attention are, on any view, extraordinary and we are satisfied that in the exercise of the *nobile officium* this court may properly examine the allegation of injustice made by the petitioner."

The apparent similarity between the third head under which the civil *nobile officium* is exercised and the criteria outlined in *Anderson v. H.M. Advocate* is misleading. Over 10 per cent of the civil petitions to the *nobile officium* which are granted are the result of procedural errors or omissions on the part of solicitors (McBryde, 1978). The High Court of Justiciary takes a stricter approach to such cases.

***Fenton, Petitioner* 1982 S.L.T. 164**

> **Opinion of the Court**: "The *nobile officium* . . . is the power of the High Court to redress all wrongs for which a particular remedy is not otherwise provided . . . The petitioner's complaint is not that the legislature has not provided a means whereby he could appeal against a refusal to grant interim liberation. His complaint is that the legislature has not provided him with a statutory remedy to appeal when he has failed to observe the strict time-limit which the legislature had imposed for the lodging of an appeal. In our view it is not for the court to exercise its power under the *nobile officium* simply because an accused or his legal advisers have been mindless of a statutory time-table. If it were otherwise the court could be flooded with petitions to the *nobile officium*. If the legislature intended that failure to obtemper a strict statutory time-table could be excused on cause shown, that could have been provided for in the statute, as is the case in other procedural matters. That was not done and there is no justification for considering that this was a *casus omissus*. A statutory procedure was enacted, and in the absence of any provision to excuse non-compliance, non-compliance is fatal. The exercise of the *nobile officium* should not be regarded as the kiss of life in such circumstances.
>
> We are accordingly of the opinion that this attempt to invoke the *nobile officium* is not justified and we accordingly dismiss the petition."

***MacLeod, Petitioner* (High Court, September 1975, unreported)**

The petitioner had been convicted of two motoring offences. He appealed against sentence but due to an error on the part of his Edinburgh solicitors no appearance was made on his behalf when the case called and the appeal was dismissed. Although the solicitors accepted full responsibility for the error, the High Court of Justiciary refused to exercise the *nobile officium* to reopen the case.

[See also *Ferguson, Petitioner* 1980 S.L.T. 21.]

It seems that the High Court of Justiciary is prepared (in some cases) to exercise its *nobile officium* to correct judicial and court administration errors (see *H.M. Advocate v. Keegan* 1981 S.L.T. (Notes) 35; *Rae, Petitioner* 1981 S.C.C.R. 356, *Ferguson v. P*, 1989 S.L.T. 681; and Heywood, Petitioner, 1998 S.C.C.R. 335) and sometimes also those of the prosecution (see *H.M. Advocate, Petitioner* 1990 S.L.T. 798). Unlike the Court of Session, the High Court has traditionally declined to use the *nobile officium* to correct errors made by the petitioner's legal advisers. Such a policy runs the danger of not appearing to be reasonable or fair. This situation may, however be changing following the decision in *McIntosh, Petitioner* 1995 S.L.T. 796, in which the High Court exercised the *nobile officium* to allow an appeal to be heard which had been abandoned on the inaccurate advice of the petitioner's legal advisers.

[For additional recent cases where an accused has benefited from the nobile officium see *Welsh, Petitioner*, 1992 S.L.T. 903 and *Schavione, Petitioner,* 1992 S.L.T. 1059. Interestingly, in 1997 the High Court exercised the nobile officium to recall a finding of contempt of court against a solicitor made during his conduct of a case (*Blair-Wilson, Petitioner*, 1997 S.L.T. 621).]

INDEX